Laurence Smart

from

Richard Alle

D1340307

IMPERIALISM AND NATIONALISM IN THE FERTILE CRESCENT

IMPERIALISM AND NATIONALISM IN THE FERTILE CRESCENT

Sources and Prospects of the Arab-Israeli Conflict

Richard Allen

New York
OXFORD UNIVERSITY PRESS
London 1974 Toronto

Copyright © 1974 by Oxford University Press, Inc.
Library of Congress Catalogue Card Number: 73–90373
Printed in the United States of America

Contents

Maps

Preface

After all that has been written on the tragic collision between Jew and Arab in our day, my only justification for another book is the hope of providing, especially for undergraduates and the ordinary reader, a reasonably clear, simple, and dispassionate account of the deep historical origins of this complex conflict in its wider Middle Eastern setting. Its basis is my brief but illuminating experience as a junior official of the Palestine Government in Jerusalem in the mid-1920s, more recent visits to the area, and nearly ten years of college teaching in the United States. In 1925-27 peace still reigned in the Holy Land, and it was possible to weigh the issues confronting the country with little of the distortion caused later by strife and passion. For that reason this earlier spell of practical involvement may have some value. My subsequent work in the British Diplomatic Service in other parts of Asia beset by ethnic and communal problems was useful to me as a frame of reference; yet none of these problems were as refractory and unique as those that arose in Palestine.

Much has been written by distinguished scholars and men of action about Western imperialism in the Middle East, the nationalist movements it encountered, Zionism, and the rise of Israel. But much of this writing concentrates on, and specializes in, a particular aspect, or espouses one side or the other with deep conviction. My aim has been to offer a general picture of the origins of the main issues and the course they took, for the non-specialist rather than for the experienced expert; and I have sought to avoid obtruding my personal views.

In my experience, however, many who have dealt with the issues arising in and around Palestine or Israel have tended to focus rather too much on purely local issues and somewhat to neglect the decisive role, in the destinies of the area, of the ancient and modern rivalries and ambitions of the great powers. In this context the role of Britain was of course, for a time, of capital importance. But while the British have taken credit—on the whole, justly—for bringing order, stability, and progress to various parts of the world, Palestine must be accounted (with Ireland) one of their more obvious failures. It is small consolation that nearly all others concerned have committed errors of justice, judgement, and performance which have till now kept bitterness, hatred, and tension so painfully alive in this precious and unique region.

The term *Middle East* (now generally preferred to, e.g., *Near East*) is variously defined. Thus, one current American textbook (Armajani's *Middle East, Past and Present*), from which I have quoted, regards it as covering Iran, Turkey, Arabia, the Fertile Crescent, and Egypt, but not the Arab world as a whole. On the other hand, the 1973 edition of an authoritative British text, *The Middle East: A Political and Economic Survey*, edited by Peter Mansfield, includes, in addition to the above, the Sudan and the Emirates of the Persian Gulf with Oman, but excludes the North African countries. The U.S. State Department, however, in its booklet of 1969 called *Issues in United States Foreign Policy, No. 1—The Middle East*, defines the term as covering all the Islamic countries of the Arab world, including Morocco, Algeria, Tunisia, and Libya; the non-Arab Islamic countries, Iran and Turkey; and three non-Islamic countries of the eastern Mediterranean: Cyprus, Greece, and Israel. For the purpose of this book I have followed in general the State Department's wider definition, though for obvious reasons I have concentrated on the Fertile Crescent with Israel and Egypt. It would in fact be hard to omit such North African countries as Libya and Tunisia at this juncture when both have adopted a position of some importance in relation to the Arab-Israeli conflict, a main theme of this book.

I am particularly grateful for all I learned about the problems of Palestine—from two somewhat differing standpoints—from those who were my two immediately senior officials in the Jerusalem Government in the 1920s. One is Mr. Mordekhai (Max) Nurock, later Israeli Minister to Australia, who is still active in the Israeli Ministry of Foreign Affairs. The other is Sir Alec Kirkbride, former British Ambassador to Jordan and Libya, whose early experiences as a British officer fighting in the Arab Revolt of World War I, and during his years with King Abdullah, are delightfully recorded in his two books to which I have referred.

I am indebted also to General Sir John Glubb for his kindness in reading and commenting on some passages in this book; to Mr. Ze'ev Suffot, Counsellor and Consul General at the Israeli Embassy in London, for help on some factual points, and for a fascinating tour of parts of southern Israel, on which he took me in 1971; and to Mr. John Snodgrass, British Consul General in Jerusalem. I would thank also Mr. Arthur Whitman, Director of Development of the American University of Beirut for his comments on certain passages, especially in connection with the development of American cultural work in the Middle East; and also Mr. Bernard Cheeseman, Librarian of the Foreign and Commonwealth Office, London, and his colleagues, for the facilities generously placed at my disposal. I owe a special debt to Mr. Peter Mansfield, author of *The British in Egypt* and editor of the *Middle East Handbook*, and to Professor Oleg Smolansky of Lehigh University (Bethlehem, Pa.), who has written extensively on Soviet strategic aims in the eastern Mediterranean and the Middle East. Both have given generously of their time and made many valuable suggestions. Finally, I could have done nothing without the exemplary patience of my wife, who, apart from her valuable help with the Index, showed exceptional tolerance toward a husband whose mind was constantly on other things.

I would add a plea for indulgence. This is a work with many exotic words, and there is, I fear, some unavoidable inconsistency— for example, where two or more equally respected authors use different spellings in their transliteration of Oriental, and especially Arab, names; or where it has become customary in recent years to use a more correct but sometimes less familiar version. One example is the Albanian founder of the Egyptian Royal House, whom most of us of an older generation have known as *Mehemed Ali*. This version of his first name is Turkish, however, and instead it should now, I am told, properly be spelt like the name of the Prophet. In general I have used the more familiar versions of names except where I have been advised to change by publishers or friends

—with reference to Oxford University Press *Middle East Survey* in case of doubt. For Hebrew and Jewish names I have used either those in a modern version of the Bible or in the recent one-volume *Jewish Encyclopedia* of Roth and Wigoder. A special difficulty is Iran, which in quotations from older works is so often referred to as *Persia*, while *Persian Gulf* is still general usage. Here I confess that I have used one name and the other in different places—*Persia* more generally in dealing with earlier centuries, and the more correct *Iran* in modern times.

As readers will see, this work was finished before the fourth Arab-Israeli war was. A brief Epilogue covers in outline the dramatic final months of 1973 and first months of 1974.

Richard Allen

Linfield College, Oregon

London

March 1974

IMPERIALISM
AND
NATIONALISM
IN THE
FERTILE CRESCENT

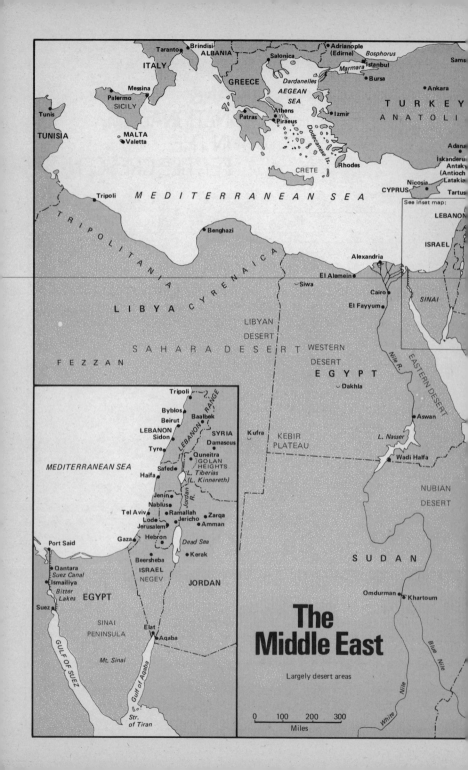

The Middle East

Largely desert areas

0   100   200   300
Miles

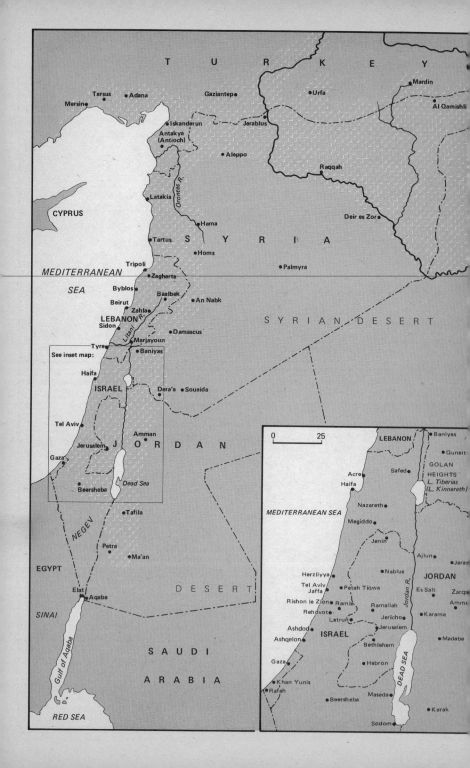

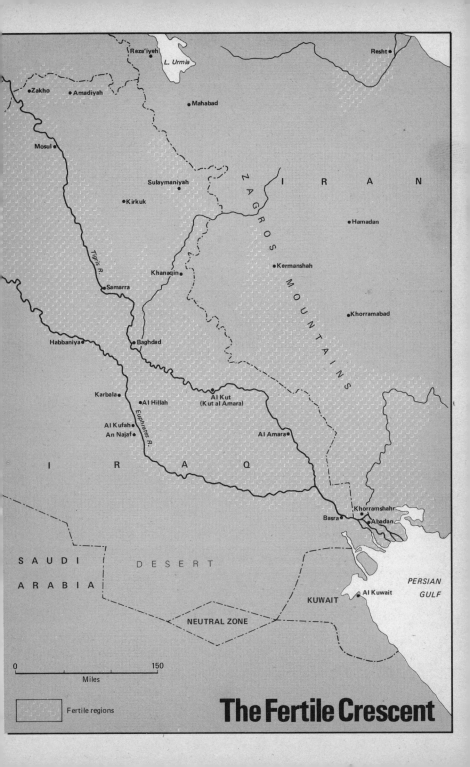

The Fertile Crescent

Fertile regions

0   150

Miles

Reza'iyeh

L. Urmia

Resht

Zakho   Amadiyah

Mahabad

Mosul

IRAN

Z A G R O S

Sulaymaniyah

Kirkuk

Hamadan

Tigris R.

Khanaqin

Kermanshah

Samarra

M O U N T A I N S

Khorramabad

Habbaniya

Baghdad

Karbala

Al Hillah

Al Kut
(Kut al Amara)

Al Kufah
An Najaf

Euphrates R.

Al Amara

I R A Q

Khorramshahr

Basra   Abadan

SAUDI

D E S E R T

ARABIA

PERSIAN

GULF

KUWAIT

Al Kuwait

NEUTRAL ZONE

Introduction

In the 1920s the fierce conflict that was to occur in Palestine had not yet arisen, or rather was still in embryo. In the British Government in Jerusalem it was realized that there was small hope of ever reconciling the colliding goals of the long-established Arab community and the developing Jewish National Home. Most officials conscientiously did their jobs from day to day, hoping that the future would somehow justify their efforts. But the Arabs, who then formed 90 per cent of the population, saw the Mandate awarded to Britain by the League of Nations as a violation of the promises of national freedom made to them by the British to induce them to revolt against the Turks. The Zionists, on the other hand, saw the British administration as a temporary convenience until—in the unguarded words of Dr Chaim Weizmann, leader of the Zionist movement—Palestine should become "as Jewish as England is English." Meanwhile, the terms of the Mandate commanded Britain to "secure the establishment of the Jewish National Home," to "facilitate Jewish immigration" and the "close settlement by Jews on the land," while at the same time "ensuring that the rights and position of other sections of the population were not prejudiced."[1] We knew, and the Arabs knew, that this was a circle that could not possibly be squared.

When I left Palestine in 1927 none of us could foretell that in just forty years the intentions of the Balfour Declaration, the terms of the Mandate, and the subsequent plans of the United Nations, would have been mostly set aside or been "overtaken by events." The complex strands of all these binding pronouncements, with their careful reservations and qualifications, have in effect been severed by the sword. In their place, Dr Weizmann's simple and drastic programme has been almost literally carried out. In the state of Israel, which emerged victorious from the wars of 1948 and 1967, the former overwhelming Arab majority has become, in those parts of Palestine incorporated in Israel, a small subordinate minority, roughly equal, in its proportion of the total population, to the Jewish minority in the whole of Palestine in the early 1920s.[2]

After this last victory, for most Jewish people—and others—Israel stood forth as a shining creation of courage, dash, imagination, and passionate loyalty to an ancient code and a modern dream. By contrast the neighboring Arab nations deserved, it seemed, little consideration. They had been their own worst enemies. Their image was clouded and discredited by empty boasts, flamboyant provocations, and humiliating setbacks. They had fought to restore the Palestinians to the homes and country they had lost, from the refugee camps and villages into which they had been crowded in neighbouring lands; and their failure somehow cast a shadow even over the refugees, their number swollen by this new war. Some of Israel's admirers obscurely felt that here were more ineffective Arabs whose cause almost deserved to be lost.

One purpose of this book is to look more closely at this picture, which though oversimplified nevertheless reflects a fairly widespread state of opinion on the morrow of the June War; and to con-

1. Mandate for Palestine, July 24, 1922, Articles 2 and 6.
2. In each case approximately 10 per cent. If Dr Weizmann was referring to England in its frequently used loose sense of the whole United Kingdom, his goal had in fact been exceeded, since the minorities of Welsh, Scots, and Irish in the U.K. are considerably larger.

sider other consequences of Israel's victory and the Arab defeat and what may ultimately come of them. One consequence, of course, is that Israel has provisionally acquired territory reaching far beyond the land between Dan and Beersheba, which was the Palestine of the Bible. Another is that Israel, small though she is, has become the strongest military power (after Turkey) in the Middle East, and by far the most efficient. Any fear has vanished—at least for the present—that the infant Israel might be crushed or checked by the far more numerous and widespread, but less well-organized and coordinated Arabs.

A third consequence is the sharpened realization by many Jewish and non-Jewish thinkers—by all who have the welfare of the Jewish people at heart—that ultimate security for Israel can be attained only through Arab friendship, cooperation and goodwill. It has indeed been suggested that a Jewish national state—however formidable and successful—which is surrounded by implacable hostility is merely the ghetto on a more majestic scale.

One other basic factor conditions any writing on a theme like this. Because its roots are so deep in the past, the situation between Israel and her neighbours cannot fairly be judged without taking into account both legend and tradition, as well as fact, of early centuries. All are equally important. For the Fertile Crescent in its widest sense has been the seedbed of Judaism, Christianity and Islam, the three great religions of the One God, all significantly related to each other. And the passionately held beliefs and age-old aspirations inspired by these great faiths are at the very source of our conflict, however legendary in part their origins may be.

Yet in the last resort the present crisis has not been determined mainly by the goals and strivings of those small but highly gifted peoples who left their imprint on the Holy Land. In fact for centuries Palestine has been a pawn of the imperial powers, which have played, or sought to play, a decisive role in this area of enormous political and strategic importance. Zionism and Arab nationalism—and the repercussions of the one upon the other—have all been used by the powers for their own ends. These causes have been alternately supported and encouraged, or condemned, or exploited, as seemed best to suit the rivalries of those major states with the ambition and capacity to dominate all or part of the eastern Mediterranean and the Middle East; or to be required by the exigencies of the wars in which they were engaged. One example is of course Britain's promises to Arabs and Jews during World War I (even though idealism also played its part). Another is the United States' original condemnation of a Jewish state in Palestine (in the report of the King-Crane Commission despatched by President Wilson), to be followed fifty years later by almost unqualified U.S. support for Israel. A third is Russia's prompt encouragement of Israel in 1948, in contrast to her later role as defender and supplier of the Arab states when she perceived that this could lead, as it has, to a progressive strengthening of her position in the area.

It is thus these major powers rather than the smaller states and peoples immediately involved which must be held primarily responsible for what we may question or challenge today in the position and attitude of Israel or the Arab states. With greater foresight and realism the dominant countries could have prevented so dangerous and destructive a confrontation from developing as it did; and could have set things on a different course. They could have averted the present latent threat that a conflict in one small corner of western Asia might help to spark off a third world war. Even today, when Israel is relatively strong and would prefer to be left to deal with each of her Arab neighbours separately and without outside interference, this is in fact no longer a practicable course. The major powers cannot evade their ultimate responsibility. A danger to all of terrible proportions forces them to play their part in seeking to solve without disaster a situation basically of their own creation.

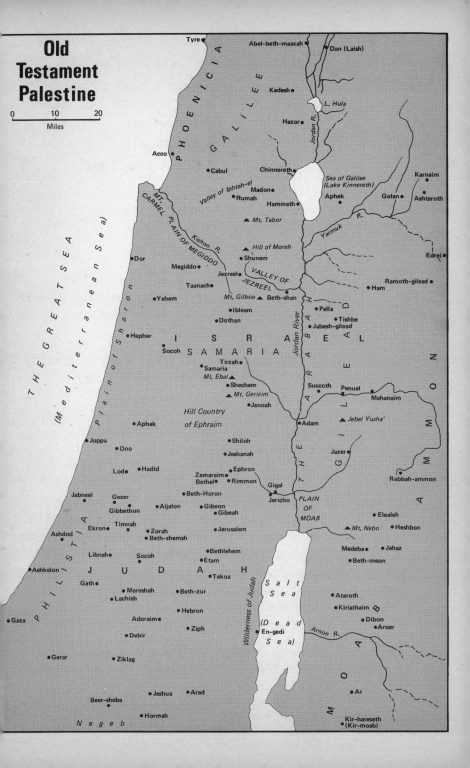

Old Testament Palestine

0   10   20
Miles

Tyre

Abel-beth-maacah

Dan (Laish)

PHOENICIA

GALILEE

Kedesh

L. Hula

Jordan R.

Hazor

Acco

Cabul

Chinnereth

Sea of Galilee
(Lake Kinnereth)

Karnaim

Valley of Iphtah-el

Madon

Rumah

Hammath

Aphek

Golan

Ashtaroth

MT. CARMEL

PLAIN OF MEGIDDO

Mt. Tabor

Yarmuk R.

Edrei

Kishon R.

Hill of Moreh

Shunem

VALLEY OF
JEZREEL

THE GREAT SEA

(Mediterranean Sea)

Dor

Megiddo

Jezreel

Ramoth-gilead

Plain of Sharon

Taanach

Mt. Gilboa

Beth-shan

Ham

Yehem

Ibleam

Pella

ARABAH

Jordan River

Dothan

Tishbe

Jabesh-gilead

Hepher

ISRAEL

GILEAD

Socoh

SAMARIA

Tirzah

Samaria

Succoth

Penuel

Mt. Ebal

Shechem

Mahanaim

Mt. Gerizim

Janoah

Hill Country

Adam

Jebel Yusha'

AMMON

of Ephraim

Aphek

Joppa

Shiloh

Jeshanah

Jazer

Ono

Lode

Hadid

Ephron

Zemaraim

Rimmon

Rabbah-ammon

Bethel

Jabneel

Gezer

Beth-Horon

Gigal

Gibbethon

Aijalon

Gibeon

Jericho

PLAIN
OF
MOAB

Ekron

Timnah

Gibeah

Ashdod

Zorah

Jerusalem

Elealeh

Beth-shemsh

Mt. Nebo

Heshbon

Libnah

Socoh

Bethlehem

Medeba

Jahaz

Ashkelon

Etam

JUDAH

Beth-meon

Gath

Tekoa

Salt
Sea

Mareshah

Beth-zur

Ataroth

Lachish

Kiriathaim

Hebron

Adoraim

Ziph

(Dead

Dibon

Aroer

Gaza

Debir

En-gedi

Sea)

Arnon R.

Gerar

Ziklag

Wilderness of Judah

MOAB

Jeshua

Arad

Ar

Beer-sheba

Kir-hareseth
(Kir-moab)

Hormah

Negeb

PHILISTIA

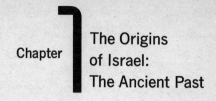

Chapter 1

The Origins of Israel: The Ancient Past

The Patriarchs

The Bible tells us that Abraham was the father of the Hebrews. Genesis suggests that he was born at Ur of the Chaldees, then capital of the Sumerian empire, in Mesopotamia or present-day Iraq. More modern scholarship believes his birthplace to have been the family's original home at Haran in northwestern Mesopotamia on the river Belikhi, a tributary of the Euphrates; and that the family returned there from Ur after the city was sacked by the Elamites around 1960 B.C.[1]

In the prevailing state of turmoil and insecurity, his father, Terah, appears to have decided to set out with his family of "Aramean nomads" for the distant land of Canaan, corresponding broadly to the Palestine of modern times. But his father died in Haran, and Abram (as he was originally named) became head of the family. We are told that he broke with the idolatrous, polytheistic beliefs of his father and turned to the service of the one God. Thereafter the Lord appeared to him in a series of visions, urging him to con-

1. Isidore Epstein, *Judaism: A Historical Presentation*, p. 11. All works cited in the footnotes without full details of publication will be found in complete form in the Bibliography.

tinue the journey and promising that his descendants should become a great nation. He would seem to have entered Canaan around 1900 (or possibly 1700) B.C. After he reached Shechem, near the modern Nablus north of Jerusalem, it was revealed to him that the land of Canaan would be theirs. Moreover, the nation he would found would bring the knowledge of God to all the world.[2]

The family lived temporarily in Egypt, to escape a famine in Canaan, and then returned north to the Negev and settled in the plain of Mamre, near what later became Hebron. Some of the revelations Abram subsequently experienced have been described as a Divine Covenant, the significance of which was both national and universal. For the new nation he was to found had been chosen by God for the sake, not of domination, but of universal service. While the rite of circumcision ordained as part of this covenant was a national mark of consecration to the service of God, it provided for the inclusion of all strangers who were willing to join the Abramic nation in this service. It was at this point that Abram's name was changed to Abraham, meaning literally "father of a multitude (of nations)." All the families of the earth were to be blessed in him and in his seed.[3] These revelations predicted that Abraham's off-

---

2. *Ibid.*, pp. 11–13. See also Cecil Roth and Geoffrey Wigoder, eds., *The New Standard Jewish Encyclopedia.* The chronology of the Old Testament is vastly complicated in terms of our modern reckoning, and there are wide divergencies in the dates assigned by different authorities to certain key events. The whole problem is carefully studied in Jack Finegan's *Handbook of Biblical Chronology* (Princeton, N.J.: Princeton University Press, 1964). Thus, Epstein's date for the destruction of Ur and the return of Abram's family to Haran is generally in accord with the date mentioned by Finegan (p. 193) for Abraham's entry into Canaan as being that indicated by the figures in the Hebrew text of the Bible record. On the other hand Finegan concedes that, according to the figures in the (Greek) Septuagint (see below), this event would have occurred nearly two hundred years later, around 1700 B.C. And this latter date would accord generally with the chronology given in Zev Vilnay's scholarly *Guide to Israel,* pp. 41–45. Vilnay's dates in any case show the contemporary Israeli view of what is probably correct, and they have been generally followed in the chronology at the end of this book for most of the later events in the Old Testament story.

3. Epstein, p. 14.

spring would suffer captivity for four hundred years "in a strange land," but would subsequently be given not just Canaan but also the "land from the River of Egypt [i.e., the Nile] to . . . the river Euphrates" belonging to various other tribes.[4]

For some Jews who have set themselves nationalistic rather than universal goals, this last prediction has seemed to justify territorial ambitions far transcending Palestine. In the days of modern Israel's strength it has been an understandable source of anxiety to their neighbours. Fortunately this interpretation has by no means gained general acceptance, being as it is somewhat strangely at variance with those other sacred precepts condemning "domination." We also have a glimpse of Abraham meeting Melchizedek, king of Jerusalem, and being blessed by this high priest of the pre-Judaic religion at the time being practiced there.[5]

According to tradition, two events now mark the close parentage of the two main branches of the Semitic race and carry the seed of their future dissensions. Abraham had grown old, and his wife Sarah had born him no children. So she gave him, the Bible tells us, her Egyptian servant Hagar as wife, and Hagar bore him a son, Ishmael, who has come to be identified with the Arab peoples. But eventually by God's providence Sarah too bore a son, Isaac. When Isaac was weaned, Sarah saw Ishmael laughing at him. She then urged Abraham to drive out Ishmael and his mother because she would not have the slave girl's son sharing the inheritance with hers. Though Abraham was "vexed," God comforted him, saying that he would make a great nation of Ishmael's descendants as well, because he was Abraham's child.

Hagar was then banished to wander in the wilderness of Beersheba. When she feared that the child would die from lack of water, God created a miraculous well from which they drank, and repeated the promise of a great destiny for Ishmael's descendants.

4. Genesis 15:18–21 (*New English Bible*). See also *Jewish Encyclopedia*, p. 84.
5. Teddy Kollek and Moshe Pearlman, *Jerusalem, Sacred City of Mankind*, p. 17.

When he grew up "he became an archer, and his mother found him a wife from Egypt."[6] One of the ceremonies of the Muslim pilgrimage to Mecca today commemorates Hagar's desperate search for water in the wilderness. Furthermore, the Prophet Muhammad "claimed Abraham and Ishmael as the founders of Arab monotheism pure and undefiled, and thus independent of, and prior to, both Judaism and Christianity.[7]"

Thus Isaac, who in his turn became the father of the Jews, was the half-brother of the banished Ishmael, invoked by the Arabs as their ancestor and founder of what they believe to be the true religion of the one God originating with Abraham. But, for the Jews, Isaac was Abraham's only legitimate successor, having been established and acknowledged as such by the Patriarch and being the child of Abraham's original wife. We are told also that God tested Abraham's faith by commanding him to sacrifice Isaac. When he had shown his readiness to obey, Isaac was spared, a ram was sacrificed in his place, and the Lord once more proclaimed the glorious future that lay before the family of Abraham.[8]

Abraham died near Hebron, which has been specially sacred to Jewish people ever since. Before his death he was concerned to preserve the family links and racial purity of his stock. He would not hear of Isaac's taking a wife from the women of the Canaanites, the earlier inhabitants of Palestine, one branch of whom, the Phoenicians, were the ancestors of the modern Lebanese. Instead, he sent his servant to his family in Mesopotamia to find a wife, and the servant brought back Rebecca, Abraham's great-niece. She married Isaac and became the mother of twins, one of whom, Esau, was persuaded by the other, Jacob, rashly to renounce his birth-

6. Genesis 21:8–21 (NEB). For a careful analysis of this tradition of close relations between those who later became identified as Jews and Arabs, see S. D. Goitein, *Jews and Arabs: Their Contacts Through the Ages*, pp. 3–32. This regards as a "pseudo-scientific myth" the notion of a Semitic "race," but explains the real affinities—and differences—between the ancestors of the Jews and those of the Arabs.

7. Alfred Guillaume, *Islam*, p. 44.

8. Genesis 22:1–19 (NEB).

right.[9] But despite Abraham's concern this ethnic aloofness of the family from the Canaanites of Palestine was not destined to endure.

It was to Jacob that the name *Israel*, meaning "champion of God," was first given. This happened after he had undergone a mysterious experience of wrestling with an angel. Jacob had twelve sons, and they became the fathers of the Twelve Tribes of Israel, ten of whom were destined to disappear through assimilation and other causes, leaving only those of Judah and Benjamin. One of Jacob's younger sons, Joseph, became a slave in Egypt, yet rose there to high court rank under a dynasty allegedly related to the Hebrews. His family joined him and greatly multiplied; but when this friendly dynasty was expelled by a hostile one, they were all reduced to slavery. In the fifteenth century B.C. the new dynasty conquered most of the Fertile Crescent and, when Syria and Palestine revolted, the Israelites in Egypt were ruthlessly oppressed. They were saved by Moses, whom they came to regard as their national liberator and whose later pronouncements, as tradition has recorded them, became the laws by which all good Jews are still supposed to regulate their lives.

The Exodus

Moses was not himself a slave, being the adopted son of an Egyptian princess. But we are told that he stood up for his unhappy countrymen despite his fortunate position. He was then forced to flee to Midian, where he became a shepherd. On Mount Horeb he saw a flaming bush which the fire somehow did not consume, and heard God ordering him back to Egypt. He was to bring his people out of bondage and lead them to Canaan, the land they had been promised.[10] On his return, Moses was able to convince the

9. Genesis 24 and 25:24–34 (NEB), and *Jewish Encyclopedia*, pp. 84–85.
10. Epstein, pp. 15–16. Midian lay east of the Gulf of Aqaba in present-day Saudi Arabia, and some authorities consider that Horeb may be identifiable with the Arabic place name El Khrob near ancient Madian in the southwest corner of this area, not far from the Strait of Tiran. It is, however, more usual to identify it with Mount Sinai in the Sinai Peninsula between the gulfs

Israelites that it was indeed God who had given these orders, the same God who had made himself known to their patriarchs, Abraham, Isaac, and Jacob. The ruling Pharaoh opposed, we are told, the departure of the Israelites until a series of calamities, attributed by believers to divine intervention, "broke down his hardness of heart and obduracy."[11] It may have been around 1350 B.C. that the Israelites were able to leave Egypt with many non-Jews from the slave camps. These earliest refugees seem to have been led by Moses to Suez where they crossed the Red Sea. The ensuing ruler of Egypt may have regretted any concessions made to the Israelites, since they were pursued by Egyptian forces. But the pursuers suffered yet another calamity, when drowned near Suez through some miraculous or natural phenomenon.[12] It is significant that nearly three and one-half thousand years later the forces of Israel should have managed to prevail over those of Egypt in just this area. Nothing could mark more vividly the tragic length of the strife between the associates and descendants of Ishmael and those of Isaac.

The Exodus is the dramatic if highly confusing story of the wanderings of the tribes of Israel and their fellow refugees in the semi-desert regions between Egypt and Palestine until, after crossing the Jordan from the east, they reached the land of Canaan and assaulted Jericho. Again, thirty centuries later the name *Exodus* was to be applied, in a work of fiction strongly condemnatory of British rule, depicting the plight of Jews seeking to enter Palestine from Central Europe after World War II. In any event the central factor in the story of the original Exodus is, in the words of a distinguished Jewish scholar recently deceased, "the revelation . . .

---

of Suez and Aqaba, the Arabic name for which is Jebel Musa (Mountain of Moses); and this region, nearer to Egypt, may have been the true area of Moses' initial wanderings. The Old Testament is ambiguous on the point. For these two conflicting views see, e.g., Emil G. Kraeling: *Rand McNally Bible Atlas*, and G. E. Wright and V. F. Filson, *Westminster Historical Atlas to the Bible* (rev. ed.). Mount Sinai is also the site to which is attributed Moses' Covenant with God during the Exodus.

11. Epstein, p. 16.
12. *Ibid.*, p. 17.

made . . . to Moses on God's sacred mountain and transmitted by him to the Children of Israel and through them to all mankind."[13]

It is also usual to regard these revelations to Moses upon Mount Sinai as a further Covenant with God, one that stressed and sanctified the special destiny of the Jewish people. This is strikingly emphasized in Deuteronomy, which later recapitulated the laws of Moses. One passage there addressed to Israel is particularly significant. "For thou art a holy people unto the Lord thy God and the Lord hath chosen thee to be a peculiar people unto himself above all the nations that are upon the earth"; or, in an alternative translation, "You are a people holy to the Lord your God and the Lord has chosen you out of all peoples on earth to be his special possession."[14] With the unquestioning traditional faith bred in successive generations by these age-old assurances of divine election presented to them as dogma defined and edited by their religious authorities, it was almost inevitable that the Jewish people, even in modern times when many have abandoned religious orthodoxy or even observance, should have developed an intimate instinct of superiority over the non-Jewish world. However keen one's sense of all that the world has owed to the Jews, this is a constant factor in the problem considered in this book and one with which it is imperative to reckon.

At the time of the Exodus there seems to have been something of a power vacuum in Sinai as well as in the Negev, which stretches in a great wedge from around Gaza and Beersheba to the head of the Gulf of Aqaba. This vacuum was due to movements of expansion and withdrawal of the more developed peoples, including the Egyptians, concentrated along the coastal road between the Nile

13. Nelson Glueck, late President of the Hebrew Union College, Cincinnati, *Rivers in the Desert; A History of the Negev*, p. 65.
14. Deuteronomy 14:2 (Authorized Version and NEB). It must be borne in mind that very few manuscripts of the books of the Old Testament survived the destruction of Jerusalem in A.D. 70. Thereafter the Jewish religious leaders set about defining the canon—i.e., the laws of their faith—and finally standardizing the text. This "resulted in the production of an eclectic text based on arbitrary rather than scientific principles." See Introduction to NEB, p. xi.

Delta and Gaza. Thus the Israelites were able to wander at will throughout the area, camping where there were good springs as at Kadesh-barnea, the modern Ain Qudeish, some forty-five miles south-southwest of Beersheba.

Nearby, to the north, the border area of the hills of Canaan, with a fertile soil and fairly abundant water, was then intensely cultivated. A direct route, with wells and available grazing, led northward from Kadesh-barnea into Canaan. But all the scouts sent out to reconnoitre except Joshua and Caleb advised against an attack in this area—the Canaanites and their allies were too strong—and this stirred up something of a rebellion against Moses. Nevertheless, the Israelites attacked, and were badly mauled.[15] They had to withdraw eastward through Edom and Moab (southeast and east of the Dead Sea) into what is now Jordan. There they managed to defeat the local tribes and to establish themselves securely before again attempting to break through into Canaan. And it was at Mount Nebo in Moab, only some eighteen miles southeast of Jericho, that Moses died. According to tradition the wanderings of the people he had led from Egypt had lasted forty years. They were literally within sight of the land which they were told God had promised them, but Moses was fated never to enter it himself.

The Conquest of Canaan

By now, of course, the Egyptian Empire, which had stretched to the Fertile Crescent, was beginning to decline, and Canaan was in turmoil, with several of its vassal kings in treacherous communication with outside invaders. This was the chance for Israelites hardened in adversity. Under Joshua's command they captured Jericho and occupied in succession south-central, southern, and finally northern Palestine,[16] the wholesale massacre of the local populations being zestfully recounted in the Book of Joshua.

Not all were killed, however. There was anarchy after Joshua's

15. Glueck, pp. 109, 112–14.
16. Epstein, pp. 32–33.

death, and the Israelites, weakened by this, resorted, as we are told, to "peaceful penetration" of the new land. There was some acculturation in a settled and more sophisticated society, and probably some intermarriage even at this early stage. Concessions to the local religions led certain chieftains, the Judges, to fight against this trend.[17] But even while the Israelites under Joshua were conquering the hill country of Canaan, the Philistines, a sea people apparently from Crete and Asia Minor, were entrenching themselves in the coastal regions. They had a fairly high material culture and were the first in the area to use iron weapons—which gave them a distinct advantage.[18] They remained an important element in the country, and it was after them that Palestine (Land of the Philistines, or, in Arabic, *Falastin*) was named.

In the time of Samuel, last of the Judges, the Philistines defeated the Israelites, invaded the highlands, and captured the Ark of the Covenant, which contained "the two tablets of stone which Moses had deposited there . . . , the tablets of the covenant which the LORD made with the Israelites when they left Egypt."[19] This disaster stressed the need for centralizing authority, and Samuel was eventually persuaded that Israel needed a king, though one with strictly limited powers. Around 1025 B.C. the choice fell upon Saul, and he freed the Israelites temporarily from the Philistines but was eventually killed in battle after Samuel, dissatisfied with some of his actions, had anointed David in his stead. According to Biblical scholars, two hundred fifty years had elapsed between Joshua and David.[20]

David and Solomon

It was David who first effectively unified the tribes of Israel and proclaimed Jerusalem to be their capital; and it was here that his

17. Epstein, pp. 33–34.
18. Kollek, p. 22.
19. Kings 8:9 (NEB).
20. Kollek, p. 22.

son Solomon built the first Temple, in the inner shrine of which the Ark of the Covenant was preserved. Thenceforward, Jerusalem was poetically known to Jewish people as Zion or the City of David. David also shattered the power of the Philistines.[21] Jerusalem had been a hostile fortress between the two portions of the Israelite kingdom. It was also near the head of one of the passes leading up from Philistine territory. Its capture was thus necessary to secure the independence of the Israelites from the Philistines and to unify their northern and southern tribes.

"David ruled an increasingly vigorous kingdom, perhaps the most powerful state . . . between the temporarily weakened rival empires, the Egyptians in the south and . . . the Babylonians in the north. Subduing the Philistines gave him complete control of the Mediterranean coastal plain. Capture of Damascus brought his dominions up to the Euphrates. Conquest of the eastern and southern territories gave him an outlet to the Red Sea, through the Gulf of Aqaba. His son . . . Solomon was to reap the full benefits of these military and political achievements." There is special significance in this account by Jerusalem's present Mayor. It depicts in traditionally exalted terms one of the supreme, if transient, moments in the story of Israel, and one that has inspired Jewish people ever since. He adds, "Jerusalem was now not only the political and military capital of the country. It became, and was to remain for all time, the religious centre of the nation."[22] A similar note is struck by Dr. Glueck: ". . . a nation had been hammered out on the anvil of war . . . its dream of becoming its own master in the Promised Land fulfilled. The forms of this reality would be altered . . . but the phenomenon of Israel's being rooted in the Holy Land would remain unchangeable. Israelites might henceforth be dispersed and the kingdoms of Israel and Judah disappear, but Israel itself would remain. A new entity had been fashioned whose faith in God made it resistant to the attrition of time."[23]

21. Kollek, pp. 11, 27.
22. *Ibid.*, p. 34.
23. Glueck, p. 148.

Solomon's reign of forty years is regarded as a golden age in Jewish history. And yet "Israel shone in Solomon's glory at the expense of having foisted upon it a despotic Oriental monarchy. The evil he did lived after him. Much of the good perished with his passing."[24] From all accounts he was a wise and skilful statesman with a keen eye for economic opportunity. He opened up the Negev, the key to Egypt and Arabia. He built the port of Ezion-geber at the head of the Gulf of Aqaba, with a smelter to exploit the copper resources of the Wadi Arabah running down from the Dead Sea to the Gulf. And from that port he traded with Arabia, India, and Africa. At the same time, he was on close and friendly terms with most neighbouring peoples including the Egyptians—having married a daughter of the reigning Pharaoh—and the Phoenicians (of modern Lebanon), who specialized in trading with the Mediterranean and the countries of Western Europe. Indeed, the Phoenician king provided much of the material to build the Temple. Having long been harsh, semi-nomadic tribesmen, the people of Israel had become part of the sophisticated Oriental world surrounding them, and many were to lose in the process the uncompromising faith inherited from Moses, and even their Israelite identity.

Solomon himself was not immune. The Bible blames this on his love of women, especially foreign ones. "When he grew old, his wives turned his heart to follow other gods." Therefore, we are told, the God of Israel decided to punish him by tearing the kingdom away from his son, leaving him only two tribes "for the sake of . . . David and . . . Jerusalem."[25] A commentary on these passages ascribes the ensuing disruption more simply to the deep dissatisfaction caused by Solomon's "attempts to reduce the free yeomen of Israel to the status of subjects of an Oriental king."[26] In any event, a rebellion against Solomon was launched by Jeroboam of the tribe of Ephraim, and the rebel was compelled to flee to Egypt. After Sol-

24. *Ibid.*, pp. 149–52. The dates of his reign are here given as 960–22 B.C. Epstein, p. 36, gives them as 971–31.
25. Kings 11:1–13.
26. J. R. Dummelow, ed., *Commentary on the Holy Bible*, p. xx.

omon's death Jeroboam established for himself the separate kingdom of Israel in northern and central Palestine, with ten of the
original twelve tribes. Only the tribes of Judah and Benjamin remained loyal to the house of David, and from then onward these
two constituted the kingdom of Judah.

Separation and Ruin of Israel

Jeroboam and his successors detached Israel from the south not
only politically but also in matters of religion. Pilgrimages to Jerusalem were forbidden, a fresh priesthood was created, heathen practices crept in. Deprived as they were of the unifying force that had
radiated from the City of David, anarchy broke out among the
tribes, but this was checked temporarily by King Omri and his son
Ahab in the ninth century B.C. Under the influence of Ahab's Phoenician wife Jezebel, however, the worship of Baal was restored. The
prophet Elijah fought vigorously to destroy this heathen revival,
and, further, foretold disaster for both king and queen as penalty for
the judicial murder of a subject whose property they had seized—
thereby affirming that the God of Israel was a God of righteousness
whose demands stood above everything, even above the interests of
the state. Finally, by instructing his disciple Elisha to countenance
the punishment of Israel by a non-Israelite, he upheld the doctrine
that the God of Israel was also the God of all nations.[27] Afterwards,
with the help of Jehu, a rebellious army leader whom Elisha had
made king of Israel, there was a massacre of Baal worshippers and
of all the house of Ahab including his heathen wife; but the religion of the northern kingdom remained tainted with heathenism
and its society with immoral practices.

The Judean prophet Amos visited Israel with solemn warnings.
God, he said, had no greater regard for the Israelites than for other
nations. He was not the God of Israel only. He was a universal God
of universal morality, and his special relation to Israel demanded
that they should make the divine standards their own. A far greater

27. Epstein, pp. 40–41.

calamity was in store for them if they did not reform. The warning was ignored; and Israel was conquered and eventually submerged by successive invasions of the Assyrians. Samaria was left to Israel for a time; then in 721 B.C. that too was overrun, and its population deported and replaced by foreigners. These "absorbed the last remnants of the Israelites to form a semi-idolatrous people known as the Samaritans," who survive today in and around the modern Nablus. The ten tribes disappeared from history with the northern kingdom that had borne the name of Israel. Thereafter the term *Israel* was used for all descendants of Abraham through Isaac wherever they might be.[28] The fate of this first state of Israel was one of the tragic setbacks that have so often recurred in the history of the Jewish people even after some of their most dramatic successes. The fate of Judah was for a time a happier one; then it too was overtaken by disaster.

Judah and the Babylonian Captivity

Idolatrous practices, particularly those of Baal and Moloch, had taken hold in Judah also. Shortly before its fall, Israel was threatened by the northern kingdom as well as by the Syrians and later the Assyrians. Here the warning voice was that of the prophet Isaiah, who helped King Hezekiah to purify religion and inspired him and his people to repel a siege of Jerusalem by the Assyrian king, Sennacherib, around 701.[29] Hezekiah's great-grandson Josiah, who died in 609, practically put an end to state idolatry. National worship was centralized in Jerusalem, which became "the shrine of the one great system of ethical and intellectual monotheism in the ancient world."[30] His inspiration had been the prophet Jeremiah. But their achievement could not avert the catastrophe that lay ahead. For shortly before Josiah died, the Assyrian empire came to

28. *Ibid.*, pp. 41–45.
29. Kollek, p. 65.
30. *Ibid.*, p. 68.

an end; and some years later Judah was crushed between the con-
tenders for the succession—Egypt, and a revived Babylonian empire
in Mesopotamia. Babylon eventually won, and by 603 had made
Judah a vassal state.

Around 588 the proud and turbulent Israelites rebelled, as they
were to do again with even more fatal results six hundred years
later. This time the invaders triumphed over beseiged Jerusalem.
The king of Judah, blinded, was carried off in chains, and with him
Jeremiah, fiercely and accurately predicting the downfall of Babylon. By Nebuchadnezzar's orders Jerusalem and its Temple were
destroyed and its people deported to Babylon. Psalm 137 records
the lamentations of the Israelites "by the waters of Babylon," their
nostalgia for Jerusalem, and their dreams of killing the children of
their enemies.

In less than fifty years Jeremiah's prophecy was fulfilled. By 538
the Babylonian Empire with Judah had been conquered by the
Persians under the enlightened Cyrus. All Jews in Babylon who so
desired were authorized to return to Judah and rebuild their Temple—with financial help from him—and he restored the many
sacred objects looted by the Babylonians. A dedicated group returned, but many remained in Babylon and later in Persia, as they
did in Egypt, where many Judeans had also found refuge. Without
a temple and without a country, the Jews in these lands developed
a vigorous religious life. "They turned more and more to the Torah
and their other sacred writings, and around these spiritual possessions they built a new polity . . . founded upon piety and learning, religion and study." Thus did they "make the divine standards
their own," as the prophets had commanded, and demonstrated
that their God was indeed the God of all the world.

The Babylonians and the Persians saw the value of allowing the
Jews to practice their religion and develop their institutions and
gave them opportunities for material advancement. Many attained
wealth and influence; and Daniel, like Joseph in Egypt, became a
great figure at court. In the Persian Empire they were prominent in

business and even politics.[31] The uprooting from Judea in 587 B.C. can indeed be reckoned as the first phase of the Jewish dispersal (or *diaspora*, in the more familiar Greek), rather than (as is commonly assumed) the sequel to the Roman destruction of Judah after A.D. 70. A Jewish presence was gradually to become a significant factor in nearly all the countries of the globe, but especially in the West. Despite the jealousies inevitably aroused by their superior gifts and intensity of achievement, these dispersed Jewish elements were to be a dynamic, creative force in the development of our modern civilization.

Judah Restored. From Persian Dominance to the Greeks

By a strange paradox of history, the devastated country of Judah to which the exiles returned, to the northwest of the Dead Sea, covered much of the area of Palestine remaining to the Arabs after the war of 1948. By 515 B.C. this Judean nucleus had rebuilt the Temple, and soon a second group from Babylon returned. But the next seventy years are historically obscure. Then, around 445, Nehemiah, a high Jewish official at the Persian court, was appointed Governor of Judah. He pushed forward the rebuilding of the city, revived morale, and strengthened administration. But it was the scribe Ezra, also from the Jewish community in Persia, who revitalized religion and strictly redefined its rules, bringing with him priests and Levites for this purpose. "Through Ezra, the Torah became the accepted constitution of the Jewish community. Henceforth . . . whether in Jerusalem or the Diaspora . . . they would preserve their own special identity; . . . Jerusalem . . . through . . . Ezra . . . became the spiritual capital of Jews in their dispersion."[32]

Little more than a hundred years after Nehemiah and Ezra

31. Epstein, p. 83. The Torah is the "teaching" or the Law, including the Ten Commandments, as recorded in the Pentateuch, i.e., the first five books of the Old Testament traditionally ascribed to Moses.
32. Kollek, p. 77.

(years that are, again, obscure), in 322 B.C. the Persian Empire was subjugated in its turn. Its conqueror was a European, the first European imperialist to intervene in the Middle East on any major scale: the Macedonian Alexander the Great. Having absorbed Greece, Alexander set the stamp of later Greek culture, art, and architecture known as Hellenism on this and other areas of the Orient. After Alexander, two Greek dynasties dominated the Middle East: the Seleucids in the Fertile Crescent, Persia, and beyond, and the Ptolemies in Egypt. A later Ptolemy ruler was the famous Queen Cleopatra, heroine of one of Shakespeare's most vivid plays. She captivated Julius Caesar and Mark Anthony in turn, and died by her own hand after Anthony's defeat by the future Augustus, founder of the Roman Empire.

Judea and the Jews in the Hellenistic World

During this new Greek age Palestine was first under the Ptolemies and then under the Seleucids, but for much of the time was contested between the two. Hellenistic culture became a mixture of Greek and Oriental elements, and gradually Greek-speaking Orientals assumed a leading role in the Seleucid and Ptolemaic empires.[33] Inevitably the many Jews in Egypt, especially in Alexandria, were attracted by Greek culture. "Under the first three Ptolemies the Jews were contented and prosperous, and extended their settlements in Egypt where they were freely permitted to build synagogues and practice their religious rites. The result was to bring them into closer touch and sympathy with Hellenism; [though they] kept in communication with Jerusalem and occasionally resorted to it for the great feasts, they could hardly avoid transmitting Greek tendencies and influences to their own people. To this period belongs the Septuagint version of the Holy Scriptures, the Pentateuch having first been translated into Greek by Egyptian

33. J. W. Swain, *The Ancient World*, I, 548–49.

Jews"[34] (apparently around 280 B.C.). The Greek version of the Old Testament was the oldest in any foreign tongue. It carried the meaning of Judaism to the outside world, attracting many converts.

In the turmoil created by the fight for Palestine, the corporate life evolved by the Jews under their scribes inevitably suffered. As the country eventually settled down under the Seleucids, a religious governing body was established known as the Sanhedrin. "Unfortunately the Hellenism that reached Palestine . . . was not [that] of classical Greece. It was a debased kind . . . , decadent, wily, voluptuous . . . [with] devastating effects. . . . The biblical ordinances were disregarded, the Sabbath . . . desecrated. . . . , circumcision neglected." Incited by a megalomaniac ruler, renegade Jews tried to Hellenize Judea by force. An aged priest of the Hasmonean family organized an insurrection. One of the priest's sons, Judas, called Maccabeus ("the Hammerer"), recovered the Temple, which he cleansed and reconsecrated in 165 B.C. In 143 Judas's brother Simon secured the independence of Judea and was elected its first High Priest and civil ruler.[35]

The strong nationalism of the Maccabees had triumphed in an age when the world trend was toward unification through imperialist expansion. The Greeks had attempted this and the Romans were to succeed. Influenced by this and other, deeper trends, some Jews seem to have dreamed of a kind of world domination based on religion, of a day when all men would accept their God as the one true God and worship him at Jerusalem. This is indeed suggested in Isaiah, though in a passage apparently of this later age. When Christianity emerged, its devotees were men influenced by this trend toward universality in Jewish thinking.[36]

---

34. Dummelow, p. xlix. It is significant that all three key words of Jewish religion here quoted are Greek. Thus *Synagogue* = place of bringing together; *Pentateuch* = the first five books (originally *implements*) of the Old Testament; and *Septuagint* = the Greek version of the Old Testament allegedly carried out by about seventy translators sent from Jerusalem to Alexandria at the request of the ruler of Egypt.

35. Epstein, pp. 89–93.

36. See Swain, II, 205–7.

The Second Jewish Commonwealth

Judea expanded under Simon's son. Samaria and Edom were reconquered and their people forced to conform to Judaism. Under the later Hasmonean high priests and kings of this second Jewish Commonwealth much of the territory once ruled by Solomon was temporarily recovered. But all this military achievement brought to a head an ever latent conflict in the Jewish world between "nationalists" and "universalists." It has indeed recurred in our day with the military triumphs of a resurgent Israel. In those earlier centuries the wealthier, upper-class Sadducees, both priests and laymen, who had absorbed many foreign ideas, were the main supporters of the nationalist trend. From their standpoint, political expediency and economic interest must be the final criterion of state policy. God was to them essentially the God of Israel only. On the other hand, the Pharisees, the spiritual heirs of the pious and orthodox *Hasidim*, believed that, in strict conformity with the *Torah*, God was a universal God, the God of all mankind. The Hasmonean rulers wavered in their support first of one side, then the other. Queen Salome Alexandra, whose reign was one of the happiest of this stormy era, supported the Pharisees. But after her death in 67 B.C. her younger son, Aristobulus II, backed by the Sadducees, supplanted his elder brother, Hyrcanus II, who thereupon turned for counsel to a wily statesman with ambitions of his own. This was Antipater, an Edomite of Arab strain who had become a Jew by religion.[37] He keenly perceived the rising power of Rome, to which both sides appealed.

Judea under Rome: Herod the Great

Inevitably Judea fell under Roman sway after 63 B.C. Antipater had been Rome's man. His former master, Hyrcanus, became his puppet after Julius Caesar made Antipater Procurator of Judea, and

37. Stewart Perowne: *The Life and Times of Herod the Great*, p. 25.

Antipater set up Herod, one of his sons, as Governor of Galilee. But a Parthian invasion placed the rival branch of the Hasmoneans on the Judean throne. The Roman Senate was then induced to make Herod King of Judea, and, with the help of Roman troops, the Hasmonean dynasty was extinguished in 37 B.C.[38] The new king, a ruthless despot who reigned for thirty-three years and took many lives, has come down to us as Herod the Great. Though despised by the Jews as an outsider, he was steadfastly loyal to Rome, whose troops protected him. Kollek has described him as "a most efficient administrator and a brilliant organizer, with a remarkable talent and passion for building." He fortified Masada on a remote peak near the Dead Sea as a refuge from his subjects. He built Caesarea on the coast so well that the Romans later made it their capital. Finally, he rebuilt the Temple and carried out other huge projects in Jerusalem. He may well have wished "to curry favor with his sullen subjects . . . and glorify his name by the physical association of his works with the great city." The rebuilding of the Temple continued long after his death, and was finished only a few years before A.D. 70, when the whole edifice went up in flames, never to be replaced. Little though the Jews loved him, they freely acknowledged the Temple to have been a thing of surpassing beauty.[39]

When Herod died, there was a Jewish rebellion, and ten years later the Romans removed his son from office. Thenceforward (with one short break) the Roman procurators ruled Judea directly as a province of their empire. One of them, Pontius Pilate, who served from 26 to 46, might be unknown to history had he not "ordered the Crucifixion of a Galilean Jewish preacher, Jesus of Nazareth, little dreaming of the effect upon mankind his action was to have." This was, it seems, during the Passover Festival at Jerusalem in A.D. 33.[40]

38. Epstein, pp. 95–99.
39. Kollek, pp. 97–106.
40. Kollek, p. 111.

Chapter **2** Judaism and Christianity:
The Early Centuries

Downfall of the Jewish State

Christians have inevitably exalted the contemporary impact of
Jesus' death. It is equally natural that non-Christians should contest
such a view, perhaps with justice. "At the time, a time of tension
and conflict and rebellion against imperialist Rome, the death of
Jesus caused scarcely a ripple in Jerusalem." Gradually, it seems, the
sites traditionally associated with Jesus' life acquired a special sanctity, but scarcely before the Roman Empire had become Christian
some three hundred years after His death. Only then did Jerusalem,
so long a centre of pilgrimage for the Jews, become one for the
Christians as well.[1]

Long before the Crucifixion, Herod the Great had died. In his
own interest he had been staunchly loyal to Rome. Once he was
removed, in 4 B.C., Roman rule in Judea was beset with troubles.
The Jews were rebellious on many grounds, political, national, cultural, economic, and religious. They were also deeply divided among
themselves, and some of the Roman procurators after Pilate were
rashly provocative toward them. The well-established Sadducees,

1. Kollek, pp. 117 and 120.

and many of the Pharisee scholars, were disposed to accept Roman imperialism. But there were activists who appealed to the Maccabee tradition, and Zealot extremists who in A.D. 66 captured the fortress at Masada near the Dead Sea, and eventually Jerusalem itself. After Roman troops sent to raise the siege had suffered a humiliating defeat, the future Emperor Vespasian committed fresh forces, leaving the final assault to his son Titus. When Jerusalem fell, the Temple and most of the city were destroyed.[2] Many Jews were executed. Thousands more were carried off to Rome, some as slaves, some to be victims in gladiatorial games. Numbers of the slaves were later able to buy their freedom and increase the Jewish colony in Rome. Masada held out longer than Jerusalem. Finally, faced with a Roman victory, the Zealot defenders chose collective suicide. The revolt had lasted five years. Strangely enough, its desperate heroism seems to have evoked little sympathy among the Jews outside Palestine, who were already far more numerous than those in Judea. So long as these communities did not rebel, they were able to retain their many privileges.[3]

As a sequel to the revolt, many Jews were dispersed, voluntarily or involuntarily. But, as we saw, this tragedy was by no means the start of the diaspora, though this has often been assumed. The Jews had lost their kingdom. Henceforth they were severely restricted from visiting the site of the Temple in what had been their capital. As a further humiliation, the tax all Jews paid for the maintenance of the Temple continued to be enforced by Rome as the *fiscus judaicus* to support the idolatrous cults of the empire. New Jewish communities sprang up in Europe, among them a notable one at Cologne growing out of the transfer from Palestine to the Rhine Valley of a Roman Legion, which took with it many enslaved Jews.[4]

2. "The site of the Temple, after lying desolate for more than 500 years, was cleansed and restored to the worship of the One God by the Children of Ishmael, the race from which Herod himself had sprung." Perowne, p. 161.
3. Swain, II, 452.
4. Frederick M. Schweitzer, *A History of the Jews Since the First Century A.D.*, p. 35.

Many also left Palestine on their own initiative to escape the new despotism of Rome. But Jewish communities surviving in Palestine evolved a new spiritual life that was to preserve Judaism as a living force throughout the world. The saviours of Judaism were the Pharisees. These have acquired for Christians a quite undeserved reputation for hypocrisy and sanctimoniousness,[5] when in fact they were the democratic and liberal element in Jewish religious leadership.

The Transformation of Judaism

"Of all the parties and sects that existed at the time of the Destruction, . . . the only one to survive the national cataclysm was the Pharisees. All the other parties failed their people in . . . dire need. . . . In Judaism, as the Pharisees conceived it, the loss of political autonomy and the destruction of the Temple broke no essential links. They had developed . . . the synagogue with its elaborate liturgy which could now take the place of the Temple for prayer and worship."[6] One of their greatest figures, Hillel the elder, came to Palestine from Babylonia in about 30 B.C. Another was Rabbi Jochanan ben Zakkai, a leader in the reconstruction of Jewish life when the Temple was no more. Escaping from Jerusalem during the siege, he seems to have secured from Vespasian permission to open a religious and cultural centre for the Jews at Jamnia (now Yavne) in the coastal plain some ten miles south of Jaffa, with those sacred texts that could be saved. He and his followers did not want spiritual progress to be subject to geographical limitations. The Jews still had the Torah, which was to become their rallying force. The academy at Yavne was a spiritual and scholarly centre designed to reinforce the national bonds now that those of the fatherland had been lost. There a new Sanhedrin was set up to take the place of the former Jerusalem Sanhedrin as the central reli-

5. *Ibid.*, p. 32.
6. Epstein, p. 112.

gious authority, with jurisdiction recognized by Jews in Palestine and outside.[7]

Rabbi Jochanan was a scholar, not a priest of the Temple. The priesthood had been open only to the hereditary aristocracy. The rabbinate admitted anyone of the requisite intellectual attainments. This new orientation of Judaism meant that in future the rabbi-scholar who "prayed through study"—and not the priest—became the leader and hero of the Jewish people. It meant also that the synagogue became far more than just a place of worship: it was now the hub of the local Jewish community, the communal assembly hall, club house, local court, and centre for charity.[8] The new course helped to stress the universal mission of world Jewry, and even gave implied encouragement to conversion. In a session of the Sanhedrin at Jamnia, Judaism declared officially that the "seed of Abraham" does not depend on blood and soil, but that Israel transcends all bounds of racialism and nationalism and that whoever is hungry for the bread of life may come and eat, regardless of his ancestry's treatment of the Jews.[9] Gamaliel, Rabbi Jochanan's successor at Yavne, was a descendant of Hillel. He was declared Patriarch, an office eventually recognized by Rome as being hereditary in Hillel's house. Of all the patriarchs who represented the Jewish community in dealings with the Roman government perhaps the greatest was Judah Hanasi.[10]

The Talmud

Rabbinic Judaism, originating in the teachings of the Pharisees, is also called Talmudic Judaism. The Talmud (or Study), as it developed between about 200 B.C. and A.D. 500, is mainly an explanation of, and commentary upon, the Torah (or Teaching), the

7. *Ibid.*, p. 113.
8. Schweitzer, p. 45.
9. Rabbi J. S. Raisin, *Gentile Reactions to Jewish Ideals, With Special Reference to Proselytes*, pp. 221–22.
10. Schweitzer, p. 46.

sacred Scripture setting forth the laws of conduct for all Jews, and concerns in particular the Pentateuch, the first five books of the Old Testament traditionally ascribed to Moses. The first body of Talmudic writing was the *Midrash* (or Sermon). Then in the four hundred years between B.C. 200 and A.D. 200 there appeared the *Mishnah* (Repetition), a digest of custom and usage that was handed down from ancient times by word of mouth, and in the production of which Judah Hanasi played a leading part. Further commentary and explanation became necessary in the application of the *Mishnah*. This took the form of the *Gemara* (or Completion). Eventually two Talmuds emerged, the Palestinian one by about A.D. 425, and the Babylonian one a hundred years or so later.

In succeeding centuries the Talmud, conceived as a single entity, was gradually edited and codified so as to establish Judaism as an integrated system of values and beliefs. It came to be divided into two main elements. The first, the *Halachah* (or Law), contained injunctions regarded as legally binding on all Jews, and is sometimes called the "bread" of the Talmud. The second (the "wine") was the Aggadah (or Tales), mainly literary material of inspirational value.[11] The two Talmuds are written in different versions of Aramaic, the vernacular language of Palestine, Syria, and much of western Asia at the time of Jesus and the destruction of the Temple. Hebrew had ceased to be a spoken language at the time of the second (Hasmonean) Commonwealth. It was not revived as such until the twentieth century, when it became the national language of the Palestinian Jews and ultimately of Israel.

The Babylonian Talmud, two-thirds longer than the Palestinian, is regarded as its superior in arrangement, text, and content, and is the one upon which all subsequent codifications of the Jewish law primarily rest. One main reason was the far easier conditions under which it was produced. In Babylon the Jews enjoyed full rights. They had a large measure of autonomy under a leader invested with great powers by the Persian kings. Their scholars could take their

11. *Ibid.*, pp. 40–41.

time. The Jews in Palestine, on the other hand, had suffered another tragic setback in the second century.

Bar Kochba's Revolt

In the reign of the Emperor Hadrian, from 132 to 135, a second Jewish revolt was launched by one Simon Bar Kochba, unhappily acclaimed as a military Messiah by one of the great Talmudic scholars, Rabbi Akiba, who was martyred when the rising was crushed. Hadrian then suppressed the Sanhedrin and the Yavne centre, forbade the study of the Torah, and banned the practice of its observances. So many preferred death to obedience that the Jewish leaders agreed that a Jew to save his life might violate any of the commandments of the Torah except those forbidding idolatry, murder, adultery, and incest. This decision became a guiding principle of Jewish life in later ages. Finally, Hadrian completed the destruction of Jerusalem. It was rebuilt as a purely Roman city, called Aelia Capitolina. No Jews might visit it save once a year on the anniversary of the Destruction. They then might come to weep (as they still do) at the fragment of the Temple wall which had survived. There was still a community in Palestine, but the failure of their second revolt had deprived the Jews of the last vestige of self-government.[12] Fortunately, there was a revival of tolerance under Hadrian's successors, and the Patriarchate somehow survived for nearly three centuries more.

The disabilities against the Jews were removed by Caracalla in 212, when all freemen were made citizens of the empire.[13] Nevertheless, early in the fourth century, when Christianity became the official religion of the Roman Empire, danger and suffering again befell the Jews. Judaism was now a political as well as a religious heresy, and a militant Church backed by the state set about making life unbearable for the Palestine Jews. Under such conditions the compilers of the Palestine Talmud had little peace of mind in

12. Epstein, pp. 117–18, 126–27.
13. Schweitzer, p. 38.

which to do their work. Their Patriarchate was abolished in 425, and the centre of Jewish life eventually shifted to Babylonia. In spite of all these tragedies the Jews had been able, "to fashion for themselves a new nationhood, not bound up with a national territory or fixed homesteads, but with a national literature, religion and culture . . . to . . . ensure their survival as one distinct people among the nations of the world."[14]

Babylonian Jewry

In ancient as in modern times successive empires disputed the Fertile Crescent. The fight was as fierce for the lands between and beyond the Tigris and Euphrates as it was for Syria, Palestine, and Egypt. Babylon on the lower Euphrates was, as we saw, the capital of the Babylonian Empire from which Nebuchadnezzar forcibly exiled the Jews in 586 B.C. But soon afterwards Babylonia fell to the Persians, and in 538 those Jews who wished to return to Jerusalem were permitted to do so. Most, however, struck roots and prospered in the "land between the rivers." Then in 332 B.C., Alexander the Great overran the Persian Empire, which twenty years later fell to Seleucus Nicator, one of his successors. In 171 B.C. the Seleucids were evicted by the Parthians, and they in turn (from A.D. 226) by the Sassanid dynasty of Persia. The Sassanids ruled until the rise of Islam in the seventh century, when they were conquered by the Muslim Arabs.

The Jews enjoyed varying degrees of tolerance under all these empires. Their bad moments were few and usually of short duration. During their four-hundred-year rule, the Parthians, who had no state religion, were markedly generous toward their Hebrew subjects. Jews could proselytize, and freely did so. They could enter all professions and enjoyed, as we saw, local self-government under their *Exilarchs*, men of dignity at the royal court. Tolerance was less secure under the Sassanids, since the Persians had an official religion—the ancient fire-worshipping cult of Zoroastrianism, still

14. Epstein, pp. 119 and 126. See also Schweitzer, p. 48.

practiced today by their descendants, the Parsees of western India. There was some interference with Jewish practices that conflicted with state orthodoxy—such as lighting candles and burying the dead; and around A.D. 500 a wave of persecution reached its height, accompanied by some killings and forced conversions.[15] By 600 this grim phase had eased, but largely owing to the strains and stresses inside and outside the huge Sassanid empire, which stretched from present-day Iraq to western Pakistan.

During this century Persia was constantly either at war or in a state of uneasy peace with the rival empire of Byzantium, which controlled Asia Minor, Syria, Palestine, and Egypt, as well as parts of North Africa and the Balkans. In the first half-century the Sassanid monarch Khosro Anushiravan successfully confronted the famous Emperor Justinian. Then early in the seventh century Khosro Parviz fought his way against Heraclius into Syria, Palestine, and Egypt. He took Jerusalem and carried away the "True Cross," only to be pushed back to Mesopotamia by the resurgent Byzantines, who recaptured the holy relic from their enemies. Both empires, desperately weakened by their long struggles, would become the victims of their own primitive vassals from the Arabian Peninsula, soon to be fired by a new faith.[16]

Through everything the Jewish community in Persia survived as a vital force. Its three academies, founded by scholars trained in Palestine, become renowned. Until around A.D. 220 Babylonian scholars had looked to the academies of Palestine and deferred to the Palestinian Patriarchs. From that time, however, the arrival of Judah Hanasi's Mishnah seems to have helped the Babylonian academies to become strong and independent centres of scholarship, while the Jews of Palestine were increasingly beset by insecurity and danger. The Babylonian Talmud seems to have been completed while persecution was still rife; but from about 589 a new and happier phase began. The academies were reopened. Their heads, the *Gaonim*, had gradually come to overshadow the Exil-

15. Schweitzer, pp. 49–52.
16. Yahya Armajani, *Middle East, Past and Present*, pp. 26–27.

archs, and the Gaon's council assumed the role of a new Sanhedrin looked up to by the Jews in the Dispersion as the Palestinian Patriarchate had been before its abolition in 425. The Gaonate was to preserve and strengthen the identity of the Jews as one people, not only while it was subject to the Persians, but also under the great Islamic empire of the Arabs, which was soon to dominate Persia and the Fertile Crescent as well. Its pronouncements on questions not covered by the Talmud became a great supplementary volume known as the *Responsa*.[17] At its height, around 900, the Gaonate was involved also in combating the dissident Karaite sect, which rejected all Talmudic interpretations in favour of a personal return to the Scriptures (somewhat in the spirit of Luther and other Protestant leaders). Judaism must also be preserved from any foreign defilement.

The Jewish-Christian Confrontation

Although it originated among their own people, Christianity was, as we know, rejected as a heresy by the Jewish religious leaders. Nevertheless for its own followers it represented a universalization of some of the finest elements in the Jewish faith, made applicable to all mankind. Christianity—more particularly with the advent of Protestantism—drew its inspiration from the Old Testament as well as the New. In time, also, many Christians came to feel keen remorse for their mistreatment of the Jews in later ages, especially in Europe. Hence the deep concern of some leading Christians of our day for the national regeneration of the Jewish people. And this in turn was one of the many complex motives underlying the fateful Balfour Declaration of 1917.

For their part the Jews, in spite of everything, eventually took credit for Christianity, and later for Islam, as "daughter faiths." This came to affect their attitude towards the conversion of other peoples, which had been, as we saw, a constant feature of Judaism

17. Schweitzer, pp. 52 and 53.

throughout its earlier history. "All that Judaism was concerned with in its missionary work was to substitute the religion of humanity . . . for the false gods and false morality of the pagan world. But when paganism gave place to Christianity and later also to Islam, Judaism withdrew from the missionary field and was satisfied to leave the task of spreading the religion of humanity to her daughter faiths. The reason for this was, not indifference to the fate of other peoples, but the recognition that Christianity and Islam, though lacking the true vision of the one and only God, shared in common many truths, religious and moral, with the mother faith."[18] Yet proselytism, though gradually de-emphasized, was never abandoned. It has continued until now, and some ascribe to it the marked differences between European Jews (especially those from Eastern Europe), and the Oriental Jews, which have become a source of tension in Israel today.

At the same time the links of Judaism with its "daughter faiths" present a startling paradox. While the Christian world has been the chief source of Jewish suffering, Israel in the twentieth century owed its birth and continued existence mainly to the initiative and support of Christian nations. On the other hand, the recent enforced repopulation of the Holy Land by Jews has brought down upon Israel the enmity of those (mainly Muslim) Arab people whose historic treatment of the Jews was on the whole incomparably more fair and just than that of the Christian West both in the Middle Ages and in our own time in Hitler-dominated Europe. Indeed, during many of the dark centuries of Christian oppression, Muslims and Jews were on terms of mutual understanding and creative cooperation.

One of the main factors in the tragic Jewish-Christian breach was of course the rooted conviction of Christians that the Jews in general—the whole Jewish people—were guilty of the death of Jesus. The early Christian Fathers such as St. John Chrysostom depicted the Jew "as a being perpetually betraying God and ultimately aban-

18. Epstein, p. 144.

doned by Him."[19] Not until the Second Vatican Council of our day has the Roman Catholic Church officially sought to disprove this as a charge against all Jews; and only now has the Church started to make up its mind where it stands with regard to Judaism.[20]

Another factor was the Christian belief in the divinity of Jesus. On the condemnation of Jesus a Jewish scholar exonerates even the Jewish authorities immediately involved. Pilate, he says, had ordered the political Sanhedrin to hand over to the Romans subversive persons against whom there was a clear capital charge. On examining Jesus the Sanhedrin judged that there was such a charge. Fearing that what remained of Jewish nationhood would suffer if the prescribed procedure were not followed, Jesus was handed over and crucified on Pilate's order. "The earliest adherents [of Christianity] were Jews in all respects but one—they regarded Jesus as the Messiah . . . ; they continued to go to the Temple and presumably to the Synagogue . . . , and to all appearances conformed . . . to the usual Jewish observances. Their belief that the Messiah had come was not a ground of division between them and other Jews. But within a few decades the Christian Church, under the influence of Paul, was altering its conception of Jesus . . . ; he was no longer . . . merely human . . . ; he was . . . a second God . . . a denial of the unity of God as Jews understood the term. Once this . . . had taken place . . . the final rift . . . became inevitable."[21]

As regards Saint Paul, another Jewish writer is more explicit

19. Cited in James Parkes, *The Conflict of the Church and the Synagogue*, p. 375.

20. "Authorities of the Jews and those who followed their lead pressed for the death of Christ . . . ; still, what happened . . . cannot be blamed upon all the Jews then living, . . . nor upon the Jews of today. . . . The Jews should not be presented as repudiated or cursed by God." Second Vatican Council, *Declaration on the Relationship of the Church to Non-Christian Religions*. Promulgated by Pope Paul VI, October 28, 1965. Also see Schweitzer, pp. 72 and 304.

21. Epstein, pp. 106–7.

still. "It was a strictly orthodox Jew and rabbinical student, Saul of Tarsus . . . who did more than anyone else to spread the gospel of Christianity. He is known . . . as Paul the Apostle. This 'Pharisee of the Pharisees' . . . was converted to Christianity and went around the Middle East and eastern Mediterranean on fiery missionary journeys. . . . The doctrines he espoused were largely Hebraic, but he dropped the restrictive and irksome regulations of the Old Testament. His appeal made little impact on the Jews. . . . In the end Paul . . . took his message to the wider non-Jewish world. He found ready ears and thus began the universal spread of the new faith. It is commonly accepted that without the labours of the Jew, Paul, it is unlikely that Christianity would have become a world-wide religion."[22]

As the mood of mutual rejection grew, the Christians, originally regarded by the Romans as just another Jewish sect, were soon at pains to differentiate themselves as sharply as possible from the Jews. Eventually, in the third century, "the bonds between church and synagogue were sundered at last in a war of words." With the triumph of Christianity, the Christians in time sought to assimilate the ancient Hebrew heritage. At one stage they even arrogated to themselves the name "Children of Israel." They claimed to have inherited the Biblical promises that the Jews had allegedly forfeited by their refusal to accept Jesus; and a form of Christian Zionism underlay the appeals with which Pope Urban II launched the First Crusade.[23]

High though feeling often ran, for many centuries the Christian rulers generally, and the Christian Churches of both the Eastern Orthodox and Roman Catholic rites (the breach between which was not final until 1054) were on the whole far more zealous in crushing heresies than in ill-treating Jews. Some seem to have believed that the Jews would ultimately be converted to Christianity and that this would herald the Second Coming of Christ. Jews must

22. Kollek, pp. 118–20.
23. Schweitzer, pp. 70–71.

be curbed and watched but not exterminated, for they were to be present at the Last Day.

The Early European Persecutions

In these earlier centuries the source of Jewish suffering in Europe was, as we saw, primarily religious, not racial or economic, though both these factors have played a grim part in our modern era of supposed enlightenment. The reign of Charlemagne (771–814) may be said to close the first phase in the drama of European Jewry. Until then, despite much discrimination and restriction, Jews were not marked by the abnormal characteristics forced upon them in later times. Though many were traders and financiers, they were found in every walk of life, from soldier to official, from artisan to peasant. They were often prosperous intermediaries between the Orient and the West, especially after the rise of Islam and its penetration of Spain and Portugal. Religion excluded, they were a normal segment of society. But the abnormalities became inevitable once legislation was consistently and ruthlessly used to coerce them as a religious group opposed to the Christian establishment. It became impossible for Jews to hold public office, as some had done. Other careers were gradually closed to them. Eventually they would be confined to one or two professions, segregated into separate areas, and made conspicuous by a special badge.[24] The resentments provoked by Jewish hostility towards Jesus and the Christian faith in no way mitigate or excuse the infamous historical record of most Christian nations in their dealings with the Jewish people.

In the fourth century the newly converted Emperor Constantine decreed that Jews, under penalty of death, could neither proselytize nor discourage their people from becoming Christians. They could not intermarry with Christians, nor even dine with them. New synagogues could not be built nor old ones repaired. In principle they were barred from military service and from professions like

24. Parkes, pp. 371–76.

medicine. Eventually it was decreed that they could not own slaves, the basic work instruments of the ancient world. Moreover, along with heretics, they were not "good witnesses" in suits against orthodox citizens. Naturally there were many evasions. Later in the century the Jewish position was happily reversed by the Emperor Julian, accursed among Christians as The Apostate, who again gave them full toleration and autonomy, and even promised that they should be allowed to rebuild their Temple. This is one of the many phases of history which present in total contrast Christian and Jewish pictures of events. Thus the thirteenth century, regarded as one of the greatest by the Catholic Church, was one of the most terrible for the Jews; yet the French Revolutionary and Napoleonic age, one of persecution and humiliation for the Church, was that of Jewish emancipation and equality.

In 438 the anti-Jewish legislation was revived in the Code of Theodosius II, who abolished the Patriarchate in Palestine. This code became the basis for the legal codes of the Germanic kingdoms that conquered the Roman Empire in the West, and thus a determining factor in the status of the Jews under the Eastern (Ostro-) Goths, and later Lombards in Italy, the Western (Visi-) Goths in Spain, and the Franks in Gaul and western Germany. From these last emerged the Merovingian kings of France, and the Carolingian dynasty under which all Western Europe was at one time ruled by Charles the Great, or Charlemagne. And he in turn paved the way for a new Western empire: the Roman Empire of the German Nation, or Holy Roman Empire. Thus the restraints and barriers imposed upon the Jews were gradually "woven into the legal and constitutional fabric of medieval Europe."[25]

The Jews, officially, had their rights. Judaism was recognized and tolerated. Suits brought by Jews, whether relating to their own faith or not, could be heard by the ordinary tribunals, but by consent they might have them heard by an arbitrator who was a Jew. And they were liable to prosecution only if they broke the law. Indeed,

25. See Schweitzer, pp. 14–15, 69, 74–75.

Theodosius found it necessary to condemn both Christians and Jews for destructive or provocative actions, pointing out that the Jews were protected by the law and could be tried in the courts for any crimes alleged against them.[26] Around A.D. 500, Theodoric the Ostrogoth (himself an Arian heretic)[27] sought to curb excesses against the Jews and to ensure that they should be treated strictly in accordance with the law. They were to keep their own judges, and their privileges were to be preserved. Their synagogue at Ravenna, destroyed by Christians, was to be rebuilt. A century later, Pope Gregory the Great condemned forced conversion and insisted that the Jews should be allowed exactly the privileges prescribed for them under the Theodosian Code. Yet these efforts to do justice were powerless to curb the arbitary cruelties of those in authority both great and small, and the savagery of those beneath them. Even under the great Byzantine lawgiver Justinian, Jews suffered persecution along with heretics, especially after a revolt of the Samaritans in Palestine in 529. "A Theodoric and a Gregory might see that [Jewish] rights were not ignored, but usually bishops, kings and barons were free to do what they willed. There was no appeal against them."[28]

In Merovingian France, and for a time in the Rhineland, the Jewish position was somewhat happier than in many parts. Commerce in France seems to have been chiefly in the hands of Byzantine Syrians and Jews, who had prosperous colonies in various parts of the country. The Jews extended their business by keeping in touch with their fellow Jews in Italy, Spain, and the Orient. Since, moreover, the Church at the time forbade Christians to lend money at interest, the Jews had also something of a monopoly in

26. Parkes, pp. 235–36.
27. The Arian heresy was held to deny the full deity of Christ. The fact that this belief was closer to the Jewish standpoint than to that of orthodox Christianity is considered by some writers to have disposed Arian rulers to greater indulgence towards the Jews.
28. Parkes, pp. 206, 208, 211, 213, 376. See also *Cambridge Medieval History,* II, 44.

finance and banking.[29] Restrictions upon Christian participation were in practice later relaxed. One reason Edward I of England was able after several centuries to expel the Jews in 1290 was that by then they had begun to be supplanted by Italians from Lombardy, and by Englishmen who had acquired the financial skills.[30]

The Visigoths of Spain and Portugal had been Arians and as such notably tolerant of their Jewish subjects. Around 600, however, they abjured Arianism for Roman Catholicism and from that time systematically persecuted the Jews. Amongst other things, Jews were forbidden to hold public office, though this and the other bans seem to have been evaded in practice. At one point the King ordered the baptism of all Jews under penalty of banishment and confiscation of property. This was later confirmed by the Sixth Council of Toledo in 637, which decreed that all Jews who had not been baptised should be driven out of the kingdom. Expulsion from particular lands was to be a recurring tragedy of the Jewish people in Christian Europe. Meanwhile, threatened as they were by the surge of Islam from northern Africa, the Visigoth kings suspected the Jews of collusion with their Muslim enemies, and as an alternative to banishment ordered their enslavement. Their Christian slave-masters were to take Jewish boys at seven and educate them in the Christian faith. (As late as the nineteenth century the Emperor Nicholas of Russia tried by similar methods to force Christianity upon Jews recruited as children for his armies.) In these circumstances it is hardly surprising that the Jews of the Iberian Peninsula should have welcomed the conquering Arab-Moorish armies of Islam.[31] And it is to the phenomenon of Islam—this new religion of the One God—that we must now turn.

29. *Cambridge Medieval History*, II, 156.
30. Schweitzer, p. 94. For the background and consequences of the expulsion from England, see Cecil Roth, *History of the Jews in England*, pp. 68–90.
31. *Cambridge Medieval History*, II, 174, 181, 185.

Chapter 3

Islam: Victories of a New Creed

As the earlier chapters have shown, the current Middle East crisis can be understood only against a complex background of ancient, interrelated faiths and feuds. One source of this was the partial Jewish conquest of Palestine from its original inhabitants[1] and the later struggles—particularly of the kingdom of Judah—against the other races within the country and the empires that at one time or another dominated the area. Another source was the Jewish conflict with pagan Rome, then with the Judeo-Christians, and eventually with the converted Gentiles of the Roman world and its successors.

In the seventh century, both Jews and Christians were faced with

1. It may be objected that David and Solomon conquered all of Palestine and much beyond. But their rule lasted only eighty years. To base a modern claim to all of Palestine or areas beyond upon this kingdom would be in some ways similar to England seeking to sustain a permanent claim to the areas of France she dominated in the Middle Ages. After the collapse of the kingdom of Israel around 700 B.C., the only part of Palestine which remained until A.D. 70 a lasting possession of the Jewish people was the kingdom of Judah. By a strange paradox of history, its former area approximately corresponds to that portion of the area of Palestine allotted to the Palestinian Arabs by the United Nations in 1947 which the Arabs managed to retain after the first Arab-Israeli war of 1948.

a new and powerful phenomenon: the strong faith of Islam inspired by elements in both their own religions. Like Judaism at the time of Joshua, this was a fighting creed, one that believed in the righteousness of conquest. On the other hand, like Christianity but unlike Judaism, it had no special link with one people convinced of its election by God. All who professed the new faith and observed its austere and simple rules of life were accepted as Muslims, whatever their race, colour, or geographic origin. So far as this study is concerned, the sequel to Islam (as to Christianity) was an initial but on the whole brief conflict with those Jews who rejected the new revelation. This, however, was followed by a far longer and more bitter conflict with the Christian world—one that continued for most of the next twelve hundred years.

The first phase of the struggle was the Muslim advance into Western Europe. This started with the invasion of Spain in 711 and later of southern France. But Western Europe was saved from Muslim subjugation by the victory at Tours in 732 of the Frankish leader Charles the Hammer (Charles Martel), grandfather of Charlemagne. Thrown back beyond the Pyrenees, the Muslims occupied slowly diminishing areas of Spain and Portugal. They were finally driven out by the "Catholic Kings," Ferdinand of Aragon and Isabella of Castile, in 1492 (also the year of Columbus' first landfall in America). Thus the Islamic era in the Iberian Peninsula greatly exceeded the time that has elapsed since the reconquest, and to this is due the visible influence of Muslim-Arab culture upon Spaniard and Portuguese. For much of this period, the Muslims dominated the Mediterranean as well as the Red Sea, the Persian Gulf, and the Indian Ocean and, during the so-called Dark Ages and after, largely cut Europe off from the profitable commerce with the Orient which had flourished throughout Roman times.

A second phase was the Crusades (1095–1291), a series of military expeditions inspired by the Popes and kings of Western Christendom to wrest Palestine from the Muslims who had conquered it in 637. By the time of the First Crusade the Church had decided that the Jews had forfeited their ancient Hebrew heritage. The

Christians were the true children of Israel and as such should bring the Holy Land under Christian rule.[2] After a spell of brief and partial success, which saw the rise and fall of a Latin Kingdom of Jerusalem, this venture in Christian Zionism failed; and after two hundred years the last Crusaders were expelled from the Muslim world.

A third phase covers the erosion and final conquest by the Muslims of the Byzantine Empire, and their invasion of Eastern Europe. Southern Russia was sealed off and the Black Sea turned into a Muslim lake. This irruption was not checked until 1683, after Vienna had been twice besieged. Meanwhile, conflict had inevitably emerged between the Muslims themselves. For some four hundred years the leaders of their world had been the Arabs. But the Arabs were gradually subjugated by the Turks from Central Asia. In the year 1055 the Seljuk Turks captured Baghdad, and in 1517 the Ottoman Turks brought under their rule most of the Arab areas, including the Fertile Crescent. Sixty years earlier, in 1453, they had extinguished the Byzantine Empire by taking Constantinople; and it was their armies that had nearly captured Vienna.

From the end of the seventeenth century, Eastern Europe was gradually reconquered from the Turks, partly by the Austrians but even more forcibly by the Russians. From the days of Peter the Great to modern times, Russia was determined to free her southern flank and gain access to the eastern Mediterranean and the Fertile Crescent by weakening and reducing the Ottoman Empire. In later stages of this process, when Turkey had become a lure to predators rather than a menace, the Christian powers confronted each other in competition for the spoils. For most of the nineteenth century Britain and France usually backed Turkey, at a price, against the rapacity of Russia. Then Germany became Turkey's ostensibly disinterested friend. The last act of this drama was World War I, in which Germany, having outbid the other powers, was ranged with Turkey against Russia, Britain, and France. The upshot was

2. Schweitzer, p. 70.

the destruction of the Ottoman Empire and Arab liberation from Turkish rule. The Arabs found other tests and trials awaiting them.

After some initial clashes in Arabia with the founders of the new faith in the seventh century, for most of the ensuing 1300 years the Jews in the world of Islam lived on generally tolerable, and often easy and profitable, terms with their Muslim neighbours. There was little of the hateful cruelty and discrimination which for centuries were the pattern in Christian Europe. One of the fateful consequences of the emergence of Israel in its present form has been to stir up, virtually for the first time, a bitter and persistent conflict between two groups of peoples—the Jews and Muslim (or Christian) Arabs—of closely related faiths between whom there had been an age-long tradition of understanding, tolerance, and good will.

The Prophet

Of the founders of the three great monotheistic religions, only Jesus is regarded by his followers as the Son of God. No such quality invests the Patriarchs of the Old Testament. The founder of Islam seems even closer to the hard and simple facts of life. To the faithful he is a prophet, in the succession of Moses and Jesus himself, and the Messenger or Apostle of God. In other respects he is a very human figure, a man of shrewdness, tenacity, and common sense, with his feet firmly on the ground. No Arab has ever succeeded in holding his countrymen together as he did.[3]

He is held to have been born around A.D. 570 in Mecca in the Hejaz in western Arabia. His father was already dead, and his mother died six years later. His family were, it seems, from an impoverished group of the powerful tribe of Quraish, and he was brought up by relations. His great-grandfather, Hashim, had the name borne in our century by the royal families of the Hejaz, Jordan, and Iraq.[4] He was also related through Hashim's wife to the

3. Guillaume, pp. 23 and 25.
4. Of the Hashimite dynasties, only that of Jordan survives, under King Hussein. His own great-grandfather, Husain, appointed Sharif of Mecca by

tribe of Khazraj of Yathrib (later known as Medina). Mecca was a center for the caravan trade and also a pilgrim shrine for the pagan religions then still powerful in this remote land. Both were highly profitable. One of the departure points for the caravans was southern Arabia (roughly the area of the Yemen and known in classical times as "Fortunate Arabia" or *Arabia Felix*). Here were both fertile soil and a highly developed civilization, based on agriculture and the spice trade with the Indies. As they moved northward to Mecca some caravans continued onward to the head of the Gulf of Aqaba, then farther north to Gaza and Palestine, or westward into Egypt, or northeast to Damascus and beyond. On this last route two flourishing Arab kingdoms whose monuments have survived to this day were that of the Nabataeans at Petra in Jordan and that of Queen Zenobia at Palmyra in the Syrian desert, both conquered by the Romans. Other caravan routes branched off from Mecca directly eastward to the Persian Gulf and northeastward to Hira on the Euphrates, south of ancient Babylon.[5]

The Bedouin nomads of the Hejaz were predominantly pagan, but some of the surrounding tribes had become Christian. A focus of the pagan pilgrimage to Mecca was the idols, preserved in a building known as the Ka'ba. One of these, in the form of a black stone, continued to be venerated in Islamic times, having allegedly been placed there by Abraham himself. Other pre-Islamic elements, including the month of daylight fasting known as *Ramadan*, were also later incorporated into the practices of the Muslim faith. But even when they were idolaters the Arab peoples seem to have been aware of a supreme deity, rendered in Arabic as *Allah*.

By the time of Muhammad, Jews as well as Christians had an established position in Arabia. Some Jews may have come there at

the Turks, launched the revolt against them in 1916 and afterwards made himself King of the Hejaz. The principal leader of the revolt was his son Faisal, afterwards King of Iraq. The Hashimite dynasty of the Hejaz was displaced in 1924 by King Saud, leader of the puritan Wahabis from eastern Arabia. That in Iraq was overturned by revolution in 1958.

5. *Ibid.*, pp. 3–6, 9, 24. See also Sir John Glubb, *The Great Arab Conquests*, pp. 22–24. P. 23 contains an excellent map of the caravan routes.

the time of the Babylonian captivity, some after the Roman suppression of their two revolts in the first and second centuries of our era. There was a large Jewish colony in the Yemen, where at one time the ruler himself had become a Jew. Indeed this group lasted as an organized community until brought in recent years to Israel, where their problems of adjustment have been far from simple in view of the political and material domination of West and East European Jews in the new state. In the seventh century the Jews may have formed as much as half the population of Medina. In any event they dominated the economic life of most of the Hejaz, though not of Mecca. The Yemen was also a center of Christian influence, as were Syria in the north and Hira in Mesopotamia to the east.

The Christians in the pre-Islamic Arab world were divided broadly into three groups. There were the Greek Orthodox, who belonged to the dominant faith in the Byzantine Empire, the Monophysites (or Jacobites), and the Nestorians.[6] Both the latter sects had proselytized actively among the Arabs, but were liable to persecution or condemnation by the Orthodox authorities at Constantinople. The Yemen was in constant touch with, and shortly before Muhammad subordinate to, the African kingdom of Ethiopia across the narrow Bab Al-Mandeb Strait, where the religion of the dominant group was Monophysite, like that of the Egyptian Christians known as Copts. Although inevitably there was intermingling between the sects, the Monophysites seem to have had a strong position in Syria, where the Arabs, particularly the Beni Ghassan, were frequently recruited as mercenaries by the Byzantine Empire during Constantinople's long and exhausting wars with Persia. At Hira the Nestorians seem to have been firmly established,

6. The Monophysites held that there was but one, composite, nature in Christ; the Nestorians maintained that there were two persons in Christ, and placed strong insistence on His human nature. Their doctrines are discussed more fully in the New Catholic Encyclopedia (New York: McGraw-Hill, 1967), IX, 1064–65, and X, 346–48. Another valuable map showing the pre-Islamic distribution of the different religious denominations will be found in Glubb, p. 29.

but the eastern Arabs of this region, the Lakhmids, were often recruited by the Persian Empire and normally fought with zeal against their countrymen on the Byzantine side.

For our purpose the importance of these divisions, both religious and military, is that they helped to prepare the ground for the astonishingly rapid and brilliant Arab conquests that followed the emergence of Islam. Around the time of Muhammad, both groups were turned into enemies of the empires employing them by the cessation of subsidies and the killing or arrest of their rulers. Another factor in the swift success of Islam seems to have been the subtle complexity of Christian doctrine as interpreted by the Greeks, a subtlety beyond the reach of simple desert dwellers who were largely nomads. We are told of one Monophysite Arab chieftain who sought with scant success approval in Constantinople for a simple and basic interpretation of the doctrine of the Trinity "stripped of the subtle refinements of the Greek theologians."[7]

It was against this background that the life of Muhammad ran its course. In his early youth, according to one scholar, "one may safely assume that he got a job with one of the business enterprises in which the Quraish tribe was engaged. He probably travelled as a caravan boy to the Fertile Crescent, Egypt and perhaps Iran."[8] He evidently acquired some trading skills, for in 594 a rich widow named Khadija engaged him as her business manager, and he seems to have travelled for her on a successful commercial venture to Syria. Soon after he returned they were married—at her suggestion, it is thought. Although she was then 40 and he only 25, they seem to have been extremely happy. Through her wealth she had a prominent social position, and hence, from his modest beginnings, Muhammed found himself not only with ample means but also with some influence among the Quraish. Khadijah bore him six children, two sons and four daughters; but only the girls survived. While all the girls married, the only marriage of importance from

7. Guillaume, pp. 9, 11, 13–19.
8. Armajani, p. 30.

the standpoint of the future of Islam was that of Fatima, whose husband was a cousin of Muhammad's called Ali.[9] Muhammad had contact with both Jews and Christians and learned of the doctrines of their sacred books, even if perhaps in a somewhat confused form. His wife had a Christian cousin, Waraqa, and Muhammad himself became attached to a Christian slave named Zeid from southern Syria and given to him by his wife. Having freed this young man, he adopted him as one of his sons.[10]

In the desolate landscape surrounding Mecca there were volcanic caves that were acquired and furnished by those who could afford it to escape the heat and noise of the city. One night in 610, toward the end of Ramadan, Muhammad, in his cave, heard a voice commanding him to speak out in the name of the Lord. In consternation he thought at first that he had become deranged or possessed. He planned to kill himself by jumping off a precipice, but was checked by a voice from Heaven hailing him as the Apostle of God, and a vision of the Archangel Gabriel astride the horizon. When he told his wife, she consulted her Christian cousin. Waraqa's response was that Muhammad was to become a prophet to his people. When the voice and visions were renewed, Muhammad knew himself to be indeed the Messenger of God and recognized that it was the Archangel Gabriel who dictated Allah's words.[11] The Muslims call this first supernatural manifestation "The Night of Power." Among the few who early believed in his mission were his wife, his cousin Ali, his adopted son Zeid, Abu Bekr (a close friend who was also a substantial merchant of Mecca), and one Othman ibn Affan of the wealthy Umayya clan of Quraish who were traditional rivals of the Hashim. Both Abu Bekr and Othman were to be future Caliphs of Islam.[12]

Three years after his first vision, at the age of 43, Muhammad

9. *Ibid.*, pp. 30–31. See also Guillaume, p. 27.
10. Glubb, p. 43.
11. Guillaume, p. 29. Armajani, p. 31.
12. The word *Khalifa* means Successor, and after Muhammad's death it was used generally for those who were regarded as having succeeded to his religious and secular authority.

felt that he had been called upon to preach his faith publicly in Mecca. This he did in the simplest terms. God was One. The idols must be swept away. He was God's Messenger. One day the dead would rise again, the righteous to Paradise, but the wicked and idolators would be consigned to eternal fire. He based his teaching upon the words of God dictated by Gabriel and gradually collected and embodied in what became the Q'uran. He made no claim to have founded a new religion. As we saw in Chapter 1, he regarded his teaching as the religion of Abraham, founder of the monotheism of the Arabs. He alleged that the pure revelation made to Abraham had been distorted by the Jews. "Jesus had been sent to bring religion back from Judaistic heresies to the true faith. Muhammad believed in the Virgin Birth and . . . that Jesus had been the Spirit of God and had once again preached the pure faith of Abraham. Subsequently, however, the Christians had also adulterated the true faith. Now he, Muhammad, had been sent by God, in order that once more mankind be recalled to the purity of the original true religion."

Muhammad seems to have hoped in the early stages that Jews and Christians would acknowledge their errors and rally to him. His contact with Jews may have been closer than with Christians for he seems to have been somewhat more familiar with the Old Testament than with the New. Thus there are passages in the Q'uran urging the faithful to fight against unbelievers much as the Israelites were ordered in the Pentateuch to destroy their uncircumcised enemies. At the same time a special feature of the Q'uran— one that may have been a powerful factor in promoting the great conquests by the Arabs soon to occur—was the promise of immediate admission to Paradise of all who fell in battle against unbelievers, and a detailed description of the delights awaiting them in the next life. Muhammad's reference to passages in both Testaments are sometimes at variance with the original. This may be because (as seems probable) he could not read or write and therefore repeated them from memory.[13]

13. Glubb, pp. 44–45.

It is perhaps natural that the Jews of Arabia and elsewhere, who felt themselves materially and spiritually more advanced—to say nothing of the Christians—should have been sceptical of the new revelations, sometimes at heavy cost to themselves. According to one Jewish historian of our day, "the Biblical phraseology which Muhammad gleaned from Jews and Christians was fragmentary and inaccurate. . . . He was broad enough to recognize the genius of the religious leaders of the past, . . . but he felt that he, the last of the prophets, transcended them all. . . . Westerners find little that stirs the soul in the record of Muhammad's revelations, collected reverently after his death and incorporated in the hundred and fourteen suras of the Q'uran. It seems to be an incoherent rhapsody of fable, precept and declamation. But behind the confused messages was a powerful personality, an ardent, passionate soul capable of carrying his followers through every impossible sacrifice. Muhammad was his own greatest contribution to his faith."[14]

In the early years not only were converts few; many Meccans were strongly hostile to the new teaching. They resented the implications that their revered but idolatrous ancestors were in hell; and they feared a loss of profit if pilgrimage to the pagan shrines were discontinued. Although the Quraish converts were protected by tribal law, some who were not, such as slaves and servants, were attacked. In 615, after five years of scant achievement, Muhammad advised a number of his followers to emigrate to Christian Ethiopia. He even momentarily paid tribute to three of the Meccan's favorite idols, but afterwards recanted, convinced that this had been a work of the devil. The elders of Quraish urged the uncle who had been his guardian to withdraw tribal protection from him so that he could be punished; but they were rebuffed. Although a few converts —among them some substantial persons—continued to be made, a boycott of the Hashim clan was enforced for three years by the remainder of the tribe. After it was lifted, Muhammad announced

14. Abram Leon Sachar, *A History of the Jews* (New York: Knopf, 1948), pp. 156–57.

that in one night he had flown with the Archangel to Jerusalem and thence to Heaven, where he had seen Adam, Abraham, Moses, and Jesus. The Meccans met this news with mockery and insult. In Taif, forty miles away, he was stoned. Then in 619 his wife died, and also his guardian uncle.

In March 620, during the pilgrimage to Mecca's pagan shrines, Muhammad preached his doctrines to a small group of seven pilgrims from Yathrib, and won them to his views. By the next pilgrim season the Yathrib converts had increased to twelve. These, with the aid of Meccan converts, seem to have achieved some swift success in the northern city. At the end of a third pilgrim season, in March 622, seventy-three believers from Yathrib met secretly with their Prophet in a dry watercourse some miles from Mecca, to swear allegiance to him and make a pact of mutual protection. His new companions then unobtrusively returned, leaving him in Mecca. The elders of Quraish sensed that Muhammad might leave to join this new nucleus of followers. On the proposal of another of his own uncles, they decided that he must be killed, but in such a way that the blood guilt would be generally distributed. One from each clan of Quraish would together strike him down. When he heard of this, Muhammad escaped with Abu Bekr, his closest friend, and hid in the desert. They were not found, although the Quraish offered a large reward and searched intensively. Camels were brought, and the small group, joined by his cousin and son-in-law Ali were guided through the desert to Yathrib by unfrequented ways. After arriving in Yathrib, Muhammad married Abu Bekr's daughter and later a number of other women—some, it seems, chosen for political reasons, i.e., to conciliate their relatives. None, however, produced a son.[15]

This flight from Mecca, known as the *Hijra* (Emigration) changed the history of the world. It was to ensure the triumph of Islam, and from its year, 622, the Muslim calendar was eventually dated. Yathrib was later renamed the City of the Prophet—*Medinat al-Nabi*—or, more familiarly, Medina. The faithful who made their

15. Glubb, pp. 46–60.

way from Mecca to Medina were thenceforth known as the Emi-grés (*Muhajirun*); the supporters of Muhammad from Medina as the Helpers (*Ansar*).

Medina was the centre of a far more fertile and flourishing area than that around Mecca, its traditional rival. It had originally been settled by three Jewish tribes—some, it seems, from the Fertile Crescent, others, local converts. Their language was Arabic and their way of life largely Arab. These Jews had been partly displaced by two heathen Arab tribes, to one of which—the Khazraj—Muhammad's family was related. There had been fighting between these Arab tribes, though shortly before the Hijra they had agreed on a common chief. In any case Muhammad was welcome to the Medinans, not merely as the Messenger of God (for those who responded to his doctrines) but also as an arbiter of their differences and as one who, having feuded with the Quraish, might lead them in their rivalry with Mecca.[16]

In these new conditions Muhammad necessarily became a political as well as a spiritual leader. Indeed, he and his followers may have seen the two roles as one. "The legislation of Muhammad as political leader, and his various judgments and declarations, were considered . . . also the solemn commands of Allah. . . . Government and religion merged. . . . Islam became a theocratic institution and has remained so, at least in theory, to this day." Thus Allah's commands in the Q'uran regulate the life of Muslims in specific and concrete terms, and the modern Muslim, who wants to separate religion and state, is caught in a dilemma. Turkey has become a secular state, but it has been hard for her people to adjust to this. The Islamic tradition is again making headway: as one example, non-Muslim citizens are not really considered Turks.[17]

Muhammad, as we saw, felt somewhat closer to the Jews than to the Christians. He had followed certain Jewish practices such as turning toward Jerusalem for prayer, and thus expected Jewish acceptance of his teaching. But the Medina Jews, strongly en-

16. Armajani, p. 34.
17. *Ibid.*, pp. 35–36.

trenched as they were, rejected and ridiculed his doctrines. "They accused him of garbling the Scriptures and refused to accept an Arab as the Messiah." They paid heavily for their scorn. One tribe was banished from Medina in 625; later, some six hundred members of another tribe were massacred and the rest exiled. A further group north of Medina was also expelled. In each case their land was given to those of the new faith.

Rejection by the Medina Jews may have been decisive in launching Muhammad and Islam on an independent course. Without rejecting the Judeo-Christian tradition, from this time onward he seems to have proclaimed that it was the Jews and Christians who had falsified the true religion. In future, Muslims were to pray facing Mecca rather than Jerusalem, in the belief that the Ka'ba was built by Abraham at the behest of Allah. The idols were to be destroyed, the worship of Allah restored there. Dealing with Mecca and the Meccans became a vital goal. He would not, like Jesus, leave the fate of his message solely to his followers and to God. War, conquest, and diplomacy were needed to establish God's rule on earth. Islam was to be imposed upon the Arabs; and so for the last ten years of his life—from 622 to 632—Muhammad was constantly at war.

His first battle—against a Meccan caravan, at Badr—was won against considerable odds. During the next year he was defeated and wounded at Uhud by a Meccan force led by Abu Sofian of the rival Umayya clan. Medina itself had to be defended against a Meccan assault. But Mecca lost much by this new warfare, while Muhammad had less to lose. Furthermore, once Mecca became for the Muslims a place of reverence and pilgrimage, its people no longer needed to fight to save the profits brought by pilgrims. So peace was made in 628; Muslims and Meccans were put on an equal footing, and Muslims could make the pilgrimage to Mecca.

Two years later, without fighting, Muhammad approached Mecca with his army. There had been further important conversions; even his chief adversary in the war came over. Muhammad entered as a victor, and had the idols round the Ka'ba destroyed. He then returned to Medina, his political capital (Mecca, however, remained the religious capital of Islam). But he still went to war, with the goal of making Arabia one. All that was demanded of the different tribes was a verbal confession and payment of a tax for the poor. Soon even the fringes of the area—Oman, Hadramaut, the Yemen—had acknowledged the new faith. In 632, in a last pilgrimage to Mecca, he took leave of his people in a memorable speech. Ties of faith, he said, must be more binding than ties of blood or tribal loyalties. Loyalty to Islam was all. Every Muslim was brother to every other Muslim. Raiding was banned; there must be no stealing from one's brother. Three months later, on June 8, he died in the arms of Abu Bekr's daughter, Ayisha, his favorite wife, and was buried under the floor of her room.[18]

The Spreading Fire of Faith

As we have seen, Islam, born in Arabia, was a fighting creed. Special merit was attached to war against unbelievers, especially idolaters, to convert them to the faith, and there was the prospect of instant Paradise for those killed in battle. At times, and in extreme circumstances, this duty was magnified into a *jihad* or holy war. Thus Islam was "a religious community which was at the same time an armed encampment. Its house of worship was also a court of law as well as headquarters for military command. . . . Every believer was also a military conscript, and the leader in worship was also the commander in battle." Islam as it developed was without a priesthood. Muslim seminaries trained preachers, but also lawyers and teachers of Arabic, the sacred language of the Q'uran. Those who led the congregation in prayer in the mosque were called in Arabic *imam*, and those who were specially learned, *ulama*. The most important discipline in Islam was the study of the *shari'a*, the laws of God as revealed in the Q'uran. An important element in the system was an offering, equivalent to a tax, called *zakah*—customarily some 2½ per cent of every Muslim's income. This was

18. *Ibid.*, p. 39.

obligatory for all Muslims and was used for community purposes. Non-Muslims were exempt from military service, but paid instead a special poll tax called *jizya*. Voluntary offerings in real estate or cash were collected by the government and devoted to religious endowment (*waqf*), administered in later Muslim countries by a special office or ministry. Every Muslim was expected to make the pilgrimmage to Mecca once in his lifetime if he could afford it.

When they spoke of non-Muslims, the first leaders of Islam thought primarily of Jews and Christians—of whom, as we saw, there were many in Arabia—and the Q'uran specifically invokes the Judeo-Christian tradition. Both Jews and Christians were held to have strayed from the true religion revealed to them in the Bible by the patriarchs and earlier prophets such as Abraham, Moses, and Jesus. Amongst other things the Christian doctrine of the Trinity was rejected by Muslims, as it was by Jews, as a blasphemous deviation from the absolute unity of God. On the other hand, the Muslim concept of the next world and life after death was closer to Christianity than to Judaism.

While Muhammad was considered the last of the prophets, Jews and Christians were placed in a special category as "People of the Book," i.e., the Bible. They were not to be forced to accept Islam. If not converted by persuasion, they could remain in their own faiths under Muslim protection. This assurance of religious freedom was one reason that Jews, when persecuted in Christian lands, went to Muslim countries and lived there in peace. It was also the basis for the system of autonomous religious communities (the *millet* system) that later developed in the Turkish Empire. This doctrine caused special difficulty when the surge of Islam led to the conquest of countries with organized religions that were neither Jewish nor Christian, since there could clearly be no question of killing all those who declined to accept Islam. Thus gradually an elastic though unofficial interpretation prevailed, and the Zoroastrian fire worshippers of Persia and the Hindus and Buddhists of India were tacitly accepted as "People of the Book."[19]

19. *Ibid.*, pp. 39–47.

Although there is no evidence that Muhammad meant his message for the world beyond Arabia, by the time of his death his armies were reaching out to the border areas. One of his last expeditions was an unsuccessful assault on the Byzantines north of Ma'an in present-day Jordan.[20] Just before his death another expedition was to set out to the Syrian frontier. As we saw earlier, the Persian and Byzantine empires were drained by their long wars, and the Arabs, who had been their clients, had turned against them. Despite the latent opportunities this offered, the small Muslim world was bitterly confused and divided after the Prophet's death. The men of Medina (the Helpers of the Prophet) sought to have as leader and Caliph—as spiritual and temporal ruler—a man from one of their own tribes. Abu Bekr insisted that the Arabs would not accept a leader except from Quraish and, with a pledge of loyalty from his fellow Meccan Umar, swung opinion to his side.[21] Thus he became the first of the four orthodox or legitimate Caliphs to rule the Muslims for nearly thirty years after Muhammad's death (until 661).

All Caliphs were chosen by some kind of consensus, or after designation by their predecessor, and had some valid claim to the succession by reason of close connection or relationship with the Prophet. The others were Umar himself, Othman of the Ummayya clan, and Ali, the cousin and son-in-law of Muhammad. Abu Bekr survived only two years, and it is a significant sign of the turbulence and intense rivalries of the Muslim world that his three successors all died violent deaths. Indeed, the rifts in Islamic leadership from this early period have never truly healed. For some time after 661 the Caliphate became the prize of the strongest or most astute claimant; later it was inherited by puppets of strong rulers; and finally it was captured in the sixteenth century by the Turkish Sultans, who had not even the title of being Arabs. It then remained in the hands of the Ottomans until the last Sultan was deposed in 1922.

20. Glubb, p. 93.
21. *Ibid.*, p. 106.

Characteristically, after the Prophet, many of the tribesmen, convinced that they had given their allegiance to Muhammad personally, judged themselves to have been freed by his death from the Arab unity he had imposed. Something like this unhappy pattern was to be repeated in modern times. This movement of rebellion is known as the Apostasy. Had Abu Bekr and his fellow leaders been less vigorous, Islam might never have spread to half the world. But he immediately attacked the rebels, and the campaigns against them carried the wild Arab armies up to and into the fringes of the great Persian and Byzantine empires. There thus developed, almost by accident and without previous intention, the Arab conquest of the settled lands to the east, north, and west of Arabia.[22]

By June of 633, a year after Muhammad's death, the Apostasy had been suppressed. This meant the enforcement of his ban on intertribal warfare. Providentially—or disastrously from the standpoint of their enemies—there lay before the Arabs a unique chance of diverting their martial ardour against the wealthy and sophisticated Persians and Byzantines, weakened by their wars, softened by luxury, and burdened by the elaborate organization of their armies and civil government. There was adventure and loot for the asking, and a meritorious work of God to be accomplished. In ten years the Arabs conquered and occupied most of the Fertile Crescent up to the Taurus and Zagros mountains shielding Asia Minor and central Persia. In 634 and 636 two decisive battles took place on the river Yarmouk in the Dera'a gap, then as in modern times the key to Syria. Damascus, Jerusalem, Antioch had been taken. In Jerusalem the Greek Patriarch Sophronius surrendered the city personally to the austere, threadbare, barefoot Caliph Umar. The Muslim conqueror, however, declined to infringe the sanctity of the Holy Sepulchre, and said his prayers upon the ground outside.[23]

In 637—the year of the fall of Jerusalem—the Persians under their legendary general Rustum were decisively defeated by the Arabs in the desert fringes of the Euphrates at Qadasiya. Here the

22. See Guillaume, pp. 78–79.
23. Glubb, p. 183.

Arabs were in their element, and, with their camels, could manoeuvre easily and escape pursuit. The Persians, without camels, were gravely hampered in the desert, and their cautious general had crossed the river only against his better judgement, being urged on by his young king, Yezdegird. The Persians had the advantage of elephants, the tanks of ancient armies. But the Arabs seem to have learned how to stampede the beasts by piercing their eyes. After the Arab victory the twin cities of Ctesiphon and Seleucia on the Tigris fell to the Arabs, who knew them as *Medain* (The Cities). Ctesiphon had become the capital of the Persian Empire after Alexander the Great. Following a further defeat, Yezdegird and his forces withdrew behind the mountains, leaving Mesopotamia—the Land between the Rivers, the original home of Abraham and nucleus of the Jewish people, and the modern Iraq—in Arab hands.[24]

The Caliphate of Umar, who has been called the St. Paul of Islam, lasted ten years. Under him the faith spread indeed like fire, and the short period under Abu Bekr and himself is looked on as the golden age of Arab regeneration and expansion. No one disputed his orders or authority, or his fundamental goals. However wide and diverse the areas conquered, Arabia was to remain the centre of power of this new Muslim theocracy. It was to be a completely Muslim land, and all non-Muslims were banished from it. Wherever his armies carried the faith, Islam was to be the dominant religion, and Arabic, the language of the Q'uran and thus of God himself, the prevailing tongue. In most of this he and his followers were astonishingly successful. Iran and Byzantium had been unable to conquer each other; the Arabs defeated them both. A vast majority of the peoples of Syria, Palestine, Egypt, and Iraq became Muslims, adopted Arabic, and remembered the new course of their history with pride. They may have welcomed the change from Byzantine domination, with its intolerant pursuit of heresy. But the Persians had already a long, proud national history, and they remembered their defeat with bitterness. While they adopted Islam

24. *Ibid.*, pp. 197–203.

they generally set themselves apart from their conquerors.[25]

Although for a time Umar's administrative policies were successful, his very personal methods of dealing with the vast empire he had suddenly inherited, and his arbitrary treatment of the victorious army commanders, alike contributed to the growing disunity bedevilling his successors. Yet there was no loss of vigour; fresh victories continued to expand the empire both before and after he died. By 644 the Arab conquests had spread to the Nile Delta and much of central Persia, and to North Africa as far as Tripoli. The surrender of Egypt was hastened by the death of Heraclius, the ill-fated Byzantine Emperor whose reign, though initially victorious against the Persians, had ended in conflict and defeat. Nevertheless, the winning of Egypt was a remarkable feat. Characteristically, Umar, who had already dismissed the conquerors of Syria and Persia, called the conqueror of Egypt severely to account—on the charge that he had become wealthy, and paved the way for his rejection by the next Caliph.

The rough and ready methods originally sanctioned for the distribution of booty made it hard for the conquerors not to become rich. Glubb tells us that, under Abu Bekr, "the fifth of all plunder was sent to Medina . . . , but no sooner was it received than it was distributed. Some might be used to acquire weapons, horses or . . . chain-mail . . . , while the remainder was distributed to the needy among the Muslims. No accounts were kept and the constant emptiness of the treasury was . . . remedied by the arrival of the loot of fresh victories." The other four-fifths of the plunder was distributed among the victorious troops. It was hard for the first Caliphs, still living in stark simplicity, to appreciate the temptations of their soldiers in the rich lands they overran. Umar decreed that they were not to settle there, but were to remain a dominant, dedicated master race, simple and austere, aloof from, and uncontaminated by, Byzantine or Persian luxury and sophistication, ever ready to fight the unbeliever. To ensure this, military bases were set up at

25. Armajani, pp. 51, 54.

Jabiya in Syria, at Ramlah in Palestine, at Kufa and Basra in lower Mesopotamia, and at Fustat, now part of Cairo in Egypt.[26]

It was, however, utterly unrealistic to suppose that contacts with the subject races would not develop to a degree that in the long run would profoundly transform the ruling Arab elite. These "garrison towns generally on the edge of the desert, became the centres of Arab government. To them the inhabitants . . . came to market their produce . . . and through them the knowledge of Arabic gradually permeated the country. All non-Muslims had to pay a tax, and this disability not unnaturally led to a vast access of converts to Islam. . . . Civilian employees from the occupied country . . . performed such services as a military community requires of its civilian dependents. The policy . . . was to allow the natives to administer the country very much as they had always done."[27]

The Arabs could not supply a competent civil service, and thus the accounts in the former Byzantine provinces continued to be kept in Greek, and in the former Persian areas, in Persian. The early Caliphs had no means of minting money. Byzantine currency remained in circulation in Syria and Palestine; so did that of Persia in Iraq. Whatever rules the conquerors might make about taxes, their actual assessment and collection from the conquered peoples must still have been done by the former imperial officials. In other ways the early Caliphs had soon to provide for contingencies far beyond the scope of their simple patriarchal outlook. So long as their warriors collected four-fifths of the spoils, they needed no pay. But once the fighting was over in any particular area and there was no more loot, they had to be paid like armies everywhere.

Umar decided that all real estate in the conquered lands belonged to the Muslim Arabs. Apart from this, the revenue of the state in cash and kind came from the fifth of all booty, the *jizya* (poll tax) paid by non-Muslims, and a land tax paid by all non-Arab peasants. The total revenue was so large that Arabs were exempted from the *zakah* levy. Furthermore, while all proceeds be-

26. Glubb, pp. 150 and 258.
27. Guillaume, p. 80.

longed to the Muslim *umma,* the surplus left after paying government expenses was distributed to the Arabs, who thus benefited doubly from privileged status. Finally, on the basis of a census of their service, position, and religious standing, all Arabs were given regular emoluments, from the Prophet's widow to the lowest soldier.[28]

A further problem faced by Umar was that the Muslims had no code of civil law. Their law was the Q'uran, which Christians, Jews and Zoroastrians could not be expected to accept. Ultimately the Zoroastrians of Persia ceased to be a problem, since most of them embraced Islam—although *shi'i* Islam, adopted as the official religion of Persia in the sixteenth century, is usually held to be less orthodox than *sunni* Islam, which became the dominant version of the faith. For the Christians and Jews, the Muslims adopted the simplest and most sensible arrangement: they were allowed to keep their own separate judicial, as well as religious, systems administered by their own judges. When the Arabs were finally conquered by the Turks in the sixteenth century, this *millet* system was, as we saw, taken over by the Ottoman Empire and lasted until that empire collapsed at the end of World War I.

Meanwhile, the privileged status of the Arab conquerors and their pride of race were gradually modified by the many new factors implicit in their victories. Thus, for example, during the first century of Islam, non-Arabs gradually worked their way into positions of authority, and Arab pride gave way to a sense of interracial pride based on loyalty to Islam. This lasted until our day, when the first attempts were made to divorce religion from politics even in Muslim countries. Moreover, in practice intermixture with the local populations could not be prevented and was a strong contributory factor in the development of this new type of community. The Prophet authorized Muslims to have four wives. But he had sanctioned also the use as concubines of women captured in war and—of course—of slaves. "With the fantastically rapid conquests of the fertile and civilized provinces of Syria and Iraq, an almost unlimited

28. Armajani, pp. 57–58.

supply of women . . . became available to the Muslims, together with the necessary wealth . . . to maintain them. As a result, an immense number of children was born to Arab fathers, mostly in the military bases, and these children were classified as Arabs, although most of their mothers were captive foreign wives or concubines. Within a single generation, the ethnological character of the Arabs who had conquered Syria and Iraq was already becoming different to that of the Arabs of Arabia."[29]

The difference was indeed profound. Iraq, under Persia, had been Oriental in its culture, though this contrasted sharply and in many complex ways with the life of Arabia. For their part the peoples of the Nile Delta and the coastal regions of Syria were not then "Orientals" in any meaningful sense, but rather were part of the Mediterranean Greek and Roman world, and profoundly influenced by the subtle cultures of these two ancestors of European civilization. Thus in those regions the simple Arab conquerors tended gradually to acquire many of the characteristics we associate today with the sharp-witted, sophisticated peoples of the Levant. On the other hand, those in the desert areas, or its fringes in eastern Syria, Jordan, and much of Iraq, have tended to retain the simple, downright directness of their forebears.

The Worldly Phase Begins

In 644 Umar was stabbed at prayer by an incensed Persian. As he lay dying he appointed a committee including Ali and Othman (both sons-in-law of the Prophet) to select the next Caliph. After prolonged dispute Othman, then past seventy, was chosen. Unlike his two predecessors, Othman was an Umayyad from the Quraish clan, which had been the most distinguished and influential before Muhammad. Many Umayyads were worldly and properous merchants, and some of its leaders, notably Abu Sofian, had fought the Prophet in his early years. Later they were converts to the faith, and one of Abu Sofian's sons (Muawiya) had become governor of Syria in Umar's later years.

29. Glubb, pp. 216–18.

Othman was rich, genial, and easygoing, and for a time more popular than the stern Umar. But he was a deplorably weak ruler, and under him much of the governmental structure built by Umar collapsed. When he became Caliph, the old Umayyad Meccan aristocracy saw their chance to recover their position, which, since the Prophet, had been overshadowed by Hashimite prestige, and to check the hopes and claims of the Medinans who had contributed decisively to Muhammad's success. They prevailed on Othman to fill many of the chief posts with members of their clan, and it was the Umayyads rather than the Caliph who took over the Arab empire. Despite Umar's ban on such things, Othman allowed his kinsmen to acquire land in the conquered territories; and there emerged a growing trend, denounced by the fundamentalists, toward luxurious living and laxer moral standards. Eventually his twelve-year rule, discredited by nepotism and corruption, became a source of spreading discontent. This was inevitably encouraged by Ali, his Hashimite rival, whose hope of succeeding Umar had been dashed.[30]

Despite vacillating and erratic guidance from Medina, the Arab conquests somehow continued of their own momentum. The victorious ruler of Egypt was replaced by Othman's foster brother, recalled at that point to expel the resurgent Byzantines from Alexandria, then again dismissed. Thus powerful enemies were made of men who, had they been better treated, could have saved the Caliph when the final crisis came. But it was characteristic of the spirit and fighting qualities of nearly all Arabs of that age that, even under new and relatively untried Umayyad leaders, they were hardly less victorious than under the veterans of Umar's time. The Caliph's able but money-loving foster brother reconquered Tripolitania and invaded Tunisia. Othman's young appointees on the northeastern front completed their conquest of a rebellious Persia and carried the Arab banners into Afghanistan. Yezdegird, the last Sassanid King, was hunted into central Asia and ignominiously killed there. Until the Safavids some eight hundred years later,

30. See Guillaume, p. 81; Armajani, pp. 58–59; Glubb, pp. 273–74.

Persia did not again have a dynasty that was truly her own. Zoro-astrianism was almost totally displaced by Islam, though, as we saw, it was preserved by a Persian remnant—the Parsees—which settled in Bombay. In the north, Azerbaijan and parts of Armenia were taken. In Syria, Muawiya, with help from Egypt, built and launched a fleet, and with it captured Cyprus. In this and subsequent engage-ments, the Muslims checked the Byzantine command of the sea. In later phases of the struggle with the Christian world, the Medi-terranean was to become virtually an Arab lake, while, to the south, Arab dominance of the trade routes to India and China was to con-tinue also for some eight hundred years until the age of European discovery initiated by the voyages of Vasco da Gama and Co-lumbus.

In Othman's time, however, the Muslims suffered one notable reverse: in the eastern Caucasus, one of their armies was destroyed by the Khazars, a people of Turkish origin that for centuries had dominated the region between the Black and Caspian seas. Nearly a hundred years later, when the Arabs succeeded in subjecting the Caucasus, the Khazar ruler temporarily accepted Islam but later changed his faith. His sister was married to the Byzantine Emperor, who pressed him to accept Christianity. Hesitating between the Byzantines and the Arabs, he decided, around 740, to adopt Juda-ism as a sign of his neutrality. When attacked from the East at the end of the tenth century, the Khazars scattered over what is now southern Russia and Poland, and carried their Judaism with them. Thus the Jews of Eastern Europe, some of whom had migrated thither from persecutions in the West, were increased and strength-ened by a new ethnic element, totally non-Jewish in origin, which had embraced their faith.[31]

Othman had been one of the earliest converts to Islam, and even the Prophet had extolled his piety. Yet his ultimate tragedy was caused by his insistence on a definitive, authorized version of the sacred text: all alternative versions were to be destroyed. But a for-

31. Glubb, *Peace in the Holy Land*, pp. 209–10. See also Schweitzer, pp. 79–80.

mer personal attendant of Muhammad's, then in Kufa, claimed that he could recite the Q'uran just as the Prophet himself had done. Since Othman's version differed from this in some respects, he therefore charged that the Caliph had suppressed verses unfavorable to the Umayyads, and, by his destruction of all readings at variance with his own, had burned the word of God. This and other factors brought the sedition against Othman to a head. Only Syria was kept in order by its competent and long-established Umayyad governor, Muawiya. Eventually, in 656, three groups of insurgents from the military bases at Kufa and Basra in Iraq and Fustat in Egypt converged upon Medina. When a relief force despatched by Mauwiya was approaching, a group led by Abu Bekr's son Muhammad forced its way into the Caliph's house and killed the old man while he was reading the Q'uran. Ali, with ambitions of his own, had done nothing effective to stop this, and, a week after Othman's death, was proclaimed Caliph in his place.

As a member of the Prophet's family by blood and marriage, no one had a better claim. But the harsh charges against Othman and his shocking murder by one of the inner group of the faithful had changed Islam. After twenty-five years the Caliphate had ceased to be the sacrosanct pinnacle of a theocracy. It had become a prize to which any ruthless and ambitious leader might aspire. In any event, there were by now two main schools of thought on how the succession should be settled. One held that all Caliphs should be from the Quraish; the other, that the Caliphate should be restricted to the family of the Prophet and its descendants. The "legitimists" of this second school were Ali's partisans (*shi' at Ali*, or later simply *shi'a*). On this issue the *shi'is* were later to diverge from the mainstream of *sunni* Islam (that which is held to conform to the *sunna* or practices of the Prophet). Theirs was the version of the faith later adopted in Persia and in parts of Iraq and India.[32]

Once in office, and against the weightiest advice, Ali made two cardinal mistakes. One was to leave unpunished those who had killed Othman. This exposed him to the later charge of complicity

32. Armajani, pp. 59–61. Glubb, *The Great Arab Conquests*, pp. 298–304.

in the murder. The other was to send out orders summarily replacing the provincial governors. Muawiya ignored the summons, then replied in insolent terms; the blood of his kinsman was to be avenged. At this juncture Ali was deserted by two companions whose advice he had disregarded; both had aspirations of their own and, while Ali prepared a campaign against Mauwiya, they joined a Mecca faction that also took the field against Ali. The struggle culminated in a battle on the Euphrates between Ali and Muawiya. Faced with defeat, Muawiya astutely appealed for arbitration based on the Q'uran. Ali seems to have been forced by his troops to accept;[33] and yet to submit the Caliphate to arbitration fatally compromised his own position as well as the remaining sanctity of the office. And many of Ali's followers left him, rejecting his decision, and, on the leadership of Islam, formed a third doctrinal group, the Kharijites or ("seceders"). These would accept no claim based on family or tribal links; the purity of the faith demanded piety above all. One of them killed Ali in 661 in the fifth year of his contested rule, and his elder son Hasan was proclaimed by the "legitimists" in his place.

Meanwhile in 660 Governor Muawiya had proclaimed himself Caliph in Jerusalem. Hasan submitted to him, having no relish for a further struggle.[34] Muawiya and his followers had long since abandoned their military bases and made Damascus their capital; Medina ceased to be the centre of the Arab empire. The Umayyad Caliphate of Damascus inaugurated a new and brilliant imperial era in sharp contrast to the homespun methods of the first Caliphs. Though gradually absorbed by the subtle and sophisticated culture of the eastern Mediterranean, the Arabs brought to it their language, their vigour, and their faith. The outcome was a civilization that combined creatively some of the finest elements of classical antiquity and the legacies of the Orient, and far outshone the Dark Ages to which Western Europe was condemned after the fall of Rome by the barbarian invasions and other causes.

33. Glubb, pp. 326–27.
34. Armajani, p. 62.

Chapter 4   The Arab Empires

The Umayyads

By the year 661, when Ali, last of the orthodox Caliphs, was murdered, Islam had spread by conquest over most of the Middle East, carrying with it the language and many of the customs of its birthplace, Arabia. In so doing, it gradually created, and with surprising speed, the Arab world we know today. But in the next hundred years—those of the Umayyad Caliphate—the Arabs spread far beyond this "Arab World." "In the east they reached the gates of China, in the west they thrust a wedge into Gaul beyond the Pyrenees, in the north they knocked at the gates of the capital of the Byzantine Empire, and in the south the limit of their expansion was the Indian Ocean and the African desert."[1]

The Umayyads had their capital at Damascus, which had been within the fold of Graeco-Roman civilization for a thousand years. Thus, although the Arabs remained the dominant strain, in its developing methods of administration the empire was largely Byzantine and to some extent Persian rather than Arab. Muawiya preserved the easy egalitarianism of Arab tradition, being constantly accessible and moving freely around without escort—and yet his

1. Nejla Izzeddin, *The Arab World*, p. 34.

chief secretary was a Syrian Christian.[2] Some of the main problems of the empire were internal and stemmed from the characteristic Arab proneness to feuding—a trait that has endured into modern times—intensified in those early years by fundamentalist religious fervour.

The Arabs were habitually reluctant to accept any preordained order of succession: in their view, amongst those obviously available the most capable should take over. Thus many of the Arab leaders saw no special sanctity in the claims of Muawiya's own son and designated successor, especially at a time when Islam was no longer a theocracy and the Caliphate had become the prize of the most determined seeker after power. There were, after all, surviving sons of other Caliphs who might prove equally capable, if not more so. This conviction produced an abortive revolt in favour of Husayn, a grandson of the Prophet and younger son of Ali, the last orthodox Caliph. In 680 Husayn and his followers were massacred by the Damascus forces in Iraq. His dramatic martyrdom produced an intense reaction against the Umayyads in the Muslim world, and elicited the passionate partisanship of the "legitimists," the *shi'is*, in favour of Ali and his descendants, and gave permanent strength to the separatist movement which has divided *shi'a* from *sunni* Islam to this day.[3]

For many years the Umayyad monarchy was wracked by civil war. It was consolidated as an effective empire over all Muslims only in the reign of Abdul Malik (692–705), after Mecca had been captured by his troops. This remarkable ruler still governed in patriarchal Arab fashion, dealing with grievances in person. Arabic replaced Greek for all official purposes. Yet under him this new state, forged by the simple peoples of Arabia, acquired a sophisticated public organization with specialized ministries and secretariats, a system of archives, and postal service to all corners of the subject

2. Bernard Lewis, *The Arabs in History*, p. 66.
3. *Ibid.*, p. 67. See also Sir John Glubb, A *Short History of the Arab Peoples*, pp. 75-77.

lands.[4] Moreover, conquest and expansion were resumed. Under his immediate successors, in 711, the Muslims successfully invaded Spain. Then for the second time they unsuccessfully besieged Byzantium. The forces of the empire reached out to occupy Bokhara and Samarquand in central Asia, and Sind, in what is now western Pakistan. But the peak was soon passed. The abortive attack on Constantinople has been called "the last assault by the Arabs in the grand style."[5] The fleet and army of Syria were destroyed and the finances of the empire gravely strained.

Discrimination between Arab and non-Arab Muslims was another source of tension and discontent. Despite the theoretical equality of the non-Arabs, and their higher status than the *dhimmi* (non-Muslims), they were known by the condescending name of *mawali* ("clients"), and were excluded from the inner circles of power. From the days of the Prophet, non-Muslims had been subject to a poll tax, and this later produced much of the revenue of the expanding Arab state. Although all Muslims were in principle exempt, as the number of converts grew with every new conquest the state would have gone bankrupt if none of them had paid. "In practice, therefore, converts were, more often than not, obliged to continue payment. Exemption had . . . become largely an Arab privilege, which Muslims of other races did not enjoy."[6] Discontent was heightened when one pious Umayyad ruler abolished the tax on non-Arab Muslims, in strict accordance with the Prophet's injunctions, and his successor re-imposed it.

The Abbasids

A principal centre of disturbance was Khurasan, the northeastern province of Persia. It was from here that, in 747, a Persian-led rebellion was launched against the Umayyads in behalf of their

4. Glubb, p. 79.
5. Lewis, p. 76.
6. Glubb, p. 85.

Hashimite rivals, a rebellion that gained the support of the Shi'is since Ali was of the Hashim clan. In 750 the Umayyads were decisively defeated. A descendant of Abbas, the uncle of the Prophet, then became the first Caliph of a new dynasty, the Abbasids, with its centre no longer in Syria but in Iraq. His successor was to build himself a new and resplendent capital on the site of a small village on the Tigris named in Persian the "God-given" (Baghdad). The Umayyad leaders who could be caught were massacred; as was, by treachery, the Persian leader whose rebellion had helped to place the Abbasids on the throne. By now all Arabs of whatever dynasty were strongly resented by the Persians. But the Abbasids, during their scant century of strength and glory lasting until 842, became past masters at playing off against each other the different factions among their supporters, rivals, and foes. Meanwhile, one Umayyad chieftain who managed to escape founded a state of his own in Spain. Originally based on Córdova, this, like the empires based on Damascus and Baghdad, was to become the focus of a brilliant civilization, Arab in tongue and tone and yet enriched by the impact of other older and more complex cultures.

The overthrow of the Umayyads resulted in the orientalization, not only of the Arab empire, but of Islam itself. The Umayyad state had been essentially a Mediterranean power, since not only Damascus but also Syria, Palestine, Egypt, North Africa, and Spain had all been part of the world of Greece and Rome. During the Arab conquests the Persian Empire, including Iraq, as well as the territory gained by the Muslims in Afghanistan, India, and central Asia, had become colonies of this Mediterranean empire. But the Abbasids, having achieved power mainly with Persian help, made Baghdad their capital in an area that had been Persian and thus decisively Oriental for just as long as Syria and the other "Mediterranean" regions had been part of Graeco-Roman civilization. It was in a rich river valley, at the junction of many trade routes, which had been the traditional focus of the great cosmopolitan empires of the Middle East. As a result, the Arab-dominated empire of the Umayyads became transformed under the Abbasids—Arabs though they were—into a multi-racial Muslim state in which advancement was open to all races alike. One sign of the expanding influence of the Orient was that "the Caliph now became an autocrat claiming a divine origin for his authority, resting it on his regular armed forces, and exercising it through a salaried bureaucracy. The increased importance of force . . . is . . . exemplified in the important position held by the executioner. . . . Pedigree was no help to advancement, but only the favour of the sovereign, and the Arab aristocracy was replaced by an official hierarchy. The new dignity of the Caliph was expressed . . . in the . . . title 'Shadow of God upon Earth'." While any man could approach the early Caliphs, "the Abbasids surrounded themselves with the pomp and ceremonial of an elaborate . . . court."[7]

The revolution that brought the Abbasids to power was, as we saw, a revolution of the discontented. There had been discontents among the Arabs themselves, as well as among the *mawali*. Some supporters of the revolution had been Arabs from the southern tribes of the Arabian peninsula who were less firmly established in the aristocracy of the conquerors than the northern tribes. Another discontented element was the underprivileged town population, especially the *mawali*, merchants and artisans of diverse ethnic origins. In any event, as the conquests ended, this Arab aristocracy of fighters became essentially redundant. An era of peace produced a cosmopolitan ruling class of officials, merchants, bankers, landowners, scholars, jurists, and teachers. While Abbassid administration was a development of that of the late Umayyads, the influence of Persia became increasingly strong. A new office, possibly of Persian origin—that of *wazir* or chief minister—was created by the Abbasids to control, under the Caliph, all the operations of government.[8]

Despite Persian influence, the most determined opponents of the Abbasids were the Persians themselves, both the masses and the upper classes. They showed their general dissent in the religious

7. Lewis, p. 83.
8. *Ibid.*, pp. 81, 84.

field through espousal of the Shi'a creed as well as by heterodox movements outside Islam. The Persian nobility were more devious. They "occupied positions of power and responsibility, and Persian culture, customs and even costume became the vogue." They felt that they "could accomplish their anti-Arab aims subtly from within and through political control." Another form of opposition was a Persian-influenced literary movement to combat the claims of the Arabs to national superiority. Many of those concerned were non-Arab secretaries in government offices. In the Persian spirit, these encouraged scepticism in religion and morals and backed heretical causes.[9]

Harun al-Rashid, the Abbasid Caliph who was a contemporary of Charlemagne, reigned from 786 to 809. His years of rule were in many ways the high point of the imperial regime. By now Baghdad had become a by-word for cosmopolitan luxury and sophistication. A vivid picture of it is painted in the widely known tales of Scheherazade, called *The Thousand and One Nights*. It is only unfortunate that the exotic aspects of these "Arabian Nights" of the distant past, and, at the other end of the scale, the image of the primitive Beduin in his long robes, seem to be all that the less-educated Westerner cares to know about "the Arabs" and "the Arab World" today. Baghdad was in any case the centre of a prosperous and highly civilized society far in advance of that of contemporary Europe. As we saw, the European Dark Ages coincided with this age of Arab imperial enlightenment. This was no accident, for the Arabs now dominated the Mediterranean and the Indian Ocean. Before the Atlantic had been crossed, or Europeans had settled or subjected any part of Asia, Europe was largely cut off from overseas trade and the wealth flowing from it. Moreover, at its height, this civilization we call Arab was, as we saw, a product of the cross-fertilization of Arab native vigour with the subtleties and refinements of far older cultures that had passed their prime.

The Abbasid Caliphate, and other shining centres of this earlier

9. Armajani, pp. 80–83.

Arab world, helped to preserve the heritage of Greece and Rome for the West in Arabic translation. Furthermore, many branches of human activity that we like to think of as those in which the West excels were a specialty of these cosmopolitan, Arab-dominated realms. Much was preserved, conceived, or developed by them in such fields as navigation, industry, commerce, banking, mathematics, medicine, zoology, geography, chemistry, and other natural sciences. While arithmetic, with the decimal point and zero, came originally from India, the men of this first Arab world went on to invent trigonometry and algebra (this last an Arabic word, like admiral from *amir*, commander). They even measured the circumference of the earth some six hundred years before the Europeans acknowledged that it was not flat.[10]

"It was in Syria . . . that that great flowering of culture known as Arab or Muslim civilization began—a culture which, for the next five hundred years, was to spread throughout western Asia, north Africa, and Spain, giving light to the Middle Ages . . . and sowing some of the seeds of the Renaissance. . . . Mixed it certainly was . . . both in regard to its materials and to the race, religion and geographical environment of the thinkers, scientists and artists who collaborated in creating it. . . . From their Peninsula the Arabs brought two great contributions, Islam and the Arabic language, together with their code of desert chivalry. They also brought the psychological stimulus of . . . a vigorous, conquering people [to] the stagnant, if more civilized . . . outside world. In this world there was Greek philosophy, Roman ideas of law and government, Byzantine and Persian art, Christian theology and Judaic tradition. Arab civilization was a product of all these factors. . . . Christians and Jews played a prominent part in all the learning and culture of the new universal society . . . [but] the Arabs created the conditions for the new civilization and brought together the various resources out of which it developed . . . and Islamic thought, whether expressed in law, theology, or mysticism, played a funda-

10. See Majdia D. Khadduri, (ed.), *The Arab-Israeli Impasse,* pp. 24–25.

mental part in directing their thought and shaping their life. . . .
Islam itself . . . came from the Arabs and was propagated by Arab
arms."[11]

The Arabs: Fragmentation, Decline, and Ultimate Subjection

We have traced in broad outline the origins of Judaism, Christianity, and Islam, the links between them, and the special relations
to the Holy Land of the followers of all three faiths. We have also
outlined the causes and circumstances of the Jewish Dispersion, the
triumph of Christianity in the West, the spread of Islam through
the Middle East, and, more specifically, the creation of the "Arab
World" in the Fertile Crescent, Egypt, and North Africa. Finally,
we have noted the sharp contrast in earlier centuries between Jewish sufferings in many Christian lands, and the relative tolerance
of Islam. This contrast has become tragically significant today in
the light of the present hostility of the Arab world, not to Judaism
or the Jews as such (though the former secure position of the Jewish communities in these countries has been largely destroyed) but
to the militant state of Israel, which has arisen in their midst. It
has been essential to describe as we have the ancient roots of the
present Arab-Israeli conflict, but since the conflict itself is our main
concern, the scope of this work debars us from pursuing in comparable detail the transition from the ninth century to modern
times. The main phases of this transition were indicated at the
start of the last chapter and these will now be considered somewhat
more fully, but in reduced detail and at a swifter pace.

A notable aspect of the centuries following the Abbasid triumph
was, as we know, the fragmentation and gradual decline of the
Arabs as a dominant, imperial race. The seeds of this decline were
in fact sown as early as A.D. 750, when the Abbasid failed completely to eliminate the Umayyads. The ultimate phase was to come

11. Edward Atiyah, *The Arabs*, pp. 39–41.

in 1517 when the Ottoman Turks completed the subjugation of the Arab world by the conquest of Egypt and the Fertile Crescent.

The Muslims in Spain. The Muslims invaded Spain in 711 and, some forty years later, in 755, the escaped Umayyad leader established what he claimed to be a separate Caliphate in Córdova. The Jews of the Peninsula, harassed by the Visigoths, had looked forward to the Muslim invasions, and in fact these invasions initiated one of the happiest phases of Jewish history in Europe. The golden age of Islamic Spain was one in which the wealth of the Jewish genius played a brilliant role, as it had in Baghdad itself, in bringing to full flower the multi-faceted civilization born of the Arab conquests.

The Shadow of the Turks. It was the conquests in central Asia that led to the long and fateful Arab intercourse with the Turks, originally with the Seljuq branch. Converts to Islam, these future Turkish masters were at first slaves and mercenaries, and only later became a kind of Praetorian Guard of the Baghdad Caliphs.[12] In any event, by the latter part of the ninth century they had become the effective rulers of the Abbassid empire, and the Caliphs themselves were puppets in their hands.[13] As so often in history, and as the earlier Arab conquests had shown, a more primitive, vigorous race was able to impose its will on a society militarily weakened by luxury, sophistication, and interbreeding with softer and more civilized peoples. In 1055 the Seljuqs entered Baghdad in force, and only sixteen years later defeated the Byzantine armies and gradually overran most of Asia Minor—a feat that even the Arabs at their height had never achieved. This success, and an appeal to the Pope by the Byzantine Emperor, was indeed the starting point of the

12. "The Turks were as brave and obedient as they were uncouth and unlettered. . . . In any event [they] proved to be a Frankenstein monster." Armajani, p. 89.
13. Atiyah, p. 43.

Crusades. But a relic of the former servile status of the Turkish soldiery was the name *Mamluk* (meaning "owned" or "slave") attaching to many of them. Despite this ostensible stigma, a group of Mamluks was to rule Egypt and Syria as an independent dynasty from 1254 to 1517, and later to play a dominant role in Egypt under Turkish suzerainty until they were crushed in 1811.

The Fatimids. Long before this, yet another dynasty of rulers also claiming to be Caliphs had established itself in Egypt and other parts of North Africa. The Fatimid rulers, descended from Fatima, daughter of the Prophet and wife of Ali, and being thus Shi'is, controlled this area from 969. They founded the city of Cairo as their capital, and the famous Muslim university of Al Azhar, which claims to be the oldest university in the world.[14] After two centuries, in 1171, they in turn were supplanted by a Kurdish officer, Salah al-Din, who had served as their chief minister or *wazir*. This leader was successful also against the Crusaders, whom he defeated at Hattin in Palestine in 1187, and thus became famous in Western legend as Saladin. The process of fragmentation was also conspicuous in North Africa, and in Spain after the break-up of the Umayyad Caliphate in the tenth century as the result of Berber incursions from North Africa. It was equally rapid and significant to the east of the Fertile Crescent, in Persia, Afghanistan, India, and central Asia, but with these areas we are not specifically concerned.

The Mongol Onslaught. In the thirteenth century, even the Turks temporarily succumbed to the incursions of a people more primitive than themselves—the Mongols, to whom they were distantly related. In their initial attacks these nomadic central Asian tribesmen generally wrought the total destruction of settled communities, which they saw as the natural enemies of their way of life. Thus in 1258 they captured and destroyed Baghdad, and the enfeebled Abbasid Caliphate in that city came to an end. The Abbasids

14. Armajani, p. 92.

were invited by the Mamluks to re-establish the Caliphate in Cairo, but there too the office remained the shadow it had become. Somewhat later the Mongols sacked Damascus and were checked only by the Mamluks from Egypt, who defeated them in Syria and Palestine.

The Ottomans. The Mongol victories over the Seljuqs in Asia Minor and beyond paved the way for the later rise of the *Osmanli* or Ottoman Turks, who were named after the ruler of a small principality near the Bosphorus. These finally conquered Constantinople and extinguished the Byzantine Empire in 1453, renaming the imperial city Istanbul. This Turkish victory carried a new tide of triumphant Islam into southeast Europe, but it was no longer an Arab tide. It brought the Crescent to the gates of Vienna, and only in the seventeenth century did Islam begin markedly to recede in Europe.

The Muslim Recession. Expansion of the Western Powers. In contrast to the Ottoman victories, in Spain and Portugal, at the other end of Europe, Islam had far earlier been forced onto the defensive. Fighting back from the North, the resurgent Christians recaptured Toledo in 1085, Córdova itself in 1236, and Granada, the last Muslim or "Moorish" stronghold, in 1492. Similarly Sicily, which had been captured by the Arabs in 827, was lost by them to the Normans in 1061. Save for a time and in its eastern waters, by the year 1500 the Mediterranean had long ceased to be a Muslim lake. And what naval superiority the Muslims possessed was destroyed by the victory of the Christian powers over the Ottomans at Lepanto in 1571. But it was not only in European waters and the Iberian Peninsula that Islam was being checked. While the Ottomans were still surging forward in the Balkans and the Fertile Crescent, the Western Christian powers had discovered America. Spain and Portugal had settled their first colonies in the Western Hemisphere; and the Portuguese had landed on the coast of India. Between them the Western powers gradually supplanted the Arab mastery of the Indian Ocean and the Persian Gulf, and launched the long drama of Western dominance in Asia.

For many years this was on a most modest scale. These first Western pioneers were still respectful of the rights and authority of the more powerful Asian kingdoms. Later, as Western military and material skills prevailed, the Dutch and British and other Western peoples also came to give the law to much of Asia and Africa. The Western powers, fired by the Renaissance, freed from feudal constraints and the barriers to expansion imposed by the Islamic empires, traded in all the seas and learned to produce wealth on an unprecedented scale. These and other factors were to reduce the Fertile Crescent and other regions of the Orient, once envied for their riches, to the humble status of "underdeveloped areas" in modern times.

Ottoman Conquest of the Arab World. Meanwhile the Ottomans had subjugated the Arabs and their allies and had won the Middle Eastern and North African empire they were to hold until the twentieth century. They were greatly helped in this by the acquisition from Europe of Western firearms and artillery and the skills to handle them. By 1468 they had completed the reconquest of Asia Minor. They then confronted the Mamluks in Syria and Egypt and the Persian Empire. The Persians were defeated in 1514 but recovered—thanks to their new unity under the vigorous Safavid dynasty. In 1516–17, the Mamluks, deficient like the Persians in firearms, were defeated, first near Aleppo, then near Cairo. The Abbasid puppet-Caliph was carried off to Istanbul.[15] The Mamluk victory had also given the Ottomans possession of the Muslim Holy Cities, and later the Caliphate was assumed by the Turkish Sultans. They retained this dignity until its abolition by Kemal Ataturk's Republic in 1924, the Sultan's rule having been abolished two years earlier.

A few years passed before the Ottomans acquired Iraq. After the destruction of Baghdad in 1258 by the Mongols who had established their Ilkhan Empire in Persia, and subsequently by Timur (Tamerlane) in 1401, the city was held by the Mongols and Turk-

15. George E. Kirk, *A Short History of the Middle East,* p. 56.

mans until the Persian revival under the Safavids. After the Persian and Mamluk defeats in 1514–17, however, the territory was conquered by the Ottoman Sultan, Suleiman the Magnificent, in 1534, when he was at the height of his power. Repeated wars with Persia gave it little peace thereafter. It also long remained a land of divided loyalties in view of the preponderance of pro-Persian Shi'is south of Baghdad. After the Persians had briefly recovered and lost Baghdad in the early seventeenth century, in 1639 the frontier between Iraq and Persia (or, more correctly, Iran) was fixed roughly as it is today.[16]

Decadence of the Fertile Crescent

Much has been written about the thousand-year decline of the Arabs, in the Fertile Crescent and elsewhere, into squabbling, sterility, and general ineffectiveness, after the glorious achievements of their early years of rule. Through various vicissitudes, in fact, the Arab imperial structure lasted as a dominant, civilized, imposing force for some two hundred years—broadly from the start of the Umayyad Caliphate in 659 to the sharp decline of the Abbasids after 842, when their Turkish soldiery gradually assumed control. This was by no means an abnormally short span compared with that of other empires, such as Britain's, which lasted as a significant force also for two hundred years, from the mid-eighteenth to the mid-twentieth century. Moreover, the Arabs, like the British, manage to implant their language, religion, laws, and ways of life, in regions where these had been unknown before. Yet the two achievements were strikingly dissimilar.

The Arabs succeeded to a marked degree in absorbing and transforming many of the areas they conquered even when these were closely inhabited by other peoples. This was never achieved to any comparable degree by the British, for example in India. On the other hand the British succeeded in settling many of their own people overseas in largely empty lands with many fertile areas. Their

16. Glubb, pp. 231–35.

descendants evolved, alongside other Europeans, into powerful independent nations, with a high degree of social and political solidarity. Such was the case with the United States, Canada, Australia, and New Zealand. No comparable opportunities were either sought by, or available to, the Arab conquerors, nor, had they been, would the results have been the same. An Arab scholar, in assessing his people, writes that "it is open to question whether the extreme and turbulent individualism of the desert inhabitants did not . . . impart strong centrifugal tendencies to the whole Arab empire, and remain the basic social weakness of Arabs even after centuries of settled life in fusion with other races. . . . The stubborn individualism and unwillingness to accept the leadership of another . . . is still present in all Arab communities, sedentary as well as nomad, Christian as well as Muslim. . . . As the first fervour of the victorious faith cooled, the pre-Islamic weaknesses which the Arabs had brought with them from the desert began to assert themselves."[17] One striking consequence may perhaps be seen in the story of the Iberian peoples. For nearly eight hundred years of Muslim rule or influence seem to have imparted to the Spaniards and Portuguese some of these Arab traits—reflected to this day in the turbulent rivalries of the Latin-American lands they colonised.

Ottoman rule at least preserved the common qualities of the Arab countries, diverse though these might be. It imparted few new cultural values or creative impulses, but it did not absorb the Arabs, nor did it impinge upon the essential qualities of Arab life.[18] On the other hand, under this rule the wealth and administrative standards of these regions suffered. Strangely enough, this downward trend was more marked under the Ottomans—though they were mixed to some extent with more sophisticated European races, and operated from the great Byzantine capital—than it had been under the Mamluks, recruited from the wild nomad tribes of central Asia. But the Mamluk rulers were on the spot and took a personal interest in promoting the prosperity of their dominions.

17. Atiyah, pp. 46–47.
18. *Ibid.*, pp. 47–48.

Again, the Mamluks, a purely military ruling class, had been content to leave the details of administration in the hands of the skilled and experienced local peoples. The Ottomans, on the other hand, despite the partial autonomy of the Christian communities, in time imposed a pattern of their own—loose and corrupt though it was—on these remote provinces. Moreover, the Ottomans in general took little or no interest in the development of culture, science, commerce, or industry, "contemptuously abandoned by them to the subject races."[19]

In any event this administrative and economic recession in the Fertile Crescent and beyond accentuated the general political and social decline of the conquered Arab world caused by those failings of character we have just noted. One consequence of all these factors was that, in Syria, by the early nineteenth century, "the literature of the classical ages had vanished from memory and lay buried in oblivion. The patterns of literary expression were lost and the spiritual influence of a great culture removed . . . minds remained starved and ideas stagnant."[20]

19. Glubb, p. 230.
20. George Antonius, *The Arab Awakening*, p. 39. Opinions differ, however, on the extent to which Ottoman rule "suffocated Arab progress." Armajani, p. 156, rejects this as a myth. "The Turks did not bring the Fertile Crescent and Egypt under the direct administration of Istanbul. . . . [They] were content to send a governor-general just to keep an eye on the affairs. . . . [They] honoured the religion of the Arabs, [their] language . . . and . . . laws. In these and other fields the Arabs were freer than some Turks."

Chapter **5** Development and Vicissitudes of the Jewish Diaspora

Chapter 2 dealt with the varied and troubled destinies of the Jewish communities in Europe in the early centuries of the Diaspora. Under the Byzantine Empire and the Germanic kingdoms of the West they had suffered the restrictions of the Theodosian Code. In general, they were less harshly treated in the heretical Arian kingdoms than in those that had become Roman Catholic. Yet in Merovingian France they had on the whole prospered, having been able to play a large part in commerce and finance. In general, in spite of oppressive laws and rules the Jews had been a normal segment of society covering most walks of life until after the reign of Charlemagne, from 771 to 814. After the rise of Islam they also became valuable intermediaries between the Orient and the West.

The Iberian World

The "golden age" for the Jews in Spain was not solely linked with Islamic rule, though it was fostered by the Muslim presence. The Christians had held on in the mountains of Asturias and from the eighth century onwards progressively recovered territory. Tolerance was essential in Islamic Spain if a recalcitrant Christian majority was to be effectively controlled. But the Christian rulers themselves felt bound to tolerance until the Muslims had been finally eliminated, when harsher counsels prevailed. Thus the Jews were able to benefit in both areas, though only so long as the Christian-Muslim struggle continued. The Umayyad Caliphs employed leading Jews in high positions of trust, and used their international knowledge and skill in languages for diplomatic negotiation. The break-up of the Caliphate around 1030 was not in itself a setback for the Jews, since their scholarship and skills were thereafter diffused, and were in demand in the independent Muslim kingdoms that took over in different parts of the Peninsula. Inevitably the importance of the Jewish role in many of these kingdoms led to a kind of cross-fertilization of Semitic cultures. This was all the more natural in view of the ethnic and linguistic affinities between Jews and Arabs. Arabic was then the international language of Mediterranean culture. But Hebrew and Arabic are, it is said, as close to each other as French is to Italian. According to Roth, "The most important section of Jewry became Arabised. They flaunted Arab names, spoke Arabic only among themselves and adopted Muslim intellectual fashions and standards."

The capture of Toledo by the Christians in 1085 darkened Jewish prospects. The Muslim rulers in the south appealed for help to North Africa. The result was an invasion by the fervidly puritanical Berber Muslim tribes known as al-Moravides. These reunited Muslim Spain and attempted to gain converts from Judaism to Islam. When their puritanism and reforming zeal relaxed, they were succeeded in the twelfth century by even more fundamentalist Berber groups, the al-Mohades, who insisted on conversion, extermination, or expulsion. Toward the end of this century, therefore, it was the Christian kingdoms that received and tolerated the unconverted Jews and afforded them one last creative period in the Peninsula.[1] In one rare and brilliant case the current of Jewish scholarship flowed back toward its Oriental origins. The famous Moses ben

1. Cecil Roth, A History of the Jews, pp. 158–64.

Maimon (Maimonides), born in Córdova, escaped with his family from al-Mohadan fanaticism and found a home in Cairo, where he became physician to Saladin. He put forward a wholly rational philosophy of Judaism, one that was highly controversial for a while but formed the groundwork of Jewish philosophy in later times.

European Predominance in Jewish Life

Yet the medieval flowering of Jewish life in the Iberian countries, and in France, Germany, and other northern lands meant in general a shift in the centre of gravity of the Jewish people. "The first half of the 11th Century witnessed the final stage in the intellectual and political supremacy of Mesopotamian Jewry and the interruption of the chain of tradition which dated back to the First Exile. But before the torch of learning fell from their . . . hands, the Gaonim had succeeded in passing it to a new, vigorous colony in the West." Egypt and North Africa were, it seems, the connecting link in this process, the ancient communities there having been rejuvenated by the surge of Islam. From the mid-eleventh century, northern France, Germany, and the adjacent countries were to share with Spain and Portugal the hegemony of Jewish life, with Provence acting as a kind of bridge between them.

Hebrew poetry, we are told, flourished in Spain as it has done nowhere else outside Palestine. The method of Talmudic study characteristic of the Mesopotamian schools was transferred to Andalucía around the year 1000 and matured in the northern Franco-German communities. The Jewish communities in Provence excelled in the translation into Hebrew and other languages, for the benefit of the Jewish masses, not only of Jewish literature in Arabic, but of outstanding works of Gentile authors, ancient and modern. Translations by Jewish scholars of the ancient Greek scholars for certain European rulers also played their part in helping to give birth to the Renaissance.[2] One of the many misfortunes of the Jews is, however, that—except in Italy—they had little share in, or benefit from, the

2. *Ibid.*, pp. 156–57, 169–79.

enlightenment brought about by this "rebirth." In a sense indeed it stacked the cards against them, since the Renaissance raised the level of Christian education above that of the Jewish, which had formerly been superior.[3] It must be added that the Jewish Middle Ages cannot be said to have ended until the French Revolution of 1789 was in sight.[4] Nevertheless, the achievements of the Jewish communities in Europe during these prolonged Middle Ages meant, according to one Jewish scholar, that the Oriental communities were no longer destined to be of crucial importance in the destinies of the Jewish people. "That section of the Jewish people which was to count for something in . . . history . . . was henceforth to be associated permanently with . . . European culture [and] with the European outlook."[5] Israel today bears striking witness to this prediction. Possibly, however, its validity may be impaired with time, since this new Jewish state, hitherto under European leadership, has now acquired an ethnic majority of Oriental Jews.

By the year 1100 Jews were to be found in every town of any significance in Christendom. As European leadership came to the fore, so did the terms *Ashkenazim* to define transalpine, mainly German, Jews, and *Sephardim* for Iberian or Mediterranean Jews.[6]

3. Israel Abrahams, *Jewish Life in the Middle Ages*, ed. C. Roth (new ed.), pp. 364–65.
4. *Ibid.*, pp. 13–14, 19.
5. Roth, p. 168.
6. Schweitzer, p. 83. See also Roth and Wigoder, pp. 1715–176, who point out that the difference between Sephardim and Ashkenazim was basically one of synagogal rite and tradition, that of the Sephardim going back ultimately to Babylonian Jewry, and that of the Ashkenazim to Palestine. The term "Sephardim" came to be applied to the Jews of Spain and Portugal, many of whom after their expulsion settled in the Turkish Empire, which then covered North Africa, Egypt, Palestine, and Syria, as well as the Balkans. The great centre of Sephardi life until its destruction by the Nazis in 1943 was Salonika, the chief city of northern Greece. But in view of the fact that many Sephardim from Spain and Portugal settled in the Orient and that many Oriental communities follow the Sephardi ritual, a tendency has developed in recent years to regard as Sephardim all members of Oriental communities and even all non-Ashkenazi Jews. When used later in this book, the term "Oriental Jews" should thus be taken to include the Sephardim from the Orient and the eastern Mediterranean.

The former eventually developed a dialect based on German (Yiddish), the latter one derived from Spanish (Ladino). Perhaps in view of the specially privileged position they for a time enjoyed, the Sephardim came to be regarded as something of an aristocracy in World Jewry.

During most of the 11th century there was hope for some permanent accommodation between the now flourishing Jewish communities in northern Europe and the Christian world. It was also the period during which the Talmud was made thoroughly intelligible and relevant to Jewish life in Europe, since the Aramaic in which it was written was being forgotten there. This was achieved by the commentaries and explanations of one outstanding Jewish scholar among many, Rabbi Solomon bar Isaac (Rashi), who died in 1040 but whose work is still authoritative.[7] Where toleration prevailed, its pattern varied. The Jewish masses were less tolerant towards Christians than their spiritual and intellectual chiefs. But in normal circumstances the Christian masses were more tolerant of the Jews than were their priests and rulers. This was mainly because the leading Christians wanted to convert the Jews, while the Jewish leaders had no corresponding desire to convert Christians.[8]

The Crusades: A Tragedy for the Jews. In any event, the hopes of accommodation were dashed. The start of the two-hundred-year period of military and spiritual adventure known as the Crusades launched an era of disaster and tragedy for the Jews only exceeded by the Hitler holocaust of our day. Strangely, the First Crusade and the ensuing cruelties coincided with the spell of greatest Jewish prosperity in Christian Spain, under Alfonso VI of Castile, the conqueror of Toledo. Indeed, the savagery induced by the Crusades in northern Europe contrasted sharply with the more humane atmosphere of southern Europe. These more tolerable conditions tended to endure in Italy even when they ceased in Spain, since the Popes set an example of formal toleration in their own domin-

7. Schweitzer, p. 84.
8. Abrahams, p. 434.

ions, however much they might call for the application of restrictive measures to the more distant Jewish communities.

There were massacres in Lorraine, the Rhineland, and Central Europe, and in Jerusalem after its capture by the Crusaders, who maintained their Latin kingdom in Palestine for a hundred years. (One other consequence of this conquest was that it severed for centuries what had remained of the Jewish link with the ancient capital of Judah.) Later there were massacres in England and elsewhere backed by sinister fantasies, like those accusing the Jews of murdering children and using their blood for ritual purposes, of desecrating the Host, and other supposed outrages. They were also charged with inciting to heresy—and Abrahams suggests that the emergence of the Albigenses and Hussites may have been partly the result of friendly intercourse between Christians and educated Jews.[9] Finally, they were taxed with responsibility for all major disasters such as fire and plague, and particularly for the Black Death in the mid-fourteenth century. After the sweeping Christian victory over the Muslims in Spain at Las Naves de Tolosa in 1212, the position of the Jews in the Peninsula also gradually worsened. There was no longer the same need for conciliation, or for Jewish services as intermediaries or in other fields. The privileges the Jews had enjoyed were progressively cut down in deference to the decrees of the Church, notably those of the Third and Fourth Lateran Councils of 1179 and 1215, which in one Christian scholar's view "constitute the high-water mark of anti-Jewish legislation in the Middle Ages."[10]

Restrictions on Employment. Before the reign of Charlemagne, and afterwards, the Jews, as we saw, functioned in nearly all normal walks of life, including farming. "Even in northern Europe the Jews were not entirely divorced from the soil until the Middle Ages were well advanced. In the south, a minority remained attached to it to the end."[11] They had no prejudice against manual labour as

9. Abrahams, p. 426.
10. Schweitzer, p. 88.
11. Roth, p. 189.

such, but they believed in working with their heads rather than merely with their bodies, and tended to be contemptuous of unskilled labour.[12] The slave trade was another field of their activity. In the early Middle Ages the Jews, with their international connections, were able to play a major role in this profitable traffic, to which little or no moral stigma attached at the time. So far as the Jews were concerned, Christian Europe distinguished between slave-holding and slave-dealing. Slave-holding was forbidden to the Jews, but not slave-dealing. Indeed Charlemagne had readily allowed Jews to act as his intermediaries in this trade.[13] But in the thirteenth century—so great for the Church, so terrible for the Jews—slavery was forbidden by Rome.

The Distinguishing Badge. These two Lateran Councils renewed and extended all prohibitions going back to Constantine. The Jews were to live apart from Christians—a rule heralding the ghetto system. Christians were not supposed to employ Jewish maids, nurses, midwives, or physicians. Usury was condemned. No Jew should hold public office—a measure aimed at the privileged posts assigned to them by many kings and magnates. Worse still, from 1215, the Jew had to wear a distinguishing mark or badge, sometimes a yellow or crimson circle. It was "symbolic of the Dantesque circle of hell to which he or she was presumably condemned." This infamous practice, converting the Jew—the supposed prime source of evil—into a pariah whom all were free to torment, was revived under Hitler only forty years ago.

The Inquisition. The Inquisition, established primarily under the Dominican Order after the suppression of the Albigenses in 1233, was another major source of tribulation for the Jews, as for dissidents of every kind. The inquisitors censored Jewish books and burned them publicly if they were found heretical. Thus most

12. Abrahams, p. 247.
13. Abrahams, p. 114.

copies of the Talmud were destroyed, and Talmudic studies became a crime.[14]

Arbitrary Power of the National State. In the thirteenth century, another development was to have fateful consequences. By then the concept of Europe as one Christian commonwealth under the spiritual leadership of the Pope—however fictitious in practice— was being overshadowed by the rise of highly competitive nation-states, for the most part under arbitrary and grasping kings. The rulers of England, France, Spain, and the Holy Roman Empire each claimed to exercise the power over Jews that had once been the prerogative of Constantine and Charlemagne. The Jew came to be regarded as the property of the king, who could do with him what he wished.

In England the Jews who had settled there in the wake of the Norman Conquest were mercilessly fleeced until they were no longer a worthwhile source of profit to the king, and others had acquired their financial skills. They were then expelled, in 1290, by Edward I, and were not readmitted until the days of Cromwell in the mid-seventeenth century. King Louis IX of France, known as a saint, was notorious for his rigour against the Jews. They had been expelled under his grandfather in 1182, then re-admitted. They were expelled again under his grandson, Philip the Fair, in 1306, after he had cancelled his debts to them and taken over the monies they were owed—a classic manoeuvre frequently repeated. Some Jews were recalled later, when France was in serious financial straits, then once more expelled in 1394. After this they played no significant role there until the Revolution. In Provence, home of the Albigenses, the crushing of this movement helped to wreck the happier conditions that had prevailed for the Jews, and, by the mid-fourteenth century, the harsh regime of the North had spread to the South, except in Avignon, the home in exile of the Popes.[15]

14. Schweitzer, pp. 90–91.
15. *Ibid.*, pp. 92–97.

Germany, the Land of Martyrdom

Even before Hitler's genocide—on a scale far exceeding the crimes of the Middle Ages—Germany had been called the classic land of Jewish martyrdom. Here the main cause of suffering was not expulsion from a given area. That would have been impossible in view of the political fragmentation of Central Europe before the nineteenth century. When driven out of one territory, the Jews could, on harsh terms, usually find refuge in another. Yet killings and persecution constantly occurred. The hysterical conviction that the Jews had somehow brought about the Black Death led to the extermination of numerous communities in Switzerland and the Rhineland, and even in Austria and Poland. After these onslaughts German Jewry never recovered its numbers or wealth; only the settlements in Worms and Frankfurt-on-Main remained without a break to modern times. The hegemony of German Jewry passed to Eastern Europe, whither many had fled.[16]

Spain and Portugal: the Final Phase

In spite of the dominant Christian position in the Peninsula after 1212, the oppressive legislation of the Church, and the abuses they suffered elsewhere, the Jews in Spain and Portugal largely retained their favourable status for another hundred sixty years. Some attempt was made to enforce the decrees of the Third and Fourth Lateran Councils,[17] but this was only intermittently effective. Unfortunately for them, the Jews supported the losing side in the Castilian civil war of the mid-fourteenth century. Pedro the Cruel, who had been good to them, was beaten. Many Jewish communities were sacked during the war, and at its end the victorious king, Henry, enforced the repressive legislation as a mark of his resentment; but even he showed some restraint.

16. Roth, pp. 213–17.
17. Notably by the *Siete Partidas* of Alfonso the Wise of Castile (1252–84).

In 1391, the year after Henry's death, an outbreak of mob savagery stirred up by fanatical sermons in Seville was followed by anti-Jewish violence in other parts of Spain. Some fifty to seventy thousand died. Most seem to have been faced with the choice of death or baptism, and a very large number chose baptism. The number of so-called New Christians was soon reckoned at two hundred thousand, but the total must have grown later, since the process of enforced conversion continued throughout the fifteenth century. This compliance was in marked contrast to the heroism of Jews elsewhere who had in general accepted death rather than abandon their religion. This paradox has been variously ascribed to the advanced assimilation of the Jews of the Peninsula and their loyalty to the host society, or to a break in their morale.[18]

All doors were in principle open to the New Christians. They attained high posts in the government and even the Church, and intermarried with the great, even with the royal house of Aragon. But they seem to have remained in surreptitious contact with those of their community who still practiced their religion. This and other factors made them an object of suspicion and insult. They were called *Marranos* (pigs). In the last stages of the Reconquest, in 1478, the Inquisition was called to Spain to root out all imperfect orthodoxy. Its proceedings were directed by the pious Queen Isabella's confessor, Torquemada, himself of Jewish descent, who has become the archtype of the ruthless interrogator. But although many went to the stake, and the Marranos were shadowed by the Inquisition until the French Revolution, somehow they managed to survive, and with them survived those elements of Judaism they had retained, for they were "Jews in all but name and Christians in nothing but form."[19]

Soon after their work began, the Inquisitors foresaw that the survival in Spain of practicing Jews would be a constant threat to the converted. They therefore sought, and in 1492 obtained, a Royal Decree expelling from Spain all Jews unwilling to be bap-

18. For the former view, see Schweitzer, p. 105; for the latter, Roth, p. 220.
19. Roth, pp. 223–25.

tized. After the capture of Granada, the last stronghold of Islam, this decree was issued by the Catholic Kings Ferdinand of Aragon and Isabella of Castile, from the Alhambra, the exquisite surviving palace of the Muslim rulers. Later the open practice of Judaism became punishable by death. Inevitably the measure was applied to other Spanish dominions, such as Sardinia, Sicily, and (later) Naples, although these had no comparable problem of crypto-Judaism. In the same period the Jews were expelled from Navarre and from Provence (though still with the exception of Papal Avignon). In the rest of France, declared Jews were still banned, but Marrano settlements grew up in certain ports such as Bordeaux and Bayonne. Portugal was initially receptive to the Jewish exiles, most of whom sought refuge there. But Ferdinand and Isabella made the marriage of their daughter to King Manuel conditional upon their expulsion from Portugal as well. Relatively few Jews were in the event allowed to leave. Rather than lose these potentially valuable subjects, the King resorted to mass conversion of the most drastic kind, beginning with the children, who were severed from their parents and brought up in Christian surroundings. The upshot was the creation of "a class of Portuguese Marranos comparable to those of Spain in their crypto-Judaism, except that they were even more steadfast."[20]

Even more serious was the general picture in Western Europe, which was "devoid of professing Jews by 1500 except for a few huddling communities here and there. Thus the migration of the 8th to the 10th century and after, that had carried Jews as far west as England, had been arrested and flung back. Jews streamed eastward to seek refuge in Christian Poland and the . . . Turkish Empire where, after a period of autonomy and prosperity, they again suffered persecution upon the partition of Poland and the virtual demise of the 'Sick Man of Europe' in the eighteenth century."[21] The Sephardim in particular found a haven in the Muslim-

20. Schweitzer, p. 109.
21. *Ibid.*, p. 111.

Ottoman world, and they brought to it their Spanish customs and language. There, under the Sultans, many of them filled important posts comparable to those they had held in Spain. One of them, ennobled as Duke of Naxos, was even permitted by the Sultan to attempt the resettlement of Jews in Palestine. Though unsuccessful, he rebuilt the city of Tiberias. In general the Jews, together with the Greeks and Armenians, played a dominant role in the economic life of the empire, not only in Istanbul but also in other great trading centers such as Smyrna and Salonika, the last of which became a preponderantly Jewish city. "The Jewish people must always remember the Turkish Empire with gratitude because, at one of the darkest hours of its history . . . , Turkey flung open its doors widely and generously . . . and kept them open."[22]

Transition to the Modern Age

To understand the goals and outlook of a Hebrew people henceforth dominated by European Jewry, it has been necessary to trace in some detail the cruel fate of its European communities in the crucial period up to 1500, culminating in the supreme tragedy of the Iberian Jews. Many hard blows lay ahead before the dawn of freedom in the late eighteenth century, but with these we must deal on broader lines.

The sixteenth century was another black age in Jewish life, yet it saw the consolidation of important communities of Marranos (many of whom reverted to their original religion) in such prosperous ports as Antwerp, Amsterdam (the "Dutch Jerusalem"), and Hamburg. It was also from the communities of the Low Countries, which produced the famous philosopher Spinoza, that many Marranos and Jews came over to settle in England in the seventeenth century when this was sanctioned under Cromwell and Charles II. Here acceptance and assimilation brought them eventually social equality and paved the way for their political emancipation in the nineteenth century. Strangely, England and Holland, where conditions had been most adverse, were the first to treat the Jew with

22. Roth, pp. 253, 256.

real tolerance.[23] But the sixteenth century saw also the consolidation of the ghetto system, and the degradations that entailed. The system lasted for nearly three hundred years, through the sixteenth, seventeenth and eighteenth centuries, and Europe has never known less about the Jews than it did while the ghetto endured. Indeed, it has been said that the Jewish Middle Ages began just when the medieval cloud vanished from Christian society.[24] Another paradox is that Judaism became more mystical as Europe became more rational.[25] Many thought that the Iberian disaster must herald the final deliverance promised by the prophets. Thus Safed in Palestine became a centre for the study of mystical lore, particularly that of the *Cabala* and *Zohar*. But traditional, especially Talmudic, studies, retained a strong foothold in northern Europe and Poland.[26]

The Renaissance lasted some two hundred years, from 1350 to 1550, and the scholarship of the Jews made a notable contribution to it. The spirit of humanism alleviated their lot, though mainly, as we saw, in Italy. In Mantua and Ferrara, in Florence under the Medici, in Rome under the Medici Popes, and especially in Venice, which long remained the capital of the Marrano dispersion, their gifts were highly valued and they played a role of high value in local cultural as well as economic life. The scholars of the Renaissance placed Hebrew alongside Greek and Latin as a "sacred" language, and there was a revival of Hebrew studies to which many great Christian thinkers and writers contributed. But then in Italy as elsewhere the Reformation and the ensuing Counter-Reformation intensified intolerance and once more darkened their lives. Moreover, the Reformation, launched by Luther in 1517, was fated to come only a generation after the expulsion from Spain. Forty years later, in 1555, Pope Paul IV, imbued with the spirit of the Counter-Reformation, renewed the previous oppressive legislation and or-

23. See Schweitzer, pp. 136–41, and Roth, p. 304.
24. Abrahams, pp. 80, 101, 365.
25. *Ibid.*, p. 176.
26. For an explanation of the *Cabala* and the *Zohar* (Book of Splendour), and the emergence of Safed as a "Holy City," see Roth, pp. 258–63.

dered that thenceforward the Jews were to be strictly segregated in quarters of their own.

The ghettos, as they came to be called, took their name from the old Jewish quarter in Venice near the *geto* (foundry). They were surrounded by a high wall, with two gates closed at night and on major Christian festivals. From then on Jews were excluded from the professions, their commercial activities were severely curbed, and the special badge or hat rigorously enforced. Throughout Italy and outside it ghettos were set up in these humiliating conditions. Even inside them Jews in their houses were at the mercy of Christian landlords, since they were forbidden to own real estate.[27] While some Jews rejoiced that they were a bulwark against assimilation, confinement to the ghetto led to an inbred life and outlook, and to physical and mental degeneration.

The Reformation took its lifeblood from a rational Hebraism, which however had no special appeal to the Jews.[28] Luther had initially protested against the inhuman treatment they suffered. He seems to have imagined that his "rational Hebraism"—his direct appeal to the Word of God—would somehow bring about the conversion of Israel to Christianity as he conceived it. He became violently hostile to them when this did not occur, urging rulers to suppress and expel them. The Catholics, on the other hand, were prone to hold the Jews responsible for the Protestant rebellion. Thus, for the Jews—with one or two notable exceptions—there was eventually little to choose between Protestant and Catholic Europe.

Poland

Poland is a special chapter in the story of World Jewry. It acquired, within the frontiers of the ancient kingdom, and retained until World War II within those of the pre-1939 Republic, one of the largest Jewish concentrations in the world. These massive commu-

27. *Ibid.*, pp. 247, 248–76.
28. Abrahams, p. 176.

nities of Poland and western Russia, almost totally exterminated in the Hitler holocaust, have nevertheless furnished some of the most gifted leaders of the Jewish people in the twentieth century, among them Dr Chaim Weizmann, the first President of Israel.

For some two hundred years—from 1450 to 1650—Poland, united with Lithuania, was the largest country in Europe, running from the Baltic to the Black Sea and covering most of the Ukraine. To the south of that area, the remains of the Khazar kingdom, converted to Judaism in the eighth century,[29] survived into the eleventh. Then the Tartar invasions of the thirteenth century subjugated much of Russia and severely damaged—although they did not conquer—Poland, bringing inevitable chaos and dispersion in their train. Thereafter, Ukraine and Lithuania had special need of economic development, and were therefore opened up to Jewish settlement by the Polish kings. With the Germans, Jews helped to build up Poland's commerce, industry, and finance, and frequently acted as estate managers and financial agents for the Polish nobility.[30] By 1650 the Jewish community had reached half a million. Poland had become the principal country of refuge, as the United States was to be in a later age.

Unfortunately "the economic motives which had evoked anti-Jewish feeling in western Europe . . . , [and] the resentment . . . against the Jewish money-lenders and their usury, conducted for the benefit of kings and princes, had its inevitable outcome also in Poland."[31] The overwhelming mass of Ashkenazic Jewry came to be concentrated there and in the surrounding Slavonic territories, just as the expulsion from Spain concentrated the majority of Sephardic Jewry in Turkey and its dependencies. At the same time the Jews in Poland enjoyed for the time being a degree of self-government quite exceptional in the Diaspora.[32] From 1580 to 1764 the Council of

29. See Chapter 3.
30. Schweitzer, pp. 147–50.
31. Norman Bentwich, *The Jews in Our Time*, p. 36.
32. Roth, pp. 268–71.

the Four Lands (or Provinces) formed a kind of Jewish Parliament, which collected taxes due to the government, regulated the affairs of the community, and represented it before the Polish authorities. But this relatively happy state of affairs was doomed. It endured in the early seventeenth century because Russia was weak and divided and Germany decimated by the Thirty Years' War. Later in the century, however, Prussia and Russia, Poland's two most formidable neighbours, gathered strength. Just over a hundred years later it was they who, with Austria, ruthlessly split up Poland and wiped it from the map.

From the mid-seventeenth century the disintegration of Poland was progressive. The Ukrainian Cossacks rebelled in 1648–51. Seeking escape from Polish Catholic domination and union with their Russian Orthodox co-religionaries, they recovered most of the Ukraine for Russia. Their resentment against the Poles and their Jewish agents led to wholesale massacres in which some two hundred thousand Jews were killed.[33] Later Poland became a pawn of Russia, Sweden, Prussia, and Austria. Her kings could no longer control their provinces nor protect the Jews, who suffered constant persecution. In 1764, shortly before the first partition in 1772, the Council of the Four Lands was abolished, and the communal life of Polish Jews was shattered. After the second and third partitions in 1793 and 1795 most of them fell under Russian rule so that they passed from a fairly tolerant Roman Catholic, to a bigoted and hostile Orthodox state. Also during the eighteenth century the smaller Jewish communities around the Black Sea passed from the tolerant Ottomans to harsher Russian rule. In Prussia and Austria, on the other hand, the Jews in their newly acquired territories gradually obtained civil rights and acquired the culture of their environment.[34] Meanwhile, however, after the Ukrainian massacres, the tide of European Jewry, which had set eastward from the close of the eleventh to the close of the fifteenth century, once again set

33. See Schweitzer, p. 150. Roth, p. 306, gives the figure as 100,000.
34. Bentwich, p. 37.

westward. It continued to flow for nearly three centuries and in the process recast completely the distribution of Jews throughout the world.[35]

The New World

With the discovery of America the prosperity of the Mediterranean waned. In the great trading ports of Northern Europe, especially those under Protestant rule, people of Jewish stock tended to find themselves in a relatively tolerant environment. The Marranos were often in a commanding position and before too long were able to organize themselves into open and undisguised Jewish communities. By 1600 many Marranos had settled in Brazil, Mexico, and Peru. These were afterwards harassed and, in the Spanish colonies, largely suppressed through the Inquisition by 1650. At the time, however, a small group of Marrano refugees from Brazil made their way to New York, then still under Dutch rule. Some went on to Newport, Rhode Island. In general there was religious toleration in British and Dutch territories, so that by the eighteenth century, this Newport community had become openly Jewish with its own synagogue, and a similar community had been established in Georgia. Such were the modest beginnings of what was to become in our day the most powerful and affluent concentration of Jews in the world—that of the United States.

The Dawn of Freedom

By the time Poland had been crushed, the French Revolution had started to change the face of Europe. But even before this the walls of the ghetto were breaking down. The growth of international trade enhanced the value of the Jews because of their cosmopolitan connections, and this was progressively realized by the statesmen of the West. Colbert, who controlled his country's economy under Louis XIV, had encouraged their return to France. Benevolent

35. Roth, p. 307.

despots like Joseph II of Austria and Frederick the Great of Prussia, and even Russia's German Empress, Catherine the Great (the latter two influenced by the great freethinker Voltaire), sought to end state interference with religious belief. In Germany Moses Mendelssohn (grandfather of the composer) launched the Enlightenment (*Aufklärung*). This movement sought to draw Jews into participation in European culture. In Germany itself it linked "Jewish with German culture as it had been linked in previous ages with Hellenistic and Arabic culture. The essential aim of the Enlightenment was to integrate Jewish life in that of the people among whom they lived."[36] The movement was encouraged by the response from such German thinkers as Kant and Lessing.

It was not, however, German rulers or thinkers who played the decisive role in securing for European continental Jews the proper rights of man. This was achieved by the French Revolution and its Napoleonic sequel. In the territories conquered for France by Napoleon, and in the name of the principles of liberty he often overrode, the ghetto barriers were thrown down and full enfranchisement was formally secured. As might have been expected from a man of the Emperor's stamp, this was by no means pure idealism. As a condition of complete liberation, a Jewish Council, renamed the Sanhedrin, with representatives from Italy, Holland, and Germany, had to agree that the Jews were purely a religious community. They must drop their national aspirations, including their urge to return to Zion, and their separate community laws. Henceforward they were Frenchmen, Germans, or Italians of the Jewish faith.[37]

Happy though the general results were, both of the German *Aufklärung* and of Napoleon's dictates, they raised for the Jews a problem of growing gravity as time went by. The implied degree of assimilation with the world around them might risk the integrity, even the survival, of the Jews as a separate community.

36. Bentwich, pp. 38–39.
37. *Ibid.*, p. 39.

Chapter 6

Christian Imperialism in the Turkish Empire and the Arab World

From the fall of the West Roman Empire in the fifth century until the Crusades in the eleventh, Europe as such played no significant part in the Fertile Crescent, save in pursuit of trade and pilgrimage to the Christian Holy Places. For most of this time Europe proper was plunged in the Dark Ages, while the Fertile Crescent was, as we saw, dominated first by the Byzantine and then by the Arab empires. Although the Byzantines were Christians mainly of the Greek Orthodox rite, their empire was more Oriental than European.

From the earliest years the guardianship of the Holy Places was to cause strife in Christendom as well as among the non-Christian powers. The rivalries, anxieties, and resentments this engendered were to last into the nineteenth century—indeed, until our own day. The safety of the Holy Places and assurance of access to them was always crucial to Christians, particularly in the Age of Faith. Charlemagne, king of the Franks and Catholic Emperor of the West, was permitted by the Arabs to establish his protectorate over them, but in 1010 this privilege was abolished by the Fatimid Caliph, Hakim (still held in special reverence by the Druses), and the

Church of the Holy Sepulchre was destroyed. Thereafter the protectorate passed to the Greek Orthodox Church. Later in the century the Arabs succumbed to the Seljuq Turks. The pilgrimage to
Jerusalem became hard and dangerous, and this was one of the
main causes of the First Crusade.

The Crusades were an international enterprise, but one in which
Catholic Western Europe, and especially the French, stood out. In
1230, when Jerusalem had been militarily lost but temporarily restored by treaty to the Christians, the Pope entrusted the custody of
the Holy Places to the Franciscan Order, and later this custody
passed to Catholic France. This trust, and France's prominence in
the Crusades, were later invoked in support of her claim to a special
role not merely in the Holy Places but also in the neighbouring
areas of Syria and Lebanon, where the Crusaders had been based.
France also claimed the right to protect Christians in the Turkish
Empire—at least those in communion with Rome.

Of these three claims, the second was eventually to lead to the
establishment of a French Mandate in Syria and Lebanon from
1920 to 1946. Far earlier, however, the first and last of these tended
to clash with those of the Greek Orthodox Church, centered in
Istanbul under the wing of the Ottoman Government. Since the
Turks ruled Palestine for four hundred years, from 1517 to 1918,
this lent added weight to the Orthodox claims. But a far more
powerful source of support came eventually from imperial Russia,
which regarded itself as a principal pillar of the Orthodox Church,
the true successor of the Byzantine Empire, indeed as the Third
Rome. For various reasons Russia's role did not become effective
until the eighteenth century. Later, however, with Russia's support,
the Orthodox managed to win the principal rights with respect to
the physical occupation of the Holy Places, particularly after
the Holy Sepulchre was burned down in 1808 and rebuilt. From the
same period Russia emerged with massive pretentions to be the
principal protector of the Ottoman Christians, most of whom were
either Orthodox or members of one of the Eastern Churches that
rejected Rome.

Turkey: Zenith and Decline

The decline of the Ottoman Empire, remote though its origins are, is highly relevant to our theme. For, had the empire maintained its vigour, as did, for example, that of Japan, and ordered its modern alliances on different lines, there might well have been no "Palestine Question" and Israel could hardly have emerged as she is today. The Ottomans reached their height under Suleiman the Magnificent between 1520 and 1566. He annexed most of Hungary and, though he failed to take Vienna, his empire stretched from the Danube to the Persian Gulf and from southern Ukraine to Egypt. Habsburg Austria, still formally the Holy Roman Empire, Venice, and Genoa, which had dominated much of the eastern Mediterranean and parts of the northern Black Sea coast, had all been defeated and reduced. Not until 1571 did these powers and others, including Spain, secure partial revenge by inflicting a severe defeat on the Turkish fleet at Lepanto.

In 1535, however, France, in rivalry with the Hapsburgs, had allied herself with Suleiman and thereby secured important privileges known as "Capitulations." These included freedom of trade and navigation in Turkish ports, the removal of French merchants from Ottoman jurisdiction to that of French consular officers, religious liberty for French settlers and "custody of the Christian Holy Places," indeed a quasi-protectorate of France over Christians of the Latin rite within the empire. For some three centuries after this, France's policy was one of support for and collaboration with the Turkish Empire, a policy culminating in the Crimean War of the mid-nineteenth century. "A strong Ottoman Empire was a conscious aim of France, and the maintenance of its integrity became an axiom of French foreign policy."[1] At this time neither Russia nor Britain was a factor of importance in the Balkans or the Middle East.

The Ottoman decline, which ensued with surprising speed after Suleiman's death, was due partly to factors common to most Orien-

1. George Lenczowski, *The Middle East in World Affairs*, p. 5.

tal monarchies including the Arab Empire, partly to special features of the Turkish system. A basic reason was one that had affected the Arabs. "As a military organisation, the vitality of the Ottoman state depended upon warfare and its economy was based on loot and tribute from the conquered nations. Because of . . . the rise in power of the nations of Europe and Asia . . . military conquest became more expensive and . . . difficult. By the end of the 16th century, conquest had virtually stopped and the army became restless. . . . The . . . machinery of government . . . oiled and fuelled by war, gradually came to a grinding halt."[2] Other general causes were the constant uncertainty about the succession to the throne, the spread of corruption with the sale of important offices to the highest bidder, and the emasculation of vigorous leadership through the lure of the harem. Partly through feminine influence Suleiman himself ceased to preside over his Council and ordered the killing of two of his sons, leaving a dissolute drunkard to succeed him. Other degenerates followed, and it has been said that "most of the Sultans preferred the harem to the halls of government."[3]

One of the features special to the Turks was the Janissaries or New Army. These were originally an elite and celibate corps, recruited from boys of Christian families, and devoted to the personal service of the Sultan. But after the Janissaries were permitted to marry and enlist their sons in the corps, their New Army acquired the outlook of a privileged caste, since their sons, being born Muslims, were no longer slaves. In time it became a kind of Praetorian Guard of limited efficiency in war, politically demanding, and a menace to the state. Another potentially weakening factor was the Turkish application, and evasion, of the theocratic principles of Islam. This resulted in a dual system of authority. On the one hand there was a Muslim Institution of *ulama* learned in the Shari'a, on the other a Ruling Institution recruited almost entirely, like the Janissaries, from converted slaves of Christian de-

2. Armajani, p. 158.
3. *Ibid.*, p. 151.

scent, and chosen for their intelligence. The ulama, extremely reactionary and powerful, ran the judicial, educational, and religious systems. They could veto the Sultan's decisions as not being in accordance with Islamic law, and at least eleven Sultans were deposed by them. The Ruling Institution covered the army and administration. The fact that its members were slaves gave the Sultans in principle absolute control of both and enabled them to order many matters independently of the Shari'a. But this led to conflict with the ulama, who opposed all such potential evasions of Islamic law. In the nineteenth century, despite their reactionary views, the ulama even backed the constitutionalists against the power of the Sultan and the Ruling Institution.[4]

Finally the *millet* system, which gave a large measure of autonomy to the non-Muslim religious communities (despite its advantages for the Turks and their subjects in the early years), developed into another divisive and controversial factor. When the European powers came to use the Christian minorities as tools of their imperialism, the suspicious Turks tended to abandon toleration and in some cases resorted to cruel persecution.[5] The Armenian community was a principal victim. Suspicion of their links with Russia led to their decimation by massacre within the last century and in consequence to the damaging hostility of many leading European powers towards the Ottomans. In the last resort, however, it was less the internal weakness of the empire than the strength of its external enemies which led to its progressive disintegration.

Turkey's Threat to Europe
Becomes Europe's Threat to Turkey

The weakness of the Ottomans and the growing strength of the European powers were dramatically marked when the Turks failed a second time to capture Vienna in 1683, thanks to decisive intervention by the king of Poland. Their subsequent defeats and the

4. *Ibid.*, pp. 153–55.
5. *Ibid.*, p. 155. See also Chapter 3.

cessions of territory secured from them by the treaty of Carlowitz in 1699 (including most of Hungary and much of present Yugoslavia) ended the Ottoman threat to the Austrian Empire and indeed to Europe.[6] While the following centuries saw Austria expand further into the Balkans at Turkish expense, her role in the disintegration of the Ottoman Empire was from then on relatively small. One of her most critical problems in modern times was the fierce conflict between Austrian imperialism and south Slav nationalism, which helped to spark off World War I.[7] And Slav nationalism was traditionally backed by her neighbour and rival Russia. From the eighteenth century onwards Russia's designs on the Turkish Empire became manifest in many fields.

The Rise of Russian Imperialism

As we saw, Russia claimed to be the heir of the Byzantine Empire. The prince who became Grand Duke of Muscovy in 1462, after the fall of Constantinople, had married the niece of the last Byzantine Emperor, and adopted the double-headed eagle of the Byzantines as his emblem. The Russians never accepted *Istanbul* as the capital's new name. For them it remained *Tsargrad*, the Imperial City, and to it in the days of their strength they felt they had a presumptive claim. Despite these pretentions, Russia was in the fifteenth century a weak, landlocked state, surrounded by powerful enemies, notably the Poles to the west, the Tartars (who had dominated much of Russia since the thirteenth century) to the east, and the Turks to the south.

Over two hundred years later, in 1682, when Peter the Great came to the throne as a boy of ten, Russia was still weak. The power of the Tartars was broken in the mid-sixteenth century by Ivan the Terrible, who had occupied Kazan and Astrakhan. Moreover, before Peter, Russia had reached the Caspian, the edge of the

6. See Lenczowski, p. 9.
7. As a result of the murder of the Austrian Crown Prince, Franz Ferdinand, at Sarajevo in Bosnia in 1914.

Sea of Azov, the White Sea, and the Arctic Ocean and, by penetrating Siberia, the Pacific. Poland was weakened, but Sweden had
become strong, and barred Russia from the Baltic seaboard and the
Gulf of Finland. The Black Sea was still beyond Russia's reach,
but by the end of Peter's reign in 1721 he had broken the power
of the Swedes. He had acquired the eastern Baltic coast and the
head of the Gulf of Finland, where he built St. Petersburg as Russia's new capital and "window on Europe." He made great efforts
against the Turks but in substance failed. Though he had captured
the fortress of Azov, he was soundly defeated by the Turks later in
his reign and compelled to return it. He was thus left with barely
a foothold on the Black Sea, and, had the Turks exploited their
victory, Russian military power might have been annihilated.[8] But
Russia's advance southward was soon resumed.

By the end of the reign of Catherine the Great (1762–96) Russia
had secured, by the treaties of Kuchuk Kainardji (1774) and Jassy
(1792), direct access to the northern Black Sea between the
Dniester and Dnieper, the Crimea, the Strait of Kertch leading
from the Sea of Azov to the Black Sea, and, in the eastern Black
Sea regions, territory almost up to the Caucasus. Catherine had also
obtained a protectorate over the Christians of Moldavia and Wallachia (which eventually became autonomous and then independent, under the name *Roumania*), as well as the right to intervene on behalf of an Orthodox Church with Russian priests which
Catherine was allowed to establish in Istanbul, while the Sultan
promised to "protect" the Christian religion. These clauses were
later interpreted to imply a Russian protectorate over the whole
Christian population of Turkey,[9] one that embraced not only the
vassal Slav races related to the Russians themselves, such as the
Serbs and Bulgars, but also Roumanians and Greeks, and the Christian inhabitants of Asia Minor and the Fertile Crescent, including
Armenians and many Arabs. For the rest, Russia gained much the

8. Lenczowski, p. 10.
9. Bernard Pares, A *History of Russia*, p. 309.

same rights as France had two hundred and fifty years earlier, in particular the right to establish consulates, and freedom of trade and navigation.

By 1800 Russia had become a great European power. In the south, much of the Ukraine was hers and she was able to establish naval bases and fortifications in Odessa and Sevastopol, and thus gain a firm grip on the Black Sea. Moreover, she was poised to dominate the Caucasus and later much of central Asia. In the north she controlled the eastern Baltic. She had vastly expanded in the west as a result of the territory annexed from Poland in the three partitions of 1772, 1793, and 1795. St. Petersburg, built at perhaps the most graceful period of European architecture, had become a centre of power and ruthless statecraft, with influence reaching throughout the Continent. And here the great Empress had exchanged ideas with some of the leading thinkers of the day. Yet by the time she died Catherine had become a relic of the past. The French Revolution had not only freed the Jews from oppression. It had overturned the world of the eighteenth century, and an upstart Corsican general, Napoleon Buonaparte, having conquered Italy, was far ahead of Russia in seeking to take over key regions of the Middle East.

Napoleon in Egypt

Napoleon, like most earlier and some later leaders with imperial ambitions, sought possession of perhaps the most strategic region in the world, namely Egypt, at the junction of Asia, Africa, and Europe. In one respect he was pursuing one of France's most traditional goals, which was to cripple her old enemy Britain, if not at home at least in her imperial possessions. Only fifteen years earlier the France of the old regime had helped to destroy most of Britain's empire in North America by aiding the colonies in the American Revolution. Now, if Egypt could be held, Napoleon could block the direct communication of the British with India and perhaps revive France's plans of the mid-eighteenth century for an East Indian empire of her own. But in another respect his policy was a break with tradition, since it brought France into conflict with Turkey, which she had supported since the sixteenth century. Although the Mamluks—now under Turkish suzerainty—were powerless to prevent the French occupation of Egypt, Napoleon's plans were wrecked in 1798 when the French fleet was destroyed by Admiral Nelson at the Battle of the Nile. His army failed also to capture Acre, and could advance no farther than southern Lebanon. In 1799 Napoleon slipped away to France, where he soon became First Consul and later Emperor. The British took the surrender of the French army and restored Egypt to the Turks.

There were two important consequences of this French expedition. Some of France's best orientalists accompanied it and greatly contributed to the fine tradition of French scholarship in the Levant.[10] Coupled with the centuries-old work of the Catholic missions, this scholarship helped to spread the French language and culture in much of the Arab world in modern times. Meanwhile, even before Napoleon, the French Revolution had stimulated ideas of human equality and individual rights, and these stirred up discontent and desires for self-assertion among peoples subject to the blunt autocracy of the Turks. Another consequence was to arouse the British. France was, as always, a formidable danger to Britain, being a country twice her size and, in the late eighteenth century, with three times her population. Apart from this, the British had become acutely sensitive to the safety of their newly acquired Indian dominions. There was a new realization that these were threatened by something more serious in the long run than the campaign of a European power operating far from its base. This was the expanding might of Russia, which was already threatening the stra-

10. One important discovery of the expedition was a slab of black basalt with inscriptions found near the Rosetta mouth of the Nile, and named the Rosetta Stone. Containing versions of the same text in Greek and the local languages, it eventually made it possible for the great French scholar, J. F. Champollion, to decipher ancient Egyptian hieroglyphic writing.

tegic communications through Turkish territory, and also reaching out in central Asia towards the borders of India itself. From now on, Britain was keenly interested in the fate of Turkey and her subject lands, and their protection from any predatory moves by Russia. In the nineteenth century this was to bring Britain close to the traditional standpoint of France. Indeed the middle of the century was to see France, Britain, and Turkey combine to defeat Russia in the Crimea.

Napoleon: Triumph and Downfall

Meanwhile Napoleon's conflict with Turkey ended with the brief peace of Amiens in 1802. Thereafter, and while at the height of his power, he used Turkey for his own purposes as he did other nations. When war resumed and he faced a European coalition initiated by Russia and Britain, the Turks were persuaded to join him in fighting Russia. But they were in effect jettisoned when he made friends with the Russian Emperor Alexander at Tilsit in 1807, Alexander having turned against his English ally, whom Napoleon now regarded as his chief enemy.

After a short truce between Russia and Turkey, arranged through Napoleon's mediation, Russia and France discussed the division of the Ottoman Empire in conjunction with a plan of Napoleon's for their joint invasion of India through Turkey and Persia.[11] Nothing came of this, but war broke out again between Russia and Turkey and continued until May 1812. The Treaty of Bucharest then advanced Russia's borders farther south, with gains in the region of the Caucasus and acquisition of the eastern portion of Moldavia known as Bessarabia (an area lost by Russia after the Bolshevik Revolution but regained by her from Roumania after World War II). It also contained a clause promising self-government to the Serbs, which the Russians were later to invoke on their behalf.[12] By

11. Hugh Seton-Watson, *The Russian Empire* 1801–1917, pp. 115–16.
12. *Ibid.*, pp. 125, 181. See also Lenczowski, p. 13.

the end of 1812 Napoleon had suffered a disaster in Russia. His final defeat at Waterloo came only two and a half years later, in June 1815.

Russian Influence at Its Height.
The Greek Insurrection

Her victories in the final campaigns against Napoleon brought Russia greater influence in Europe than ever before and Alexander expected her to play a leading part in the affairs of Europe, and elsewhere. He became progressively more reactionary and took the lead in the formation of the Holy Alliance with Austria and Prussia. While invoking Christian precepts, this alliance came to regard its principal mission as the suppression of revolution.[13] In the Levant this posed a critical problem for Alexander when the Greeks were in revolt against the Turks from March 1821 onwards. And it was serious for the Turks in that the Greeks were scattered all over the Empire and played a leading role in commerce, navigation, and the learned professions. The rulers of Moldavia and Wallachia were Greeks; and so, not unnaturally, was the upper hierarchy of the Greek Orthodox Church. One uprising, initiated in Roumania by Alexander Ypsilanti, a Greek officer in the Russian army, was disavowed by his Emperor and crushed by Sultan Mahmud II (1807–39), who also had the Orthodox Patriarch hanged in Istanbul.[14]

Despite this savage act, Mahmud[15] was "the last effective and forceful ruler in the Ottoman Empire, . . . the man who inaugurated many reforms of far-reaching consequences." One of these was the suppression by massacre of the Janissaries on whom the Turkish reactionaries depended. They had got completely out of

13. Seton-Watson, pp. 174–75.
14. *Ibid.*, pp. 179–81.
15. According to Lesley Blanch, *The Wilder Shores of Love* (London: Murray, 1966), Mahmud's mother was Aimée Dubucq de Rivière (a cousin of Josephine Beauharnais, Napoleon's first Empress), who had been captured by Barbary pirates and brought to Istanbul. Bernard Lewis, however, regards the widespread belief in Mahmud's French antecedents as of doubtful authenticity.

hand and proved ineffective against the Sultan's many enemies.[16] More Greek revolts occurred in 1821 in the Peloponnese, on the mainland north of the Gulf of Corinth, and in some of the neighbouring islands. There were massacres of Turks which were ruthlessly repaid. In January 1822 a body calling itself the National Assembly met and declared the independence of Greece. The Serbs also made a bid for autonomy, and this was eventually successful. These movements were serious enough for the Turks, and aroused a wave of anti-Christian fury. At the same time they were a great embarrassment for the Emperor Alexander who was "torn between sympathy for the Orthodox and hostility to rebellion, between concern for Russian aims . . . and a desire to support a sovereign menaced by revolutionaries."[17]

Meanwhile, the other major European powers were at odds among themselves over the problem. In the post-Napoleonic settlement Britain had acquired Malta and the Ionian Islands off the west coast of Greece. She had thus extended her power base from Gibraltar to the east-central Mediterranean and was now keenly involved in the crises of the Middle East. Some of her idealists, such as the poet Lord Byron, were fervently pro-Hellene, and he died defending the Greek cause. Even the Foreign Secretary, George Canning, famous for his liberal attitude when Spanish America revolted against Spain,[18] favoured the Greeks. His brother, Stratford Canning, became Britain's powerful Ambassador at Constantinople and one who strongly supported the Greek case. But the even more powerful Duke of Wellington backed the Turks, as did the Austrian Chancellor, Prince Metternich.[19] The French as well as the British were eventually forced by public opinion to press the Sultan to make concessions to the Greeks. "All Europe seemed to be aroused . . . by the fact that Greece, the birthplace of democracy,

16. Armajani, pp. 203–5.
17. Seton-Watson, p. 181.
18. Canning's name is associated with the famous passage in the Royal Message of December 12, 1826, "I called the New World into existence to redress the balance of the Old."
19. Seton-Watson, pp. 181–82.

had declared her independence. . . . European liberals, classical scholars and lovers of democracy . . . raised money . . . and encouraged their governments in favour of the Greeks." Something similar was to happen a hundred years later in the case of Zionism, though the impulse and motives were obviously different in many ways.[20]

Muhammad Ali

As the insurrections continued and the Janissaries and other armed forces showed their weakness, the Sultan appealed in 1824 to the Pasha (Viceroy and Governor-General) of Egypt, Muhammad Ali. From 1805 this illiterate but shrewd and ambitious Albanian had made his mark in Egypt. He had sought French help in training an efficient army along European lines, building up a navy, and reforming the economy and administration of the country.[21] In the process, the land was nationalized, and natural resources such as cotton developed on modern lines and exploited by state monopolies under his control. Save for the absence of socialist and nationalist idealism, his goals, and even some of his reforms, were not unlike those of President Nasser in our day. On behalf of the Sultan, his son Ibrahim had subdued the puritan Wahabis of Arabia.[22] He recovered Mecca and Medina from them, and later conquered most of the Sudan. Muhammad Ali settled scores with the Mamluks by massacre and became in effect sole ruler of Egypt under the Sultan's somewhat nominal authority. Ibrahim was now sent to Greece in response to the Sultan's appeal, and had almost completely crushed the rebellion there by 1826, the same year in which the Janissaries were killed off.

20. Armajani, p. 204.
21. *Ibid.*, p. 211.
22. The Wahabi sect of Islam was founded in the mid-eighteenth century by Mohammed ibn-Abd-il-Wahab to restore the pure faith of Islam. The powerful and astute King Ibn Saud, the Wahabi Sultan of Nejd, again took over the Holy Cities and most of the Peninsula in 1924–26; and it has remained Saudi Arabia ever since.

Meanwhile Emperor Alexander of Russia had been succeeded in 1825 by his brother Nicholas I. Alexander had done nothing to help the Greeks, and his reactionary brother professed to have no sympathy for these rebels. Nevertheless he insisted that the Sultan should withdraw his troops from Roumania and should confirm the autonomy of Serbia. Mahmud eventually agreed and, by the convention of Akkerman of October 1826, gave autonomy to the princes of Serbia, Moldavia, and Wallachia, under Turkish suzerainty, and permission for Russian ships to sail in Turkish waters and to pass through the Straits (the Bosphorus and Dardanelles) leading from the Black Sea to the eastern Mediterranean. After Ibrahim's successes and the suppression of the Janissaries, which strengthened the Sultan's position, Russia, France, and Britain, by the Treaty of London of July 1827, tried to mediate between him and the Greeks. The allies sent a joint fleet under a British admiral, and he, failing to negotiate a truce with Ibrahim, attacked and destroyed the Turkish fleet in the Bay of Navarino without specific authorization from the three governments concerned. Thereupon Mahmud repudiated the Akkerman Convention, and in April 1828, Russia again went to war with Turkey.

The Sultan had had no time to reorganize his army, and Russia again scored striking successes in the Caucasus and the Balkans, finally capturing Adrianople (Edirne—perilously close to Istanbul) in 1829. By the ensuing Treaty of Adrianople Russia extended her European frontier with Turkey down to the southern branch of the Danube Delta, and the autonomy of Serbia and the Roumanian principalities was confirmed. Under the jealous eye of Austria, and despite Turkish suzerainty, Russia had acquired a predominant position in these areas. The Treaty confirmed also the main conditions negotiated at Akkerman, and provided that Russia could trade freely in the Ottoman Empire and in the Black Sea and the Straits. The Straits would be open to all ships at peace with the Turks, who were now forced to recognize the independence of Greece. Meanwhile the French had landed troops in Greece, and Russian influence there was marked by the election of a former Greek adviser of

Emperor Alexander as President of the National Assembly. Finally, by the London Protocol of February 1830, Greece was formally declared independent under the guarantee of Russia, Britain, and France.[23]

Despite his strength of character and dedication to reform, the reign of Mahmud II was marked as we saw by dramatic reverses. There was the loss of Greece and the partial enfranchisement of Serbia and Roumania. Then in 1830 the French occupied Algeria, on the pretext that it had long been a dangerous base for pirates. It was eventually incorporated into Metropolitan France, and in the mid-twentieth century was one of the last Arab countries to become independent. At an opposite end of the empire—in the extreme south of the Arabian Peninsula—the British occupied Aden in 1839, the last year of Mahmud's reign. This was the first Arab territory of which Britain acquired control, and the British turned it into a strongly fortified outpost of their Indian dominions—thus again marking her new consciousness of the importance of the Middle East in imperial communications. Aden's eventual independence came even later than that of Algeria.[24]

Meanwhile another sequel to the Greek struggle was to shake the empire to its foundations and produce a far more forceful and arbitrary intervention of the European powers in Turkey's affairs than any before. One apparent cause was the hostility felt by Mahmud for Muhammad Ali and his son, subordinates who had done so much better than the imperial forces. For his part, Muhammad Ali seems to have thought little of the Sultan's grant of Crete as a reward for his services in Greece, and was determined to acquire Syria. He possibly dreamed of replacing the house of Osman as ruler of the empire. Between November 1831 and June 1932, on the pretext that the Governor of Acre had misbehaved, Ibrahim occupied Palestine and captured Damascus. By this time both father and son had been declared outlaws by the Sultan, who decided

23. Seton-Watson, pp. 298–302.
24. Algeria became independent in 1962, as a result of the courageous policies of President de Gaulle; Aden, in 1967, under the name of South Yemen.

to fight rather than come to terms with these formidable vassals. But Ibrahim, after taking Aleppo, defeated one Turkish army in the approaches to the Taurus Mountains, and another at Konia in central Anatolia. Still protesting loyalty, he then advanced another one hundred and fifty miles to Kutaya and from there requested the Sultan's leave to move his forces on to Brusa near the Sea of Marmora, where they would have been an imminent threat to Istanbul.[25]

By this time the Sultan had appealed to the European powers— who, as usual, were divided. At first only Russia seemed disposed to take any decisive action to check Muhmmad and Ibrahim, for the possibility of their replacing the Osmanlis threatened the privileges Russia had already secured or still hoped to obtain. Two naval squadrons and two contingents of Russian troops were sent to Istanbul and to Scutari on the opposite bank of the Bosphorus. They were not to be withdrawn until Ibrahim had evacuated Anatolia. But as a condition of this evacuation, Muhmmad demanded all Syria, part of Iraq, and the district of Adana in southern Anatolia. These terms were finally conceded by the Convention of Kutaya in April 1833. The Russians then profited by their military presence to force upon the Sultan an agreement that in effect imposed a military protectorate and marked the zenith of Russian influence in Turkey.[26] This was the Treaty of Unkiar-Skelessi, which committed Russia to providing military and naval assistance to the Sultan when requested. By way of reciprocity, the Sultan was required (in a secret clause which of course became known) to close the Dardanelles against the warships of any other power if Russia so requested.

Thus Russia, blocked in Europe by the land-locked Baltic and Black seas from easy and open passage to warm water ports, had obtained one of her most valued traditional goals—assured access to the eastern Mediterranean, a goal now secured in different circumstances by the Soviet Union. At the same time, the Black Sea

25. J. A. R. Marriott, *The Eastern Question* (4th ed.), pp. 231–32.
26. *Ibid.*, p. 235.

would be closed to the warships of other powers that could threaten her.[27] Britain and France protested, and Russia and Austria hedged, but there was a lull in the crisis from the beginning of 1834 to the summer of 1838, when Mahmud concluded a commercial treaty with Britain, and this diminished Muhammad's gains from his economic monopolies.

The Albanian rule in Syria was not popular, and the Sultan, against expert advice, tried once again to crush his over-ambitious vassals. For Muhammad Ali and his son, already in possession of the Muslim Holy Places, sought to make all their possessions hereditary and, failing any chance of ruling all Turkey, planned the revival of an Arab empire under their dynasty.[28] With this purpose they sought, prematurely and in vain, to revive Arab national pride and solidarity. In any event the third Turkish army despatched against Ibrahim also met with a resounding defeat near the Euphrates on the Syrian frontier. Soon afterwards the Turkish fleet surrendered to Muhammad Ali. Mahmud's successor, a boy of sixteen, then opened direct negotiations with Muhammad. But the powers stepped in collectively and, with unprecedented high-handedness, demanded that these negotiations should be stopped. The new Sultan seems in fact to have been relieved that the European powers were taking upon themselves the task of dealing with the Pasha of Egypt, who had brought so many humiliations on the house of Osman. There ensued the usual period of dissension. Finally, the policy of Lord Palmerston, Britain's forceful Foreign Secretary, prevailed: to maintain the future integrity of the Ottoman Empire, to invalidate the Treaty of Unkiar-Skelessi, and to confine Muhammad Ali and his heirs to Egypt.

By now France was to some extent at odds with the rest. Muhammad Ali had relied heavily on French expertise, and France's government saw in him an instrument for the restoration of French

27. Seton-Watson, p. 303, suggests that while the treaty was essentially defensive, if Turkey had become completely dependent on Russia a more dangerous situation, e.g., for Britain and France might have arisen.
28. Antonius, pp. 25–34.

prestige, shaken by the downfall of Napoleon. The French position in the Mediterranean had been strengthened by the acquisition of Algeria, and France already seems to have contemplated taking the lead in building a canal across the Isthmus of Suez. Britain sensed that, if France expanded her ambitions in the Middle East, Russia would resume her grip on Istanbul, and the Turkish Empire might be split into dependencies respectively of France and Russia. The result therefore of French ambitions was a rapprochement between St. Petersburg and London, based on a Russian offer to allow Unkiar-Skelessi to lapse. This was followed by the Convention of London of July 1840, between Turkey, Russia, Britain, Prussia, and Austria, to "pacify the Levant." France was excluded, much to her indignation. Had she known in advance of these negotiations "Muhammad Ali would . . . have been encouraged to thwart the will of Europe."[29] After a change of government, France calmed down and was eventually readmitted to the Concert of Europe.[30]

Meanwhile the hitherto triumphant Albanian leaders had at least been checked, though not by Turkey. By the Convention of London, Muhammad Ali had been offered the hereditary rulership of Egypt and southern Syria, but this was subject to a time limit for acceptance, which in effect, he ignored. Instead, he appealed in vain to France for protection. In August 1840, the British Mediterranean squadron together with some Austrian warships appeared off Beirut with orders to cut communications between Egypt and Syria. Shortly afterwards the Sultan declared Muhammad Ali deposed. The formidable Ibrahim was defeated by British and Austrian marines, and Beirut and Acre were captured. The British fleet then sailed to Alexandria, and Muhammad Ali was at last forced by the powers to come to terms. In a second Treaty of London of July 1841, to which France was a party, Muhammad was confirmed as hereditary ruler of Egypt and the Sudan under the suzerainty of the Sultan who recovered Syria, Crete, and Arabia. A special part of the

29. Marriott, pp. 238–42.
30. The conventional term adopted, from the early nineteenth century, for the major powers of Europe acting collectively.

settlement known as the Straits Convention closed the Straits to all foreign warships while Turkey was at peace.[31] After his death in 1849, followed by that of Ibrahim a few months later, the next Viceroy was Muhammad Ali's grandson Abbas I. "Unfortunately for Egypt, the successors of Muhammad Ali were mostly incompetent and extravagant." After six years of misrule Abbas was murdered in 1854.[32] The title of Khedive was accorded to later rulers from 1867. The position of Egypt remained anomalous. While she was almost totally autonomous in her own house, the Sultan's suzerainty limited her freedom of action in the international field, particularly with regard to the European powers. These contradictions were to be a further source of conflict in the future, a conflict that the powers were destined to exploit.

Reform in Turkey

For some eleven years after the settlement of 1841, there was no major crisis in the Middle East. The young Sultan who had succeeded Mahmud[33] pressed on with a policy of reform known as the *Tanzimat*. This had its roots in the eighteenth century, when government officials were sent abroad to study the systems of the West. Educated bureaucrats of this type had brought Mahmud II to power in 1808. With their help he had started a program of modernization which bypassed or brought into line the ulama of the Muslim Institution. The Tanzimat went considerably further. The dual system of Muslim Institution and Ruling Institution was replaced by a council of ministers under a Prime Minister controlling a reorganized army. Secular schools were set up alongside the religious ones. The ulamas' former monopoly of law was broken. A judicial system based on that of France was gradually brought in

31. See Marriott, pp. 243–44.
32. Armajani, p. 215. According to P. J. Vatikiotis, *The Modern History of Egypt*, p. 76, Ibrahim Pasha reigned after his father for six months.
33. Abdul Mejid (1839–61).

so that eventually only matters of personal status (e.g., marriage, divorce, personal property) came under the Shari'a.

In 1863 Robert College near Istanbul was opened by American Protestant missionaries, and this eventually enrolled Muslim as well as Christian students. Three years later, in the Arab regions of the empire, other American missionaries founded the Syrian Protestant College at Beirut. As the later American University there, this was to play a role of capital importance in the new life of the Arab peoples. In the same area, following the conflict between Druses and Maronites (whom France claimed to protect as Roman Catholics), an organic statute was granted to the Lebanon. This gave each class of the population a wide measure of autonomy under the suzerainty of the Sultan.[34] An even more striking feature of the Tanzimat was the declared equality of all the Empire's subjects of whatever religion (making Christians for the first time liable to military service), the shaving of beards, and the replacement of the turban by the fez.[35] The reforms were designed partly to impress the Western powers, but grave misgovernment in fact continued. In any case some of the powers were less concerned to modernize and strengthen Turkey than to profit by the weaknesses that remained.

An Anglo-Russian understanding had paved the way for the second Treaty of London and for a time it looked as if this might endure. Nicholas sought agreement also with Austria. In the event of the collapse of Turkey, all Russia wanted, he said, was the Roumanian principalities. He did not wish to take Istanbul and he would not accept the restoration of the Byzantine Empire. He made himself agreeable when he visited London in 1844. Turkey was dying, he explained; there was a lot of explosive material about, but the only country he was really worried about was France.[36] He seems to have convinced the British that he had become a man of peace and (wrongly) to have convinced himself that Britain would never go to war over this eastern question.

34. *Cambridge Modern History*, XI, 276.
35. Armajani, pp. 232–35.
36. See Seton-Watson, p. 309, and Pares, p. 387.

The European Revolutions of 1848:
Background to the Crimean War

Soon afterwards, in 1848, there occurred a series of European revolutions highly disturbing to so conservative an autocrat as Nicholas.
The ensuing chain of events was to lead to the grossly mismanaged
Crimean War in which Britain, France, Turkey, and others eventually defeated Russia and curbed for the time being her powerful
influence in Europe and the Middle East.

The upheaval in Austria swept from office Prince Metternich,
who since 1815 had been a main upholder of "legitimacy" in Eu-
rope. The Hungarians revolted with the aid of some Poles, and
Russia helped Austria to suppress the insurrection. When Louis
Kossuth and other Hungarian and Polish leaders fled to Turkey,
Russia and Austria demanded their extradition, and Turkey, with
British support, refused.[37] Equally disturbing to Nicholas were the
revolutionary changes in France. In 1848 Louis Philippe, the last
Bourbon King, was overthrown and a second Republic set up.[38] At
the end of the year Louis Napoleon, nephew of the first Emperor,
was elected President. Three years later he acquired dictatorial powers and, at the end of a further year, became by plebiscite Napoleon
III, Emperor of the French.[39] Napoleon and Nicholas were soon on
the worst of terms, the Tsar refusing to accord him the royal style
in formal communications.

In any case, as a ruler from a self-made dynasty, Napoleon had to
be sure of the support of the two pillars of mid-nineteenth-century
France, the army and the Catholic Church. The army needed the
kind of military prestige that could be won only by an adventurous
foreign policy, in contrast to the pedestrian and material goals

37. *Cambridge Modern History*, XI, 276–77.
38. Louis-Philippe, of the junior (Orleans) branch of the Bourbons, became
King as the result of an earlier French revolution during Nicholas' reign, that
of 1830.
39. It is not without interest that General de Gaulle, after he came to power
in France in 1958, revived the plebiscite system in order to strengthen his
authority.

pursued under Louis Philippe, the "bourgeois king." To show his attachment to the Church, Napoleon restored to Rome Pope Pius IX, evicted by Republican forces, and asserted French claims to the custody of the Holy Places in Jerusalem. The rights of custody granted to France by Suleiman the Magnificent had last been formally confirmed in the mid-eighteenth century. Since then, however, through a period first of the sceptical Enlightenment and then of constant revolution, the French had done little to keep the Places in good order. The Orthodox clergy, with the Sultan's permission and Russia's support, had occupied and repaired the shrines that France had allowed to fall into decay.[40]

Napoleon's demands, put forward in 1850 while he was still President, were conceded in substance by the Turks after some delay. When Russia objected, the Sultan equivocated by giving assurances in somewhat different terms to the Orthodox Patriarch and to the French. In January 1853, Nicholas was still making conciliatory approaches to Britain, but in March he put forward peremptory demands in Istanbul designed to re-establish Russian predominance. Had they been accepted, there would have been a formally acknowledged Russian protectorate over the fourteen million Orthodox subjects of the Sultan. The Turks, however, rejected these terms in May. They had, it seems, been persuaded by Stratford Canning,[41] the powerful British Ambassador, once so friendly to the Greeks, acting without express authority from home.

The War Breaks Out

The drift into an unnecessary war then gained pace. In July Russian troops moved into the Roumanian principalities. France and Britain ordered their fleets to the Dardanelles. This was the first occasion in modern times when these two traditional enemies acted as allies in a major war; they were to do so again with varying success in the two world wars of the twentieth century. But through

40. *Cambridge Modern History*, XI, 311.
41. By now Lord Stratford de Redcliffe.

these wars, and after them, dissensions inevitably persisted in view of the clash of national temperaments and ambitions. Meanwhile Austria, disturbed by Russian moves in the Danubian region, tried conciliation without success—with the backing of Prussia, Britain, and France. In October 1853, Turkey demanded Russian evacuation of the principalities and, failing this, declared war. In November the Russians destroyed the Turkish fleet. In January 1854, the French and British moved their fleets into the Black Sea and asked the Russian navy to return to port. In February France and Britain insisted on the evacuation of Moldavia and Wallachia and, when this was rejected, declared war themselves on Russia in March. Austria, without actually going to war, gave strong diplomatic support to the two Western allies, and later in the year joined the alliance. Prussia, though neutral, favoured Russia, to whom she was under various obligations; years later she was able to repay her debt in full.

Britain was determined not to allow Russia exclusive domination over the Black Sea and the eastern Mediterranean, nor over the Sultan and his Christian subjects. By April, French and British forces had arrived in the Straits; later they moved to the Black Sea coast. Faced with this new threat, the Russians in August withdrew from the principalities, which were occupied by Austria. But by then France and Britain had decided to attack the main Russian power base in the Black Sea—the port and fortress of Sevastopol in the Crimea.[42] After initial allied successes in September the chances of quickly taking Sevastopol were lost. With its fortifications greatly strengthened, it held out for a year and was only partly captured in September, 1855. Meanwhile the allies had been joined in January 1855 by the kingdom of Sardinia, led by Count Cavour, one of the principal builders of Italian unity. He thus ensured that the Italian voice would be heard at the subsequent peace conference. During the campaign, the allied troops faced terrible losses from disease, lack of supplies, and general muddle, especially during the first win-

42. The general background to, and course of, the war is usefully presented in *Cambridge Modern History*, XI, 309–24; Seton-Watson, pp. 319–31; and Marriott, pp. 249–84.

ter of the war. The care of the wounded was deplorable and the start of modern nursing is usually credited to the determined efforts of Florence Nightingale at the time. But even after the victory at Sevastopol the war dragged on. Then in January 1856, Nicholas having died, his less inflexible successor, Alexander II,[43] agreed to discuss peace.

At a conference in Paris a new settlement was drawn up, one "unpleasant for the Russians but not disastrous."[44] The Black Sea was neutralized, so that neither Russia nor Turkey could keep fleets there. This was a set-back only for Russia, however, for the Turks could keep a fleet of any size in the Aegean and bring it into the Black Sea when needed. The principalities—Moldavia and Wallachia—were freed from the protectorate of Russia, which had to cede southern Bessarabia. Under Turkish suzerainty their autonomy and that of Serbia was thenceforth collectively guaranteed by all the signatories of the Treaty of Paris. As a check to Russia's developing grip on the lower Danube, navigation on it was made free for all nations. The Straits Convention was upheld, closing them to foreign warships in time of peace. Turkey was admitted to the Concert of Europe, and the European powers renounced all right to intervene in her internal affairs. Britain, Austria, and France separately guaranteed the integrity of the Ottoman Empire. It seemed as if this might now look forward to a future of new strength, progress, and reform; but the actual sequel was to be very different.

Russia After the Crimean War

With the Treaty of Paris of 1856 Russia's European predominance came to an end.[45] She was able to revive her power in the Black Sea

43. Later famous as the Tsar Liberator for his reforms, in particular the emancipation of the serfs. After he was murdered by revolutionaries in 1881, the reactionary policies of his successors contributed significantly to the revolutions of 1917, the second of which brought into existence the Soviet-Communist regime of Russia today.
44. Seton-Watson, p. 239.
45. Pares, p. 390.

and the Balkans after Prussia defeated Austria in 1866 and France in 1870. In 1877–78 a further war between Russia and Turkey was sparked off by insurrections of the Slav peoples in the Balkans. The result was another sweeping victory for Russia, who dictated humiliating terms. Yet Russian designs on this eastern Mediterranean area were once again curbed by the Berlin Treaty of that year, though she recovered southern Bessarabia and increased her territory in the Caucasus. For all their professions about Turkish integrity, most of the European powers continued to diminish her empire. Bulgaria became autonomous; Serbia, Roumania, and Montenegro, independent. Austria occupied Bosnia—where Sarajevo would become the starting point of World War I and of Austria's own destruction—and also Herzegovina. Britain took over Cyprus.

Turkey, however, soon acquired a new friend. After her defeat by Prussia, Austria had been forced to reshape her empire as a Dual Monarchy in partnership with the Hungarians. She ceased to be a rival of Prussia and became the junior ally of the German Empire, founded after France's defeat as the strongest military power in Europe. Germany thus became committed to Austria's ambitions in the Balkans. At the same time this new empire of the north gradually developed the strongest influence of any European power at Istanbul. Germany trained the Turkish army, constructed and invested heavily, and refrained from the general condemnation of the Armenian massacres in the 1890s. Hence Turkey's fateful alliance with Germany, Austria, and Bulgaria during World War I.

After 1878 Russia pursued her ambitions in central Asia rather than in the Middle East, and became predominant in parts of Persia. She also expanded in the Far East—helped by the new Trans-Siberian Railway—until this was checked by Japan's victory in 1905–1906. But over-all—and especially in Europe—there was a slow decline in Russian strength and influence in the late nineteenth and twentieth centuries, a decline which became more marked after 1905 and the abortive revolution of that year. World War I was a period of loss and suffering, prolonged through the Bolshevik revolution and the early years of the Soviet regime—

losses and sufferings repeated in World War II, until the final victory. Only with Russia's later emergence as a superpower, with formidable nuclear and conventional capacity, did her ambitions and imperialist designs, in the Middle East and elsewhere, become formidable once more. But much was to happen before then, both to the Turkish Empire and its subject peoples and to Russia's imperialist rivals in the Middle East.

The Other Imperialist Powers

Russian imperialism had aimed at the heart of the Turkish Empire or (in her claims to protect the Orthodox) at the body as a whole. With other Christian imperialists, such as Britain, France, and later Italy, it became rather a case of detaching or controlling one of the Empire's outer limbs, as France had done in annexing Algeria in 1830. Significantly it was during the Crimean War, in November 1854, that an agreement was signed between a French Consular Officer, Ferdinand de Lesseps, and the Viceroy of Egypt for the construction of the Suez Canal, and this was finished fifteen years later. For a whole century, and long before Palestine, Jordan, or Iraq became a matter of concern to Britain, this was to be a main focus of British imperial strategy and intervention.

The United States

One other country was a major source of Christian influence in the Ottoman Empire (though this was not its official policy)—the United States. Despite a record of highly successful and even ruthless expansion, Americans were strongly anti-imperialist by tradition and, in a tribute by the British writer, "a people which used power with purpose and restraint, and with motives generally more trustworthy and disinterested than those of the European nations."[46] In

46. Alastair Buchan, Director of the Institute of Strategic Studies, London, in *Encounter*, January 1968. It is a tragic paradox that the United States, whatever the errors of its Vietnam policy, should today be branded as the archimperialist by many countries deeply in debt to America's practical idealism and generous help.

the nineteenth century and after, the influence of the American missionaries, especially in the field of education, was a powerful stimulus to the awakening of Arab nationalism, which Muhammad Ali in his own interests had vainly tried to rouse. The main thrust of Arab nationalism came after his day and has continued to the present. It is indeed one of the vital factors in our problem, and one we should examine at this stage.

Chapter 7

Nationalism in the Turkish Empire and the Arab World

Arab nationalism was only one facet of a general phenomenon. For the American and French revolutions had stirred national consciousness in most corners of the world. They had proclaimed human equality and dignity, and the right of man freely to decide his fate. The great upheaval of the Napoleonic wars had spread these doctrines far and wide, even among peoples that passionately rejected domination by Napoleonic France. The German war of liberation of 1813 was one striking example. The conquest of freedom by the Spanish colonies, by the Greeks, the Roumanians, the Serbs, the Bulgars, the Italians and others, were further results. The European revolutions of 1830 and 1848 kept the Continent in ferment in defiance of the reactionaries and legitimists who dominated for so long the post-Napoleonic scene. All elements in the Ottoman Empire felt this ferment, not merely its European peoples—though, thanks to their closer links with the Christian powers, these were earlier successful in gaining some autonomy and ultimately freedom. The *Tanzimat* of Abdul Mejid, with its proclamation of equality between creeds and peoples, was in part a response to these stirrings. During the second half of the nineteenth century and the first years of the twentieth, however, two other movements emerged successively, those of the Young Ottomans and of the Young Turks. Both contested the system and methods of the Tanzimat and invoked the principles of nationalism, but differed in their doctrines and their goals.

The Young Ottomans

The Young Ottomans, originating around 1865, wanted to be the leaders of the Empire, with the Sultan transformed into a constitutional ruler. They complained that the Tanzimat, while copying the West, had not renovated Ottoman society. The individual was still subject to autocracy, and foreign imperialists still dominated the state. They aimed at forging an Ottoman nation out of its diverse peoples, but one based on the supposedly pure Islam of the first Caliphs. The Q'uran was their main inspiration. All this implied the exclusion of the non-Muslims, but most of these already had their own nationalist aims. One of the foremost statesmen of the movement was Midhat Pasha, who came to prominence with a new campaign of reform in 1869 under the weak and half-mad Sultan Abdul Aziz. But conditions were such that the movement achieved only limited success.

In 1875 a fresh source of foreign intervention emerged when Turkey was unable to continue paying full interest on her debt. In the following year—by which time the Empire was virtually bankrupt—Midhat and other Young Ottomans were responsible for bringing to the throne a Sultan, thought at first to be liberal, but proved to be one of the cleverest and most devious autocrats Turkey has ever had. This was Abdul Hamid II, who ruled for over thirty years until removed by the Young Turks in 1909. Sultan Hamid was at heart a strong reactionary and correspondingly suspicious of the reforming zeal of the Young Ottomans. A patriot by his lights, he became adept at minimizing the effects of foreign intervention by playing the rival Europeans off against each other. In his first year, when the European powers were meeting in Istanbul to seek a solution to the Balkan insurrections and Turkish misgovernment, he approved a constitution put forward by Midhat (who had been made Prime Minister). After the conference ended, he shelved the constitution, exiled Midhat, and proceeded eventually against the other leaders.

The Young Ottomans had been stifled by 1878. For a time many of the literate Arab elite had been attracted to them, but this was a passing phase since from the mid-nineteenth century the Arabs had been developing a nationalism of their own.[1] For all the Sultan's cleverness, the erosion of the Empire and of its internal sovereignty continued. In 1881 the French annexed Tunisia. In the same year the whole country "went into receivership. The British, French, Dutch, German, Austrian and Italian creditors set up the Council of Administration of the Ottoman Public Debt and took control of the major phases of its economic life."[2] By 1853 Britain was growing dominant in the Persian Gulf as the result of a treaty for the suppression of piracy with the chiefs on the Arabian coast. In 1878 she acquired Cyprus. In 1882 she occupied Egypt, and this will be the subject of our next chapter.

The Young Turks

The Young Turks were a branch from the same stem as the Young Ottomans. They too, inspired by the West, sought to remodel the empire on the basis of a liberal, constitutional monarchy. In 1889 a group of medical students formed a "Committee of Union and Progress." Forced into exile when their plans were discovered, they split into factions. One was attracted to Pan-Islamism as the Young Ottomans had been. When the Sultan himself sought to emphasize the secular as well as spiritual prerogatives of the Caliphate as it had originally functioned, and thus strengthen his position politically and internationally through Islam, their leaders made their

1. Armajani, pp. 235–37.
2. *Ibid.*, p. 207.

peace with him.[3] Another group with markedly liberal ideas was headed by members of the Sultan's own family. They were attracted by what they conceived to be the distinctive qualities of Anglo-Saxon society—namely, the development of personality and individual initiative. They were for a federalized, decentralized Ottoman state. In it, "the different peoples and communities of the empire could satisfy their aspirations and safeguard their rights in regional and local government and in a public life emancipated from collective or governmental control."[4] The liberals continued to be influential after the first Young Turk Revolution of 1908, but the revolution itself was primarily the work of a third and ultimately dominant group.

This group had been based in Paris in the 1890s. Without rejecting Islam, its followers believed in positivism—that is, in the primary importance of exact science and experience. This made them favor a secular state, and one based on Turkish rather than Ottoman nationalism;[5] and they rejected the decentralized, multinational empire of the liberals. After the Young Turk revolt the Turks came to see themselves as a master race and sought to impose a Turkish imprint on the minority peoples. A Pan-Turanian movement gained some ground, advocating the regeneration of the Turks by reunion with the Turkish peoples of central Asia, most of them under Russian rule. This policy of Turkish nationalism was easier to apply in areas such as Syria, where the feudal order had been broken up by Ibrahim Ali and later replaced by a centralized administration dependent on Istanbul. But "Turkification" sat badly with the Christians, and also with the Muslim Arabs, in spite of Abdul Hamid's efforts to win over these Muslims by stressing his role as their Caliph. For the Arabs had again become deeply conscious of their role in history as the founders of Islam, and of the brilliant superiority of their great age to the meagre cultural contributions of the Turks. In fact an essentially Turkish state was

3. See Antonius, pp. 68–70; and Armajani, p. 239.
4. Bernard Lewis, *The Emergence of Modern Turkey*, pp. 199–200.
5. Armajani, pp. 239–40.

achieved only when the Empire had been destroyed—It was created by Kemal Ataturk in the Republic forged by him after the defeat and expulsion of the Greeks from Anatolia in 1922 and the exchange of populations that followed.

The army became the spearhead of the Turkish nationalists. In 1906 a group of young officers formed a society that later merged with and strengthened the Committee of Union and Progress. Three of these men—Enver, Jemal, and Talat—were to become leaders of the Ottoman Empire in its last phase. A fourth, Mustafa Kemal, played no major role before World War I, but was to become, as Ataturk, the father of Turkey as she is today.

Two Revolutions and Two Balkan Wars

In the Turkish revolution of 1908, originating chiefly in Macedonia, the army forced the Sultan to restore the constitution of 1876. But in 1909 a reactionary counterrevolution, engineered, it seems, by Abdul Hamid, proclaimed again the supremacy of the Sultan and of the law of Islam. This rising was crushed by an army from Salonika which deposed the Sultan and publicly hanged some of the chief figures in his entourage. But the high expectations of a dawn of enlightenment were soon dashed, partly as a result of external pressures and severe reverses. Austria-Hungary annexed Bosnia and Herzegovina; Bulgaria declared her independence; Albania revolted in 1910; Italy occupied Tripolitania and the Dodecanese Islands, including Rhodes, in 1911–12. Also in 1912 Crete, which had become autonomous in the late nineteenth century, was annexed to Greece. In 1912 and 1913 Bulgaria, Serbia, Montenegro, and Greece fought the Turks in two Balkan wars and did some fighting among themselves. The upshot was that Turkey lost in Europe all but the small bridgehead of territory, including Adrianople, which she still retains.

These dramatic events also brought the Enver-Jemal-Talat triumvirate firmly into power in 1913 and they ruled Turkey as a military dictatorship until her final defeat in 1918. Talat, by far the ablest, was judged a man of swift and penetrating intelligence, forceful when necessary but never fanatical or vengeful. Enver, however, was flamboyant, reckless and self-indulgent, Jemal a man of high professional competence, personal authority, and responsibility, and at times of a cold, fanatical ruthlessness.[6] Whatever their qualities, this combined regime became in time no less oppressive than that of Sultan Hamid. A measure of its cruelty was the fate of the Armenians. In the ninth century theirs had been a separate and important kingdom and a bulwark of Christianity in Asia. Later they had come under the Turks, Persians, and Russians. In Turkey, around 1800, the Armenians were still noted for their loyalty to the empire. Later, however, when Christian Russia conquered the Caucasus and created a Russian Armenia, a nationalist movement came to life among the Armenians in Turkey. This seemed a deadly threat to the Turks, since, unlike the remote peoples of the Balkans, the Armenians stretched across their homeland from the Caucasus to the Mediterranean. To their misfortune, part of this area was shared with the fiercely Muslim, anti-Christian Kurds, who were incited against the Armenians by Abdul Hamid. Thus some hundred thousand Armenians were massacred in 1894–97; but under the Young Turks a million and a half may have perished in 1916 alone.[7]

All that now remains of Armenia, once a vast kingdom, is the small Soviet Republic of that name. But it is significant that today, in their traditional drive southward toward the eastern Mediterranean, the Russians no longer need the Armenians as one chosen instrument of potential penetration across the Anatolian land mass. For, as we shall see, the land barrier has now been bypassed by Communist Russia—thanks to the misjudgements of the major powers; and the Soviet Union has gained easy access for her fleets and forces to most of the warm-water ports of the Arab world. But in those days before and during World War I, the Arab nationalists were also victims of the fierce intolerance of the Young Turks. It is

6. Lewis, pp. 221–22.
7. *Ibid.*, p. 350.

fair to add that this last government of the Ottoman Empire did carry through a number of modernizing measures paving the way for the unification, secularization, and westernization of Republican Turkey, measures that Kemal—also with marked ruthlessness—enforced.

The Rise of Arab Nationalism

The story of Arab nationalism, sometimes referred to as Pan-Arabism, is complex and controversial, and hard to clarify in simple terms. Many different peoples of widely divergent character had come to be counted as Arabs, having absorbed their culture and language. The Egyptians are one example. They are ethnically distinct from the Arabs east of Sinai and, with their many attractive human qualities, have never excelled in the military field.[8] The leaders and many of the soldiers who gave Egypt renown and stature in the modern age were foreign: Turks, like the Mamluks, or Albanians like Muhammad Ali. Traditionally Egypt has been concerned primarily with the Nile Valley and her own affairs. Only in recent years has she claimed the role of leader of the Arabs as being the most advanced Arabic-speaking Muslim state.[9] And this has aroused fierce rivalry in others. Historically and in modern times Egypt's main rivals have, as we saw, been Syria and Mesopotamia (Iraq). It is these countries of the Fertile Crescent, and particularly Syria, which were the main focus of the Arab resurgence in the nineteenth century, and it is with them that this chapter will be chiefly concerned.

Inevitably the Arab revival meant conflict with the Turkish patriotism of the Young Turk triumvirate. The Arabs were the largest racial group in the Empire, outnumbering the Turks in a ratio of roughly three to two. Their position was also special in many ways. The Turks honoured their religion and language, and had traditionally allowed them a wide measure of autonomy. For their part

8. Glubb, p. 243.
9. P. J. Vatikiotis, *The Modern History of Egypt*, Preface, p. xiii.

most Arab Muslims, before the rise of nationalism, had normally felt loyal to the Sultan-Caliph because of their common faith. Yet the two peoples were basically out of tune. The Turks, brave, simple, and direct, seem to have lacked sympathy and understanding for the subtle, temperamental, and complex Arabs.[10] Their remedy when difficulties arose was to use force. But there were striking differences between "Arabs" even in the same land. Thus in Syria—that incomparable crossroads between West and East—the townspeople had inherited the legacies of successive civilizations, faiths, and conquerors. These conquerors had for the most part garrisoned only the larger centres, where intermarriage had changed the ethnic stock. But there was a limit to the distance the conqueror's writ could run. Among the country people—settled villagers or desert nomads—there was a deep continuing conservatism and an inborn suspicion of the government, whatever it might be. They were sporadically victimized and exploited, and repaid this by raids upon the towns. The population of many of these countries thus tended to be split into two antagonistic groups of very different character and outlook.[11]

Religion was another divisive factor. Under the Turks, Syria covered Lebanon and Palestine as well, and there was a high proportion of Christians, especially in the two latter regions so closely associated with the early years of the faith, and later with the Crusades. Most of the Christians of Lebanon were Maronites, whose Church, pronounced heretical under the Byzantine Empire, had entered into communion with Rome. From 1625 the Jesuits, and later other Orders such as the Capuchins, Carmelites, and Vincentians, pursued the long tradition of Western missionary education there. A Maronite college was opened in Rome, thus reviving Lebanese links with the West for the first time since the failure of the Crusades, and in the eighteenth century the Maronites had colleges of some importance, which kept alive the study of Arabic literature.

10. Glubb, p. 246. See also Armajani, p. 156; and Antonius, p. 104, for the ratio of Arabs to Turks.
11. Glubb, p. 238.

France, with her leading role in the Crusades and in the Holy Places, assumed a protective interest in the Maronites and other Roman Catholics, and this intervention was to have significant political consequences. Meanwhile, here as elsewhere, Russia sought to take the Christians of the Orthodox Churches under her wing. When the Jesuits were suppressed by the Pope in 1773 most of their establishments were shut down, but other Orders maintained the tradition of Catholic education. In 1831 the Jesuits returned after their revival, in part to face the challenge of American Protestant missionaries who had started work in Syria and Lebanon in 1820. Under Ibrahim Ali this missionary work was stimulated by his policy of tolerance and abolition of anti-Christian discrimination,[12] and more than thirty schools were soon founded. He also launched a system of Muslim primary and secondary education to further the teaching of the Arabic language and literature, which had degenerated under the Turks.[13] For until 1729 when a press was started in Istanbul, the Ottoman Sultans had banned printing in Arabic or Turkish. Seventy years later Napoleon had brought an Arabic printing press to Cairo for his own publicity; but the first Muslim printing press in the Arab world had been that of Muhammad Ali in Egypt. Then, encouraged by Ibrahim's policies, the French Catholics and American Protestants in Syria established Arabic printing presses, and with these reprinted for the Arabs their half-forgotten classics and produced translations of some of the sources of Western knowledge.[14]

When Ibrahim was forced out of Syria in 1840 and the Turks returned, his Muslim schools and colleges were closed, but, for fear of offending the now largely dominant European powers, the Turks dared not threaten the Catholic and Protestant foreign missions. The Christians were thus given a marked advantage over the Muslims,[15] so that one unfortunate sequel to the years of Egyptian rule

12. Antonius, pp. 33–36.
13. Anthony Nutting, *The Arabs*, p. 266.
14. Lewis, p. 172.
15. Nutting, p. 267.

and to constant foreign intervention at that time was intensified rivalry between the religious communities. In any event the Muslims, who remained on the whole loyal to the Sultan, were themselves divided between Sunnis and Shi'is and a somewhat exotic offshoot of the Shi'is, the Druses, who believe the Fatimid Caliph Hakim to have been a manifestation of the Deity, and who constitute a separate religious group.

Administratively the Lebanon, barred by difficult mountains and with its varied patchwork of religions, achieved a special degree of autonomy from the early days of Turkish rule, under two successive dynasties of local princes. "In the struggle among the three religions, the dynasty managed to belong to all three. They changed their religion whenever the situation demanded."[16] After 1840 the last of the Lebanese princes was exiled. In the general Syria-Lebanon-Palestine area the Turks imposed a tight rule requiring increased use of the Turkish language. Meanwhile the Latin and Orthodox Christians tended, as we saw, to look to France and Russia, while the Druses sided with the British. At that time, however, neither the Sultan nor the Russians had much power in the Fertile Crescent. Instead, there developed in Syria a Franco-British rivalry, the French supporting the Maronites in the north and the British supporting the Druses in the south. In 1860, when the Druses massacred many Maronites, the French sent a force to protect the Christians.[17]

At this juncture the French wanted to declare a protectorate over the country, but the Sultan refused, with British support. In 1861, however, he issued an organic statute, approved by the European

16. *Ibid.*, p. 213.
17. Despite the different attitude and motives of the two powers concerned, there is a curious parallel between this French expedition of 1860 to protect the Christians of Lebanon and the landing of U.S. Marines there in 1958, almost exactly a century later, in response to a request from the Christian President of Lebanon. This was at a time when President Chamoun feared that the safety of the Christian community and other pro-Western elements might be endangered by the chauvinistic nationalism of certain near-by, predominantly Muslim countries.

powers, formally giving autonomy to Lebanon under a Christian governor chosen by Istanbul. This autonomy continued until 1914,[18] but in World War I Lebanese sufferings were intense. Turkish hatred of the Christians, with whose protectors they were at war, led to a virtual blockade of this mountainous area (which produced little food) and massive death by starvation. It is worth adding, before we return to our main theme, that the religious patchwork in the Lebanon has continued to this day, with the Muslim and Christian elements in the country now reckoned to be roughly equal. The present Republic has therefore developed a unique formula for the distribution of power. The President is always a Maronite, the Prime Minister a Sunni Muslim, and the Speaker of the Parliament a Shi'a Muslim, while the Cabinet would normally include an Orthodox minister and a Druse.[19]

The Educational Impulse

The Arab awakening in the nineteenth century, like other national movements, was stimulated largely by Western education. Yet only to a very limited degree and in certain special cases did this inspire attachment or gratitude to the countries from which it came. Historically the image of the West—and especially of those countries beyond the Mediterranean—had been for the Arabs obscure and of small account. In their great age they had ruled Spain and Sicily and had taught Western students in their own universities. The Crusaders had learned from them some elements of civilized living and had then been thrown out. The West, it seemed, had little or nothing to teach them. "The . . . literature of the medieval Arabs reflects their complete lack of interest in western Europe, which they regarded as an outer darkness of barbarism from which the sunlit world of Islam had little to fear and less to learn. . . . This attitude was at first justified, but with the progress of western Europe it became dangerously out of date."[20]

18. Armajani, p. 214.
19. *Ibid.*, p. 11.
20. Bernard Lewis, *The Arabs in History*, pp. 164–65.

By the time the Jesuits started teaching in the Fertile Crescent the West had far outstripped the Arabs in skill and power, and the Arabs had become a conquered and subordinate people. As Western imperialism developed, fear and deep mistrust replaced the earlier contempt. The Turks were bad enough, but for most Arabs they were co-religionists. The Arabs had seen the European powers humiliate the Ottomans and the Sultan, their Caliph. And in the Fertile Crescent, by the mid-nineteenth century, it was France and Britain rather than the Sultan who had acquired a decisive voice in their affairs. On the other hand the United States with its professed anti-imperialism did not inspire the resentment provoked by French and British intervention. Whatever the forcefulness of its own expansion, it posed no threat to the Arabs in those years. To all the good and valuable things its missionaries brought there were, in today's phrase, "no strings attached." There was only the marginal risk, discerned by fanatical Muslims, that some of the faithful might backslide into Christianity. For these reasons the educational programme developed by American Protestant missionaries tended to be more acceptable to many Arab nationalists than those offered by missionaries from the European powers. Yet there were complicating factors. One was that the less popular British were also involved in the Protestant missionary work. Moreover, whatever the policies of the French Government, Catholic missionaries could rely on the Maronite Christian majority's traditional loyalty to Rome and could strengthen their following by stressing the dangers of heresy inherent in Protestant proselytism.

In general the goal of the Arab movement, like those of other countries that had failed to keep pace with the modern world, was to seek the skills and learning of the West in order to be able to stand with assurance on their own ground. For the Arabs were determined with these weapons to resist, and if necessary, revenge, any future attempts to invade and dominate their lands, or establish alien strongholds in them as the Crusaders had done and as the French had tried to do in 1860. It is in the light of this goal, so passionately sought and in the event only partially attained, that we must judge the tumultuous Arab reactions to the founding of Israel, and much else besides. By reason of the educational advantages retained by the Christians over the Muslims after Ibrahim's downfall, it was the Christian Arabs who first led the national movement. Thus both the French and American educators were its foster parents. But the Americans were generally counted friends of Arab national aspirations, whereas one of the main goals of the French was to spread French culture. For this reason, from the mid-nineteenth century, American influence on the Arab movement was specially significant. It is another irony of history that America's policies since World War II should now have made her appear, in the Fertile Crescent and elsewhere, as the main champion of Israel at the expense of those Arabs she once taught and inspired.

The American Contribution

While the story of the Fertile Crescent in the early nineteenth century was thus a dramatic one of internal struggle and international complications, against this complex background a simple conclusion has been drawn. "The Arab national movement opens . . . in 1847 with the foundation in Beirut of a modest literary society under American patronage."[21] In fact the contribution of the United States to education and cultural revival in the area had started nearly thirty years earlier. Presbyterian, Congregational, and Dutch Reformed denominations, working under the American Board of Commissioners for Foreign Missions, had come to Beirut in 1820.

Malta, in the centre of the Mediterranean, had been their local base. For this highly strategic island, for centuries a Catholic stronghold of a Crusading Order, the Knights of St. John of Jerusalem, had come under British rule in 1814, and thus for the first time into

21. Antonius, p. 13. The late George Antonius was a Palestinian Christian educated in Egypt. After being Deputy Director of Education in Jerusalem under the British Palestine Government in the 1920s, he became a protagonist of the Arab cause as a member of the Arab delegation to the Round Table Conference of Arabs and Zionists in London in 1939.

the possession of a Protestant power. But in the Fertile Crescent of that time the Americans were under a double handicap. Not only did they face the always latent suspicion of the Muslim rulers and subjects of the Ottoman Empire, but they had also to break fresh ground at the expense of the faiths already established in the area. There were no Protestants, and a Protestant community could be built up only by converting those of other beliefs and thus incurring the resentment of their spiritual leaders. Moreover, for some time they were confined to Beirut; whereas the Catholic missions, with their long head start, were already in Damascus, Aleppo, and other parts of Lebanon. But Ibrahim's rule gave all foreign missions a chance to spread, and Catholics and Protestants were soon in vigorous competition. One gain from all this was as we saw, a regeneration of the Arabic language and the renewed diffusion of literature in Arabic, covering both the great classics of the past and modern knowledge, as well as works of religion and manuals of education of every kind. This in turn generated a movement of ideas which soon transcended literature and sought, through new political awareness, to regain for the Arabs the freedom they had lost.

In all this the Arabic printing presses played a vital role. Yet even early in the nineteenth century such presses were practically non-existent in the Ottoman world save in Istanbul and Cairo. It was thus a highly significant step forward when the American Mission transferred its Arabic press from Malta to Beirut in 1834.[22] The missionary in charge of this, Eli Smith, later had a new fount of type cast in Germany after researches in Cairo and Istanbul. This became known as American Arabic, and in time the Americans became pioneers of teaching in Arabic with adequate modern texts. The French on the other hand tended to stress their own language and literature. An Arabic translation of the Bible was one of the first goals of the American press, and in this and other projects Dr Cornelius van Dyck, a medical missionary who became a great Arabic scholar, and Eli Smith, were powerfully helped by two remarkable Lebanese Christian scholars, Nasif Yazeji and Butrus

22. *Ibid.*, pp. 36-44.

Bustani. Moreover, in 1834 Mrs Smith opened a school for girls, the first in Syria specially built for this purpose. In the same year at 'Aintura the Catholics reopened an important college which had been closed when the Jesuits were suppressed and was to play an important part in inspiring writers and thinkers of the Arab movement. Though somewhat slower in their response to the new opportunities, the Catholics were in no way behind-hand in meeting the Protestant challenge. Their Arabic printing program, developed in the 1840s and 1850s, was eventually marked by the outstanding quality of their classical texts and other books of learning.

The most valuable, and permanent, legacy of American missionary work in the Fertile Crescent was the Syrian Protestant College, founded in 1866 under the presidency of Dr Daniel Bliss, who after some forty years in that post was succeeded by his son. Under its later name, the American University of Beirut, and in what has become one of the choicest and most central areas of that city, this has remained to this day an institution of great distinction and achievement. As a symbol and instrument of Arab-American friendship it has weathered all the storms in that relation caused by the creation of Israel eighty-two years later. In 1875 a Catholic college transferred to Beirut became the University of St. Joseph. According to Antonius this was "an institution which, like its American sister . . . , exerted a decisive influence on the rising generations."[23]

First Plans for Arab Freedom

The nationalist plans for freedom from the Turk were to culminate in the Arab revolt of 1916, described in a later chapter. How did these plans originally take shape?

We have seen how—prematurely and in vain—Ibrahim Ali had tried to stimulate Arab nationalism for his own ends, and how, after his removal, Abdul Hamid made a special bid for the loyalty of his Muslim Arab subjects by a display of austerity and piety and

23. *Ibid.*, p. 44.

by stressing his role as their Caliph. But his policy had wider goals, and in pursuing these, he sought to profit by the Pan-Islamic campaign of Jamaluddin al-Afghani which had captured the attention of the Muslim world in the late nineteenth century. This fiery and controversial figure, who became, with the Wahabis, a spiritual father of the Muslim Brotherhood of our day, urged the union of all Muslim countries, freed from alien rule, under one universally acknowledged Caliph.[24] After expulsion from Persia he lived his later years under the protection of Sultan Hamid, who, without genuinely espousing his ideas, saw a possible advantage in becoming a universally acknowledged leader of Islam, for in that capacity he could hope to undermine the loyalty to their respective countries of the many million Muslims under Britain, France, and Russia, and thus strengthen his status in the world.

In any event, his refurbished role as Caliph required him to show favor to the Arabs and especially to the descendants of the Prophet. He made generous grants to Arab institutions, and for upkeep of the sacred shrines of Islam in Arab custody. A number of Arabs acquired special influence at court, and even (before the Young Turks) in the affairs of the empire. At the same time the stirrings of Arab nationalism aroused his keen suspicion. He had potential troublemakers closely watched and where necessary removed, if not by murder, by enforced residence under his eye in Istanbul. One of those thus invited to reside in Istanbul arrived there in 1893 in his late thirties—a descendant of the Prophet, Husain ibn Ali of the Hashim clan of Quraish. In view of their special status, many of his ancestors had been custodians of the Muslim Holy Places as Grand Sharifs of Mecca, and this was eventually to be Husain's destiny as well. Husain's three sons, Ali, Abdullah, and Faisal—all to attain royal rank within thirty years—were sent to school in Istanbul.

24. See Armajani, pp. 244–45, where he describes Afghani as an agitator who claimed to be from Afghanistan though he was actually a Persian, and who represented himself as a Sunni though he was a Shi'i. Antonius, pp. 68–69, is somewhat more complimentary in his evaluation. Unlike the Wahabis, Afghani believed in the importance of reason in Islam and thus in the possibility of reconciling it with the modern world.

Quietly though Husain lived, the Sultan suspected him, not without reason, of having an independent mind and character.

Meanwhile, from 1895 until the downfall of Abdul Hamid in 1909, another Arab, the Syrian 'Izzat Pasha, became the pivot of the Sultan's Arab policy. This was at a time when the influence of the German Empire, then at the height of its power and prosperity, was becoming predominant in Turkey, and that of Britain, France, and Russia was waning. This German predominance was to be of fateful significance, for it was to bring Turkey into World War I on Germany's side. And this in turn was to lead to the downfall of the Empire and the creation of a truly Turkish state. It also led to the embitterment of the Arabs, denied their promised freedom by their supposed champions, Britain and France; and to the separation of Palestine from Syria for the purpose of creating there a Jewish National Home.

The German Role in Turkey

Germany's new strength in Turkey was dramatized by the visit to the Sultan in 1898 of her Emperor, William II, the flamboyant grandson of Britain's Queen Victoria. The Kaiser afterwards visited Damascus and Jerusalem and proclaimed his friendship for the three hundred million Muslims throughout the world who revered the Sultan as their Caliph. This overture was in sharp and astute contrast to the chorus of condemnation directed at Abdul Hamid by the other imperialist powers for his supposed instigation of the Armenian massacres a few years earlier. Germany had in fact had a stake in Turkey as early as 1838, when a young Prussian officer was lent to train her armies. He was later destined, as Field Marshal von Moltke, to lead German forces to victory over Austria and France.[25] This tradition continued, and from 1883 to 1896 the Ottoman army was modernized by Colonel von der Goltz as efficiently as Turkish conditions permitted. He did much for military education in special staff colleges, and this attracted an elite of Arabs as well as Turks.

25. Marriott, p. 237.

Some became leaders of the Young Turk Revolution, others of the Arab revolt against the Turks in World War I. One of Abdul Hamid's cleverest projects, inspired, it seems, by Izzat and directly related to the Arabs, was also carried out by Germans—the Hejaz Railway (built between 1901 and 1908), which ran nine hundred miles from Damascus to Medina. This was presented as an act of piety on the part of the Sultan-Caliph, since it facilitated pilgrimage to the Holy Cities; and contributions flowed in from the Muslim world. But the Sultan seems also to have aimed at controlling more effectively his southern Arab territories, since troops could now be swiftly moved as far as Arabia to deal with any disaffection. Ironically, this railway was to prove of great benefit to the Arab insurgents when their turn came.

The Ottoman Empire was also an underdeveloped area of great economic potential; and the Germans were intent on opening it up for their own gain. They obtained concessions to build a railway through Anatolia to Baghdad and the Persian Gulf, and soon to be known as the Berlin-Baghdad Railway. After reaching Konya from the Bosphorus the line skirted the southern fringe of Anatolia roughly along the ethnic border between Turks and Arabs. It constituted a clear threat to Britain's then dominant economic and strategic position in the Middle East and the Persian Gulf. But this second German-built railway was also, for the Sultan, another means of keeping the Arabs in check and averting the Arab rising he so much feared.[26]

The Scientific Societies

The starting point of the Arab movement was the Society of Arts and Sciences, formed by a small group in 1847, chiefly of local Christians including Yazeji and Bustani. Such was the strength of religious feeling at the time that Muslims and Druses declined to join, but Smith, Van Dyck, and several other Americans belonged. Shortly afterwards the Jesuits started an Oriental Society on similar

26. Antonius, pp. 76–78.

lines. Both societies broke new ground, for their collective pursuit of knowledge was something quite new for the individualistic Arabs. While both organizations died out after a few years, by 1857 an important successor had emerged—the Syrian Scientific Society. This included not only Christians but Druses and Muslims too—the Muslims having made it a condition of membership that missionary influence should be removed. In 1868 (before the stifling censorship under Abdul Hamid) this association obtained official recognition and recruited members from Istanbul, Cairo, and elsewhere. Nationalist goals were first voiced by one of its members in a patriotic ode exalting the glories of the Arab race and denouncing Turkish misrule. But so effective was Abdul Hamid's espionage, censorship, and repression, and so skilful his appeal to Muslim loyalties, that little more was heard of the Society during his reign. Moreover, there were only a couple of limited manifestations of Arab hostility to his regime,[27] although these were significant as the first organized political efforts of the national movement.

The First Secret Society.
The Migration to Egypt

In 1875 a small Arab secret society took shape. Composed originally of a few Christian graduates of the American college in Beirut, it then made a point of recruiting Muslims and Druses as well, and of branching out (around 1880) to other cities such as Damascus, Tripoli, and Sidon. By means of anonymous posters it campaigned for self-government for Syria and Lebanon, abolition of press censorship, and use of Arabic as an official language. Midhat Pasha, the progressive former Prime Minister who had been exiled to govern Syria, was suspected by the Sultan of complicity in this campaign— it appears, quite falsely—and recalled. After a few years, discouraged by the severities of the Ottoman police, the group dissolved and its leaders moved to Egypt. There, as we shall see in the next chapter, British rule had just been established. Despite the "Olympian

27. Nutting, p. 270.

paternalism" of the British, the air was considerably freer in Egypt than in Hamidian Turkey. Arab cultural life could develop unhindered. So, within reason, could Arab nationalist activities.

Apart from the nationalist leaders, however, from the mid-nineteenth century many Arabs left Turkey to seek a better life and fuller economic opportunities elsewhere. Some went to Egypt, others farther afield, and notably to the Americas. Most were Christians, since Ottoman rule was far less tolerable to them than to the Muslim Arabs, for whom, even at its worst, it was the rule of a leader sanctified by their religion. In Egypt and the Sudan the mainly Western-educated Christian Arabs from Syria and Lebanon were valuable to the British in government and professional services and also in general as intermediaries between them and the Muslim, Arabic-speaking, local populations of these now Christian-dominated lands.[28] While it was harder for Christians, and took longer than it did for Muslim Arab immigrants, to become fully integrated into Egyptian life, they played a prominent part in the cultural life of the country, and eventually in the Egyptian nationalist movement. It was Christian Arabs from Lebanon who launched the first Egyptian newspapers and magazines, some of which are outstanding in the Arab world today.

The Intellectual and Literary Revival

There was indeed a striking Arab intellectual and literary revival during the late nineteenth and twentieth centuries, not merely in the Fertile Crescent but in most parts of the Arabic-speaking world. Thanks to the sanctity of the Q'uran, classical Arabic had been preserved as a vital element in daily life. The great variety of local dialects spoken in countries as different and as far apart as Morocco and the Sudan had not become separate written languages as, say, French and Spanish had evolved from Latin. They were still recognizably Arabic even if the local peoples had some initial difficulty understanding one another. Thus the linguistic unity of the Arab

28. Atiyah, pp. 83–87.

world was preserved, and with it a community of ideas. New scholars, writers, and poets developed a modern Arabic, and in this current, speech produced striking works reflecting the influence and inspiration of contemporary Western philosophy, science, political thought, and literature. Western science in particular seemed to hold the key to the secrets of the universe, and for most of them the idea of progress had the same fascination that it did for Victorian England and other developing societies of the West. In this Arab intellectual revival Cairo and Beirut played a leading role, as did certain Lebanese emigrants to the United States writing in both Arabic and English; such was the mystic Kahlil Gibran, whose works have enjoyed widespread success in America and elsewhere in our day.[29]

The revival embraced also religious and social reform. Two leaders in these fields were produced by Egypt. One was Mohammad Abduh, an Egyptian patriot who took part in the nationalist rebellion of the 1880s leading to the British occupation. Abduh, was also a Pan-Islamist disciple of Afghani, but one who in general avoided politics and concentrated on educational and other reform. He was less hostile to Christianity than was his teacher, and believed that Islam should respond to the challenge of the West not so much through a renewal of political unity and power as through reform of Islam itself. He was a pioneer in modern social service among Muslims and he sought to liberalize and rationalize Muslim theological interpretation in opposition to the dogmatic conservatism of the ulama at the University of al-Azhar. Muslims, he felt, must borrow European methods, and his own commentary on the Q'uran was tolerant, moral and pragmatic. Although he became critical of doctrinaire Arab nationalism, he believed in the unity of all citizens, whether Muslims or non-Muslims, of the same state.[30] A second

29. *Ibid.*, pp. 85–86. Gibran, born in 1883, settled in America in 1912 and died there in 1931. He also illustrated his own books. One of his most popular works is *The Prophet*, originally published in 1923 and republished by Knopf in 1963. See also Armajani, p. 248.

30. Armajani, pp. 245–46.

leader was a courageous social reformer, Qasim Amin, who appealed for the liberation of women.[31]

From Christian to Muslim Leadership

One problem for the Muslims—even for those as tolerant and progressive as Abduh—was the demand of Christian nationalists for a secular state in which they would share all rights and duties with the Muslims on an equal footing. For although equality of all creeds existed in principle in the Muslim Ottoman Empire, a secular state would imply a denial of the supremacy of Islam over other religions. The progressive disenchantment of the Muslims—first with Abdul Hamid and then with intensified Turkification under the Young Turks—gradually induced the young Arab Muslim nationalists to make common cause with their fellow Christians. Indeed, around 1900 one of the most important developments in the movement to gain freedom from Turkish rule was the transfer of leadership from Christian to Muslim hands. Another was the gradual spread of these visions of freedom from Syria-Lebanon, where they were born, to all corners of the Arab world. In keeping with the Arab temperament, however, the whole process was spasmodic and impetuous rather than systematically planned.

The change to Muslim leadership was, rather strangely, another by-product of that Western education, which had at first been so vital an inspiration to the Christian nationalists. For, as Western education expanded, it actually hampered the growth of true nationalism. For one thing, it added to the tensions and rivalries in a land already of marked diversities and frequent strife, when Russian, German, and Italian missions came to compete with the established French, American, and British ones. Then, too, as the teaching of modern science and technology developed, it was hard to adapt Arabic to the new terms. The foreign missions found it easier to teach in a Western language. Even the Americans, who had done so much to revive Arabic as a teaching medium, adopted Eng-

31. Atiyah, p. 87.

lish as the language of instruction from about 1880. In time, the students of foreign institutions began to feel more at home in French, English, and other European languages, than in Arabic and were less and less imbued with the culture of their own people.

The Muslims were far less subject to these cosmopolitan trends. There were few of them at the foreign mission schools, since their families and spiritual leaders had a natural fear that they might lose their faith. They were less well taught, but the language in which they learned was Arabic and they were in constant tune with Arab life and tradition. By the time Abdul Hamid fell, the leadership of the national movement had become predominantly Muslim.[32] One who contributed to this transference of leadership was a Syrian Muslim writer from Aleppo named Abdul-Rahman Kawakebi, who died in 1903. Like others he left for Egypt after suffering for his denunciations of the Turkish regime. His passionate appeals for Arab independence seem to have produced little reaction at the time,[33] but they were a significant departure from the views of leading Pan-Islamists such as Afghani, by whom he had been influenced. For he regarded the Arabs, by reason of their history, as a people apart and entitled to a special place in the Islamic world. He rejected the Turkish Sultan's right of the Caliphate and urged the reestablishment of the Caliphate in the Holy Cities of Mecca and Medina in the person of an Arab from the Prophet's tribe of Quraish. This was to have repercussions in the aftermath of World War I.[34]

Arab Disillusion with the Young Turks

With the illusion of freedom, the Young Turk Revolution of 1908 produced an initial wave of inter-communal enthusiasm. An Ottoman-Arab fraternity was founded, and Husain ibn-Ali, against the warnings of Abdul Hamid, was appointed custodian of the

32. See Antonius, pp. 92–95.
33. Nutting, p. 271.
34. Antonius, p. 98. See also Armajani, p. 312. The reference is to the abortive assumption of the Caliphate by King Husain of the Hejaz in March 1924.

Holy Places as Grand Sharif of Mecca. Since the Arabs were more numerous than the Turks, they expected to have a majority in the forthcoming parliament, but the elections were in effect rigged by the Committee of Union and Progress, and the Arabs found they had little over one-third of the total seats. After the second revolution of 1909 they were further embittered when the by now all-powerful C.U.P. banned their fraternity and other non-Turkish ethnic groups. Thereafter the boldest elements in the national movement were forced underground, though there remained two overt Arab groups tolerated for the time being by the C.U.P. The first was the Literary Club in Constantinople, with branches in Syria and Iraq. It was ostensibly non-political and essentially a meeting place for the exchange of ideas. The second, the Ottoman Decentralization Party, was out of Turkish reach in Cairo. It rejected the tighter centralization imposed by the Young Turks and urged home rule for the non-Turkish provinces. In spite of these respectable objectives, a number of their leaders were seized and hanged by the Turks during World War I.

Home Rule Agitation. More Secret Societies

There were also two important secret societies and eventually a third—formed when the first had to be abandoned. The first, *al-Qahtaniya*, was named after a remote ancestor of the Arab race and aimed at turning the empire into a dual, Turkish-Arab, monarchy on the lines of Austria-Hungary. Its recruits included some high Arab officers in the Turkish army. Without being actually dissolved, it was soon abandoned when one member was suspected of having betrayed his trust. The second, *al-Fatat* (in full, Young Arab Society), was started by Arabs studying in Paris. It moved later to Beirut and then in 1914 to Damascus. Mostly Muslim, it aimed at complete Arab independence from Turkish or any other foreign domination; and so well was its secret kept that its existence was not revealed until the Turks had been overthrown.

Meanwhile in 1913, an Arab congress with a preponderance of

Syrian delegates met in Paris and openly discussed home rule for the Arab provinces, as well as other moderate demands such as the use there of Arabic as the official language. When unable to persuade the French to ban the congress, the Turkish Government promised to satisfy some of the demands. Thus Arabic would become the official language of the Arab provinces; Arabs would be taken into the cabinet and other top posts; and there was a vague promise of decentralization. But when the imperial decree was issued purporting to carry out these promises, most of the prospective concessions had been sidetracked. This trick was followed by repression.[35]

After the lapse of *al-Qahtaniya* some of the army officer members formed another secret society essentially for the military—*al-Ahd* (the Covenant), which, according to Antonius, "became to the soldiers what *al-Fatat* was to the civilians." The Iraqis as the major Arab group in the Turkish army, had a strong voice in this. Neither society knew of the other until 1915, when they merged in Damascus in aid of the Arab Revolt, which broke out the next year. The founder of *al-Ahd*, an Arab major on the Turkish general staff and a member of the C.U.P. with a fine military record, was arrested on suspicion and condemned to death. He had been born in Cairo, however, and, thanks in part to agitation in Egypt and to British intervention, he was eventually pardoned. He returned to Egypt, where many years later he became Inspector General of the Army.[36] This incident, typical of the clumsy bad judgement and intolerance of much of Young Turk policy, caused further deep resentment among the Arabs. Thenceforward they gave up all hope of a compromise settlement that would keep them in the Turkish state, and set their sights on ultimate revolt and independence. The instrument of that revolt was to be the quiet, pious, Husain ibn-Ali, descendant of the Prophet and now Sharif of Mecca, helped by the British from Egypt. This rule of Britain in Egypt was one of those foreign influences so hated by many Arab nationalists, yet

35. Antonius, pp. 102–117. See also Nutting, pp. 272–73.
36. Antonius, pp. 118–21. The officer in question was Major Aziz Ali al-Masri.

necessary to them to gain their immediate object—freedom from the Turks.[37]

The Eve of World War I

We have been concerned mainly with the Arab provinces of the Empire such as Syria, where the centralizing rule of the Young Turks could be reasonably effective. But the Arab Revolt broke out in Arabia, where the Ottoman hold was patchy and intermittent. For that reason, before considering Egypt we should perhaps look briefly at the situation in Arabia and the other outlying regions of the Empire on the eve of the first World War.

In Libya, while the Italians had taken Tripoli and Benghazi and other coastal regions, the plateau country of Cyrenaica was still unconquered. This was the home of the fundamentalist Senussi sect of Islam, with influence stretching down into central Africa. Although its leader had his reservations about the C.U.P., the Senussi had helped the Turkish forces to resist the Italians in 1911 and had continued to resist them since. Meanwhile the British— mainly through their Indian empire—dominated most of the southern and eastern fringes of Arabia and the Persian Gulf to an extent that virtually ignored the Sultan's rights. They had also extended their hold on Aden to establish a protectorate over nine small states in the hinterland. Elsewhere their position was affirmed by treaties with the rulers of Muscat and Oman and Bahrain, and with other rulers on the Arabian side of the Persian Gulf—notably Kuwait, at the door to Iraq. These rulers were advised by British political officers from India under the direction of a British Resident at Bushire on the Persian Gulf. A British company had been given the right to develop the oil fields in southwestern Iran, and the large potential oil resources here and in other parts of the area gave it great economic as well as strategic and political importance.

In the Hejaz the Turks were reasonably secure after the completion of the railway to Medina. As Sharif, however, Husain clashed

37. Nutting, p. 274.

with them when he tried to revive prerogatives of his office which had been allowed to lapse. Moreover, the C.U.P. wished to administer the area on the centralized pattern applied elsewhere. When he objected, they tried to depose him, but the risk of an insurrection eventually restrained them. To the south, between the Hejaz and Yemen, the high country of Asir (named for its inaccessibility) was in the hands of a dynasty known as the Idrisi, of Moroccan origin and pious reputation. Having unsuccessfully fought the Turks in the early 1900s, their chief had remained a nominal but discontented Turkish vassal. As for the Yemen, the Turks complained that it took as many forces to control it as were needed for all the rest of the Empire. Between 1872 and 1911 no less than four attempts were made to keep order in the interior as well as in the capital, San'a. Finally, the Turks compromised and gave the Imam Yahya wide autonomy and generous funds.[38]

In the center of Arabia between the Hejaz and the Persian Gulf lay Nejd, a territory dominated by the Wahabis under Saudi rule, from the eighteenth century until their defeat by Muhammad Ali in 1818. By 1843 the Saudis had regained Nejd and ruled it again for over twenty years. Later it was the cockpit of a triangular struggle. In 1871 the Turks seized the Hasa area bordering the Gulf, and for a time occupied all of Nejd. Then a family of chieftains named Rashid managed to take over Nejd until 1901. In that year a Saudi leader took Riyadh, the capital, and re-established Saudi rule in southern Nejd, the north remaining under the Rashids. When Ibn Rashid sought help from the Turks, they sent troops in 1904 and 1905, but without success; and in 1912 Ibn Saud ejected the Turks even from the Hasa. Yet this Turkish help to Rashid had one important result: Rashid stood by the Sultan while Ibn Saud sought help from the British when, two years later, Britain and Turkey were at war.[39]

38. Antonius, pp. 121–25.
39. Glubb, pp. 253–55, 275.

Chapter 8 Great Britain Takes Over Egypt and the Sudan

Of the major Western countries, Britain was one of the last to intervene decisively in the Middle East. While she had shared in the Crusades with the rest of Western Christendom, from the angle of politics and strategy these had been of small permanent importance. France had pursued her ambitions there from the sixteenth century onward, normally by cultivating the friendship of the Turks. In the seventeenth century Austria threw back the threat of the Ottomans and gained some ground at their expense. From the eighteenth, Russia sought, not merely to free her southern flank but to dominate the Turkish Empire; and had annexed vast outlying areas. In the early nineteenth century American missionaries came upon the scene, and the effect of their quiet zeal to do good, especially in the educational field, was out of all proportion to its ostensible scope. Since Germany and Italy did not become nations until the second half of the century, they made no striking impact on the Middle East until the late nineteenth and early twentieth centuries.

Britain's increasing concern with the area from the nineteenth century was, for a long time, more specialized than that of these other powers. She was less interested in the Ottoman and Arab worlds as such than in safeguarding the security of, and communications with, the vast Indian empire she had gradually acquired after 1757.[1] These communications passed through Egypt, which was thus one of her principal concerns long before the Suez Canal was opened in 1869. For with the building of a railway between the Mediterranean and the Red Sea, this land link offered the advantage of speed over the long voyage to India round the Cape of Good Hope which Britain had conquered from the Dutch. Earlier, Napoleon had tried—and failed—to supplant Britain in India by breaking her link through Egypt. Then there was a double Russian threat that might have proved even more serious than any France could offer after Napoleon fell. For if Russia could have gained free access to the eastern Mediterranean before 1856,[2] she might herself have grasped Egypt and cut those vital communications. At the same time, by expanding into central Asia, Russia posed an immediate threat to India from a near-by power base on land.

The Canal

A canal across the Isthmus of Suez had been a goal of Egypt's rulers since the days of the Pharaohs. The French revival of this project in modern times was by no means welcome to the British, who tried to have it stopped. Yet it took definite shape under Napoleon III.[3] It seemed that "Strong in possession of Algeria, cordially united with Spain, France might . . . hope to convert the Mediterranean into a French lake . . . , [and] cutting a canal across the Isthmus of Suez might neutralize the advantages secured to England by the possession of Cape Colony."[4] Again, such a canal might enable other countries to threaten Britain's hold on India, and with it her substantial trade with Egypt and the Persian Gulf.

1. Date of the battle of Plassey, which led to her occupation of the key territory of Bengal.
2. A goal the Soviet Union has now in effect achieved.
3. See Chapter 6.
4. Marriott, p. 239.

As a young Vice-Consul and son of the French political agent in Egypt, Ferdinand de Lesseps had won support from Muhammad Ali for his plans for a canal across the Isthmus. Britain favoured an alternative plan—for a canal and railway from Cairo to Suez[5]—at a time when her trade with Egypt was increasing. Muhammad had greatly increased the cultivated area of Egypt (especially for such crops as cotton and tobacco) and had created a class of landowners by giving estates confiscated from the Mamluks to his family and friends. In 1838 the British managed to nullify his large profits from state monopolies by an Anglo-Ottoman Commercial Treaty under which monopolies were barred and the British could buy from the Egyptians direct. As a result, by 1868 Britain was supplying 41 per cent of Egypt's imports and taking 49 per cent of her exports.[6]

After the death of Muhammad and Ibrahim the short rule of Abbas, who hated foreigners, partly undid their work. But Said, who succeeded in 1854, was again favourable to European influence and expertise. He promptly granted the Suez Canal concession to De Lesseps, who was something of a personal friend. By reason of Britain's non-cooperation, the Suez Canal Company was formed with capital from France, Holland, Spain, and Italy, with a concession running for ninety-nine years from the date of the canal's completion. The Viceroy, who undertook to provide four-fifths of the labor, held preferred shares yielding him 15 per cent of the net profit; but since he was still an Ottoman vassal, the Sultan's consent was needed, and this had not been obtained when digging started.[7] Britain, despite considerable influence at Istanbul, failed to bring matters to a halt; Said ignored the Sultan's objections and at his death in 1863, the building of the canal was pursued even more vigorously under his nephew and successor, Ismail.

When the Sultan, under British pressure, faced the Company with an ultimatum on the ground that he had not ratified its concession, de Lesseps appealed to Napoleon III. It was then agreed

5. Peter Mansfield, *The British in Egypt*, p. 4.
6. Armajani, p. 215.
7. *Ibid.*, pp. 215–16.

that the French Emperor should head a Commission of Arbitration, and under its award the Company gave up its right to free forced labor, as well as to certain lands and navigation facilities, in return for substantial compensation from Egypt. The Sultan then formally sanctioned the concession. In 1869 the canal was opened by Napoleon's Spanish Empress, Eugenie. This was one of the last manifestations of France's outstanding European position, which had lasted for more than two hundred years.[8] In 1870, after her humiliating defeat by Prussia, the German Empire, proclaimed in the palace of Versailles, became the Continent's strongest military and political power.

Ismail, though a man of courage, vision, and intelligence, was obsessed with the idea of changing Egypt into a European country, and Cairo into an elegant European city. By modern standards the country in fact advanced remarkably during his reign. Apart from the Suez Canal, irrigation, railways, and port facilities were greatly extended, much land was reclaimed from the desert, exports more than trebled, and there was impressive reform of the legal, administrative, and educational systems. An observatory, and a national library, and a museum were founded, and learned societies revived and encouraged. European skills were recruited as never before, and by 1876 more than a hundred thousand Europeans were settled in Egypt. Under the Capitulations in force throughout the Ottoman Empire they were virtually above the law. The French archaeologist Auguste Mariette was put in charge of the National Museum, and another Frenchman, Dr Antoine B. Clot, of public health and medicine. But an American officer, General Stone, became Chief of Staff of the Egyptian army, while British officers were sent with indifferent success to extend Egypt's power into the Sudan and beyond. Ismail even experimented with representative government by establishing an indirectly elected Consultative Assembly that was to last from 1866 to 1879.[9]

Through bribery and flattery of the Sultan, who conferred on him

8. Since around 1660, the beginning of the great age of Louis XIV.
9. Vatikiotis, pp. 85–89, 97, 129.

the title of Khedive in 1867 (giving him quasi-royal standing), Ismail secured more independent authority and a change in the succession in favour of the eldest son in his immediate family.[10] He could now make treaties on certain technical matters, and could raise loans and grant concessions in Egypt's name without reference to Istanbul. He substituted European methods of administration and public organization for an Islamic-Ottoman system. But he kept highly Oriental methods of political manipulation and power control. In this last respect, Egypt has somewhat lagged behind Europe till today.[11]

In any event the cost of Ismail's grandiose projects and achievements, in addition to his ostentatious extravagance and the debt of $15 million he had inherited from Said, was enormous for those days. Moreover, before he was able to raise state loans, Ismail's debts had been his personal liability rather than that of Egypt, and the rates of interest at which he could borrow were ruinously high. He had squandered freely because of the high price of Egyptian cotton during the American Civil War, and yet when prices fell after the war, he did not spend less. By 1869 Ismail owed about $125 million at rates of interest varying between a nominal 7 and 12 per cent, but actually amounting to between 12 and 26 per cent. To make matters worse, in 1875 the Turkish Empire as a whole was as we saw, virtually bankrupt, and the effect on Egypt's credit was disastrous. But the Suez Canal was the decisive factor in bringing about foreign control of Egypt.

Under Napoleon's award, Egypt owed some $25 million in compensation to the Canal Company, and this was to be recovered from the interest on the Khedive's shares until 1895.[12] Then Ismail spent further vast sums on lavish entertainment for all the guests who attended the Canal's inauguration, among them many from

10. See Mansfield, pp. 5–7; and Vatikiotis, pp. 78–79. The normal Ottoman practice was for the succession to go to the oldest surviving male heir in the ruling family.

11. Vatikiotis, pp. 88–89.

12. Mansfield, pp. 4–6.

the royal families of Europe. While an international conference in 1873 fixed the tariffs for passage, the Canal did not show a profit until 1875, and by that time Ismail had decided to dispose of his shares in order to raise money (he held 44 per cent or 176,602 out of 400,000). Learning of this, England's Prime Minister Disraeli bought them for Britain for £4 million[13]; the British Parliament was told only after the deal was closed. This gave Britain, as the largest single shareholder, a preponderant voice on the company's board. It also started the decline of French influence in Egypt. This was also one of many causes of the bad relations which developed between Britain and France in Egypt until, in 1904, they agreed to sink their differences in face of the German threat to both. The conference of 1873 had decided that the Canal would be open to ships of all nations, and this was confirmed by a convention of 1888, which laid down that it should apply to warships as well as merchant ships without distinction of flag and in times both of war and peace.[14]

Egypt Faces European Control

The sale of his Suez shares brought Ismail only a short respite from his financial troubles. He asked Britain to send him a Treasury expert to suggest improvements in the Egyptian financial system, but was then persuaded to accept a British financial adviser, whom the French insisted on matching with an adviser of their own. Accord-

13. Slightly under $20 million at the old parity of $4.82 to the pound. Benjamin Disraeli, later Earl of Beaconsfield (1804–81), one of the most fascinating figures in nineteenth-century politics, was from a Venetian Jewish family settled in England. His father, after a difference with the local synagogue, had adopted the Christian faith. Conquering the prejudice aroused by his exotic appearance when he first entered Parliament, he eventually became the leader and rebuilder of the British Conservative party, and a great favourite of Queen Victoria. He was also a noted wit and author. His reputation has survived, despite the efforts of adversaries such as Gladstone, the great leader of the Liberal party, to belittle him as an unprincipled adventurer.
14. Armajani, p. 216, points out that Britain violated this principle both in 1882 and in World War I.

ing to a British report Egypt could meet her debts if her resources
were properly managed and a reasonable interest charged. In 1876,
following French advice, Ismail converted all Egypt's debts, floating
and funded, into a Unified Debt of about $450,000,000 at 7 per
cent, secured on many of the state revenues and on his personal
estates. The British objected that this was too favourable to the
French and secured from Paris a compromise more satisfying to
Britain. Egypt's total debt charges would be some two-thirds of the
country's revenues. The Finance Minister strongly resisted this
foreign intervention, and a burden which seemed more than Egypt
could bear. But Ismail accepted the new plan and dismissed his
Minister. The Anglo-French Dual Control of Egypt then began.[15]

One British and one French Controller-General was appointed,
the British for revenue, the French for expenditure. A special department, the *Caisse de la Dette*, was set up to service Egypt's obligations, with commissioners from the various European creditor
states. Britain's commissioner was a young army officer, Captain
Evelyn Baring, former private secretary to the Viceroy of India.
After a further spell in India Baring was to return to Egypt and in
effect rule the country from 1883 to 1907. The British occupation,
which brought him into prominence, occurred more as the result of
a series of muddled compulsions and misunderstandings than of any
sinister plan for further British imperial expansion. Similar muddles
and cross-purposes were to occur during World War I in connection with Britain's promises to the Arab freedom movement and to
the Zionist movement. It is therefore important to relate in some
detail how Egypt ever became, through British intervention, the
vital link in advancing both these causes.

The Egyptian debt was fully serviced in 1877, but an intolerable
burden fell on the peasants, the *fellahin*, when during that year a
low flood of the Nile led to crop failure with ensuing starvation and
grave distress. Thus even after the Dual Control was established,
the Treasury was badly depleted. While most Egyptian government
officials and army officers were months in arrears of pay, the higher

15. Mansfield, pp. 8–9.

officers, who were for the most part Turks or Circassians, and the Europeans, went on drawing handsome salaries. In view of the continuing financial crisis, Baring persuaded Ismail to accept an international commission of enquiry into revenue and expenditure. Charles Gordon, a British officer with Sudan experience, was appointed Chairman at the instance of the Khedive. He proposed that all interest payments should stop until the arrears of pay had been met. Over this he clashed with Baring, and was again relegated to the Sudan. The two men disliked each other, and this was to have fateful consequences later.

The commission condemned the corruption and abuses of the Government—and especially Ismail's autocratic rule—without conceding that the Dual Control was in part to blame. Ismail was induced to delegate his power to a cabinet headed by an Armenian Christian with a French and a British Minister, and to cede his personal estates (about one-fifth of Egypt's cultivated land) in return for a civil list to cover his personal expenses, which were to be kept strictly separate from the state budget. More European, predominantly British, officials were appointed to government posts.[16] Characteristically Ismail set out to undermine this government, which played into his hands by retiring a number of officers on half pay. The Assembly created in 1866 was re-convened. It demanded control over the cabinet and government expenditure and resisted the proposal of the British Finance Minister to declare Egypt bankrupt. General protest demonstrations, inspired by nationalist resentment and encouraged by the Khedive, led Ismail to dismiss the cabinet and, after an interregnum under Crown Prince Tewfik, to appoint one composed entirely of Egyptians. The European officials resigned in May of 1879. Yet at that stage neither Britain nor France contemplated direct intervention.

Matters came to a head after a sharp protest by Germany and Austria against the new Government's proposal to reduce the in-

16. *Ibid.*, pp. 10–12. The chief minister was Nubar Pasha. The Minister for Finance, Sir Rivers Wilson, was British. The Minister for Public Works, M. de Blignières, was French. See also Vatikiotis, pp. 132–34.

terest on the floating debt to 5 per cent. London and Paris then persuaded the Sultan to order Ismail to abdicate in favor of Tewfik, and also to modify the authority given to the Khedive to raise loans: in future, loans could be raised only with the consent of his creditors. When Britain took over the administration of Egypt this was found to be a most awkward restriction. Later in 1879 the Dual Control was revived and Baring became one of the Controllers. A Law of Liquidation of 1880 lightened the tax burden on the fellahin and shifted some of it to the wealthy, but the Government was still left with no more than 34 per cent of a reduced revenue.[17]

The First Nationalist Movement

Three elements competed in the Egyptian nationalist movement of the 1870s and early 1880s. A first group were politico-religious reformers like Mohammed Abduh who were disciples of Afghani.[18] Among them was Saad Zaghlul, who was to emerge as Egypt's strongest nationalist after World War I. This group declined, however, when Afghani was exiled by Tewfik soon after he had assumed power. A second group were constitutionalists, who believed that the Assembly should become a genuine parliament. These tended to be men of property; their leader, Sherif Pasha, was a Turk and a big landowner who had headed the last government of Ismail but resigned when Tewfik threw out his plans for a constitution. This left the army, in particular its Egyptian elements of peasant stock, as the effective nationalist leaders.

Unlike Said, Ismail had given most of the top jobs to Turco-Circassians, to the embitterment of the *fellah* officers. In response to a protest against such favoritism, their leader Ahmed Arabi and two colleagues were arrested in 1881 but rescued by army units that supported them. Arabi became a national hero.[19] The groups who

17. Vatikiotis, pp. 135–44; Mansfield, pp. 11–16.
18. See Chapter 7.
19. Of humble origin like the late Gamal Abdul Nasser, Egypt's most effective leader of our day.

rallied to him, became known as the National Party, and had a gifted pro-nationalist Turk as their brains, as well as a sweeping programme of reform. After a public confrontation between Arabi and the Khedive, a new, nationalist government was formed under Sherif.[20] Arabi accepted its orders, and it looked at though Egypt's future was assured on the basis of a bloodless revolution. But things went wrong for several reasons. Arabi had integrity and moral courage, and great appeal for the masses; yet "he lacked decision and . . . political and military skill."[21] Tewfik, weak but autocratic, wanted to get rid of the colonels. Sultan Hamid, while eager to restore Turkish authority in Egypt, was characteristically devious. While prepared at one time to send Turkish troops, he also established contact with Arabi and flattered him with the title of Pasha. The British gave no very clear counsel; most of them were uncertain what was happening.

The British Consul-General, Edward Malet, was hesitant, naïvely optimistic, and lacking in judgement. Auckland Colvin, the British Controller-General who had succeeded Baring, was a stronger character, and came to favour the overthrow of Arabi and British intervention. Yet both the British Conservatives (in power till early 1880) and the Liberals under Gladstone[22] (who had then taken office) were genuinely opposed to British armed intervention. They wished to keep in step with France, both powers being already concerned over the growing strength of Germany. If intervention were necessary, they preferred that it should be by Turkey, the suzerain power.

A third prominent British figure strongly favoured the nationalists. This was Wilfred Scawen Blunt, a romantic idealist of distinguished family who seems to have taken at their face value the anti-

20. See Chapter 7. The gifted Turk was Mustafa Sami, Minister for War in this Cabinet and later Chief Minister with Arabi as Minister for War.
21. Mansfield, p. 19.
22. William Ewart Gladstone (1809–98). Originally a Tory and adherent of Prime Minister Peel, he led the Liberal Party from 1867 to 1894. He is considered by many the outstanding British statesman of the later nineteenth century. For his relations with Disraeli, the Conservative leader, see above.

imperialist declarations of men like Gladstone.[23] But, despite his high principles, Gladstone had a politician's capacity for shifting his ground and masking the change with high-flown oratory. When Gladstone declared that he favoured Egypt for the Egyptians, Blunt misled the nationalists into believing that people like this would never occupy their country. Yet Gladstone was to be forced into occupation by the compulsion of existing imperial commitments, which made the Suez Canal and Egypt the British Empire's "lifeline."

The British Invasion

In January 1882 a new Government in France prevailed on Britain to join in issuing a warning to the Egyptians, to the effect that both powers would strongly support the Khedive in maintaining the established order in Egypt. This was taken as a threat by the nationalist government, which thereupon drafted, and forced the Khedive to promulgate, an Organic Law introducing parliamentary rule. In May, however, the Khedive, encouraged by the British Consul-General, broke with the nationalists, and their government resigned. Soon afterwards a second Anglo-French note demanded that Arabi and some of his fellow officers should go into voluntary exile. This was backed by an Anglo-French naval squadron in Alexandria. The result was an outburst of popular fury that forced the Khedive to recall the nationalist government with Arabi. In June many Europeans and others were killed in riots in Alexandria. It was promptly assumed by the British that Arabi and the military were behind this and that the country was in chaos. In July Glad-

23. Blunt's wife was a grand-daughter of Lord Byron, who had fought for the independence of Greece. Blunt was following a characteristic trend of many prominent British persons in denouncing imperialism and devoting himself to the national cause of another people. Thus, during the American Revolution, Burke and a number of public figures condemned the war Britain was waging against the colonists. A closer parallel with Egypt is India, where Allan Octavian Hume abandoned a successful official career to be, in 1885, one of the principal founders of the Indian National Congress, which became dedicated to the overthrow of British rule.

stone publicly condemned the Egyptian military; theirs was not, he said, a genuine popular movement. A powerful group in the British cabinet now favoured intervention, since the supposed chaos endangered the Suez imperial link. In fact Arabi had on the whole shown restraint in his dealings with Europeans, and he at once issued an appeal for peace and obedience to the law. Moreover, for the next two months the machinery of government seems to have worked reasonably well.

In London the Government still hoped that Arabi would be turned out by the Turks. Though a conference of the powers in Istanbul requested the Sultan to send troops, he did not comply until it was too late. In July 1882 matters came to a head. The British admiral, disturbed by the build-up of fortifications at Alexandria, presented an ultimatum demanding the surrender of the forts. Upon receiving only partial satisfaction, he bombarded and destroyed them, together with part of the city. Much of the rest of Alexandria was burned during its evacuation by the Egyptian troops. The French, disturbed by developments in Europe, had refused to join, and withdrew their fleet—a decision they keenly regretted later, since it left them with no voice in Egypt's future.

British forces landed after the bombardment, but Arabi, far from giving in, declared that Egypt and Britain were at war. The Khedive, who had moved to Alexandria, decided that the British should prevail, placed himself under their protection, and denounced Arabi as a rebel. Arabi retorted that Tewfik had defected to the enemy, and the nationalists set up a rival government to the Khedive's. The British then sent an expeditionary force, ultimately of thirty thousand men, in principle to uphold Tewfik's authority. Unlike Nasser later, Arabi failed to block the Suez Canal, trusting that its neutrality would be respected. The British, however, closed it for three days and sent troops to its central point at Ismailia. From there they advanced westward and attacked the relatively uncovered flank of the Egyptian army at Tel el-Kebir. They won a sweeping victory over Arabi's forces, which had divided leadership and barely ten thousand trained men. Yet the Egyptians fought with great courage

and had very high casualties. The nationalist rival government submitted to the Khedive, and Arabi surrendered to a British general.
When subsequently tried, he was defended by a British lawyer,
escaped execution, and was exiled to Ceylon.[24]

The Veiled Protectorate

With no legal title and no clear plan, Britain suddenly became
master of Egypt, a land still nominally part of the Turkish Empire.
Although this had not been the intention of her Government,
Egypt had fallen so neatly into Britain's hands that her rivals and
enemies were prone to think that she had schemed to achieve this
from the start.[25] In any case, the Gladstone Government insisted
that the British presence should be only temporary, until the Egyptians could satisfactorily govern themselves. The main occupation
force was in fact promptly withdrawn, and only a small garrison
was left behind. But the British invasion had shattered what remained of the weak Khedive's authority, and the National Party
disintegrated. Without either, Egypt actually had little potential
for self-rule. At the same time it was unfortunate for Egypt that the
late nineteenth century was the high noon of imperialist presumption. Despite the brilliant Asian empires of the past, many otherwise admirable Western leaders were convinced that Orientals were
incapable of governing competently. While they paid lip service to
the notion of helping Asians and Africans to govern themselves,
they were convinced that they needed the benefit of prolonged
"guidance" by the enlightened West. This same arrogant and un-
founded assumption was to bedevil Britain's and France's dealings
with the Fertile Crescent after World War I and helps to explain

24. Mansfield, pp. 30–52. See also Vatikiotis, pp. 151–61, who takes a less
sanguine view of the motives and character of Arabi and his followers. He states
that the Arabi revolt "was largely motivated by the personal disaffection and
ambition of certain officers. . . . There was no articulate or organized understanding of an Egyptian political entity seeking national emancipation" (p.
160).

25. Armajani, p. 218; Mansfield, p. 56.

why the "temporary" British occupation lasted for seventy-two years.

During this time the fermentation of ideas brought by foreigners inspired Egyptians to seek an end to foreign domination and to gain power themselves. But the conquest of power by educated Egyptians from the formerly dominant Turco-Circassian elite did not create solidarity between the Egyptians themselves. The rich remained sharply divided from the poor; and the new elite made no special effort to reduce the poverty and injustice suffered by the *fellahin*. Although much was done by the British to improve the peasants' lot and help the country to prosper, the task of fundamental social reform was to fall in our day to men like Nasser, another breed of revolutionary soldier sprung from the people, like Ahmed Arabi.[26]

A system of rule for Egypt was gradually evolved by Britain after a careful mission of investigation.[27] Faced with the contradiction between Britain's democratic ideals and sense of imperial destiny, this mission urged that the British should not administer Egypt from London. Annexation was excluded, as was any drastic reorganization such as the British had carried out in India. Yet, as the occupation developed, Egypt was in fact largely reorganized on the pattern of the British system in India, with the difference that British advisers were placed alongside each Egyptian minister and each governor was flanked by a British inspector. In theory the advice of the British could be ignored; in practice, obedience to it was expected and if necessary enforced. The façade of Egyptian self-government was maintained by two representative bodies. The upper chamber was known as the Legislative Council. Just over half its members were elected by provincial councils, all the others being appointed by the government. In the lower house or General Assembly, forty-six out of eighty-two members were elected on a restricted franchise, the rest being ministers and members of the

26. See Vatikiotis, pp. 159–61.
27. Headed by the Marquis of Dufferin, Britain's Ambassador at Istanbul and later Viceroy of India.

upper house. The chambers could neither initiate legislation nor control ministers. The Egyptians saw them for the sham they were; and many were exasperated by the British claim to be there in aid of Egypt's independence. Some would have preferred outright annexation because then they would have known just where they stood and what they had to fight.[28]

British "guidance" to Egypt was on the face of it of the most unassuming kind. Until World War I the effective ruler of the country was the British Agent and Consul-General, who retained the modest title held by British representatives in Egypt before the invasion, when he was merely one of several agents of foreign governments in Cairo. The fact that it became a post of decisive power was largely the work of the man to whom in 1883 it was assigned.

The Cromer Era Begins

This was Sir Evelyn Baring, later Lord Cromer,[29] who had already gained experience of Egypt as Debt Commissioner and briefly as British member of the Dual Control. A soldier by training, from a family of prominent bankers, Baring had administered the finances of India with great success before returning to Egypt. With little diffidence about his own gifts, he saw it as his job to put Egypt right by applying the methods that had worked in India. He had a keen sympathy for the peasant, and was serenely convinced of the rightness of Britain's mission to better his lot and that of Egypt generally by paternalistic regulation rather than by constant consultation with the moods of local opinion. In general he had small sympathy with nationalist agitation that might hinder efficient government rather than promote it. He had, it seems, little interest in the Orient as such. India and Egypt were essentially a challenge to his superb administrative abilities. His path was not smoothed

28. Mansfield, pp. 57–58.
29. Although Baring did not become Lord Cromer till 1892, it will be convenient to refer to him by this later title now.

by his unflattering opinion of the social system of Islam, and he never bothered to learn Arabic, though he demanded very high standards of local knowledge from his staff. He was a figure of a past age, and what he did in Egypt has been warmly praised by some and critically judged by others.[30]

According to one positive judgement, "The regeneration of Egypt was largely the work of . . . Lord Cromer. . . . By 1888 he balanced the budget. As the revenue increased, the tax burden on the peasants was lightened and more money was spent on public improvements which in turn brought more revenue, and prosperity. . . . The *fellahin* were treated like human beings. . . . It had been the custom to force them, with whips and without pay, to toil . . . cleaning out the canals. Now a . . . decree abolished flogging, and wages were found for this . . . labor. Now too the *fellahin* . . . got their fair share in the distribution of water, which . . . the great landowners had manipulated in their own interest. The productivity of the ordinary peasant holding was doubled. New irrigation works . . . , pushed all the time, brought more and more wasteland into profitable cultivation."[31] A less enthusiastic view maintains that: "The direct and indirect British rule which lasted until 1936 (according to some . . . until 1952) was a mixed blessing. . . . The British . . . , more efficient than the Ottomans . . . , were anxious to create a viable Egypt for the safety of the route to India, for purposes of trade, and incidentally, for good public relations. . . . Cromer abolished forced labor, revised taxation in favor of the *fellahin*, and improved irrigation, sanitation and other services. These reforms were . . . made . . . in an orderly and efficient manner. He did not concern himself with reforms which had to be carried out through social revolution, such as land tenure, *waqf*, education and the like. . . . The British relied on a one-crop agricultural policy, and ignored the problem of population growth. . . . They were against industrialization. Cro-

30. Approval of his work was expressed by Arabi, of all people, when he returned from exile in 1901.
31. Alfred Leroy Burt, *The British Empire and Commonwealth*, pp. 515–16.

mer's successors were less efficient. . . . [He] kept the number of British officials to a minimum, but under Gorst and Kitchener they increased in number and decreased in quality."[32]

Cromer's first year was his worst. London required him to do three conflicting things: to stave off bankruptcy in Egypt; to instal a strong Khedivial regime so that the British could withdraw; and to face a disastrous situation in the Sudan. This last was to be one of the chief reasons why the British remained.

The Sudan Crisis

The Sudan was Egypt's lifeline, as the Suez Canal was the British Empire's. But while there are alternative routes to India and the Far East—a fact we have rediscovered since the Canal was closed— Egypt has no alternative sources of water, only the Nile. Its main original branches (the White Nile rising in Lake Victoria Nyanza, and the Blue Nile rising in Ethiopia) flow through the Sudan, joining at Khartoum, its chief center. As in Iraq, the land between the two rivers, known as the Gezira, is of exceptional richness. Any damming of these rivers in the Sudan, whether to intensify crops or out of enmity towards Cairo, could bring Egypt swift impoverishment. All rulers of Egypt have therefore sought to conquer the Sudan—or at least to ensure its friendship and cooperation. It had been subdued by Muhammed Ali, and Ismail's insolvency was in part caused by expeditions under British officers to extend Egyptian control. After the explorer Sir Samuel Baker, Colonel Charles Gordon had been in charge, but he resigned in 1881.[33]

---

32. Armajani, pp. 218–19.
33. Colonel, later General, Charles Gordon became known as "Chinese" Gordon for his efficient help to the Peking Government in suppressing the Taiping rebellion. His deep religious convictions and tragic death have made him a romantic legend. He seems in fact to have been a very difficult man of strong prejudices and marked tactlessness in personal dealings, and also of erratic and impulsive judgement based on inadequate assessment of the local situation, and an almost total ignorance of Arabic. The antipathy between him and Cromer, the careful realist and efficient administrator, was perhaps inevitable, but there

During that same year an insurrection started under the leadership of one Mohammed Ahmed, who called himself the Mahdi in the belief that he was divinely guided to bring justice to the world. A more immediate cause of his revolt was Ismail's attempt, with British help, to suppress the slave trade—such things were after all sanctioned by the Q'uran. The Mahdi profited by Egypt's weakness during Arabi's clash with the British, and defeated Egyptian forces at many points.[34] In September 1883—about the time Cromer arrived in Cairo—the Egyptian Government on its own initiative sent into the Sudan a poorly-trained army under a British general.[35] When two months later this was destroyed by the Mahdi's forces, there was fear that Egypt itself might be invaded by the Mahdi. British troops would surely be needed, and there could be no further question of Britain's leaving Egypt soon. The London Cabinet felt forced by fate to remain as Egypt's protector. At the same time Cromer drew the only sensible conclusion: If Egypt were to be saved, and were ever to become solvent, she must concentrate on her own defence. The eternal drain of the Sudan must be stopped. The whole territory must be abandoned for the present, with the hope that Egypt's flow of water would not suffer after all. But someone had to attempt an orderly withdrawal of the Egyptians and Europeans in the area. In the end it was mainly pressure of public opinion and the press in England that led to the choice of Gordon for the job against Cromer's better judgement. With muddled enthusiasm, the British public saw in Gordon a Christian hero who could somehow save the situation in this savage land of alien faith, and Gordon seems to have done little to discourage the belief. Having been formally invested as Governor-

---

were other good reasons for Cromer's extreme reluctance to have Gordon selected for his final mission to the Sudan. For a candid but well-documented evaluation, see P. M. Holt, *The Mahdist State in the Sudan*, 1881–1898, pp. 87–95. Mansfield, p. 69, says of Gordon that he had "given abundant proof of his courage, endurance, military skill and electrifying personality. At the same time he was so alarmingly eccentric as to border on dottiness."

34. Mansfield, pp. 65–66.
35. William Hicks.

General of the Sudan, he arrived in Khartoum in February 1884. But he carried confusing instructions that allowed him far more leeway to make executive decisions than had been intended. Thus he decided that he would "smash the Mahdi," and save Egyptian rule in the Sudan, rather than simply conduct a withdrawal.

One of Gordon's wiser plans was to restore the position of certain traditional rulers and magnates as a counterpoise to the Mahdi's new movement, and to suspend the suppression of the slave trade, which the Sudanese who lived by the trade had so resented. Despite Cromer's support for these moves, London refused to agree to the restoration of the key man among the local potentates, a slave-trader who might have helped Gordon effectively.[36] In any event, Gordon gravely misjudged the Mahdi's strength, and was eventually cut off by him in Khartoum both from Egypt and from the Red Sea. During 1884 the British public and many even of Gladstone's Liberals pressed for an expedition to relieve Khartoum, but Gladstone obstinately refused. When he finally gave way, it was too late. By the time the relief force approached, Khartoum had already fallen and Gordon had been speared to death. The new British troops were themselves not strong enough to defeat the Mahdi and eventually they too had to withdraw. A few months later the Mahdi himself was dead. His successor, Abdullahi al-Taashi, was known as the Khalifa—a revival of the ancient title from the early days of Islam. He made three attempts to invade Egypt, all of which were checked, but remained master of the Sudan for thirteen years, till 1898.[37]

His rule was harsh and primitive, though many officials of the Egyptian regime continued to serve. Coming from a backward tribe of herdsmen, he had virtually no understanding of economic factors or of trade. He seems to have tried to help the peasants but could do little against the rapacity of his troops. The population was gravely reduced.[38] But Egypt's water supply did not in fact

36. Zobeir Pasha.
37. See Mansfield, pp. 67–76.
38. Holt, pp. 253–55. Burt, p. 515, paints the population decimation and general conditions in extremely black, but possibly exaggerated, terms.

suffer, for the skills needed to build dams and expand irrigation were lacking in the Mahdist state. This threat revived, however, from the late 1880s, when the European powers, who had such skills, scrambled to absorb the unconquered parts of Africa. Britain was concerned mainly with the Italians and the French. The Italians took over Eritrea but were defeated by the Ethiopians in 1896. The French hoped by annexing part of the southern Sudan to link their central African possessions with French Somaliland on the Red Sea.

Thus, by the mid-1890s Britain had decided to help Egypt reconquer the Sudan. This was accomplished in 1898 by an Anglo-Egyptian force under General Herbert Kitchener, Sirdar or Commander of the Egyptian Army, who was to be a successor of Cromer in Cairo, and one of the chief planners of the Arab revolt during World War I. In September, the Mahdist forces were finally defeated at Omdurman, near Khartoum, with the help of new mechanical weapons such as the machine gun.[39] Two months earlier a French expedition under a Major Marchand had reached the Upper Nile at Fashoda and had planted their flag there in token of occupation. After Omdurman, Kitchener arrived in Fashoda to claim the area for Britain. After some tense weeks of hostility, the French Government gave way. The conquest had been planned and led by the British and they were determined to have the main say in the Sudan's future, free from the trammels on their action in Egypt imposed by the Capitulations and the country's international creditors. On the other hand, the troops and money for the campaign had been largely Egyptian. Finally a condominium was established by an agreement of 1899. In the Anglo-Egyptian Sudan, both flags were flown but, under successive British Governors-General, the country was essentially run by Britain. This was to be a special source of conflict with the Egyptian nationalists in the years to come.

39. Winston Churchill, who took part in the battle as a young cavalry officer, has left a vivid description of it in *My Early Life*, pp. 178–202. Churchill was of course famous later as Britain's Prime Minister in World War II.

Cromer: the Later Years

In restoring Egypt to solvency, Cromer had to gain at each step the cooperation of the creditor powers. This was hard, for, jealous as they were of British influence, these powers—and especially France, the other main creditor—sought to keep their voice in Egypt's affairs and looked to Britain's early withdrawal. This international control of Egypt's affairs was once more formalized, by a London convention of 1885, and lasted in effect till the Anglo-French Entente Cordiale of 1904, by which France renounced her rights and interests in Egypt in return for Britain's doing the same in Morocco. The convention did arrange a loan for Egypt at low interest, and this just enabled the country's finances to pull through. But in general the first ten years of the occupation meant parsimony in expenditure together with much skilful, and at times short-sighted, improvisation by Cromer and his highly gifted team. One of their best moves was to set aside from the loan $5 million for improving irrigation. In some areas this brought an increase in the cotton crop worth forty times the outlay. Greatly expanded irrigation, marked by the construction of the first Aswan dam around 1900, was perhaps Britain's most solid achievement in Egypt.

The prospect of early evacuation soon became more and more unreal. Yet even the normally imperialist Conservatives (in office for most of the years from 1885 to 1905) felt impelled to make a gesture of this kind, though with no real intention of renouncing Britain's supremacy. In 1887 their leader after Disraeli, Lord Salisbury, promised Turkey that the British garrison would be out in three years—unless, however, Egypt's situation seemed "dangerous," in which case there would be no withdrawal. Much to Cromer's relief, Abdul Hamid refused to ratify this somewhat devious deal.[40]

---

40. Mansfield, pp. 83–116. The third Marquess of Salisbury was succeeded as Conservative Prime Minister in 1902 by his nephew Arthur James Balfour, who later as Foreign Secretary in David Lloyd George's coalition Government in World War I, signed the Balfour Declaration of 1917, promising the establishment of a Jewish National Home in Palestine.

The first phase of Cromer's rule ended in 1892. This had consisted chiefly of manipulating the government operations from behind the scenes, with the help of complacent Egyptian Prime Ministers or those who found it expedient to conform to his views. By the 1890s Egypt's finances were much improved. Forced labour had been stopped; wages were paid instead. The increasing cost of public works was met from revenue, not borrowing; and a start had been made to reduce taxation. Yet the burden of debt from Ismail's day was still extremely high. The Caisse de la Dette had inflated its powers, and without its consent no part of Egypt's now considerable reserve fund could be used for the benefit of the country. Nor could new loans be raised. A large part of the revenue was assigned directly to the Caisse. After the Anglo-French agreement of 1904, however, the Caisse's powers were again cut back, loans and administrative expenditure were freed from its control, and, by 1914, "Egypt had finally escaped from the financial bondage of Ismail's debts."[41]

Cromer's policies emphatically benefited the fellahin, one of his main goals, and wrought wonders in raising the country from poverty and confusion to a state of considerable prosperity. But more could have been done for the fellahin—and generally to correct the uneven distribution of wealth and the predominance of the foreigner in Egyptian enterprises—had it not been for his typically Victorian faith in laissez-faire, in a minimum of government intervention. For all his hopes of increasing small proprietorship and cutting rural indebtedness, the fellahin, when Cromer left, still owned less than a quarter of the cultivated land, and still had a burden of debt not reflected in the statistics. Again, the scientific development of agriculture was left to private initiative; there was no department to deal with it till some years later. Also just is the charge that industrialization was not pursued; Egypt was an excellent market for free-trade England's manufactured goods. Even less was done by Cromer for education. In 1910 the literacy rate was only 8.5 per cent for men and 0.3 per cent for women. He had

41. *Ibid.*, pp. 104–5.

the Victorian imperialist's instinctive fear that nationalist agitation by frustrated intellectuals would only damage good government, which the Egyptians were in any case unlikely to be able to furnish for themselves. Paradoxically, crime increased under Britain's modernizing rule—by reason partly of the changes wrought in the traditional structure of society, and partly of the less ruthless sanctions meted out to the offenders.

Nationalist resentment in fact recurred when the shock of Arabi's failure had worn thin. Indeed it became manifest in the highest quarter. In 1892 Tewfik, who for ten years had passively accepted British rule, suddenly died. His son Abbas II, well-educated in Europe, was determined to show his independence. When he challenged Kitchener and Cromer over the state of the Egyptian army, he was forced to back down, and this left him with an abiding grudge against them both. For a time he gave money and encouragement to the new nationalist groups. Many of their recruits came from the school of law—a legacy from Ismail's day, like those of medicine and engineering. The school was largely resistant to British influence, for it was under French control and taught French law, the basis of the Egyptian code. A group of young lawyers under the leadership of Mustafa Kamel[42] founded a new National Party that sought support in Europe, in the Pan-Islamic fold, and from the Sultan of Turkey. They were greatly helped by a clash between British officers and villagers in the Delta in 1906, in which both the behaviour of the British and the very harsh punishment of the villagers caused enduring bitterness.[43]

Another more moderate nationalist group—the People's Party—had members of the Egyptian establishment, together with some spiritual disciples of Mohammed Abduh. When Mustafa Kamel died young in 1908, it was one of the young leaders of the People's Party, Saad Zaghlul, well thought of by Cromer and a member of

42. This charismatic figure has been somewhat uncharitably judged by Sir Ronald Storrs, Oriental Secretary to the British Agent and later Governor of Jerusalem, as a corrupt charlatan of discreditable private life. See Storrs' *Orientations*, p. 74.
43. This became notorious as the Denshawai incident.

the government in his day, who was to dominate Egyptian politics after World War I in strong hostility to the British.[44]

The Liberal Experiment

Cromer was succeeded in 1907 by his financial adviser, Sir Eldon Gorst, a man of high intellect, dynamic energy, and far more open mind, though of less commanding personality and not always politically shrewd. Gorst sensibly made friends with the Khedive and thus helped to bring on a break between the nationalists and the palace at a time when Abbas was disturbed by the Young Turk Revolution. He pursued with zeal London's new plans to develop Egyptian self-government.[45] He did his best to revive the moribund provincial councils—which did eventually come to control state primary education—and to breathe new life into the Cairo General Assembly and Legislative Council. Ministers were to be present in the assembly whenever important matters were discussed, and it was in fact allowed to reject an advantageous offer of funds by the Suez Canal Company in return for an extension of its concession.

Gorst moreover encouraged the founding of an Egyptian university, and invited Egyptians in generous numbers to his table. He also sought to cut the numbers and diminish the predominance of British officials—a policy keenly resented by the local British, who falsely regarded him as weak because he tried to fulfil some of the terms on which Britain had occupied Egypt. Mustafa Kamel had worked to bring the Christian Copts into the national movement and, on Gorst's advice, the Khedive appointed a distinguished Copt as Prime Minister.[46] But this able statesman had signed the Condominium treaty establishing the Anglo-Egyptian Sudan and, for such an act, was regarded by the nationalists as the Christian stooge

44. Mansfield, pp. 163–70.
45. Storrs, p. 66.
46. Boutros Ghali Pasha. The Copts are native Christian descendants of the ancient Egyptians. Though often cruelly oppressed after the Muslim invasion of the seventh century, they survived as a separate community and are in general the best educated section of the population.

of a Christian occupying power. Gorst's liberalizing plans suffered a tragic blow when the Prime Minister was murdered in 1910, and his bid for Anglo-Egyptian friendship and cooperation was ended by his death from cancer in the following year. The Khedive made a special journey to England to be with him before he died.

Autocracy Revived

To succeed Gorst, Kitchener was brought back "to keep Egypt quiet."[47] A man of totally different stamp, he did this by invoking his own brand of paternal autocracy. He was on poor terms with the Khedive as a result of their earlier clash over the army. He limited Abbas's powers in various ways and helped to prepare his exclusion from the throne in 1914, when Turkey and Britain were at war. Known to some nationalists as the "Butcher of Khartoum," Kitchener was in many respects the blunt, unsubtle soldier, a man of firm, unyielding action, with few intellectual gifts or interests save the collection of antiques. Yet he had a feminine flair for atmosphere and the working of another's mind, and an intuitiveness that could be uncannily right.[48] He had glamour and style and was more capable than Gorst of exploiting the British Agency's power of independent action. Unfortunately, this meant that British officialdom again became predominant. London had not wished him to reverse Gorst's liberal policies, but he characteristically stressed practical reform as of far greater import to most Egyptians than "abstruse political questions."

Under new restrictive legislation, he dealt severely with the more hostile nationalists, but he cultivated the moderates in the People's Party, who had been alienated by Gorst's friendship with the Khedive. Like Gorst, he opened his house generously to Egyptians, but in more regal style. He replaced the feeble representative bodies by a legislative assembly, but for the most part elected on a very restricted franchise. While this assembly had certain powers to veto

47. Mansfield, p. 192.
48. Storrs, p. 105.

and delay legislation, and call Ministers to account, it yet remained essentially advisory.

In a more practical way than Cromer, Kitchener was deeply concerned for the fellahin and the agricultural prosperity of Egypt. He turned the new department of agriculture into a full-fledged ministry, and sought by somewhat rash and drastic means to lift the burden of debt from the mass of peasants; thus the debts of those with less than five *feddan* (roughly five acres) could not be recovered in a court of law. This and other rural improvements won for Kitchener the trust of the fellah. He did not seem to think that the ardent nationalist youth and urban intelligentsia mattered very much. Time was to prove him wrong and, from this angle, it was perhaps good for his reputation that the crisis of 1914 removed him from Egypt to other spheres.[49] When World War I broke out, Kitchener was on leave in England. He was stopped from returning to Cairo and appointed Secretary for War. Huge volunteer armies were raised by his commanding presence in that post. While on a mission to Russia in 1916 he was drowned when his ship was sunk.

The War with Turkey Starts

During the war of 1911 between Italy and Turkey the British had kept Egypt neutral. There could be no question of this in August 1914. Britain herself was involved and, thanks to the skill of German diplomacy and penetration in Turkey, and to the clumsiness of British dealings with Istanbul, that country was rapidly drifting into military alignment with the Central Powers.[50] On August 5th, 1914, Egypt was forbidden to trade with Britain's enemies, and thus suffered severe financial loss from the restrictions on her cot-

49. Mansfield, pp. 193–202.
50. Germany, Austria-Hungary, and Bulgaria, at war then with France, Russia, and Britain. Italy, which had been allied with the Central Powers, had declared her neutrality, and subsequently joined their enemies. For a vivid, popularly written account of how the alignments and actions of the powers evolved at this juncture, see Barbara Tuchman, *The Guns of August*. The initial involvement of Turkey is described in pp. 161–87 (paper ed.).

ton sales. In November 1914—as so often in past centuries—Russia declared war on Turkey, which had been manoeuvred by German armed pressure into hostile acts against the Russian Black Sea coast. The war with Turkey then spread to Russia's allies, Britain and France. Egypt was placed under British military control, and in December was declared a British Protectorate, with the proviso that future consideration would be given to her self-government.

Once again, as in 1882, the Egyptians were led to assume that Britain's new status was merely temporary, and counted on its being changed after the war. Thus Egypt's link with Turkey was broken by Britain after four hundred years. At the same time, to minimize adverse Muslim reactions it was stressed that no hostility to the Caliphate was implied. Independently of Istanbul, Prince Hussein Kamel, Abbas's uncle, was invited to become the new ruler of Egypt with the title of Sultan.[51]

Eve of Revolution in the Arab World

From the standpoint of the issues in this book, Britain's occupation of Egypt and the Sudan was the most important incursion of Western imperialism into the Middle East. By 1914, with the strongest navy and bases in Malta, Cyprus, Alexandria, Port Said, Suakin, Aden, and India, Britain dominated the most strategic region in the world: the eastern Mediterranean, the Suez Canal, Red Sea, Indian Ocean, and Persian Gulf. It was particularly vital for our story that she now lay close to Arabia and the Fertile Crescent, where the Arab Revolt was to take shape, and commanded the borders of Palestine, where the pioneers of Zionism were planting

51. See Vatikiotis, pp. 242–44, and Mansfield, pp. 205–208. There had been a secret alliance between Germany and Turkey from August 2, 1914. The Turks were incensed with the British for retaining two British-built battleships for which Turkey had paid. The Germans astutely sent two of their warships, the *Goeben* and *Breslau*, to replace them, the British fleet having failed to prevent their arrival in Istanbul. With a Turkish crew and under Turkish colors but under a German admiral, these were ordered to bombard Russia's Black Sea ports, thus giving Russia grounds for declaring war on Turkey. War with Britain and France followed.

their roots and unfolding their aspirations. Within a few years, and with fateful results, Britain would seek to follow in Palestine, Jordan, and Iraq the general pattern of her policies in Egypt and the Sudan, though subject to many local variants and special circumstances. Chief among the last was the evolution of world Zionism and its initial impact upon the Holy Land, and to this we must now turn.

Chapter **9** Zionism:
Dream Into Reality

For the Jews the dream of a return to Zion—to Jerusalem the City of David[1]—went back to the destruction of the Temple and of the Jewish state in the early years of the Christian era. It inspired them through the Middle Ages. Their sufferings during that grim age were intensified by the Crusades, based on a kind of Christian Zionism claiming that the Jews had forfeited the heritage of Abraham.[2] When the Crusaders captured Jerusalem and massacred its inhabitants of other faiths, they broke for the time being the last living link between the Jews in the Diaspora and their Holy City,[3] which had meanwhile become sacred to the Christians and Muslims as well. Later, in the sixteenth and seventeenth centuries, messianic figures had arisen among the Jews claiming a mission to lead them back to Eretz Israel.[4] There were also, as we saw, more prac-

1. See Chapter 1.
2. See Chapter 2.
3. See Chapter 5.
4. One of the strangest of these was Sabbatai Zevi from Smyrna, who managed to visit Jerusalem and in 1665 proclaimed himself the Messiah. Arrested in Istanbul, he embraced Islam under pressure from the Turkish authorities. Despite this, his followers remained loyal, some even into our modern age. See Roth, pp. 310–12.

tical gleams of hope when an ennobled Jewish magnate in favour at the Turkish court was permitted by the Sultan to try to resettle Jews in Palestine. Though this project failed, one small new Jewish contact with the Holy Land was the contemporary rebuilding of Tiberias.[5] Moreover, Safed in Palestine became a center for Jewish mystical studies.[6] Thus "physical contact between the Jews and their homeland was never completely broken. Throughout the Middle Ages sizeable Jewish communities existed in Jerusalem and Safed, and smaller ones in Nablus and Hebron. . . . Individual migration to Palestine never ceased; it reached a new height with the arrival of groups of Hassidim in the late 18th century."[7]

Meanwhile the dream persisted in the Diaspora. Jewish families would drink toasts to "Next Year in Jerusalem," and turn towards Zion when they prayed. But a Zionist movement with force, purpose, and achievement did not emerge until the late nineteenth century, as a late sequel to Jewish emancipation. Apart from its religious and mystical appeal, Zionism was more specifically a response to three factors. One was the danger of assimilation created by emancipation. Then, too, grave restrictions on emancipation persisted in certain areas, notably Eastern Europe. Finally there were the sporadic outbreaks of anti-Jewish feeling[8] which continued even in the most progressive countries. One such outbreak was to inspire the launching of a world-wide movement by certain dedicated Jewish groups seeking to return to Palestine. For many years the movement enrolled only a minority of Jews throughout the world, since most Jews were concerned to safeguard the often privi-

5. See Chapter 5.
6. *Ibid.*
7. Walter Laqueur, A *History of Zionism*, pp. 40, 42. The Hassidim or Chassidim were followers of a powerful movement of Jewish religious revival originating in the Ukraine in the mid-eighteenth century after the massacre of Jews by Cossacks in the mid-seventeenth century. It stressed feeling and emotion rather than mind and intellect and had a special appeal for the uneducated masses. See Epstein, pp. 270, 271.
8. It will be convenient and more accurate to avoid where possible the conventional term *anti-Semitism*, since the Jews are only one branch of the Semitic race, to which the Arabs also belong.

leged and successful status they had attained in their countries of adoption.

Emancipation and After

As we saw in Chapter 5, emancipation was primarily a product of the French Revolution, which in turn owed much to the French Enlightenment and the American War of Independence. By 1789 Jewish emancipation had already advanced some way in Germany under the impact of the *Aufklärung,* which sought to integrate the Jews into German life. Integration was also the goal of Napoleon when he revived a Jewish Sanhedrin. While the Congress of Vienna, which reshaped Europe after Napoleon's fall, in general confirmed the freer Jewish status established during the revolutionary and Napoleonic era, it also ushered in a reactionary phase. Thus it was still possible for the states of the new German Confederation to revoke their liberal legislation if they could prove that it had been imposed by foreign pressure. There was also an attempt to revive the ghetto in Italy. But, in most of early nineteenth century Europe, Jews mixed with their fellow men on an equal footing, and full rights of citizenship were not long delayed, since the reactionary phase was tempered by revolutionary waves (notably in 1830 and 1848) mainly seeking greater freedom and constitutional government; and in these movements the Jews played a full and vigorous part.

By 1871 a formal and legal constitutionalism prevailed throughout Western Europe, even in the German Empire. The Jews had now acquired in these countries the privileges and obligations of full citizenship, which had been assured to them by the Constitution of the United States some eighty year earlier. In Britain "their social emancipation had been complete almost from the beginning";[9] and Benjamin Disraeli's career as Prime Minister and Conservative leader was a mark of this exceptional tolerance. For, al-

9. Roth, pp. 329–33.

though baptized, he gloried in his Jewishness and, in his writings, constantly stressed the superior qualities of the Jewish people. As the century progressed, Jews played an increasingly prominent part, not only in politics but, as always, in business and intellectual life; and notably in art, literature, law, philosophy, science, medicine, and music. Some of the most gifted and accomplished families, such as the Rothschilds, Hirschs, and Montefioris, became wealthy, titled pillars of society. Loyalty to their adopted countries and substantial assimilation to Gentile ways of life seemed at last to promise a happy and acceptable ending to the long chapter of hideous injustices the Jews had suffered in the past.

Yet even at the height of the liberal nineteenth century, there were trends and circumstances threatening to undermine these hopes. Dangerous jealousies—even hatreds—were aroused by increasing Jewish prominence and success. With their outstanding qualities, and the traditions of ethnic solidarity and mutual help bred by centuries of oppression, this success was inevitable in all those countries where they now enjoyed the full protection of the laws and a share in public life. Indeed anti-Jewish prejudice was more swiftly aroused when Jews had become efficient rivals and competitors in every field, than when they were an oppressed, segregated minority at the mercy of arbitrary persecution. At the same time all supporters of the established order tended to be deeply suspicious and resentful of the extent of Jewish participation in revolutionary movements, not all of them constitutional. The fact that Karl Marx, a Jew, was the scholarly theoretician of Communism in the nineteenth century and that from then on individual Jews were prominent in the Russian revolutionary movement and the subsequent Soviet State,[10] has been a pretext for damning the

10. The outstanding figure among these was Leo Trotsky (formerly Bronstein). By his brilliant organization of the Red armies he saved the infant Soviet state in Lenin's day. Stalin's jealousy of a man who had towered above him, and Trotsky's non-conformity with the Stalinist version of the Marxist-Leninist Communist doctrine, led to his exile and eventual murder in Mexico on Stalin's orders.

Jews in our own age—even though, it is said, Marx would have been horrified at the Communist totalitarian dictatorship his theories were invoked to justify. A further cause of the emergence of a Zionist movement with concrete goals and programme was the continuance of severe restrictions and cruel persecutions in Eastern Europe.

Eastern Europe Still a Land of Suffering

The kings of Poland had encouraged the settlement of Jews for their own ends, and given them a wide measure of autonomy.[11] But, when Poland was partitioned, Europe's densest concentration of Jews came under the rule of Russia, a land of harsh autocracy that had never shown comparable tolerance. One policy of the Emperors was to keep the Jews as far as possible within the newly acquired Polish territories in what was known as a Pale of Settlement. Another, more marked from around 1800, was to facilitate their integration—through conversion, as it was hoped. While steps toward liberalizing the lot of the Jews were taken by the Emperors Paul I and Alexander I, under Nicholas I (1825–55), the pressure was far more harsh. The area of settlement was reduced by the exclusion of the western frontier region, kosher food was taxed, and synagogues could not be built near churches. Jews were conscripted into the army for the first time, and for a spell of twenty-five years beginning at the age of twelve and eventually of eight.

These inhuman rules were repealed by the relatively liberal Alexander II. More scope was given to the Jews in the context of his new policies of westernization and industrialization, this last being a field to which the Jews, with their financial skills, could make a substantial contribution.[12] But the respite was no guarantee of real and lasting emancipation. The murder of Alexander by revolutionaries in March 1881 led to a fresh wave of cruelty and oppression under his successors. This new oppression was formalized by the

11. See Chapter 5.
12. Roth, pp. 334–36.

May Laws of 1882, following anti-Jewish outbreaks in southern Russia. Under these laws Jews were excluded from all villages and small-town or rural centers even in the Pale of Settlement. In the great cities where university education was available, Jewish women were allowed to live only if they could produce the label of a prostitute.[13]

Conditions were hardly better in Roumania, which had gained full independence in 1878. A condition required by the Treaty of Berlin was that all citizens of whatever religion should have equal rights. But discrimination against Roumanian Jews continued on the pretext that, however long their residence, they were essentially alien. Nearby, at Kishinev in Russian Bessarabia, there were fresh attacks and killings in 1903, spurred on by terrorist groups[14] hostile both to the Jews and to the modernization of Russia with their aid. Two years later came the disastrous war against Japan and an abortive revolution in which constitutional reforms were tried and failed. Between 1905 and 1911, pogroms in hundreds of Russian cities claimed many thousands of Jewish victims.

On the eve of World War I, Russia was still, for the Jews, a land of suffering and degradation. It had harboured over half the Jewish population of the world, but many by then had left. Yet the harsh conditions in the Russian Empire had by no means stifled Jewish genius, for some of their people's most gifted figures came from this environment. While Jewish scholarship and achievement had reached new heights in the Western world where Jews were fully free, this record had been in general harmony with the Gentile environment and had expressed itself in the languages of the adopted countries. In Eastern Europe, there had been a cultural revival in Hebrew—the *Haskalah*—and somewhat later in Yiddish.[15] Through the Haskalah the sacred language was rendered more flexible and

13. *Ibid.*, pp. 351–52. Such outbreaks are usually described by the Russian word *pogrom* (massacre), which clearly indicates how sinister they were.
14. "The Black Hundreds," a name grimly foreshadowing the "Black September" Arab terrorists of our day.
15. See Chapter 5. See also Roth, pp. 337–40.

better adapted to the modern world, and Hebrew became the medium for bringing European culture and contemporary thought to the Jewish masses.

Fresh Jewish Emigration and Resettlement

A significant consequence of their still grim lot in Eastern Europe was another great wave of Jewish emigration to the West. Though emancipation had been a reality in Western Europe, and many went there, disturbing currents of antagonism and practical discrimination in the Continental nations still gave cause for alarm. The Anglo-Saxon world, including the self-governing countries of the British Commonwealth, offered more generous opportunities and richer chances of success. Streams of emigrants from Eastern Europe therefore made their way to Britain, the leading industrial country until about 1870; to the United States, the swiftly developing economic giant; to Canada, Australia, and New Zealand—themselves growing at a comparable rate—and finally to South Africa, then still in the British sphere and with the world's most extensive deposits of gold and diamonds.

The Jews in America

The Jews (the Marranos included) had had a stake in America from the start, since Columbus's expedition had been financed by a Marrano loan. From their founding to the War of Independence, the North American colonies had attracted Jewish settlement, since they were free from the Inquisition, which hunted heresy in the colonies of Spain and Portugal. As early as 1654 Jews settled principally in what became New York, and spread out mainly from there. A hundred years later there were Jewish communities in many of the chief colonial cities. They suffered few disabilities. While it is true that, despite the generous provisions of the American Constitution (which barred a religious test for public office), full emancipation was delayed in one or two states, by the 1870s it was everywhere complete. Napoleon's defeat and the reactionary sequel to the revolutions of 1830 and 1848 brought greatly increased Jewish immigration mainly from Central Europe; and the German Jews dominated in culture and wealth. The Gold Rush carried Jewish settlers to the Pacific. During the Civil War, apart from those Jews who fought on either side, one of the most influential figures was Jewish—Judah Benjamin, Secretary for War and then Secretary of State in the Confederate Government.[16]

Reform Judaism

Some of the later Jewish settlers brought with them a fresh movement in Judaism, one that originated in Germany with a disciple of Moses Mendelssohn, and found a fruitful soil in England and America. Its goal was "to adjust the old forms of Jewish life and practice to the spirit and culture of the peoples into whose history the Jews were being drawn."[17] Although one motive was to stop the drift from Judaism, Reform Judaism (as it came to be known) sought to eliminate from it whatever might hamper friendly relations between Jews and their neighbors or call in question their loyalty to the state. In practice it paved the way for at least partial assimilation of Western Jews to their Gentile environment.

The language of the adopted country was used for prayers and sermons; and the first place of worship of Reform Judaism was called a "temple," a name hitherto reserved for the Temple in Jerusalem. The early reformers thus paid tribute to their hope for the restoration of Israel's national shrine. Eventually however, the prayers for Jewish national restoration and that of the Temple were dropped as were references to the then Messianic hope of an "ingathering" of exiled Jews in Palestine. By the later nineteenth century the reformers were insisting on an essentially universal conception of Judaism, since it was, they said, purely a religion, with no national implications. Some even took to holding services on Sun-

16. Roth, pp. 354–59.
17. Epstein, pp. 291–92. For Mendelssohn see Chapter 5.

day instead of Saturday, the Jewish Sabbath, and to denying the authority of the Bible and Talmud.[18]

Orthodox and Conservative Judaism

There was considerable divergence among the followers of Reform, and it was strongly opposed by the traditionalists, whom they labelled *Orthodox*. But Orthodoxy also evolved in the nineteenth century, and the present Orthodoxy of the Western world, in effect a revival of that of the Arabic-Spanish period, combines strict adherence to tradition with full participation in the science and culture of the age. The divergences in the Reform movement brought it in 1846 to a halt in Germany, but not in the United States, where it made rapid and radical strides. A conference at Pittsburgh in 1885 called for the rejection of all Mosaic and Rabbinic legislation, and a few years later even the requirement of circumcision was dropped. A reaction to these far-reaching changes was the Conservative movement, which accepted the whole structure of Rabbinic tradition, restored worship in Hebrew, upheld the special revelation of God to Israel, and looked to the fulfilment of Jewish national aspirations in Israel's ancient homeland. Conservatism, too, produced its divergencies, but with these we are not here concerned.

Judaism Revitalized. Growth of American Jewry

By the late nineteenth century, as a result of emancipation, Reform, Conservatism, and other trends of change, Jewish communal life in Western countries had been gravely weakened through conversion to Christianity and assimilation to Gentile society. What revitalized Judaism in such countries was the wave of Eastern European Jewish immigrants fleeing from the cruelties and abuses occurring mainly after 1881, when pogroms and the May Laws imposed fierce new pressures on the Jews. The strong impact of these refugees on their host countries was due to their higher standard of

18. *Ibid.*, pp. 292–94.

religious scholarship and traditional Jewish piety, and this in turn was a result of the vast network of rabbinical schools (*Yeshivoth*) in countries such as Russia, Poland, and Hungary.[19] The renewed oppression of the Jews of Eastern Europe coincided with a labour famine in America. In consequence, between 1881 and 1900, over six hundred thousand Jewish refugees landed in the United States. Three years later the total number of U.S. Jews was reckoned at one and one-half million. By 1928 there were about three million. Today there are some six million.[20]

From often very modest beginnings in such industries as tailoring, furniture-making, tobacco, and fur, the successive waves of Jewish immigrants during the half-century between the 1880s and the first world war gradually learned to prosper in many instances by organizing strong trade unions.[21] They also spread to other great American and Canadian cities such as Chicago, Boston, Baltimore, Cleveland, Philadelphia, Montreal, and Toronto. But New York remained the main point of concentration for American Jews, and by 1925 there were one and three-quarter million in that city alone. Never before had so large a number of their people been gathered together in one spot.

As time went by, a brilliant role was played by the Jews of these new Western lands in all branches of industry and in all professions. They attained the heights well-known to all in the field of entertainment and publicity media; and especially in the cinema, stage, radio, television, and the press.[22] Thus the Jewish communities of North America became—especially after the first World War—the most wealthy, powerful, and influential in the world.

19. *Ibid.*, pp. 295–97, 303.
20. There were 5,870,000, according to the figures of the Jewish Statistical Bureau in the *World Almanac* (1973).
21. One example was the predominantly Jewish Amalgamated Clothing Workers of America.
22. A few outstanding examples would be Charlie Chaplin, the Marx Brothers, and Danny Kaye. In the press it was largely Jewish inspiration and leadership that gave the *New York Times* its pre-eminent position.

The Jews in Britain

In Britain the Jews were a smaller group than those in North America or Germany and, partly for that reason, their path in modern times was exceptionally smooth. The British had no feeling of insecurity such as was aroused for example in Germany by the substantial numbers of Jews in their midst and the intensity of their identification with German life. The baptized Jew, as we saw from the case of Disraeli, could reach virtually any heights, however strong his loyalty to Jewry. But, from the early nineteenth century, and long before their full and formal emancipation, even Jews who made a point of practicing their religion were socially acceptable to a degree little known elsewhere, even in the United States, where marginal discrimination in society and even in educational institutions still exists.

The tone had been set by King George III as early as 1809, when he visited a London synagogue by invitation on the Sabbath eve. British Jews became members of exclusive clubs and intermarried with the aristocracy. Some were themselves ennobled for special service and distinction. One of the first was Moses Montefiore, who had been Sheriff of the City of London and was knighted on Queen Victoria's accession in 1837.[23] He became prominent at a time when the advanced Jews of the West felt it their mission to help and guide their fellow Jews in the harsher and more primitive conditions of Eastern Europe and the Muslim world. In France, Adolphe Crémieux, appointed Minister for Justice in 1870, had earlier organized the *Alliance Israélite Universelle* to defend Jewish rights wherever attacked, and this was eventually matched in England by the Anglo-Jewish Association and in Germany by the Association for the Help of German Jews (*Hilfsverein der Deutschen Juden*).[24]

23. Laqueur, p. 34. See also Roth, pp. 344–45.
24. See Roth, p. 346. In somewhat changed conditions, this paternalistic attitude towards Oriental Jews is still on the whole that of the predominantly European leadership of Israel.

Montefiore visited Jerusalem repeatedly and, with permission from the Sultan of Turkey, launched various building projects there, including a quarter for Jewish artisans outside the walls of the old city. With Crémieux and other European Jewish leaders he effectively intervened with the Sultan to secure the release of Damascus Jews who had been falsely accused of the abduction of a Christian prelate. In this kind of activity Montefiore, "the stately patriarch, . . . to the end of his phenomenally long life, became as familiar in the courts of Russia and Roumania as in the Jewish quarters of Palestine and Morocco."[25] He and other distinguished leaders of their community in Britain had much traditional sympathy for the resettlement of Jews in Palestine, but it was essentially an idealistic sympathy with small practical drive and content. The initial translation of the dream into reality was to be the work of others.

Zionism: Plans, Experiments, Setbacks

Moses Hess, born in Germany in 1812, has been called the first prophet of the new movement known as Zionism. He had tried assimilation and found it wanting. In his book *Rome and Jerusalem* of 1862 he saw as the only solution to the Jewish problem the rebirth of an autonomous national identity in Palestine. This must precede any hope of Messianic deliverance. He could not, like many, believe that anti-Jewish prejudice was a dying relic. For him the racial antagonism of Germans towards Jews was deep and instinctive and beyond rational argument. He was convinced also that the Jew in exile who denied his nationality would never earn the respect of his adopted country. Although Hess apparently never became genuinely religious, he had nothing but contempt for Reform Judaism, with its claim to recall Christianity to the moral principles it had abandoned; such a goal, he believed, could be achieved only by an organized Jewish nation unifying morality and life in its own social institutions. The state was needed as a spiritual center

25. Roth, p. 345. See also Kollek, pp. 228–29.

and as a base for political action,[26] and it did not matter how many Jews it would contain.

His book, uneven but brilliant, broke new ground, and later theorists of Zionism developed similar ideas without, it seems, having first read his work. At the same time other voices were raised in favour of Jewish settlement in Palestine, and in 1862 (the year of its publication) a rabbi from eastern Germany proclaimed that the settling of Jewish colonies there must precede the Messianic era. To this end the German rabbi sought the help of Moses Montefiore and two English Christian friends of the Zionist cause, Lawrence Oliphant and Lord Shaftesbury, the great social reformer. As a result of their efforts an agricultural school was founded near Jaffa at Miqveh Israel in 1870, and the first Jewish agricultural colony at Petah Tiqvah in the same area in 1878.[27]

In 1881 the pogroms following the murder of Alexander II convinced a Jewish doctor of Odessa named Leo Pinsker—one who like Hess had believed in assimilation—that the Jews must help themselves and secure a land of their own. Pinsker set down his ideas in a pamphlet called *Self-Emancipation*.[28] Without a country, he wrote, the Jew must remain an eternal foreigner; yet unlike other foreigners with lands of their own, he was a beggar for hospitality he could not repay. According to his plan, the various Jewish societies should call a national congress and arrange to buy a territory for the settlement of several million Jews. "It must not," he insisted "be the Holy Land, but a land of our own." Thus he was not at first a Zionist in the strict sense of the word, but was converted to Zionism towards the end of his life, and played a leading part in a campaign for Jewish agricultural settlement in Palestine, called The Lovers of Zion.

Independent projects were promoted in various Russian towns,

26. Laqueur, pp. 46–53.
27. Epstein, pp. 306–7. Originator of the plan was Rabbi Kalisher of Thorn. Another notable Christian friend of the Jewish people was the novelist George Eliot. The hero of her *Daniel Deronda* is a Zionist seeking fulfilment of the movement's goals.
28. *Autoemanzipation*, published in Berlin in 1882.

but they suffered from lack of funds, preparation, experience, and expertise, and the Lovers of Zion movement as a whole was a failure, though its backers seem to have kept their faith that one day their dreams would come true. Against all the probabilities of the time, this did in fact occur some sixty years later.

Typical of the odds faced by these early settlements was the lot of one small group of students from Kharkov, founded in 1881, and known as the *Biluim*.[29] They settled at Gedera south of Jaffa, and are reckoned as the first wave (*aliya*) of Zionist immigration. Gedera was organized on socialist lines, like the *kibbutzim* and other agricultural colonies in Israel today. The orthodox Jews in Jerusalem looked askance at the *Biluim*, whom they regarded as "Russian anarchists"—mainly it seems, because of their lax religious practices. This reaction again was to typify the conflict between the practical dynamics of colonization and traditional Jewish piety, which persisted throughout the expansion of Zionist settlement and still exists in Israel today. The Turks also were suspicious of these Russian immigrants as possible agents of the Russian Empire, and in 1893 banned Russian Jews from Palestine. But the ban was evaded by bribery and false registration.

By the late 1890s some eleven settlements had been founded, mainly in the Jaffa area and the coastal zone running north to Haifa (paradoxically, the original land of the Philistines, traditional enemies of the Israelites); in Galilee and the far north; and between Jerusalem and Jaffa.[30] But the adverse factors were great, and many settlers suffered terribly from malaria before the marshes were drained. Moreover, the faltering settlements in Palestine held few attractions for the main stream of Jews hastening from Eastern Europe. When failure threatened, a leading Russian rabbi joined

29. From the initials of the Hebrew phrase meaning "O house of Jacob, come ye, and let us go."
30. These were (in the Jaffa area and coastal zone to Haifa) Petah Tiqva, Gedera, Rehovot, Hadera, and Zikhron Ya'akov; (between Jerusalem and Jaffa) Moza and Har Tuv; (in Galilee and the far north to the present Lebanese border) Rosh Pina (a venture of the Roumanian Jews), Yessod Hama'ala, Mishmar Hayarden, and Metulla.

with Lawrence Oliphant in appealing for help to two of the wealthiest Jewish philanthropists in Europe, Baron Edmond de Rothschild and Baron Maurice de Hirsch.[31] Before he would help the Palestine colonies, Hirsch insisted that the Jews of Russia must raise a substantial contribution. When this was not done, he concentrated initially on Jewish agricultural settlement in Argentina. For this and other schemes he founded the Jewish Colonization Association with a capital of some $40,000,000. Rothschild was prepared to help the Palestine colonies, subject to keeping a tight control through his agents on the way they were run. Thus the settlements survived, and by 1900 had increased to twenty-one, with forty-five hundred inhabitants. In this embryo Jewish world, two-thirds of its people were working on the land. But it all amounted to little more than a miniature social and cultural experiment, and was quite inadequate as the basis for a national revival. This could be accomplished only by political Zionism, a mass movement promoting mass immigration.

Cultural Zionism

Significantly, this goal did not appeal to all, not even all of those involved in the settlement program. Asher Ginzberg, a gifted member of the Odessa Committee of the Lovers of Zion who had been sent to Palestine in 1891 and 1893, sharply criticized what his organization was doing. "Palestine," he wrote, "could not absorb the Jewish masses; it should be a cultural and spiritual center but not the political or economic basis of the Jewish people."[32] Under his pseudonym Ahad Ha'am (One of the People) he thus became the founder of a movement known as Cultural Zionism.

Ginzberg did not take his stand upon religion, but saw as the main problem the progressive disintegration of Jewish spiritual life through the pressures of a non-Jewish social and cultural environ-

31. Baron de Rothschild was head of the French branch of the Rothschild family; Baron de Hirsch was by birth German.
32. Cited in Laqueur, p. 80.

ment. Since most Jews would have to remain in the Diaspora, a Jewish state would still leave the Jewish problem unsolved. What he urged was the establishment in Palestine of an autonomous Jewish community, gradually built up by an intellectual elite imbued with the historic culture of their people. They would no longer have to conform to alien patterns and would therefore be able to give full play to the characteristic qualities of the Jewish genius with its insistence on "the primacy of absolute ethics, based on ethical equality of men and spiritual unity of mankind. . . . Such a community . . . would serve as a spiritual center for all the scattered Jewries of the world, radiating to them spiritual influence and unifying them . . . into one new national bond. In this way, the Jewish people would become equipped . . . for the building of the ideal Jewish state in the future."[33]

Despite Ahad Ha'am's opposition to political Zionism, Dr Chaim Weizmann, future Zionist leader and first President of Israel, valued his inspiring faith. "For Ahad Ha'am, Zionism was the Jewish Renaissance in a spiritual sense. . . . He measured both the organization in the Diaspora and the colonies in Palestine by their effect upon Jewry. His first concern was with quality, perfection. He was what Gandhi has been to many Indians."[34] Also as with Gandhi, Ahad Ha'am's words continue to find an echo today. Among those who shared his views was the distinguished Jewish philosopher Martin Buber, who lived to teach at the Hebrew University in Jerusalem before and after the creation of the State of Israel, though his outlook was more mystical and religious.[35] Other thinkers remained strongly opposed to Jewish political *nationhood* while upholding the distinctive nationality of the Jews. Thus the German-Jewish philosopher Hermann Cohen held that this nationality could be maintained within the framework of the adopted

33. Epstein, pp. 312–13.
34. Chaim Weizmann, *Trial and Error*, pp. 36–37. See also note 44 below.
35. Martin Buber (1878–1965) was, amongst other things, the recreator of Hassidic legend and thought, and transformed this little-known communal mysticism of Eastern Europe into one of the great mystical movements of the world. He was also an outstanding advocate of Jewish-Arab cooperation.

countries, that the quintessence of it lay in the Messianic ideal that made Israel a living emblem of the unity of mankind. He rejected all Zionism, asserting that its goal of a separate Jewish state in Palestine was in conflict with this ideal.[36] Significantly, Cohen died fifteen years before the emergence of Hitler.

Others again continued to be disturbed by the exceptionally grave geographical, economic, and moral problems facing any attempt at really large-scale Jewish settlement in Palestine. The land was tiny, much of it desert and bare mountain, with relatively small areas of naturally fertile soil—and most of this already under cultivation. From the moral standpoint, there already lived in Palestine people who had been there continuously from before, during, and after the Jewish Dispersion. Some were descended from the Canaanites, whose land it had been before the original Jewish settlement; some, from the Philistines and other non-Jewish peoples of ancient times; some, from new settlers who had arrived at the time of the Arab conquest and during the thirteen hundred years since then. Most had been converted to Islam, others had remained Christian from the days of the Christian Roman Empire. But the claim of these established Palestinians to the soil of Palestine was, by any modern standard of right and law, no less valid than that of the Jews themselves, and could not justly be ignored or set aside.

Theodor Herzl Launches Political Zionism

In consequence of these scruples, obstacles, and dissensions, by the last years of the nineteenth century it looked as though the Zionist plan for recreating a Jewish national presence in Palestine might falter and break down. "If its history had ended in 1897 it would now be remembered as one of the less important sectarian-Utopian movements . . . , an unsuccessful attempt at . . . grafting the ideas of the Enlightenment on to the Jewish-religious tradition. . . . Zionism was . . . comatose when in 1896 Theodor Herzl appeared.

36. Epstein, pp. 314–15.

Within a few years he was to transform it into a mass movement and a political force."[37]

Herzl was a man of two worlds. He was born in Budapest in 1860 and lived the first eighteen years of his life in Hungary—a country on the edge of eastern Europe where much was still backward, a land of pogroms, ritual-murder allegations and brutal anti-Semitism. After moving to Vienna with his family, he became a doctor of laws, a playwright, a man of wit and fashion, with an acquired cosmopolitan background, and a first-rate journalist, in the service of the *Neue Freie Presse*, Vienna's most important newspaper, in Paris from 1891 to 1896, and its literary editor in his later years.

Herzl placed small stress on his Jewish background, admired the Gentile aristocracy, and was anxious to shine in the society of the great. One of his strong ambitions was to become an outstanding writer—which he was not. Where he made his mark was in the political field, which he professed to regard as less important. Yet even here he failed to achieve any decisive success during his lifetime. For he was not an original political thinker; he lacked any shrewd sense of political reality, naïvely exaggerated the potential impact of his undoubted charisma and charm—and the burning convictions he acquired—on the rulers, statesmen, and men of affairs he met. Indulged by devoted parents, he was seen by some critics and adversaries as a wrongheaded autocrat demanding blind obedience, an unstable egoist, an amateur diplomat who made promises he could not fulfill in pursuit of a goal that seemed beyond all hope of achievement.

Yet in his short life, this strange, uneven, compelling man, who gained small credit from the great and wealthy among his people, acquired a unique grip on the Jewish masses, who came to regard him as a kind of prophet, almost as a king. His early death in 1904 at forty-four, worn out by his efforts in his chosen cause, helped to foster a cult which became a sort of legend. He had predicted that the Jewish state would be established within fifty years, and Israel

37. Laqueur, p. 83.

was founded fifty years later, almost to the month. For this and other reasons he is regarded as the national hero and founding father of his country to a degree not vouchsafed to others who did far more in a practical way for its creation; and Israel has made a shrine of his remains.

The Dreyfus Case

Herzl's years in France changed this man of many parts into one fired by an overwhelming, single-minded conviction that he was called upon to lead his people—at least a representative number of them—out of oppression and ultimately back to nationhood in the Promised Land. The catalyst was the Dreyfus case, in which a French officer of Jewish origin, Captain Alfred Dreyfus, was framed, degraded, and very severely sentenced for a crime of treason he was later found not to have committed. Herzl, already keenly aware of the oppression and discrimination still suffered by the Jews of Eastern Europe, was shattered by the realization that someone, by reason of his Jewishness, could be the victim of such vicious injustice in France. This was, after all, the land of the original Enlightenment; and ever since Napoleon the Jews had been integrated as Frenchmen to a quite exceptional degree, and were second to none in their French patriotism.[38] If this could happen there, no Jew could ever be really safe anywhere.

It was perhaps characteristic of Herzl's nature, and of his new sense of concentrated dedication, that doubts and qualifications were given little weight, especially those suggested by others or by events that did not fit the image he had formed. Had his mind been more open and more thoroughly informed, he would in justice have perceived that France in the 1890s was quite literally not herself, and that the Dreyfus case was a shocking exception to the normal course of things. The morale and sense of security of the French had been terribly shaken by their defeat in 1870 and the sub-

38. *Ibid.*, p. 35.

sequent scandal over the building of the Panama Canal.[39] Certain reactionary elements in army and church seem to have connived at the inculpation of an innocent man from a not-always-popular group. But the liberal elements, headed by the writer Emile Zola, by the socialist leader Jean Jaurès, and by Georges Clémenceau, the fiery left-wing statesman who was to lead France to victory in World War I, mounted on behalf of Dreyfus a magnificent campaign of vindication in which the really enlightened elements in France did in fact triumph.

"The Jewish State"

By 1895 Herzl was convinced that there was only one solution to the Jewish question, and this he set forth with eloquent intensity in a booklet published in Vienna in the following year. This was called Der Judenstaat (in translation: The Jewish State: An Attempt at a Modern Solution of the Jewish Question). Much of it was on similar lines to the ideas of other thinkers whom he had not read. Thus he proclaimed that the Jewish question was neither social nor religious but national; assimilation had not worked; anti-Semitism was growing. However loyal to their adopted countries, the Jews continued to be pilloried as aliens. This was the work of the majority peoples, on the basis that might made right. The Jewish state was not a Utopia, but a necessary step by which the Jews might escape their plight.

Domineering though he was in some respects, Herzl's approach to the Jewish state was that of a nineteenth-century liberal. So, no

39. This was designed in 1879 by Ferdinand de Lesseps, who however failed to repeat his success with the Suez Canal, a simpler proposition since it was a tide-level construction. The French Panama Canal Company was forced into liquidation in 1889, as a result of mismanagement, corruption, and fever, when less than a quarter of the work had been done, and with an outstanding debt of some $350 million. The United States bought the French rights and assets in 1902 and completed the canal. This was opened to traffic in 1914, its formal completion being announced by President Wilson in 1920.

one would be forced to migrate there; those who felt happy in their present situation could stay where they were. The essential thing was that Jews be given sovereignty over a corner of the earth adequate for their national requirements. If the state (to be built by European Jews) were established in or near Palestine, it would bring civilisation to backward Asia. Agencies would be set up with adequate funds to supervise the building of the state, which would be run on progressive lines, with complete liberty of faith and conscience. In contrast to Israel's situation today, it would be neutral and have only a small army. It would be a "democratic monarchy or an aristocratic republic," not an unlimited democracy, since the Jews were no more fitted for this than other peoples.

Herzl was confident that anti-Semitism would cease once the scheme got under way. He mentioned neither the Lovers of Zion nor the already established Jewish colonies in Palestine[40] and made no reference to the existing inhabitants of the country. Indeed, he was later to refer to Palestine as a "land without people" and to urge that it be given to the Jews as a "people without land." This omission was, however, repaired in a later work, *Altneuland* (*A Country Old and New*), published in 1902 shortly before his death. In this he foretold that the new society in Palestine would be realized in harmony with the Arab Palestinian population, which would greatly prosper as a result of Jewish immigration.[41] Thus Herzl can hardly be blamed for Israel's failure to achieve this goal, which was also the implicit basis of the Balfour Declaration of fifteen years later.

The World Zionist Congresses

Herzl followed up *The Jewish State* by organizing the first World Zionist Congress at Basle in Switzerland in 1897, attended by some two hundred delegates. While this was largely the result of his own

40. Laqueur, pp. 90–96.
41. Hans Kohn, "Theodor Herzl," *Encyclopedia Britannica* (1971), XI, 459–60.

efforts, he received valuable support from one or two outstanding men. One was Max Nordau, an older man, also from Budapest, and a prominent writer on social problems who remained active in the Zionist movement until 1914. Another was David Wolffsohn, a leader of the German Lovers of Zion but originally from Lithuania. It was Wolffsohn who made Herzl realize the vital importance of support from the Jewish masses in Eastern Europe.

During the first and subsequent Congresses (which were held annually for some years) reactions crystallized to Herzl's scheme for a Jewish state. Many sophisticated Jews were critical, particularly of course the more wealthy, comfortable, and assimilated. The religious leaders were split. The Chief Rabbi of Vienna declared that Zionism was incompatible with the teachings of Judaism, though other rabbis joined the movement. Among the leading thinkers, Ahad Ha'am was predictably opposed. Amongst other things he objected to the lack of specific Jewish features in the new state, such as provision for the use of Hebrew. Two of his Eastern European disciples, Nahum Sokolow and Chaim Weizmann,[42] were critical also. Both stressed the importance of a spiritual renaissance, but Weizmann urged Herzl not to give too much weight to the pro-Zionist rabbis who were trying to impose their religious views on the whole movement. A socialist left wing of Zionism also emerged, led initially by Nahman Syrkin; and socialism was later to have a conspicuous part in Israel's development. In general, however, the less fortunate Jewish masses from Eastern Europe and

42. Nahum Sokolow (1861–1936) became Secretary-General of the World Zionist Organization and editor of *Die Welt* in 1906; was Chairman of the World Zionist executive 1922–31; and President of the World Zionist Organization 1931–35. His *History of Zionism 1600–1918* was a standard work, but Walter Laqueur's admirable *History of Zionism* (1972), *q.v.*, brings the story up to date.

Chaim Weizmann (1874–1952) became reader in biochemistry at Manchester University in 1904, the year Herzl died. He was President of the World Zionist Organization 1917–30, and again 1935–46. At first strongly opposed to the socialist elements among the Zionists, he later became more friendly towards them. First President of Israel from 1949. *Trial and Error, q.v.*, is his autobiography. Both he and Sokolow became naturalized British subjects.

elsewhere were captivated by the new vision and by Herzl's handsome, regal bearing and commanding presence at the Congresses.

World Zionism. The Jewish National Fund and Colonial Trust

Despite many rows and splits, the early Congresses took certain concrete steps that were to have far-reaching consequences for the future. A World Zionist Organization was set up with headquarters in Vienna and an official paper *Die Welt* (The World), originally published in German. Moreover, the first Congress adopted a programme declaring that Zionism sought to secure for the Jewish people a publicly recognized, legally secured, *home* in Palestine. The word *home* rather than *state* seems to have been adopted for obvious reasons of diplomacy, Palestine being then an integral part of the Turkish Empire. The distinction was, however, to gain marked significance in later years.

Jewish agricultural workers, labourers, and those of other skills would be settled in the National Home. In accordance with the official programme of the Zionist movement all Jewry would be organized and unified in accordance with the laws of the various countries. Jewish "self-awareness and national consciousness" would be strengthened. An annual contribution known as the shekel conferred the right to vote in the elections to the Congress, which became the supreme authority of the movement. In 1901 a Jewish National Fund was established for the purchase of land in Palestine as the inalienable possession of the Jewish people. The Fund was—and continued to be—raised entirely by voluntary contributions from Jews throughout the world. Before World War I the Fund had its headquarters in Berlin. Another early creation of the Zionist Organization was a banking institution known as the Jewish Colonial Trust. While neither the Fund nor the Trust obtained at first more than a fraction of the money needed for the Zionist programme yet they enabled the Organization gradually to pursue further Jewish settlement in Palestine through an office and Land Development Company established there in 1908.

Abortive Overtures to Turkey

At the first Congress Palestine had been adopted as the Zionist goal, and Herzl went there in 1898. He thought that the hills of Judea between Jaffa and Jerusalem looked "dismal and desolate,"[43] but did not let this discourage him. He made elaborate efforts to obtain Palestine from the Sultan of Turkey on the basis of some kind of charter by which it would remain a vassal state of the Ottoman Empire, and tried to invoke the German Emperor's support during the Kaiser's visit to Abdul Hamid. As an inducement he even hinted to the Sultan that the Jews might assume part of the Empire's debts—though this seems to have been a somewhat risky bluff, since Herzl had secured little effective backing or sympathy from the wealthy Jewish magnates. In any event the wily Abdul Hamid was not prepared to make over any portion of his dominions, though he commented, prophetically, that if and when the Turkish Empire were dismembered, the Jews might get Palestine for nothing. Meanwhile, he said, they could settle in scattered groups in the various provinces of Turkey, provided they became Ottoman subjects. But he was reluctant to let them do so in Palestine.

Thus Herzl's efforts in Istanbul ended in costly failure, and yet he felt that the Jewish masses needed immediate help. He had to consider other areas of possible Jewish settlement as a temporary expedient, and so turned to Britain.

Possible Alternatives to Palestine

The fourth Zionist Congress, in 1900, was held in London because, Herzl maintained, England was the only country in which Jews were not confronted with anti-Semitism.[44] The moment was not

---

43. Laqueur, p. 110.
44. *Ibid.*, pp. 108, 112–19.

unfavourable for seeking British help over Zionist plans, since the British were disturbed over Eastern European Jewish immigration to their country, and the threat of cheap labour it implied. Some of their leaders were prepared to consider finding a home for the Jews in some part of the territories they ruled. This could not be Palestine, since it was not theirs. It might be somewhere far off in Africa, or conceivably—despite all obvious objections—an area close to Palestine and under British control. Certainly no one at the start of the twentieth century could have predicted that in less than twenty years Britain would have become master of Palestine itself and could pave the way for the Jewish return to the Promised Land.

An approach to the British Government thus offered ground for hope. But the attitude of leading British Jews was less encouraging —and their support was needed to convince the British authorities of the need to help. Lord Rothschild declared that he did not believe in Zionism. He disliked the implications of Herzl's views. These seemed to suggest that a Jew could never really be an Englishman. He was also convinced that Herzl would never get Palestine. Rothschild however proposed Uganda—in order, it seems, to take the wind out of the Zionists' sails. Herzl countered by proposing Sinai, "Egyptian Palestine" (meaning apparently the approaches to the Holy Land within the frontiers of Egypt, including El Arish), or Cyprus. In October 1902 Herzl saw Britain's strong Colonial Secretary, Joseph Chamberlain,[45] who believed that something might be done for the Zionists in the southeastern Mediterranean—but the Greeks and Turks could not be turned out of Cyprus for their sake. He urged Herzl to discuss the El Arish area with Lord Lansdowne, who as Foreign Secretary was responsible for Britain's dealings with Egypt. And Lansdowne was obliged to defer to the all-powerful Cromer, whose experts decided that irrigation of the El Arish area would take too much water from the Nile. Herzl visited Cromer and found him arrogant and disagreeable.

45. Father of Austen Chamberlain, Foreign Secretary 1924–29, and Neville Chamberlain, Prime Minister 1937–40, when he was succeeded, in the disastrous early stages of World War II, by Winston Churchill.

The British seemed to Herzl blind to the future dominance of Egyptian nationalism, for which he felt some sympathy.

East Africa and the Sixth Zionist Congress

Meanwhile, after a visit to Africa Chamberlain decided that Uganda might be suitable.[46] Herzl reluctantly considered this after the El Arish failure. In 1903, at the start of the sixth Zionist Congress (again in Basle), Herzl produced a lukewarm message from the British Government, to the effect that facilities would be given for a Zionist study commission to visit Uganda and see if there were suitable vacant lands. If there were, and if London agreed, there would be a "good chance" of a Jewish settlement's being established "under a Jewish official as chief of the local administration"; and the settlers would be able "to observe their national customs."

Herzl's prestige enabled him to push through a decision to send the commission to East Africa, but he had a rough passage, even though Uganda was envisaged only as a temporary measure of relief. It became plain that the Eastern European Jews—even the most recent sufferers—would not go there; they would accept no substitute for Palestine. Many were in any case indignant with Herzl because he had visited Plehve, the Russian Minister for the Interior, and Witte, the Russian Prime Minister, whom they regarded as their natural enemies, in an attempt to secure alleviation of the Jewish lot. At this juncture Weizmann prophetically said that Britain would make the Zionists a better offer.

Herzl's Death and Achievement

Herzl died in July 1904, after further embittering skirmishes with the Russian Jews, who continued to insist that the Congresses should not consider territorial projects outside Palestine and Syria.

46. Since he referred to Uganda as being "hot on the coast," and Uganda as eventually constituted has no coast line, it is clear that Chamberlain was considering also part of the area that became Kenya.

For his part Herzl had insisted that political Zionism, in contrast to such earlier movements as the Lovers of Zion, had proved to be the only effective way of advancing the Zionist cause. He had promised not to exert pressure in favor of East Africa; and this scheme was gradually allowed to drop. For all Herzl's misjudgements and short-comings, the special honour paid to him by Israel today is not mis-placed. By his often extravagant actions he had fired and concen-trated the hopes of all his people who were at odds with, or felt themselves misfits among, the Gentile societies in which they lived. He had dramatized the Jewish plight by creating a world organiza-tion which all could hear and see. And, in the aftermath of World War I, the reverberations of his movement were to throw down for the children of Israel the barriers to the Promised Land, with con-sequences which were themselves dramatic for the Middle East and of critical moment to most other nations of the world.[47]

The Interregnum. Reorientation towards Britain

Nevertheless, in the years immediately after Herzl's death it looked as though political Zionism had failed. It had become clear that the Zionists could not hope to gain any guaranteed, substantial foot-hold in Palestine before the break-up of the Turkish Empire. One result was that between 1904 and 1914 the movement was taken over by the "practical" Zionists, who believed that its ultimate goal would not be achieved by some sudden turn of fortune, or inspired manipulation of the world's leading statesmen. Only by slow, steady progress with Jewish colonization in Palestine might the base be created for some future political victory.

47. See Laqueur, pp. 119–35. One further reason for the demise of the East African scheme was the objection of the white settlers there to Jewish immigra-tion. Nobody seems to have given a thought to the Africans. From the vantage point of the 1970s, it is interesting to consider what would have been the re-actions of the assertive rulers of Uganda and Kenya—already troubled by their large and unpopular Asian communities—if they had also had an autonomous Jewish settlement in their area.

During these years of what was sometimes called the interregnum, Zionism had no clear foreign policy, and dissension smouldered between the Eastern European Jews and those of the West. The East Europeans claimed with some justice that theirs was the heartland of Zionism, since it was there that the Jewish question was most acute. Herzl's immediate successor as President of the World Zionist Organization was Wolffsohn from Cologne (to which the headquarters of the movement were transferred). He was a man of more limited imagination but far greater practical sense; and he managed to put the movement on a sound financial basis. Unfairly criticized by many, he was ousted in 1911. From then on the East Europeans, including Weizmann and Sokolow, were dominant in the movement, although the new President was Professor Otto Warburg, a distinguished scientist from Hamburg. The interregnum was marked by the gradual reorientation of Zionism towards Britain, a change of course that assumed capital importance with the outbreak of World War I, when the official headquarters of the Zionist executive were still in Berlin. From 1904 Weizmann himself had been a lecturer at Manchester University, and in 1906 he had met Arthur Balfour,[48] with whom his later association was to be critically important for the Zionist cause. Sokolow also moved to England.

Progress in Palestine

The Zionists continued to be active in Istanbul, for Turkey still held the key to Palestine. They had hopes of the Young Turk Revolution, since it had been initially encouraging to the minorities in the Empire. Later, Turkey's defeats in her war with Italy and in the Balkans had also made her for a while more responsive to Zion-

48. Arthur James Balfour (1848–1930), a nephew of Lord Salisbury, *q.v.*, succeeded him as Prime Minister 1902–1905. He became Foreign Secretary in Lloyd George's coalition cabinet in World War I and after (1916–19). In that capacity he signed the Balfour Declaration, on behalf of the British Government, promising Britain's support for a Jewish National Home in Palestine.

ist approaches. But the large sums Turkey had been encouraged by Herzl and others to expect from Jewish sources were not forthcoming, and, in the long run, the Young Turks were, as we saw, even more nationalistic than the old regime. After 1911, however, the restrictions on Jewish immigration were partly lifted, and foreigners could more easily buy land in Palestine.

A second wave of Jewish immigrants arrived there between 1905 and 1914, and from 1908 colonization was systematically organized through the new Palestine office in Jaffa run by a capable special agent of the Zionist executive, Arthur Ruppin. To implement this program, a Palestine Land Development Company was set up to train workers for settlement on the land bought by the Jewish National Fund and by Baron Hirsch's Jewish Colonization Association. It also founded the cooperative and communal settlements (*Moshavim* and *Kibbutzim*), later a characteristic feature of the Jewish National Home and of Israel today. These training programmes obviously could not be judged by purely business standards as some demanded, since they produced no ready profit on the money spent. Yet Ruppin insisted on such programmes and other not obviously "profitable" expenditure for long-term goals, since it was essential to train the new arrivals to become citizens of an emergent nation. To this end a plot was acquired in 1913 on Mount Scopus, on the outskirts of Jerusalem, as the site of the future Hebrew University. Hebrew schools emerged, and a National Library. In 1909 a specifically Jewish city called Tel Aviv (the Hill of Spring) was founded on land north of Jaffa. By 1914 and the start of World War I, it had 1,500 inhabitants.

Balance Sheet of Early Zionism

Indeed by that time Zionists had gone far in Palestine despite the early setbacks. There were forty-three Jewish agricultural colonies, with a population of some twelve thousand, and covering a hundred thousand acres. Afforestation had been started in the Judean hills. Basic industries founded by the settlers were producing cement, bricks, beet-sugar, and the like. Hebrew had again become a living, public language; and there were Hebrew newspapers in Jerusalem. Moreover, Palestine had more Jews to the total population than any other land; and the Jew had returned to the soil and made a success of it. Even Ahad Ha'am was impressed. For one who rejected power politics, emerging Zionist Palestine could hardly be the pure, regenerative, universalistic, centre for Jews and Judaism that he had envisaged as a beacon to the world, but still a cultural centre was taking shape in Jerusalem and Jewish values were being revived in the land of their birth. In 1912 he prophesied in the *Jewish Review* that Palestine would be a national spiritual centre of Judaism, of study and learning, literature and language, bodily work and spiritual purification, a true miniature of the people of Israel as they ought to be. Ten years later he moved to Tel Aviv to be near it all, and died there in 1927.[49]

In spite of all this progress, on the eve of World War I the basis of the new Zionist creation—of this gradual and strenuous remoulding of a Jewish national identity in Palestine—was still weak and in some respects disturbingly unsound. Ruppin condemned in particular the extent to which the colonists had continually to be supported by outside funds, by the annual contributions to Palestine of the Jews dispersed throughout the world. He held strongly that this *halukka* system should stop; the Zionists who had returned to Zion must become self-supporting through their own work. In this, he and successive leaders of Zionism failed. For all its victories and achievements, contemporary Israel is still a nation that those outside it must support.

49. See Laqueur, pp. 136–54. See also Norman Bentwich, *Palestine*, pp. 70–71. Bentwich, one of the young British disciples of Weizmann mentioned below, was later Attorney-General of the Palestine Government under British rule, then Professor of International Relations at the Hebrew University. He lays particular stress on the role of Ben Yehuda in the revival of the Hebrew language as a modern medium of communication. Ben Yehuda settled in Jerusalem from Russia in 1882 and worked there for some forty years on his dictionary of modern Hebrew.

The New Zionists of the West

Before the critical upheavals of the first World War, a younger
generation of Zionists was arising, especially in the West, and they
were less affected by the discords of the past. The younger German
Zionists, some from recently settled Eastern European families,
were gradually won over to practical Zionism by Weizmann and
the Russian leaders. Strangely, most German Jews remained actively anti-Zionist. They had no premonition of the Hitler holocaust, and apparently believed that they and their children would
always be secure in a Germany permanently wedded to the rule of
law. In England after 1912 some dedicated young leaders gave
strength to Weizmann's "Manchester School of Zionism" and to
the Zionist Federation of Great Britain. For them the old controversy between "practical" and "political" Zionism had virtually
disappeared.

Meanwhile, the Jewish community in the United States had
become progressively more prosperous and influential. Yet Zionism
made little impact until America's involvement in World War I
in 1917 awakened what had been a society securely and somewhat
primly isolated from strife-torn Europe—and even more so from
the stresses and stirrings of the ancient Middle East—to the realities of world affairs. There was a federation of the various local
groups, but a shortage of money and weight. The leaders tended
to be from liberal, Americanized Jewry, men such as Rabbis Stephen Wise and Judah Magnes, of whom the latter eventually became President of the Hebrew University in Jerusalem and, like
Buber, a strong advocate of Arab-Jewish cooperation. *Hadassa*, the
Zionist Women's Organization that was to gain great strength, was
started in America in 1912 by one Henrietta Szold, a lady of exceptional determination whose Zionism predated Herzl's. One of
the most valuable adherents to Zionism was the great lawyer, Louis
Brandeis, who had lost touch with Judaism until his conversion to
the cause. He lent respectability and weight to the Zionist movement by his presidency of it from 1914 to 1916, in which year he

was appointed the first Jewish Justice of the Supreme Court. By the time the Zionist Organization of America was founded in 1917 the movement had become a great potential force in the United States and elsewhere. Even so, it would have been difficult at that juncture to predict that in some thirty years American Jewry and the American Government would have become the main hope and security of the new state of Israel.

Zionism Wins News Friends.
Zionism and the Arabs

By 1914 Zionism had spread beyond Europe to most countries of the world. It was said that the little blue cash box of the Jewish National Fund could be found in more than a hundred thousand Jewish homes. But Zionism was something more than a highly organized movement of ideas and practical achievement, reaching out to wherever Jews could be found. It had also managed to make new and powerful Gentile friends by methods of persuasion and diplomacy less ingenuous and more effective than those Herzl had used. Thus the closely-knit Zionist community of South Africa won the sympathy of the Boer leader, General Smuts, and of Lord Milner, the great imperial administrator, who was British High Commissioner in South Africa in the early twentieth century.[50] Both were to become highly influential statesmen of the British Empire during the imminent world war.

50. Laqueur, pp. 156–62. Smuts and Milner had been deeply involved in the Boer War (1899–1902) between Britain and the Dutch-South African territories, the Transvaal and Orange Free State, and its aftermath. Milner was Governor of Cape Colony and High Commissioner for South Africa before the war, in which Smuts fought against Britain. During and after the war Milner became governor of the defeated Transvaal and Orange Free State, and supervised their reconstruction after the ravages of the conflict. After self-government was restored to them, and the Union of South Africa was formed in 1909 as an autonomous nation of the British Commonwealth, Smuts became a convinced supporter of Britain. Milner became a member of Lloyd George's war cabinet. After commanding the Commonwealth forces fighting against Germany in Africa, Smuts became Prime Minister of South Africa and led its delegation to the Peace Conference in 1919.

Like Balfour and the Welsh Liberal, David Lloyd George, who became British Prime Minister in 1916, these men saw in Zionism the chance to redress the cruel wrongs done by the Christian nations to the Jews. By supporting the Jewish return to Palestine they sought to ease the burden on the Christian conscience in a way that they decided was right and just. As the future unfolded, it became clear that they could satisfy what was in fact their genuine idealism at small cost to themselves but possible at grave cost to others—the Palestine Arabs—for whom also the Holy Land was home. Here was a factor that had in general been overlooked or deemed of very secondary importance, and yet Palestine was part of Syria and neighbour to Egypt.

As we saw from the foregoing chapters, in the whole Fertile Crescent as well as in Arabia and Egypt, nationalism was astir, agitating to free this sector of the Arab world from alien rule. Within four years, the moment of deliverance came, and went. The resulting bitterness was one of the main causes of Arab hostility to the ever-growing volume of Jewish immigration to Palestine; and this in turn was the principal source of the conflict we face today. With the hindsight of the 1970s, however, it seems likely that this hostility could in large measure have been avoided. The major powers—in particular Britain and France—could have been less confused about potentially contradictory objectives and obligations, less ambitious to promote what seemed their immediate interests, and less convinced than they were by the long tradition of imperialism that their continued tutelage was essential, that the natives of, or migrants to, these less-developed regions could not be trusted to work out their own salvation. The next chapters will chart this involved and dramatic sequence of events.

Chapter 10
The Middle East and the First World War

The first world war and the ensuing peace settlement transformed profoundly the face of Europe and the Middle East. New stresses and uncertainties were introduced into what had been the relatively stable and prosperous world of the late nineteenth and early twentieth centuries, dominated by the great powers of that day. The "war to end wars" (as it was called) overturned the political system and leadership of most of the countries of those areas. It also bred a whole series of minor and major conflicts culminating some twenty years later in a second world war of even vaster proportions. This in turn led to further conflicts and insecurities, many of which we still live with today. In the inter-war period, the nineteenth-century liberalism, which had found an echo even in Russia, was replaced there, and eventually in much of Central, and parts of Southern, Europe by more or less totalitarian regimes. Two of them—those of Nazi Germany and Soviet Russia—proved to be of a ruthless effectiveness unparalleled in the earlier history of the world.

All this was of course hidden from the statesmen and soldiers who, in the late summer of 1914, faced with relative confidence and optimism the drift of the nations into a war that would surely soon be over. To many it might be just another of those gallant encounters—mainly between professionals—of which Europe had seen so many; and afterwards the world might revert to much what it had been before.

In the Middle East the key factor in the conflict was Turkey's involvement as the ally of Germany, Austria, and Bulgaria, against Russia, Britain, France, and eventually Italy and other nations. As we saw in Chapter 8, Turkey had hesitated to become drawn in, and not until November 1914 did she find herself at war with Germany's foes. Britain, France, and Russia had hoped to keep the Ottomans neutral, but had in effect been outmanoeuvred by the Germans. An ironic paradox is that, had the British succeeded in their aim—as they did in World War II—Palestine might have stayed under the rule of a modernized Muslim Turkey, and Britain would not then have been able to make it available for the Jewish National Home.

Turkey's Role

In 1914 the ten million Turks were a minority in their empire of twenty-five million subjects. They faced an equal or greater number of Arabs, some two million Armenians, one and a half million Kurds, and about the same number of other nationals, including Greeks. As we saw from Chapter 7, after the Young Turk Revolution the new leadership made some illusory gestures of conciliation towards their minorities, particularly the Arabs. These soon realized, however, that there was no question of being treated on an equal footing. Arab nationalist resentment was further aroused when the Triumvirate[1] increasingly resorted to centralization and Turkification of the empire.

1. Enver, Talat, and Jemal. In spite of Talat's abilities and Enver's personal failings, Enver as Minister for War and Chief of the General Staff proved to be the most effective leader of the three, and his pro-German leanings had been largely responsible for bringing Turkey into the conflict against the Western Allies.

Although most of the non-Turkish peoples were in fact of dubious loyalty, Istanbul seems to have had considerably more confidence than events justified in the loyalty of the Arabs, who were fellow Muslims and numerous in the armed forces. At the same time Jemal Pasha, who became military governor in Syria at the beginning of the war, did his best to cow the Arab nationalists in the Fertile Crescent by ruthless measures against all suspected of conspiracy, and many of such suspects were hanged. Thus the Arab Revolt, when it occurred in 1916, deeply shocked and surprised the Young Turk leaders. The Greeks in the Empire caused no trouble during the war, Greece itself being for a time favourable to the German powers. The Kurds, too, were no problem—chiefly, it seems, because their predatory instincts were let loose on the Armenians, who, as we saw,[2] had lived near them for centuries in one of the most strategic regions of Turkey. The Armenians were accused of disloyalty, not without justification, since many were strongly sympathetic to Russia, their supposed protector. The upshot was their forcible removal to other parts of the Empire in circumstances of extreme cruelty which caused the death of six hundred thousand, or, as some reckon, far more.[3] Another smaller Christian minority, the Assyrians, formerly sharing with the Kurds parts of eastern Turkey and northwestern Persia,[4] were also victimized and displaced during the war, since they had, like some Armenians, helped the Russians in their advance into eastern Turkey.

Apart from crushing disloyal minorities, the Turks were determined to rid themselves as far as possible of the foreign tutelage they so much resented. Thus, in her treatment of the Armenians and Assyrians, Turkey ignored the guarantees required by the Concert of Europe for the welfare of national and religious minorities.

2. Chapter 7.
3. See Lenczowski, p. 49. There is considerable discrepancy between the estimated figures given by different authorities for the number of victims. It has been pointed out that Russian reprisals against tribesmen of Turkish stock in central Asia were hardly less savage.
4. Notably the region of lakes Van and Urumia.

The European powers had also limited Turkish tariff autonomy, and required the assignment of certain revenues for the services of the public debt. But there was now no Concert of Europe to enforce these rules, or those relating to passage through the Straits, which could now be closed to ships of other nations. Moreover, as early as September 1914, Turkey abolished the capitulations granting foreigners immunity from her civil and criminal jurisdiction.

The Germans, who were entrenched in her armed forces, demanded that Turkey should take the pressure off the European fronts, where they and the Austrians were hardest pressed, by hostilities against Russia and against Britain in Egypt. Turkey could —and did—tie up many Russian troops in the Caucasus area, and Britain sent strong forces to defend the Suez Canal, which repulsed an attack upon it by the Turks and Germans in February 1915. The Germans believed that if the Canal could be cut, and with it Britain's imperial communications with India, Germany might win over the Hindu and Muslim nationalists and turn that whole vast country against the British. This was known as the Zimmermann Plan, after the man who became German Foreign Minister in 1916 and who, a few months later, was notorious for his abortive scheme to involve Mexico against the United States.[5]

As regards the Muslims in general and the proposed attacks on neighbouring areas, Turkish and German war plans coincided. The Turks hoped to reconquer Egypt, Cyprus, and other lands they had lost to Britain, Russia, France, and Italy. Then, in pursuit of the Pan-Islamic policies originally stressed by Abdul Hamid, they aimed to make their Sultan the Caliph of all Islam, as the first Caliphs had been. The old, weak ruler whom the Young Turks had put in Hamid's place was readily induced to declare a holy war (*jihad*) against the enemy powers that had so many Muslim sub-

5. The Mexico scheme is usually known as the Zimmermann Telegram, which contained instructions to the German Minister in Mexico to work for an alliance between Mexico and Germany. Intercepted and deciphered by the British, it was published by the U.S. Government on March 1, 1917, and was one important factor in bringing the United States into the war. See Barbara Tuchman: *The Zimmermann Telegram*.

jects. The Germans backed Turkish Pan-Islamism, and the Turks were prepared to support German plans to win over Persia and Afghanistan and eliminate Russian and British influence there. These plans looked hopeful at one point, but were eventually a failure, partly through Turkey's insistence on playing a leading part in all the moves undertaken in the Muslim world, where many local peoples—notably their traditional rivals and adversaries the Persians—had no love for the Turks.

The jihad also was a failure. The Yemenis, the Rashidis of central Arabia, the Senussis of Libya, and the Mahdists of the Sudan, made some response. The Muslims of India were impressed, but there was no rising against the British, who were doing everything possible to avoid offending Muslim susceptibilities. So far from keeping the Arabs loyal, the jihad was ignored by the most prominent living descendant of the Prophet, the Sharif Husain, custodian of the Holy Cities Mecca and Medina. In his case nationalism proved stronger than religion. With his sons and in collusion with the British he launched the Arab Revolt and thus helped to precipitate the downfall of the Turkish Empire. It was characteristic of British efforts to avoid offending their own Muslims that, when they invaded Iraq to try to join up with Russian forces operating from the Caucasus, they accepted no help from the guerrillas of the Arab Revolt. Their expedition was organized from India and largely with Indian troops; and some of them were Muslims for whom the Arab insurgents against their Caliph were traitors to their faith.

These somewhat discordant British operations were conveniently handled by different British authorities. The Mesopotamian campaign was, as we saw, essentially the affair of the Government of India, while the negotiations with the Sharif Husain, the military collaboration with the Arab insurgents, and the eventual invasion of Palestine by a regular British army from Egypt were dealt with by the London Government. As at other times in history a country at war was not unduly concerned with harmonizing what its right and left hands were doing. Unfortunately, uncertainty about ultimate goals and interdepartmental divergencies were seriously to bedevil Britain's dealing with the Arabs and Zionists as the war drew to a close, and afterwards.

Divergent policies of the same government were not, however, a monopoly of the British. One aspect of Ottoman policy in effect contradicted Turkey's other, Pan-Islamic, aims, and was a source of embarrassment and resentment to the Germans. This was Pan-Turanism, which sought to promote the union of all peoples of Turkish blood. Its leaders were basically secularists who resisted (as did later Kemal Ataturk) the reactionary, traditionalist influence of Islam upon Turkey, and who therefore opposed Pan-Islamism and also the policy of Ottomanization designed to keep all peoples of the empire loyal to the Turkish state. After 1917, and especially after the Russian revolutions of that year, the Turks increasingly favored Pan-Turanism. They were understandably fired by the hope of linking up with and liberating the groups of Turkish blood in Russia which had suffered severely at Russian hands. By 1918, therefore, Turkey was for concentrating her war effort on the Caucasus front, from which (before their revolutions) the Russians had managed to invade northern Turkey and Persia. But this by no means suited the Germans, who hoped to bring Turkish pressure to bear on other fronts where the British were doing too well.

At the same time Pan-Turanism made no real sense either to the Germans or to the Turks themselves in the context of Turkey's appeals for solidarity to their fellow-Muslims—the Persians and the Arabs. For one thing, it would have implied Turkey's eventual absorption of Persia's Turkish-speaking province of Azerbaijan. As for the Arabs, if Istanbul was aiming at a Greater Turkey, more or less all-Turkish by blood, then the Arabs had no place in it and could justifiably hope to go their own way. As it was, the Turkish Government intermittently pursued these two inconsistent policies, hoping—vainly, as it transpired—to gain from both.[6]

6. See Lenczowski, pp. 39–55. In tracing this outline I have been much indebted to his admirably concise analysis of the complex developments during this early part of World War I.

The Years of Decision

The middle years of World War I—1915, 1916, and 1917—were the decisive ones for the future of the Middle East. In March 1915, following the abortive Turkish attack on the Suez Canal, the British fleet tried, and failed, to force the Dardanelles. Between April 1915 and January 1916 British, New Zealand, and French land forces sought to occupy the tongue of Turkish land north of the Dardanelles after landing at Gallipoli and elsewhere in the area. These promising moves, inspired by Winston Churchill, then First Lord of the Admiralty (Minister for the Navy) in the British Cabinet, were repulsed.[7] Allied action against Turkey in the Balkans was resumed in the following year, when a fresh front was opened in the region of Salonika in support of a new, pro-Ally, Greek Government, which had risen against the former pro-German regime.[8]

The year 1915 saw the decisive phase of the secret negotiations between the British High Commissioner in Egypt and the Sharif Husain of Mecca; June 1916, the start of the Arab Revolt. In July 1917 the Arab insurgents captured Aqaba and in December a British army captured Jerusalem. Meanwhile on November 2, 1917, the British issued the Balfour Declaration, which promised, on certain conditions, their support for a Jewish National Home in Palestine. Five days later the Bolshevik Revolution broke out, and this installed the Soviet-Communist regime which made peace with Germany, and took Russia out of the war.[9]

---

7. Churchill, relegated to a less important post, subsequently resigned and then fought for a time in France as an ordinary army officer. He was brought back into the Government as Minister for Munitions in July 1917.

8. The new Greek Government was headed by Eleutherios Venizelos, responsible, after Turkey's defeat, for Greek expansion into southern Turkey, which ended in disaster in 1922.

9. By our calendar, the date of the revolution was November 7, 1917. By the older calendar then in use in Russia, it was on October 25. This is why it is called in Russia the October Revolution. The Soviets afterwards adopted the Western calendar.

The Arab Revolt: the Background

While he was High Commissioner in Egypt, Lord Kitchener apparently became convinced that in the event of break-up of the Turkish Empire the general area of Palestine (then often known as southern Syria) down to the Gulf of Aqaba would be "on political and strategic grounds an indispensable asset to the British Empire."[10] This conviction was to become an important factor in Britain's future policy. Yet Britain already controlled both shores of the Suez Canal, the western shore of the Red Sea, Aden, and the Persian Gulf. For some of her people it was hard to see what further imperial advantages Britain could gain from the possession of Palestine to offset the obvious complications of extending her control into the Fertile Crescent. Yet others saw in the Palestine plan, not only imperial profit but also a work of righteousness if thereby the Jews could be helped to return to the land where they once had lived. Another scheme which appealed to Kitchener and was also to have considerable weight in Britain's Middle Eastern policies was the eventual formation of an autonomous Arab state or states friendly to Britain to serve as a dyke against the expansion southward of other imperialist powers, whether Germany with Turkish support or, one day, Russia again.

The first approaches which eventually led to the Arab Revolt came from the Sharif of Mecca. They were of course oblique, and they were met at first with characteristic British coolness and caution. In February 1914 the Turks sent a new governor to the Hejaz to apply conscription and other unpopular measures of centralization. The Sharif then sent his second son, Abdullah, who was a deputy in the Turkish Parliament, to visit the Khedive in Cairo

10. This appears in the report of a committee set up by the British Government (H. M. Stationery Office, Cmd. 5974, 1939, p. 12) to consider the correspondence between the British High Commissioner in Egypt and Sharif Husain of Mecca early in World War I. For further details see Zeine N. Zeine, *The Struggle for Arab Independence*, p. 3, and Antonius, pp. 126–29.

and to see Lord Kitchener in secret. He also met Kitchener's principal expert on local affairs, the Oriental Secretary, Mr (later Sir Ronald) Storrs. Abdullah complained of Turkish measures, among them a plan to depose his father, which might prompt the Hejaz Arabs to revolt. What would the British do then? Could they supply some arms? Abdullah was told that there was little hope of British intervention, since Britain and Turkey were traditional friends. Nevertheless, from these talks Britain knew who might be counted on if and when Turkey should become her enemy.

When the European war began, one further factor turned the British towards Mecca. Their Muslim subjects must be able to make the pilgrimage there even if it were in enemy territory. While Kitchener was now Secretary for War, he continued for some time to play a leading role in these affairs; and it was now his turn to ask the Sharif's intentions. Accordingly, in October 1914 messages from Kitchener were delivered to Husain by way of Cairo and Abdullah. If Turkey should go to war with Britain, which side would Husain be on? If his people were to help Britain, the British Government would guarantee that there would be no intervention in Arabia, and would give them every assistance against external aggression. At this point the British were solely concerned with the Arabs of the Hejaz, and primarily with access to the Muslim Holy Places.

As the Sharif perceived, war between Turkey and the Western powers would raise issues far broader and more fundamental than access to Mecca and Medina. At stake was the future of all Arabs who aspired to rid themselves of Turkish rule. But there were many dangers, and his own family was divided. His third son, Faisal, was for standing by the Turks in the hope of earning their gratitude and some concessions for their people. The Arabs were ill-prepared, and the revolt might fail. Moreover, Husain suspected, as did many other Arabs (and not without reason), that Britain and France had designs on parts of the Fertile Crescent; and on that score he found nothing reassuring in the British offer. Abdullah was more sanguine about the prospects of a rising; why not test whether Britain would guarantee Arab independence? Husain sent a temporizing reply to gain time while he sounded Arab opinion elsewhere.

By the time Kitchener's answer reached Mecca, Turkey was at war, so that in addition to the pledges already made, the British promised to support the emancipation of the Arabs if they became their allies, and even referred (in the Arabic translation of the English text) to the "Arab nation." The Sharif saw this as a definite invitation to launch a revolt of all Arabs, and his reply showed him prepared to become the unavowed ally of Britain. But time and discreet preparation would be needed before he could face a breach with the Turks.[11] In January 1915 a new British High Commissioner, Sir Henry McMahon, arrived in Cairo, and in July, when Husain had completed his soundings of the Arabs, these tentative approaches took more definite shape. Meanwhile Sir Reginald Wingate, the British Governor-General of the Sudan, had also conveyed to Husain his readiness to help. Moreover, in and around the Arabian Peninsula the Amir of Kuwait, Ibn Saud of Nejd, and the Idrisi ruler of Asir had aligned themselves with the British; and forces from India had occupied Basra at the start of the Mesopotamian campaign.

While his soundings went on, Husain evaded with considerable skill any open support for the Caliph's holy war. While paying it lip service and organizing ceremonial demonstrations, he excused himself from more by the threat of British forces in Egypt and the Sudan. Knowing that the Turks were plotting against him, he sent Faisal to Istanbul with complaints against the local governor. Yet Faisal's main purpose lay in Damascus. While there he had talks with the nationalists both on the outward and return journeys, and was admitted to al-Fatat and al-Ahd. The conspirators now agreed on conditions for collaboration with the British; they were embodied in a so-called Damascus Protocol, the gist of which was sent by Husain to McMahon in a note of July 1915.

This was the start of a highly significant and controversial corre-

11. See Antonius, pp. 127–34.

spondence lasting into 1916. The Arabs sought British support and recognition for their independence within an area bounded on the north by the approximate ethnic frontier between Turk and Arab, on the east by the Persian border, on the south by the Indian Ocean, and on the west by the Red Sea and the Mediterranean. But Aden, Egypt, the Sudan, and the other Arab countries under foreign rule, were not included. In the north, the Arabs asked for Adana and Mersin in southern Turkey, and Alexandretta (Iskanderun) at the junction of Anatolia and Syria. They were induced by British objections to drop their claim to the first two, but not the third. The British also had reservations about the "portions of Syria . . . west of the districts of Damascus, Homs, Hama and Aleppo." These, they said, were not purely Arab—a point rejected by Husain. It subsequently appeared that Britain was more concerned about possible "detriment to the interests of her ally France" in those regions.

Britain proposed also, in view of her interests in Iraq, some kind of Anglo-Arab administrative partnership in the provinces of Baghdad and Basra. Husain would agree only to a temporary British post-war occupation; and in return the British should pay a subsidy to the Arab state. Britain promised to support Husain in the event of the establishment of an Arab Caliph; and not to conclude any peace which did not provide for Arab freedom. In this context, and subject to the modifications discussed, Britain was prepared to "recognize and uphold the independence of the Arabs in all the regions lying within the frontiers proposed." Trusting apparently to Britain's sense of fair play, Husain was prepared to shelve the problem of French interests until after the war, while making it plain that there could be no question of ceding any part of the Arab homeland to France or any other power.

Was Palestine included in the area in which the Arabs were to be free? The Arabs are convinced that it was; and this was part of the understanding on the basis of which they launched their revolt. The British argue that it was not; and here lies the source of one of the bitterest aspects of the present conflict. For by the actions of the major powers after the first world war, the Arabs were also cheated of most of the other prospects held out to them when they revolted. Yet their freedom *was* ultimately achieved, a generation or so later. But in the case of Palestine this crucial territory ceased to be theirs in any real meaning of the word.

The Arabs argue with some force that, since the British agreed to Arab independence in the whole area defined by the Sharif, except where they made specific reservations, and since no such reservation was made in respect of Palestine, this must have been part of the area to become independent. Palestine was not in fact mentioned in the correspondence, and the British contend that it was excluded by implication as one of those "portions of Syria . . . west of the districts of Damascus, Homs, Hama and Aleppo." But Palestine actually lies not west but south-southwest of Damascus, and the areas reserved by McMahon are elsewhere defined as being in the Turkish *vilayets* (administrative divisions) of Aleppo and Beirut. Now the vilayet of Beirut did not include the most vital part of Palestine—namely, the region of Jerusalem. Under the Turks this was a separate administrative area, the Sanjaq of Jerusalem; and the Arabs stress that it would have been essential to mention the Jerusalem Sanjaq if Palestine were to be excluded. If the contention of the British is valid, they failed to make their meaning clear and thus failed the test of all sound diplomacy, which is precision.[12]

12. There is a current impression, especially in the United States, that the British definitely intended to include Palestine within the promised area of Arab independence. Thus Armajani, p. 294, says "this celebrated controversy was perhaps settled in 1964 by the 'Westermann Papers' opened for research by the Hoover Institute at Stanford University. The collection contains two documents prepared by the intelligence department of the British Foreign Office for use by the British delegation at the Paris Peace Conference. These . . . fell into the hands of William Westermann, Professor of History at Columbia University and a member of the American delegation. . . . The documents state categorically that Palestine was included as part of the British Pledge to the Arabs."

These papers were in fact memoranda embodying the views of departmental advisers. However well-founded they might be, they do not constitute the offi-

The Arab Revolt: the Campaign

Husain had hoped to synchronize a revolt in the Hejaz with a rising in Syria and an allied landing at Alexandretta. After their failure at the Dardanelles and a setback in Mesopotamia,[13] however, the Allies were in no mood for further thrusts at the Turkish heartland. Meanwhile Jemal Pasha, in the hope of a more successful attack on Egypt, was pressing Husain to levy recruits for him, and insisted on Faisal's return to Damascus. Increasingly suspicious of nationalist intrigues, in May 1916 Jemal resorted to savage repression, culminating in the execution of many distinguished persons, some of whom were suspected of separatist activities because their names appeared in papers seized in the French consulates in Beirut and Damascus. He failed, however, to discover the plans for impending revolt.

The executions killed all Faisal's doubts, transforming him into a skilful and passionate leader of the rising and eventually into its principal commander. When his father ordered him to return, Faisal persuaded Jemal to let him do so on the pretext of heading the Hejazi recruits who were supposed to fight for Turkey. After coordination between his father, his brother Ali in Medina, and the tribal chiefs, the revolt was launched on June 5. By the middle of the month, Mecca and Jedda had been taken, but the Turks at Medina held out until the end of the war.[14]

From then on, British help came increasingly into play, and

cial and considered standpoint of the British Government, any more than similar memoranda by the State Department would represent that of the U.S. Government.

The British Government did not publish the full text of the Husain-McMahon correspondence for many years, but the texts were of course available to the Arabs through Husain, and the relevant ones will be found in English in pp. 413–27 of Antonius. See also his pp. 164–83.

13. This culminated in the surrender of the British garrison at Kut al-Amara.

14. Sir Alec Kirkbride, *An Awakening*, p. 102. Kirkbride was a British officer who served in the revolt. He was also one of the author's immediate superiors in the Palestine Government in 1925–27. The other was Mr Mordechai ("Max") Nurock, later Israeli Minister to Australia.

before long was an indispensable pivot of the revolt. General Wingate of the Sudan was made responsible on the British side for the operations in the Hejaz. Arms were of course supplied, as well as officers for training and liaison, staff work, supply, and administration. Available also were various technicians, a squadron of armoured cars, some light artillery, a few aircraft, and one or two naval vessels. Among the liaison officers was T. E. Lawrence (Lawrence of Arabia), who had worked as an archaeologist in the area, a man of remarkable power of endurance, with a genius for guerrilla warfare and a flamboyant style that appealed to Arab tribesmen. Yet there were many other officers who made a remarkable contribution but on whom less fame has been thrust.[15]

Gold, too, was generously supplied; and it has been estimated that the revolt cost Britain over $50,000,000.[16] There was also a small but quite effective French mission. Moreover, there were some regular Arab forces operating with the revolt. Without them it might have failed. Nearly all had served in the Turkish forces and had either deserted to join the insurgents or had volunteered after

15. *Ibid.*, p. 118. See also Antonius, pp. 320–24. According to Antonius, Lawrence had only a limited knowledge of the background of the revolt, and there are various inaccuracies in his *Seven Pillars of Wisdom*, including his claim to have planned and played a leading part in the capture of Aqaba, which was first suggested to Faisal by a chieftain of the Huwaitat tribe. His knowledge of Arabic was also limited, and his own reported attempts to pass for an Arab doomed to failure by this and his very English appearance. Kirkbride suggests that he would have made an excellent *condottiere* of the Italian Renaissance, and, incidentally, that he was by no means bloodthirsty (as a certain well-known film portrays him), but a man who believed that war should if possible be avoided and fought if at all with a minimum of harm to either side. A harsher critic is Souleiman Mousa, who refers at the end of his *T. E. Lawrence: An Arab View* (pp. 275–78) to Lawrence's suppression of certain untrue stories in his *Seven Pillars of Wisdom* when his shorter *Revolt in the Desert* was published. He links this with his later service in the Royal Air Force as an enlisted man, and sees in him a dual nature, one part of which drove him to brag and falsify, another being his conscience as an educated man driving him to atonement.

16. Zeine, pp. 14–16.

being captured. All realized that they were liable to be shot as traitors if taken by the Turks. Most were Iraqis, the largest Arab contingent in the Turkish army; and among the senior commanders were three who were later to be Prime Ministers of Iraq.[17] The tribal units were of varying quality. Many turned out for a specific operation and then went home, their chiefs being given lump sums in gold to distribute among them. They were brave but without discipline or military training and far better at hit-and-run attacks than at obstinate defence when things were tough. More useful were the mercenary camel units, chiefly from the nomads of the Hejaz and Nejd who gave more continuous service.[18]

A turning point of the campaign was the capture of Aqaba by the insurgents in July 1917. Thenceforward they were based on a point adjacent to Sinai and Palestine. Aqaba could be supported and supplied from Lower Egypt, and from there they could attack northward roughly parallel to the operations of the British forces from Egypt. The Sharif Husain now took the title of King of the Hejaz, having been dissuaded by his allies from calling himself King of the Arabs, since that would have upset other rulers of the intensely individualistic Arab peoples. Meanwhile a regular British army had advanced from Egypt to invade Palestine, but this was twice defeated before Gaza, in March and April 1917. This deadlock was broken after the appointment of General Sir Edmund (later Lord) Allenby as Commander. In October, by the capture of Beersheba, the Turks were outflanked and Gaza fell. Before the end of 1917, Jaffa, Jerusalem, and Jericho had been taken. The British line was then stabilized just north of these cities, with an open right flank facing the Turks in Transjordan and along the Hejaz Railway, which they garrisoned down to Medina. Faisal's army, based on Aqaba, had its command posts about thirty miles to the north, with some detachments considerably ahead of this.

17. Jaafar el Askari, Nuri es-Said (killed, with Faisal II, in the revolution of 1958), and Moulud Mukhlis. See Kirkbride, p. 4.
18. *Ibid.*, p. 5.

By this time the Turks had suffered an important defeat in Mesopotamia also, with the loss of Baghdad.

Meanwhile, in November 1917, the Balfour Declaration—to which we shall return—had been issued by the British Government. One of the motives for this timing was the revolution in Russia, which had brought about the collapse of that ally, and an impending offensive of the Germans in France, strengthened by troops from their eastern front. When this offensive, early in 1918, inflicted severe losses on the allied armies in France, many British troops were transferred there from Palestine and replaced by Indian troops. All this stalled the Palestine fighting until September 1918, when the offensive was resumed. The British plan was to break the Turkish line near the coast and then push through to the northeast and sever the enemy's communications. Meanwhile, a secondary attack would seize the Jordan crossings and distract the Turks by advancing into Transjordan while the Arabs, in coordination with these movements, sabotaged the three branches of the Hejaz Railway converging at Dera'a—those north and south to Damascus and Amman, and westward to Haifa. If the plan came off, Dera'a would be the bottleneck holding up the Turkish retreat.[19]

The operations were a complete success. Dera'a was taken near the end of September and many of the retreating Turkish forces were caught and captured. Damascus was occupied on October 1. On October 3, Allenby and Faisal entered the city by different routes and, after a brief and formal meeting, never met again. Aleppo in northern Syria was taken on October 26. A Turkish commander who fought with distinction during this last disastrous phase was Mustafa Kemal, who a few years later became the national leader of a diminished but regenerated Turkey. On October 30 the Turks signed the armistice of Mudros and the war for the Middle East was, it seemed, over.

19. For the outline given above I am indebted to Kirkbride's clear and vivid picture of these operations, in which he personally participated. See in particular his pp. 3–5, 56–57, 77–83, 99.

The Arab Revolt: the Aftermath

In fact by this time a far more intricate and embittered struggle had begun, and any real peace has eluded the Middle East for more than half a century. One main reason was that, under the stress of a war the British feared to lose and the compulsion of allied solidarity, the London government assumed other Middle Eastern commitments that could not be squared with its pledges to the Arabs. The upshot was a damaging series of contradictions which, for those who trusted Britain to fulfil all her divergent undertakings, inevitably clouded her good name.

While their enemies were still doing well, the Allies were planning to dissect the Ottoman Empire in anticipation of Turkey's defeat. There was of course still to be a Turkish state in the areas predominantly Turkish, but elsewhere, even in Anatolia, the various interested powers had each their own designs of imperialist aggrandizement. Thus Russia, the self-entitled successor of Byzantium, claimed the imperial city of Istanbul (Tsargrad) together with the Straits and areas adjacent to the Caucasus. Greece, with her own claims on the Byzantine heritage, had designs on Smyrna and its hinterland, where the Greeks were in some strength. The Italians, already in Rhodes and the Dodecanese, sought part of southern Anatolia. The French wanted Cilicia and parts of northern Iraq, including Mosul, as well as the coastal regions of Syria and the Lebanon. It would have been hard for Britain, with a far more extensive empire and a traditional concern for the strategic links with India, to let herself be excluded from the scramble for power bases in this vital area.

The Sykes-Picot Agreement

Discussions between France, Britain, and later Russia, took place early in 1916, soon after the pledges to Husain and before the Arab Revolt. At the start the British Foreign Office seems to have been genuinely concerned that any arrangements they reached should not clash with these earlier commitments. It is therefore strange that the French do not seem to have been told specifically what Britain's commitments to the Arabs were,[20] and that only the vaguest hints about these inter-allied dealings were given to Husain at the time. Yet some of the British who served with his people were painfully aware that Britain was not going to be able to honour the full letter of her bond. Lawrence in particular felt "bitterly ashamed."[21]

Once the main points were settled between the governments concerned, the final stages of the negotiations were conducted on the British and French sides by Sir Mark Sykes and M. Georges-Picot.[22] Since Russia's concern with the Fertile Crescent was the relatively minor one of her religious communities and the Holy Places in Palestine, the ensuing pact is usually known as the Sykes-Picot agreement. As regards the Fertile Crescent, this curious document provided for French and British spheres. The French sphere covered most of Syria with a slice of northern Iraq, and also stretched into Cilicia and parts of southern Anatolia. The British sphere ran roughly from the borders of Sinai (from Aqaba to south of Gaza), covering what is now Jordan and the rest of Iraq from the region of Kirkuk to the Persian Gulf, and included the ports

20. It is the general view that no clear and definite picture of these commitments was given to the French. Yet Robert John and Sami Hadawi in their *Palestine Diary*, I, 54, say that "the British Foreign Minister . . . told the French Ambassador in London . . . on October 21, 1915, of the exchanges of correspondence with Sharif Husain."

21. ". . . instead of being proud of what we did together, I was continually and bitterly ashamed. . . . It was evident that . . . if we won the war these promises would be dead paper, and, had I been an honest adviser of the Arabs, I would have advised them to go home and not risk their lives. . . . I salved myself with the hope that . . . in the final victory expediency would counsel to the Great Powers a fair settlement of their claims. . . . Arab help was necessary to our cheap and speedy victory in the East . . . , better we win and break our word than lose." T. E. Lawrence, *The Seven Pillars of Wisdom*, p. 24.

22. Sir Mark Sykes was a Member of Parliament and Assistant Secretary to the War Cabinet with ministerial rank. M. Georges-Picot had been French Consul-General in Beirut.

of Haifa and Acre. Most of the rest of Palestine, excluding the extreme south and the Negev, was, by agreement with Russia, to be placed under an international regime.

These spheres were themselves divided into two zones. In the first the two powers could set up their own administration. Annexation was not mentioned, but this left them free to annex any area if they saw fit. France was to have authority in the coastal regions of Syria and the Turkish areas, Britain in central and southern Iraq, plus Haifa and Acre. The remaining regions were largely poor land or desert, though they did include the cities of Aleppo, Hama, Homs, Damascus, and Amman in the west and Mosul and Kirkuk in the east. This more arid second zone was to be the area of the Arab state on condition that in the northern part of it (adjacent to the French-run areas) the Arabs would give France economic priority and turn to her for such officials and advisers as they might need, while in the southern zone (adjacent to the British area) they would similarly bind themselves to Britain.

The strangest part of this arrangement was that the most fertile, advanced, and sophisticated areas of the Fertile Crescent—those most capable of organizing a government of their own—were denied autonomy and were to come under foreign rule. On the other hand, the least developed parts—precisely those where the population outside the few cities was least well-educated and largely nomad— might try to establish their own rule, subject to the kind of guidance the imperial nations had become expert in imparting in return for special advantages for themselves. Flagrantly cynical though these arrangements were, in the light of the promises to which the Arabs had so trustingly and effectively responded, had they been honourably and generously carried out, the upshot might have been far preferable for the Arabs to the mandate system ultimately applied.[23] This last was a key factor in the enduring bitterness of many Arabs towards the West with which we are faced today.

After their revolution in November 1917, the Bolsheviks promptly published the Sykes-Picot agreement and other secret

23. This was T. E. Lawrence's view.

pacts, thus giving Turkey a unique chance to discredit the Western powers with their Arab allies. The Turkish leaders made a peace offer to Husain, who thereupon demanded explanations of the British. In February 1918 London assured him that what was published did not constitute an actual agreement but rather provisional talks designed to avoid difficulties between the Allies. In distorting its meaning, the Turks had overlooked the fact that the Allies were bound to secure the consent, and safeguard the interests, of the populations concerned. Husain still had sufficient faith in Britain to credit her somewhat halting words. The Turkish overtures were ignored, and the Arabs pressed forward with the British to victory.

Meanwhile, however, Britain had publicly undertaken yet a third Middle Eastern commitment of immense significance—the Balfour Declaration of November 2, 1917. Once again, this seemed to the Arabs something that could not possibly be reconciled with the pledges Britain had given. Yet once again, whatever their doubts, they consented for the time being to accept such assurances as Britain was able to produce.

The Balfour Declaration

As we saw from Chapter 9, when the project for Jewish settlement in Uganda lapsed, Dr Weizmann predicted that Britain would one day make the Zionists a better offer. The prospects for this brightened once Turkey and Britain were at war, for should Britain win, Palestine, on Egypt's borders, might well become hers. Since Weizmann's skilful diplomacy had disposed some British statesmen to favour Zionist plans, Britain might then be persuaded to sponsor and protect the establishment in Palestine of the Jewish National Home. One step toward this goal was the formation of Jewish units to serve with the British forces. Thus, a Zion Mule Corps took part in the Gallipoli landings and three Jewish Battalions of the Royal Fusiliers fought in the Palestine campaign.[24]

24. There is a detailed and interesting account of the British-sponsored Jewish military effort in the first World War in Leonard Stein's massive and authori-

Independently of any conviction about the rightness of a Jewish return to Zion, the British were realistically aware that a declaration of sympathy for this goal might help to win the war. Indeed, it might bring the United States into the fight on Britain's side, in view of the wealth and power of American Jewry. But there were snags to surmount. Many American Jews were of German or Russian origin. Some of German background pathetically believed that anti-Semitism was dwindling in Germany, the spiritual home of so many of the Ashkenazim. On the other hand, many Russian-American Jews were indignant that the Western powers were allied with a country they loathed, and so tended to be pro-German on that account. The Germans knew how much their country might gain by exploiting these feelings, and sought to prevail upon the Turks, without success, to hold out some prospect of Zionist settlement in Palestine. Finally the French, in the early negotiations over Turkey's future, had hopes—which they were persuaded to abandon—of getting Palestine for themselves.

In any event, winning American-Jewish sympathy for the allied cause was an important factor in bringing the United States into the war against Germany in April 1917. While American Jews were sharply divided about Zionism, many had been moved by Britain's visible solicitude for the future of the Jewish people. The question constantly discussed between British and American statesmen and the Zionist leaders of both countries was how to cast this concern into a public declaration of policy encouraging to the Zionists and yet acceptable to the non-Zionists and the Jewish masses in all

---

tative *The Balfour Declaration*, pp. 484–501, and the intense controversy this aroused with non-Zionists. These Jewish forces were of course the initial step in the evolution of a formidable Israeli army thirty years later. Stein also stresses (e.g., on pp. 167–72) the valuable diplomatic work achieved at this time and later by Nahum Sokolow in collaboration with Weizmann, not only in Britain (despite initial difficulties) but also in France and Italy. From the same East European background as Weizmann, Sokolow was fourteen years older and, as a member of the Zionist Executive, his senior in the Zionist hierarchy. As we saw, Sokolow's *History of Zionism* (London: Longmans, 1919) held the field until the publication of Laqueur's in 1972.

parts of the world. A form of words was needed that would win generous support for the Allies from Jews in their own and neutral countries, and would at the same time shake the loyalty of the powerful Jewish elements in the enemy camp. The form finally adopted succeeded in the first objective but largely failed in the second. Before this form was reached, every word—and many alternatives—had been minutely checked on both sides of the Atlantic to an extent that would have been hard to guess from the smooth, informal phrasing to which Balfour put his name.

Many deep divisions of opinion had somehow to be squared. Significantly, in the British political circles of 1916-17, Edwin Montagu, the one Jewish member of the Cabinet,[25] did his best to defeat the Zionist plan, which was strongly supported, not only by his co-religionary, Herbert Samuel,[26] but also by Prime Minister Lloyd George, Foreign Secretary Balfour, and, to some extent, by Winston Churchill. In America the divisions were scarcely less striking. The *New York Times* and many prominent and influential Jewish leaders, such as Henry Morgenthau Sr., who had been U.S. Ambassador to Turkey till 1916, were definitely anti-Zionist for the same kind of reason as Montagu—i.e., that any Jewish national identity in Palestine would tend to cast doubt upon their first loyalty, which was to the United States.[27] Foremost among American Zionists were Justice Brandeis and Felix Frankfurter, another distinguished lawyer who was also to become a Justice of the Supreme Court.[28] Balfour visited America specially to meet them. President

25. Edwin Montagu (1879–1924), Secretary of State for India, 1917–22, in which capacity he helped to sponsor the concessions to Indian nationalism embodied in the Montagu-Chelmsford Report.

26. Sir Herbert (later Viscount) Samuel (1870–1963), Montagu's first cousin, had resigned from the Government in 1916, but was afterwards High Commissioner for Palestine. Lloyd George had been a legal adviser to the Zionist organization before World War I.

27. Such people, perhaps with some injustice, tended to be labelled "assimilationists" by the Zionist organization.

28. Felix Frankfurter (1882–1965). In 1919 he was legal adviser to the Zionist delegation at the Paris Peace Conference, and collaborated closely with Dr Weizmann in his negotiations with the Amir Faisal.

Wilson was hesitatingly benevolent toward the plan for a pro-Zionist statement, especially after the United States entered the war.[29]

The Declaration was in the form of a personal letter from Mr Balfour to Lord Rothschild, as head of the Jewish community in Britain, and Rothschild was asked to convey its contents to the Zionist Federation. It first stated that the British Government "view with favour the establishment in Palestine of a national home for the Jewish people and will use their best endeavours to facilitate the achievement of this object." The Zionists had pressed for the adoption of far more definite wording, which would have recognized Palestine as "*the* national home of the Jewish people." The British refused to make so unlimited a commitment. At the time they felt it prudent to mark the fact that a Jewish national home would be only one element in Palestine.

There followed two qualifications, the first intended to convey some assurance principally to the Palestine Arabs, the second to reassure non-Zionist Jews. Together these read: ". . . it being clearly understood that nothing shall be done which may prejudice the civil and religious rights of existing non-Jewish communities in Palestine, or the rights and political status enjoyed by Jews in any other country." The Declaration was endorsed, though without marked enthusiasm, by the Allies still in the war. But as a result of the Bolshevik revolution Russia ceased at that stage to be concerned.

The second of the qualifications in this offer was, as we now know, on the whole superfluous. Save in the case of the Arab countries, the rights and status of Jews throughout the world were in general little affected by the National Home or, later, Israel. The Hitler holocaust before and during World War II cannot be

29. Woodrow Wilson (1856–1924); U.S. President (1913–21). His position at the Paris Peace Conference was weakened by the fact that his Democratic Party had by then lost its majority in the Senate. He suffered a thrombosis and partial paralysis in October 1919. His rigid refusal to accept Republican reservations to the Versailles Treaty and League Covenant led to their rejection in November 1919 and again in March 1920.

called a consequence of the Jewish presence in Palestine. As regards the first reservation, some judge that "non-Jewish communities" was hardly a tactful or adequate description of the Palestinian Arabs who formed over 90 per cent of the population. An obvious though inadequate reason for the term was the existence of small but important religious communities of non-Arab Christians and others.[30]

More important was the fact that the Declaration guaranteed only the civil and religious rights of the existing owners of the country, when any really reliable guarantee would have had to cover their political and economic rights as well. Despite centralization and authoritarian rule, the Arabs of Syria, Lebanon, and Palestine had had some limited political rights under the Turks—especially since the Young Turk Revolution had introduced a parliament and constitution—and normal economic rights, subject to the casual irregularities usual in any Oriental state. Moreover, all the Arabs had just been promised by the British full political rights of nationhood and freedom. The British may or may not have meant to include Palestine in their pledge at the time it was given, some three years before the Balfour Declaration; but the Arabs definitely believed it to be included. Finally, by the end of 1917, the educated and intelligent among them knew of the gospel of self-determination which President Wilson was resolved to enforce.

In these circumstances, for Britain to make it publicly plain that the political and economic rights of the Palestinian Arabs were to be ignored was gratuitously to invite a future of strife and conflict such as has in fact occurred. Balfour himself, a man of high intelligence and personally of fastidious integrity, was fully aware of the dilemma. In a memorandum for the Cabinet in 1919[31] he stressed the contradictions between Britain's pledges to the Arabs and her commitment to Wilsonian self-determination, and the Zionist pro-

---

30. Such as the Bahais, whose principal centre was at Haifa.
31. E. L. Woodward and R. Butler, eds., *Documents on British Foreign Policy, 1919–1939*, IV (1919), pp. 340–47.

gramme she had undertaken to support. And then he added, ". . . in Palestine we do not propose even to go through the form of consulting the wishes of the present inhabitants of the country. . . . The four Great Powers are committed to Zionism. And Zionism, be it right or wrong, good or bad, is rooted in age-long traditions, in present needs, in future hopes, of far profounder import than the desires and prejudices of the 700,000 Arabs who now inhabit that ancient land." He gives no further explanation of this lofty and somewhat cavalier pronouncement both on the Palestinians and on Zionism, but concludes by saying that in his view this was right and that "Zionism would not hurt the Arabs." It can hardly be said, therefore, that Britain did not enter into her Zionist commitment with her eyes open. Whatever Zionist pressure may have been brought to bear on her leaders to ensure that the door should be left open in Palestine, not merely for a National Home, but also for an eventual Jewish state, the responsibility for making this ultimate goal possible must be laid essentially at Britain's door rather than at that of the Jewish people.

Had the political and economic rights of the Palestinian Arabs in fact been guaranteed by Britain from the beginning, the National Home in Palestine could have emerged—as some, including Herzl, foresaw, and in spite of the Hitler holocaust—as a state for both related peoples, each of whom could have developed in conditions of tolerance and mutual benefit. In view of their special qualities of drive, and modern skills, the European Jewish elements would almost certainly have played the leading role, and the great goal of a Jewish return to the Holy Land could have been accomplished with a minimum of controversy, bitterness, and suffering to the weak. This would have been one solution to the problem of adjusting Zionism to the reality of the large majority of Palestinian Arabs whose land it then was. But as things turned out, by the time a plan for an Arab-Jewish state was produced by the British some twenty-two years later,[32] too much had happened and it was already too late.

32. In the British Government's White Paper of 1939. See below.

The Arab Revolt: the Epilogue

Nineteen eighteen was the year of victory. It was also the year of more or less skilful prevarication by the Allies to counter a variety of protests and to mask the contradictions between the promises they had made. Significantly, King Husain was told by a British emissary sent to Jeddah that, under the Balfour Declaration, Jewish settlement in Palestine would not be allowed to prejudice the political and economic freedom of the Arab population. He thus received an informal assurance, never officially underwritten by the British Government, that those political and economic rights of the Arabs on which the Declaration was silent would in fact be preserved. Indeed, on condition that "National Home" did not mean a Jewish state in Palestine, Husain was prepared to accept the policy of the Balfour Declaration, and to welcome Jews to all Arab lands.[33]

On the strength of these exchanges and Dr Weizmann's conciliatory approaches to certain leaders, Arab opinion in many quarters was momentarily set at rest. The doubts persisted, however; and in the spring and early summer of 1918 seven Arab leaders in Cairo sought, and were given by Britain, more definite assurances. This time they were told, in the most encouraging terms, that Britain recognized the complete independence of those Arab territories which had been independent before the war or had been liberated by the Arabs themselves (that is, the independent states of the Arabian Peninsula and the Hejaz to Aqaba). In the case of those territories liberated by the Allied armies (at that time most of Iraq and southern Palestine) their future government would be "based upon the principle of the consent of the governed." As for those parts of Iraq and Syria still unliberated, Britain would work for their freedom and independence.

At that point a fresh crisis during the Turkish retreat demanded

33. Christopher Sykes, *Crossroads to Israel*, pp. 44–45. See also Antonius, pp. 244–70. The emissary on this occasion was the distinguished orientalist Dr D. G. Hogarth, afterwards head of the Ashmolean Museum at Oxford.

swift action by the Allies. On October 3, 1918, just as Faisal was entering Damascus, the Arab flag was hoisted in Beirut and removed on British orders after a French protest. The local populations were incensed by this, and also increasingly aware of French plans to occupy the Syrian coast, as well as of British plans to instal the Zionists in Palestine. To avert a rising, an Anglo-French Declaration of November 7 promised "the complete and final liberation of the peoples . . . oppressed by the Turks, and the setting up of national governments and administrations deriving their authority from the . . . choice of the indigenous populations." France and Britain would help in setting up these governments in Syria and Iraq and would recognize them when established. They had, they insisted, no wish to impose any particular system, only to help ensure the smooth working of these freely chosen governments, equal justice for all, economic development, better education, and an end to past dissensions exploited by the Turks.[34] Once again, Arab faith in their allies was momentarily restored.

The Post-War Settlement

For many, the Paris Peace Conference seemed a dawn of hope that would lead to the realization of new ideals. In fact, its methods of negotiating and the settlements it achieved were a depressing story of greed, muddle, and hurried compromise prevailing over the high idealism that President Wilson and others were unable to sustain. It sowed, as we saw, the seeds of continuing conflict, of local and eventually world dimensions.[35] Pending the outcome of the conference, and the implementation or repudiation of allied promises,

34. Antonius, pp. 270–75.
35. This story is vividly told by Harold Nicolson in his *Peacemaking, 1919.* A prime example of the fatal lack of coordination and clear purpose was the fact that until almost the last moment no one was really clear whether the peace with Germany was to be negotiated or imposed. Eventually, mainly through lack of time, the latter system was adopted. Germany was thus given a pretext for disregarding and eventually overthrowing the Versailles Treaty on the grounds that it was a *Diktat.*

the Fertile Crescent was split by the victorious Western powers into four zones of military control called Occupied Enemy Territory Administration (OETA). The first two zones, covering Iraq and Palestine, were under the British; a third, covering Lebanon and the Syrian coastal region, was under the French. The fourth zone, which covered the interior of Syria (in the wider sense of the term then generally used) from Aleppo to Aqaba, was known as OETA East and was assigned to the Arabs under Faisal.

When Faisal protested against the splitting of Syria, he was solemnly assured that these arrangements were ones of temporary convenience and that the country's future would be settled by its people's choice. The Hejaz under King Husain was now an independent Arab state. In central Arabia, Ibn Saud had been strengthened and Ibn Rashid weakened by the Turkish defeat, and in a few years Ibn Saud was to take over all central Arabia and the Hejaz as well, transforming his kingdom into what is now Saudi Arabia. South of the Hejaz, the Idrisi continued for the time being to control Asir, and the Imam Yahya retained the Yemen. The smaller rulers on the Persian Gulf and south Arabian coast kept their former autonomy but were no longer nominal vassals of Turkey.

In November, only a few weeks after his entry into Damascus, Faisal went to London and later Paris to press for Arab independence and to represent the Hejaz at the peace conference. He now found that the Sykes-Picot agreement, contrary to all assurances, did in fact set up French and British spheres of influence in the Fertile Crescent. The British wanted to annul it on the grounds that one party, Russia, had denounced it. Moreover, it did not suit Britain that France should receive Mosul with its oil resources; and London wanted a British-controlled, rather than an internationalized, Palestine in order to implement the Balfour Declaration. But the French insisted on keeping the agreement, since it was their only clear title to anything in the area. Finally, however, Prime Minister Clémenceau agreed to give up Mosul (in return for a large French share of the oil production) and Palestine to the

British, in order to ensure France's grip on the other areas she claimed. The French had no love for Arab nationalism, since they feared it might lead to subversion in Algeria, Tunisia, and Morocco;[36] and they resented Britain's encouragement of it. Partly for this reason, they strongly objected to Faisal's being head of OETA East, and to his representing the Hejaz at the Conference.

Faced with this French hostility, the Arabs still regarded Britain as their best friend. Faisal seems to have been convinced by the British Foreign Office and others that the British could best help him if he adjusted his policy to theirs to the extent of giving, before the Peace Conference, some recognition to Zionist aspirations in Palestine. For their part the Zionists wanted Faisal to put his name to a formal agreement with Weizmann, whom he had already met during the Arab Revolt. Faisal had strict instructions from his father to accept nothing less than complete fulfilment of the promises made to the Arabs. On the other hand, he knew that Husain himself (in his statements to Dr Hogarth) had shown some readiness to welcome Jewish settlement in Palestine and elsewhere. Moreover, Weizmann had assured Faisal at their first meeting that his people had no intention of working for a Jewish government in Palestine. Finally, Lawrence, on behalf of the British Government, seems to have urged him to sign an agreement with Weizmann with the argument that this could do no harm so long as Arab independence was fully achieved. In these circumstances and on this condition, Faisal was prepared to believe that Arab-Jewish cooperation in connection with Palestine might work, and so, with Lawrence's support, he approved and signed a pact with the Zionist leader on January 3, 1919. Although this was destined to remain a dead letter, and has been somewhat neglected for that reason, it is nonetheless a highly significant document, and makes it plain how events in the Holy Land could have taken a far happier turn had those in power been more resolute and far-sighted in grasping the opportunities it offered. For it shows how far the Arab leaders were prepared to go to meet these Jewish dreams and

36. As it did, to their cost, after World War II.

hopes, so long as their own promised goal of freedom was met and they could settle the destiny of their lands and peoples as they chose.

The agreement was clearly intended to accept the Zionist programme in Palestine, subject to certain conditions. It calls for the closest collaboration between Palestine and the Arab state, each with boundaries settled after the Peace Conference by mutual agreement, and each with accredited agents in the other's territory. The Balfour Declaration would be carried out, with large-scale Jewish settlement in Palestine, but Arab peasant and tenant farmers would be protected in their rights and helped with their economic development. There would be freedom of religion there, and no religious test for public office. The Muslim Holy Places would remain under Muslim control. The Zionist Organization would send out a commission to survey Palestine's capacity for economic development, but this commission would be at the disposal also of the Arab state, the development of which the Zionists would help in every possible way. Britain would arbitrate any matters in dispute. A clause was added by Faisal, and signed also by Weizmann, by which the agreement would be void if the Arabs did not get their promised independence.[37]

With the dimensions that our conflict has assumed, and the hindsight of more than fifty years, it would seem that, if the British leaders had been bolder, clearer-headed, and more single-minded about the wisdom of honouring their pledges to the Arabs, much hatred and misery could have been spared. If the Faisal-Weizmann pact had not been voided by Britain's failure to do this, the Zionist programme could have been implemented on a far more secure basis than that offered by the Balfour Declaration since, if

37. See Antonius, pp. 278–86. Full text of the agreement is at pp. 437–39. Article IV reads specifically, "All necessary measures shall be taken to encourage and stimulate immigration of Jews into Palestine on a large scale, and as quickly as possible to settle Jewish immigrants upon the land through closer settlement and intensive cultivation of the soil. In taking such measures the Arab peasants and tenant farmers shall be protected in their rights, and shall be assisted in forwarding their economic development."

Faisal had been able in the long run to carry the Palestinian Arabs with him, the National Home would have had their eventual if reluctant acceptance. And meanwhile the neighbouring, and sovereign, Arab state could have dealt from strength with all the problems of justice and adjustment raised by Jewish settlement in Palestine, with appeal to British arbitration when the inevitable storms arose. There need have been neither the desperate resentment nor the bitter resistance aroused by the imposition, in Palestine and elsewhere, of the rule of others, and of drastic changes without democratic consultation or what today would be called regard for human rights.

There are various reasons—none entirely conclusive—why things happened as they did, why the men of Europe who reshaped the world after the first world war failed to implement freedom in the Middle East as they had promised, and in a way that has become universal in our day, when new nations of every size and kind abound. One reason was that, in spite of the lip service paid to self-determination and other Wilsonian principles embodied in the Covenant of the League of Nations,[38] most of the men of that age still lived in an aura of nineteenth-century imperialism. For them, the Asians, whatever the glories of their past, or the promises made to win them over and keep their support, could not really be trusted to govern themselves effectively without further "guidance" from the West. Even President Wilson indirectly sanctified these

38. Foundation of the League of Nations, predecessor of the United Nations, was due largely to the idealism and inspiration of President Wilson and of certain British and French statesmen. It in turn owed much to the Hague Peace Conferences of 1899 and 1907. The President insisted on its being one of the first questions dealt with by the Paris Peace Conference, and the Covenant of the League was published as a draft on February 14, 1919. It created the Mandate system under Article XXII, to provide for the administration of former German and Turkish territories. After World War II it developed into the Trusteeship system of the United Nations. The Mandates were supervised by the Permanent Mandates Commission of the League, to which the Mandatory Power had to report each year. Iraq, Palestine, and Syria were placed in the highest (A) category of mandate, of which the independence was to be recognized provisionally until they were "able to stand alone."

attitudes by the League of Nations Mandates system, under which British and French rule was ultimately imposed on all the Fertile Crescent. For others there were also economic factors (the most important being oil) and strategic considerations.

For the British, however, neither of these was decisive. At that time oil flowed freely to the West from countries like Persia that were not under Western rule. In any case, under the Sykes-Picot agreement, Mosul with its oil was to have been included in the area of the Arab state. As regards strategy, there were those who saw Palestine as an alternative base from which to protect the Suez Canal if and when the British were forced out of Egypt; and it did in fact play a useful role as a garrison area in World War II. But at the time when the original decisions were taken, strategic considerations were, it seems, repugnant to Balfour and only a minor factor for those in power in Britain, including the military, in determining the policy he announced.[39]

In India and elsewhere, despite the still engrained traditions of the past, the British were in fact gradually moving towards policies of ultimate liberation. Hence it is possible that, had they alone been concerned, they might have found it right to redeem their word and support real independence for the Arabs, and thus to have entrusted the implementation of the Zionist programme to the operation of the Faisal-Weizmann agreement. There is small doubt that Israel would still have been created, but on a basis that the Arabs would have been pledged to accept; and Britain would have escaped most of the odium which she incurred. The final consideration was her relations with the French, who were far more traditional in their thinking and who saw Arab independence as a dangerous trend that might unsettle their North American empire.

Britain had done almost all the fighting in the area and at the time was far stronger than France. She could have forced the French to renounce their somewhat farfetched claims, or to have adopted a more liberal line. (She was indeed to do something of

39. See Sykes, pp. 20–22.

this kind in 1945-46, though with not very happy results.[40]) In any event, with a precarious peace settlement to be forged and tested, and the dominating threat of a resurgent Germany, Britain was not prepared to face a dangerous breach with a difficult but essential ally. Unfortunately—and this was the most fatal misjudgement of all—Palestine, Zionism, Arab embitterment, the whole post-war chaos in the Middle East, seemed to the world arbiters in Paris rather a minor affair.

The Peace Conference

The hostility of the French to Faisal persisted in Paris, though they reluctantly agreed to his being the delegate of the Hejaz at the Peace Conference. Faisal formally claimed sovereign independence for all the other Arabic-speaking peoples of Asia, except those of British Aden. He made no mention of the Arabic-speaking peoples of Africa, since they were all dependencies of the victorious Allies. He condemned the Sykes-Picot agreement, invoked President Wilson's principles, and urged that a Commission of Enquiry be sent to Syria and Palestine to discover the wishes of the people. This plan was backed by President Wilson and officially approved.

The Commission's members would be French, British, Italian, and American. America and Britain appointed their delegates; the others dragged their feet. The French knew that the Syrians would not want them as masters, and suspected Faisal's proposal of being a British trick to keep them out. Though this had no foundation, the British themselves were not too keen on the plan. Of course, opinion in Iraq and Palestine might well be adverse to Britain's receiving any mandate to rule there; and hostility to the Zionist programme was virtually certain. The scheme for an international enquiry was ultimately sidetracked. A French campaign against it, coupled with Zionist hostility and Italian indifference, gave the British a pretext for withdrawal. Only the Americans on the com-

40. See Chapter 13.

mission, Dr King and Mr Crane,[41] proceeded on the President's orders with their task.

The King-Crane Commission

The American Commission reached Syria at a time of intense effervescence. Faisal had returned there in May 1919, cheered by the prospect that the international commission would soon arrive and find in his favour. Meanwhile, elections were held throughout Syria, Lebanon, and Palestine, including the areas under French and British occupation. The initiative lay with former members of *al-Fatat*, who had formed an Independence Party. The upshot was a General Syrian Congress meeting at Damascus—though some of its members were prevented by the French from attending.

In July this Congress passed a series of resolutions demanding the independence of all Syria (including Lebanon and Palestine) under Faisal as King, and of Iraq, together with cancellation of the Sykes-Picot agreement and the Balfour Declaration, and all that they implied. The delegates rejected any implication that the Arabs were among the less developed peoples and needed the tutelage of a mandatory power. They would, however, accept technical and economic help, preferably from America, or otherwise from Britain, but for not more than twenty years, and only if their independence were not infringed. They would accept nothing from France and rejected all French claims to authority in their country.

The King-Crane Commission accepted some but not all of these views. Despite the repudiation of mandates by the Damascus Congress, the commission advocated a mandatory system for the countries of the Fertile Crescent, though for a strictly limited time. In the then prevalent mood in Syria, the consensus of opinion they

41. Dr Henry C. King was President of Oberlin College in Ohio. Mr Charles R. Crane, a prominent business man and Oriental traveller, was a political supporter of President Wilson, who appointed him U.S. Minister to China in 1920.

consulted naturally led them to recommend that Syria, Lebanon, and Palestine should remain united under Faisal, preferably with the United States as the mandatory power, or Britain if Washington would not undertake this. The Mandate should on no account go to France. While they did not visit Iraq, on the strength of their consultations in Syria they recommended that the Mandate for Iraq should go to Britain.

The two Americans seem to have been impressed by the strength of anti-Zionist opinion and the views of British officers in Palestine that the Zionist programme could be imposed only by force of arms. They were also struck by Jewish statements foreshadowing the "practically complete dispossession" of the non-Jews as the result of Jewish purchase of their land. They therefore saw no way of safeguarding the non-Jews' civil and religious rights unless the extreme Zionist programme were greatly modified by definite limitation of Jewish immigration. In this context they doubted whether the Zionist claim to Palestine, "based on an occupation of 2,000 years ago," could be seriously considered; and whether Jews, to whom the Christian Holy Places were "abhorrent," could be the proper guardians of those shrines.

Thus the French and the Zionists had some reason to be disturbed by this enquiry. They need not in fact have worried. The King-Crane report, dated August 28, 1919, did not reach President Wilson until he was on the verge of the grave illness that overshadowed his last years. It was sent to the Allied Governments; but, with the repudiation of the Versailles Treaty by the U.S. Congress, America temporarily ceased to play a role in this aftermath of World War I. The report was not published for three years and had meanwhile been ignored.[42]

42. Texts of the Syrian Congress's resolutions and of the recommendations of the King-Crane Commission are in appendices G and H of Antonius, pp. 440–58. The Versailles Treaty was the peace settlement imposed on Germany, of which the Covenant of the League of Nations was an integral part. It was the principal act of the Paris Peace Conference. See notes 35 and 38 above.

Liquidation of the Arab State

Meanwhile a peace settlement with Turkey still hung fire, as did the disposal of the territories she had lost. Faisal, foiled of his international commission, was called again to London in August 1919, just as the King-Crane Commission was finishing its work. The French were still convinced that the British were intent on using Faisal to cheat them of their claims under the Sykes-Picot agreement and their expectation of a League of Nations mandate to rule western Syria and Lebanon. To appease the French and relieve the British taxpayer, Prime Minister Lloyd George decided to withdraw the British troops who remained in the French and Arab zones of occupation, but to retain them in Palestine. Without explicitly recognizing the French claim in their area, this British concession smoothed the path for its acceptance.

Although the move was welcome to Paris, the French reserved their position as regards the final boundaries of the mandates. It was clear that Clémenceau had his eye on eastern as well as western Syria, and was ill-disposed to any independent Arab state there. In protesting against this new betrayal of his cause, Faisal urged that a fresh conference of Britain, France, and the United States should be held to settle the future of the Arab lands in the sense of all the assurances the Arabs had received. This met with no response; instead, the British pressed him to come to terms with the French. Now virtually defenceless, Faisal had no choice but to give in.

At the end of November 1919, Clémenceau met Faisal and consented to a provisional deal pending the final peace settlement. Under its terms the Arab Government would respect French occupation of Lebanon and the Syrian coastal region, and the plain between the Lebanon and Anti-Lebanon mountains would be a neutral zone. Beyond this, the Arab state would have to turn to France for such help as it might need. Faisal had conceded far more than he could justify either to his father or to his supporters in Syria. But he could not, it seems, bring himself to break with his ally, Britain, who had stood by him after a fashion until now. He stayed on in

Europe for some weeks, apparently hoping that the new conference he had asked for might take place and that he might finally
win better terms through American and British support. Unhappily, since the defeat of the Versailles Treaty Washington had lost
the motive and capacity for effective intervention. Moreover, for
Lloyd George's Government, immediate expediency and what
loomed as more vital obligations at home and elsewhere far out-
weighed any war-time promises to Husain and Faisal and the
quarrelsome family of Arab peoples.

Out of the fifteen months since his triumphal entry there in
1918, Faisal had spent only some five in Syria. He returned to Damascus in January 1920, to find the French firmly installed in the
coastal regions, and the British out. Stirred by frustration and insecurity, the extremists prevailed. They denounced all Europeans
and, since they knew that Faisal had discussed an agreement with
the French, some accused him of being a French agent. His father
added his reproaches. When he failed to obtain a mandate from
his people to conclude the Paris negotiations, the French became
more hostile than ever. Then rumours of his deal with Weizmann
led to further charges that he was in Jewish pay. He tried to discredit these charges by sponsoring anti-Zionist resolutions just when
the Damascus Congress had, it seems, encouraged an attack on a
Jewish settlement. And this attack killed any hopes the Zionists
might have placed in him. Finally he risked the hostility of his old
friends the British by abetting the incipient rising in Iraq against
them. By now he had many enemies and few friends left.

On March 8, 1920, the Syrian Congress defiantly proclaimed the
independence of Syria, with Palestine and Lebanon, with a proviso
for Lebanese autonomy within the framework of Syrian unity. It
was a dangerous and futile move to force the hand of Faisal, who
was to be its constitutional king. The independence of Iraq was
similarly proclaimed at a meeting of Iraqi leaders, who chose
Faisal's elder brother, the Amir Abdullah, as their king. The proc-
lamations presumed to take at their face value the repeated Allied
assurances about Arab independence and popular consent, and

ignored the hard fact that, faced with other priorities, the Allies had long since dropped any intention or pretence of keeping their word. The British and French at once rejected the Syrian Congress's decisions, and in April called a meeting of the Supreme Allied Council at San Remo, Italy, to press on with the treaty with Turkey and other matters. Somewhat irregularly, the Council resolved to settle the future of the Arab territories in advance of the final treaty, which was not signed until August, and was soon thereafter nullified by the vigorous action of the Turks themselves. Mandates were assigned to France for Syria and Lebanon, and to Britain for Iraq and Palestine. The last of these incorporated the Balfour Declaration and the solemn obligation to carry it out.

Faisal was now at the mercy of the French, with whom he had failed to come to terms. His own people urged him to fight against them—a war he could not win. He refused, apparently still hoping that somehow the United States and Britain would come to the rescue. Britain, however, had urged him at all costs to avoid hostilities. He was preparing to return to Europe in July when he received from the French Commander-in-Chief an ultimatum demanding an unqualified acceptance of the French Mandate, the punishment of those hostile to the French, a reduction of the Arab forces, and the French occupation of Aleppo and other key points within the neutral or Arab zones. The ultimatum was accepted, though it seems doubtful whether the French wanted this. In any case, the acceptance was ignored. French troops invaded what remained of the Arab state and occupied Damascus after crushing the Arab resistance that Faisal had tried to prevent. Faisal was ordered out, and he left for Haifa execrated by the people who had acclaimed him less than two years earlier. He was received in Palestine with embarrassed courtesy by the first British High Commissioner, who had just taken up his duties under the Mandate. After an exile in Italy he was again invited to London, where the British explored fresh plans for his future.

As we have seen, the essentials of the Zionist programme—whether in the form of an Arab-Jewish state embracing a Jewish

National Home, or even of a Jewish-ruled state of Israel—might have been eventually achieved on some basis of acceptance by the Arabs, if their claims to nationhood and independence had been met at the time when freedom was promised to them. They could then have had some inducement to make generous and voluntary provision, in agreement with the Zionists, for those displaced by Jewish immigration and land purchase, even when critical pressure on Palestine resulted from the Hitler holocaust. But the bitterness of the Arabs' resentment at being cheated of those rights in 1920, and the long struggle against Western imperialism which followed, killed all hope of this. When nationhood was finally achieved in most of the Arab world a generation later, there was no longer any early chance of Israel's developing in peace and mutually beneficial contact with her Arab neighbours. Instead she is faced with hatred, rejection, and retaliation. Whatever reasons of state, ambition, or confused purposes governed the actions of the Allies, and particularly the British, in those crucial years, the treatment of the Arab peoples during and after World War I—and the consequences for the Jewish return to the Holy Land and for Western standing in the Middle East—lay a heavy burden on those responsible, and one in which their descendants can take no pride.[43]

43. It is symptomatic of the heart-searching of certain British participants in these events that, by the time he reached the Paris Peace Conference, Sir Mark Sykes had conceived serious doubts about the Sykes-Picot agreement, and seems to have aimed at getting it modified. But he died soon afterwards. T. E. Lawrence's post-war choice of obscurity as an aircraftman in the Royal Air Force, and his refusal of the decoration awarded to him for his war services, seem also to have been partly dictated by his sense of the failure of his Government to keep faith with his Arab friends.

Chapter **11** British Rule
in Palestine:
The Early Years

In the last chapter we dealt with the modern sources of our conflict and considered whether and how it could have been avoided. What happened during World War I in the Middle East and Europe is fundamental for an understanding of our current troubles. But the present chapter and the two to follow have a more restricted theme. They deal chiefly with the thirty years of British rule in Palestine.[1] These three decades fall into three phases. During the first, from 1918 to 1929, the situation was generally under control. The second, from 1929 to 1939, covers another Arab revolt, this time in Palestine, the tragic clashes caused by the massive build-up of Jewish immigration and the incipient Hitler holocaust, a final attempt by Britain to stem this tide in fairness to the Palestinians and to preserve Arab friendship under the threat of World War II; and finally the outbreak of the war itself. The third, from 1939 to 1948, deals with

---

1. Christian rule in Jerusalem seems to have been fated to be of relatively short duration compared with the earlier Jewish presence and the thirteen hundred years of Muslim domination. It lasted for roughly three hundred years from Constantine to the Arab conquest, for one hundred under the Crusaders, and for a mere thirty after Allenby's conquest.

the course and outcome of this second war, the recourse by certain Zionist groups to anti-British terrorism once Britain and her allies had saved them from the threat of Hitler, America's new prominence in the Palestine conflict, the intervention of the United Nations, and the proclamation of Israel as Britain's mandate ended.

The start of the Mandate saw an end to many hopes and also to some uncertainties that had prolonged the state of flux and chaos in the Middle East when no one quite knew what the victorious powers were going to do. But the die was cast in 1920 after the San Remo conference, the expulsion of Faisal from Damascus, and the liquidation of the Arab state. There was little hope now of any Arab regime voluntarily accepting the Zionist programme. On the other hand, the British rulers of Palestine were committed to its fulfilment. Indeed the provisions of the Balfour Declaration were incorporated and elaborated in the mandate; and this was a great triumph for the Zionists, second only to the issue of the Declaration itself, which was at the time a good deal more than they had expected. But, in the circumstances described in the last chapter, the Zionist programme had to be imposed by force on the overwhelming majority of the Palestine population.

The question remains whether the Jewish National Home could ever have emerged—as Britain hoped and planned and as Herzl himself had envisaged in his later years—without sacrificing the Arab Palestinians' basic interests and continued presence, and with their eventual if reluctant consent. One can guess that this might just have happened had it not been for the vastly increased flow of immigrants fleeing the Nazi holocaust—but it is by no means certain. One further consequence of the eclipse of Faisal in 1920 was, however, unfavourable for Zionist expectations. For eventually, as we shall see, this débâcle had the indirect result of withdrawing Transjordan from the area to which the Zionist programme was to have been applied. Indeed its inclusion in that area had been foreseen by a number of leaders, including Balfour.

In any case, our main focus will now be Palestine. While relating events there to what occurred in the rest of the area, we shall concentrate on the background and essential causes of the eventual emergence of a powerful state of Israel with a predominantly Jewish population, and the consequences this has entailed, rather than attempt any detailed record of the British period. This has been authoritatively done by writers better qualified than myself.

The Military Administration

Although the final fate of Palestine was then still unknown, Britain gave initial support to the Zionist programme as soon as she had conquered the southern part of the country. General Allenby's first proclamation was issued in Hebrew as well as in English, French, Italian, and Arabic. Martial law was imposed, and strict orders given to uphold the status quo in all secular and religious matters, with the exception of those measures which the adoption of Zionism was going to require. Thus, departmental and public notices and, as soon as possible, official and municipal receipts, were set forth in English, Arabic, and Hebrew. The Occupied Enemy Territory Administration (OETA) employed Jewish officers, clerks, and interpreters. "For these deliberate and vital infractions of military practice, OETA was criticised both within and without Palestine. They were . . . justified by the . . . almost universal endorsement of the Balfour Declaration . . . , which gave any occupying power the right to assume, though the League of Nations was then unborn and mandates hardly conceived, that the ultimate government would have to reckon with Zion."[2]

In other respects the maintenance of the status quo produced further complications for the British. Thus France continued for some time to assert her claim to protect all Latin Christians despite Italian objections and those of the Vatican, now that the Holy Land had come under Christian, albeit Protestant, rule. These claims were relinquished only when the Mandate was approved by the League of Nations in 1922. From the outset, however, the Or-

2. Storrs, p. 301.

thodox Christians came under the care of the British administration, Communist Russia having at that time abandoned interest in her religious heritage.[3]

The next step in the implementation of the Balfour Declaration was the despatch of a Zionist Commission with the blessing of the British Government. Its official mission was to form a link between the British authorities and the Jewish population, to coordinate relief work, to organize the Jewish population and help it to resume its activities and restore and develop its colonies, to establish friendly relations with the Arabs and other non-Jewish communities, to report on the possibilities of further developing Jewish settlement, and to look into the feasibility of establishing a Jewish university.[4] On orders from London, the Commission was made welcome upon its arrival in Jerusalem in March 1918, but the ground had not been properly prepared, since its arrival came as an almost complete surprise to a harassed and hastily improvised military administration. Though far from being anti-Zionist or anti-Jewish, senior British officers felt that its arrival at so early a stage was premature and inopportune.[5]

In any event, the administration still regarded itself as officially bound by the terms of the Anglo-French Declaration of January 1918, and, partly for that reason, decided not to publish the Bal-

3. During and after World War II the Soviet Union reasserted some of Russia's traditional claims in Palestine, having found it convenient to utilize the Orthodox Church in Russia as a pliant tool of the Communist state.

4. Nevill Barbour, *Nisi Dominus* (London: Harrap, 1946), pp. 69–70.

5. Storrs, pp. 296–97, 354, 340–42. The Commission included Dr Weizmann, Edwin Samuel (son of the future British High Commissioner), Israel Sieff, Leon Simon, Dr Eder, and Joseph Cowen. It was accompanied by Major Ormsby-Gore, later British Secretary of State for the Colonies, and Major James de Rothschild, as Political Officers. An anti-Zionist French Orientalist, M. Sylvain Levy, was attached but soon withdrew.

Storrs became Military Governor of Jerusalem from the beginning of 1918 and retained a similar post under the later civilian administration until 1926, when he was appointed Governor of Cyprus. His account of these years (pp. 275–440) paints a brilliant and vivid picture of the impact of Palestine in the early years of Zionism upon a highly intelligent British official in exceptionally bewildering circumstances.

four Declaration in Palestine at that juncture. This attitude was accepted by the Zionists while the war continued. It did not, however, deceive the Arabs, who were aware of the Declaration from outside sources.

The Zionist Commission's task was complicated by the fact that by no means all Jews in Palestine favoured Zionism. Jerusalem in particular, where the Jewish population formed a majority,[6] contained strongly orthodox Jews to whom it was something of a sacrilege. And the Zionists themselves were in effect divided between those (however unorthodox) who believed with religious fervour that the Return was the accomplishment of biblical prophecy, and those who rejected the religious motive and desired that in Palestine the Jews should become a nation like any other.[7] As the Commission got into its stride and the more extreme and dynamic elements from Eastern Europe assumed an ever more dominating role both in its ranks and in those of the new settlers, relations with OETA became uneasy.

Whatever his ultimate objectives, in those early years Dr Weizmann was firmly wedded to a policy of "gradualness," and his statements both to the Arabs and the British were filled with reasonableness and reassurance. At an initial meeting with local notables after the Commission's arrival, he urged them to disregard any insinuations to the effect that the Zionists were seeking political power. They and the local peoples would progress together, he said, until they were ready for joint autonomy. Zionists, he assured them, had the deepest sympathy for the struggles of the Arabs, and the Armenians, for their freedom. All three peoples could mutually assist one another to regain that freedom. And this at once evoked a friendly and welcoming response from the senior Muslim dignitary, the Mufti of Jerusalem. But fellow Zionists were less patient, tactful, or understanding. Certain of their leaders had idealized and

6. According to Storrs, pp. 280–81, there were then some 30,000 Jews in Jerusalem, including 16,0000 Ashkenazim, and 14,000 Sephardim and Oriental Jews from the Yemen and Bokhara.
7. Sykes, p. 35.

positively welcomed the prospect of living under what they envisaged as the wise paternalism of British colonial rule. The reality was a good deal more distasteful. Many of the eastern Ashkenazim, who had suffered constant (and recent) Russian oppression, had imbibed anarchist and revolutionary ideas. With their deep suspicion of authority, they saw in the well-meaning improvisations of a casually recruited team of British officers, many with little experience of administration, and of the most diverse civilian origins,[8] the fierce and arbitrary abuses of their Tsarist tormentors.

Stirred by such ideas, the Commission was urgently concerned to establish certain visible signs and facts to demonstrate to the world that the Zionists had now begun the creative organization of the Return to Eretz Israel. Early in 1918 twelve foundation stones of the Hebrew University on Mount Scopus—one for each of the tribes of Israel—were laid in the presence of the British Commander-in-Chief. There was also a considerable increase in the number of Jewish schools with a modern, Zionist outlook and curriculum. Meanwhile strong pressure was exerted on all Jews in Palestine to drop Yiddish and speak Hebrew. Yet the orthodox Rabbis continued to refuse to speak anything but Yiddish, since they held Hebrew to be a holy tongue only for sacred purposes. Dr Weizmann further sought to acquire for his people the space in front of the Wailing Wall in Jerusalem, an area inhabited in part by Arab families, whom he proposed to rehouse. The British Governor of the city explored this project but was forced to drop it in view of Muslim fears, since this ground, adjoining the sacred Haram al-Sharif, was part of a Muslim *waqf*.[9]

For the first time in modern history Zionists could now enter the

8. Apart from a few professional soldiers OETA included "a cashier from a bank in Rangoon, an actor-manager, two assistants from Thomas Cook, a picture-dealer, an army coach, a clown, a land valuer, a bo'sun from the Niger, a Glasgow distiller, an organist, an Alexandria cotton-broker, an architect, . . . a . . . London postal official, a taxi-driver, . . . two schoolmasters and a missionary." Storrs, p. 360.

9. Storrs, pp. 346–47. After the war of 1967 this area was taken over in depth by the Israeli authorities.

Holy Land with the official blessing of the ruling power. But this very fact opened vast vistas of misunderstanding. The new arrivals, led by their Commission, were keyed up with tense, eager, thrusting, expectation of immediate settlement in the land that had been promised them as theirs. Nothing else really counted. They had come to Eretz Israel bringing their national emblems—the blue and white flags with the Shield of David—and chanting their national anthem, *Ha-Tiqvah* (The Hope), many quite unaware of any serious obstacles beyond those obviously created by hostile officialdom. Few had any clear notion that the "land without people" was in fact the home of others with a title to it no less substantial than their own. The pioneers knew of course that the Arabs existed, and in the earlier years many Arabs were employed by them as labourers. Again, some had been forcibly struck by a sense of coming as strangers to the land of another race; one of these was Ben Yehuda, the father of modern Hebrew, on landing at Jaffa from Russia in 1882.[10] Even so, to them the Arabs were a very minor factor, and the few there were would, they thought, necessarily welcome Zionism because it meant "progress."

Except for the port regions of Jaffa, Haifa, and Acre, much of the coastal plain was indeed sparsely inhabited when the Jewish settlers first came. Some areas were marshy-malarial, and modern drainage—still not widely practiced even in the West—had not been applied. Thus the advance vision of the average Ashkenazi from Europe was of a Palestine which had once been a fertile land but had been allowed to degenerate into a desert or semi-desert by a handful of more or less primitive natives who knew no better. That Jerusalem was a vital centre of faith and inspiration for Christianity and Islam; that it was the Arabs who had started the citrus fruit industry in coastal Palestine which the Jewish colonies later developed, that the Palestinians had their own educated upper class and, in common with other Syrians, parliamentary representation, potential access to high office while under Turkey, and strong

10. Amos Elon, *The Israelis: Founders and Sons*, p. 155.

nationalist aspirations—all these things were either unknown or weighed little in the balance.

Thus in 1918 and the ensuing years the mood of the Commission and some of its newest followers was one of bewilderment, frustration, and resentment. They resolved to stand up to a Government which, they convinced themselves, was anti-Zionist, and to pitch their demands as high as possible in the hope of obtaining as many as they could. The Eastern European leaders, with the notable exception of Dr Weizmann, who by now had long experience of living among and working with the British, were simply not interested in tactful, friendly coexistence with the Arabs or the British, or even with their Sephardic and Oriental brethren, with whom a fierce rivalry soon broke out. For, had these newcomers wished to use their Sephardic brethren's services for such a purpose, there were many distinguished and intelligent Sephardim living in or near Palestine who would have been ideal agents for dealing or negotiating with the Arabs, having in general maintained close and friendly contact with them since the expulsion of their forefathers from Spain.[11] From the standpoint of those dominant in the Commission, however, tact and tolerance and conciliation might, it seemed, entail a grave risk for the Zionists—that of becoming just another community in Palestine, doomed to assimilation or to a minor role in the country. This all helps to explain what seemed to the equally bewildered British officials the Commission's inadmissible presumption (supported by Justice Brandeis from America) that the policies of the British administration should first be submitted for its approval.

Both the Zionists and the Palestinian Arabs blamed OETA for its characteristically British, and often somewhat muddled and clumsy, efforts to be fair to all concerned. The Palestinian Arabs held that their country was being illegally invaded—since they had not been consulted about, and had not given their consent to, the establishment of a Jewish National Home; it was therefore the busi-

11. Storrs, p. 365.

ness of the British to put a stop to it. For the Zionists, on the other hand, "equality of obligation" between the Arabs and themselves was a betrayal of the promises they had received. Some Zionists recognized, but others were hardly aware, that they were demanding a revolution in Palestine such as had never been brought about in short order in any populated country by peaceful means. Ironically, the main target of the accusations, especially by the Zionists, was the dedicated and accomplished Governor of Jerusalem, Sir Ronald Storrs, who in fact wished both sides well.[12] But he was a distinguished specialist in Arab affairs, the friend of many leading Arabs, and had taken part in the negotiations for the Arab Revolt. This at once damned him in Zionist eyes.[13]

Another cause of the exasperation which developed between the Commission and OETA was that neither had been given any concrete, factual definition of what the Balfour Declaration meant. Since Britain was traditionally sceptical of logic and prided herself on her empiricism, this vagueness may have been deliberate, and indeed Balfour's own intention.[14] It is true that in the early years it was not known how many Jews would in fact come to settle in their National Home. And today we can all guess that the Home might never have developed into a predominantly Jewish state, had

12. See his *Orientations*, pp. 275–440 *passim*. From the author's own observation as a junior officer during the last year of Storr's governorship, his only real failing was a desire to be all things to all men. This tended to lead him into conflicting promises, not all of which could be fulfilled.

13. Dr Eder of the Zionist Commission informed a British Commission of Enquiry in 1921 that in his view there could be "no equality in the partnership between Jew and Arab, but a Jewish predominance as soon as the numbers of that race are sufficiently increased. . . . The Jews should, and the Arabs should not, have the right to bear arms and . . . this discrimination would tend to improve Arab-Jewish relations." Sykes, p. 50. See also p. 35.

14. Balfour had told the British War Cabinet that he understood the words "National Home" to mean "some form of British, American or other protectorate, under which full facilities would be given to the Jews to work out their own salvation and to build up a real centre of national culture and focus of national life. It did not necessarily involve the early establishment of an independent Jewish state, which was a matter for gradual development in accordance with the ordinary laws of political evolution." See Barbour, p. 68.

it not been for Hitler's holocaust, which no one at the time foresaw. Nevertheless, the degree of vagueness allowed to surround this
revolutionary statement of British policy seems to have been far
greater than the circumstances justified. The price was heavy in
conflict and confusion, and ultimate loss of British power and
prestige.

Three generals headed OETA as Chief Administrators during
its two and a half years. Under the last of them,[15] tension with the
Zionist Commission came to a head, and he recommended its abolition. The Commission had by now come to regard itself as entitled to decide the future, if not the present, government of the
country. It resolved that Palestine should be called Eretz Israel,
with the Jewish flag as its national emblem; and, since it was the
Jewish homeland, that the Jews should have the determining voice
in its affairs. After Dr Weizmann's departure, OETA found itself
subject to indirect Zionist pressure through London or America—
and increasingly resented it. As General Bols complained, the
forces of law and order were being ignored; in any court case involving someone Jewish, the Commission sought from the occupying power, not justice, but discrimination in favour of their
countryman. Meanwhile, Muslims and Christians had become
restive over the infringements of the status quo in favour of the
Zionists, while the Zionists charged the British with anti-Zionism.
The Zionists, Bols stressed, seemed bent on committing a temporary military administration, which had observed strictly the rules
laid down for it, to a "partialist" policy before the issue of the
Mandate. While officially claiming nothing more than a National
Home, they would in fact be satisfied with nothing less than a
Jewish state, with all that this politically implied.[16]

The British Government, however, was loyal to its Zionist policy.
The general's plea was rejected, and his administration ended. This
was in the fateful year 1920, which we have already described. We
have seen how at that time the erosion of Faisal's throne and the

15. Major-General Sir Louis Bols.
16. Barbour, pp. 96–97.

defiance of the Syrian Congress were factors leading to the conference at San Remo which assigned mandates for Syria and Lebanon to France and for Palestine and Iraq to Britain. In the very month —July 1920—in which Faisal was expelled from Damascus by the French, the first British High Commissioner under the new Mandate took up his duties in Palestine. This was Sir Herbert Samuel, a leading British-Jewish statesman and former minister in the London Cabinet, and one of the most powerful advocates of the Zionist cause. His deputy, the Chief Secretary, Sir Wyndham Deedes, although Gentile, was also a convinced Zionist. The Attorney-General, already in office under OETA, was Mr Norman Bentwich, a distinguished British-Jewish lawyer and scholar who, as we saw, had been one of the younger generation of Zionists in England. Finally, a small but capable team of newly recruited British-Jewish officials was distributed among the government departments. When the High Commissioner attended the synagogue and read from the Law in Hebrew, many Zionists felt that they were present—or soon would be—at their hour of fulfilment.

The Samuel Era I

What Was Britain's Mandate? Sir Herbert's appointment had been strongly favoured by Dr Weizmann, and the terms of the Mandate he was to enforce were, for the Zionists, a good deal more specific and encouraging than the bland generalities of the Balfour Declaration. In the twenty-seven articles of the text finally approved by the League of Nations[17] (the Mandate came officially into force in September 1923), Britain was required to place Palestine under such political, administrative, and economic conditions as would secure the establishment of the Jewish National Home and the development of self-governing institutions. Furthermore, an "appropriate Jewish Agency" would be recognized as a public

17. For full text see Appendix. "Close settlement" meant the settlement of relatively large numbers on a small area after its productivity had been enhanced by intensive cultivation.

body to advise and cooperate with the administration in regard to the Home, and the Zionist Organization would for the present be recognized as that Agency. Jewish immigration would be facilitated "under suitable conditions"; and, in cooperation with the Jewish Agency, close settlement by Jews on the land, including state lands and waste lands not required for public purposes, would be encouraged.

The acquisition of Palestinian citizenship would be made easy for Jews taking up permanent residence in Palestine. The special privileges and immunities enjoyed by foreigners under the Turkish Empire would lapse during the Mandate. The Mandatory could take over the natural resources, public works, services, and utilities of Palestine and arrange with the Jewish Agency to construct or operate any of these works, services, and utilities, and to develop the country's natural resources, so long as the government did not undertake these tasks itself. The government would also introduce a land system "appropriate to the needs of the country, having regard . . . to the desirability of promoting the close settlement and intense cultivation of the land." It would assume all responsibility for the Holy Places subject to study by a special commission approved by the League. There would be complete freedom of religion and conscience. Each community could run its own schools, and Hebrew would be an official language.

Most of the other provisions were the essential constitutional framework for the normal functions of government. But a special feature was that the Mandatory would report each year to the League of Nations on the fulfillment of its charge. This of course foreshadowed the reports required by the United Nations after 1945 in respect of the Trust Territories, as the Mandates were renamed. In 1924, by agreement with Britain, the United States was granted all rights and benefits under the Mandate as though it had been a member of the League.

There was small comfort for the Palestinian Arabs either in this document or in the messages delivered by the new High Commissioner on his arrival. The Mandate indeed required Britain, as had the Declaration, to safeguard their civil and religious rights, to respect the Muslim *waqfs*, and to refrain from interference with Muslim sacred shrines. Moreover, a message from King George V assured the Arabs of the "absolute impartiality toward every race and creed" which the government would observe. They were also told that the Jewish National Home, not only would not affect their civil and religious rights; it would not "diminish the prosperity of the general population." In a further message of his own the High Commissioner stressed British loyalty to the principle of equal justice for all, regardless of station, race, or creed.[18]

This was not a great deal by contrast with all that the Zionists could claim, and yet, in conveying these assurances, Sir Herbert seems to have been perfectly sincere. For, as a result of his environment and upbringing, he was in fact imbued with that British compulsion to be fair to all which had so exasperated the Zionist Commission in the former military administration. With considerable courage he sought to pursue this goal against the odds created by the provisions of the Mandate during his five years of rule. For this and other reasons, this great Jewish figure, who rendered such signal services to Zionism, has never been a national hero in Israel. Inevitably suspect to the Arabs because of his race and faith, he became extremely unpopular with the Jews before his time was up.

The Samuel Era II

External Stresses in the Fertile Crescent and Egypt. Comprehensibly, Arab restiveness mounted as Jewish immigration rose.[19] In

---

18. Norman Bentwich, *Palestine*, pp. 99–100.

19. Only 1,806 Jewish immigrants seem to have arrived in Palestine in 1919. Their numbers increased to 8,000–8,500 per year in 1920–23. But even these figures, quoted in Sykes, p. 56, from Mark Wischnitzer, *To Dwell in Safety*, (Philadelphia, 1948), were regarded as disappointing by the Zionists. That they were not larger seems to have been due to the fact that for most of this time the United States stayed open to Jewish immigration, while Soviet Russia, from which so many Jews wanted to go to Palestine, was closed to emigration, as it still largely is today.

the spring of 1920 there had been, as we saw, Arab attacks on Jewish settlements, and these were followed by Arab-Jewish riots with bloodshed in Jerusalem. External events helped to keep the country astir. Less than two weeks after Samuel took over, the Arab state collapsed and Faisal arrived as a refugee in Haifa. The demise of the Arab state left a power vacuum in the south-Syrian area east of the river Jordan, and so this area was now included in Britain's Mandate, under the name Transjordan (later Jordan). This region had been casually governed from Damascus, but with the collapse of Faisal's rule it had splintered into local autonomous units. The sequel was equally casual yet decisive for the future of the area. Early in 1921 it ceased to be a potential adjunct to the Zionist programme, either as a region for Jewish settlement, or as one to be set aside for Arab landowners and cultivators who might part with, or be forced out of, their land in Palestine.

Samuel's main concern was to prevent civil war. He visited the Transjordan area in August 1920, and set up local councils in the three main districts. British officers with police were attached to them to give advice and keep order. One such council, which called itself "The National Government of Moab," adjoined the Hejaz and had its capital at Kerak southeast of the Dead Sea. Representing the High Commissioner there was a young British officer who had fought in the Arab Revolt.[20] After Faisal's overthrow, his elder brother, the Amir Abdullah, who had earlier been chosen King of Iraq, resigned his post as Hejaz Foreign Minister and announced that he would march north with an army, defeat the French, and take over Syria for himself. In January 1921 he reached Ma'an near the border of Moab. When the British adviser pressed Jerusalem for instructions he was told it was "most unlikely" that Abdullah would advance into the British zone. Immediately afterwards the Amir and his army arrived.

With the initiative thus thrust upon him, the British representa-

20. Major (afterwards Sir Alec) Kirkbride. See his *A Crackle of Thorns*, pp. 21–28. An additional note of genial unreality was the insistence of the local sheikhs on choosing him as President of their Governing Council.

tive with his fifty policemen saw no alternative but to welcome his distinguished visitor. The Amir soon gained acceptance as ruler of all Transjordan; and, having thus arbitrarily won a position of personal power, this not very warlike prince let himself be persuaded not to attack the French. At the same time his unexpected presence in Transjordan achieved Britain's goal of keeping the country quiet.

Meanwhile the imaginative and dynamic Winston Churchill had become responsible for Britain's mandates as Colonial Secretary. At a conference in Cairo in March 1921, he did his best to clear up the tangle of Britain's conflicting obligations. Iraq was the most urgent problem. After San Remo the country had risen against the British in a bloody and costly revolt. London now realized that here, where there was no Zionist commitment, concessions to Arab nationalism must be swiftly made. The first was to give Iraq a king of its own. A plebiscite was held and this time the choice fell, as Britain wished, upon Faisal, who thus exchanged the throne of the Umayyads for that of the Abbasid Caliphs. He and his descendants then reigned in Iraq from August 1921 until the revolution of 1958. Britain had at least taken one short step to redeem her debt of honour to the Hashimites. A more important concession followed in 1922, when the Mandate for Iraq was transformed into a treaty of alliance between Baghdad and London.

One further consequence of the Cairo conference was Britain's eventual recognition of Abdullah as ruler of Transjordan. This has been seen by some as a wise choice, by others as a devious denial of Zionism's potential scope. But since the conference aimed at allaying Arab fears and resentment, there was virtually no choice but to accept this accomplished fact. Iraq, which had once wanted Abdullah as king, had gone to his younger brother. To have denied Abdullah this modest compensation would have fostered an abiding grudge in one who became one of Britain's loyal friends and, much later, almost the only Arab ruler to show some moderation and understanding towards Israel. Indeed it was this that earned him a tragic and violent death.

Recognition, officially confirmed in 1923, gave Churchill also the chance to insist on some important points. In return for a measure of British guidance, and the subsidies he needed, Abdullah accepted the British Mandate. But Transjordan became administratively separate from Palestine and was formally exempted from application of the provisions for establishment of a Jewish National Home. A formal agreement between Britain and Transjordan followed in 1928. After settling the future of Abdullah, Churchill met a delegation of Palestinian Arabs in Jerusalem, who demanded self-government and the cancellation of the Zionist programme. He refused, but assured them that the Home did not mean a Jewish government to dominate the Arabs.[21] This assurance was elaborated in a British White Paper of 1922 which is discussed below.

At the time of the conference, Cairo was itself in a state of tension and suspense. In World War I—as later in World War II—Egypt was a strategic base for British operations involving large concentrations of Commonwealth troops. While the money spent by the forces, together with the high prices paid for the country's products (especially cotton), profited landowners and business men, many suffered from inflated prices. At the end of the war the nationalist movement was more vocal than ever. Just after the Armistice in November 1918, the extremists, led by Zaghlul Pasha,[22] insisted that the British Protectorate must go, and that Egypt should send a delegation (*wafd*) to London for negotiations. Complete independence was demanded. When this was refused and Zaghlul exiled against the British Agent's[23] sensible advice, an outbreak of subversion and murder had to be harshly suppressed; the name *wafd* became thenceforth the slogan and emblem of the Egyptian nationalist party.

General Allenby was sent out as Special High Commissioner; and he, too, had the wisdom to see that the Protectorate must go,

---

21. Sykes, pp. 61–69. See also Kirkbride, pp. 25–27.
22. See Chapter 8.
23. This was now Sir Reginald Wingate, former Governor-General of the Sudan and one of the original organizers of British support for the Arab Revolt. He had succeeded McMahon in December 1916.

and eventually forced his views upon the British Cabinet. But negotiations with the Egyptians for a treaty to replace the Protectorate
broke down over Britain's insistence on safeguards for her own and
foreign interests. In February 1922, therefore, Britain made a unilateral declaration that Egypt was an independent, sovereign state,
and that the Protectorate, and martial law, were abolished. Until
agreement could be reached between Britain and Egypt, however,
four matters were "reserved to Britain's absolute discretion": "the
security of the communications of the British Empire in Egypt"
(i.e., the Suez Canal), the defence of Egypt, the protection of foreign interests and minorities there, and the Sudan. The Sultan,
Ahmed Fuad, who had replaced his elder brother, Hussein Kamil,
in 1917, was declared King of Egypt as Fuad I.

Egypt thus became semi-independent in 1922, with diplomatic
representation abroad, and a new constitution on democratic lines.
Fresh elections then produced a large Wafdist majority and put
Zaghlul temporarily into power as Prime Minister. But in effect it
was still Britain who determined how independent Egypt should
be; and the King himself, with autocratic ambitions and hostile to
the constitution and the Wafd, played to some extent into Britain's
hands. Thus, while the new dispensation was for the present broadly
acceptable to the moderates, nationalist agitation led in 1924 to a
fresh crisis with the murder of General Sir Lee Stack, Governor-
General of the Sudan, who commanded the Egyptian army. This
led in turn to severe British countermeasures, including the withdrawal of all Egyptian troops from the Sudan, and to the replacement of Allenby by a convinced imperialist, Lord Lloyd, who had
made his name as an Indian Governor. Now, as a highly intelligent
man, Lloyd too realized that further major concessions would have
to be made to Egyptian nationalism. It was, however, more than
ten years before a treaty could be signed between the two countries, a treaty that provided a workable arrangement until after
World War II. Even before the Egyptian treaty was signed, the British mandate for Iraq had lapsed and that country had become a
member of the League of Nations.

Meanwhile, the French were embarking on the first and most sterile phase of their Mandate, from 1920 to 1926. They were, as we saw, hostile to the Arab national movement for fear of subversion in their politically less advanced North African territories of Morocco, Algeria, and Tunis; and they were deeply suspicious of Britain's close relations with Arab leaders such as Feisal and Abdullah. One of their countermeasures was the political and administrative fragmentation of the mandated area. Thus Lebanon was roughly doubled in size at the expense of Syria and came to include a comparable number of Muslims to Christians. North of Lebanon the regions of Latakia and Alexandretta were made into separate divisions. All three came under a French governor with extensive powers. Two further divisions were the states of Syria and of the Jebel Druze in the mountains between Damascus and Transjordan. With firm French control of the coastal regions, these potentially hostile areas were largely shut off from their natural outlets to the sea. This did not prevent another damaging revolt against the mandatory power; this one, erupting in 1925, spread from the Jebel Druze into Syria and inflicted serious initial reverses on the French.

With far less recent experience of the area, the French were a good deal slower than the British to realize the need for quick and serious concessions to nationalist feeling at a time when the defeated Turks were confounding the European powers by a strong and effective national resurgence under Mustafa Kemal.[24] Only

24. Later known as Kemal Ataturk. After May 1919 he organized in Asia Minor, a nationalist congress and armed resistance to the dismemberment of Turkey in defiance of the collaborationist government in Istanbul, which accepted the humiliating treaty of Sèvres in August 1920. By then he had become President of a new provisional government at Ankara. The Armenian Republic, independent under the Sèvres treaty, was defeated and confined to the province of Erivan, which became a Soviet Republic. In 1921 the renewed military strength of Turkey induced the Italians and French to evacuate southwestern Anatolia and Cilicia. Meanwhile, the Greeks, who had occupied Smyrna and attempted to take Ankara, were decisively defeated in September 1922 and expelled from Asia Minor. In 1922 the Turkish Sultanate was abolished, and in 1924, the Caliphate. A republic was proclaimed in 1923, after the Treaty of Lausanne had given Turkey far more favourable terms than those

after some sixteen years did the French adopt the path of compromise pursued by Britain in Iraq and Egypt. In this slow adjustment to Arab nationalism the French were hampered by a colonial system, evolved in North Africa, that was far more Roman in tradition than that of Britain. Its highest goal was the projection of French civilization overseas; and assimilation to French life, and eventual citizenship, was one of the greatest privileges to which some of their dependent peoples might aspire. But the Arabs of the Fertile Crescent, who had in the past developed a civilization and a subtle, sophisticated language both older than those of France, did not always see it in that light. A major cause of resentment was that the supremacy of Arabic, previously threatened by Turkish nationalism, was now endangered by French insistence on the teaching of French in all state schools, by a certain neglect of Arabic-speaking schools, and by the use of French on an equal footing with Arabic in the courts of law.

The Samuel Era III

Internal Developments. In spite of the disturbances early in 1920 and the stir caused by Faisal's passage through Palestine in the following July, during the next months the Samuel regime gradually settled down. In spite of the many tensions, a useful start had been made by OETA, especially in such fields as public health and communications, with the creation of a modern administration in a land still subject to Turkish law and practice. Although, under the Mandate, good government was constantly bedevilled by political problems—and it is with these that we shall be chiefly concerned—progress and modernization were in fact achieved in nearly all fields. While there was a flow of new legislation, some of it ini-

---

imposed at Sèvres. Though renouncing all non-Turkish territories, she recovered eastern Thrace and certain islands, abolished the Capitulations, paid no reparations, and recovered the (demilitarized) Straits, which were to be open to all ships in peace time, and in war if Turkey were neutral. If Turkey were at war, enemy ships but not neutrals might be excluded. Turks in Greece and Greeks in Turkey (except in Istanbul) were compulsorily exchanged.

tially disconcerting to the local peoples accustomed to the harsh and simple autocracy of the Turks, certain familiar landmarks and practices were retained from Turkish days. Thus, taxation continued to be based mainly on customs revenues and agricultural tithes. But adjustments were made to reduce its burden, and this was further relieved by the general elimination of corruption. In line with their measures to deal with the over-all problem of security, the British inevitably carried out a reform of the judiciary in accordance with the traditions of British law; and this task was simplified by the abolition of capitulations. Here there was swift adjustment to the new standards and methods, for soon British judges were appointed to preside only over the Court of Appeal, the four District Courts, and two Land Courts. All other judges and magistrates were Palestinians, drawn from the three religious communities.

Before 1914 there had been no telephones and only one car. Here again, as in communications generally, modernization was swift. The country had been infested with malaria; rabies and eye diseases were a scourge. All were effectively tackled with the help of various international medical and missionary bodies. Education was another striking field of progress; and during these early years over three hundred government schools were balanced by some four hundred private ones, including all the Jewish and mission schools. Significantly, when after thirty years British rule foundered in chaos and strife, many of the Palestinian Arabs had become in some respects educationally better qualified than the Arabs of surrounding countries before the Palestinian dispersion during and after 1948.[25] A consequence of the new order was that the archaeo-

25. This may seem surprising in view of the fine educational work done over a long period by, for example, the French institutions in Syria and Lebanon and the American University of Beirut. The fact remains that Palestinians are in considerable demand for responsible jobs in these and other Arab countries. One rather negative reason could be the language conflict in Syria and Lebanon between alumni of institutions teaching in French or English. Another, more positive, reason might be the British emphasis on character training in the educational system in Palestine.

logical riches of Palestine started to be opened up as never before, and Sir Ronald Storrs' Pro-Jerusalem Society developed an international campaign to preserve and enhance the beauties of the Holy City. Tourists became a valuable source of revenue.

The land was to be one of the acutest areas of conflict under the Mandate. Palestine covered some ten thousand square miles, perhaps half of it cultivable, and two-thirds of the population lived off the soil. Before 1914 there were, as we saw, some Jewish colonies, and these colonies owned about 177 square miles. By April 1925 the Jewish-owned area had expanded to 319 square miles, but was still only some 6 per cent of the cultivable area. Nearly all the rest was in Arab hands, and their land was cultivated on a traditional pattern. Successive areas were left fallow and little fertilizer was used. Erosion was widespread, due to long deforestation, and much poverty had been caused by Turkish wartime felling of the olive trees (for burning in their trains), and the commandeering of farm stock. Remedial measures included loans to farmers and the creation of a Department of Agriculture and Forests. Special encouragement and training was also given in the use of fertilizers, conquest of pests, the production of fruit, poultry, and honey, and the planting of trees. Tobacco, which had hardly been grown in Palestine under the former Turkish monopoly system, became a valuable addition to agricultural wealth.

Under Turkey, titles had been in confusion from lack of a cadastral survey. Such a survey was now made. Small industries were developed, based mainly on local products and resources, amongst them wine and tobacco, and soap from olive oil. A start was made with electrification and the exploitation of chemicals from the Dead Sea. Jewish enterprise was prominent in this modest expansion of industry, and some small manufactures of consumer goods were launched in Tel Aviv. Thus much was achieved in a material sense through these and many other measures during the first eight years of the Mandate, under Samuel and his immediate successor. There was some bloodshed and much occasional bitterness, but there were also gleams of hope of a peaceful and creative future.

In spite of the ground swell from World War I, the initial up-heavals and uncertainties in Syria and Transjordan, and some ugly killings in May 1921, between 1922 and 1925 a fairly swift pacification of Palestine was achieved. For this purpose the police were strengthened by two newly raised corps of gendarmerie, one local, of Arabs, Circassians, and Jews; and one British. Apart from them, the only British forces retained in Palestine by 1925 were one regiment of cavalry, one squadron of aircraft, and one company of armoured cars. Indeed, in his own report on the five years of his administration, Samuel was able to state that "for some time past, Palestine has been the most peaceful country of any in the Middle East."[26]

The Stresses and Measures of 1921 and 1922

The riots of May 1921 were basically the result of a tragic misunderstanding, since they arose out of a clash between Communist- and Socialist-oriented Jewish immigrants on the border between Jewish Tel Aviv and Arab Jaffa. Ever since Britain had undertaken to implement the Balfour Declaration, the Arabs of Palestine had been convinced that they would be faced with mass Zionist immigration that would lead in the long run to Jewish domination of their country. In the light of events some twenty years later, their instinct was hardly at fault. But in the early 1920s they ignorantly and rashly presumed that this mass invasion might occur at any moment; and for this reason the more primitive and fanatical among them were easily stirred up to desperate courses. The local Arabs may also have feared that the rioters from Tel Aviv were moving to attack them.[27] In any event these Arabs raided an immigrant hostel in Jaffa and murdered a group of Jews awaiting settlement. During the following days the violence spread; Arabs

26. *Report of the High Commissioner on the Administration of Palestine,* 1920–25 (Colonial No. 15, 1925), p. 5. Much of the earlier summary of the work done in the first years of the Mandate is based upon this.
27. Sykes, p. 69.

attacked Jewish settlements, and some of the Jews effectively retaliated with the illicit arms and training they had managed to
acquire. By the time security forces stopped the fighting nearly one
hundred Jews and Arabs had been killed, in almost equal proportions, and over two hundred wounded. The pattern set in 1921 was
to be repeated years later on a far more formidable scale.

Concessions to Arab Opinion

Meanwhile, however, Sir Herbert seems to have been convinced by
this tragedy, and by all he had witnessed since he came, that it was
vital to meet the resentment of the Arabs with concessions. He
sought to reduce their bitterness and fear by showing regard for
their leaders and institutions, and by keeping Zionist expansion
within moderate bounds. When the Arabs ceased to fear and saw
how much the country might benefit from it, the National Home
would, he thought, gradually become acceptable; and the whole
country could then progress in peace. In line with these policies,
the status of the Muslim community and their Holy Places had
been generously regulated.

Under the Turks, these affairs had been settled in Istanbul by the
Ministry of Waqfs, which had sequestrated considerable funds
from ancient endowments. Now the local Muslims were given
full authority over their affairs, and these funds were restored to
them. They chose by election their own Supreme Muslim Council, which cared for the religious buildings and charitable endowments, supervised the religious courts, and administered its own
revenue. Then, only two months before the riots, Sir Herbert had
appointed as Grand Mufti of Jerusalem—and thus as the senior
Muslim dignitary—a young man still in his twenties who had been
sentenced *in absentia* for helping to stir up the earlier violence
against the Jews. Haj Amin el-Husseini belonged to one of the
great families of Palestine and was half-brother to the late Mufti
who had died. In this case, however, the often successful British

policy of giving to a hostile extremist a post of high importance and distinction, in the hope of inducing moderation and responsibility, failed to work. Haj Amin, though slow to show his hand, became in time one of the bitterest enemies of Britain and the Jews.

Proposed Extension of Representative Government

In the aftermath of the May killings the High Commissioner took two further steps. To the indignation of the Zionists, he temporarily suspended Jewish immigration. Furthermore, realizing that uncertainty was one of the main causes of unrest, he sought from London a formal, authoritative statement of the exact meaning and implications of the Balfour Declaration. But first there were discussions of the possibility of more representative government in Palestine. In spite of the doubts of the Zionists (in view of the Jewish minority in the country) and even of Prime Minister Lloyd George, the High Commissioner and Mr Churchill insisted that broadened representation would be right.[28] The chief stumbling block was the Arab Executive, which had sent a delegation to London. This body, though unofficial, represented a large volume of organized Arab opinion in the country.

During his visit to Jerusalem the previous year Churchill had made it plain that the instant autonomy demanded by the Arabs could not be conceded in view of the special circumstances of Palestine and Britain's specific commitments to Zionism, but that, as in all their dependent territories, the British had been concerned from the start to have some element of popular representation which could lead by degrees to genuine self-government. The High Commissioner had set up an Advisory Council, and it had functioned with reasonable smoothness from 1920 to 1922. In addition to ten officials, it consisted of four Muslim and three Christian Arabs, and three Jews, all nominated by him. All legislation was submitted to this Council, and "on no occasion did the govern-

28. Sykes, pp. 82–83.

ment find itself unable to accept the considered opinion of the non-official members."[29]

Now, as the time approached for the official application of the Mandate with League approval, plans were made for a somewhat larger, Legislative, Council. Apart from the same number of officials, it would have twelve unofficial members (eight Muslims, two Christians, and two Jews), indirectly elected in two stages under the old Turkish system.[30] These proposals were rejected by the Arab representatives. They insisted that the Council must either consist entirely of elected members or there must be a clear majority of Arabs over the official, and non-official-Jewish, elements. But since the Palestine Government would then have faced a deadlock with its legislature in seeking to establish a Jewish National Home in accordance with the Mandate, the Arab conditions were rejected by the British. This led to a boycott of the primary elections, and the proceedings had to be nullified. An attempt was then made to reconstitute the Advisory Council with a somewhat larger unofficial membership in the proportions proposed for the Legislative Council. Eight Muslim and two Christian Arabs duly agreed to become members, but most of them were forced by extremist pressure to withdraw. In view of this second failure to secure proper representation of the Palestinian majority, the Advisory Council was revived with official membership only. A year later the Arabs were invited to form an Arab Agency to deal with the Government on the same footing as the Jewish Agency. But this also was turned down.

Britain's Official Statement of Policy on Palestine

The statement of Britain's policy interpreting the Balfour Declaration and the Mandate was issued on Mr Churchill's authority in a

29. *Report of the High Commissioner* . . . , p. 44.
30. This involved a primary election of delegates by all men over 25. Members of the Council were then to be elected by the delegates so chosen.

White Paper of June 1922,[31] which reproduced the correspondence with the Arab delegation and the Zionist Organization. According to this Paper, the Declaration was never meant to create a wholly Jewish Palestine. This would be quite impracticable, and Britain had no such aim. Nor did she contemplate "the disappearance or subordination of the Arabic [sic] population, language or culture in Palestine," or that the country as a whole should be converted into a Jewish National Home. Moreover, the statement read, the Zionists at their Congress in 1921 had shown their determination to live with the Arabs in unity and mutual respect; each would have full scope for their national development.

The White Paper added that the existing Jewish community of eighty thousand already had national characteristics, with its political organs and distinctive social, religious, and intellectual life. The National Home meant the further development of this community with the help of Jews elsewhere, so that it might become a centre in which the whole Jewish people would take pride. There was no question of imposing a Jewish nationality upon the people of Palestine. In any case, Jewish immigration could not exceed the economic capacity of the country to absorb it. It would not be a burden on the Palestinians as a whole, and would not deprive any of them of their employment. The contention was then repeated that Britain had always regarded Palestine as excluded from the area of Arab independence promised to the Sharif of Mecca in the McMahon correspondence.

In response to this statement, Dr Weizmann assured the British Government that the Zionist Organization's activities would conform to its policy; and he stressed particularly the Zionists' understanding that immigration must be regulated by the economic capacity of Palestine. The Arab delegation inevitably objected to various passages in the White Paper and the Mandate, stressing that their historic rights were stronger than those of the Jews, since

31. Correspondence with the Palestine Arab Delegation and the Zionist Organization (Cmd. 1700, 1922), pp. 17–21.

"Palestine had a native population before the Jews even went there, and this population had persisted all down the ages." They also exposed the weakness of the British argument for the exclusion of Palestine from the promises to the Arabs,[32] and demanded a national government responsible to a parliament elected by all the people of Palestine—Muslims, Christians, and Jews. Unless British policy changed, they said, they must continue to fear that the Jewish National Home would in fact mean the subordination of their people, language, and culture in Palestine. In the light of what Israel has in our day become, it will be clear why Britain's solemn assurances of the 1920s—and those of the Zionist organization—have long rung hollow in Arab ears, why the Arabs of Palestine ceased to value Britain's word, and why, for this and other reasons, British influence in the Middle East is now largely a thing of the past.

But during the later years of the Samuel regime and the short rule of his successor (1925–28), the future was still hidden and things were in fact relatively calm. Despite continued Arab intransigence and protest, and the failure to achieve any kind of representative government, there seemed some hope that moderation and compromise might in the long run prevail. For there was little, at that stage, to support the worst Arab fears. There was no mass Jewish immigration. For many years, indeed, from the Zionist standpoint immigration was disappointingly small, despite various resourceful devices to overcome the restrictions of the British authorities.[33] There were no Jewish armed attacks, no affront to Islam

32. See Chapter 10, above, and Sykes, pp. 84–88. Even Sykes, a writer on the whole sympathetic to Zionism, calls Britain's interpretation of the McMahon correspondence, which became the basis of her claim to implement Zionism in Palestine, "absolutely indefensible." He is convinced that the feeling that the British had established themselves there "by clever swindling," as the Arabs maintained, sapped the confidence and sense of dedication of most British officials in Palestine. He also regards it as short-sighted that the Zionists should have used so dubious an interpretation so extensively in their propaganda, for by so doing "they accepted a humiliating position: that of people whose station in life was based on a piece of sharp practice" (p. 86).

33. "The years 1923–1929 were relatively quiet. Arab passivity was partly due to the drop in Jewish immigration in . . . 1926–1928. In 1927, Jewish emi-

or Christianity or their Holy Places. Moreover, most—though by no means all—British officials tended to be sympathetic towards the Arabs as the traditional element in the country, and as those most in need of help if modernization and progress were to be achieved. Both in the districts and the central government it became clear that the British were at pains to do at least as much for the Arabs as for the Jews, if not more, for the Jews were far more capable of looking after themselves, and did in fact advance largely by their own efforts. Thus, e.g., the burden of Jewish education and health rested almost entirely upon the Jews themselves, and yet they regularly paid taxes for the support of public health and education mainly for the benefit of the Arabs. And even the British-Jewish High Commissioner, in an important dispute over state land in the Jordan valley, faced further unpopularity with his fellow Jews by adjudicating in favor of the Arabs, who were legally on weak ground.[34]

The Zionists, on the other hand, despite their written agreement[35] were by no means happy with the White Paper of 1922. True, the British Government had now officially disavowed its promises of independence to the Arabs so far as Palestine was concerned. This had, of course, been implicit in the Balfour Declaration; yet its confirmation in a statement of British government policy could be used effectively in Zionist publicity with the world at large, which had little if any knowledge of the actual background

---

grants exceeded immigrants, and in 1928 there was a net Jewish immigration of ten persons only." See Denis Bailey, "Palestine," *Encyclopedia Britannica* (1971), XVII, 169. There is a useful account of the immigration system in *Palestine under the Mandate*, by A. M. Hyamson, a distinguished British-Jewish scholar who was Director of Immigration of the Palestine Government for many years. The general purpose of the British authorities was to ensure that those entering the country had some means of support, or prospect of gainful employment, or could cite persons who would accept responsibility for them. But members of families could at one stage be admitted without limit, and there were many fictitious claims on this score. See pp. 52, 53, and 66.

34. *Report of the High Commissioner*, 1920–25, 41–42.

35. The full text of the Zionist Organization's letter will be found in *Correspondence* . . . (Cmd. 1700), pp. 28–29.

of the Arab Revolt. What was more serious was that the White Paper formally committed the Zionists to a policy confining Jewish immigration to the economic capacity of Palestine, and to a definition of the future which, if literally followed, would have permanently prevented the Jewish National Home from ever becoming the dominant factor in Palestine. Meanwhile they were committed to the acceptance of a Legislative Council in which they would necessarily have been in a minority. They could not know at that stage that Arab intransigence would play into their hands through the boycott of the elections, the enforced withdrawal of the Arabs from the enlarged Advisory Council, and the later abandonment of the whole project for more representative government. Despite this intransigence of a vocal minority, however, most of the Arabs either took no interest in politics or had gained enough faith in the performance and assurances of the British for them to go along tacitly, for the present, with the existing regime.

These factors, coupled with the fall in Jewish immigration, produced a spell of fairly general peace during and after the later years of Samuel's rule. The calm was little disturbed even by the British Government's decision in 1923 that a British presence in Palestine was necessary also for the defence of the Suez Canal in case Egypt were abandoned; and that Britain must continue to implement the Balfour Declaration for reasons of "consistency and self-respect." Nor was peace compromised to any serious degree in Palestine even by Balfour's arrival in 1925 to open the Hebrew University in Jerusalem. In Syria, however, his life was in danger from the bitter hostility encountered, and the French hurried him out of the country.[36]

The Plumer Years

Sir Herbert Samuel's successor, Field Marshal Lord Plumer, was in most ways a complete contrast, but like him was an extremely capable, clear-headed man of strong character, with an equally determined sense of fairness. Unlike Sir Herbert, he had no special link

36. See Sykes, pp. 95–97.

with or feeling for Zionism—or indeed for the Arabs—but he hated injustice and oppression of every kind and, having been deeply moved by the horrors of World War, was reluctant to use force if this could be avoided. From the grinding war of attrition on the Western European front, Lord Plumer had emerged as the British general with perhaps the highest and least controversial reputation of them all. He was also a man of devastating honesty and a directness that was often effective in defeating any obliqueness of approach in others. When asked on arrival what his policy was, he said he had not got one; his job was to carry out his Government's instructions as best he could. When faced with an Arab protest against his standing for the Zionist anthem at a Jewish gathering, he pointed out that, as a guest, it was his duty to respond to the hospitality of his hosts. Had he been *their* guest, he said, he would have shown them equal respect.[37] The Zionists, at first deeply suspicious of what looked like another military government, and resentful of his strict application of the immigration rules, appreciated his integrity and fairness when things soon after became hard for them.

Jewish immigration might indeed have caused another bloody conflict in 1925. For an economic slump and other harsh conditions prevailed in newly revived Poland,[38] where three million Jews formed 10 per cent of the population. There was also a temporary relaxation of the emigration laws in Communist Russia—and this meant that nearly 34,000 Jews, mostly from Eastern Europe, en-

37. These incidents are recorded in Sykes, pp. 107–108. The general evaluation of his character, and the deep impression made by this small and physically unimpressive man, are fully borne out by the author's own experience of serving under him and enjoying on occasions his hospitality and kindness.
38. Poland recovered her independence after 123 years in 1918, though her territory was considerably less than before the partitions. As we saw, the kings of Poland had attracted Jews to their country and given them at one time various privileges. These were later eroded, but the Jews suffered a good deal more in those parts of the country that came under Russia than they had before the partitions, or than they did when Poland was restored. Nonetheless there were painful restrictions and discrimination after 1918. Things improved, for the time being, when Pilsudski became Dictator in 1926.

tered Palestine in that year.[39] Yet there was virtually no protest or agitation in the territory or the surrounding Arab countries. One reason was that Palestine was firmly ruled. Then, as the Arabs could see, the Polish slump and currency restrictions in Eastern Europe were weakening the embryo National Home by causing distress and failure to Jewish businesses and individuals in Palestine, with widespread unemployment in consequence. Moreover, a substantial re-emigration of Jewish immigrants had been going on for some years.

At that stage, Continental Europe was not for Jews the place of fear and danger it later became. In the German Weimar Republic, for example, Hitler was still just a discredited agitator, and the Jews were conspicuously prosperous and successful. This being so, many who had come to Palestine left again with the prospect of better conditions elsewhere. And even in Poland the advent of the dictator Pilsudski in 1926 led to a temporary easing of the Jewish lot and a notable fall in emigration in 1927. In the following year the surplus of immigration over emigration was only ten. Thus, so long as there were still flourishing prospects for Jews in Europe and elsewhere,[40] the prospects for a large expansion of the National Home were correspondingly dim.

When Lord Plumer left in 1928, in spite of many troubles there had been a long spell of relative peace, chiefly because of that enforced pause in the build-up of the National Home. But the causes of conflict, though muted, were still alive. One of the most basic was the inevitable, though then still gradual, displacement of Arab cultivators from their land by Jewish purchase. This development,

---

39. According to the *Report by His Britannic Majesty's Government to the Council of the League of Nations on the Administration of Palestine and Transjordan for the Year 1925* (Colonial No. 20), p. 51, this number included many Russian converts to Judaism.

40. Jewish immigration to America was adversely affected by the U.S. Quota Law of 1921, which was stiffened in 1924. But this did not in itself produce any marked increase in immigration into Palestine. There were still good opportunities for Jewish people elsewhere, including Germany. Only after the onset of Nazi persecution in 1933 did Jewish immigration into Palestine rise dramatically.

in itself perfectly legitimate, was merely an intensification of what had been going on since the late nineteenth century. The trouble was that most of these farmers were tenants of absentee Arab landlords, many of whom lived in larger cities of the surrounding lands. The Jewish organizations were ready to pay high prices, and most landlords were very humanly content to be well paid and not specially concerned to keep their land in Arab hands.

Sir Herbert Samuel and his successors were all aware of the explosive risk of having a landless and resentful Arab peasantry exploited by nationalist leaders who hated the whole Zionist experiment. This threat was to become a grim reality in the 1930s, and was intensified by the growing boycott of Arab labour in the Jewish settlements. Yet careful measures had been laid down by the British from the start. Under a Land Transfer Ordinance of 1920, when an estate was sold the tenant was to retain enough land to keep himself and his family. Realizing that this had not worked, Lord Plumer appointed a committee to devise remedies, and more legislation with the same object appeared in 1929, 1931, and later years. But all these well-meant measures had little effect; and landlord and buyer, neither of whom had any real interest in safeguarding the tenants, got round them by various devices.

Since the Jewish organizations insisted on vacant possession, the peasants were paid to leave their holdings before the transfer took place, or (until this evasion was stopped) were granted a short tenancy of less than a year. Though in some cases tenants (real or fictitious) exploited the situation, in general the problem of the displaced and landless Arabs continued to grow, especially after 1931, when large-scale Jewish land purchases resumed. One root of the trouble appeared when the Government, much later, put forward a scheme to organize and finance the provision of new land for landless Arabs. Neither the Arab nor Jewish political leadership would have anything to do with it, and very few Arabs came forward to claim the government help. In this they were following an old tradition. We have seen how much was irregular and arbitrary in the Ottoman Empire in regard to land titles and other things. If a poor man wanted to live in peace, he kept as clear of the government and officialdom as he could.[41]

In another context Lord Plumer misjudged the signs of the times. The 1920s in general were years of hope. Many felt that perhaps the first Great War had not been fought in vain. In 1923 Turkey's future had been settled by the Treaty of Lausanne. In 1925 the Treaty of Locarno provided for Germany's reintegration into Europe.[42] Concessions to local nationalism in Iraq and Egypt had, after all, produced a certain equilibrium; and Palestine had somehow not been infected by the bitter struggle in Syria against the French. Moreover, during the Field-Marshal's tranquil spell of office, Dr Weizmann had been conspicuously tactful and moderate. In 1923, in a speech in America, he stressed that, however successful the National Home, it would remain an island in a sea of Arabs, with whom it was imperative to reach an understanding. In 1925, at the Fourteenth Zionist Congress, he said that, from the standpoint of the world's sense of justice, the Arabs had the same right to their homes in Palestine as the Jews had to their National Home, that the Arabs' legitimate interests must not—would not—be harmed.[43]

In this general mood of confidence, Lord Plumer decided that the size and cost of the Palestine security forces could be reduced. The gendarmerie, both British and Palestinian, was disbanded and the military presence reduced to a squadron of armoured cars. Thenceforward for any swift crisis only the normal police was immediately available. A newly-formed and highly mobile Transjordan Frontier Force was in principle available for service in Pales-

41. Hyamson, pp. 86–89. See also Sykes, pp. 115–19. The extent of the abuse the Government was trying to remedy became notorious in the case of one large sale of some 50,000 acres in Jezreel Valley to the Zionist Commission in 1920. About 8,000 tenants were evicted, with compensation worth only some $17 a head.

42. For the background and substance of the Treaty of Lausanne see above. For a brief and useful summary of the Treaty of Locarno see, e.g., William E. Langer, *Encyclopedia of World History* (Boston: Houghton Mifflin, 1960), pp. 959–60.

43. Sykes, p. 121.

tine as well as Transjordan; but it was needed chiefly on its home ground.[44] Furthermore, if absolutely necessary, troops could be moved up from Egypt in a few days. Lord Plumer could not know that a year after he left, there would occur a tragic clash—far more serious than any before—which could simply not be handled by the depleted local forces. A few days for reinforcements were simply not enough.

44. *Report by His Britannic Majesty's Government to the Council of the League of Nations on the Administration of Palestine and Transjordan for the Year 1926* (Colonial No. 26, 1927), p. 8.

Chapter **12** The Palestine Conflict
and the Drift
to World War II

In spite of some ugly moments, the first ten years of British rule in Palestine were on the whole years of hope. In the decade from mid-1929 to the outbreak of World War II in 1939, however, the issues at stake became increasingly explosive, and Britain's handling of them less firm, consistent, and effective. Very soon after Lord Plumer's departure Arab violence broke out, as we shall see, over a trivial incident, misjudged by British officials on the spot, and at a time when there was still a pause in Jewish immigration and in the expansion of the National Home. It showed how illusory and fragile the spell of peace under Samuel and Plumer had been, how quickly raw nerves, and threats that were largely exaggerated at the time, could spark off a sudden, irrational, and primitive outburst. Indeed, many Arabs were already up in arms by 1931, before the resumption of large-scale Jewish land purchase had made the threat to the Arab position a far more real one.

As it happened, 1929 also ushered in the world economic slump, which was to intensify "autarky"[1] and national barriers even in the advanced nations, and thus render harder the acceptance of alien immigrants just at the time when emigration from Central Europe

1. Strictly speaking, an economic system relying on national self-sufficiency. In practice, lack of such self-sufficiency was supplemented by what in effect were barter deals rather than the normal processes of trade and finance.

was becoming an urgent and critical compulsion for the Jews. In September 1930, Adolf Hitler's National Socialists (the Nazis) first emerged as a major political party committed to free Germany from the dictated Treaty of Versailles. Their programme, launched in 1920 and soon to be seriously carried out, stressed that no Jew could be a member of the nation, and that non-Germans must leave the Reich. Its propaganda appealed to many of the middle classes hard hit by the post-war inflation as well as to some of the nationalist upper classes burning to avenge Germany's humiliation, and it had a special message for masses of young men whose prospects of jobs had been ruined by the world slump. It declared war on "the Jewish-materialist spirit within us and without us." The Jews, it alleged, were responsible for the evils of both capitalism and Communism, and wielded sinister international power through their alleged control of the world press, the communications, and entertainment media, and of much else besides.

In 1933, soon after Hitler became Chancellor, the Nazis secured absolute power through the abolition of all other parties and the drastic reorganization of Germany; and on the President's death Hitler became head of state as well as of government. The persecution of the Jews, starting with a boycott of their businesses and professional activities, was formalized in 1935 by the Nurnberg Laws. All with one quarter or more of Jewish blood lost their citizenship, and pressure mounted to drive their community of some five or six hundred thousand out of the country—while their considerable properties went to the Nazi state. Intermarriage or sexual intercourse with Jews was forbidden, synagogues were destroyed, and increasing numbers victimized in concentration camps.[2]

2. At the root of Nazi racial theories was the borrowed myth of "Aryanism," which regarded the Aryans as large, blond, long-skulled peoples more or less equivalent to the "Nordic" races of Western, Central, and Eastern Europe, of which the Germans were the supposed leaders. In reality, Aryan is the term applied to the tribes which lived originally between the Hindu Kush mountains and the Caspian Sea and were ancestors of the leading races of Persia, India, and Europe, including among the latter the Mediterranean peoples and, e.g., the Celts and the Slavs.

After consolidating his power internally, Hitler, by a series of bold and ruthless moves, and swift rearmament, had built up a position of considerable strength for Germany before the outbreak of World War II on September 1, 1939. The anxiety of France and Britain to avoid a second world war played into his hands. In 1936 Hitler denounced the Locarno Treaty and reoccupied the demilitarized Rhineland, formed an "Axis" with the Italy of Mussolini[3] (which had its own grievances against the Western powers), and made a pact with Japan, which strengthened this combination. In March 1938 he annexed Austria, and in September the German-inhabited regions of Czechoslovakia—after a conference at Munich at which Britain and France agreed to Hitler's demands.[4] In March 1939 what remained of Czechoslovakia became a German protectorate. In August Hitler made a pact with Russia—a step that ten days later led to the start of the second world war with the invasion of Poland, which was then partitioned, for the fourth time, between Germany and Russia. Britain and France declared war on Germany but were unable to give Poland any effective help, being mainly concerned with the protection of their own lands from Hitler's now powerful and well-trained forces. By this time Palestine had been rent by strife for ten years, and much had happened in the surrounding countries. Meanwhile, the oscillations in Britain's policy for the mandated territory had reflected the unresolved con-

3. Benito Mussolini (1883–1945) instituted "Fascism," another form of totalitarian rule, in Italy, when he became head of the Rome Government in 1922. He clashed with Britain and other members of the League of Nations over Italian invasion and annexation of Ethiopia in 1935–36. He brought Italy into World War II on Germany's side after Germany had defeated France. He was killed by the Italians at the end of World War II.

4. The Munich surrender was the culmination of the policy of "appeasement" of the Nazi-Fascist Axis by the Western powers. Widely and comprehensibly condemned though it has been, there was virtually no alternative for Britain and France but to "buy time" if Hitler were ever to be defeated. Intensive rearmament in the year remaining before the outbreak of World War II just enabled Britain to hold out in 1940–41, after the defeat of France, until eventually a reconstituted Western alliance, with America's powerful help and the eventual victories of the USSR after Russia's invasion by Germany in mid-1941, brought about the total defeat of the Axis countries.

tradictions between the commitments her people had assumed there.

The Broken Peace

A year after Plumer left, there was fresh bloodshed, this time over a flimsy and movable screen. But the screen was at the Wailing Wall, a focal point of religious fervour, since it adjoined the great Mosque, the Dome of the Rock, but was at the same time the relic of Herod's Temple at which Jews had prayed for some two thousand years.[5] The screen served merely to separate men and women during their prayers, but it was in no sense a fixture and had been used on earlier occasions. The row had started in September 1928, when the Jerusalem District Commissioner drew the attention of the Muslim religious authorities to the screen. Yet the Muslims had not protested earlier on the grounds of its infringing the religious status quo which Britain was supposed to preserve. A wise course would have been to ignore the screen unless and until such a protest had been made. As it was, the Commissioner had given the Muslims a pretext for making trouble—and they understandably exploited it. When the screen had not gone by a stated time, as ordered by the British authorities, the police removed it. A brawl resulted between the Jewish worshippers and Arabs who invaded the area. The Muslim Supreme Council, under the Grand Mufti, made the issue into a campaign. As a symbolic encroachment upon the area sacred to the Jews, the Mufti's house above the Wall was enlarged, and Jews praying were distracted by new and nearby Muslim calls to worship. Then too, the Muslims—as was their right—changed the pavement facing the wall from a blind alley into a thoroughfare.[6] The row died down, but simmering hatreds led to a far more tragic outbreak in August 1929.

In spite of the faltering growth of Jewish settlement, the Zionist position had meanwhile been strengthened by the formation of a

5. See Chapters 1 and 2.
6. Hyamson, pp. 117–18. See also Sykes, pp. 125–29.

Jewish Agency. In principle this represented non-Zionist as well as Zionist elements in World Jewry and, after its formal establishment at the Sixteenth Zionist Congress in 1929, a wider measure of support both moral and financial was secured for the Jewish community in Palestine. Although the governing body was originally composed half of Zionists and half of non-Zionists, the Zionist element continued to dominate. The proportion of non-Zionists was gradually reduced until in the end the Executive of the Jewish Agency (in Palestine) consisted of seventeen Zionists and three non-Zionists. There was no election of non-Zionists at all after 1937, and henceforth the Jewish Agency was an undisguised *alias* for the Zionist Organization.[7]

By a somewhat oblique course Dr Weizmann's diplomatic skill had once again secured a striking success. The British Government had hoped that the victory of Weizmann at the 1929 Congress, with his proclaimed preference for "practical" courses, over the Zionist extremists, and the association of non-Zionist elements with the movement, would be a permanent guarantee of moderation. It might have been, had the Arab leaders realized how firmly the Zionist moderates were in the ascendant at that stage, and had they been willing to strengthen such elements by compromise with, and constructive response to, their goals. But they were adamant in rejecting anything of the kind, relying upon the unquestioned strength of their case.[8] But their refusal to compromise—however sound in

7. Hyamson, pp. 115–16.
8. It may be useful here to recall the main points in the Arab case. Some Arabs claimed to descend from the ancient Canaanites who were in Palestine before the Jews arrived; many again were there continuously from Hellenistic and Roman times and throughout the Jewish Diaspora; others came with the Muslim conquest in the seventh century, and even they lived in Palestine for an unbroken period of 1300 years, until the mid-twentieth century. Then the Arabs were convinced that Palestine was included in the promises made to them by Britain in 1915. Although Britain subsequently denied this, they felt that there was no excuse for the British to ignore the principles of democracy and self-determination by not first consulting the people of the country and securing their agreement before deciding on the foundation of a Jewish National Home that was bound to affect their future profoundly.

doctrine and logic—and their determination to reject any surrender of their traditional rights in the country, were in the long run fatal to their cause. In 1929 their violent intransigence seems also to have been bred by a kind of despairing fear of ultimate disaster. From the speeches of the extremists at the Sixteenth Zionist Congress and the formation of the Jewish Agency it looked to them as though World Jewry was forming a menacing front against the Palestinian Arabs. Vladimir Jabotinsky, leader of the Revisionists,[9] had told the Congress that the National Home could only mean a state with a Jewish majority, and one in which the life of the community would be directed by the Jews. Moreover Palestine meant both sides of the Jordan, and it was the duty of the British to open up all this territory to settlement. He called upon the Jews to repudiate the White Paper of 1922 and give up any attempt to appease the Arabs until a Jewish majority had been achieved.[10]

On August 15, 1929—a day sacred to the Jews, recalling the destruction of the Temple—the Revisionists held a demonstration which gave point to Arab fears. When the demonstrators demanded that the Jews should become owners of the Wailing Wall, many Arabs seem to have thought that the Zionists planned to seize the Mosque and its precincts too, that being the very site on which the Temple had stood. During a week of rising tension a Jewish boy was killed by an Arab and there was a further Zionist demonstration at his funeral. It was usual for villagers to flock into Jerusalem on Fridays, the Muslim holy day, for worship at the great Mosque. On Friday, August 23, they arrived with clubs, knives, and some firearms. After a mass meeting with the Mufti—

9. There is a valuable, detailed account of Jabotinsky's life (1880–1940) and the evolution of Revisionism in Laqueur, pp. 338–83. He had promoted the formation of Jewish fighting units in World War I, and resigned from the Zionist Executive in Palestine in 1923 in protest against Weizmann's policies of compromise. The Revisionists' goals and attitude are broadly indicated in the quotations from Jabotinsky below. Later, they were responsible for the terrorist fighting group, the Irgun Zvai Leumi. Their political heirs are the Herut Party of Israel. See in this connection Armajani, p. 378.
10. Sykes, pp. 134–35.

at which, however, nothing provocative seems to have been said—there were widespread Arab attacks on Jews in Jerusalem, as well as in Hebron, Jaffa, Haifa, and Safad, many of a most savage nature. Since the security forces, depleted as we saw under Plumer, were quite inadequate, more troops had to be summoned from Egypt and Malta, but they arrived too late to prevent the worst tragedy, up to that point, in the history of modern Palestine. Before order was restored, 133 Jews had been killed by Arabs, and 116 Arabs had been killed, almost entirely by soldiers and police. Many more were injured and there was widespread destruction and looting of Jewish property. Especially serious was the fact that for the first time the fear and hatred of the Arabs had fallen not just upon the Zionists but also on old-established Jewish religious groups with which they had long lived in peace and which had small sympathy for Zionism.[11]

The British Labour Government Enquires and Wavers

There followed a series of enquiries into, and pronouncements upon, these events. The variable judgements formed by the British could in part be explained by the replacement of the Conservatives by a Labour government in Britain, with different policies, shortly before the disturbances occurred. But they were chiefly due, as in the past, to the basically insoluble contradictions in Britain's Palestine commitments. In any event, they did little to reduce the tensions and resentments created—and this was another tragedy, for in the mid-1920s, when Jewish immigration was slack, as we saw, a sense of common interest between the two related races had been slowly awakening. Now Jews boycotted Arab enterprises, and in retaliation Jewish businesses were boycotted by the Arabs not only in Palestine but in the surrounding countries, which were their natural markets.

On the other hand the killings, while they bred hatred, also im-

11. See Hyamson, pp. 120–21. There is also a vivid account in Sykes, pp. 136–38. The religious occasion was the Fast of Ab.

pelled to fresh efforts those Jews who deplored the extent to which the extremists and many new immigrants had arrogantly ignored Arab susceptibilities and the reality of Arab national feeling. These Jews saw as the only just solution the formation of a bi-national state with equal rights for each people, whether a majority or a minority, on the general analogy of Switzerland, and a link between such a state and the neighbouring Arab countries. The group—*Brit Shalom*—was small and its goals have not been realized, but it had distinguished leaders such as Dr Judah Magnes, the American reform rabbi who became President of the Hebrew University, and the philosopher Martin Buber; and, as the *Ihud* (Union) Association, it continued to raise its voice in Israel. After 1929 Magnes urged the Zionists to renounce force and even the goal of a Jewish majority, provided that the Arabs would accept some continued Jewish immigration and settlement and the further development of Hebrew culture in Palestine. As the Ihud perceived it, to repay violence with force, to seek no agreement with the Arabs, would lead to perpetual strife (as it has done), and perhaps to the deterioration, even the ultimate ruin, of Zionism. But all this met with little response from Zionists embittered by the clash, and, for the reasons we have seen, virtually none from the Arab side.[12]

The Commission sent from London to investigate the outbreak[13] recommended that the Palestine Government should clearly state its policy, that pending an agricultural survey no more peasant pro-

12. See Laqueur, pp. 221–53. His chapter "The Unseen Question" (pp. 209–69) is a close and important analysis of this vital issue. It is sadly ironical that, after the Arab-Israeli war of 1967, certain leaders of the Palestinian Arabs should have declared their readiness to accept this idea of a bi-racial—or multi-racial—state when it is almost certainly too late for any such plan to have a chance of success. Unfortunately this is only the most recent example of a tendency on their part to disdain chances of compromise and practical advantage until the advantageous moment has passed.

13. Usually called the Shaw Commission, this had members from each of the three British political parties, Conservative, Liberal, and Labour, under the chairmanship of Sir Walter Shaw, a former Colonial Chief Justice. The full text will be found in *Report of the Commission on the Palestine Disturbances of August, 1929* (Cmd. 3530, 1930).

prietors should be evicted when their lands were sold, and that a League of Nations body should pronounce on the conflicting claims to the Wailing Wall. The Commission stressed further that the Zionist Organization—which had incidentally held its own enquiry strongly criticising the Palestine authorities—had no claim to share in the government, with which its relations should be more clearly defined. The troops sent for the emergency should be retained and the police organization overhauled. While no justification was found for the Arab attacks (though these were spontaneous and not previously planned) the Arab leaders were criticized—some for stirring up the troubles, others, including the Mufti, for not doing enough to prevent them. On the other hand, according to the Commission, Jewish land policy was leading to the creation of a landless and frustrated class, and Jewish immigration had at times exceeded the economic absorptive capacity of the country; "in normal times," however, the Arabs had benefited from Jewish enterprise and industrial activity.[14]

In the light of the Shaw Commission's report a further enquiry was set on foot into immigration and land purchase. When this second report was available the Labour Government published a third statement in the form of a White Paper defining its policy.[15] Although these three documents were attacked from both sides, the Zionists found them even more discouraging than did the Arabs. According to the second report, more and more Arab peasants were

14. Hyamson, p. 123.
15. The immigration and land purchase enquiry was entrusted to Sir John Hope-Simpson, a British official with Indian experiences, who had recently done well in the resettlement of over a million Greek refugees from Turkey. The White Paper of 1930, which in general adopted the recommendations in the Hope-Simpson report, is usually known as the Passfield White Paper after Lord Passfield (formerly Mr Sidney Webb) Colonial Secretary under the Labour Prime Minister, Ramsay Macdonald. Webb and his wife were distinguished socialist theoreticians and pioneers of the Fabian Society, which believed in the gradual attainment of socialism. They had small sympathy for Zionism, which they seem to have associated with Jewish large-scale capitalism. The full text of the White Paper will be found in *Palestine: Statement of Policy by His Majesty's Government in the United Kingdom* (Cmd. 3692, 1930).

approaching destitution as the existing amount of cultivable land became scarcer, by reason of high natural increase in the Arab population[16] and Jewish purchase of areas from which Arab labour was then excluded in order to build up a sturdy breed of Jewish agricultural and industrial pioneers. The solution recommended was government expenditure to make other land cultivable. Then proper provision could be made for the existing population, and considerable immigration could be allowed.

This proposition was accepted by the British Government. Its 1930 White Paper confirmed the salient points in that of 1922, and stressed that Britain's obligations towards the two races were of equal weight, and could be reconciled. Once again, London proposed to set up a Legislative Council on the lines previously planned. Pending the implementation of the Hope-Simpson scheme, Jewish settlement would be confined to land already owned by Jews, who had "a large reserve of land not yet settled or developed," although Jewish immigration would continue. But tenants (i.e., the Arabs) must be protected "by some form of occupancy right, or by other means, . . . against ejectment or the imposition of excessive rental."[17] One main objection of the Zionists was to Britain's stand on equal obligations, since they contended that Britain's obligation to the Zionists was the primary one and that to the Arabs secondary. Another was to Hope-Simpson's view that, even when his scheme was operating, there would hardly be room for more than another hundred thousand people in Palestine, and only part of this number would be Jews.

The Arabs were soothed temporarily by the White Paper. But when Jewish immigration continued unchecked they felt betrayed. They continued to press, without success, for an autonomous re-

16. "The population of Palestine on the British occupation was about 673,000, of whom less than 60,000 were Jews and the remainder, with few exceptions, Arabs" (Hyamson, p. 108). By 1946 there were 1,269,000 Arabs and 678,000 Jews in Palestine (Bailey in *Encyclopedia Britannica*, 1971, XVII, 171). The twofold increase in the Arabs was of course mainly by natural growth; the elevenfold increase in the Jews, mainly by immigration.

17. Cmd. 3692, pp. 18–19. See also Hyamson, pp. 125–26.

gime with an elected parliament and a government responsible to it, the abolition of the Declaration and Mandate, and a stop to further sales of Arab lands and Jewish immigration. But the Zionists, with their far readier access to sympathetic leaders of British public life, secured a letter from Prime Minister Ramsay Macdonald assuring them *inter alia* that the Balfour Declaration was an unchangeable principle of British policy, and in effect repudiating the White Paper. Dr Weizmann, who had resigned from the Presidency of the Zionist Organization, was stimulated to fresh activity. Mr Macdonald said nothing about the land development scheme or the Legislative Council. A financial crisis produced by the slump forced Britain to stall over providing funds for the land scheme, and it eventually lapsed. And no progress was made on the constitutional issue. If the Arabs had played their cards with skill and had accepted a Legislative Council of the kind proposed by the British at a time when they still had a dominant majority of the population, they could have placed the Zionists at a grave disadvantage. For the liberal principles proclaimed by most Zionists precluded them from rejecting this step toward democracy, whatever anxieties they felt. But the Arabs themselves relieved them of their anxiety. When invited by the British Government to discuss these matters with the Zionists at a Round Table conference, they refused—and thus lost another invaluable chance of influencing policy while they were still in the lead.[18]

The Last Spell of Uneasy Peace

After the Jerusalem Government had firmly enforced the League of Nations ruling on Muslim and Jewish rights in the Wailing Wall, this issue died down, and another spell of uneasy peace prevailed in Palestine when the next High Commissioner arrived at the end of 1931.[19] One reason for it was that, although agriculture was hard hit, an economic upturn had been felt there during one of the

18. Hyamson, pp. 126–28; Sykes, pp. 147–49.
19. General Sir Arthur Wauchope.

worst spells of the world depression, and this in turn may have been due partly to the expansion of the Jewish Agency. There was in any case considerable British and American Jewish investment in Palestine in the early 1930s, together with a revival of Jewish immigration that brought in fresh skills and wealth. Besides, the world was still at peace and Germany still a land of opportunity for the Jews. But the mood was sullen, positions had hardened since the riots, and both sides felt a sense of grievance.[20]

Before 1929, whatever the complaints, the British administration had on the whole been tacitly acceptable to both sides for, with all its failings, it was probably the best government Palestine had known in its history. But in the 1930s there was a growing tendency towards violence not only among the Arabs but among the Zionists too, as Hitler approached and conquered power; and under the threat of destruction the divisions among Jews became more and more acute. One further factor was to become highly significant in future. After the outbreak of 1921, the Palestine Government itself had facilitated sealed supplies of arms to outlying Jewish settlements for their defence in case of need. The Arabs were quick to see in this a move by the British government to arm the Jews to attack them.[21] Many of these arms had been withdrawn by the authorities while peace prevailed, but after 1929 some had been restored.

Of graver import for the future, the whole character of the Arab movement gradually changed as the Mufti became its leader. Jews and Christians in general had been traditionally acceptable to the Muslims as People of the Book; only the Zionist Jews had counted as the enemy. Now the Arabs were incited against the non-Muslims in the name of Islam. The core of the Mufti's simple and effective message seems to have been that this small Arab homeland was being overrun by infidel Jews in league with an infidel Christian government. The only remedy was a holy war. By invoking Islam, Haj Amin gained the sympathies of the whole Muslim world. More

20. Sykes, p. 150.
21. Hyamson, p. 128.

concretely, in 1933 he was able to inspire an Arab rising directed for the first time specifically against the British.[22] Yet for years the British had given Haj Amin the benefit of many doubts. His air of quiet and modest courtesy in dealing with them convinced many of them, until the evidence was too strong, that he must be a man of genuine moderation. But in retrospect many of the Arabs themselves see his policy of unyielding hatred as an evil influence upon their destiny.

The New Surge of Jewish Immigration

In the 1930s the Arabs had more concrete grounds for fearing the growth of Jewish power than any wild, extremist claims at the 1929 Zionist Congress. Between 1931 and 1935 Jewish immigration showed a steady and startling increase. In 1935 it was more than fifteen times as large as in 1931.[23] One powerful reason was Hitler's advent to power in January, 1933. The Zionists would have been less than human if, while doing all they could to help their fellow Jews they had not also sought to wrest the maximum political advantage from this tragedy. It gave, after all, new point and urgency to their central theme, that a National Home—or, as they hoped, a Jewish state—was a vital and immediate need. They could now argue that in justice the world owed this to the afflicted Jewish people; and that no "secondary" considerations, such as disrupting the lives of the Palestinian Arabs, should be allowed to interfere. The Arabs could—and did—retort that since the Jews had never suffered under Islam as they were now suffering in Europe, it was the Europeans who must solve this tragedy, not the Arabs, who had no guilt whatever in the matter. Why, they asked, should Britain and such countries take only a few thousand refugees apiece while the mass of them were thrust upon the Arabs of one small and backward land?

22. Sykes, pp. 155–56.
23. There were 4,075 Jewish immigrants in 1931; 9,550 in 1932; 30,327 in 1933; 42,359 in 1934; 61,854 in 1935. See Israel Cohen, *The Zionist Movement*, pp. 231 and 321.

One important aspect of the tragedy was indeed that the Western nations failed at this juncture—and later when the tragedy spread with Hitler's invasion of Eastern Europe—to organize a massive enough programme of resettlement of Jews on their own soil. This could have saved Palestine from a pressure of immigration that made nonsense of Britain's immigration policy—earlier agreed with the Zionist leaders—since it was far in excess of the country's economic capacity at the time. That the Western nations did not do so can be ascribed to the world economic crisis, to the threat and then outbreak of another world war and the desire to avoid further international complications, and above all to the skill of the Zionist Organization in making it appear that, because of this crisis, Palestine had become the only proper refuge for all persecuted Jews.

There was one further anomaly during the early years of Hitler. In the period 1932–35 only about one-eighth of the immigrants came from Germany, and nearly half were from Poland, as they had been in earlier times. This may have been in part because many German Jews felt a special affinity with the ordered, efficient, sophisticated Germany they had known, and were slow comers to Zionism; so that when they could leave Hitler's Germany (usually after forfeiting their wealth) their natural goal was the advanced countries where they could rebuild their lives in a world of familiar opportunity, rather than poor, arid, strife-torn Palestine. Another reason may well have been that "most of the Jews in Palestine were Slavs and, as the choice of immigrants was democratically controlled . . . , the Slav majority saw to it that Slav preponderance was not lost in the suddenly changed circumstances of the Nazi era."[24] In any event the tension and sense of provocation produced among the Arabs by the mounting wave of Jewish immigration were very real, however deplorable their actions during the next major outbreaks in 1933 and 1936 and the sporadic unrest continuing to the eve of World War II.

24. Sykes, p. 169. The predominance in Israel's post-independence leadership has also been Slav, and some feel that a similar urge to preserve this may be reflected in the Government's present concern to secure immigrants from Soviet Russia.

The Killings of 1933

The new bitterness between the two communities, and between them and the Government, frustrated the well-meant efforts of Palestine's new ruler, General Wauchope, a determined yet broad-minded and conciliatory soldier who in quieter times might have had real success. The Zionists seem to have been thankful that the plan for a Legislative Council, in which they would have been a minority, had been dropped—as it had, at the end of 1930, because of Arab intransigence. They were furious when Wauchope did his best to revive it; and the Arabs for their part decided to boycott the Jews in every field. In October 1933 a demonstration by Christian and Muslim Arabs in Jerusalem was broken up by the police, but it was soon followed by similar outbreaks, in Jaffa and other Arab centres, in the course of which twenty-five Arabs were killed.

This time no Jews were victims,[25] the Arabs having resolved that, since Zionist expansion in Palestine was essentially the work of Britain, the British must be their principal target of attack. If the British could be forced out, the Zionists could be destroyed. By now, however, the more extreme Zionists were also turning against the British—despite the fact that it was Britain who had conquered Palestine and paved the way for the creation of the Jewish National Home. This new anti-British trend was marked by the murder in April 1933 of the Socialist leader, Chaim Arlosoroff, then head of the political department of the Jewish Agency. He was generally believed to have been killed by the Revisionists, not just out of ideological hate but also because he was on excellent terms with the British, and had "a freedom from chauvinism and an abil-

25. Hyamson, p. 132. It is somewhat ironical that Wauchope should have been so unpopular with the Jews, since his policy was to approve as large a Jewish immigration as the country could possibly bear. But the Zionist leadership wanted considerably more, and illegal immigration became a marked feature of the period.

ity to see what is real and unalterable in Arab political aspirations."[26]

Labour Zionism

Jewish socialism of various schools had in fact become active in the Zionist movement soon after the original Zionist Congress of 1897, and by 1933, after many conflicts, it was becoming a dominant force in Zionism. It was to remain so in the state of Israel, through the *Histadrut* (General Federation of Jewish Labour), and *Mapai* (Israel Workers' Party), which has been the core of most Israeli Governments, and to some extent the more extreme *Mapam* (United Workers' Party), which however has tended to subordinate its Zionism to its socialism.[27]

Jewish socialism in Palestine had a rural as well as an urban and industrial base and evolved on somewhat unique lines. Since there was originally no Jewish proletariat there, jobs had to be created, and the Histadrut became a large-scale employer of labour as well as a defender of its rights. In agriculture there were collective and cooperative settlements (*Kibbutzim* and *Moshavim*), the first being essentially an enlarged version of the *Kvutzot*, small experiments in communal colonization started in 1910. The main feature of them all was that they managed their own affairs. With their extreme independence and individualism and their usually high standard of education, these Jewish workers had small patience with the normal system of managers, overseers, and daily wages. In these new types of Jewish settlement, operated by men and women

26. Before the murder there had been a campaign in the Revisionist press accusing Weizmann as well as Arlosoroff of being "traitors" and "despicable lackeys of the British"; see Laqueur, p. 319. Dr Weizmann had his own differences and difficulties with Labour Zionism, but both were condemned by the right-wing extremists. The quoted description of Arlosoroff is by Col. F. H. Kisch, a British-Jewish officer of great ability who was also prominent in the Zionist Executive, and was later killed in World War II; see Hyamson, p. 135.
27. Armajani, p. 378.

bred on theories of the sanctity of manual work, there was small room for Arab labour. To hire Arab workers—as had been done in some of the older colonies—would from their standpoint have been to compromise with the evils of capitalism and to ignore the vital task of training Jewish pioneers.

Labour Zionism was for years in conflict both with the "gradualism" and "practical Zionism" of Dr Weizmann and his followers, whom they affected to despise as "bourgeois Zionists,"[28] and with the semi-fascist agitation of the Revisionists, who wore brown shirts like Hitler's strong-arm men. The Revisionists declined politically after 1933, but their military wing, the *Irgun Zvai Leumi* (National Military Organization), split from the *Hagana*, the labour-dominated defence force, and was prominent in terrorism first against the Arabs and, in the later stages of the second world war, against the British. Meanwhile, the leadership of the rising labour movement fell more and more into the hands of David Ben Gurion, who joined the Jewish Agency Executive with other top socialists in this same year, 1933. Fifteen years later he was to become the first Prime Minister of Israel, while his elderly rival Chaim Weizmann, who had perhaps done more than any other one person to bring the new state about, was relegated to the powerless if distinguished functions of its President.

The Arab Rebellion

As we saw, a peak of Jewish immigration, both legal and illegal, was reached in 1935. Moreover, tension grew with the discovery of a large shipment of arms disguised as cement and consigned to a

28. The Socialists had been forced to resign from the Zionist Executive in 1927, and a somewhat unsuccessful attempt was then made to stimulate the recovery of the Zionist economy in Palestine by adopting sound traditional methods of finance in place of "socialist experimentation." This phase was known as the "Sacher regime," after one of Weizmann's trusted supporters in Britain, who was then on the Executive—Harry Sacher, a journalist, lawyer, and business man. See Laqueur, pp. 270–337, which gives a full account of the rise of left-wing Zionism.

Jewish agent. For the Arabs, another embittering factor was that such gains as the Legislative Council would have brought them in view of their larger numbers were lost when, early in 1936, the project was virtually dropped. Their leaders had once again put forward extreme demands and, when these were refused, had hesitated too long over discussing compromise proposals in London. For they realized that, if they agreed to them, they would have to accept also the Zionist goals of the Mandate. Moreover, the debates in the British Parliament at that time of torment for the Jews in Europe gave disturbingly little thought to the local agitation and darkening prospects of the Arabs. So once again hatred and violence grew.

In April 1936 sporadic attacks on the Jews developed into a country-wide Arab rebellion, mainly against the British, accompanied by a general strike lasting until mid-October. At the time of the double outbreak an Arab Higher Committee had been formed, representing the four Muslim and two Christian parties, under the Mufti of Jerusalem. The general strike had been launched by this Committee, but was eventually called off, in response partly to an appeal by the rulers of Iraq, Transjordan, Arabia, and the Yemen. But the Committee lost control of the rebellion to certain ruthless outside Arab elements—with which, however, there seems to have been collusion—while the increasingly unhappy Palestinian peasants bore the brunt of the fighting. The rebellion had been largely suppressed by the end of the year, but at the cost of some three hundred deaths and more than three times that number wounded.[29]

In November yet another British commission of enquiry—this time under Lord Peel, a former Secretary of State for India—had arrived to probe the causes and prospects for solution of a conflict which in its latest phase had spread from Palestine to the Arab world beyond. Since the start of the Mandate this world had itself changed in many ways. In various countries independent Arab sovereignty had become, or was becoming, a reality; and for the

29. See Sykes, pp. 178–87, and Hyamson, pp. 136–38.

Palestinian Arabs this trend threw into harsher relief their own contrasting lot. Not only were they deprived of self-determination; from their standpoint they were faced—by decision of the British Government—with the erosion of their stake in their own country in favor of predominantly European settlers of formidable drive and capacity.

The Arab World: Arabia, Iraq

In the Arabian Peninsula the most striking development had been the rise of Ibn Sa'ud of Nejd as ruler of nearly the whole area, which was thereafter known as Saudi Arabia. In 1924-25 the Saudi forces defeated those of the Hejaz and dethroned first King Husain and later his son Ali. Before that, Husain had failed to negotiate a treaty with the British after pressing for guarantees for the political and economic, as well as civil and religious, rights for Palestinian Arabs. He was also resented by his fellow Arabs for his tactless assumption of the Caliphate in March of 1924.[30] The rulers of Arabia had been completely independent since the collapse of Turkey, but in Iraq and elsewhere the attainment of sovereignty was a process of gradual relinquishment of control by the dominant Western power.

In Iraq the 1922 treaty of alliance with Britain was succeeded by three others negotiated by King Faisal, Husain's son, who successfully persuaded the British to relax their obsession with "safeguards," and the Iraqis to set some store by voluntary cooperation with Britain. The decisive treaty was that of 1930, by which the Mandate was abolished and Iraq, two years later, became a member of the League of Nations. There were provisions for mutual consultation, for Britain's use of certain Air Force bases, and for a British military mission to build up the Iraqi army. Despite criticism from both sides, the new treaty notably eased Britain's relations with the Arab world.

30. Antonius, pp. 331–36.

Egypt

The year 1936 was significant for Egypt as well as for Palestine, marked as it was by the conclusion, after many false starts, of an Anglo-Egyptian treaty to replace Britain's unilateral declaration of Egyptian sovereignty in 1922. The Wafd had been eclipsed for many years after General Stack's murder in 1924, the King's suspension of the 1923 constitution, and a spell of semi-dictatorship. But the King, for his own ends, had restored parliamentary government in December 1935, and the Wafd had been returned to power at the next elections. A few months later the Wafd's old adversary, Fuad I, died and was succeeded by his sixteen-year-old son, Farouk, the last king Egypt was destined to have. In the final anti-British demonstration before the Wafd was restored, the leader of the Cairo secondary school students was grazed by a bullet. This was Gamal Abdul Nasser,[31] who was to unseat King Farouk some sixteen years later, to introduce many badly-needed social reforms, to become the most vocal leader of the Arab world, and finally to eliminate British power from Egypt.

Meanwhile, the Wafd were happy to be back in power. They had gained in wisdom and lost in revolutionary ardour; and they saw another imperialist threat in Italy's designs upon northeast Africa.[32] They were now prepared to be relatively moderate towards Britain. The new treaty brought Egypt far closer to real independence. The Capitulations were abolished, Cairo secured full rights of jurisdiction and taxation over all residents, and also gained control over Egypt's security forces for the first time since 1882. Europeans in the police force were drastically cut.[33] In the army, now un-

31. Mansfield, pp. 258–63.
32. In 1935–36 the Italians, advancing from Eritrea, conquered Ethiopia and incorporated it into their northeast African possessions. This was done in defiance of the League of Nations and gave the Italians an extended and powerful position on the flank of the Sudan.
33. A British officer was retained as head of the Cairo police until 1946, chiefly because of his effectiveness in supressing narcotics, a traffic which had flourished under the Capitulations and had made addicts out of a quarter of the population.

der an Egyptian general, the officer corps ceased to be a preserve of the land-owning classes. As in the days of Arabi Pasha, men of modest origin were trained at the Military Academy; and one of these was Nasser. British troops were to be gradually withdrawn to the Suez Canal zone and Sinai, and limited in peace time to 10,000 land forces and 400 Air Force pilots. In the event of war— which was to come only three years later—the British could reoccupy the country, with full use of its communications. There were some British concessions in respect of the Sudan, though the Condominium remained and the question of sovereignty was shelved for the time being. The harsh measures of 1924 were abandoned. Egyptians could normally immigrate there freely. Egyptian troops would be used there once again, as would Egyptian officials when Sudanese were not available.

The treaty would expire after twenty years, in 1956. After that there would be a further alliance, but Cairo would then ask a third party to decide whether British troops in Egypt were still needed. Actually, as we shall see, by late 1956 British troops had been out of Egypt for two years, Nasser had seized the Suez Canal, and Britain's attempt to reoccupy it had been a fiasco.

Transjordan, Syria, Lebanon

After Britain's recognition of the Amir Abdullah as ruler of Transjordan in 1923, his position was further formalized, and a degree of semi-independence granted, by subsequent arrangements. A treaty of 1928 recognized the sovereign independence of the country on condition that its Government was constitutional. This treaty was ratified after acceptance by a Legislative Assembly, comparatively backward Transjordan having paradoxically acquired this weapon of democracy at a time when, for special reasons, it was denied to Palestine. In 1936 the Government became a Council of Ministers responsible to the Amir. After World War II Abdullah was to be formally proclaimed King, and the country, though still leaning heavily on its alliance with Britain, established normal relations with the outside world.

By 1927 France had suppressed the two-year rebellion in Syria. It had been even more costly and prolonged than the earlier Iraqi rising. From 1926 the French slowly grasped the need to come to terms with Arab nationalism, though they still clung to their authority as long and completely as they could. In that year the enlarged Lebanon was proclaimed a republic, as was Syria in 1930. Though there were many clashes over constitutional forms and rights, in the latter part of 1936 France concluded treaties with both countries on the general lines of the Anglo-Iraqi treaty of 1930. Both were to come into force in three years when Syria and Lebanon would become members of the League of Nations and the Mandate would lapse. By that time, unfortunately, World War II had broken out. Some of the fighting spread to the two republics; and there could be no progress towards real independence until the war was over. The final stages of emancipation were then marred by a sharp clash between the French and their British allies.

The Peel Commission

The Arabs of Palestine had been persuaded by Arab leaders elsewhere to call off their strike and trust Britain's intentions. Yet they boycotted the Peel Commission until the last moment, on the grounds that Jewish immigration had not been stopped. This was another grave mistake for, when the Arabs did appear, the Commission had already spent seven or eight weeks hearing British and Jewish evidence and only five days were left for that of the Palestinians. Some of the commissioners, however, also met the Amir Abdullah in Amman.

Despite these difficulties, the Peel Report is an impressive document of over four hundred pages, analyzing the sources of the conflict from the days of the Patriarchs, and conditions in Palestine from Turkish times through the years of the Mandate.[34] The Zionist case was skilfully presented, orally and in writing, by Weizmann, Ben Gurion, and others. They maintained that, in spite of all the violence, Jews and Arabs could live and work together; neither should dominate or be dominated by the other. The Zionists would accept the principle of parity. If and when there were a Legislative Council, they would never claim more than an equal number of members, whatever the future ratio between Arabs and Jews. Ben Gurion stressed that it was not their goal to make Palestine a Jewish state. On the other hand, they argued that peace could be attained only if the Mandate were interpreted at every point in accordance with the full Jewish claims. There must be no further restriction on Jewish immigration (to the full economic capacity of the country) or acquisition of Arab land. "No measures," they said, "must be taken to prevent the Jewish population from becoming in due course a majority in Palestine"; and, if and when this occurred, "no veto should be put on Palestine becoming a Jewish state, in the sense that the Jews would have a major voice in its government."

The Mufti, as spokesman for the Arabs, was no match for Weizmann's diplomatic skill. He quietly and tenaciously put the uncompromising arguments on the Arab side. As expected, however, the Commission would not agree that Palestine was included in the area of Arab independence promised by the British during World War I. Less predictably, it refused to accept in evidence the report of President Wilson's King-Crane Commission. One of the Mufti's colleagues asked how, if Germany with sixty million people found six hundred thousand Jews too much, the Arabs of Palestine could manage with four hundred thousand Jews in a land so small in area and population—they just could not be absorbed. When asked whether some would have to be removed, the Mufti replied that that must be left to the future. About that future he was pro-

34. Palestine Royal Commission, *Report* (Cmd. 5479, July 1937). A curious slip on p. 16 describes the Syrian Protestant College as becoming "Roberts" College (Robert College being in Istanbul) instead of the American University of Beirut.

phetic in another sense: he claimed that the influence of the Zionists was such that they would be able to do what they liked with Palestine, and perhaps bring the Mandate to an end.[35]

On the strength of such evidence and other facts emerging from their enquiry, the Peel Commission concluded that there was virtually no hope of the two communities' settling down together in harmony. Even an Arab-Jewish government based on cantonization[36] (a scheme favored by the Palestine administration) did not seem to them likely to work. The Commission proposed instead a plan abolishing the Mandate and splitting Palestine into an Arab state, a Jewish state, and an area remaining under British administration. It was virtually a counsel of despair, complicated and unsatisfactory in many respects, and of mainly historical interest, since it was never to be adopted.

The Jewish state would have included most of what is now northern Israel, and notably the coastal region from south of Tel Aviv to north of Acre, the valley of Esdraelon running southeast from Haifa, and Galilee. The Arab state would have covered most of the rest of Palestine, including the Negev, and would have been joined to Transjordan, as the hill regions west of the Jordan were in fact joined to the Kingdom of Jordan between 1948 and 1967. But the British would still have controlled an enclave covering Jerusalem, Bethlehem, and a corridor to the Mediterranean at Jaffa (although Jaffa itself would have been within the Arab state), as well as Haifa (the main port), Acre, Safad, Tiberias, and Nazareth—all within the Jewish state—of which Safad and Tiberias were of special sanctity to the Jews. Another city sacred to the Jews as well as Muslims—Hebron, with the tombs of the Patriarchs—would be in the Arab state. A further anomaly was that the Jewish

35. See Laqueur, pp. 514–16, the Peel Commission's Report, pp. 140–43, and Sykes, pp. 192–200. The quotation is from p. 143 of the Commission's report, and is at first sight a little hard to reconcile with Ben Gurion's disclaimer of any aim of making Palestine a Jewish state.

36. The plan entailed a constitution on the model of that of the Swiss Confederation, a multi-racial nation composed of various cantons, each with some autonomy, yet all accepting the authority of the federal government.

state with 258,000 Jews would also contain 225,000 Arabs, while the balance of the Jews would be in the Arab state or in the British areas. To remedy this the Commission proposed an exchange of population and land ownership. Yet another curious aspect of their plan was that the Jewish state would have held all the most fertile land, and for that reason it was supposed to pay a yearly subvention to the Arab state, enlarged by Transjordan, next door.

The Fate of Partition: Bloudan and Zurich

The Peel plan met with sharp criticism from many quarters and was gradually dropped. It was "contemptuously rejected by the Arabs."[37] The Palestinian Arabs held a conference soon after, at Bloudan near Damascus, with other representatives of the Arab world; and here once again the Declaration and Mandate, and any alienation of Palestine territory, were roundly condemned. The conference called for an independent Palestine with safeguards for minorities, on the basis of a treaty with Britain.

There was much feeling against partition amongst the Zionists as well, though Dr Weizmann was for a time strongly attracted by the imminent prospect of a Jewish state, however small. But he failed to secure even a conditional acceptance of the Peel plan by the Twentieth Zionist Congress at Zürich in August 1937.[38] All that was conceded was that the Jewish Agency's Executive should find out Britain's terms for establishing a Jewish state. If a definite scheme should emerge, it would have to be submitted to a new Congress for decision. Meanwhile, the publication of the Peel Report in July had been followed by further Arab violence, involving the murder of a British District Commissioner; it amounted to a revival of the rebellion and continued until 1939. The British re-

37. Laqueur, p. 518.
38. The author had the interesting duty, as British Chargé d'Affaires in Switzerland in 1937, of attending the formal opening session of this Congress on behalf of the British Government.

sponded by coercion and a measure of martial law. The Arab
Higher Committee was dissolved and those members caught were
deported. The Mufti was deprived of his non-religious functions.
Soon afterwards he fled to Lebanon, where he remained a powerful force behind the insurgents. In December 1937 the London
Government stated that it did not consider itself bound to a policy
of partition, and this amounted to a burial of the Peel scheme.

The Year of Appeasement

Nineteen thirty-eight acquired an ugly fame as the year of "appeasement" of Nazi Germany. In fact, Britain and France were
forced, as we saw, to gain time at the expense of weaker countries.
They had at all costs to gather strength for the decisive challenge
to Hitler in World War II, which started the following year.[39] As
this new war approached, Britain was also forced to take stock of
her position in the Middle East. This was to mean yet another
change in Britain's policies in the direction of concessions to the
Arabs as she perceived the full risk, not just to her imperial position
but to the future of the whole free world, should the Arab countries, exasperated by London's Zionist commitments, align themselves with her Axis foes. For there would have been small hope of
defeating Hitler and his allies if the whole Arab world, including
Egypt, Iraq, Syria, Morocco, and Algeria, had also fought upon
the Axis side. Britain's greater consideration for the Palestinians
and other Arab peoples was of course condemned by the Zionists as
appeasement of the Arabs at the cost of the Jews.[40] In the mood of
desperation born of Hitler's initial campaign to "cleanse" the German Reich of Jews, many were persuaded that the National Home
in Palestine was the one hope and solution for suffering Jewry. The

39. See Chapter 13.
40. It was argued that the revolt which in fact occurred in Iraq would have
been suppressed anyway and that the Arab rulers would not have come out
openly for the Axis unless and until Hitler's and Mussolini's victory had been
certain. See Laqueur, p. 524.

restrictions which Britain now sought to place upon its growth in what she judged to be the interests of fairness to, and good relations with, the Arabs of Palestine and elsewhere, seemed to them, as their vision narrowed to a passionate preoccupation with their own plight, to be an evil and totally unjustifiable conspiracy against the Jewish people. In a number of Zionists this conviction engendered towards Britain a deep hostility which largely erased any feelings of appreciation for her original efforts to promote the Return. This in turn was to lead to some acts of sinister violence against the British the memory of which has clouded Anglo-Zionist and Anglo-Israeli relations ever since.

Development of the Zionist Fighting Forces

The period of the Arab rebellion led to significant developments in the Zionist defence forces. Even before 1914 these had existed in embryo in the settlements in the shape of watchmen's associations. After the British occupation they had developed, as we saw, into the Hagana. By a masterpiece of British illogicality, this body had no legal status and was sometimes called a secret army (though everyone knew of its existence). Yet the right of the Jews to self-defence was tacitly recognized by the British, who intermittently provided the Zionist colonies with sealed supplies of arms. Illegal supplies were also secured, as were the elements of military training. But "with the outbreak of the Arab revolt in 1936 Hagana [became] a tightly organised and reasonably effective defence force . . . of thousands of part-time soldiers. . . . The command and the great majority . . . belonged to the labour movement. . . . Those opposed to labour Zionism opted for the *Irgun Zvai Leumi* which, following Jabotinsky's lead, had split away from the Hagana in the early 1930s. . . . The *kibbutzim* played a particularly significant part in Hagana, both as strategic strong points . . . and as bases for . . . training and . . . arms."[41] A further devel-

41. Laqueur, pp. 329–30.

opment of the Zionist armed forces (during World War II) was the *Palmach*, an elite corps—also of left-wing complexion and based on the Kibbutzim, and without uniforms or badges of rank—intended to become the nucleus of a standing army. The Palmach was to provide Israel with many senior army commanders when it and the other para-military groups had been dissolved and incorporated into the regular Israeli forces.[42]

In the earlier stages of the struggle with the Arabs the Hagana were induced by the Zionist leaders to confine themselves on the whole to the defensive. Later they became considerably more aggressive. The special training given to small Hagana groups by a British officer, Orde Wingate, who had become an enthusiastic pro-Zionist[43] contributed much to their self-confidence and professional skill. Since the Arab guerrillas operated usually at night, Wingate organized and commanded night squads for counter-operations manned mainly by Jews, though with some British officers and men. It was two thousands years since the Jews had displayed military prowess specifically in the cause of their own people, and their largely sedentary pursuits during the Diaspora had bred some self-doubt of their capacity in this brutal and basic activity. But the success of some of these operations showed the Jewish fighters to be equal to any in the world.[44]

Hitler's "Solution" of the Jewish Question

During the first five years of his rule Hitler's victimization of the Jews was a gradual process. While many were thrown into concentration camps for alleged offences, one of his main goals at that

42. *Ibid.*, p. 330.
43. Wingate, killed in World War II, was a cousin of Sir Reginald Wingate of the Sudan, where he had served. During the war he organized the Ethiopian partisans against the Italians and, as a Major-General on the Burma front, the "Chindits," special forces operating beyond the river Chindwin against the Japanese during their occupation of the country.
44. Sykes, pp. 219–22.

time seems to have been to drive them out of the country by depriving them of status and livelihood. The pressure was drastically stepped up in November of 1938. During the so-called *Kristallnacht*, most synagogues were burned, there were mass arrests, and a huge collective fine was imposed on them. From this time onward, the Jews of Germany became virtually outlaws, and yet it was not until January 1942, more than two years after the beginning of the war, that Hitler decided "finally to solve the Jewish question." The Nazis carried out his orders by massacring all the Jews they could in Continental Europe, which, from Norway to Greece, and the French Channel coast to central Russia, was by then largely under Hitler's domination. Nearly six million Jews are reckoned to have perished before the Allies finally stopped the most massive and systematic slaughter in history.[45]

In the last two years before the war, either absorption into the Reich or Hitler's pressure and example had infected Germany's neighbours in Central and Eastern Europe, and smoothed the path for these colossal crimes. "The process of eliminating Jews from German society and economic life, which had taken five years . . . , was telescoped into as many weeks in Vienna and Prague." In Roumania the Jews were told that half of them would have to leave; in Hungary three hundred thousand were to lose their jobs. In Poland, where there were three million Jews out of thirty million people, "it was the declared policy of successive Polish governments to make the position of Polish Jewry intolerable and compel them to emigrate."[46] Even Italy, where anti-Semitism was an alien growth, was induced to promulgate anti-Jewish laws, though their application was a good deal milder at that time than elsewhere in the Nazi orbit.[47]

45. The Jews were not the only victims. Attempts were also made to exterminate the gypsies and people of other supposedly "inferior races."
46. Laqueur, pp. 505–6.
47. The author was told this by Georg Szell, former Musical Director of the German Theatre in Prague and later famous as Conductor of the Cleveland Symphony Orchestra in America, who was living in Italy at the time.

The Evian Conference

In July 1938, a conference of thirty-one nations met on President the refugees in Western Europe fell victims once again when Hit-Roosevelt's initiative at Evian in France to seek a solution to the threat overhanging Hitler's victims through emigration to countries beyond his grip. Represented, in addition to the United States, were the nations of Latin America, Canada, Australia, New Zealand, and Britain, the Scandinavian countries, Holland and Belgium, France, Ireland, and Switzerland. Britain had asked that Palestine should not be discussed, and that Weizmann should not be allowed to speak. In their new concern with the coming war, the British were, rightly or wrongly, determined to avoid what they saw as the impending flooding of Palestine with Jewish refugees far in excess of the number the land could absorb without provoking fresh and dangerous conflicts with the Arabs of Palestine and elsewhere.[48] Moreover, there was still scope and time for saving and resettling in better material conditions than in Palestine hundreds of thousands of Jews—perhaps all who would have been able and willing to leave Central and Eastern Europe in the last year before the war—if real generosity and imagination had prevailed and if America and Britain had taken a firm and creative lead. What mostly prevailed was narrow self-interest.

The conference failed, and those who might have been saved were doomed. In the three years 1938-40 the United States took about 100,000 Jews (a little more than the normal U.S. immigration quota for Germany). Britain took 65,000 Jewish refugees in the whole ten years 1933–43. Palestine being within the British orbit, London was reluctant to take more for fear that this would increase Jewish pressure on Palestine. The tiny Dominican Republic

tr-p 324

48. In these years the immigration issue had of course become highly political. It had ceased to be simply a question of the economic absorptive capacity of Palestine, which, as the Peel Report (p. 85, para. 82) conceded, had been increased by the high rate of Jewish immigration in 1934 and 1935. See in this connection Laqueur, pp. 508–9.

offered to take 100,000. But Australia took only 15,000, and Canada very few; South Africa barred all but close relations of Jews already there. The Western European nations were more generous in proportion to their size. France took 35,000; Belgium, 25,000; Holland, 20,000. But all this was a drop in the ocean; and most of ler's armies conquered it in 1940. By some accounts the Zionist leaders were not too keen for the conference to succeed. For there would have been less vital urgency about building up the National Home if the bulk of the refugees had managed to settle elsewhere. The Home would no longer have been—as they were convinced it should be—the main beacon of hope and safety for the afflicted Jews.[49]

The Round Table Conference

The British Government's provisional abandonment of the Peel partition scheme in December 1937 became more definite a year later. A technical commission appointed to study the matter produced an inconclusive and discouraging report,[50] in which it was proposed that the area for the Jewish state should be greatly reduced from that proposed by Peel. Meanwhile, in October 1938 the Arab and Muslim countries had held an inter-parliamentary congress in Cairo "for the defence of Palestine." This was a weightier affair than the meeting at Bloudan and one that seemed to Britain—increasingly concerned with the balance of forces in the coming war—to hold a more serious threat of Arab-Axis collaboration. At this juncture the London Cabinet decided to try to bring about some Arab-Zionist compromise through a Round Table conference in London. A conference of sorts met in February and March of 1939, and it included not only the Palestinian Arabs, but also delegates from Egypt, Iraq, Saudi Arabia, and Transjordan. On the Jewish side, non-Zionist as well as Zionist leaders were invited,

49. Sykes, pp. 223–29. See also Laqueur, pp. 507–8.
50. Known as the Woodhead Report, from the name of the Chairman of the Commission, Sir John Woodhead.

some of them from Europe and the United States. But it was really two separate conferences, since the Palestinian Arabs refused to meet or sit round a table with the Jewish delegates, and, apart from two informal meetings between the Jews and the Egyptians, Iraqis, and Saudi Arabians, such contact of ideas and plans as existed was the work of British and other intermediaries. The meeting failed to bridge the gulf between two standpoints implacably opposed.

For the Arabs, the cause of the strife was the deep attachment of the peasants to their soil and culture. The rebellion had been essentially a revolt of villagers against schemes envisaging their displacement "to make room for the immigrant citizens of the proposed Jewish state." The peasants blamed the Arab landowners who had sold their land and agreed to their displacement, as much as Britain, under whose aegis all this was done. While the economic development produced by Jewish capital and initiative had enriched Arab landowners and middlemen, for the Arab masses the rise in wages was offset by that in the cost of living, so that their economic position was scarcely better (if no worse) than it had been for generations.

In the early years of the Mandate the Arabs had resented being denied their independence. Now it was a question of self-preservation. The wave of Jewish immigration in the mid-1930s had raised the spectre of a Jewish majority. The partition proposals had "translated Arab fears of eventual dispossession into a certainty." There was no room for a second nation in a country already inhabited by people whose national consciousness was strong and real. A Jewish state could be established only by dislodging the peasantry, and the peasants would fight rather than give up their land. But if Palestine became an Arab state, the Jews could be assured of having "a national home in the spiritual and cultural sense, in which Jewish values could flourish, and the Jewish genius have the freest play to seek inspiration in the land of its ancient connection." Meanwhile, to place the burden of Hitler's outrages upon Arab Palestine was a miserable evasion of the duty of the civilized world, for nothing could justify the persecution of one people to relieve the persecution of another.[50a]

The Arab fears were indeed borne out by subsequent events. But the Zionists pointed to the world's guarantee of their rights in Palestine,[51] and to the fact that the National Home, so far as it had been created, was the only spot on the globe to which, at a moment of horror and disaster, the Jews could go with a claim to be made welcome. For at that juncture they felt even more helpless and isolated than the Palestinian Arabs, who at least had ostensibly strong support from their Arab neighbours.

In October 1938, in consequence of "appeasement," Hitler annexed the predominantly German areas of Czechoslovakia. Then in March 1939, while the London Round Table conference was still in session, he took over the rest of the country and reduced it to a protectorate. The Nazis and the Italian Fascists were pro-Arab, and the Mufti was later to broadcast from Berlin against both Britain and the National Home. Soviet Russia and its satellite Communist parties were also for the Arabs even in this early phase. The Jews above all felt that Britain was betraying her promises and obligations to them. How could Britain sacrifice them at a moment of life and death and after the "miserable evasions" of Evian? Yet after the Woodhead Report they knew that there would be no Jewish state in Palestine based on partition, since no such state could be devised which would be large enough to allow for the new Jewish immigration at the rate its leaders might decide. Most Zionists had anyway been unhappy about partition. On the other hand, they were determined not to accept the permanent minority

---

50a. Antonius, pp. 406–12. The above is the gist of the concluding passages of a work usually judged to be the best presentation of the Arab position. It had been published shortly before the Round Table Conference, at which Antonius, formerly in the Palestine Government, was an adviser to the Arab delegates. Its inclusion of the McMahon-Husain correspondence seems to have prompted the British Government also to publish this correspondence for the first time. See Sykes, p. 234.

51. This of course referred to approval of the Mandate by the League of Nations, backed by the United States.

status implicit in an Arab state with guarantees for the Jews, or a bi-national state with shared government, as proposed by some of the non-Palestinian Arabs. The Zionists had gone to the London conference after assurances by the British Colonial Secretary[52] that Britain was still bound by the Balfour Declaration and the Mandate, that she did not contemplate an Arab state, and that she would not stop Jewish immigration. They also put some faith in direct contact with the Arabs. Ben Gurion, for all his strong nationalism, hoped that something useful might emerge from such contacts; if the Arabs would only accept the right of the Jews to immigrate, they might agree to a Jewish state within an Arab federation[53]—an idea Sir Herbert Samuel had backed when criticizing the Peel Report.

But all these hopes were dashed, and the conference broke down. Britain had warned both sides that if this should happen, she would impose her own solution. The British solution took the form of yet another White Paper, that of May 1939,[54] regarded by the Zionists as a repudiation of the Declaration and Mandate. Britain did not of course see it as that, and "repudiation" was hardly just or accurate. But the White Paper did suggest that the National Home was an accomplished fact, and impose certain limitations on its expansion—limitations that implied leaving the Jews a permanent minority in the country. It betokened in any event yet another change of course in Britain's policy, and one which went some way towards meeting the Arabs on those issues they most bitterly resented.

This extremely concise White Paper—of twelve pages—envisaged the creation of an independent bi-national State of Palestine in ten years, in treaty relations with Britain that would provide guarantees for the Holy Places, foreign interests, and British strategic needs. It reckoned the Jewish population at the time as 450,000 or "approaching a third of the entire population," and provided for

52. Then Malcolm MacDonald, son of the former Prime Minister, Ramsay MacDonald.
53. See Laqueur, pp. 523–25.
54. *Palestine: Statement of Policy* (Cmd. 6019, 1939).

the immigration of 75,000 more Jews over five years so as to bring the Jewish proportion up to one-third. "As a contribution towards the solution of the Jewish refugee problem," twenty-five thousand would be admitted as soon as the authorities were satisfied that the newcomers could be maintained, and ten thousand a year during the five years. Illegal immigrants would be deducted from the annual quota. In the terms of the White Paper after these five years the British "would not be justified in facilitating, nor would they be under any obligation to facilitate the further development of the Jewish National Home by immigration regardless of the wishes of the Arab population." So later Jewish immigration would be subject to Arab agreement.[55]

Further transfer of Arab land in certain areas would also have to be stopped, since there was "no room" for such transactions. In other areas transfers would have to be restricted if Arab peasants were to keep their present standard of life and if many were not to become landless. In a third area land purchases could be freely made. The British High Commissioner would have powers to regulate or prohibit such transfers, but the British would retain authority only during a transitional period.[56] They would be prepared immediately to put Palestinians in charge of certain government departments, with British advisers, and these Palestinians would sit on the High Commissioner's Executive Council, i.e., the Government of Palestine. Arab and Jewish representatives would be asked to serve roughly in proportion to the size of their population. All branches of government would increasingly be placed under Palestinians carrying out the administrative and advisory functions of the former British officials. They might then acquire Ministerial status, and the Executive Council would become a Council of Ministers.[57] An elected Legislative Council might be established later, should public opinion favour this. After five years an Anglo-Palestinian

55. Cmd. 6019, pp. 5, 10, 11.
56. *Ibid.*, pp. 11–12.
57. As we saw, this had occurred in Transjordan several years earlier.

body would review the working of these arrangements and consider what should be the constitution of independent Palestine.[58]

In spite of the concessions to their standpoint, this last plan was at first rejected by the Arabs as well as by the Zionists. But as the Arab statesmen from neighbouring countries obtained some influence over them, these Palestinian Arabs became more reasonable. Indeed the new British plan, with minor modifications, was accepted by their moderate party before the White Paper was published.[59] Whatever its vices, the plan does seem to have achieved one important goal, which was to minimize Arab hostility and subversion against Britain in a war in which she—and Palestine—came close to destruction. It reduced the sway of extremist Arab agitators and helped to ensure fairly tranquil bases for British troops in Egypt and Palestine at the most critical period of the war. Indeed the 1941 revolt of Rashid Ali in Iraq might have led to an enemy takeover there and in Syria had Britain's new policy of adjustment to Arab claims and susceptibilities not given encouragement to the pro-British elements in both countries at this stage.[60]

For their part the Zionists were bitterly hostile; and the White Paper seems ultimately to have killed Anglo-Zionist cooperation in the peaceful development of the National Home. They saw the ending of the Mandate and the proposed establishment of an independent Palestine as a cowardly and cynical surrender to their adversaries. For in the Zionist view the Arabs would continue to regard Palestine, even if it were nominally bi-national, as essentially an Arab state, and would seek to dominate it. The Arabs could hope to do so because Britain was determined to keep the Jews a permanent minority and thus thrust them into a new ghetto. They would not even become 40 per cent of the population, as Lord Samuel had at one point proposed—this had been whittled down to one-third. And Britain had ignored Dr Weizmann's plea

58. Cmd. 6019, pp. 6–7.
59. Hyamson, p. 145.
60. Sykes, pp. 239–40.

for parity and non-domination of one race by the other. Since the Jews had been penalised for Arab rebellion and bloodshed, Ben Gurion urged them to show their own nuisance value; Britain would have to use force against them. Hence, sabotage by the Hagana, violation of the restrictive laws, and stepped-up military training for Jewish youth.[61]

For all Dr Weizmann's talk of parity, it was becoming clear that the Balfour Declaration, which they had accepted, fell far short of the Zionists' ultimate goal. It had promised them *a* National Home *in* Palestine—not, as they had hoped, that Palestine would be *the* Jewish National Home.[62] What the Zionists had attained by 1939–40 could in fact be called *a* National Home *in* Palestine, and the British were taking advantage of the fact. In twenty years the Jewish community had grown from a small fraction to a third of the total population and was in many respects dominant in the country's economic and cultural life, with its own autonomous institutions. Under the White Paper a solid share was reserved for it in the over-all government of the country; and the Jews would in fact have dominated this government also, by reason of their exceptional gifts, even if Palestine had continued to have an Arab majority. Yet all this would not be—as the Zionists were determined it ultimately should be—a Jewish state in a land that was, or might become, "as Jewish as England is English."

Inevitably, however, when Hitler's armies invaded Poland in September 1, 1939, everything acquired a new dimension. The Jews in Palestine and elsewhere had no choice but to fight with Britain against the greatest enemy their race and European civilization had ever known. With one exception,[63] the Jewish armed groups in

61. Laqueur, pp. 529–31; see also Sykes, pp. 235–41.
62. For the first, Zionist, drafts of the Declaration referring to Palestine as *the* National Home of the Jewish people, and submitted to Balfour in July, 1917, see Stein, pp. 462–72. See also Weizmann, p. 256. These drafts made no mention of the non-Jewish majority in Palestine.
63. Jabotinsky had promised that Irgun, and Jews generally, would join the war effort against the Axis and forget their grievances against the British "for the duration," a promise Irgun later broke. In any event a minority in Irgun,

Palestine—even the Irgun Zvai Leumi—dropped their sabotage and terrorist activities and, while the war was still in the balance, joined forces with the British. The Jews, Ben Gurion said, would fight the White Paper as if there were no war; and they would fight the war as if there were no White Paper.[64]

headed by Abraham Stern, rejected this, believing that imperialist Britain was the enemy (see Chapter 13, n. 2). Later he favored the Soviet Union and the liberation of the whole Middle East from the imperialist yoke. His group, officially called *Lehi* (Israel Freedom Fighters) were known to their opponents as the Stern Group or Gang. They murdered Lord Moyne, British Minister of State in the Middle East, in Cairo in November 1944. On both these bodies see Laqueur, pp. 374–78.

64. Armajani, p. 323.

Chapter **13** The Second World War
and After

In the earlier chapters we have seen how in the first world war a series of complex events and fateful British moves in the eastern Mediterranean and the Middle East sowed the seeds of the Arab-Israeli conflict in its present form. By 1939, when the second world war broke out, the issues at stake had become clearly defined and sharply contested. Yet, throughout this new struggle and for some three years after it, no one could tell just what the final shape of Palestine would be. From the start of the war the country had some years of uneasy calm. The Allied campaigns against the Germans and Italians, which spread to Egypt and Syria, never reached Palestine, though at times they threatened to do so. The Arabs halted their revolt on the strength of a White Paper that went some way —though from their standpoint not far enough—to meet their views. They resumed cooperation with the British authorities and for the time being lived in peace with the Jews. The local conflict between the two communities was temporarily eclipsed by the larger struggle.

For their part the Zionists were in conflict among themselves. They were determined to fight the White Paper, which they regarded as illegal since the Permanent Mandates Commission of the League of Nations held that it was not in accordance with the Mandate.[1] In the first years they fought it by all means in their power short of armed contest with the British.[2] Yet, as London had foreseen, they had no choice but to join forces with Britain and her allies so long as Hitler was triumphant. For his ultimate victory would have meant not only the total destruction of the Jewish communities in Europe but also the fall of Palestine and the end of the National Home. Once the defeat of the Nazis seemed assured, however, the clash with Britain in Palestine took a more violent form despite the dangerous disruption of the still vital war effort that this involved. Meanwhile, in the first phase of the war, Palestine, which had weathered the world depression, was hit by a disastrous slump. There was small demand for her citrus fruit and other products, and, by the end of 1939, half the workers in her infant industries were unemployed. But some prosperity returned when the country became a major allied military base.

The Palestine War Effort

On the eve of the war, Dr Weizmann assured Prime Minister Chamberlain that the Jews stood by Britain and the democracies. Jewish manpower, technical ability, and resources would, he said, be put under Britain's coordinating direction. Their political differences would give way before the pressing needs of the time. This

1. This decision was unanimous. When asked whether their interpretation might be so revised as to accept the policy of the White Paper, the Commission turned this down also, though by a close vote (4 to 3). At the same time the Commission could not veto the proposals of a mandatory government; it could only advise the Council of the League. After the outbreak of war the Council did not meet, and London therefore held that the White Paper was legally in force. See Sykes, p. 259.
2. The exception was the Stern Group. "Abraham Stern, for years one of the central figures in the Irgun, . . . believed that Britain, not Germany and Italy, was the main enemy. Consequently he refused to stop the fight against the mandatory power." See Laqueur, p. 376. Irgun itself, however, refrained from armed attack against the British until 1944, when it allied itself with the Stern forces.

of course left open the conflict over the White Paper, but the Zionists seem to have hoped that these assurances might induce Britain either to modify it or postpone enacting it. In this they were disappointed. The mandatory could not and did not implement the constitutional provisions of the Paper during the war; but it did its best strictly to enforce the restrictions on land transfers and immigration—though with very qualified success, due to Zionist resistance and evasion.

In spite of this continuing tension, 136,000 young Jews volunteered for the war effort, and by late summer of 1944 there were 23,500 Palestinian Jews in the British defence forces,[3] their hope being to form a Jewish army under British command and thus revenge themselves on the Nazis under their own colours. At the same time the Zionists reckoned with the value of a well-trained, battle-toughened fighting force to promote the fortunes of the National Home in the years of decision after the war, and perhaps to force the issue and become the nucleus of a national army if and when the chance should occur of converting the Home into a Jewish state. The scheme got off to a fair start, with the blessing of Winston Churchill, after he became Prime Minister in 1940, and of some of Britain's top military leaders. Dr Weizmann was officially informed in September 1940 that the British Government had decided to organize and train such an army, which "to begin with" would be 10,000 strong, including 4,000 from Palestine.

This was at the start of the Battle of Britain, a moment of dramatic urgency in which the survival of the whole Allied cause— indeed of Western civilization itself—was at stake.[4] But after the

3. For the first figure see Laqueur, p. 535; for the second, Israel Cohen, p. 282.

4. This battle was an all-out attack on Britain by the German Air Force, to prepare the way for the invasion of the British Isles and a victorious end to the war in 1940, since, from the fall of France in June 1940 until the Nazi invasion of Russia in June 1941, Britain remained the only major power fighting Hitler. The battle began in early August and lasted until the end of October 1940, when the *Luftwaffe* was forced to abandon further massive attacks for the time being. It is usually reckoned as one of the most decisive battles of history.

main crisis passed, the plan bogged down in local obstruction and delays, caused partly by the genuine difficulty of finding the necessary equipment for such an army at a time of multiple military commitments, and partly by the Palestine Government's understandable concern over the future intentions of the Jewish army and Arab reactions to the placing of so powerful a weapon in their adversaries' hands. In 1941 it fell to the British Colonial Secretary, Lord Moyne, to tell Dr Weizmann of these delays. The Zionists seem to have assumed that Moyne was in some way responsible for Britain dragging her feet; and, although this was without foundation, it was to have tragic consequences for him later. In the end a special Jewish force was not set up until 1944; then all that was permitted was a Brigade Group—not even a division—and, by the time it was in combat, only a few weeks of the war against Hitler remained.

The long frustration which this scheme had met helped further to sour relations between the Zionists and the mandatory power. From the beginning these relations had been uneasy, and from 1939 the Zionists never forgave the British for their belated attempt in the White Paper to do at least partial justice—as Britain saw it —to the Arab side.[5] For their part "the Arabs came to regard the White Paper as a right acquired not only by the Palestinians but by the Arab world in general, of which Palestine was a small but essential part. . . . Though Palestine's status as an independent state had not been formally manifested, this should not debar the country from taking part in the counsels of [the independent] Arab states."[6] In the later stages of the war this general concern of the Arab states for Palestine—which remains to this day Israel's most crucial problem—was to be given formal status and substance by the formation of the Arab League. Meanwhile, at the start of the war, the Palestine Government was concerned to restrict expansion of the Zionist stake in Palestine in the spirit and intention of the White Paper. Even the Hagana came under attack, although this

5. See Sykes, pp. 246–55.
6. Nevill Barbour, *Nisi Dominus*, p. 208.

force had been tacitly recognized by the British authorities for years. There were seizures of arms and the arrest late in 1939 of forty-three of its officers, including Moshe Dayan (later the famous Israeli general and Minister for Defence). Long prison sentences were imposed that were not quashed until more than a year later.[7]

All this did not mean that the Palestinian war effort was in any sense ineffective. Another reason for the delays over the Jewish army had been the ingenuous faith of many British (itself a source of the White Paper) that Arabs and Jews working together for what had become their common country would form a basis for cooperation and mutual respect, a common Palestine loyalty, the embryo of a national consensus. To that end, in September 1940, a Palestine force was formed by adding a Palestinian battalion to a British regiment. While each company was supposed to be half Arab and half Jewish, in fact, Jews predominated over Arabs largely because they felt themselves far more vitally concerned with the war against Hitler than the Arabs, and were consequently subject to strong pressure from their community to enlist in what remained a voluntary force. In practice these Jewish-Arab companies worked surprisingly well within the disciplined framework of an essentially British military system. The force was expanded to fourteen companies instead of the traditional eight and in 1942 was renamed the Palestine Regiment. It was the nearest approach to a Jewish-Palestinian force permitted to them pending the ultimate constitution of the Jewish Brigade. In it the Jews gave of their best, but they also gave excellent service in the various British fighting forces they had joined as individuals.[8] Unfortunately, whatever Arab-

7. Laqueur, p. 535.
8. Dayan, for example, lost an eye while serving with the British forces in Syria against the Vichy French, i.e., the French authorities in Syria and Lebanon controlled by the Government set up at Vichy in central France by those French elements who accepted France's defeat in 1940 and were prepared in effect to take their orders from the Germans. They were led by Marshal Pétain and were strongly hostile to the Free French, who continued to fight the Germans under General de Gaulle, formerly one of Pétain's officers. The Free French fought with the British in this campaign and took over Syria and Lebanon after the defeat of the Vichy forces.

Jewish collaboration existed on a day-to-day basis in military and other fields did nothing to narrow what seemed to be an unbridgeable political gulf between the two communities. This dissension persisted in its most acute form over land transfers and immigration.

Land Transfer

Land transfer regulations were issued under the White Paper in February 1940. On this question as well as immigration the mandatory "showed no willingness to adjust [the White Paper policies] in the light of the tragic fate of European Jewry." Jewish purchase of land was barred in nearly two-thirds of Palestine, and restricted in nearly one-third. Only in 5 per cent of the country—largely in the areas where Jews were already closely settled—could they buy land as they wished. Not even ground officially classed as uncultivable was exempt from these restrictions. Zionists contended that Jews were being virtually confined to a new Pale of Settlement as in Russian Poland, and there were violent anti-government demonstrations. More might have been made of this issue had not the organizations responsible for Jewish settlement, such as the *Keren Kayemeth*, managed to get round the regulations in collusion with individual Arabs willing to sell. Between 1940 and 1947 they thus nearly doubled their Palestine land-holdings, in great part with land acquired outside the "free" area.[9] The Government's measures against illegal immigration, widely evaded though they were, caused far more bitter feeling among the Zionists.

Immigration

Passions have long run high over this complex and tragic issue. So tellingly has it been presented by writers and news media favourable to the Zionist cause, that Britain has emerged in the blackest colours as the evil and ruthless villain of the piece. It would perhaps be

9. See Laqueur, pp. 534–35; Sykes, pp. 258–59.

nearer the truth to say that, in carrying out the policies of the White Paper judged necessary to minimize hostile wartime reactions from the Arab states, London and Jerusalem often showed, like all Governments, a bureaucratic rigidity and a lack of sensitivity, flexibility, and imagination which had no place in coping with the huge European-Jewish disaster. Illegal immigration flourished in spite of everything. The Zionists maintained that it was legal, since the White Paper had been rejected by the Permanent Mandates Commission—indeed, they now considered unlimited immigration to be justified quite independently of the economic absorptive capacity of Palestine as judged by the British authorities. As we saw, however, London held the Paper to be legal, since it had not been condemned by the League Council, and accordingly deducted the number of illegal immigrants from the legal quota. Thus in 1944, at the end of the five-year period after which Jewish immigration was to cease except with Arab consent, only some two-thirds of the promised 75,000 regular immigration permits had been issued; and this inevitably became another grievance.

A further complication was the fact that, from the years before the war until 1942, enforced Jewish emigration to Palestine from Germany and the German-dominated countries of Central and Eastern Europe was largely organized—in shocking conditions of discomfort and danger—by the Nazis themselves, who provided their victims with forged Palestine permits found to be worthless on arrival. The British naturally suspected that their foes were using this convenient channel to send in spies and agents disguised as Jewish refugees, and this increased their determination not to admit those illegal arrivals whom they were able to catch and detain, though a few, such as the sick, pregnant women, and orphan children were often allowed in, and a number inevitably slipped through their fingers.

In a deplorably rigid interpretation of these rules in March and April 1939, when the enormity of Nazi crimes against the Jews was still not accurately known, three ships which arrived from the Danube with illegal refugees were ordered by the Palestine authorities to return to their port of embarkation, despite the risk that their passengers might again fall into Nazi hands. This caused a storm in the British Parliament and, despite allegations to the contrary, no substantial cases of this kind seem to have recurred.[10] The incident happened nearly five months before the war broke out, and from then on Britain adopted a different policy towards the refugees. Those without permits were kept out of Palestine whenever possible, but provision was made for them elsewhere in British territory, such as Cyprus and Mauritius. While, for Hitler's victims such places were no substitute for Palestine, neither was a land of hardship. Whatever their protests and disappointments, the refugees knew that these were but temporary halts and that every option could be open for them and their people after the war. Meanwhile they were free from Nazi persecution—or indeed any other.

The new British policy did not prevent some appalling disasters. Yet only a share of blame for them can be laid at Britain's door. In November 1940 the British intercepted and brought into Haifa two unseaworthy ships loaded with refugees; a third arrived soon after. Since those aboard had no valid permits, they were not allowed to land. The British commandeered a French liner, *La Patria*, to take all three shiploads to Mauritius. The Jewish Agency, through Hagana men, arranged to wreck the ship's engines. Too much explosive was used, and the ship itself was wrecked and sank with the loss of 250 lives. The Jewish Agency then announced that the sinking was an act of mass suicide designed as a protest against British inhumanity. The odium for a tragedy caused by their own misjudgement was thus skilfully cast upon the Palestine Government, despite the fact that most of the survivors of the disaster were allowed to remain.[11]

Another heart-rending event, amongst others less known, became notorious a year later. The *Struma*, with more refugees, reached Istanbul from Constanza in Roumania. The Turks ordered

10. Sykes, pp. 265–66.
11. Sykes, pp. 267–70; Laqueur, p. 535.

the ship back on hearing, only after two months, that its passengers would not be admitted to Palestine or taken elsewhere. Here both the British and the Jewish Agency were guilty of inhuman rigidity and delays. The British might have relented over permits for Palestine for all concerned, and eventually did so—but too late —for the children between eleven and sixteen on board. The Agency, instead of insisting that these people should be sent nowhere but Palestine, could have agreed to their transfer to Cyprus or Mauritius and thus, in the event, saved their lives. Better still, the Palestine Government could have taken its own decision about transfer without deferring to the Jewish Agency. Again, the Turks could have given these unhappy human beings at least war-time refuge in their own uncrowded country, where so many Jews had settled in tolerable conditions in the past. Finally, however, and before arrangements could be completed for the children's admission to Palestine, the Turks had the ship towed into the Black Sea, where she sank after an explosion and nearly all were lost.[12] Once more, in an involved case of multiple responsibilities, Britain found herself saddled in Zionist publicity with the entire blame.

In the following year, 1942, the dimension of tragedy within Europe vastly increased. The Nazis were then at the height of their power, with most of the Continent, including western Russia, in their grip. They were no longer content to harass and expel the Jews; now they adopted a policy of mass extermination called "the final solution of the Jewish question." The upshot was that, during their twelve years of power, some six million Jews were done to death. The world's gradual awareness of this ghastly phase, of the stark and brutal outlines of the holocaust, gave new intensity and drama to the plight of those who managed to escape. Britain and the United States tried to mitigate these horrors by

12. Laqueur, p. 535; Sykes, pp. 271–74. The former says that the *Struma* was torpedoed; the latter that the cause of the explosion is unknown. Sykes also attributes the line taken by the Turks to the influence there of a strong pro-German party and the growth of anti-Semitism.

organizing a conference of all concerned at Bermuda in April 1943, but except in one respect the results were as meagre as those of the Evian conference before the war. The Zionists seem to have taken little notice of or interest in the meeting, since its main purpose conflicted in a sense with their own. For at Bermuda as at Evian the goal was to find a refuge in any land to which the persecuted could be sent—and preferably not in Palestine. Madagascar was one of the possibilities explored, and, from the Zionist standpoint, this seemed almost as objectionable as nearby Mauritius. The conference did, however, lead to the organization of a body that later did most valuable work—namely, the Relief and Rehabilitation Administration of the United Nations (UNRRA).

In general, however, despite the "final solution," the refugee problem remained essentially the same after 1942, though it acquired far vaster and more urgent dimensions. Many successfully entered Palestine by clandestine means. Others were interned elsewhere for the duration of the war. Some were victims of enemy action or of accidents in overcrowded, unseaworthy boats. It may be convenient at this point to anticipate our story and mention a later incident, one of the most notorious refugee dramas for which Britain has been blamed. This was the affair of the former American ship, *President Garfield*, bought by Hagana sympathisers and renamed *Exodus*. With 4,500 permit-less refugees on board this vessel reached Haifa in June 1947 just when the special commission appointed by the United Nations to settle the future of Palestine (UNSCOP) was meeting in the country. The British would have been wise to defuse the dramatic potential of these refugees by letting them land, since they arrived just at the time when Britain was ceasing to be responsible for Palestine's fate. Instead, they played into Zionist hands by ordering the ship back to the southern French port from which it started. When the refugees, at the behest of their political leaders, refused to land there, they were taken to Hamburg in the Germany they loathed, and disembarked by force. Public opinion was whipped up as had been intended—

especially in America—and Britain was pilloried as guilty of the worst of crimes. It was as though she had sent the victims back to death in the Nazi camps.

Such charges had by then become part of a general campaign to ensure the swift departure of the British from Palestine and to gain American sympathy and support for the early realization of a Jewish state. Many believed them, and the campaign was a resounding success. In fact, however—unlike some earlier ventures—the voyage of the *Exodus* had never been a matter of life and death, since it all happened more than two years after the end of the war. The Nazis had long since been defeated, their leaders punished, the concentration camps emptied or destroyed. Europe was being rebuilt in peace. Whether or not they were still temporarily refugees, and whether or not they could enter Palestine at once, there was no longer any hostile threat to the survivors of Hitler's scourge.[13]

Inter-Communal Relations in Wartime Palestine

During the sombre years of the war, and in view of the crisis of European Jewry, it was perhaps human that, in Palestine as elsewhere, the Jews should have been almost exclusively concerned with the fate of their own people. Even in peace-time those Jews (such as the members of the *Brit Shalom*) who favored tact, compromise, understanding, and collaboration in dealing with the Arabs had met with small response from their own people and extremely little from the Arabs. Since the Arab revolt in Palestine of the 1930s and the incipient holocaust in Europe the self-concentration of the Yishuv[14] had hardened, sharpened, and dangerously

13. For the general account of these incidents I have relied mainly on passages already referred to in Laqueur and Sykes (with addition of pp. 568–70 of Laqueur and pp. 381–84 of Sykes with respect to *Exodus*), as well as upon the archives of the British Government now available. The dramatization of the *Exodus* voyage in novel form is the popular *Exodus* by Leon Uris (New York: Doubleday, 1958).

14. In this context, the Jewish community in Palestine in its relations with World Jewry.

simplified the issues as they saw them. For most Jews the time had passed for heeding Dr Weizmann's cautious warnings in the 1920s of the importance of the Arab issue. What did not contribute to the salvation and ultimate independence of the Jewish people seemed less and less to count. This widespread lack of perception of what was genuine in the Arab case, this militant insensitivity to the feelings of their less dynamic and successful neighbours, is still one of the principal psychological barriers to peaceful adjustment between present-day Israel and those around her.[15] Few paused to reflect that the Arabs, having never been consulted, had just as good a right to fight what they saw as the ultimate confiscation of their country as the Jews might have to fight the White Paper. By this time, the recent Arab revolt, and such Arab resistance as continued to the expansion of the National Home, seemed to most of the Yishuv just lawless brigandage and sabotage, to which force was the only answer.

During the war, meanwhile, British relations with the Zionists, and especially with their armed forces, underwent strange and fateful changes. Right at the start, as we have seen, the policies of the White Paper had seemed to require strong measures against the Hagana. Soon, however, the Hagana's value to the war effort became clear, and there ensued a kind of honeymoon with local civil and military authorities on a paradoxical basis of semi-recognition of a force that was never explicitly legalized. Thus the Palestine Government formed the Jewish Settlement Police, which was drawn from and run by the Hagana though nominally under British command. Then, from the spring of 1940, special Hagana units later known as *Palmach* were recruited by a secret organization controlled by the British Government for dangerous tasks behind the enemy lines.[16] Here the Hagana did fine work, often at great

15. A later and notable exception to these attitudes was that of the late Mr Ben Gurion after he had been Prime Minister of Israel.
16. See Sykes, pp. 261–62, 313. *Palmach* meant Shock Companies in Hebrew. The main British organization concerned was Special Operations Executive (S.O.E.), roughly equivalent to the American O.S.S.

cost to themselves. There was similar under-cover collaboration between the British and the—from their standpoint far more irregular—forces of the Irgun.

The years 1942–44 were the key period of the war in the Middle East and most other areas. In 1941, as we saw,[17] the pro-German Vichy forces in Syria and Lebanon had been defeated and these countries taken over by the Free French allies of the British under General de Gaulle. Also in 1941, an anti-British revolt broke out in Iraq, inspired by the Prime Minister in Baghdad, Rashid Ali, and by the Mufti of Jerusalem, and supported by the Germans. This was suppressed a few weeks later by a British column from Palestine which crossed the desert and captured Baghdad, accompanied by the Arab Legion (the Transjordan Army) under the command of Colonel John Glubb,[18] who was later to play a highly significant role during Israel's fight for independence in 1948.

In 1942 the British were defeated in North Africa by the Germans, who then invaded western Egypt.[19] Had Egypt fallen, Palestine inevitably would have fallen too, and the half-million Jews who by then had settled there would have been exterminated by the Nazis. The common peril drew the Yishuv closer to the British, virtually for the last time. But the immediate danger seemed to have passed by November, with the British victory over the Germans at El Alamein and the landing in western North Africa of American forces under General Eisenhower and further British troops.[20] Thereafter the Zionists could breathe more freely; and,

17. See Note 8, above.
18. Sometime known as Glubb Pasha. Later he became Lt.-Gen. Sir John Glubb, author of a number of authoritative works on the Arabs, with whom most of his long military career was spent.
19. Britain, the United States, and other allies were even more disastrously defeated in this year by Japan in the Far East, following the Japanese attack on Pearl Harbor in December 1941. The year 1942 saw the fall also of Singapore, the Philippines, and the Netherlands East Indies (Indonesia). But this aspect of the war is of only marginal relevance to our story.
20. This was achieved by the British Eighth Army under General Montgomery. The same month saw the equally decisive Russian victory over the Germans at Stalingrad.

for some of them, the pursuit of their special goals—even if it meant bloody conflict with the British—became far more important than continued prosecution of the war they had so far fought together.

Jewish Extremists Go to War with Britain

Also in 1942, Irgun and the New Zionists or Revisionists acquired a new leader to replace Jabotinsky, who had died in 1940. This was Menachem Begin, a man unquestionably of great courage and dedication who had escaped from Poland and, as a member of the Polish forces, had reached Transjordan via Russia and Persia. He had then entered Palestine illegally, and with an unswerving hostility towards the British there, having formed, largely on hearsay, the most unflattering views about Britain's policies towards dependent peoples. From his declarations and writing, he clearly could not believe that Britain's motive in issuing the Balfour Declaration and assuming the Mandate could have been other than purely selfish imperialism, or that she could have had any genuine concern for justice in seeking through the White Paper to forestall the displacement of the Arabs by curbing the unlimited expansion of the National Home. He was in any event determined to destroy the mandate system when the time should be ripe. He judged this moment to have come by early 1944, even though some of the crucial battles of the war against Hitler remained to be fought.

By this time the German forces in North Africa had surrendered, and the Allies, after taking Sicily, had launched their invasion of Italy, which had a new pro-Allied government. Yet the Germans, while retreating also in central Russia, still held most of Italy and the rest of Europe, and were fighting tenaciously and effectively on this southern front with the help of a subsequent pro-Axis, Italian Government loyal to Mussolini, whom they had managed to release from prison. Moreover, the critical test for the Western Allies was still to come when, in June 1944, with General Eisenhower as supreme commander, they set out to breach the Atlantic "wall" by landing troops on the Normandy beaches in France. Finally, Hitler still hoped to produce an atom bomb before the United States, and his experts had been collecting the materials for it ever since the invasion of Norway in 1940. Had he done so, he could even then have won the war in spite of all his military setbacks.

None of these considerations carried any weight with the Irgun in Palestine. They now dropped collaboration with the war effort and in effect declared war against the British. By so doing they became allies of the Stern Group,[21] which had been working against the British from the start. Between them they set on foot a programme of terrorism, certain incidents in which will be mentioned later. Whatever opinions our generation may hold, it will be for the future to judge whether or not their deeds contributed to the good name of the Jewish people. Such activities could not of course be sanctioned officially by the Jewish Agency or the Hagana, who were still at war with Hitler rather than with the British and, however much they protested against and sought to circumvent the policies of Britain, were still in day-to-day relations with the Palestine Government. Indeed, they were acutely embarrassed by certain terrorist excesses which made grave difficulties for the policies they were pursuing in the interests of the National Home.[22]

21. Known also as Israeli Freedom Fighters, or *Lehi* in Hebrew.
22. Some time later the Irgun leader wrote a book to explain and justify his activities during these years. This was Menachem Begin: *The Revolt* (English trans., 1951). In parts penetrating and intelligent, it is elsewhere ingenuously blind to all considerations other than his highly subjective vision of the British enemy, and their supposed tools—the Arabs, and also of what he saw as the only proper means—through inspiring fear of Jewish fighting ruthlessness—of attaining the supreme goal of a Jewish state. He ignored the point, earlier conceded even by Dr Weizmann, that the Arabs had as good a claim to Palestine as the Jews. His editor ascribes to him the decisive role in the successful emergence of Israel, and the book tends in fact to belittle the role of the Jewish Agency leaders such as Ben Gurion, and the Hagana, whom the author seems to find not ruthless enough. In an ominous passage directed at the Arabs (pp. 49–50) he maintains that while the Irgun had no desire to fight or harm them, if they heeded British propaganda designed to influence them against the Jews, and raised a hand against the Jews, they would be dealt with swiftly and with the utmost severity.

Nevertheless, from 1944 there developed for nearly all Zionists in Palestine the vision of a clear-cut double struggle over which there must be no relenting or turning back. First, by making things hard for the British, they sought radically to change their Palestine policies or to get them out of the country. There was no longer any place for the British policies—preposterous to most of the Yishuv —of fairness to both sides, of safeguarding the interests of the Arab majority, of preserving a balance between the largely immigrant Jews and the Arabs who had been there during the Jewish Dispersion—policies that had been a stumbling block to the Zionists from the start. Second, by handling the Arabs roughly the Zionists sought to subdue them, and thus to reduce their presence in Palestine so as to make room for an eventual majority of their own people.

What with the European catastrophe and the masses of Jewish survivors who now were, or would be, knocking on Palestine's door, the goal of a viable Jewish state had come closer to realization than ever before. From the Zionist standpoint it would have been a crime to fail, through softness or excessive scruples, to seize the chance of achieving this goal in unique circumstances that might never recur. The fate of others somehow took second place. Thus, although certain deeds of murder and destruction were condemned by the official Zionist leadership at the time, the irregular forces responsible for such acts were incorporated into the Israeli army as soon as the struggle for independence started. The leader of the Sternists had been killed in 1940, but others had carried on his work. As regards Irgun, after independence Menachem Begin was to become the leader of the extreme right-wing Freedom Party (*Herut*), and for some time a minister in the Israeli Cabinet.

Winning Over the United States

While they sought to eliminate the White Paper and if necessary Britain herself, and to overcome any threat from the Arabs, a third goal of the Zionists at this time was to win the goodwill and support of the United States, which they knew to be essential to the achievement and maintenance of a Jewish state. This entailed, on the one hand, gaining the political support of the U.S. Government, with a view especially to bringing pressure to bear on Britain, and, on the other, securing the interest, approval, and financial help of American Jewry. This had long been the wealthiest and most substantial community in the Diaspora. Now it had acquired a key role. Many American Jews had been strongly anti-Zionist in the early years of the movement, but more and more of them had become Zionist once they realized that the primacy in Diaspora Jewry had fallen on their shoulders after the massacre of European Jews.

While Menachem Begin was giving an aggressive new direction to Irgun and the Revisionists, the official Zionist leadership had been by no means idle in these three fields, and especially in that involving the United States. In the same year of 1942, in which Begin had arrived in Palestine, important policy decisions had been publicly reached in New York which were to be the basis of their programme until independence. In May of that year a conference mainly of American Jews who were also Zionists but including some non-Zionists and Zionists from elsewhere, took place at the Biltmore Hotel in New York. By this time the official leadership of the Zionist movement, long at odds with the Revisionists, was itself to some extent split into two camps. There were those, chiefly of the older generation, who believed with Dr Weizmann that the best results might still be achieved by patience, caution, and slow, steady progress; by continuing to negotiate with the British for a Jewish army and (with American support) for the reversal of the White Paper; and by gradually building up a Jewish majority in Palestine on the basis of the immigration of several thousands a year. Mr Ben Gurion, although only twelve years younger,[23] had a bolder, more impetuous outlook. Less polished, subtle, and diplo-

23. Dr Weizmann was born in 1874, Mr Ben Gurion in 1886. Although only 68 at the time of the Biltmore Conference, Weizmann was aging swiftly and rather prematurely. His son Michael, an officer in the British Air Force, had been killed in action only three months earlier and he seems never to have recovered completely from this blow.

matic than the somewhat autocratic Weizmann, he had a greater belief in collective decision-making, in the cut-and-thrust of brashly modern democratic process. He wanted to impress and win over the Americans by "thinking big" and proposing simple, dramatic goals even if they were quite impracticable for the present. He astutely used an article written by Weizmann for the American review *Foreign Affairs*, calling for a Jewish state in which the Jews would govern themselves and control their own immigration, to launch a more resounding and vivid resolution. This was adopted without opposition, although some Jewish groups which objected to it abstained from voting. The militant ring of its eight-point programme brought the official leadership closer to the Revisionists, who claimed that Ben Gurion had been influenced by Jabotinsky in the past.[24] Indeed the Revisionists approved his new course and only deplored what they regarded as his subsequent lack of necessary ruthlessness in executing the program.

The key passages in the Biltmore resolution called for the fulfilment of the "original purpose" of the Balfour Declaration, rejected the White Paper, demanded a Jewish army, and, in the final part, declared that there could be no peace, justice, and equality in the post-war world "unless the problem of Jewish homelessness was fully solved." The "gates of Palestine [must] be opened . . . , the Jewish Agency . . . vested with control of immigration into Palestine and . . . the necessary authority for upbuilding the country; . . . and . . . Palestine . . . established as a Jewish Commonwealth[25] integrated in the structure of the new democratic world." Ben Gurion publicly criticized Weizmann's style of leadership and sought to have him removed as President of the World Zionist Organization for being too pro-British, weak, and unreliable.

24. Begin, pp. 136–37.
25. There was of course a contradiction in terms here, since the establishment of Palestine as a Jewish Commonwealth was certainly not in accordance with the Balfour Declaration, which contemplated a Jewish National Home *in* Palestine. But few of those who heard the resolution at the time would have had the background knowledge, or the desire, to challenge this.

Sharp letters were exchanged between them. Dr Weizmann seems to have been personally offended and, perhaps for this reason, makes no mention of the Biltmore conference in his memoirs. Yet the draft of the resolution had been written by one of his closest helpers, and the fact that he was not unduly worried by British or Arab reactions seems to be borne out by his endorsement of the programme in December 1942.[26] In any case, by then, as a result of

Allied victories, the Yishuv in Palestine was safe and future prospects seemed vastly brighter. Weizmann's prestige as the unquestioned leader of World Zionism was fully upheld. But in Palestine itself Ben Gurion's influence was predominant. Weizmann had not been to Palestine since 1939 and, by not returning there at this juncture, may have sacrificed his earlier power to impose counsels of moderation and caution. On the other hand, there was hardly anyone who could replace him in the role—still so necessary—of international spokesman and ambassador, in which over the years he had achieved so much.[27]

The Arab League

Long before World War II, as we have seen, the surrounding Arab states had come to regard the fate of Palestine as a close concern of their own; and some of their people had taken part as individuals in the Palestinian Arab revolt of the 1930s. As the Jewish National Home grew in size and strength before, during, and after World

26. Laqueur, pp. 545–47; and Sykes, pp. 280–85.

27. The ideal person to have taken over this diplomatic activity—or rather to have resumed it—would have been Nahum Sokolow, but he had been dead since 1936. He had been one of the chief figures in diplomatic negotiations surrounding the Balfour Declaration, as well as those conducted in the interests of Zionism at, and after, the Paris Peace Conference. He appears to have been a born diplomat, especially in dealing with the Latin countries. Having been born fifteen years earlier than Weizmann, in 1859, he did not always take him very seriously. Only for a few years—from 1931 to 1935—after Weizmann had deliberately stepped down, was Sokolow able to satisfy one of his main ambitions, to be President of the World Zionist Organization.

War II, many of the stronger Arab nationalists evolved their own interpretation—an inverted version of the Irgun assessment—of the sinister motives of Western imperialism, particularly of Britain's. For such people the White Paper, though a step in the right direction, was quite inadequate since it did not aim at removing the National Home, but merely at limiting its scope. For them too, Britain, like the other colonial powers, was in the Middle East from purely selfish imperialist motives; but in their judgement the imperialists knew that sooner or later they would have to retreat and give complete independence to all the larger states of the Arab world. So they were using the Jewish National Home—now striving to become a Jewish state—as a chosen instrument through which to maintain their power and influence while appearing to relinquish them.

After the establishment of Israel, these Arab suspicions came to be held even more strongly though in a somewhat new form. The old imperialists such as France and Britain were in retreat. The Arabs and other Asians saw that the United States had been the mainstay of these declining imperialists during the war; and they were prompt to conclude that America had assumed their mantle when the war was over. After all, the United States was the stronger and wealthier of the two new superpowers, and had vast oil interests in the Arab world. In their belief the United States had been mainly responsible for the establishment of Israel, and Israel could not survive without American financial, military, and political support. But since in their opinion America had always been hardheaded in her own strategic interest, they were certain that Washington would never have been so generous towards the Jewish state if Israel were not in fact the instrument and spearhead of the new imperialism. The long and deep U.S. involvement in Vietnam seemed only to confirm this image of her as the arch-imperialist, with the old imperialists such as Britain (also with oil interests), sheltering under her wing. The role of the other superpower, the Soviet Union, was to be more variable and enigmatic, as we shall see. In the middle of the war all this lay in the future, and yet the

Arabs of the world already saw the Jewish National Home as a potential danger to them all, within the framework of imperialist ambitions, and thus made a determined effort to close their ranks.

In their urge to achieve greater unity, the Arabs found an ally in Britain in spite of the recriminations caused by London's Zionist policies during the past twenty-five years and of the suspicion of many Arabs that Britain's readiness to help might spring from a desire to expand the scope of Zionism to their countries too. In 1941, after the defeat of the Vichy French in Syria and Lebanon, Britain was once more in military control of the Fertile Crescent, as she had been in World War I after the defeat of the Turkish Empire. Before 1914, as we know, her traditional policy had been to back the Turkish Empire as a barrier against the southward expansion of Russia, and as a zone of security on Britain's route to India. Her Arab policies in 1915–16 had aimed at replacing the Turks by a united or federated Arab state. But these failed because of the Sykes-Picot agreement with France and the Balfour Declaration. Now, however, there might be a chance of trying again. Unification could now achieve the additional goal of helping to safeguard Britain's considerable oil interests in the Persian Gulf. It might incidentally help her to regain some of the credit she had lost with the Arabs by her sponsorship of the Jewish National Home.

Accordingly, as early as 1941, when Pan-Arabism already had wide support in the Fertile Crescent, Mr Anthony Eden,[28] then Foreign Secretary in the London Cabinet, promised Britain's support for any move towards Arab unity. The Zionists' Biltmore programme gave fresh impulse to the scheme; and in October 1944 Iraq, Syria, Lebanon, Transjordan, Egypt, Saudi Arabia, and Yemen signed the Protocol of Alexandria in which they agreed to form an

28. Anthony Eden, now Earl of Avon, born 1897, had been Foreign Secretary between the wars and was then considered one of the best younger men in the Conservative Party. He was chosen to succeed Churchill as Prime Minister in 1955. He had been a strong earlier supporter of the League of Nations, but his policies during the Suez episode of 1956 were severely judged as having flouted the United Nations, as well as for other reasons, and ended in failure. He resigned in 1957.

Arab League. The final pact was signed in Cairo in March 1945. A representative of Palestine was invited and also signed, since the other countries held Palestine to be legally an independent Arab state, though one that could not yet exercise its rights. Those who formed the League therefore decided that they had the right to choose a Palestinian representative. Unfortunately for Arab prospects, the League turned out to be a loose affair. Each state retained its full sovereignty, and the decisions of the League were not binding on its individual members.[29]

The Fertile Crescent and Egypt during World War II

We have already noted the three most dangerous moments survived by Britain and her Allies in the Middle East during the war—namely, the revolt in Iraq, the campaign against the Vichy French in Syria and Lebanon in 1941; and the successive Italian and German invasions of western Egypt, the most serious being that of 1942. For the rest of the war, the Allies could on the whole count on the friendly attitude of Iraq, Transjordan, and Saudi Arabia, and the general passivity of Egypt despite a good deal of restless discontent. While Transjordan was autonomous and had the apparatus of parliamentary government under the Amir Abdullah, it was still in effect a British dependency, and its full sovereignty as an independent kingdom was not recognized until 1946. After its abortive rebellion, Iraq, with a boy king, Faisal II (grandson of Faisal I), and a regency, came under the rule of Prime Minister Nuri Said, a veteran of the Arab Revolt against the Turks in World War I, and an old comrade-in-arms of the British. Baghdad declared war against the Axis in 1943, and in the following year, Nuri was a prime mover in the formation of the Arab League.

A link between Transjordan and Iraq, and between both of them and Britain, was as we saw the descent of their kings from the Hashimite dynasty of King Husain of the Hejaz, with whom Britain had negotiated during World War I. It was therefore some-

29. See Armajani, pp. 343–44.

thing of a paradox that the other most friendly ruler in the area should have been King Abdul Aziz ibn Saud, of Saudi Arabia, who had ejected King Husain and given the whole country his own name. While remaining neutral, however, he "put his great moral influence unreservedly on the side of Great Britain throughout the war; at all important moments he counselled moderation to his fellow Arabs and urged them to cooperate with . . . Britain."[30]

Before taking over Syria and Lebanon from the Vichy regime in 1941, the Free French had promised both countries immediate and complete independence. These promises were endorsed by the British, who had to provide for the economic needs of the area through the Anglo-American Middle East Supply Centre in Cairo. The Syrians and Lebanese regarded the promises as real and valid, and were encouraged by the British to do so. It became clear, however, that General de Gaulle had no intention of implementing these promises for the time being, since his local representative, General Catroux, forthwith appointed French governors for Syria and Lebanon. But both countries now had republican constitutions and in 1943 both elected prominent nationalists as President. There were strikes and disturbances, and the Lebanese in particular took a determined stand for the integrity and independence of their country, making it plain besides that they would cooperate closely with the Syrians and with the Arab world in general. At that stage the French could not bring themselves to accept this. They arrested the President and his whole Cabinet, though they released them subsequently under British pressure. Later in the war the French were pressing both countries for treaties similar to the Anglo-Iraqui and Anglo-Egyptian treaties. But these were already considered to be out of date by Iraq and Egypt, especially by the latter. In any case, with their sights set on real independence, Syria and Lebanon were quite unwilling to grant France the special rights still implied by treaties of this type. By the end of the war they had received powerful support: they had been recognized as independent nations by the United States as well as by the Soviet Union. Further-

30. Barbour, p. 209.

more, they had declared war upon the Axis and afterwards became charter members of the United Nations.[31]

Important though all these countries were, Egypt was the key to the British war effort in the whole Middle East and, before the Allied landings in Morocco and Algeria in 1942, in North Africa as well. Egypt became the focal point of the Arab League, and was later to be the chief centre for the successive Arab coalitions against Israel. Although the Egyptians are ethnically mixed and very different from the true Arabs of Arabia, Cairo with its famous al-Azhar university had for many centuries been a great centre of Arab culture. In the past, the nationalist movement in the country had been essentially Egyptian; during World War II, however, Pan-Arabism became a powerful force and, placed as the Egyptians were at the junction of North Africa, Arabia, and the Fertile Crescent, their nationalism gradually acquired this new complexion. They proclaimed their solidarity with the other Arab nations and came to see themselves as leaders of the Arab world. But this was not a claim the Arab peoples of the Fertile Crescent were very ready to concede. Syria had been the nerve centre of Arab nationalism under the Turks and after World War I. As for Iraq, there was an age old rivalry between the peoples of the Tigris and Euphrates basin and those of the Nile valley. Moreover the Iraqis, who had formed the largest Arab element in the Turkish army, were superior militarily to either the Syrians or the Egyptians. Here were some of the many sources of Arab disunity in the years to come.[32]

Because of the strategic importance of Egypt the British had in-

---

31. Armajani, pp. 340–41; Barbour, p. 211.
32. See Glubb, A *Short History of the Arab Peoples*, pp. 13–19. These introductory pages contain an illuminating analysis of the characteristics of the different Arab peoples. He says, *inter alia*, "in Arabia . . . the great open spaces have produced individuality and initiative [but] the density of population and the enervating climate of the Nile Delta have been destructive of initiative and self-reliance." Of the Syrians, including the Lebanese and the Palestinian Arabs, he says "their characteristics resemble those of the Greeks, particularly their extreme intellectual subtlety. . . . They are racially unrelated to the Arabians."

serted a clause in their treaty with Cairo of 1936 placing all that country's facilities at Britain's disposal in the event of war. This clause was duly invoked and Egypt fully carried out her obligations under the terms of the treaty.[33] Still for nearly the whole war Egypt remained neutral, and this suited the British for various reasons. For one thing, it freed Cairo from air attacks by the Axis; then too, it would have been hard to spare war equipment for Egyptian troops when this was in short supply for Britain's own forces. Only in February 1945—and then chiefly in order to have a voice in the peace settlement and to join the United Nations—did Egypt declare war on the Axis. The politics of these years were chiefly a struggle between the Wafd—the once-fiery nationalists who had become older and more accommodating—and their opponents, who were in general favoured by the young King Farouk as they had been by his father. Unlike Faisal II of Iraq, Farouk had attained his majority before the war and now reigned in his own right. A special problem was that the King, in spite of his British education, strongly disliked the British Ambassador to Egypt, Sir Miles Lampson,[34] who although in principle merely a diplomatic representative, treated the young man with something of the condescension and high-handedness shown by Cromer towards the young Khedive Abbas Hilmi.[35]

Another problem was that between June 1940 and June 1941, when Britain was fighting the Axis virtually alone, many in Egypt believed that Britain was doomed and that Egypt might do well to prepare for a German and Italian victory.[36] Then early in 1942 a crisis occurred in Britain's relations with Egypt, and particularly with the King. Although, since the war started, Egypt's successive

33. Mansfield, p. 271.
34. Later Lord Killearn. Prime Minister Churchill was himself lacking in sympathy for Egyptian nationalism.
35. Mansfield, p. 272.
36. *Ibid.*, p. 274. One of those who so believed was the Egyptian Chief of Staff, afterwards removed under British pressure; another was Captain Anwar al-Sadat, later President Nasser's right-hand man and now himself President of Egypt.

governments had generally done what Britain had required, it was not judged to be enough. Her leaders had been in general opponents of the Wafd supported by the King. The Axis were still winning, and there was some danger of a pro-Axis government in Egypt. The British decided that the Wafd under Nahas Pasha, who had signed the 1936 treaty, would be the party most likely to give their war effort the unstinted help they needed; and forced this decision on the King in a way most humiliating for Farouk and for the Egyptians in general. The King was given an ultimatum to agree by a certain time to appoint a Wafd government. When this deadline expired, the palace was surrounded by British troops, and the British Ambassador arrived to present him with a document of abdication, the intention being to appoint his pro-British uncle in his place.

Farouk surrendered, appointed Nahas, and was allowed by the British to continue as Egypt's King. But the humiliation of their country was not forgotten by Egyptians. In the army most officers felt it keenly, and two of them who recorded their anger at the time—General Naguib and Lieutenant Nasser—were ten years later to expel Farouk and impose on Egypt the greatest social and political revolution in its history. Indeed, ultimately the results of this act of force, apparently dictated by the immediate needs of the war, were also to destroy both the Wafd and the power and influence of the British in Egypt.

Meanwhile, although shaken by revelations of corruption, Nahas Pasha and the Wafd did in fact keep Egypt firmly in the Allied camp in the dark days preceding the British victory at El-Alamein. But they hardly seemed to be aware of the forces rising against them. Egypt's key role in the Allied war effort multiplied her social problems. A huge army of occupation, serviced by the Anglo-American Supply Centre, boosted inflation and widened the gap between rich and poor. In this restless period two movements gathered strength. One, the Muslim Brotherhood founded in the 1930s, sought to eliminate alien Western systems, to create an essentially Islamic state on the basis of the Q'uran, and to bring freedom to the whole Islamic world—the British being among their most obvious targets. The Brotherhood gave its members para-military training, denounced the Wafd as a tool of Britain, and practiced terrorism and murder to achieve its ends. In October 1944 the King felt able to dismiss the Wafd—discredited by the Brotherhood by reason of its corruption and failure to cope with the social hardships caused by the war—and to restore a government more to his own taste. In opposition, the Wafd sought to justify its nationalist credentials by being increasingly anti-British. By August 1945 with the Allies victorious both in Europe and the Far East, all Egypt's political leaders were pressing for the complete evacuation of the British, and for the unity of Egypt and the Sudan. They also wanted Egypt to confine her membership of regional arrangements under the United Nations to her Arab neighbours and thus avoid commitments to the larger powers, of which Egypt might become the tool as so often in the past.

The Moyne Murder

In November 1944, meanwhile, Cairo saw the murder of Lord Moyne. The former Colonial Secretary was now stationed in Egypt as British Minister of State in the Middle East, a post of Cabinet rank created to coordinate all British activities in the area. Paradoxically, this murder was the work, not of the Egyptians, whom Britain had frequently angered and humiliated over the last sixty years, but of extreme Zionists from a movement decisively helped by Britain—even if some Jews judged that she had done too little. It was a tragedy not only for the victims (for Lord Moyne's driver was killed, too) but also for the two young Jews—one of seventeen, the other of twenty-two—who were hanged for the deed, persuaded to the end that it was a great thing to have done. They had been recruited by the Stern Group and had become so imbued with its grim fanaticism that they were convinced that they were advancing the cause and hastening the freedom of their people by killing an elderly man whose removal, as they had been told, would "change the course of history."

Had the organizers of the murder made an objective study of their proposed victim and his work, they would have known that Lord Moyne, though a fine and capable public figure, was in no sense irreplaceable. Nor was he the ultimately decisive author of the policies they rejected. He had no special prejudice against Zionism, and his only crime was his determination to do his duty as he saw it to both sides. Unfortunately, for some Zionist extremists, any consideration given by the British to the Arabs was at that stage a kind of crime. There was indeed some truth in the remark attributed to the Stern leader who allegedly planned Moyne's death—that Britain could not carry out her promises to both Jews and Arabs. But from this he drew the startling conclusion that the British must be forced to abandon Palestine and its Arabs, and that a murder which, in his view, might help to achieve this was fully justified.[37]

In any event the immediate result was a setback to the Zionist cause, for Moyne was a personal friend of Winston Churchill, who had always been pro-Zionist and who, in 1939, had "delivered against the White Paper one of the great speeches of his career."[38] At the time Churchill was planning to replace the White Paper after the war by a new partition scheme more favorable to the proposed Jewish state than that of Peel, since it would have gained the Negev, and of course full scope to admit any number of immigrants it wished. Significantly he stressed that active American participation was needed. Only two days before the murder the Prime Minister and Dr Weizmann had had a friendly and constructive talk

37. See Gerold Frank, *The Deed*, p. 190, a vivid, dramatic account of the whole background and course of the murder, by an American journalist who was present at the trial of the two boys. As might be expected, it reflects an almost total condemnation of British policy and ascribes to this unhappy event an importance for the future of Palestine and the birth of Israel which is hardly justified by the facts.

38. Weizmann, p. 506.

about this, and, at Churchill's suggestion, Weizmann was to have discussed it with Moyne in Cairo.[39] Although the murder was immediately condemned by Weizmann and all responsible leaders of Zionism, it was only human that Churchill, until he fell from power in July 1945, should have become more negative towards the movement. On November 17 he declared in Parliament that if Zionism tolerated such crimes he and others who had supported it would have to "reconsider their attitudes." Discussions between the Zionist Executive and the British Government were suspended, and memoranda from the Jewish Agency and Weizmann appealing for increased immigration as the preliminary to a Jewish state met with virtually no response. The Zionists pinned their hopes, however, on the new Labour Government under Clement Attlee, which in opposition had made some most encouraging statements.

The Aftermath of the Second World War

Germany surrendered on May 7, 1945. While the struggle against Japan continued until the following August, so far as the Middle East and Europe were concerned, the war was over. Hitler's third German Empire lay in ruins. He was dead, and his chief collaborators were promptly tried and punished. Less than a month before, Harry S. Truman had become President of the United States on the sudden death of Franklin D. Roosevelt, and from the moment he began to deal with the post-war settlement, the United States had an increasingly decisive influence on the fate of Palestine. This was to lead in just three years to the proclamation of the state of Israel.

When the European war ended, there had been for some months a lull in the strife between the main Zionist body in Palestine—the Jewish Agency, headed by Ben Gurion—and the Palestine Government. Despite the White Paper and continuing difficulties in London, they had been drawn together—up to a point—by the shock of Lord Moyne's death and by the determined efforts of both the

39. Sykes, pp. 301–3, 310; Laqueur, pp. 542–43.

Agency and the government to curb Jewish terrorism. Another factor had helped during the autumn of 1944. This was the departure of the intensely unpopular High Commissioner, Sir Harold Mac-Michael, whom the extremists charged with personal responsibility for the deaths of all illegal immigrants barred from Palestine. His successor, Field Marshal Lord Gort, who had held the top post in the British Army,[40] had a personal gift for inspiring trust and liking which won over many otherwise hostile people even in the immensely difficult circumstances of his day. He could not have his orders from London changed, but he made certain concessions and gestures that pleased the Zionists even if they were inevitably unwelcome to the Arabs. And the Arabs, as in the days of Plumer, tended instinctively to respect and defer to an outstanding military chief. Had Gort ruled Palestine for the full five years of his term it is just possible (though the chances were extremely slim) that he might have been able to inspire and effect some peaceful settlement. But he left after a year, suffering from terminal cancer, and died almost at once. One of Gort's concessions was to allow the settlement in Palestine of the Jewish immigrants who had been diverted to Mauritius for lack of valid papers. One of his gestures was to call formally on Dr Weizmann when he visited Palestine for the first time since 1939. This was in November of 1944, only a week after the Moyne murder.

Weizmann's Visit to Palestine

Weizmann's visit was indeed something of a royal progress. The Yishuv knew that at last it could pay tribute to the man who had laid the foundations for The Return by practical steps and shrewd negotiation that had proved far more effective than the dreams and schemes of Herzl and those before him. Weizmann had, after

40. Chief of the Imperial General Staff. Gort had also been Commander-in-Chief of the British Expeditionary Force in France 1939–40, and Governor of Malta when it managed to survive as a vital point in British Mediterranean strategy during the years of Axis victory. He held the highest British decoration for bravery, the Victoria Cross.

all, played the key role in securing the Balfour Declaration and, after this, the agreement with Faisal which, a generation earlier, might have smoothed the path for the National Home without conflict with the Arabs. That this last chance was lost had not been Weizmann's fault, but that of the powers who had failed at the time to give the Arabs the independence they had promised. Then there had been years of disturbance and bitter strife, and more recently the sudden and urgent expansion of the National Home by reason, above all, of Hitler's diabolical courses. On the other hand, without the Balfour Declaration Palestine—the former southern Syria—would have become, in combination with Transjordan, another Arab state. After a period of direct mandatory rule, it would have been in treaty relations with Britain similar to those of Iraq and Egypt. And like them, and like Syria and Lebanon, it would have attained complete independence as a founding member of the United Nations soon after World War II. Meanwhile, there would in all probability have been a steady increase in Jewish settlement on both sides of the Jordan, and perhaps even to the limits of the ancient kingdom of David and Solomon, on some agreed and peaceful basis. But this would not have been the return of the Jews as a nation to Eretz Israel, which the Zionists saw as the only proper fulfilment of Jewish aspirations.

Weizmann was deeply touched by his reception and by the spectacle of what his people had achieved. But some things disturbed him, which he ascribed to the "bitter frustrations of legitimate hopes." He called these "a relaxation of the old . . . Zionist purity of ethics, a touch of militarization, and a weakness for its trappings; here and there, something worse—the tragic, futile, un-Jewish resort to terrorism . . . and worst of all, in certain circles, a readiness to compound with the evil, to play politics with it . . . to treat it not as . . . an unmitigated curse to the National Home, but as a phenomenon which might have its advantages."[41] He still stood for moderation and restraint. He wanted the Zionists to accept Churchill's new partition scheme. There might then be a

41. Weizmann, *Trial & Error*, p. 539.

Jewish Commonwealth after five, or possibly ten, years, during which they would aim at a hundred thousand immigrants a year.

With all the sense that lay in such proposals, time had really passed them by. They had not the ringing, dramatic immediacy, nor the full sweep, of Ben Gurion's Biltmore programme, which claimed the whole of Palestine—and right away. Before the end of the year, the Jewish Agency publicly declared to the British Government and the world at large, and with the support of the Va'ad Leumi,[42] that it opposed partition. Politically, Weizmann was a father figure but a spent force. Had he kept his strength and vitality and been able to come to Palestine earlier, during the crucial years of the war, things might have taken a less turbulent course.

Britain's New Labour Government

The Labour Government under Mr Attlee that displaced Churchill's coalition in July 1945 did some wise and necessary things. It liquidated Britain's stake in India—on the whole, with success—and gave up other parts of the Empire, to which traditionally Labour had been opposed. But this was done at a time when the continued burden of all British overseas commitments would have been, as they fully realized, economically beyond the country's strength.[43] In any case, the Empire was something they knew of old, but Palestine was not part of it. The Mandate had been entrusted to Britain by an international body, the League of Nations,

42. National Council. This was in effect the parent of the Israeli Knesset. See in this connection Sykes, pp. 308–11.
43. This point was tellingly made by a distinguished American economist and former Ambassador to India, Mr John Kenneth Galbraith, in an interview with a representative of the London *Observer* on November 27, 1966. Under the heading "You Lucky British," Mr Galbraith said, "The British people, perhaps along with the Japanese, were the first in history to benefit from the shedding of an empire. . . . You could have been saddled for generations with the burdens of providing assistance, administration, education, plant and capital for the emerging nations . . . all at colossal cost. But you were allowed to get out as an act of social morality just at the moment when it was in fact an act of pecuniary self-interest."

which was itself reconstituted in another form in 1945 as the United Nations.

At that moment, however, Palestine was caught up in complex, international cross currents and conflicting obligations and responsibilities with which a Labour Government was not ideally qualified to deal. Many of its members and supporters were from the trade-union movement, and it was less experienced in the field of international diplomacy than the Conservatives. The Foreign Secretary, Ernest Bevin, was a man of great integrity, shrewdness, and strength of character, and one of the most powerful elements of working-class background in the Labour Party—yet of limited acquaintance with the involved subtleties of international affairs. And in post-war conditions it fell to him more than to any other minister to deal with Palestine affairs.

Had Palestine been simply a British territory, the Labour Government—indeed any British Government—would have left it with relief as soon as the war was over. Indeed, from this standpoint, the post-war terrorism of the Jewish extremists, intended to make Britain want to leave at once, was tragically irrelevant. Apart from the losses and deep hostility it caused, it did not affect the issue. The British wish to leave was widespread. The delay was due primarily to the new Government's tardy appreciation of some facets of the Palestine problem which they had ignored when they were not directly concerned. They then sought to ensure by some means that the Palestinian Arabs, for whom also they had an international responsibility and who were still two-thirds of the population, were not simply handed over to a Jewish state bent, as the Arabs saw it (and not without justification), on their subordination or eviction.

Labour's Election Promises

The Palestine policies of the Labour Party with which Bevin is identified from 1945 to 1948 were by no means a success. Some of the reasons are explained above. Before Labour took office, and in the usual spirit of those who aim at power, they had made some resounding statements designed to outbid the Conservatives. At the Party's conference in December 1944, Mr Attlee had secured the passage of a resolution to the effect that a Jewish National Home made no sense unless Jews could enter Palestine in such numbers as to become a majority. There were grounds for a transfer of population. The Arabs should be encouraged to move out as the Jews moved in; they should be handsomely compensated for their land and their settlement "elsewhere" should be carefully organised and generously financed. The Arabs, after all, had many wide territories of their own and should not claim to exclude the Jews from the small area of Palestine. Indeed, according to the resolution, Britain should "examine the possibility" of extending the boundaries of Palestine in agreement with Egypt, Syria, and Transjordan.

This declaration went far beyond the Biltmore resolution, so far indeed that even Ben Gurion and other leaders hastened to dissociate themselves from the transfer of population proposal. In the end it went the way of most election promises when the Labour Government discovered, once in power, that they just could not do what they had said.[44] This did not of course prevent them from being bitterly attacked by the Zionists, during the next three years, for breaking their word.

President Truman Backs Zionist Demands

Before and after Churchill's fall the Zionist leaders urged in London the prompt admission of a hundred thousand Jews to Palestine. In August 1945 Ben Gurion demanded this in the strongest terms, and insisted also that Palestine should be declared a Jewish state. The Labour Government resented this rough-shod pressure to make them honour at once the letter of their bond. But the pressure soon came from a weightier quarter. At the end of the same month President Truman endorsed the Zionist demand, having been told by his own experts that a hundred thousand was about the number of "non-repatriable" Jews in European camps

44. Sykes, pp. 311–14.

for displaced persons. At the same time, he would promise no American help to enforce a step bound to be bitterly fought by the Arab majority in Palestine. Nevertheless, the President's move showed how far the outlook and policy of Americans had changed since the isolationism of the 1920s following President Wilson's failure to remake the world as he wished.

Although Woodrow Wilson and leading Americans such as Brandeis and Frankfurter had done so much to launch the National Home, isolationism had meant not only the rejection of the Treaty of Versailles and the shelving of the King-Crane Commission's report but also an almost total lack of interest in the problems and struggles of Palestine. In the thirties, however, the powerful Jewish community of America made the country constantly aware of the sufferings of the Jews at Hitler's hands, while Zionism increasingly gained ground among them. The upshot was that "There was a steady unrelenting pressure . . . from Congress and opinion for an American solution of the Palestine Question."[45] In November 1942 an American Palestine Committee of Senators and Representatives denounced the White Paper. Then, early in 1944, both Houses of Congress passed a resolution in the general sense of the Biltmore programme.

Dualism of American Policy

This resolution was soon enough shelved, for, as had been the case far earlier with Britain, there was a growing awareness in America of other realities giving to U.S. policy an inevitable dualism that to some degree has persisted to this day. One short-term consideration was the vital importance of not having to fight the Arabs at the most crucial moment of the war, when a second front against the enemy was about to be opened in western France. A second and far more enduring factor requiring friendship with the Arabs was oil. In 1938 rich oil deposits had been found in Saudi Arabia and neighbouring areas, and these were now being exploited largely

45. *Ibid.*, p. 323.

by the Americans and British. U.S. friendship with the Arabs stemmed also, as we saw, from valuable American cultural work over more than a hundred years in such centres as Beirut, Cairo, and Istanbul—itself a powerful stimulus to the Arab national revival.

In this dilemma between pro-Zionist pressure and the need for good relations with the Arabs, President Roosevelt gave assurances alternately to both sides. In October 1944 he assured the American Zionists that he would help to bring about a Jewish Commonwealth in Palestine. Early in 1945 he assured King Ibn Saud that he would take no action hostile to the Arabs. However unwelcome this somewhat devious path might be to President Truman, to some extent he was forced to follow it. Soon he was also forced by the fatal complexities of Palestine into an anti-British course just at the time when British support was imperative in face of the new threat from Soviet Russia known as the Cold War.[46]

British Reservations: Revival of Sabotage

In his reply to President Truman's endorsement of Zionist demands, Prime Minister Attlee pointed out that the immediate admission of 100,000 Jews to Palestine would mean the complete cancellation of the White Paper without regard to the consequences for the Middle East. President Roosevelt and Mr Churchill had agreed that the Arabs would be consulted before any radical action in Palestine; no major steps should be taken before the United Nations could assume charge of the situation. Thus in the summer of 1945, with the war just over and only a couple of months' experience of the realities of power, Britain's Labour Government had already moved a long way from their sweeping pre-election pledges. They seem already to have been clear that, with Britain's reduced strength and wealth, it would be quite impracticable for her to continue to shoulder the burden of settling the Palestine issue.

Quite apart from increasing Zionist hostility, this issue was once

46. *Ibid.*, pp. 323–27.

again heading towards armed conflict between Jews and Arabs on a
far greater scale than ever before. The Mandate given to Britain by
the League of Nations in the 1920s must be taken back by its successor, the United Nations, in the 1940s. But the terrorists, incensed by Attlee's reservations over the hundred thousand, still
seem to have suspected that Britain might drag her feet and decided that an intensification of violence by them might somehow
hasten that process of winding up the British mandate which
had already by now been decided by the London Government. In
September 1945 the terrorists renewed their outrages, this time in
alliance with the Hagana. In October they made a coordinated and
damaging attack on the Palestine railway system, sank some naval
craft, and attacked the Haifa oil refinery. Meanwhile, unlicensed
immigration was stepped up with the connivance of some otherwise law-abiding people.[47]

Arab Reactions

The Arabs were not slow to react to the pressure on the British to
abandon the White Paper and sanction mass immigration of Jews
to Palestine. The Secretary-General of the Arab League, on a visit
to London in the autumn of 1945, said that, even though Palestine
was an essential part of the Arab homeland, the Arabs would accept the existing Jewish community and would give all Palestinians, of whatever religion or community, full rights of citizenship
in a Palestinian state. The problem of world Jewry, he stressed, resulted from European anti-Semitism, and was in no way the responsibility of the Arabs; yet if the United Nations produced a
scheme by which its members would each accept a quota of Jewish

47. Such as the American-Jewish Joint Distribution Committee. French officials seem also to have shown some indulgence to a movement of refugees
which was causing trouble for the British. At, that moment—and not for the
last time—France under General de Gaulle was on bad terms with Britain.
He had strongly resented high-handed British action in Syria and Lebanon
discussed below. In connection with later developments in 1945, see *inter alia*
Sykes, pp. 333–36.

immigrants, the Arab states would take part or contribute funds. He added that Palestine had already accepted more Jewish immigrants than most people considered reasonable; that Zionist agitation for more was primarily inspired not by humanitarian but by political motives; and that the Zionists were determined to discourage displaced Jews from settling anywhere but in Palestine.[48]

The Anglo-American Committee

On November 13, 1945, events took a new turn. London had succeeded in persuading Washington that the United States could not dictate a solution if it were not prepared to play a part. The British Government announced, through Bevin, the appointment of yet another Palestine Committee of Enquiry, but this one was to be half British and half American, with alternate British and American chairmen. The Committee's task would be to find out how many Jews had survived in the former Nazi areas of Europe and how they could be resettled, in Europe or elsewhere; and, to examine the political, economic, and social conditions affecting Jewish immigration into Palestine. On the basis of their report, Britain would explore temporary arrangements and then propose a final solution to the United Nations, which for the time being would substitute a trusteeship agreement for Palestine for the existing Mandate. The Arabs would be consulted on Jewish immigration, but, pending the Committee's recommendations, such immigration would continue at the then legal monthly rate of 1,500. The announcement noted that Palestine could not by itself solve the whole problem of Jewish immigration.

The Arab response was divided. Member states of the Arab League were not unfavourable, though they deplored the continuance of Zionist immigration beyond a year after this was supposed to have stopped save with Arab consent. They also resented the prospect of Palestine's continued tutelage under the United Nations when they had urged an independent Palestinian state. The

48. See Barbour, pp. 226–28.

Arab extremists in Palestine were far more instransigent, but they were something of an exception to the general Arab trend at that time. The White Paper had during the war kept the hostility of most Arabs towards Britain just below the danger point, and the only really vigorous leader of the Palestinians, the Mufti of Jerusalem, who had broadcast for the enemy from Berlin, had been discredited by his association with the defeated Axis. Moreover, the Allies' victory had brought fresh credit to Britain in Arab eyes. And this credit was further enhanced by Britain's championship, after the war, of complete independence for Syria and Lebanon at a time when the French were in no hurry to leave those states—although both of them had become founder members of the United Nations.[49]

So far as the Palestinians were concerned, Arab unity had always been questionable, and bitter rivalries had led to the murder of Arabs by Arabs during the revolt of the 1930s. Efforts to build up some kind of Palestinian unity independently of the Mufti during the later stages of the war had met with little success. The Mufti's powerful clan, the Husseinis, were determined not to let Palestine leadership go elsewhere, and in this they finally succeeded, not least by outbidding their rivals. While the moderates demanded adherence to the British White Paper, the pro-Husseini group insisted on dissolution of the Jewish National Home—an aggressive stand that may have been a predictable response to Zionist terrorism. Eventually the Mufti's chosen instrument was revived—the Arab Higher Committee, abolished by the British in 1937.[50] The violence of the extremists was not confined to words; early in November Jews had been assaulted in Tripoli and a hundred killed.

49. There was British military intervention to speed French evacuation. The removal of French and British troops from both countries was formally agreed in December 1945 and March 1946, and completed in the latter year. As we saw, General de Gaulle, Provisional President of France until January 1946, was deeply offended by Britain's action; and this may account in part for his intransigence towards Britain after he returned to office in 1958.

50. Barbour, pp. 228–29; Sykes, pp. 315–17.

The Zionists now pinned their hopes on the United States and might have been expected to welcome American association with the new Palestine enquiry now announced. Yet with their passionate sense of persecution aroused by the holocaust they were prone to see enemies in all who were not their dedicated partisans. They seem to have concluded that Bevin was irremediably anti-Jewish— which was by no means the case, as his earlier career had shown— and that his influence would somehow ensure that things did not go the way the Zionists wished. The Anglo-American Committee's work was called a great betrayal, a fresh proffer of stale evasions, and the like.[51] Still, although from this time onward extremists among the Zionists fanned a mounting campaign against the British and Bevin, comparing them to the Nazis at their worst, actual violence was limited. In spite of everything the Yishuv keenly awaited the Anglo-American report. Hence the determination to impress the Committee, when it visited Palestine, with the plight of the refugees in *Exodus*. The Committee started work at the end of 1945 and its report was published on April 30, 1946.

Meanwhile, President Truman, apparently stung by reproaches about how little in a practical way his Administration was doing, gave orders in December to hasten the admittance of refugees from Europe into the United States. This has been called "the policy which, from the very beginning of the European disaster in 1933, could alone have given the Palestine question a chance of peaceful solution," and yet, as often in such cases, orders from the top were frustrated at the official level. Ten months later, less than five thousand of these survivors had been admitted. New legislation was needed and, by the time it became effective, the future of Palestine had been settled, not in peace, but by war.[52]

51. It seems not quite accurate to say, as Laqueur does on p. 565, that in his statement of November 13 Bevin announced "that the White Paper policy would be continued." If this had been the case, the new Committee could hardly have recommended, as it did in its report, that 100,000 Jews should be admitted to Palestine.

52. Sykes, p. 341.

During their enquiry in Europe the Committee found the number of Jewish survivors there to be in fact around a hundred thousand. And, though this was to change later, none at that moment seemed to want to go anywhere but to Palestine.[53] In Cairo one Arab witness stressed that their Semitic cousins the Jews were returning from Europe as Western, not Eastern, people, and with alien imperialist, materialist, or revolutionary ideas. Like the colonialists of old, they were seeking to dominate, and claiming to civilize, an "unprogressive" area, relying on help from the imperialist powers, including the United States. In their tour of the Middle East the Committee found Palestine in a state of tension and disarray. The Yishuv was aroused by a London statement that Transjordan would become a sovereign kingdom (later to be known as Jordan), and by the continuing curbs on immigration; the Arabs, by the fact that any immigration was permitted at all. The Jordan move was a logical outcome of the stage of constitutional development that country had reached since the 1920s, and of the new status of Syria and Lebanon; but by now Bevin could do no right in Jewish eyes.[54]

In all, the unanimous Anglo-American findings were an attempted compromise that satisfied no one and had in fact no future, based as they were on the notion—long dear to the British but by now quite impracticable—that somehow the two peoples could settle down together. Partition was therefore rejected, as was any prospect of Palestine becoming an Arab or a Jewish state; the country should continue under trusteeship as a bi-national country; and since there was no hope that the United States would take on the trust, this meant continuing the British Mandate. But Britain

53. Laqueur states (p. 568) that "many survivors wanted above all a quiet life and Palestine in 1947 hardly promised this." He and others estimate that by late 1947, given equal opportunity to go to Palestine or to the United States, half would have opted for America.

54. The new status of Abdullah and his kingdom was confirmed in a treaty with Britain of March 22, 1946. The country was allied with Britain by this and a later treaty of 1948.

should immediately issue a hundred thousand immigration permits so as to settle in Palestine the Jewish refugees in Europe, and should also "facilitate further immigration under suitable conditions." The White Paper restrictions on land sales to Jews should be lifted. But as a sop to the Arabs their manpower should no longer be excluded from undertakings financed by the Jewish National Fund.[55] President Truman, blunt like Mr Bevin, had small patience with the finer processes of diplomacy.[56] When the Committee's report was published in America, he attached to it a Presidential message commending the proposed immediate admission of the hundred thousand Jews and dismissing the rest as matters for "careful study." The British Government had objections to the report and was incensed at the President's procedure. Unfortunately, however, before the Committee had done its work, Mr Bevin had promised that, if the findings were unanimous, he would do all he could to give them effect. Once again, the British Cabinet was faced with breaking its word.

However brusque Mr Truman's action, others concerned showed equal lack of judgement. Prime Minister Attlee insisted that the hundred thousand could be admitted only if all the illegal armies in Palestine—Jewish and Arab—were disbanded. This was meant to include the Hagana, which had long been tacitly accepted by the British, and with which they had collaborated during the war. The Hagana had never actually been legalized, however, and London now knew of its alliance with the terrorist groups at a time when Jewish violence was again increasing. Nevertheless, the Prime Minister's demand was excessive. If Britain had insisted only on the abolition of the specifically terrorist units, the Jewish Agency might have agreed. But they could not possibly accept the removal of the Hagana, which had been their main defence force for so long.

55. For full text see the *Report of the Anglo-American Committee of Enquiry Regarding the Problems of European Jewry and Palestine* (Cmd. 6808, 1946.
56. Mr Truman once declared: "Protocol and striped pants give me a pain in the neck." See Thomas A. Bailey, *The Art of Diplomacy*, p. 11 n.

Ironically, had Britain been flexible over the hundred thousand "the problem might then have lost its acute character . . . and thus the need for the state of Israel would have lessened."[57] With the problem of the displaced Jews in Europe solved, there might have been a swing toward moderation in the Yishuv which could have endangered Ben Gurion's policy of a Jewish state. For, in their obsessive insistence on the hundred thousand, the Zionists, too, had overreached themselves, to the point of by-passing their Biltmore program, which after all had demanded not only a Jewish state but also that immigration should be at the sole discretion of the Jewish agency.

In any event the Committee's immigration proposals were rejected by London in May 1946. This virtually ended any prospect of agreement between the Jewish Agency and the Palestine Government on some constructive settlement that the Arabs might accept. During Britain's two remaining years in nominal control, her people largely lost the power to command events.[58] For all the high hopes and ideals which Palestine had inspired in many of her leaders, Britain would finally fail to prevent the Holy Land from drifting through bitter strife to a future darkened by violence and repeated wars.

Final Phases of the Mandate

The final period of the British Mandate falls into two unequal parts. During the nine months from May 1946 to February 1947, Washington and London continued to search for a formula acceptable to both Jews and Arabs. Britain still hoped that, with the United States now deeply involved, they might between them manage to

57. Laqueur, p. 566. This view is supported by Dr Eban, present Foreign Minister of Israel. See Abba Eban, "Tragedy and Triumph," in Joel Carmichael and Meyer Weisgal, eds., *Chaim Weizmann; a Biography by Several Hands*, p. 280.

58. See Sykes, pp. 349–55, which contains an admirable picture of these tangled events.

pilot through a peaceful solution permitting Britain to wind up her stewardship and withdraw with at least some feeling of accomplishment. By the end of this time, however, the British were forced to recognize that this was hopeless and to announce that they were handing over the problem to the United Nations, with no particular solution to propose. During the fifteen months from February 1947 to May 1948, when the last British High Commissioner left and the State of Israel was declared, Britain remained in Palestine essentially as an administrative caretaker in a situation increasingly out of control, as the United Nations itself searched for a solution. The one found was also ultimately to fail.

The Grady-Morrison Plan

During the first spell, it seemed as though such chances as remained were somehow fated to be missed. The timing was wrong or some opening was "overtaken by events." A further complication was that Britain's relations with the United States over Palestine and other matters were just then subject to special strain. Impoverished by the war, the British had absolute need of an American loan. An unfamiliar sense of dependence and reduced weight in the world seems to have made them pricklier and less receptive than they might have been to certain well-meant but at times clumsily handled approaches from their far stronger partner. The United States still had some hope of persuading Britain to relent over the hundred thousand; it offered to help finance their transport and in July 1946 sent a mission to London to try to work this out. By this time, however, disturbing new developments made the prospect of any agreed settlement more remote than ever.

The Mufti had arrived in Cairo, and his strong but ruthless influence was once again dominant in Arab counsels. Then Mr Bevin (in unofficial but published statements at a Labour Party conference) made incautious and disparaging remarks about the Palestine policy of the United States, and about the Jews in America, who by now regarded him with wild antipathy. In June the Palestine Government, having failed to secure what was required from the Jewish Agency, arrested their leaders (in the absence abroad of Ben Gurion) as well as a number of Hagana and Palmach officers. Some two weeks later, apparently in response to this move, the Irgun blew up the wing of the King David Hotel in Jerusalem housing the British military headquarters and killed nearly a hundred people, including a number of Jews. The British commanding general then forbade his troops to have dealings with Jews, thus adding fresh fuel to Zionist propaganda. In July the Americans and British discussed in London yet another political solution to supplant the defunct scheme of the Anglo-American Committee.[59] It was proposed that Palestine should remain one but that there should be "provincial autonomy" for the predominantly Arab and Jewish areas. The Jewish area would have been more limited in the north than that proposed by Peel, and it would not have had the Negev, which Churchill had favoured giving to it. But the Arabs would not have had the Negev either: together with the Jerusalem Bethlehem area, it would still have come under direct British rule.

As it stood, there were few attractions for either side in this new plan, and yet, strangely enough, it did propose the admission of a hundred thousand Jews only two months after Britain had turned down the Committee's plan on that key issue. It was sadly ironical that after so short a time this major concession by the British came just too late. Having secured his main point over immigration, President Truman was keen to have the new scheme accepted, but now the Zionist leaders refused it. Although their demand for the hundred thousand had been met, they seem at last to have realized that they had made a false move in asking for a set number of immigrants, however large. Their new course was to concentrate on the main Biltmore objective—namely, unfettered control of immigration by Jewish authorities in a Jewish state.

59. This is known as the Grady-Morrison plan, having been worked out by U.S. Ambassador Henry Grady and Mr Herbert Morrison, another senior Labour Minister, in charge of the Foreign Office during Bevin's illness.

The Zionist Partition Plan

Later in 1946 there were three more moves in the search for a settlement. The British Government wanted the provincial autonomy plan to be studied by an Arab-Jewish-British conference in London. When Palestine Arabs and the Jewish Agency made difficulties the discussions were held between only the Arab League and the British. But in August 1946, before these talks started, Ben Gurion and the Zionist leaders still free produced yet another plan. They too had been shocked by the King David killings. They were at the moment in a mood for compromise and were prepared after all to agree to partition on a basis that would give them a Jewish state more or less of the size of Israel as she eventually emerged in 1948, but without Jerusalem. They would not insist on the whole of Palestine as they had in the Biltmore programme.[60]

This plan likewise came to nothing. The British refused to change the agenda for their conference with the Arabs, knowing that the Arabs objected to partition—which, in Bevin's view, could be forced on them only by British bayonets. Ben Gurion's plan did, however, lead to the resumption of talks between Dr Weizmann and the British Cabinet, while London sought to clear the air by appointing a pro-Zionist Colonial Secretary. Bevin felt that these talks were going well when in October Mr Truman suddenly endorsed Ben Gurion's partition plan—in an election-campaign move to outbid his Republican opponent, Governor Dewey. The British had implored him not to endorse it, for when he had done so the talks with Weizmann broke down. It is hardly surprising that the Zionist leaders should have decided at this point that, if the British persisted in rejecting their plan, they would reach these goals without them. They hoped that they might count on other (i.e., American) help. If not, they would manage by themselves.

60. Or *Western Palestine*, as some of the extreme Zionists called it, including of course the Revisionists. According to them Transjordan, or Jordan, was *Eastern Palestine*, and was regarded by them as *terra irredenta*, the Italian phrase commonly used for "unredeemed" parts of the national territory claimed by a particular country.

The Twenty-Second Zionist Congress

In spite of the growing breach between many British and Zionist leaders, there were still fitful gleams of hope. The new Colonial Secretary sponsored some measures of conciliation. The arrested Jewish Agency leaders were freed in November and would-be immigrants detained in Cyprus were admitted to Palestine. The Zionist Organization again condemned the terrorists, and Hagana ceased to work with them. At the Twenty-second Zionist Congress in December, Weizmann once more urged sober statesmanship and moderation. He too condemned the wild men of revolt, and not least the American-Jewish extremists,[61] who, from a comfortable distance, sent others to die and suffer in their place. He warned his people against the paths of Babylon and Egypt. Zion, he said, should be redeemed only "in judgement."

Those present showed him respect and admiration; but they did not re-elect him as their President. The key to the future lay in radical hands. The moderates had had their day. One important reason for this radical victory was that Britain could not accept the Zionist plan; and in retrospect this may seem to have been unwise. In fact this rejection was a line forced on Britain in 1946–47 by issues far larger than Palestine. India was seething with unrest as the conflict between Muslim and Hindu came to a head—a conflict soon to end in the partition of that country.[62] The Cold War was on, and in northwestern Persia the Soviet army had moved into the province of Azabaijan. Meanwhile, the British position in Egypt had reached a critical stage, with negotiations for a new treaty bogged down over the future of the Sudan and with Egypt already aspiring to the leadership of the Arab nations. More than ever, Britain needed good relations with the world of Islam, both in the Arab countries and beyond. It was simply not practicable

61. Such as the author Ben Hecht, who supported Irgun and declared that he had a "song in his heart" when British soldiers were killed.
62. On August 15, 1947, India became independent, but as two separate states: India, which was predominantly Hindu, and Pakistan, predominantly Muslim.

for her then to implement a solution for Palestine which would arouse not only Arabs but Muslims in other lands.

Britain Turns to the United Nations

In January and February of 1947 two final efforts were made to settle the future of Palestine with, or through, Britain. In January representatives of the Palestine Arab Higher Committee came to the conference in London, but were more intransigent than ever now that the Mufti had resumed his sway.[63] The Zionists held aloof from the conference but went on talking separately to British Ministers. They offered to make no public mention of their goal of a Jewish state if the Jewish immigration they demanded were allowed, and if the ban on Jewish land purchase were lifted. This seems to have been as much as they could hope the Yishuv to accept in its now aggressively demanding mood. But there was no hope of Arab agreement to these points. Then early in February Bevin put forward a variant of the provincial autonomy plan. The Arab and Jewish provinces would enjoy local self-government, and Britain would stay for five years. During the first two years, 96,000 immigrants would be admitted at a rate of 4,000 a month. Any more could come only with the agreement of the Arabs, the British, and the United Nations. This was rejected by both sides.

Britain now publicly recognized what had long been apparent to her own statesmen as well as to her extremist foes, that in the post-Hitler world the British simply could not carry out the conflicting obligations to Jews and Arabs undertaken thirty years before, when there had been at least some hope of reconciling them. In the 1920s, European Jewry had seemed prosperous and safe. The Jewish National Home in Palestine was to be for the dedicated and elect; without the Nazi holocaust it might have remained relatively small. It might even have become, as some idealists had hoped, a national centre of the highest quality, concentrating and embody-

63. The Arab League Council had given him their funds for Palestine; see Sykes, pp. 368–71.

ing all the finest elements in Jewish tradition. It could not then be predicted that Palestine would become an area of the bitterest strife, desperately claimed as a plank of salvation by a hunted race arriving in such numbers as to thrust aside those whose home it had been for thirteen centuries and more. But, as things were, the British Government announced in Parliament on February 18, 1947, that the only course open to it was to submit the problem to the judgement of the United Nations, since it had no power under the Mandate to award the country either to the Jews or the Arabs, or to partition it between them. Thus it would fall to the world body rather than to Britain to discover a solution if it could.

The United Nations Special Committee

In May of that year a United Nations Special Committee on Palestine (UNSCOP) was appointed with a membership of eleven.[64] The Swedish delegate was chairman, and the members included Dr Ralph Bunche who in 1946 had been seconded from the U.S. State Department to the United Nations. Despite its exclusion from the Committee, and its traditional hostility to Zionism, the Soviet Union was just then by no means opposed to the emergence of a Jewish state in Palestine. This favourable disposition "came exactly at the right moment for the Zionists. Without it they would not have stood a chance. . . . It was the Soviet aim to diminish western influence in the eastern Mediterranean and if possible advance its own interests in the power vacuum that was bound to follow the western withdrawal. Ten years later, Stalin's heirs were to pursue this policy in close collaboration with the radical forces which had [meanwhile] come to power in the Arab world."[65] It was a modern version of Russia's centuries-long thrust southward towards the Mediterranean and the Fertile Crescent.

64. To avoid Soviet participation, the United Nations excluded members of the Security Council. The members were from Australia, Canada, Czechoslovakia, Guatemala, India, Holland, Iran, Peru, Sweden, Uruguay, and Yugoslavia.
65. Laqueur, p. 579.

The Committee arrived in Palestine in June 1947, to find the country in growing chaos. There was a new rash of terrorism. Irgun and the Stern Group had continued their exploits from the year before, when the membership of Irgun had doubled. They boasted of murdering 373 people by the end of 1946, most of them civilians. There was ugly retaliation by the British forces, and one key terrorist was condemned to death and hanged. By March 1947 the Arabs had resumed terrorism too. Shortly before the Commission's arrival, the Mufti had managed to get joint action by Arab guerrilla groups against the Jews. Around the same time, in May, Irgun and Stern broke free a number of terrorists in Acre gaol.[66] Three death sentences were passed on those who did it, and this in turn led to one of Irgun's most deplorable murders.[67] Then, as we saw earlier, a crowd of refugees in *Exodus* arrived during the Committee's visit, and their handling by the British was another gift to Zionist propaganda. In the prevailing mood of violence and hatred, Ben Gurion himself began using the language of the extremists.

The United Nations Proposals

In September UNSCOP produced two proposals, both drawn up by Dr Bunche. The plan of the majority backed—once again—partition, though on terms rather less favourable to the Zionists than the recent plan of the Jewish Agency, even though it had certain advantages from the Zionist standpoint. Palestine would be divided into six parts, three for the Arabs and three for the Jews. The Jews received 56 per cent of the country (although they then had barely one-third of the population); the Arabs, 43 per cent. The Jewish state would cover upper Galilee and the Jordan and Beisan valleys, the coastal zone from south of Acre to some twenty miles south of

66. See Sykes, pp. 379, 381.
67. When the terrorists were executed, two captured British sergeants—obviously in no sense makers of the policy Irgun was fighting—were hanged by them in what purported to be retribution for this British act. See Begin, pp. 288-90. No other comparable incident produced in the British public so strong a reaction against these champions of the Zionist cause.

PROPOSED
U.N. PARTITION
OF PALESTINE
NOVEMBER 1947

Tel Aviv, including Jaffa and most of the Jezreel valley; and also the greater part of the Negev. The Arab state would cover western Galilee, most of the west bank of the Jordan down to and including Lydda (Lod), and the Gaza strip.[68] Although the country was divided broadly according to ethnic distribution, the plan left 100,000 Jews in the Arab state, and, 500,000 Arabs in the Jewish state, amounting to nearly half its population. Jerusalem and Bethlehem would be a separate enclave under international control. There was also supposed to be a ten-year economic union during which the Jewish state would subsidize its Arab neighbour. In the heat of debate and the hustle of events to follow, this last well-meaning but probably impracticable suggestion was forgotten and allowed to lapse.

Four members of UNSCOP objected to this rather strange plan. One of the four—the Australian—abstained, and the other three—from India, Iran, and Yugoslavia—produced a minority scheme that reverted to the illusory hope of a bi-national state. Palestine would become a federation on this basis.

The Arabs rejected both plans. The Zionists hesitated, then accepted the majority plan, and did their best to ensure its passage in the United Nations—and for this a two-thirds vote was needed. Indeed, they stuck to their acceptance even though their allotted area was whittled down by some five hundred square miles during the U.N. negotiations.[69] President Truman seems to have told his people to help the Zionists, and "great pressure was brought to bear, reportedly by American officials, on the countries which had planned to cast negative votes." When it came to the count on November 29, 1947, partition was passed by thirty-three votes to thirteen, with eleven abstentions. In spite of the Cold War, Russia voted with the United States in backing the plan. Britain had small confidence in its success, and abstained from voting. At this crucial moment, and in such a setting, the Arabs could have done much to convince the world of the strength of their case over Pales-

68. See map.
69. Sykes, p. 387.

tine. But once again they let their chances slip. When it was certain that the partition plan would pass, they asked for consideration of the minority (federation) plan, which they had rejected. By now it was too late.[70] To fight then seemed the only answer; and in December the Arab League Council declared that it would stop partition by force.

Britain Sets Date for Withdrawal

After the U.N. vote Britain announced that she would give up the Mandate on May 15, 1948. Outside the government service most Palestinians, whether Jew or Arab, looked forward to her early departure for similar though conflicting reasons. Both were intent on establishing their own state, the Jews in the area allotted to them, the Arabs in the whole of Palestine. The many who mistrusted Britain seemed convinced that the British had no real intention of leaving when they said, but would somehow cling to power. In fact, however, London was applying a policy that had recently worked in India. It had been shown there that, unless the people of a country on the verge of independence were faced with assuming full responsibility at an early and definite date, they would not face up in time to the realities of freedom. In India, however, Britain had backed a partition scheme that was put through in the end with relative success; and for this she had earned some credit.[71] In Palestine there was little credit to be earned. There was, it is true, a scheme of settlement sanctioned by the world authority, but one that, Britain knew, was bound to end in failure and bloodshed, since one side rejected it. The British have been sharply criticised for not carrying out the U.N. plan, and for letting things drift until

70. Armajani, pp. 371–72; see also Laqueur, p. 582.
71. Early in 1947 the British Government announced that it would hand over its power in India not later than June 1948. Later it brought the date forward, and India and Pakistan became independent in August 1947. Some are convinced that there would have been prolonged bloodshed if this prompt and genuine notice of withdrawal had not been served upon the peoples of India.

their departure. But before the crucial vote they had warned the U.N. Assembly that they would not impose partition by force. Indeed it is hard to see how they could have done so. Since the Arabs were determined to fight it, partition could have been carried out only if the British had fought with the Zionists against them, with those forces they had now promised to remove. Meanwhile, the commander of these forces had been told to keep the peace in the areas they held, and to ensure their orderly withdrawal by not becoming involved in the Arab-Jewish conflict.

Of course British policy in the final months of the Mandate is by no means free from reproach. Having handed over the problem to the United Nations, and being faced with a U.N. plan which they were certain had no chances of success, the British seem to have given up any attempt to secure the adoption of some alternative scheme that might—however slim the chances—have stood a better chance of keeping the peace. This, as we shall see, was left to the Americans and to the eleventh hour. This last plan also failed, since matters were by then heading for quite a different climax.

War Starts; the British Stand Aside

As it was, fighting between Jew and Arab broke out on the morrow of the U.N. vote and continued until the British left, and after. In the mounting chaos savage things were done by both sides. The British "made no preparations to transfer power to Jews and Arabs, nor indeed to the Committee of Five which had been appointed to administer Jerusalem. The most pressing task facing the Jewish population was to strengthen its defences, since the Arab countries had already announced that their armies would enter the country as soon as the British left; . . . [in fact] an Arab Liberation Army inside Palestine was established in February [1948] with the help of Syrian officers as well as irregulars. . . . While Britain continued to supply arms to the neighbouring Arab countries, . . .

America had declared a general arms embargo [and] the Jewish forces had great difficulty in obtaining supplies. By February the Arab forces were on the offensive throughout the country."[72]

Meanwhile, whatever the orders of the British troops or the motives behind them, it will always be felt as a disgrace that Britain, which still had the only regular civil and military organization in the country, should have failed to prevent such outrages as occurred in April 1948. In that month Irgun and the Stern Group massacred nearly everyone in the Arab village of Deir Yassin near Jerusalem. A few days later, in retaliation, Arab guerrillas killed the medical and academic personnel travelling in a convoy with Red Cross markings on its way to the Jewish Hadassa Hospital and the Hebrew University, also on the outskirts of Jerusalem. A nearby British military post did nothing until it was too late.

Washington Has Second Thoughts

If Palestine produced divided counsels in Britain, this was no less the case in America. President Truman was on the whole favourable to the Zionist cause, though at times exasperated by the constant pressure of its advocates. Indeed, at one point he refused to see even Dr Weizmann, who had come to America specially for this purpose in March 1948. But he was persuaded to relent, and in his ensuing talk with Weizmann the President was satisfied that they had reached full understanding.[73] But the departments of State and Defense gave high priority to America's oil and strategic interests in the Middle East and saw clearly the dangers of arousing the Arab countries against the United States by being too pro-Zionist over Palestine. For this reason they were cool towards the

72. Laqueur, p. 583.
73. Apparently the man who persuaded the President to change his mind was a non-Zionist Jewish-American from Kansas called Eddie Jacobson, who had been his partner in the clothing store they had run in earlier years. He had told the President that Weizmann was as much a hero to him as Andrew Jackson was to Truman. See Sykes, pp. 411–12.

UNSCOP plan, and this became startlingly clear the day after the President's talk with Weizmann, when the U.S. Ambassador to the United Nations announced that his Government would like action suspended on partition, and that the General Assembly should discuss instead a further, temporary trusteeship for Palestine under the U.N., without prejudice to the country's eventual political future. This roundabout language meant that the UNSCOP plan had been dropped by its chief champion, the United States.

Astonishingly, the White House had simply not been told by the State Department of the orders sent to its U.N. delegation. In view of his talk at the White House, even this did not shake Weizmann's faith in Truman, though it badly shook the Zionists. Actually, in the long run this strange incident seems to have served the Zionist cause. The President seems to have been prejudiced by what had happened against the pro-Arab policies dictated by oil and strategy; and to have been genuinely concerned not to go back upon the encouragement he and his Government had personally given to Weizmann and to the Zionists as a whole when they had earlier supported UNSCOP. This was to count decisively when, two months later, the fate of the National Home hung in the balance. When that time came, Weizmann's trust in Truman was fully vindicated.[74]

The Yishuv Arms: the Struggle for Arab Unity

With the country in a state of war and the U.S. arms embargo operating against them, the Zionists were collecting arms wherever and however they could. Through lack of arms they had suffered some early reverses against the Arab guerrillas, who by February had cut off communication between the Jewish settlements, and between Jerusalem and Tel Aviv and other parts of the country. Shortly before, as the struggle became fiercer at the start of 1948, Irgun had blown up an Arab-owned hotel in Jerusalem. But the

74. Sykes, pp. 412–15; Armajani, pp. 372–73.

Arabs had retaliated by destroying the Jewish-owned building of the local newspaper, the *Jerusalem Post*. And when Palmach had tried to relieve the Jewish settlement of Kfar Etzion southwest of Bethlehem, their whole detachment was killed by forces loyal to the Mufti under an able commander from his clan, Abd el Kader Husseini.

Meanwhile, as the British forces gradually withdrew, the Jordan army—the Arab Legion—under its British commander, Glubb Pasha, had been taking over the eastern area of Palestine allotted to the Arab state. For King Abdullah was determined, as we shall see, that the Arab state—or what eventually remained of Arab Palestine—should be part of his dominions. With this prospect and on this condition, he alone of the Arab leaders was prepared to accept, however regretfully, the fact of a Jewish state, and to come to terms with it. He even had secret meetings, on two occasions, with Mrs Golda Myerson (later Meir), representing the Jewish Agency, the lady who was destined to become Prime Minister of Israel.[75] But Abdullah's realism and ambitions were bitterly resented by the Mufti, who regarded himself as the natural leader of an Arab Palestine separate from Jordan. Eventually Abdullah was to pay for his realism, when he was murdered by an agent of the Mufti in one of the great Mosques of Jerusalem.

Abdullah's ambitions were endorsed, somewhat hesitatingly by Britain, and by Iraq, which under her related Hashimite dynasty was prepared to help in their achievement. They were by no means welcome to Egypt, which by now was seeking the leadership of Islam as well as of the Arab world. Egypt's claim to lead Islam would be gravely prejudiced should Abdullah become the guardian of the Dome of the Rock in Jerusalem, the Muslims' third holiest shrine. The Syrians were also no great friends of Abdullah, since on the whole they supported the Mufti. The unity of the Arab world in face of the threatened Jewish state was thus already something of a delusion.[76]

75. Sykes, pp. 392, 429.
76. *Ibid.*, pp. 388-92.

Anglo-Arab Post-War Adjustments

A further complication was that, at that moment, Britain's relations with Iraq and Egypt were by no means easy, and this to some extent disturbed her close relations with Abdullah. After the war the British had had somewhat stormy treaty negotiations with both countries. Britain sought mainly an updating of the earlier treaties, but the young nationalists wanted far more sweeping changes. In February 1948 a draft treaty with Iraq, agreed in London, was rejected in Baghdad and caused the fall of the Government. Its failure invalidated provisions for the further supply of British arms to Iraq, and thus potentially weakened the developing Arab war effort against the Zionists.

A draft treaty with Egypt, also agreed late in 1946, met one of the principal Egyptian demands, in that British forces were to be withdrawn from the country by stages, and completely by September of 1949. But this treaty failed also, and on the issue of the Sudan. Egypt insisted on the unity of the Nile valley—that is, on union with the Sudan, a traditional goal of Egyptian policy since the days of the Khedives. It was also, of course, a principle clearly implied in the Anglo-Egyptian Condominium agreement. But since the reconquest of the Sudan mainly by British arms, Britain had in practice governed the area as a separate British dependency and had largely disregarded Egypt's rights under the Condominium. Now that nationalism had become increasingly the order of the day, the British goal for the Sudan was self-government and eventual independence both of Britain and of Egypt. This was unacceptable to the Egyptians at the time (though Sudanese independence was later accepted) and they ineffectively challenged Britain at the United Nations in August 1947. Anglo-Egyptian relations became as bad as ever, but Britain took one step to smooth their course. She withdrew her troops from the Nile Delta to the zone of the Suez Canal.[77]

77. Sykes, pp. 406–7; Mansfield, pp. 284–89.

Prospects for Israel Improve

In March and April of 1948 the tide of war started to turn in favour of the Jews. They had been getting arms by raiding British depots, or from British soldiers whom they had corrupted. More came from America in spite of the embargo; more still from Czechoslovakia, both to Jews and Arabs. In early April the Zionist forces struggling to open the Jerusalem-Tel Aviv road captured a hilltop village near Jerusalem after some bitter fighting in which Abd el Kader was killed. Meanwhile the Arab Liberation Army—the forces mainly from Syria and Lebanon which had entered northern Palestine—had somewhat ingloriously failed. Their leader was a boastful Lebanese soldier of fortune, Fawzi el Kawakji, who had made his mark during the Arab Revolt of the 1930s, when he had had a close understanding with the Mufti. During the present fighting he was defeated in the Jordan valley and again near Haifa, when he tried to cut the Haifa-Tel Aviv road by capturing a Jewish settlement southeast of the city.

A further setback for the Arabs was Britain's tardy insistence that the Arab Legion should be withdrawn from Palestine into Jordan by the end of April. This was a reversal of London's earlier policy favourable to Abdullah, and may have been dictated by a desire to avoid further tension with Egypt at a moment of difficult relations and at a time when Egypt was jealously watching any moves that might give Abdullah special advantage in the imminent struggle for Arab Palestine. It may also have been prompted by a decision to avoid any move that could be interpreted as provocative when an all-out struggle might just possibly have still been avoided. Yet, strangely enough, nothing seems to have been done to get the Arab Liberation Army out of the country.[78]

In any event, with some checks and reverses, the tide of war would continue to flow on the whole in favour of the Jewish forces until the armistice agreements of 1949 establishing provisional frontiers for the State of Israel. Even before the end of the Man-

78. Sykes, p. 428.

date, Haifa, Jaffa, and much of Galilee were in Zionist hands. Although the military build-up of the Yishuv within Palestine had inevitably been irregular and piecemeal, many of their troops were seasoned veterans of World War II who had seen tough service with, or alongside, the British. The Zionist insistence upon building up the nucleus of a Jewish army—an army that at the end, fought with the Allies under its own flag; Jewish service in the Palestine Regiment; and the high rate of individual enrolment of young Zionists in the British forces during the war—all proved their full value during these crucial months.

Start of the Palestinian Dispersion

Many Palestinian Arabs had fought desperately to save their country for themselves. But their military training was sketchy, and their efforts, along with those of the other Arab forces, were far less well coordinated than those of the Yishuv in arms, with its modern training and single-minded, dynamic thrust. Temperamentally, also, the Arabs were somewhat more mercurial and at that stage less attuned to long and patient resistance when things went wrong. But in practice the ordinary people of both communities—those not in the front line of any current struggle—had always found it wise to move away and seek refuge in times of adversity. So in those parts of Palestine where the Jews were gaining the upper hand, numbers of ordinary Arabs, scared of the threat they faced, started to move out. In January 1948 the British High Commissioner reported a considerable Arab emigration, mainly from the middle and propertied classes. When this happened, it was the instinct of the humbler Arabs in what was still a partly feudal society to follow in the footsteps of those they were accustomed to respect.

In some cases Arab publicity took the line that the departure of their people from Palestine was a planned manoeuvre. There is little to substantiate this, however, or the Zionist charge that appeals were broadcast by Arab leaders, including the commanders of the Arab forces, urging the Palestinian Arabs to leave, with the assurance that they would be able to return after Arab victory. The commander of the Arab force that in the event did the only really effective fighting—namely, the Arab Legion under Glubb Pasha—would certainly have heard of such an appeal if it had been made; and he is positive that it was not. But the eventual Jewish conquest of Haifa and Jaffa did indeed lead to further massive Arab evacuation. And some of the more ruthless deeds of the Jewish extremists, such as the killings at Deir Yassin, may have been designed to spread panic and hasten the Arab departure. In the eyes of such people the Arabs, whatever their rights to the soil, stood in the way of the Jews' resuming possession of their Promised Land. Indeed, before the end of the struggle, some of the more ardent Zionists—those who had invoked the spirit of Masada when things were desperate—may well have felt inspired and justified by the memory of Joshua smiting the Canaanites in the dawn of Jewish history.

In any event, by the close of the British Mandate this new exodus was well under way. It is reckoned that by mid-May 1948 between 150,000 and 300,000 Palestinian Arabs had fled their country into exile.[79] And this was only the start. During the many months of bitter fighting to follow, hundreds of thousands more Arabs were moved to flee. Some with stronger nerves stayed and lived on unharmed, but by the end of 1948 only some 167,000 were left in what became the Jewish state. And in what had been their country, others had now in effect become their masters.

The End of Britain's Thirty Years

The last stage of the Mandate was one of exceptional confusion in Palestine, London, Washington, and New York. At the United Nations the U.S. delegates at first stalled over the trusteeship proposals that had so unpleasantly surprised the President after his talk with Weizmann in March—then later revived them in a rather

---

79. The lower figure is given in Armajani, p. 373; the higher by Anthony Nutting, former British Parliamentary Under-Secretary of State for Foreign Affairs; see *The Arab-Israeli Impasse*, ed. Majdia Khadduri, p. 57.

different form. There were inconclusive moves to persuade the two warring sides to discuss a truce—but the Arabs and the Zionists made conditions unacceptable to each other. Meanwhile, despite passage of the UNSCOP plan, the British in Palestine had been reluctant to hand over their authority to a U.N. body, or any other, in advance of their departure. But with the help of a U.N. Truce Commission formed in Jerusalem by the French, Belgian, and U.S. consuls-general, the Palestine Government managed during its last week to enforce a cease-fire throughout the city, though not in the whole country.

Under the new trusteeship proposal put forward by the Americans at the United Nations apparently after consultation with London, the U.N. Trusteeship Council would administer Palestine temporarily until a regime acceptable to a majority of the Arabs and Jews had been worked out. One reason why the British supported this new plan was that they were disturbed by the exodus of the Arabs and the stories of Zionist harshness towards them. Moreover, with the Americans, they were just then facing an acute Cold War crisis: the Soviet blockade of Berlin. In view of the Eastern European background and radical views of many of the top Zionist leaders, and the support Moscow had been giving Zionism at the United Nations, London apparently suspected that a triumphant Jewish state in most of Palestine might mean a victory for Communist Russia in the Middle East. In any case this newest plan was turned down by Ben Gurion and Weizmann, and Weizmann warned President Truman that partition was the only solution. By now the President seems to have resolved to put through a Palestine policy in line with his personal views and sympathies. On April 23 he had a message conveyed to Weizmann to the effect that he favoured a reversion to American support of the UNSCOP plan, adding that if this led to the proclamation of a Jewish state, he would recognize it immediately. This undertaking was kept strictly secret, but it helps to explain the resolute confidence with which the Zionist leaders took their final, decisive step.

The Arab position during these final weeks of the Mandate was equally confused. The Arab League met in Amman at the end of April at a time when, under British pressure, the Arab Legion of Jordan was slowly, but not completely, withdrawing from Palestine. As on earlier occasions, there was small evidence of Arab unity, and marked lack of harmony between the Egyptians and Jordanians. It was now that King Abdullah made a final and vain attempt to avoid war by a plan communicated secretly to Mrs Meir. There was no hope of Zionist agreement to such plan, since it revived the idea of a bi-national state, which had never been attractive to most Zionists; and this time it would have emerged in the form of a combined Jordan-Palestine state with Jewish autonomous provinces under Abdullah as King.[80] But by now the Yishuv had set up their own provisional national administration and national council in Tel Aviv, and were already using their own flag and postage stamps there, and devising their own system of taxation.[81]

As the end of British rule approached, there was a strange unreality about the final proceedings on Palestine at the United Nations. In the General Assembly the American delegation continued to discuss the Trusteeship proposal with their fellow delegates until the very moment of Britain's withdrawal. Although President Truman had already decided that he would prefer partition on the lines of the UNSCOP plan, he deliberately allowed these discussions to continue so as in effect to leave all options open. There was always just a chance that the United Nations might find a solution that would avert the almost inevitable all-out war. But the discussions on Trusteeship made no progress; and as May 15 approached, it became increasingly obvious to the President and even to the State Department that there would soon be a Jewish state, and that the United States would have to recognize it. But would it be viable? Might it later be defeated or collapse? For all that the Jewish forces had achieved, the area they actually controlled was still vulnerable and not very large. One just could not be sure.

Some such doubts seem to have assailed Mr Truman in the last

80. See Sykes, pp. 423–30.
81. Laqueur, pp. 584–85.

fateful days before May 15; and Secretary of State Marshall suggested to the Zionist leaders on his behalf that it might be best to wait. Still, strong in the President's assurance to him, Weizmann advised his people to proclaim the State without delay. Ben Gurion was equally determined, though apparently he did not know about the President's assurance. On the morning of May 14 the White House was notified by Weizmann of the imminent proclamation of the State. The British High Commissioner had already left, having advanced his departure by one day. The proclamation in fact took place that same morning (by Washington time), though the ceremony was actually held at four in the afternoon in the Museum of Modern Art in Tel Aviv, when Ben Gurion announced the establishment of a Jewish State to be called Israel. In Israel there would be equal citizenship for Jew and Gentile; and it would pursue a policy of good will towards its neighbours. Pending general elections, it would be ruled by an emergency government authorized by the national council. Two days later Weizmann was elected first President of Israel; and Ben Gurion became Prime Minister. As soon as the news of the proclamation was received in Washington, Israel was recognized by the United States; soon afterwards recognition followed by the Soviet Union and other nations. American recognition occurred while the General Assembly was still discussing Trusteeship, and the American delegation there seems to have been taken completely by surprise.[82]

The end of British rule in Palestine was the closing chapter in a dramatic course of events launched by the Balfour Declaration and the British conquest of the country some thirty years before. It was also the start of a new and equally dramatic era in the Holy Land. For there was now once again there a Jewish state, to the rejoicing of most Jews throughout the world. This was a unique achievement, a triumph of restless vitality, courage, and persistence which compelled the admiration of millions who had no special feeling for Zionism or the Jewish race. But the new era was also to be one of tragedy and despair for those displaced.

82. Sykes, pp. 430–34; Laqueur, pp. 585–86; Armajani, p. 373.

Few if any of the British statesmen of that earlier generation who had raised Arab and Jewish hopes in so arbitrary and masterful a fashion could have foreseen the shape of things now emerging in consequence of the cruel dilemma they had created by promising to one people something that was destined to victimize the other. So far as they had thought clearly about the future that had now arrived, many of those behind the Declaration had envisaged the Zionists as creating a Jewish National Home of moderate size and in a spirit of gratitude to Britain for the chance of having once more a national presence in Eretz Israel. And they had thought of the Arabs of Palestine as continuing to live mostly in their traditional homes, and gaining in prosperity and modern skills from daily and friendly contact with their dynamic Jewish neighbours. Instead, those, like Churchill, still alive in 1948, faced a Palestine seething with resentment of Britain. The Zionists strongly resented the fact that the British had been slow to give them all they asked. The Arabs were even more bitter, for Britain had given so much to the Jews that more and more of the Arab people were fleeing in panic and disorder from the land of their fathers. The confident assumptions of an imperialist age that had not reckoned with Hitler had indeed recoiled upon their authors' heads.

Chapter 14

Israel and Her Neighbours: the First Two Wars and Their Sequel

Since mid-1948 the story of Israel and her neighbours has been a constant theme of the press and other media throughout the world, and is thus broadly, if somewhat one-sidedly, known to all with an interest in public affairs. For the triumphs and problems of Israel have been presented in superbly well-organized publicity, with the support of many in key positions in Western countries who are linked by ties of race or sympathy with the struggles of the Jewish state. On the other side of the conflict, despite vigorous and dedicated championship of the Palestinian Arabs in the Arab nations and elsewhere, these special skills and opportunities in the international field have either been lacking, or so far have not been developed as they might have been. One result is that the depressing fate of the Palestinians—and the rights or wrongs of their case— have never aroused interest and sympathy in the West comparable to that aroused by the fate of Israel. This has been especially the case in America.

In any event, almost every aspect of this large field has been covered in depth and detail by many highly qualified specialists and scholars, and I have no claim to compete with them. Nor do I propose to relate in any detail the internal development of Israel; for this has been admirably done by others. A chief purpose of this book is to clarify as simply and concisely as possible the far less familiar origins and causes of the present critical situation; and the preceding chapters have sought to do this. In the rest of this book I shall be covering, up to the present, the main factors and events relating to the Arab-Israeli conflict. Finally, I hope to suggest certain conclusions that can perhaps be drawn from these for the future, in the light of the unique and complex history that lies behind them.

The key to what is still the most intractable and dangerous of all Middle Eastern problems lies in the refusal of the Palestinian Arabs, supported by most of the surrounding Arab nations, to accept the creation of the State of Israel. The case for this refusal is strong in law and logic, however lacking it may be in realism and common sense. For the bulk of the Palestinians were eventually displaced from their country by Zionist policies conceived in Europe, and sponsored by Britain, policies the Arabs were under no obligation to accept since their previous consent was neither sought nor obtained. On the other hand, in pursuing a constant attitude of rejection they have shown an obstinate courage in a losing cause which has proved disastrous for their own interests. "The Jews invariably accepted every promise or concession . . . even if it were much less than they had hoped for. . . . They then proceeded to demand more. . . . The Arabs . . . rejected categorically any concession. . . . The result was catastrophic. . . . The Arabs always demanded all or nothing—and obtained nothing."[1]

If the Palestinians had been willing to compromise with the growing National Home, the Zionists might have been forced to agree to a bi-national state in which the Jewish element would not have exceeded half the population; and the mandatory would have

1. Sir John Glubb, A *Soldier with the Arabs*, pp. 45–46. The account he gives of the war with neighbouring Arab countries which developed in 1948 is of particular weight and value, coming as it does from the commander of the regular Arab forces principally involved.

welcomed this as a fair solution. Alternatively, they could have secured, under partition, an internationally guaranteed Arab state covering roughly half the country; but in practice only Jordan has, at moments—shown some disposition to come to terms with the reality of Zionism, and such a course has been fraught with the gravest risk for her rulers. Her first King met his death largely on this account, and his grandson, Jordan's present ruler, has had to crush an incipient civil war in his determination to check what he regards as the futile and fatal resort of the Palestinians to terrorism in an effort to redress their wrongs. "Jordan and the Arab Legion were for many years to represent the moderate, practical defence of the Arab cause, and as a result they were to be anathema to Jews and Arabs alike. The Jews saw in them the principal obstacle to their complete victory. The Arabs always believed them to be but half-hearted in their cause."[2] The Mufti was particularly hostile, being, as we saw, intensely jealous of King Abdullah's assumption of the leadership of Arab Palestine, to which he himself aspired.[3]

Israel Fights for Survival

As the British withdrew and the new State was proclaimed, the Arab-Jewish fighting of the past few months took on a new intensity. As outside Arab forces came to the aid of the Palestinians, the struggle developed into a regular and bitter, but by no means inevitable, war, in which the survival or destruction of Israel was at stake. On the Arab side the brunt of the fighting fell on the Arab Legion of Jordan. This had a total strength of six thousand men

2. *Ibid.*, p. 49.
3. The solution to the Palestine problem favoured by Jordan was that Jordan absorb Samaria and Judea, as in fact happened. Galilee would join Lebanon; the Gaza-Beersheba area, Egypt. (In the event all of Galilee was taken over by Israel, and only the Gaza Strip went to Egypt.) A weakness of the Jordan plan was the almost impossible condition that British garrisons remain in Jerusalem and Haifa; though, if this had been possible, any necessary exchanges of population could have been carried out without undue hardship and without creating destitute refugees. See *ibid.*, p. 59.

(without reserves), of whom forty-five hundred were available for service in Palestine.[4] As explained above, it had been ordered out of Palestine by the British, and by May 14 its evacuation was almost complete. But arrangements were made by the Jordan Government to move the Legion back into Palestine the moment the British left, so as to ensure the fulfilment of King Abdullah's plan to take over the contiguous Palestinian areas.

In view of the King's disposition to come to terms with the Israelis and to secure under his leadership the best terms he could for the Palestinian Arabs, there need have been no general war at this juncture. This was triggered by the last-minute intervention of certain countries of the Arab League. The strongest pressure to fight came from Egypt, anxious to justify her new-sought role of leader of the Arab nations, with the support of Syria, the traditional centre of Arab nationalism, and of the Mufti, then operating from Damascus and determined to frustrate Abdullah's Palestinian ambitions. Strangely enough, nearly a year had elapsed since Britain had announced her departure and the struggle for Arab Palestine had begun. Yet it was only two days before the end of the Mandate that the Secretary-General and other Arab League representatives arrived in Amman to discuss the intentions of certain member States to fight in the Palestinian war. The Egyptians had voted money for military operations, but there had been practically no advance preparation for the invasion of Palestine, no special training, no joint military planning. King Abdullah was chosen as Commander-in-Chief of the Arab armies, but he was not informed of the plans of operation of any of the armies he was supposed to command. "The Arabs had . . . been deluded by their own enthusiasm. . . . Fond of studying . . . the Arab conquests, . . . they believed themselves . . . a great military people and . . . the Jews a nation of shopkeepers [whom] they would find no difficulty in defeating. . . . The Arab governments did immense harm to . . .

4. *Ibid.*, pp. 89–90, 47–48. It had been reduced to this figure from 8,000 at the end of the war.

the Palestine Arabs. . . . They encouraged them to be defiant
. . . and failed."[5]

Given the haphazard and uncoordinated approach to the Palestine fighting of most of these outside Arab forces, their distance
from their bases (while the Israelis had the advantage of short, inside lines of communication), and the political jealousies between
them, there was in fact no grave risk of the extinction of the new
state of Israel. The dramatic picture presented to the world of tiny
Israel in deadly danger from "a concerted assault by the regular
armies of five Arab states"[6] with a total population of some forty
million, was in fact greatly, and perhaps deliberately, exaggerated.
The Iraqis, with a more effective military tradition than the Egyptians or Syrians, entered central Palestine with some 3,000 men and
for a time gave useful support to the Arab Legion by holding Samaria—the region of Jenin and Nablus—against Israeli attacks. The
Egyptians invading from the south had about 10,000 men. The
Syrians and Lebanese mustered 4,000 between them. They briefly
entered Palestine but had been forced to retreat by mid-July. The
Saudi Arabians did virtually nothing.[7]

The Israeli Forces

On the Israeli side, the Palmach—the special units of the Hagana
with commando training—were reckoned to have 5,500 men in
1948, and thus on their own outnumbered the Arab Legion troops
available for service in Palestine. In the Hagana itself, 30,000 men
had served with the British forces during World War II and its
total strength was considerably more. In addition the Irgun fought
with the national forces and its strength in 1946 had been assessed

5. *Ibid.*, pp. 78–79; see also pp. 82, 84–85.
6. Roth, p. 417.
7. For these figures of the Arab armies, see Glubb, pp. 93–94. He says that
Saudi Arabia "was rumoured to have contributed 2–300 men, who joined the
Egyptians."

at 3,000 to 5,000.[8] Arms procurement for the Israeli forces had (as noted earlier) been sketchily but skilfully improvised by various unorthodox means. Also, many weapons and much ammunition were locally made. The Arab Legion was itself short of equipment for fighting a war. It had for instance no reserves of ammunition after the withdrawal from Palestine of the British forces, who had supplied it to the Legion as required. Two attempts were made to procure what they needed from the British forces in Egypt, but the first consignment was commandeered by the Egyptians for their own troops, and the second had to be unloaded because of the U.N. ban on the sale of warlike stores to either side.[9] In the light of all these factors the Arab-Israeli armed conflict in 1948–49 was by no means an unequal struggle, and in some respects the advantage lay with the Israelis.

The New War. First Phase. The Fate of Jerusalem

The war fell into three phases. After four weeks of fighting, a four-week truce came into force on June 11, 1948. After a further brief spell of fighting, there was a second truce from July 18. But fighting resumed in mid-October. This continued in varying form throughout the winter. Then, between February and July of 1949, successive cease-fire arrangements were made between Israel and her various enemies. These were in due course formalized as armistice agreements which kept an uneasy peace in the region for some years.

8. There is some uncertainty about the exact strength of the total Israeli forces at this time. These figures are taken from Cecil Roth and Geoffrey Wigoder, eds., *The New Standard Jewish Encyclopedia*, pp. 1491, 1815–18. Glubb considers that "the main Israeli army in May, 1948, may have been 55,000 strong. Its training, quality and armament varied considerably in different units." Elon, p. 198 n., agrees approximately with Glubb's figures for the invading Arab armies, but says that "the Israelis at this stage had some 3,000 'regulars' under arms and 14,000 inadequately trained recruits; only 10,000 rifles with 50 rounds of ammunition each, no tanks, four ancient cannon smuggled in from Mexico, 3,600 submachine guns." Elon's troop figures seem unwarrantably low in view of those given by Roth and Wigoder.

9. Glubb, pp. 91–93.

In the first phase the Old City of Jerusalem fell to the Arab Legion. The Israeli forces defending the Jewish quarter were forced to surrender, and this area of special sanctity to the Jews, including the Wailing Wall, was to remain in Jordanian hands for nineteen years. On the other hand, in Galilee, the western sector of which had been assigned to the Arabs by UNSCOP, the Israelis made considerable progress in taking over territory beyond the boundaries of the U.N.-sponsored Jewish state, capturing the port of Acre and the area between it and the Lebanese border. In the south the Egyptians captured Gaza and Beersheba, but after bitter fighting the Israelis managed to halt their advance some twenty-five miles south of Jaffa.[10] In the centre of the country, one of the main Israeli objectives was to keep open a corridor between Tel Aviv and Jerusalem and to hold the new quarters of Jerusalem, outside the walls of the Old City. These new quarters owed a great deal to Jewish effort and enterprise, and they were part of the Holy City, where the Israelis were determined to make their capital. They gained their objective, but failed at that stage to capture the country's only airport at Lydda, or the neighbouring key town of Ramleh.

The Bernadotte Mission

Meanwhile, on May 20, only five days after the British departure, the United Nations appointed as its mediator in Palestine Count Folke Bernadotte, nephew of the King of Sweden and President of the Swedish Red Cross. Israel had already applied for membership of the United Nations, but her relations with the world body were to be by no means smooth. Not only did sharp differences of view develop between the mediator himself and the Israelis but also a tendency on Israel's part to ignore U.N. authority (in which Israel was by no means alone) and to deny facilities to the observers

10. See Elon, pp. 198–200; this gives a vivid and moving account of the defence and ultimate conquest of the Jewish settlement, Yad Mordechai, which was reconquered after the fighting resumed.

brought in by Bernadotte, and later by Dr Bunche, to follow the course of the hostilities and other aspects of the situation. Having brought about the first truce on June 11, Count Bernadotte established his headquarters in Rhodes and put forward suggestions for peace negotiations. Meanwhile, officers from the three countries (the United States, France, and Belgium) composing the U.N. truce commission in Jerusalem were to control the execution of the truce.

At the end of June, Bernadotte gave both sides his own plan for a final settlement. This newest of the many plans to bring peace to the Holy Land proposed a union of Palestine and Jordan in which the two parts—one Arab and one Jewish—would each have full control over its own affairs, including immigration and foreign relations, subject to the right of the union authorities "to promote common economic interests, to operate and maintain common services, including customs and excise, to undertake development projects and to coordinate foreign policy and measures for common defence."[11] It also proposed that the Negev should be included, in whole or part, in the Arab territory, as would Jerusalem—but with "municipal autonomy" for the Jewish community. On the other hand, western Galilee would go to the Jewish territory. Haifa would become a free port; Lydda a free airport.

As might have been foreseen, this plan—somewhat less realistic than most—was categorically rejected by the Israelis; it was turned down by the Arabs also, and we are not concerned with it further. The Israeli note of rejection spoke of "wounded Jewish feelings" over the Jerusalem proposal; and these were to lead in a few months to possibly the worst crime of violence committed by the unbalanced fanatics of the Stern Group. What is remarkable is that this scheme, put forward by the authorized plenipotentiary of the U.N. Secretary-General, made no reference to the UNSCOP plan. This, it will be remembered, was rejected by the Arabs and it had been visibly overtaken by the events of the Arab-Israeli war.

11. Keesing's Contemporary Archives, p. 9408.

For the Secretary-General and his mediator it had clearly ceased to be a specific commitment of the United Nations. Nevertheless Israel described it in her answer as "the only internationally valid adjudication on the question of the future government of Palestine," although the validity or invalidity of the UNSCOP plan was clearly a matter for the ultimate judgement of the Secretary-General of the United Nations.

The Israelis were evidently determined to rely on the UNSCOP plan to secure some of their basic goals, among them virtually the whole of the Negev. On the other hand, as will be clear, they had no intention of binding themselves by this plan in any restrictive sense. They were not prepared to limit the boundaries of Israel to those laid down by the United Nations. Nor would they consent to the internationalization of Jerusalem, as UNSCOP required, though they might consent to consider the internationalization of the Holy Places.

Second Phase of the War: Israel Expands Her Frontiers

Fighting broke out again on July 8, but ten days later, on July 18, the mediator was able to arrange a second truce. In this short interval the Israelis greatly improved their military position. They took Nazareth in central Palestine as well as the airport at Lydda, and Ramleh. In this region the Arab Legion had to concentrate on defending the key salient of Latrun, commanding the main road from Tel Aviv to Jerusalem, and maintaining contact with the Iraqi forces in Samaria.[12] By the time of this second truce, the Israelis had occupied all the area assigned to the Jewish State in the UNSCOP plan except for part of the Negev and a small pocket of land near Lake Huleh still held by Syrian forces. Indeed they claimed to have taken an additional four hundred square miles, in-

12. Lying in the coastal plain, Lydda and Ramleh were harder to defend than Latrun, in the western fringes of the Judean hills. General Glubb had to make the difficult decision not to detach troops from his very limited forces to help in defending Lydda and Ramleh. See his pp. 157–72.

cluding almost all of western Galilee (allotted to the Arab state) and a wide corridor from Tel Aviv to Jerusalem.

Bernadotte Tries Again for Peace

On July 26 the Israelis made it plain that they were not prepared to respect the United Nations plan so far as Jerusalem was concerned. They announced that the new city, in view of its special Jewish character, would be regarded as Israeli-occupied territory— i.e., would not be internationalized—and then appointed a Military Governor of Jerusalem. In consequence of this Jordan eventually took a similar line with regard to the Old City by incorporating it into her territory. Early in August the Israelis asked Count Bernadotte to convey to the Arab Governments an invitation to peace negotiations. This, however, was rejected by the Arab League on the grounds that its members could not recognize the existence of a Jewish state in Palestine.

Meanwhile, there were frequent infractions of the truce, especially in Jerusalem, each side laying the blame upon the other. Bernadotte reported that both Arabs and Jews had deliberately come to ignore U.N. authority. He pleaded with some success for urgent measures to aid the Arab refugees, and also put forward fresh proposals for a settlement. There was no more talk of a union between Arab and Jewish territories. Israel, he said, was there to stay and her boundaries must be fixed, whether by agreement between the parties concerned, or by the United Nations. In any case these boundaries "should not . . . be rigidly controlled by the territorial arrangements envisaged in the resolution of November 29, 1947" (i.e., the UNSCOP plan). He then reiterated most of the territorial points in his earlier proposals. Thus, the Negev would go to the Arabs, and the whole of Galilee to the Jews; there would be a free port and airport at Haifa and Lydda; but Jerusalem, instead of going to the Arabs, would be internationalized. Moreover, "the right of the Arab refugees to return to their homes in Jewish-controlled territory at the earliest possible date should be affirmed

by the United Nations, [and] the political, economic, social and re-
ligous rights of all Arabs in the Jewish territory, and of all Jews in
the Arab territory, should be fully guaranteed and respected."[13]
The whole settlement should be supervised by a Palestine Conciliation Commission of the United Nations.

Although these proposals were backed by the United States,
they, too, were rejected by both parties to the struggle. The Israelis
would not accept the loss of the Negev, since this "would cut off
about two-thirds of Israel's territory." Western Galilee, despite its
fertility, would not be adequate compensation. They objected also
to the internationalization of Jerusalem and to the free port and
airport provisions. They claimed Jerusalem as part of Israel, Lydda
since that was linked with the "vital necessity for Israel to maintain
unbroken territorial connection with Jerusalem," and Haifa, which
must and would remain an integral part of Israel though full port
facilities would be granted to neighbouring states on a basis of
reciprocity.[14]

On September 17 Count Bernadotte was murdered in a suburb
of Jerusalem by members of the Stern Group. They took credit for
the deed in the press, stating that all United Nations observers
were members of foreign occupation forces who had no right to be
on their territory. Dr Bunche succeeded Bernadotte as acting mediator. Nothing effective was done by the United Nations to bring
this crime home to those responsible; but the Sternists were out-
lawed by the Israeli Government.

The Gaza Government of Palestine

Shortly afterward, the Mufti's organization—the Palestine Arab
Higher Committee, backed by the Arab League, and with marked

13. Keesings, p. 9532. It is striking that the proposal to guarantee the political
and economic rights of the Arabs, which had been deliberately omitted from
the Balfour Declaration, should have been brought forward by an international
authority when it was far too late for it to have any chance of acceptance.
14. *Ibid.*

support from Egypt and Syria—announced the formation, in Egyptian-occupied Gaza, of a Palestine Government claiming sovereignty over the whole country, and one in which both the Foreign and the Defence Ministers belonged to the Husseini clan. A constituent assembly would meet at Gaza on September 30. King Abdullah declared that he would oppose the formation of this new government within an area forming part of the "security zone of the Jordan Government," which zone he regarded as extending from the Egyptian to the Syrian and Lebanese borders. Actually this move was judged in Jordan to be an Egyptian attempt to gain control over all of Arab Palestine through a puppet government, and to deprive Jordan and Abdullah of all authority in that area.[15]

Third Phase of the War: Israel Advances in the South

On October 14 fighting flared up again between the Egyptian and Israeli forces in the south, and the Israelis were generally successful. They managed to link up the territory they already held with their settlements in the quadrilateral Majdal-Falluja-Gaza-Beersheba, and after a week, on October 21, captured Beersheba itself. This victory gave them control of the roads northwards to Hebron and Jerusalem, and westwards, to Gaza. The Arab Legion and Egyptian forces in the Jerusalem area were cut off from the south, and the Israelis could now threaten both them and the Egyptians in the Gaza area. A further cease-fire, ordered by the United Nations, was accepted by Egypt and Israel on October 22. This required that the combatants should withdraw from the areas they had not occupied at the beginning of the latest fighting, and also that U.N. personnel should be given facilities to observe the situation in the Negev. In practice both these conditions were largely ignored by the opposing forces.[16]

15. *Ibid*. See also Glubb, p. 190.
16. Keesings, pp. 9049–50.

The Amman Meeting and Arab Disunity

On October 23 the leaders of the Arab Governments met in Amman at King Abdullah's invitation to discuss what should now be done. In Jerusalem, in spite of the successive cease-fire, much desultory fighting had gone on ever since the Jordanians' capture of the Old City at the end of May. The initiative had then passed to the Israelis, who had tried to retake old Jerusalem by breaching the walls. Both sides were losing trained men at a rate they could ill afford, but the Arab Legion suffered particularly from the smallness of its numbers in proportion to the size of the front it had to cover. At the Amman meeting King Abdullah and his Prime Minister therefore asked for action from the other Arab forces nominally under the King's command. Could not the Egyptian forces, who were a few miles south of Jerusalem, attack the Israelis so as to draw off some of the pressure on the Arab Legion, since the Egyptians were not then actively fighting and were far more numerous than the Legion? The Egyptians thought this quite impossible; they were discouraged by the prospect of potential Israeli attacks.[17] And there was the further problem of helping their own forces in the south. These forces had been split: those in the coastal region were withdrawn to Gaza, those farther east were besieged in Falluja. Westward of Jerusalem the Arab Legion was extended as far as Beit Nabala, northeast of Lydda, and Latrun, and south of the city as far as Hebron. With a view to helping the Egyptians in Falluja, the Iraqis were asked to move south to Latrun. They too found it impossible to do what was needed. The Syrians offered to send a division to fight for Jerusalem, but all in Amman knew that their only division was fully committed on the borders of Galilee, and so again, nothing came of this. In the end the Arab Legion had to try on its own both to hold Judea and to give what help it could

17. There is an amusing yet sadly ironic account of this ineffective meeting in Sir Alec Kirkbride, A *Crackle of Thorns*, pp. 159–63. Kirkbride was at the time British Ambassador to Jordan.

to its far more numerous Arab allies in the south. Meanwhile, at the end of October, the 5,000-strong Arab Liberation Army was conclusively defeated near the Lebanese border.[18]

Further Israeli Progress

In spite of the new cease-fire, Israeli forces and the Arab Legion clashed near Beit Jibrin, roughly half way between Hebron and the coast, on October 28. The Israelis had moved south from Artuf with the aim of capturing Hebron and freeing the former Jewish settlement of Kfar Etzion between Hebron and Bethlehem, which had been taken by the Arabs several months earlier. The Arabs had moved down from Bethlehem to Hebron at about the same time, then westward to Tarqumiya. A clash ensued between a Legion reconnaissance group sent forward to the Beit Jibrin area and the Israelis advancing from the village. This minor engagement brought to a halt the Israeli advance towards Hebron and ultimately resulted in the fixing of the armistice line between Arab Palestine (later incorporated into Jordan) and Israel some ten miles west and twelve miles south of Hebron.

In November and December the Egyptian forces in Gaza advanced eastward in an attempt to reduce the pressure on their besieged garrison in Falluja. The Israelis fought back successfully, having declared themselves obliged to reserve their freedom of action. According to a report by Dr Bunche to the Security Council at the end of December, they also expelled U.N. observers from the Israeli forces. In consequence, he said, the U.N. was unable to supervise effectively the truce in the Negev. On January 5, 1949, it was announced from Tel Aviv that Israeli troops had penetrated into Egyptian territory. Nevertheless, another cease-fire was arranged on January 7. Meanwhile on December 1, 1948, the principal leaders of Arab Palestine meeting in Jericho passed a resolution advocating the incorporation in Jordan of what remained of their territory. This achieved one of King Abdullah's principal goals

18. *Ibid.*, and Glubb, pp. 200–202.

and was formally approved in Amman. Egypt, Syria, and Saudi Arabia strongly resented this development, and the rest of the Arab League refused at the time to recognize this union of Jordan and Arab Palestine. The Government for all Palestine—earlier formed in Gaza under the auspices of Egypt, Syria, and the Mufti—was moved to Cairo, and formally rejected Abdullah as ruler of the area they claimed.[19]

Israel and Britain: a New Clash

At this point Britain once more became involved in the Palestine struggle. Under the terms of her alliance with Jordan of March 1948, Britain agreed to a request from Amman to send a force to the Red Sea port of Aqaba, at the head of the gulf of that name, where the frontiers of Palestine, Jordan, Egypt, and Saudi Arabia meet. Moreover, since U.N. observers had been barred from the Israeli forces, Britain also sent reconnaissance aircraft from the Suez Canal zone to discover the depth and scale of Israeli incursions into Egypt. While their crews had strict orders to avoid combat, on January 7, the day of the latest cease-fire, five of the aircraft were shot down by the Israelis. According to London, the attack occurred several miles inside Egypt. The Israelis refused to accept the British protest, on the ground that Britain had not yet recognized Israel,[20] and contended that the aircraft had been flying over southern Palestine. They also protested against Britain's proposed despatch of a force to Aqaba, arguing that since Aqaba and the adjoining parts of Jordan were in no way threatened by Israeli forces, this "could have no purpose but to threaten Israel's territory in the southern Negev."

At the United Nations, Mr Abba Eban (today Israel's Foreign Minister) called on the Security Council to investigate Britain's

19. Glubb, pp. 205–17.
20. Britain, in accordance with traditional international practice, delayed recognition of Israel until the new state should have a functioning administration, known frontiers, and the ability to carry out international obligations.

"menacing attitude" towards Israel. Neither the Egyptians nor the Israelis, he said, had asked for British military intervention. Yet Britain had taken the part of the Arab states in their dispute with Israel, and had fomented an artificial crisis on the eve of Israeli-Egyptian negotiations at Rhodes. For its part, the British Government declared that Dr Bunche's reports "left no room for doubt" that the existing threat to stability and peace in the Middle East was the outcome of Israeli aggression, and that the Israelis had launched three military operations in violation of the truce. One had been in the Negev from October 15, another in northern Galilee later in October, and a third, again in the Negev, from December 22. And there was the risk of further such attacks. Israel had failed to comply with the Security Council's resolutions calling for an immediate cease-fire and the withdrawal of the combatants to their positions before the breakdown of the truce.

The fact was that the Council had been losing control over events, and its authority had to be re-established. In a press interview on January 12, Dr Weizmann, President of Israel, stressed his country's desire for peace with the Arab states. His personal friendship with some Arab leaders was, he said, long and honourable. He knew that in time Jew and Arab could learn to live together in peace. Israel "had no designs on the territory of others, but needed the land awarded to it by the United Nations in order to settle the tragic survivors of Nazi persecution." Israel, he added, was in no sense a puppet of either Communist Russia or of the West. Strict neutrality was her life blood.[21]

Israel's Armistice with Egypt and Lebanon

In spite of these dissensions, an armistice between Egypt and Israel was signed at Rhodes on February 24, 1949, after six weeks of negotiation; and later armistice agreements with the other Arab states were on broadly similar lines. Their stated object was to promote the return of permanent peace to Palestine. The agreement with

21. Keesings, pp. 9743, 9745.

ISRAELI BORDER AND
ARMISTICE LINES
SPRING 1949–SPRING 1967

0   50
Miles

Beirut

Damascus

Sidon

Kiswe
(Kissoue)

LEBANON

Tyre

Quneitra

GOLAN
HEIGHTS

Acre

Safed

L. Tiberias
(L. Kinnereth)

SYRIA

Haifa

GALILEE

Nazareth

Dera'a

Irbid

M E D I T E R R A N E A N   S E A

Jenin

Mafraq

SAMARIA

Tulkarm

Nablus

Jordan River

Tel Aviv
Jaffa

Lydda

Jericho

Amman

Latrun

Jerusalem

J O R D A N

Bethlehem

Gaza

Hebron

DEAD SEA

Dab'a

Rafah

Beersheba

Kerak

El Qatrana

El Arish

I S R A E L

El Auja

N E G E V

Quseima

El Ghanu

Aneiza

Petra

U A R
E G Y P T

Ma'an

El Kuntilla

Ras an Naqb

S I N A I

P E N I N S U L A

Elat

Aqaba

Gulf of Aqaba

Egypt left the Gaza-Rafah coastal strip (about twenty-five miles long and four miles wide) in Egyptian hands, but the Egyptians had to cede Falluja, while the Israelis retained Beersheba. Apart from the Gaza Strip, the final demarcation line followed in general the old frontier between Palestine and Egypt. Yet this and the lines of demarcation negotiated with the other states were not to be regarded as political or territorial boundaries. They, like the other provisions of the agreements, were without prejudice to "the rights, claims and positions" of the parties concerned in connection with "the ultimate peaceful settlement of the Palestine question."[22]

Armistice negotiations with Lebanon were concluded on March 23 at the frontier point of Ras el Nakoura. In effect the old frontier with Palestine was restored, and the Israelis withdrew from a few villages they had occupied in Lebanon. As in the case of the Egyptian and other agreements, limits were placed on the number of troops permitted to either side near the demarcation line. Negotiations between Israel and Jordan started at Rhodes on March 2. Since Syria was then on the eve of a military revolution, it was some time before Damascus was ready for negotiations. The Iraqis had asked Jordan to negotiate on their behalf pending the withdrawal of their troops. At the start of these negotiations, the Arab Legion with about a hundred men held the northern base of a triangular wedge of territory framed by the Jordan and Egyptian frontiers, at a distance of some fifty-five miles from the Gulf of Aqaba. Before consenting to a cease-fire with Jordan, Israeli forces advanced in sufficient strength to render impossible effective resistance by this small Legion group. After some fighting the Arabs withdrew, and the Israelis occupied the whole triangle down to what is today Elat on the Gulf. They justified such action, taken at a time of peace negotiations following a cease-fire, with the argument that this territory was part of the area allotted to Israel under the UNSCOP plan. Yet Israel felt justified in retaining also the other territory she had conquered despite the fact that some of

22. *Ibid.*, p. 9829.

these conquered areas had been allotted to the Arab state under the same plan.

Armistices with Jordan, Iraq, and Syria

Having obtained her strategic objective in the south, on March 11 Israel signed a cease-fire agreement with Jordan. The Iraqi forces were due to leave Samaria two days later, and the Israeli Government at that point indicated that when this occurred it would feel entitled to occupy this area also. On this account Iraq was then persuaded by Jordan to postpone the withdrawal of her forces. Plans were made for the take-over of the Iraqi area by the Arab Legion, but on March 13 the Israeli Government notified Dr Bunche that it would consider this a violation of the existing truce. At this point King Abdullah again contacted the Israelis direct. Direct negotiation with their Arab neighbours was a prime goal of the Israelis then and afterwards, and in response they agreed to the Arab Legion's replacing the Iraqis if the Legion would withdraw from a narrow belt of territory, some 112 miles in length and 1¼–2 miles wide, along the northern and western perimeter of their area. After some hesitation this was accepted, and the armistice was signed on April 3.

The Jordanians had little alternative, deprived as they now were of any effective support from their allies. The armistice left them with the important triangle in Samaria linking the towns of Nablus, Jenin, and Tulkarm. On the other hand the strip they had abandoned was an economic gain to Israel, since it took in some of the fertile, low-lying approaches to the hills. It was also a strategic gain, since it covered some of the higher ground as well and thus reduced the threat to the coastal plain of having the Jordanians entrenched in the hills immediately above it. (The general position of the line fixed in the Hebron area is noted above.) On their replacement by the Legion, the last Iraqis were withdrawn on April 28.[23] As with all the others, these agreements were supervised by a mixed armistice commission under U.N. chairmanship. In this connection, a special U.N. Truce Supervision Organization (UNTSO) developed out of the U.N. Truce Commission, which had been set up, as we saw, just before the end of the Mandate.

The conclusion of an armistice with Syria was held up for various reasons, among them the revolution at the end of March. Negotiations had opened on the Syrian frontier on April 12 and led to a cease-fire, but armistice talks broke down in mid-May and were not resumed until July. The armistice agreement signed on July 20 had no special features of geographical interest, save that it involved the return to Israel of a Jewish settlement captured by the Syrians early in the war. It followed the general lines of the other agreements, and the demarcation line was along the international frontier. This was the last of the armistice agreements, all of which had been concluded under Dr Bunche's auspices. He then retired from the field, and was later awarded the Nobel Peace Prize for his outstanding achievement. What remained of his functions were then transferred to the Palestine Conciliation Commission, which had been proposed by Count Bernadotte with the support of the United States. Meanwhile, in May, Israel had been readily welcomed into the United Nations by most of its members, despite the reluctance she had shown on various occasions to observe the rules that body had laid down.

23. The northern border of what became known as West Jordan or the West Bank ran westward from the Beisan area and eventually southward leaving the Gilboa Hills in Israel, and leaving also the whole Haifa-Tel Aviv railway in Israel, except where it touched Tulkarm. Positions were "frozen" in the Jerusalem area. There were special guarantees for the operation of the railway to Jerusalem and for free movement on vital roads, such as that between Latrun and Jerusalem. There was to be free access to the Hebrew University and the Hadassah hospital on Mount Scopus, and to the Holy Places. (In practice, however, Jews were barred from visiting the Wailing Wall and only periodical convoys were allowed up to the University and hospital until the conquest of the whole city by the Israelis in 1967.) From the Dead Sea to Aqaba the demarcation line followed the old Palestine-Jordan frontier, and thus left in Israel the potash works in the region of Sodom at the southern end of the Dead Sea. See Keesings, p. 10100; Glubb, pp. 227–37.

The Palestine Conciliation Commission

The Conciliation Commission, after appointment of its three members—one American, one French, and one Turkish—by the U.N. General Assembly, held its first meeting in Geneva in mid-January. Its headquarters were then established in Jerusalem, it held talks with Dr Bunche at Rhodes towards the end of January during the Egyptian-Israeli armistice negotiations, and then toured the Arab countries in February. In April it sponsored a meeting at Lausanne of representatives of Israel, Egypt, Jordan, Lebanon, and Syria, in the hope of reaching agreement on the outstanding issues in regard to Palestine, such as the future of the Arab refugees, the internationalization of Jerusalem, and the demarcation of definite frontiers. The talks broke down after two months, basically on a question of priorities over the first issue. Israel insisted that the problem of the refugees, and the possibility of the return of many of them to what was now Israel, should be part of a general peace settlement. The Arab states insisted, however, that the refugee problem must be dealt with before any general political settlement could be reached.[24]

The Arab Refugees

During the last months of 1948 the U.N. General Assembly had debated exhaustively the problem of the Palestine refugees. Funds for relief had been voted and recommendations for a settlement passed, based on the repatriation of refugees who wished to return or individual compensation for those who did not choose to do so. At that time their number was reckoned at a half-million; by the time the Conciliation Commission again brought the matter up at the United Nations in June of 1949, their number had risen to nearly a million.[25] There was an appeal for fresh funds for the U.N.

24. Keesings, pp. 9747, 9829, 10100, 10101.
25. According to a U.N. report of April 1949, the number of refugees had risen to 750,000 by January 1, 1949; to 770,000 by mid-February; and to 875,000 by April 1. In June the Secretary-General reported that the United Nations was caring for 940,000 refugees. See Keesings, p. 10101.

relief campaign, and the U.S. Government responded generously
with no less than $16,000,000; and other governments, in proportion
to their resources.[26] In mid-April it was estimated that 425,000
refugees were in Arab Palestine, nearly all of which had been absorbed by Jordan; 225,000 (including most of Jaffa's population),
in the Gaza Strip; 130,000 (for the most part from Haifa and western Galilee), in Lebanon; about 85,000 (mostly from the Beisan
and Tulkarm areas), in Jordan proper; and another 85,000 (from
the Safad area), in Syria. There were also reckoned to be about
11,000 in Egypt and 4,000 in Iraq. The view expressed by Israel
during the Lausanne meeting was that the best solution would be
the resettlement of the refugees in the neighbouring Arab countries "in view of the fact that the Arab population of Israel was
only about 70,000."[27]

There has been much controversy about the fate of these unhappy people during the last twenty-five years; and we shall see
later how their problem was expanded and intensified by the war
of 1967. Meanwhile, some misconceptions have been dispelled by
those who have actually dealt with them. Thus according to a
former UNRWA official, it is by no means the case that the refugees have been stagnating in idleness at international expense; and
that because many (though actually less than 40 per cent) are still
living in camps, no progress has been made towards their rehabilitation. He denies also that the countries in which they live have deliberately kept them pathetically dependent on charity as a politi-

26. Relief work for the refugees was being dealt with in Palestine/Israel by the
International Red Cross; in the Gaza area, by the American Society of Friends;
and in Lebanon, Syria, and Jordan, by the League of Red Cross and Red Crescent Societies. The U.N. Relief of Palestine Refugees Organization was buying
food supplies and handing them over to these relief organizations. Help was
also being given by the U.N. Children's Fund, especially with the care of children and of expectant and nursing mothers; and by the World Health Organization. This last established a medical programme which the relief organizations
applied. From May 1, 1950, the U.N. Relief work was concentrated in the
hands of the U.N. Relief and Works Agency for Palestine Refugees in the
Near East (UNRWA). *Ibid.*
27. *Ibid.*

cal weapon in their campaign against Israel. The neighbouring Arab nations have, it is true, opposed mass resettlement of the Palestinians, and there are many valid social and economic reasons for this. But they have on the whole a creditable record of promoting their rehabilitation as individuals through education, training, and employment.

Jordan, where the refugees became citizens and make up about one-third of the population, has made special efforts to help them, despite the great difficulty of integrating such numbers into the social fabric of a state with very limited economic resources. Lebanon has also had difficulty in view of the need to maintain a careful balance between Christians and Muslims there and the fact that some 95 per cent of the refugees are of the Muslim faith. The Syrian Government has given substantial help towards the integration of its Palestinians. Only in the Gaza Strip, where refugees make up 70 per cent of a population with a density of some 3,600 per square mile, has this kind of "normal" rehabilitation been virtually impossible.[28] There is in any case, as mentioned earlier, quite a demand for educated Palestininans for positions of responsibility in these neighbouring Arab countries, as well as in others farther afield such as Kuwait. So far as the older generation is concerned, the reason given is that the British system of education under the Mandate held the Palestinians to higher standards in certain respects than those of the Arabs of these neighbouring lands. But these educated and qualified Palestinians have of course always been only a fraction of all those living in exile.[29]

28. Harry N. Howard, a former U.S. Foreign Service officer who in 1956–61 was Acting Representative on the UNRWA Advisory Commission and later Special Assistant to the UNRWA Commissioner-General. He is now Professor of Middle Eastern Studies at the American University, Washington, D.C. These views were originally expressed in *Mid-East*, vol. 7, no. 8 (October 1967), and appear in updated form in *The Arab-Israeli Impasse* (ed. Khadduri), pp. 168–72.

29. The general attitude of educated Israelis to the Palestine refugee problem seems today to be a blend of bad conscience (rarely admitted in public) and irritation that what could have been a simple issue has been vastly complicated by the focusing of international effort and attention upon it. A young Israeli

The Bases of the Jewish State

A Jewish state was now once more a living reality in Eretz Israel. This was an achievement unique in history. For the first time a people in exile for twenty centuries had managed to fight its way back into a land that had since—and to some extent before that—belonged to others. For in ancient times, as we saw, the Jews had only briefly—under David and Solomon—dominated the whole of Palestine and beyond. For most of the Biblical period they had shared it with other peoples and kingdoms, and for much of that period they, like the others, had been vassals of the larger empires. Now, over most of the country, they had gained a domination far firmer than that of the transitory kingdom of ancient Israel, or even that of the heroic Hasmoneans of Judah. One curious aspect was the shifting impact of Jewish rule. Ancient Judah had covered very much the area of West Jordan now salvaged by the Arabs from the loss of their Palestine; whereas the new Israel, with its centre of gravity in the coastal strip, covered the ancient land of the Philistines and some parts of the Biblical kingdom of Israel that had disappeared around 700 B.C.

The Israel of 1948 meant the Return to Zion. For a century Zionists had striven for this as a practical goal; and, long before that, it had been a remote, spiritual ideal during Jewry's tribulations in the Diaspora. How far now, in these days of fulfilment, did the reality correspond to the ideals of the past? Did it match the plans and aspirations of those creative thinkers who had launched the Zionist movement in the nineteenth century? Did it meet the high standards of Weizmann himself, the former disciple of Achad Ha'am and a leading architect of the Balfour Declara-

---

professor, whom it may be preferable not to name, told the author in August 1971 in Jerusalem, that all this international fuss had kept the issue alive far longer than necessary. If the refugee problem had been left to the Israelis, they would have given money to the neighbouring Arab Governments and, before too long, there would have been a "Darwinian solution," which presumably meant that the toughest of the Palestinians would have survived, and the rest would have gone to the wall.

tion, which had given his people a national rebirth in Palestine—
of Weizmann, who had lived to become the head of the modern
Jewish state? Has the price demanded by the emergence of Israel
in the shape of injustice to others and the creation in Israel's Arab
neighbours and in other ancient lands with Jewish communities in
the Middle East of new and bitter enmities towards the Jews, de-
tracted from the greatness or value of this astonishing achievement?
Could the great goal of a Jewish Return to Palestine have been
achieved by less demanding and more compassionate Zionist approaches, and greater wisdom on Britain's part, without breeding
hatred or fostering injustice in this most vital area of the world?
And, with the militarily powerful Israel of the 1970s, can these resentments be permanently overcome by policies of far-seeing generosity and understanding towards the Palestinian Diaspora and
the Arab countries on every side? And how could this be brought
about so that Israel's neighbours might come to see her, not as an
armed camp and a menacing intruder, but as a source of benefit
and cooperation?

Israel, born in strife, is a land of contradictions. Her people, used
to violent methods and constant danger, have by no means shed
the complexes of pogrom-ridden Eastern Europe, from which most
of her leaders or their fathers came. "The price may be high, but
no one really knows the exact amount paid by Israelis in psychological entanglements, debilitating repressions, compensations, and
illusions, dangerous and otherwise."[30] There is "a spreading cult of
toughness. . . . This . . . is not as yet accompanied by a disdain
of intellect and of moral qualities. But there are times when it
comes close. . . . A spartan rigidity . . . now marks large seg-
ments of the younger adult population." In some contexts this has
reminded foreigners of German youth groups in the 1930s.[31] But
the danger, the hardness, of life in Israel has evoked a vigorous and
powerful response that might not have been called forth by settlement in a more fertile and peaceful land. In comparatively few

30. Elon, p. 235.
31. *Ibid.*, p. 243.

years the country has developed materially and culturally to an astonishing degree. Thus, in the 1970s Israel boasts of seven universities, the second highest per capita rate of university students in the world, and more medical doctors per capita than any other country.[32]

The Ingathering

A unique feature of Israel has been the unlimited immigration—the "ingathering"—of Jews from all parts of the world.[33] This is a policy that seems to make nonsense of the cautious quotas of the Mandate period, but it has of course been possible largely because of the massive clearance from the country of most of its former inhabitants. "It was an integral part of the Zionist ideal to gather in the home as rapidly as possible the dispersed tribes who were oppressed." Consequently Israel at once passed the Law of the Return, giving to every Jew the right of admission unless he had worked against the state.[34] But who, exactly, is a Jew? The traditional definition was a person of the Jewish faith. Many Zionists, however, especially the young, were non-religious. In Israel today, therefore, in accordance with Jewish religious law, you are Jewish if you had a Jewish mother; you are also Jewish if you are of the Jewish faith, even by conversion.[35]

From 1948 there were two great waves of immigrants. The first

32. The universities would include not only the Hebrew and Tel Aviv universities but also the religious university at Ramat Gan, the Technion at Haifa, the Weizmann Institute of Science at Rehovoth, and the university colleges at Haifa and Beersheba.

33. In Hebrew, *Kibbutz Galuyyot* (in full: Ingathering of the Exiled Communities).

34. Norman Bentwich, *Israel*, p. 67.

35. This is a valid definition for general purposes, though the position is in some respects rather more complex. Thus, an agnostic of Jewish descent is perfectly acceptable as a Jew and an eventual citizen of Israel. But in the case of a person of Jewish descent who had come to Israel as a Catholic monk, the courts decided that, since he had specifically embraced another religion, he did not come within the accepted definition of a Jew.

brought the survivors of the holocaust from Central and Eastern Europe, though rarely from Russia, where barely half the Jews had escaped death. The Soviet Government had always officially banned anti-Semitism, but it did not regard the Jews as a nationality, and opposed Zionism. In the 1920s it had even allotted a remote area in eastern Siberia for Jewish settlement, to be called the Jewish Autonomous Region.[36] The Soviets had supported the creation of Israel because, it seems, they had hoped for Communist influence in the new state, and also because Israel might create discord profitable to Communism in the Middle East. But when Russia found that the Communists gained little power in Israel, her basic hostility to Zionism intensified so that, around 1955, she started to back the Arab cause. Immigration from Russia to Israel is still often held up and most Russian Jews emigrating in recent years have had to pay heavily for the privilege.

Survivors of the Nazi massacres usually prepared themselves consciously for life in Palestine by learning Hebrew, studying the country, and getting some agricultural training. Unlike some immigrants under the Mandate who brought capital with them, these people came from a ruined world and had nothing but their skills to bring. By October 1949 the flow of immigrants from Central and Eastern Europe had declined, and some 70 per cent of the total were arriving from another source.

From 1949 a new wave of Jewish immigrants came from Asia and Africa, many from communities as old as the prophets. Since those ancient days they had lived, on the whole, in tolerable and sometimes in rich and honourable conditions. They were old fashioned but pious, and believed in a Messianic Return to the Holy Land, not in a modern Jewish state there engineered by man. But now those communities, especially in the Arab world, risked being victimized as scapegoats for the humiliation of the Arab forces at the hands of Israel. So many of them, with encouragement and help from Israel, left their ancient homes and arrived, bewildered, in a state that indeed was Jewish but stamped by secular ideas and

36. This was Birobidjan, bordering on nothern Manchuria.

European leadership, and thus a world largely beyond their ken. In the first years 40,000 came from Yemen and 100,000 from Iraq alone, and thousands more from Syria, Turkey, Persia, Kurdistan, Afghanistan, India, and China, and eventually some 300,000 from Egypt and the rest of North Africa.[37] Despite all the official efforts at integration, few of these darker and simpler Jews rose to commanding positions in Israel. Having been, like the Christians, second-class citizens in the Muslim world, some still had the feeling of being in a lower category in their own Jewish home. This source of social tension is aggravated by the fact that since 1962 the Oriental Jews from Asia and North Africa have become 55 per cent of the total population.

The Economy

To absorb these masses into a small and poor land meant a fantastic strain on the economy, standard of living, and the whole social structure, especially during the years 1949–51. The largest number possible had to be settled in the emptier regions (such as the Negev), which cover more than half the country, and these regions had gradually to be brought back to cultivation as in ancient times. Other people were distributed throughout the land. Former British army camps were used as reception centres pending transfer to special temporary workers' villages in which, apart from agriculture, the immigrants were used on basic public works such as road-making and reafforestation. They were sent to existing

37. Yemen had perhaps the oldest Jewish community in the Diaspora, and that in Iraq went back to the Babylonian Captivity. The population of Israel increased from 782,000 (713,000 Jews) in November 1948 to 2,657,400 (2,344,900 Jews) in 1967, 58.4 per cent of these having been born outside the country. Between 1948 and 1967 493,000 had come from Eastern Europe, 48,800 from Western Europe, 303,100 from Asia, 297,000 from North Africa, 16,500 from North America, 27,000 from Latin America, and 1,200 from Australasia. In 1971 the population was reckoned as 3,034,000. From the founding of the state to that year, 1,400,000 immigrants had entered Israel from 100 different countries. See Bentwich, pp. 68–72; Roth and Wigoder, pp. 993 and 74; and Whitaker's Almanack, 1973, pp. 887–88.

permanent settlements when they had acquired experience. Absorption on this scale meant also that productivity had to be urgently boosted with the help of massive imports of capital equipment both for agriculture and industry. The goal was a self-supporting nation; and, though great strides have been made, this is still out of reach.

Apart from the smallness of the fertile area one big snag is a shortage of industrial raw materials. Potash and other chemicals are extracted from the Dead Sea, and low-grade phosphates from the Negev. There are also great potential hydro-electric resources, apart from the Jordan and Yarmuk waters already used for irrigation and power. Indeed, the Mediterranean could be an important further source of such power, since it would fall twelve hundred feet if linked by canal with the Dead Sea, as has been proposed.[38] Some oil has been struck in the south, but it fills only a tenth of Israel's annual needs. Near Elat the copper waste from the mines worked in King Solomon's day is being turned into copper concentrates, and a cement industry has been developed with local raw materials; but there is no iron or coal of commercial value. Imports of raw materials, as well as of foodstuffs and consumer goods, are thus vital. Israel is barred by her rift with the Arab states from bringing oil from Mosul by the 600-mile pipeline to Haifa and refining it there, as Palestine did in mandate days. But a heavy-chemicals industry, using sea-borne oil, is now based on the former British refineries there.[39]

In a generation, and in spite of three wars, both agriculture and industry have made striking progress. Israel today has more than a million acres under cultivation, more than 40 per cent of it irrigated. After a grave post-war slump, citrus products are again one of the state's main currency earners, with an export of a million tons a year. Land levels and climatic conditions vary so greatly, however,

38. Bentwich, p. 84. Roth and Wigoder, p. 994. Under the Mandate, potash was evaporated at both ends of the Dead Sea. But the northern end was in Jordan until its occupation by Israel in 1967. Israel has concentrated its potash extraction at the southern end near Sodom.

39. *Ibid.*

that the country can grow temperate zone, sub-tropical, and even tropical crops, from wheat, cherries, and northern types of feed for cattle and poultry, through olives, grapes, oranges, maize, millet, bananas, and mangoes, to tobacco and medium-staple cotton.

Another industry accounting for more than a third of Israel's exports is the polishing of imported rough diamonds—a traditional Jewish skill. Less traditional is the build-up of a fishing industry,[40] a merchant marine, and civil and military aviation. Since 1965 Israel has opened two modern ports in addition to Haifa—at Elat and Ashdod, an ancient Philistine city twenty miles south of Tel Aviv. Other expanding industries are textiles, plastics, rubber, cement, glass and paper. Israel's is a mixed economy. The Government is wedded to socialist planning and cooperative or collective enterprise. But it recognized from the start the need to attract private capital, and most of the new industries have been launched by private initiative with the aid of special inducements in matters of customs and taxation, after approval by an investment centre. The Israelis have used their wealth of brains to concentrate on highly sophisticated, science-based industries, and this has enabled them to produce aircraft as well as arms, and to operate a nuclear reactor.

Israel is now recognized by virtually all the countries of the Western world and the Communist bloc, and by most of those in Africa and Asia outside the Arab world. Her people have exported their intelligence on a formidable scale by sending experts in many fields to the underdeveloped nations, often in effective competition with the Communist bloc and even with Japan.[41] In the light of this achievement, some forecast for Israel a dominant economic-industrial role in parts of Africa and Asia. But those who have grounds for opposing her predominance in Palestine itself are likely to see in this a new economic imperialism like that with which the

40. Producing nearly 23,000 tons in 1971.
41. When the author was British Ambassador to Burma (1956–62)—and particularly towards the end of this period—the Burmese placed special reliance on Israeli expertise, *inter alia* for the organization of military-agricultural colonies in frontier regions like the armed Kibbutzim on Israel's borders with her Arab neighbours.

old Western empires and the United States have so often been charged. Meanwhile, another disturbing feature of Israel's progress is the spread of an unlovely modern industrial landscape through widening regions of what is still a land holy to the three religions of the One God. Humanly enough, many Israelis want to be "a nation like any other," and seem prepared to pay the price of disfiguring Eretz Israel in the process. But can a people such as the Jews, who gave birth to, or inspired, these three great faiths, and who held to their own creed and special characteristics against all pressures during two millennia, ever be anything but unique? And if so, should not the stamp they place upon the Holy Land be unique rather than commonplace also?[42]

Finance

In spite of everything there has been an annual trade deficit of some $300 million;[43] and it has only been possible to pay for all this swift growth because the finances of the new state, like so much else in Israel, are unique.

In the days of the Mandate the build-up of the National Home depended above all on the two basic institutions of the Zionist Organization already described—namely, the Jewish National Fund (*Keren Kayemet*), which had the duty of acquiring and developing land in Palestine, and the Jewish Foundation Fund (*Keren Hayesod*), for the settlement, education, and security, of the Zionist immigrants there. Both raised funds by popular contributions from Jews throughout the world. From 1929, when the Jewish Agency was founded as such by inclusion of non-Zionist elements, the Foundation Fund became its chief financial instrument. After the

42. The unhappy consequences of industrialization and hasty modernization are particularly visible in the Tel Aviv-Ramat Gan-Petach Tiqva area and northward to Haifa and Acre. In Jerusalem there has been much criticism, some of it justified, of the commonplace character of a good deal of the new building, not least of the functional apartment blocks and projected hotel on the Mount of Olives.

43. Roth and Wigoder, p. 992.

founding of Israel, both funds continued to collect money through-out the world, but much of their work passed to the Government. In 1949–50 the Government transferred to the National Fund large areas of abandoned land, so that eventually the Fund and the Gov-ernment between them owned over 90 per cent of all Israel. Under a Land Authority and Land Development Authority, the National Fund now handles the administration and development of all these areas and has done much for drainage, afforestation, and road-building. From 1948 the Foundation Fund concentrated on financing immigration, settlement, and the absorption of new citi-zens. (The cost of settling each new immigrant was around $2,000) After 1951 it became the sole fund of the Zionist Organization. Contributions from America have been all-important to Israel as they were to the growing National Home before 1948; and for the purpose of raising money there and elsewhere the Foundation Fund was known as the United Israel (formerly Palestine) Appeal. In a wider context this appeal was linked in 1939 with various American-Jewish bodies[44] in the United Jewish Appeal, which man-aged to raise almost two billion dollars up to 1967. With such funds and those from the Government itself, 1,400,000 Jews were brought into Israel up to 1971. The U.N. International Refugee Organization also helped towards transporting the Jews from Europe. These Funds and Appeals have become an essential prop of the development budget, which has thus been largely underwrit-ten by Jews outside Israel.

The goal of development is a thousand new villages on the five million acres reckoned to be available for settlement in Israel, ex-clusive of the area conquered in 1967. Despite the use of aban-doned Arab properties, new housing gets top priority and the bulk of development funds. In the first years the Government's share in development hinged mainly upon two American loans totalling $135 million, together with the sterling balances equivalent to

44. Such as the Joint Distribution Committee, the New York Association for New Americans, and the United Hebrew Sheltering and Immigrant Aid Society (HIAS).

nearly $70 million accumulated in Britain by Jewish enterprise in Palestine during the war. In 1951, Washington also made a Point Four grant of $50 million for the settlement of refugees and a further $17 million for economic aid. In the same year Israel floated an Independence Loan with an initial target of $500 million, half of which was taken up in the United States.

Taxation in Israel is high, and consists mainly of income tax, introduced by the British in World War II and steeply raised since. Revenue from income and other normal taxes (such as those on property, customs duties, and registration fees) covers the ordinary costs of government, apart from development, and part of the military budget, which is of course substantial, but the figures are kept secret.[45] Israel has also secured reparations for the outrages committed by the Nazis. These were claimed by the Zionists in 1945, and in 1946 some German assets were allocated by the Allies for Jewish relief. Later Israel formally claimed reparation from the governments of West and East Germany. In September 1952 Bonn agreed to pay the equivalent of $175 million in goods—mostly of a capital nature, over twelve years—to help meet the cost of settling the refugees. A further sum of $107 million was paid towards settlement of Jewish material claims against Germany for the rehabilitation of Nazi victims outside Israel. As part of this process much of this money was used for Jewish intellectual and educational purposes, mainly in Europe and the United States. The reparation settlement was scrupulously carried out by the German Federal Republic, and became an important factor in the development of Israel's economy, but East Germany refused to make similar reparation. Much was also done to secure the restitution, in West Germany and elsewhere, of Jewish property seized during the Nazi period; but again in Eastern Europe little or nothing could be achieved because of the nationalization policies of the Communist regimes.[46]

45. See Bentwich, pp. 74–85. The American loans were from the Export-Import Bank of the United States.
46. Roth and Wigoder, pp. 1616–17.

Inevitably grave inflation was caused by such sweeping measures of immigrant settlement and economic expansion in a country which till now has been unable to pay its way without outside funds. The Israeli pound, successor to the Palestine pound and originally worth three dollars, sank to a fraction of a dollar. But the coins of Israel themselves are designed to recall the last dramatic Jewish foothold in Palestine eighteen centuries ago. They bear the grapes and olive branch shown on the coins struck by Bar Kochba during his revolt against the Romans in A.D. 132.[47]

Parties and Politics

Israel's proclamation of independence had promised full social and political equality to all citizens regardless of race, creed, or sex, and other general rights, and announced the drafting of a constitution. As in Britain, it was found more convenient to have no written constitution, but to define constitutional procedure in basic laws passed from time to time by the Assembly (*Knesset*). The most important of these was the Interim Organic Law, regulating the functions and powers of the President of the State, the Legislature, and the Executive. Meanwhile, the rights of citizens are held to be fully safeguarded by the laws of the State. Despite the frequent resentment towards Britain during the Mandate years, these are based on the accepted principles of English Common Law. They also include relics of Ottoman law, British enactments under the Mandate, and religious law. In general the legal measures in force when Israel was established have continued in force unless they conflict with new legislation passed by the Knesset.

A fundamental point of the new State system, apart from unlimited Jewish immigration and the guarantees usual in all modern constitutions of free, compulsory elementary education and complete legal equality for women, is national service for two years, the first part to be spent on the land, the rest in the armed forces. This system has been used to infuse national spirit into people of the

47. Bentwich, p. 81.

most diverse origins and traditions. In addition to the conscript army of all young people between 18 and 35, there is a small, elite, regular army of volunteers. After their two years' national service, citizens are called up, as in Switzerland, for a few weeks every year plus one day each month until they are no longer fit for active service. Even before the age of national service, the young have para-military exercises at school, and some of the older children help with public works in the Negev or elsewhere.

Provision is also made for the remnant of the Palestinian Arabs. Arabic is an official language, and the Arab citizens of Israel—now some four hundred thousand, excluding those in the areas taken in 1967[48]—have the same legal rights as the Israelis, including representation in the Knesset and, as Israeli officials claim, the highest standard of living of any Arabs in the world. This claim needs some qualification. The wages of Arab workers, e.g., in the building trades, are far higher than they were in the days of the Mandate, and there is a more sophisticated organization of material life. Many enjoy fringe benefits and other privileges as members of the Histadrut, and this also applies to the areas occupied in 1967. On the other hand, the cost of living is far higher than under the old regime, and, in a country in constant conflict, the liberal principles of the legal system are often overridden in the interests of state security. These precautions tend to weigh heavily on the Arabs, especially on the simple people living in areas regarded as strategic. Such persons always risk being suspected when the guerrillas organized by their fellow Palestinians raid Israel from across the border and commit acts of violence there or elsewhere.

From the early years an Israeli military administration functioned in Galilee, the Negev, and the area west of the Nablus-Tulkarm-Jenin triangle—some of it only twenty-five miles from Tel Aviv. This administration had sweeping powers to restrict freedom of movement, speech, and the press, to control transport and posses-

48. On January 1, 1971, the population of Israel proper was given as 2,999,000, of whom 2,560,000 were Jews, 326,000 Muslims, 76,000 Christians, and 36,000 Druses. Statesman's Year Book, 1972–73, p. 1078.

sion of arms; and to declare areas closed and require special permits to enter or leave them. These powers were based on the Emergency Defence Laws used by the British, first against Arab insurgents and later against Jewish terrorists, and maintained in force, with some amendments, by the Israeli Defence Laws (Security Areas) of 1949. They had been hated by the Zionists in the last years of the Mandate, and many Israelis wanted them abolished, so much so that they were only prolonged by the Knesset by one vote in 1964. Three years later, however, in the wake of a fresh war, Israeli military administration was extended to vast new areas.

For all these reasons—compounded by the dispossession and exile of most other Palestinians—the Arabs in Israel, despite their rights under the civil law, have no true sense of equal status or close affinity with the dominant sector of their Israeli fellow-citizens of mainly European origin. On the other hand, so far as the Oriental Jews are also given a sense of inferiority by the European Israelis, there is a potential fellow-feeling between them and the Israeli Arabs, especially in the case of those Jews whose original language was Arabic. At the same time this dominant Israeli element—in the excitement of success and their pressing determination to establish a firm grip on Eretz Israel—does not seem to have been much concerned to give the Arabs within their borders that feeling of welcome participation on which genuine friendship and cooperation might one day be based. And this may prove to have been short-sighted.[49] In fact, though equal rights are guaranteed to citizens of other faiths and races, Israel is intended to be in a very special sense the country of, and for, the Jews. Thus, at the Twenty-fifth Zionist Congress in 1960, Prime Minister Ben Gurion declared

49. There is an interesting study of this question by Sabri Jiryis, a Christian Palestinian lawyer and former Israeli citizen. Called *The Arabs in Israel*, it was published in Hebrew and based on official Israeli material. Objective in most of his views, this writer, in conversation with the present author, paid tribute to the integrity of the Israeli system of civil law, under which, he said, an Arab in Israel could win a case even against the Government with no more difficulty than an Israeli; but things were different when it came to the security system. His book was republished in English in 1969 by the Institute for Palestine Studies in Beirut.

that only in Israel could the Jews feel that "the soil we walk upon, the trees whose fruit we eat, . . . the schools where our children are educated, . . . the landscape we see and the vegetation that surrounds us—all of it is Jewish."[50] With such a spirit abroad, it is clearly hard for non-Jews—even those whose homeland it was and is—to feel at home.

The first general elections to the Knesset were held in January 1949, and a year later, in 1950, Jerusalem was declared the capital of Israel. During that same year Jordan formally annexed those areas of Arab Palestine, including old Jerusalem, which had been held by the Arab Legion during and after the war of 1948. Both decisions ignored the UNTSO scheme of November 1947 for the internationalization of Jerusalem; a number of countries that have recognized Israel (including the United States and Britain) have therefore declined to acknowledge Jerusalem as the capital, and have continued to maintain their embassies in Tel Aviv. Until 1967 the Old City of Jerusalem was divided from the new by a carefully guarded line of demarcation cushioned by small areas of no-man's-land. The only regular transit point was at the so-called Mandelbaum Gate.

Unlike elections in the United States or Britain, in which a candidate is chosen by majority vote for his district, Israel bases its elections on proportional representation. This means that votes are given not for particular candidates or districts but for party lists. Anyone who is over 21 and qualified to vote, and can produce 250 supporters may run for election. The upshot at the first elections was a multiplicity of candidates (1,281 for 120 seats) and parties (21), many of these only small groups, of which only nine had the minimum number of votes (1 per cent) to win one seat in the Knesset. A consequence of this system was that since no one party had an over-all majority, the first regular Government of Israel, like all subsequent ones, was a coalition.

Another feature of these first, and all later elections is that *Mapai* (Israel Workers' Party) has emerged as the most influential

50. Armajani, p. 377.

party in the country. The Mapai derives much of its power from the Histadrut, kibbutzim and moshavim, and, since 1948, has led the Government.[51] In 1949 it polled a third of the votes and secured 46 seats—just over one-third of the house. Ben Gurion, its leader, continued as Prime Minister. A second usually constant and apparently necessary feature of Israeli politics has been alliance with the Orthodox groups, and these seek a state based on Jewish religious law. To secure this alliance the Mapai has had to accept Orthodox demands for religious education, for observance of their dietary and sabbath laws, control of marriage and divorce, a ban on pig-raising, and the like. Accordingly, one of the elements in Ben Gurion's coalition of 1949 was the United Religious Party, a fusion of the *Mizrachi* and the *Agudath Israel*.[52] A third element was the Progressive wing of the General Zionists, sometimes called the Liberal Party. The General Zionists are in fact conservative in outlook and believe in individualist economic policies and free enterprise. Their strength is among urban businessmen. The Progressives, more moderate and more sympathetic to labour, had broken away and formed a separate party. Included also in Ben Gurion's coalition were the Sephardic and Yemeni groups representing broadly the Oriental Jews.

The opposition was composed of the *Mapam* (Socialist Workers' Party), the General Zionists, and the *Herut* (the political instrument of the former Irgun under its leader Menachem Begin). Mapam was more militantly socialist than Mapai, which was accused by Mapam of being pro-American and pro-British; it had opposed the Biltmore program and favoured a Jewish-Arab state. It wanted closer ties with Communist Russia and her Eastern European satellites, a more radical class struggle, and a neutral foreign policy. It

---

51. It is now called the Labour Party, after merging in 1968 with two smaller Labour groups, *Ahdut Ha'avoda* and *Rafi*.

52. The Mizrachi calls for incorporation of Jewish tradition into the laws of the state; the ultra-orthodox Agudath demands legal enforcement of Biblical law. See Keesings, p. 9774. At present the main religious group, which forms part of Mrs Meir's coalition, is the National Religious Party, which is moderate in its orthodoxy. Agudath Israel is now again separate.

was understandably accused by some of putting Marxism before Zionism; it was thus a paradox that its allies in opposition were the capitalist-conservative General Zionists and the even more right-wing Herut. With its extreme nationalism, opposition to the U.N. partition plan, and insistence on a Jewish state covering Jordan as well as Palestine, with possible further expansion and the safety of Israel secured if necessary by a preventive war with the Arabs, Herut was regarded by many as fascist. The Communists, who secured four seats in 1949, took their own line. They had some Arab members, and followed Moscow in supporting the partition plan, though otherwise generally hostile to Zionism. They have never exercised strong influence on Israel's external or internal policies.

Israel's successive Governments have been formed of varying combinations of the main parties we have described. Fresh elections were held in 1951, by which time the electoral roll had almost doubled as a result of the flood of new immigrants since 1948. This produced a swing towards the Right-Centre, the General Zionists having gained seats while Mapam and Herut lost. The new cabinet was, as always, formed around Mapai; but this time Ben Gurion enlisted the support only of the religious group. The Progressives fell out, but were prepared generally to support the Government. Since then most parties of any size have at one time or another had some part in the Government. Thus, as we shall see, Begin was brought into the Government formed by Mr Eshkol in 1967 on the eve of the Six Day War, as leader of a combination of Herut and the Liberals (General Zionists) known as *Gahal*; and into Mrs Meir's of 1969, which also includes Mapam and the Progressives, now called Independent Liberals. But Gahal resigned in 1970, insisting that Israel should retain her conquests and that there should be no peace negotiations that might lead to their abandonment. Long before this, however, Israel was again at war with her largest neighbour, Egypt, which had meanwhile acquired by revolution a dynamic new leadership and long overdue reforms in her social system. These had indeed been brought about partly by the birth of Israel.

New Ferment in the Middle East

The aftermath of World War II ended the once impressive imperial role of Britain and France in the Middle East. France had been virtually forced into withdrawal in 1945, and thereafter was deeply and painfully involved, first in Vietnam and then in North Africa, before discovering how profitable in modern times the loss of overseas empire can be. Britain, while again dominant in the Middle East after the second, as after the first, world war, lost ground there with the abandonment of Palestine in 1948; and the 1950s saw the almost total elimination of her power. For this there were many reasons. Britain had lost most of the wealth on which her power was partly based. Then too all but a few of her people—exhausted by these two great conflicts only twenty years apart and the bitter clashes that had followed them—had lost all interest in shaping other peoples' lives. More important still was the new wave of exasperated nationalism that impelled the Middle Eastern peoples to sweep away the last relics of foreign domination and—even if the economic price were high—to have at last the final say in their own affairs. This bid for complete freedom largely succeeded; but since then, as these local peoples see it, they have been faced with a new threat.

In their eyes the super powers—the United States and the U.S.S.R.—have been competing for the imperialist power vacuum created by the British and French withdrawal, the United States using Israel as its tool. Both this rivalry and the power substitution in the Middle East emerged from 1946 in the context of the Cold War between the Communist bloc and the West.[53] Greece was a battleground of this war; Turkey, a potential one. Here and elsewhere Britain could no longer afford the cost of the defence arrangements needed, and turned to the United States for help. Washington's response was the Truman Doctrine, proclaimed on March 12, 1947,

53. The Cold War was vividly brought to the attention of the American people by Winston Churchill's speech at Fulton, Missouri, in March 1946, in which the term "Iron Curtain" was first used.

in terms that forecast President Eisenhower's later domino theory in respect of Vietnam.[54] A linked and parallel development was the creation of the North Atlantic Treaty Organization (NATO) in 1949, which included both Greece and Turkey, to be followed a few years later by the Baghdad Pact.

Iraq—Iran—Jordan

Since the failure of the coup against Britain in 1941, Iraq's war-time relations with the British had been good. Much of this was due to the friendly leadership of Nuri es-Said. When Nuri retired in 1944, however, there were demands for revision of the 1930 treaty—demands which Britain was prepared to meet, though not to the point of divesting herself of all special influence in the area. By 1948, when a new treaty with Iraq was signed, India and Pakistan were independent, though still members of the Commonwealth. Moreover, since 1939 the oil industry of the Middle East had grown enormously and had become most important for Britain and Europe, as also (though rather less so) for the United States. Britain thus still believed it vital to maintain her strength and influence—or at least that of the West—in the Suez Canal and adjacent lands, for the sake of Commonwealth links, of trade and oil, and of the age-old goal of stopping Russian encroachment (now far more dangerous in its Communist guise) at one of the world's most strategic points. The new treaty with Iraq, quite acceptable to the Baghdad Government, was not so to the ultra-nationalists there; and the ensuing demonstrations led to its being dropped. There was, however, no break with Britain then. Israel's successes in her war of independence had bred uncertainty in the Arab camp; and the Iraqis found some reassurance for the present in keeping their old friends.

Further grave difficulties for Britain were created by nationalism in Iran, and were to have repercussions in her later conflicts with

54. "If Greece should fall, . . . the effect upon . . . Turkey would be immediate and serious. Confusion and disorder might well spread throughout the entire Middle East."

the Arab world, notably in Egypt and Iraq. During World War
II Iran had become a kind of joint protectorate of Russia and Britain. They had occupied the country after the German invasion of
Russia in June 1941, and the United States had also later been
involved. The Shah, suspected of Nazi sympathies, was forced to
abdicate in favour of his son.[55] Although Iran had been dominated
before, the rulers of this proud country with some two thousand
five hundred years of continuous nationhood did not readily forget
this humiliation any more than China today, with its long and
splendid past, has forgotten the modern abuses of the imperialist
powers. The Allies had agreed to withdraw their troops six months
after the end of the war; and British and American forces duly left.
The Russians, however, refused to leave the north, having staged
a pro-Communist revolution in Azerbaijan with the help of local
sympathizers—a disturbing omen of their Cold War plans for extending Communist domination in the Middle East. When Iran
complained to the United Nations the Russians were finally induced to go by pressure of world opinion and representations from
America and Britain, and by the prospect of an oil concession
promised by Iran but subsequently repudiated by the Teheran
Parliament.

This rejection of the concession had been partly contrived by a
deputy, Dr Mosaddeq, who had resolved to make oil a national
issue. Large-scale development had become imperative, and it was
hoped to finance this by means of U.S. aid and royalties from oil.
When he visited America in 1949 the Shah failed to secure aid on
the hoped-for generous scale; and he then put pressure on the
Anglo-Iranian Oil Company (AIOC) the principal oil producer in
the south. Although early in 1951 the Company agreed to a 50-50
profit-sharing plan like that of the Arabian-American Oil Company
(ARAMCO) with Saudi Arabia, the Iranians thought this too little

55. The father, Reza Shah Pahlavi, was a former officer of the Iranian Cossack
Brigade which had restored order after World War I. He became Prime Minister, and in 1925 deposed the (then absent) Shah of the former dynasty and
was himself elected Shah. His son, the present Shah, Muhammad Reza Pahlavi,
was crowned with great splendour in 1967.

and too late. Dr Mosaddeq urged nationalization of oil and this was approved by Parliament. The British then closed the AIOC refinery at Abadan, thus cutting off Iran's royalties, froze Iranian assets, and staged a naval demonstration in the Persian Gulf.

Iran was not intimidated. Mosaddeq, who had become Prime Minister, argued Iran's case at the United Nations. The World Court eventually decided that Iran was within her rights. Britain, then under a Labour Government, wisely decided to take no more forceful steps; and the oil question was eventually settled in 1954 with the creation of an international consortium to extract, refine, and market the oil on behalf of the National Iranian Oil Company.[56] The lesson was swiftly learned by the Arab states that in the 1950s a Britain of greatly diminished strength and wealth could be successfully defied to their advantage.

Meanwhile the U.S. Secretary of State and chief foreign policy maker under President Eisenhower, Mr John Foster Dulles, had been deeply concerned over Communist Russia's predatory moves in Eastern Europe, Iran, and elsewhere, and decided that NATO needed to be backed in western Asia by a pact linking the "Northern Tier" of non-Communist states near Russia. A first step, in April 1954, was a treaty of friendship between Turkey and Pakistan. There followed in 1955 a pact of mutual cooperation between Turkey and Iraq, and this was later joined by Britain, Pakistan, and Iran to form the Baghdad Pact. Its prime sponsor, the United States, thought it best not to become a member, but eventually concluded bi-lateral alliances with Turkey, Iran, and Pakistan.[57]

56. See Armajani, pp. 348–58. A clash developed between Mosaddeq and the Shah which led to Mosaddeq's elimination in 1953. His Majesty then became by degrees the effective ruler of the country. He embarked on drastic land reform and other liberal and modernization measures which seem to have won him firm support from the peasants and from a now well-trained and well-equipped national army.

57. In 1954 the ring of defensive pacts intended to contain Communist expansion was extended farther into Asia by the conclusion of the Southeast Asia Treaty Organization (SEATO) after the Geneva conference of that year on Indochina. Through Turkey the Baghdad Pact was linked with NATO, and through Pakistan with SEATO. But neither of the Asian pacts proved very effective.

Jordan had been a comparatively tranquil backwater until the war of 1948, when she absorbed the remnant of Arab Palestine. Thereafter the Palestinians—many of them poor and homeless—became a majority of her population. A number of the more educated were restless and discontented, with a tendency to look down upon the simpler Jordanians, and the ambition to take over the running of the country. Understandably, they had few kind feelings towards Britain. Some were loyal to the ex-Mufti and hostile to King Abdullah, who had frustrated the Mufti's efforts to set up an Arab Palestine state under his own leadership with Egyptian support. It became common knowledge in Amman that the Mufti's followers were resolved to kill Abdullah as a supposed traitor to the Arab cause, when in fact, had his sensible views prevailed, the fate of Arab Palestine might have been far happier. The King, a brave fatalist, refused all special precautions. In July 1951 he was shot on his way to prayer in one of the great Mosques of Jerusalem. His young grandson, Hussein, was at his side. After the brief reign and abdication of his father, Talaat, Hussein succeeded to the throne at seventeen in 1952. Despite numerous attempts to murder him also, he has survived as King for more than twenty years.

The Egyptian Revolution

During the Palestine war of 1948, one of the defenders of Falluja who keenly felt Egypt's humiliation at Israel's hands was Major Gamal Abdul Nasser, who had risen, like Arabi Pasha, from modest origins to the officer corps. Nasser and his fellow officers found that, due to corruption from the King down, the weapons they were given were faulty, old, and useless. In Falluja they discussed therefore not so much the war in Palestine as the cleansing of Egypt; and when they went home, Nasser formed the secret Free Officers' Society. Meanwhile the by now effete Wafd Government under Nahas Pasha was pressing Britain to revise the 1936 Treaty and evacuate the Suez Canal Zone, as well as to cede the Sudan to Egypt. The British were in no hurry to meet Egyptian demands.

The treaty was not due for revision before 1956, and the Sudanese must be consulted before the fate of their country could be decided. In 1951 Nahas, perhaps encouraged by Mosaddeq's bold moves, denounced the treaty unilaterally and proclaimed Farouk King of the Sudan. The Wafd moreover turned to the Muslim Brotherhood and the left-wing parties for help in harassing the British.

Egyptian labourers struck in the Canal Zone and the British were attacked by mobs in various parts of the country. In Cairo in January 1952 there was severe rioting and destruction in which seventeen foreigners and more than fifty Egyptians died. Nahas was dismissed, and short-lived cabinets succeeded each other for the next six months. Meanwhile the Free Officers, encouraged by the Syrian military coup of March 1949, had formed an executive committee for decisive action, and this, with a few changes, was to become the Council of the Egyptian Revolution. They further enlisted the sympathy of a general, the half-Sudanese Muhammad Naguib, who also felt that change was needed. General Naguib joined the Free Officers and was formally made their President, although excluded from their secret plans. If they were to make a revolution they had to do it swiftly, as the Security Police were on their track. After learning that the King planned to have a number of them arrested, they chose the night of July 22–23, when Farouk would be at his summer palace in Alexandria.

It was a smooth and almost bloodless affair. Although army headquarters had been warned, the officers there made only token resistance when the troops behind the revolution arrived to take it over. By the following morning Cairo had been occupied and the revolution announced over the radio by another Free Officer, Anwar al-Sadat, who was to follow Nasser as ruler of Egypt. A day later, Alexandria and the large garrison at El Arish in Sinai had also fallen to the revolutionaries.[58] Ironically, the last king of the reigning dynasty, which the British had treated so high-handedly, appealed twice for their intervention, knowing that their eighty

58. Peter Mansfield, *Nasser*, pp. 42–52.

thousand troops in the Canal Zone could easily have crushed the revolution. A Conservative Government was now again in office under Churchill, and some Conservatives still living in the past favoured reoccupying Egypt. But the King's appeals were not heeded. One reason, it seems, was that Washington had made plain its opposition to such action; while Britain, and the other countries of Western Europe, were still largely dependent on the United States for their recovery.

On July 25 General Naguib, who had played no part in the coup, was appointed President of the Revolutionary Command Council (R.C.C.). On the 26th, the palace in Alexandria having been surrounded, Farouk abdicated in favour of his son and the same evening sailed in his yacht for Naples. Some revolutionary leaders had wanted to have him tried and executed, but Nasser wisely persuaded them that it was more urgent to clean up the mess Farouk had left behind. Before long, however, Nasser was bitterly disappointed at the response of most Egyptians to the revolution. Instead of the great spontaneous movement of national regeneration for which the new rulers had hoped, they were faced with a flood of petitions and vindictive complaints. They themselves were open to criticism on certain obvious scores. They did little to associate with their regime the civilian elements seeking national regeneration; nor did they help the left-wing groups to power. They feared, with some justice, that if elections were held under the 1923 constitution the Assembly would once again be dominated by the big landowners and industrialists. The first task therefore was to change the structure of social and economic power. And for this neither of the two main revolutionary groups outside the army would do. The Muslim Brotherhood was too violent and reactionary; the Communists were not to be trusted, since they were loyal to an alien cause. Nasser was convinced that "Only a group of dedicated honest men, such as the Free Officers, could succeed where Arabi and Zaghlul had failed."[59]

Nasser and his colleagues saw clearly what had so long been

59. *Ibid.*, pp. 52–67.

wrong with Egypt. They faced the growing disparity between poverty and wealth, the rootless cosmopolitanism of the Egyptian elite, some of whom, for all their nationalist rhetoric, still looked down on Arabic as a "kitchen language" and on the fellahin as an almost sub-human species destined to toil and serve. They had to cure the Egyptians of a deep sense of inadequacy and inferiority engendered by the arrogant and ubiquitous foreigner. Theirs was a country repeatedly subjugated by other more skilful, tenacious, and thrusting people, from Alexander the Great to Cromer, so that they sometimes felt it was scarcely theirs. In modern times, administration had been shaped and guided by the British. Business and finance—in a land reckoned as underdeveloped but with a highly sophisticated economic infra-structure—was, if not in Western European hands, then largely in those of experienced and enterprising Greeks, Italians, Syrians, Maltese, Armenians, and Jews. Hence the R.C.C.'s understandable urge to achieve "Egyptianization" at whatever cost and however ingenuous this process might seem to others in this and many fields.

During its first year the R.C.C. abolished titles, political parties, and the Monarchy. After this, in June 1953, Naguib became President of the Republic and Prime Minister, with Nasser as Deputy Prime Minister and Minister of the Interior. The delinquents of the old regime were tried. In place of the former parties, a National Liberation Rally and a new provisional constitution were launched and these gave full authority to the regime. Before the end of 1952 land reform was decreed—a vital measure when less than half of one per cent of the landowners held more than one-third of the cultivable land and nearly three-quarters of the cultivators owned less than an acre each. The reform limited land holdings to two hundred acres,[60] the confiscated land being redistuributed in small lots to the fellahin; and the rent of the tenant farmers was reduced. But the measure was on the whole a moderate one, since the big landlords were compensated or empowered to sell their surplus land, in principle to small farmers only. There was, however, no compensa-

60. Actually *feddans*, which are slightly larger than an acre.

tion for the royal lands, much of which stayed in the Government's hands. Only some 10 per cent of the cultivated land was in fact redistributed, and this directly benefited less than 10 per cent of the fellahin; and in practice the bigger landlords managed to retain much local influence. Yet the land reform did break their power to manipulate the central government and thus cleared the way for other necessary changes with which we are only marginally concerned.

Although Nasser and his team were without diplomatic experience, he was a quick learner and was soon achieving results in the international field. In February 1953 he reached agreement with Britain by which the Sudan would become self-governing, with a plebiscite in three years to decide either for union with Egypt or for complete independence. In the event, independence was chosen. This agreement smoothed the path for a further one in October 1954, securing one of the R.C.C.'s prime objectives. Britain would withdraw her troops from the Suez Canal Zone within twenty months, with the sole proviso that the base would come again into operation if there were an armed attack on one of the Arab League states or on Turkey.[61]

By this time General Naguib was out and Nasser in supreme command. Naguib, who had become most popular, had some sympathy with the former politicians whom the R.C.C. was determined to oust. Many of the politicians were of his generation; he recalled them in their youth as ardent and promising reformers, and he planned to revive their power by reverting to parliamentary democracy. Nasser had provoked Naguib into resigning but, in view of the uproar this caused, brought him back as President, and became Prime Minister himself. The revival of parliamentary democracy and of the politicians was indefinitely postponed. By the end of 1954 Nasser had managed to dispose of his two other main adversaries—the Communists and the Muslim Brotherhood—as well as of his rival for power, Naguib. The Communists were divided and

61. The Arab League states had signed a Treaty of Joint Defence in Cairo in April 1950.

therefore relatively weak, and thus he was able to round up their key men and imprison them. In October the Brotherhood were charged with an attempt to kill him; six were hanged and their top leader imprisoned for life. Their power, too, was broken for many years. Naguib had had contacts with the Brothers and, although he was not implicated in the attempt on Nasser, he was now removed from the Presidency and placed under house arrest. Having emerged as the effective head of the country, in 1956 Nasser arranged to produce a new constitution under which he became President himself.[62]

Nasser and His Neighbours

Till now Nasser's main concern had been Egypt. His country as headquarters of the Arab League had joined with other members of the League in an effort to save Palestine for its Arab people. Yet, even under his leadership, in its first years the RCC had felt itself only marginally concerned with the politics of the Arab world. From 1954, however, Egypt's ruler was to become increasingly prominent among the Arab states and in other wider spheres. One constant problem, then as now, was the urge of the evicted Palestinians to regain, or at least resume contact with, their homeland. From the Gaza Strip and other areas beyond the provisional borders of Israel, Arab Palestinians, singly or in small groups, were crossing the armistice lines and entering the territory the new state had acquired. Then as now the upshot was that the Israelis hit back into Arab territory with raids far more severe than the incursions they had suffered.

Public opinion in Egypt and elsewhere demanded retaliation more effective than anything the refugees on their own could do; yet, as Nasser realized, Egypt and the other Arab states had small hope of winning a second all-out war with Israel. He therefore fell back upon the disastrous expedient of sponsoring raids by trained

62. Mansfield, pp. 67–90; Armajani, pp. 382–86; Ann Williams, *Britain and France in the Middle East and North Africa*, pp. 116–17.

saboteurs (*fedayeen*) picked partly from the refugees and partly from Egypt and elsewhere. Similar action has since, as we know, been frequently launched from Lebanon, Syria, and Jordan. Savage incidents and ruthless retaliation continue to this day. But these have always tended to recoil upon the innocent, and to play into the hands of Israeli publicity by darkening the Arab name and setting the Palestinians in the worst possible light. Indeed, they have masked for the world the harsh injustice originally done to these unhappy people—an injustice that Britain in the days of her power had failed either to foresee or prevent. Almost alone among Arab rulers, the kings of Jordan, where the Palestinians became a majority, fought of their own initiative to bring these murderous exchanges to a halt.

The Baghdad Pact. Egyptian-Iraqi Rivalry

Nasser was also faced with tensions and rivalries within the Arab League. At that stage, from Egypt's experience and his own he felt it imperative that the Arab states should stand aloof from the Cold War, that the Western powers should cease to have a voice in their destinies and decisions. By 1955 he was a firm admirer of India's Pandit Nehru and Yugoslavia's President Tito, and in due course all three became leaders of the group of non-aligned or neutral nations. Indeed, as his status and ideas developed he came to feel that Egypt under his leadership was destined to play a triple role in liberating first herself, then the Arab states, then Africa and the whole Islamic world, from imperialist control and influence.[63] But his convictions were in conflict with those of Nuri es-Said, now once again Prime Minister of Iraq, who was concerned less with any danger from the West than with that from Russian Communist imperialism. For that reason in 1955 Nuri laid the foundations of the Baghdad Pact in line with the United States, Britain, Turkey, Pakistan, and Iran.

63. A significant stage in this development was marked by his attendance at the Afro-Asian conference convened, also in 1955, by President Sukarno of Indonesia at Bandung.

Nasser was strongly hostile to this, and not merely because an Arab nation was now linked by a military pact with the imperialist West. His suspicion of Iraq reflected also the age-old rivalry between the rulers of the Nile valley and of Mesopotamia for control of the area between them—namely, Syria in its traditional borders, including Lebanon, Palestine, and Jordan. This rivalry had been in abeyance while Syria and Lebanon were under French mandate, but it revived after World War II when the Hashimite royal family of Iraq—related to that of Jordan and descended from Faisal, once briefly king in Damascus—had thoughts of creating a Syrian-Iraqi union under their dynasty. But Egypt had managed to prevent this; it was a key point of her policy to keep Syria out of the Iraqi orbit.

Egypt Moves Closer to the Soviet Bloc

The Baghdad Pact was made hateful to the Arabs by a violent propaganda campaign from Cairo, which incidentally prepared the ground for Iraq's revolution and rejection of the Pact in 1958,[64] and the murder of both Nuri and the King. It also ensured the rejection of the Pact by Syria and Jordan. Nasser's campaign made him into a kind of national hero of the Arab peoples. In him they saw "a leader . . . prepared to stand up and say 'no' to the great powers who had been bossing and humiliating the Arabs as long as they could remember."[65] Still in his thirties, Nasser was by no means reluctant to have this new mantle thrust upon him. He was strongly and genuinely against Communism like most Arab leaders. Not only was it the negation of Islam; it sought to undermine the patriotism in which he so passionately believed; and he had done his best to destroy its power in Egypt. But by now he was shrewd enough to sense that the West's obsessive fear of Communism, and the divisions created by the Cold War, could perhaps be used to further the causes for which he stood. There was now intense

64. The pact was then renamed the Central Treaty Organization or CENTO.
65. Mansfield, p. 94; see also pp. 91–93.

competition between the Communist and the Free World blocs, each wooing the developing countries. In such conditions it could make sense to turn to the East for help the West might be slow to give; it would certainly imply no commitment to adopt Communism as a creed.

For their part the Russians, with Stalin dead, were, from 1953, skilfully holding out just these prospects and bettering their relations with the Arab world. They had had cause to regret their precipitate recognition of Israel. For all the extreme theories of many of her Eastern European settlers, the new state had been a disappointment to Moscow as a base for influence and subversion in the Middle East. The new Soviet line was that Moscow's only wish was to see Egypt and the Arab states become genuinely independent of the Western imperialists. It had no intention of trying to draw them into the Soviet orbit, and the economic aid it could give had no strings attached.

It is against this background that the strange and gratuitous unwisdom of British and American policy in 1955 and 1956 must be assessed. One contributory factor to Britain's misjudgements was a change of government in London. In 1955 Anthony Eden succeeded Churchill as Conservative Prime Minister. He had won good opinions as Foreign Secretary, but lacked the strength of character and physical fitness to give commanding leadership and take hard and unpopular decisions in a sudden and complex crisis that neither he nor his Cabinet, nor most British people, properly understood. Once again, too many were living in the past. Another was that, for Secretary of State Dulles, the Communist threat had become a doctrinaire obsession that clouded realistic judgement. Mr Dulles, too, was in poor health and was soon to die of cancer.

Israel the Catalyst

Since the foundation of the state Israel has acted as a catalyst producing variable alignments among the countries in or concerned with the Middle East. From 1948 she was boycotted economically by the Arab states, which sought also to blacklist ships calling at Israeli ports, and refused overflying rights to aircraft landing in Israel on their way to the Far East and elsewhere. Israeli ships were stopped by Egypt from using the Suez Canal, although the U.N. Security Council ruled that this was "unjustified interference with the rights of nations to navigate the seas and to trade freely with each other." In a test case, an Israeli ship was sent into the Canal in 1954, but was confiscated and its crew imprisoned. In the same year a Russian veto in the Security Council halted an Israeli protest against Egyptian guns at Sharm el-Sheikh, at the entrance to the Gulf of Aqaba, which threatened the traffic to Israel's new port of Elat at the head of the Gulf.[66] For Russia was at that point already moving closer to Israel's Arab enemies.

On the other hand, U.S. aid poured into Israel. France, too, in those years, became a friend, embittered as she was by her eviction from Syria and Lebanon and by the independence movements in Algeria, Morocco, and Tunisia. France also became important to Israel as a supplier of arms; while Israel, as we saw, was expanding her contacts with Asia and Africa. In spite of Nasser's solicitude for the Muslim world, Israel established relations with certain key Muslim but non-Arab countries such as Turkey and Iran, and with others with a Muslim majority, such as Senegal and Mali.[67] But she and her neighbours lived in an aura of constant conflict sustained by Arab guerrilla attacks and Israel's heavy reprisals, with the likelihood that these would spark off another war however much both sides would have preferred to avoid this. Both sought to build up their military strength, and were able to procure arms from many quarters although the Western powers were officially pledged to oppose an arms race in the Middle East.[68] When, following this line (which the French were less concerned to observe) the United States and Britain refused to supply Egypt with more than very

66. See Williams, pp. 118–20.
67. These were *de facto* in the case of Iran.
68. In May 1950 the United States, Britain, and France had signed a joint declaration to this effect, designed to maintain peace and stability in the Arab states and Israel.

small quantities of arms, Nasser hinted that he might turn to Eastern Europe.

Nasser in Conflict with the Western Powers

In September 1955 Cairo made a substantial arms deal with the Communist bloc.[69] This was applauded by many Arabs as a clever evasion of Western patronage and condescension, but the United States, which had given Egypt $23 million in aid, and Britain, scrupulously carrying out her agreement to evacuate the Canal, were deeply distressed. Both assumed that Nasser might be leading Egypt into the Soviet orbit.[70] The British redoubled their efforts to induce Jordan to join the Baghdad Pact, but these misfired. King Hussein was in fact keen to join, but the visit of Britain's top general to Amman in December 1955 led to the fall of the Government and hostile demonstrations that killed all prospect of Jordan's signing. "The two-thirds of Jordanians who were Palestinians . . . wanted to have nothing to do with any pact with Britain."

Then in March 1956 the King bent with the prevailing wind and abruptly dismissed the British commander of his army, General Glubb. London was convinced that this was the result of pressure from Cairo. Resentment grew against Nasser in the Western camp, while he continued to believe that the Western powers wanted to keep Egypt in perpetual tutelage. As though to confirm his suspicions and justify his change of course, Britain just then was buying less Egyptian and more Sudanese cotton, while in 1955–56 for the first time the Soviet bloc and China bought more than a third of the Egyptian crop. And when in May 1956 Nasser recognized Communist China—to Washington an evil and dangerous move—he was further damned in American eyes.[71] A month later the Russian

69. According to Randolph S. Churchill and Winston S. Churchill, *The Six Day War*, pp. 19 and 20, the arms came from Russia, but Nasser described them to the British Ambassador as being from Czechoslovakia.

70. Apart from Secretary Dulles's fixation about the Communist danger, the 1950s were of course the period of Senator McCarthy's witch-hunt for Communists in high places in the U.S. Government and society.

71. See Mansfield, pp. 99–101.

Foreign Minister visited Cairo and was reported to have offered a large loan without interest. Nasser was evidently determined to take a line of his own regardless of Western disapproval.

The Aswan Dam

This recognition of China came just after Egypt had secured a promise of funds from the World Bank, the United States, and Britain to build a high dam on the Nile south of Aswan. The Bank was to lend Egypt $200 million on condition that the United States and Britain between them would lend another $70 million ($55 million from the United States, $15 million from Britain) to meet the hard currency costs of material and technical services. Egypt would provide the equivalent of $900 million in local services and materials. This huge scheme could increase Egypt's cultivated area by 30 per cent and add immensely to her hydro-electric power. It was a vital answer to the swift increase in her population with no corresponding expansion of the economy in sight.

From the start, unfortunately, there seem to have been doubts and reservations on both sides. The Western powers were not sure whether Egypt, after her Communist arms deal and other commitments, could meet her share of the costs. Nasser, on the other hand, was not going to accept what he foresaw as the desire of "the Americans" to control Egypt's budget and check her accounts.[72] Some critics of Western action have suggested that the offer of finance was largely designed as a political move; by holding out encouraging prospects, the West might forestall what they saw as Egypt's progressive drift into the clutches of the Communist bloc. In any case, by July 1956 Washington had decided that the scheme, from their standpoint, might not pay off. Egypt was told that the American offer was withdrawn, but those who worked with Dulles never learned why he acted so abruptly. The official reasons given

72. *Ibid.*, p. 102; see also Williams, pp. 121–23. In view of the extent of American capital in, and influence upon, the World Bank, this would have been regarded as falling within the American camp. It was a sign of the times that Nasser was already discounting any threat from British power.

were that the Egyptian economy was too unstable for so large a scheme and that Egypt had failed to secure the agreement of the other Nile states, the Sudan, Ethiopia, and Uganda.

Britain and the World Bank also backed out at once. Prime Minister Eden and eventually the French leaders—progressively concerned with subversion in Algeria—became convinced that Nasser might become some kind of Middle Eastern menace comparable to Hitler in Europe. It was hoped, both in Washington and London, that their refusal to fund the Aswan Dam might cause Nasser to fall, or, if not, to become more amenable to Western guidance—this being, however, precisely the situation Nasser was determined at all costs to resist. They did not expect him to retaliate or to seek funds elsewhere. These inept misjudgements were to be followed by disastrously miscalculated Western action.

The Suez Crisis

Nasser had just returned from a conference in Yugoslavia with his fellow leaders of the non-aligned nations, President Tito and Prime Minister Nehru. For him the rejection of the Aswan scheme was a blow to his prestige demanding quick response in kind. In a few days he announced the nationalization of the Suez Canal, the building of which, he stressed, had cost one hundred twenty thousand Egyptian lives. This was, he said, "a battle against imperialism . . . and . . . against Israel, the vanguard of imperialism, which was created . . . to annihilate our nationalism in the same way it annihilated Palestine." He added that in Egypt the Suez Canal Company, with its headquarters in Paris, would in future be managed by an Egyptian Canal Authority. Egypt would build the Aswan Dam with the revenues from the Canal, and if the imperialist powers did not like it they could "choke in their rage." For the time being any of the Canal employees who left their posts would be imprisoned.

Nasser's emotional style and daring blow delighted his Arab hearers. Unfortunately it evoked an emotional response in Britain and France as well, these being the two nations with a controlling interest in the company. All the Canal's property would in any case have reverted to the Egyptian Government in 1968;[73] yet in Britain there was a strong Suez Canal lobby that still imagined the Canal to be vital to Britain's Asian interests and responsibilities, which, apart from economic and cultural links, were now largely a thing of the past. It meant much to France also, since the French middle class had long been attracted to Suez shares as a sound investment. Both countries assumed that Egyptians could not be trusted to run the Canal properly.

Undoubtedly the Canal belonged to Egypt; and yet the immense profits on the relatively small investment of those who built it had gone almost entirely abroad. Less than 5 per cent of the shares were held in Egypt, and Cairo's revenue from the profits, even when increased in 1949, was still only 7 per cent. The wise course for the West would have been to come to terms with Egypt's desire to be master in her own house and use for the benefit of the whole nation the revenues from an installation on her soil which had many times repaid what the foreigner had originally spent on it. The valuable friendship of the world's most strategic country could have been retained by the West if Nasser, after his gesture of defiance, had been met with a generous and understanding response. Instead, the British Government, and before long the French, seem to have decided, despite all warnings, that force would ultimately be needed "to bring Nasser to his senses." They were prepared to try negotiations for a time, but all knew that there was small prospect of deflecting Egypt from her main purpose.[74]

73. Under an agreement concluded with the company by Egypt in 1949, i.e., before Nasser's revolution.

74. Soon after nationalization, Eden had told President Eisenhower that Britain must be ready in the last resort to use force against Nasser, and had been warned by the President against this. Later the President publicly declared that the United States could not in any circumstances support the use of force. (See Williams, pp. 123–25; Mansfield, pp. 103–5.) Other warnings came from within Britain. As Eden's policy developed, there were strong and vocal objections in official and political circles, including his own party, and a number of resignations. The Labour Party insisted that any firmness with Nasser must

In August 1956 a conference was held in London representing the parties to the Suez Canal Convention of 1888. Since Egypt refused to attend, her case was put by India and Russia. Proposals were drawn up for international control of the Canal, and these were presented in Cairo by the Australian Prime Minister—without success. Nasser had no reason to give way, knowing that the United States opposed the use of force. He did suggest that the Canal users could have a new treaty if the tolls were paid to Egypt, but this was rejected by London, and the Suez Canal Company announced the withdrawal of the foreign pilots from September 15. Meanwhile Mr Dulles had produced an alternative plan for internationalization called a Suez Canal Users Association (SCUA)—making it plain, however, that the United States would certainly not impose any scheme against Egypt's wishes. When SCUA was discussed at a second conference in London in September, some delegates were prepared to accept the payment of tolls to Egypt. In October Britain asked the U.N. Security Council to support SCUA, but this was rejected by a Russian veto.

The Triple Attack on Egypt

Shortly before this, France sought to interest Israel and Britain in tripartite action. Some progress was made at talks in Paris at the end of September with Mr Shimon Peres, Israeli Minister for Defence. The French Foreign Minister then sought British approval and, despite the reservations of the British Foreign Secretary, the impulses of Mr Eden prevailed. A triple accord was later reached in France, and on October 29 Israel attacked Egypt. The next day Britain and France presented ultimata to Israel and Egypt, calling

---

be shown through the United Nations. Indeed, the objections were nationwide and were heard in all circles of society. Britain's main friends in the Arab world, King Hussein and Prime Minister Nuri es-Said, were predictably opposed to the use of force, as were a number of British Commonwealth countries, especially Canada, whose Minister for External Affairs, Mr Lester Pearson, was to play an invaluable role in the sequel to these events, and to receive the Nobel Peace Prize for his achievement.

on them to withdraw from (or not proceed beyond) a zone ten miles each side of the Canal, and also asking Egypt to allow Anglo-French forces to be stationed temporarily on the Canal to separate the belligerents and safeguard shipping. The ultimatum was of course accepted by Israel but rejected by Cairo. From October 31 to November 4 the British and French bombed airfields in Egypt and destroyed most of the Egyptian air force. On November 5 British and French paratroopers and other units landed near Port Said and started to reoccupy the Canal Zone, which Britain had so recently left. Meanwhile the Egyptians had blocked the Canal by sinking ships in it. They had in fact operated it without hitch from the time the foreign employees left till then, with the help of Eastern and Central Europeans, and were to do so again once it was unblocked.

The Suez War Ends

The new war to occupy Egypt lasted only a few days. On November 5 the U.N. General Assembly, on the initiative of Mr Pearson of Canada, voted for the formation of a U.N. Emergency Force in the Middle East (UNEF) "to secure and supervise the cessation of hostilities." In response partly to this timely and helpful intervention, but chiefly to the condemnation of the United States, Soviet Russia and most of the rest of the world, on November 6 Britain called for a cease-fire.[75] Fighting ended at midnight on November 6–7.

By this time almost all the Sinai Peninsula as well as the Gaza Strip had been taken by the Israelis, including Sharm el-Sheikh, key to the Gulf of Aqaba. This foreshadowed the campaign of 1967,

75. Another and more immediate reason may have been the run on sterling caused by the crisis. The position appears to be that the United States refused to back the pound while the war continued, but that the International Monetary Fund, supported by Washington, promised a loan equivalent to £300 million if there were a cease-fire by midnight on November 6. The fact that Russia also was hostile to the action taken, in alignment with the United States, carried no decisive weight. See Williams, pp. 131–33.

but conditions were in fact different. Faced with a European attack on Egypt proper, Nasser ordered the withdrawal of his troops from Gaza and Sinai—though not before they had lost some two to three thousand men and a mass of war matériel. On November 15, when the first UNEF forces arrived, the British, French, and Israelis started to withdraw. But Israel was reluctant to leave the two vital points of Gaza and Sharm el-Sheikh, and did so only in March 1957 on the understanding that Gaza would be controlled and safeguarded by UNEF, and that the leading sea powers would ensure freedom of navigation in the Gulf of Aqaba. Israel was much disturbed when an Egyptian civil governor moved into Gaza with his staff, and broadcasts from Cairo proclaimed that the Gulf of Aqaba would be closed to Israeli ships and that the Fedayeen would "continue to sow terror in Israel."[76] In fact, on the Egyptian side, the presence of UNEF checked the Fedayeen raids for some years.

Suez: the Aftermath

The short war had been none of Nasser's seeking and, with the enemies he faced, he had inevitably suffered military defeat. But he had scored a resounding victory of prestige; whereas Britain had squandered her credit in the Middle East and elsewhere, and her influence in Egypt, like that of France, was gone. Those Arab states which still supported Britain might have found strong action against Nasser acceptable, since many of them feared and opposed him. What they could not forgive was that the British, who had at times been the Arabs' friends, and who had clashed with the Jews on that score, should now have allied themselves with Israel—the enemy in their midst—to attack a country which after all was one of them.

Egypt had also made solid gains. She now had complete control of the Suez Canal; the British civilian-manned base was there no more, and Cairo had confiscated its immense stores. All British and

76. See Williams, pp. 125–29; Mansfield, pp. 105–6; Keesings Research Report, *The Arab-Israeli Conflict*, pp. 6–8.

French property in Egypt was sequestered. The attacks had not intimidated the Egyptians, but rather had rallied them behind their leader, and given him a new power and dimension of leadership amongst the Arab nations. Meanwhile, the ensuing economic boycott of Egypt—another folly in which even the United States joined—only turned Cairo increasingly to collaboration with the Communist bloc. And, thanks to the blunders of the West, the way was now open for the Soviet Union, with her clients, to play a far more direct and effective role in the Middle East than Russia had ever done before.

While subtly promoting the Communist creed, Moscow now had the chance of securing a new imperialist stake in the Fertile Crescent, Egypt, and other parts of the Arab world, of a kind the Russian Empire had never attained. Shortly after Suez, in 1957, this new phase of Russian prominence was dramatically marked when the U.S.S.R. ahead of the United States, launched Fellow Traveller (*Sputnik*), the first man-made satellite in space. For its part the United States was prompt to realize that the eclipse of British influence put increased emphasis on its own role in the Middle East. Its response was the so-called Eisenhower Doctrine of December 1956, which named "international communism" as the greatest threat to the area. According to this Doctrine, any Russian intervention would at once be met by the United States, with force if all else failed; and some $400-500 million would be spent on aid in the Middle East in 1957 and 1958, for the benefit—that is—of those countries which resisted Communism.

Meanwhile, Israel was perhaps happier about Suez than the sequel warranted. Her Chief of Staff, General Dayan, declared that "Israel's readiness to take to the sword to secure her rights at sea and her safety on land and her capacity . . . to defeat the Egyptian forces, deterred the Arab rulers in the years that followed from renewing their acts of hostility." Actually such acts did not cease since although the border with Egypt quietened down—thanks to UNEF—Israeli and Jordanian troops clashed in the Mount Scopus demilitarized zone of Jerusalem in 1957 and 1958, and there were even more serious clashes on the Syrian border southeast of the Sea of Galilee.[77] These were to become worse in the 1960s.

From 1956 to 1959 the Egyptians allowed Israeli goods through the Suez Canal in ships not flying the Israeli flag. After that, however, ships carrying such goods were stopped and their cargoes impounded. Israel, they claimed, had no right to ship freight through the Canal since she was still at war with the Arab countries. Israel was also at odds with Jordan, Syria, and Lebanon over the division of the Jordan waters. Schemes agreed at the technical level broke down at government level—mainly because of Syrian objections. Israel and Jordan then went ahead with separate schemes, Israel piping water from Lake Tiberias to the Negev, and Jordan tapping the Yarmuk and Zarqa tributaries of the Jordan. In 1964, at a summit meeting of heads of Arab states, it was planned to reduce the flow of the Jordan's northern tributaries so that Israel would have less water to divert.[78]

The Suez adventure was bound to cause fresh ferment and far-reaching changes in the Eastern Arab world. Nasser's new prestige and Cairo's thrusting socialist-republican radio and press propaganda were by no means acceptable to the more conservative countries, which Egypt's agents were doing their best to subvert. In 1957, King Hussein of Jordan managed to throw out his own pro-Nasser Government, which had planned to move closer to the Communist bloc. King Saud of Arabia, who regarded republican Egypt with strong aversion and sent troops to help Hussein, was less lucky. In March 1958, after being accused of frustrating Nasser's plans and seeking to kill him, Saud's power was transferred to his brother Faisal, who eventually became King himself and Prime Minister and Foreign Minister as well. But 1958 was a crucial year also in the Fertile Crescent, where sweeping revolutions trans-

77. Usually known in modern times as Lake Tiberias or (to the Israelis) Lake Kinneret.
78. Keesing's Research Report, pp. 8–9.

formed both Syria and Iraq, and more or less abortive schemes failed to unify the Arab world.

Egypt, Syria, and Yemen Unite

In Syria a series of army coups had taken place from 1949 to 1954, and these brought about various ruling combinations of politicians and soldiers. Then in 1954 Constitutional rule was restored and, following elections, the Ba'ath (Renaissance) party assumed power in alliance with an army group. The Ba'ath members combined radical Arab nationalism with a programme of social reform, and appealed especially to the new educated classes. But both they and the army were deeply impressed by Nasser, and advocated union with Egypt as a step towards wider Arab union. At the time of the Suez conflict these groups blew up the oil pipeline across Syria. In 1957 they risked being outflanked by a more left-wing combination and, once arms and economic agreements had been made with Moscow, there seemed a danger of Syria becoming far more committed to the Communist bloc than Egypt, who had skilfully kept her options open. It was this trend that convinced U.S. Secretary of State Dulles that Syria would become a Soviet satellite though in fact most Syrians had no wish to be aligned with either Communism or the West. They therefore turned to Egypt and asked for an immediate and comprehensive union.

Such a union was proclaimed in February 1958 by Nasser and President Kuwatly of Syria, and called the United Arab Republic (U.A.R.). A month later Nasser launched a new experiment in Arab unity. A federal union was announced between the U.A.R. and the Yemen with the designation United Arab States. Apparently the old and reactionary ruling Imam of this backward country had been persuaded by his Crown Prince to accept Nasser's leadership in the hope of preserving their dynasty and incidentally liberating Aden from British control, even at the cost of having to bring in some measures of reform.

Nasser became President of the U.A.R., with two Egyptian and two Syrian Vice Presidents, among them Field Marshal Abdul Hakim Amer, one of Nasser's closest friends. Cairo became the capital, but the Field Marshal, now Commander-in-Chief of the United Arab States forces, functioned in effect as Nasser's Viceroy in Damascus. The U.A.R. was an uneasy partnership. There was an Egyptian preponderance in the union; Nasser kept most of the executive and legislative power in his own hands; and some Egyptian officials in Syria were tactless and overbearing. Moreover, the Ba'athists, the main promoters of the union, were brushed aside when all Syrian political parties were abolished (as they had been in Egypt), in favour of an amorphous National Union set up by Nasser in 1956 as a substitute for these parties.

The Syrians had kept a vigorous tradition of independent thought and action from Turkish days onwards. The Syrian masses continued to admire Nasser, but the pride of the army was hurt, and merchants, business men, and landowners resented Nasser's socialism as well as his indifference towards the very real agricultural, economic, and social differences between Syria and Egypt. Those who feared dependence on Moscow or the West had small relish for dependence on Egypt instead. After "three and a half years of endless trouble," as Nasser put it, Syria regained her freedom in September 1961 through another army coup. Nasser saw that it was useless to intervene. Egypt's union with Yemen was also ended and a few years later Nasser was to be involved in a long and bitter war against the dynasty with which he had been "united" there. In spite of the collapse of his double experiment, Nasser retained the title United Arab Republic for Egypt.[79]

Brief Union between Jordan and Iraq

These were not the only attempts at Arab unity. A week after the start of the radical U.A.R.—in February 1958—a similar move was

79. Since, however, the country restored its traditional name some years later, I shall again call it Egypt after the break-up of this first union in 1961.

made in the conservative camp, when Iraq and Jordan formed a union called the Arab Federation. The head of state was King Faisal II of Iraq, and his deputy was his cousin King Hussein of Jordan. The nations were united under the Hashimite flag flown by the Sharif Husain (their great-grandfather) during the Arab Revolt. In many ways this was a logical move for, while the two halves of the U.A.R. were widely separated geographically, Iraq and Jordan formed a solid block from Iran to Israel. Iraq, moreover, with oil wealth and an expanding economy, could greatly help Jordan, with her meagre resources, and become a useful field for resettling Jordan's half-million refugees. But these two young rulers, each 22, had even less luck with their union than Cairo and Damascus had with the U.A.R. After five months, in July 1958, it was destroyed by the Baghdad revolution, in which Faisal, the Crown Prince, and the pro-Western Prime Minister Nuri es-Said were killed.

Western Intervention Again. Left-Wing Revolution in Iraq

The Iraqi revolution was linked with instability in Lebanon, with its delicate balance between Muslims and Christians. At the time of the Suez crisis, Nasser became a hero to the Lebanese Muslims, and they went in their thousands to Damascus to welcome him when he appeared there as first President of the U.A.R. Many Muslims wanted Lebanon to join the U.A.R. or were dissatisfied with the government of the Christian President, Chamoun. Disturbances sparked off by Muslims led to virtual civil war by midsummer. Lest the country should become yet another satellite of Nasser, President Chamoun appealed to the United States under the Eisenhower Doctrine for help to defend Lebanon against potential outside aggression. In response American troops were sent to Lebanon for a short time; so, at King Hussein's request, were British troops to Jordan; and in both cases the danger was averted. Jordan received military and economic aid also from the United States, as she still does.

In Lebanon there was a change of President and Government, and the country resumed its quasi-neutral role vis-à-vis Arab dissensions, as a profitable investment and financial centre for most of the Middle East. Meanwhile, Prime Minister Nuri of Iraq hastened his own downfall by trying to help both Lebanon and Jordan. Early in July he ordered two officers, General Kassim and Colonel Arif, to move their troops into Jordan. While Nuri's intent was almost certainly that they should invade Syria and destroy the U.A.R., instead they seized control in Baghdad and murdered the leaders of the Hashimite regime. Kassim was supported by Pan-Arab Ba'athists (who thereupon developed an organization in Iraq) as well as by the Communists. But he soon quarrelled violently with Nasser, being essentially an Iraqi nationalist who had no wish to share his nation's sovereignty and wealth with Cairo. His colleague Arif, on the other hand, was strongly Pan-Arab and pro-Nasser, and publicly favoured a union between Iraq and the U.A.R. A link with Syria would indeed have been logical, like that with Jordan, since Iraq and Syria were continguous areas. But for these views he was arrested and condemned to death.[80] Kassim at once dropped both the Hashimite union with Jordan and the Baghdad Pact, and recognized Moscow and Peking. Once firmly in power, he used the Communists to remove the Ba'athists; and for nearly three years Communism was a force in Iraq.

Cairo at Odds with Baghdad and Washington

Meanwhile, tension between Nasser and Iraq became more acute. In 1959 a rising in Mosul was harshly suppressed, and there was an attempt to kill Kassim—both attributed to Egypt. Nasser had now come to regard Communism in Iraq as a mortal danger to the Arab countries, especially when it looked as though Moscow might help Baghdad against Cairo. He strongly criticized the Soviet Union, even at the risk of losing Soviet aid. But Khrushchev, after retort-

80. Armajani, pp. 393–400; Mansfield, pp. 108–12; Williams, pp. 131–35; Keesing's Contemporary Archives, pp. 16005, 160017, 16085–86.

ing sharply, decided it was worth Russia's while to continue this aid to Egypt. While Nasser still wanted to remove Kassim, in his pragmatic way he felt it would be risky to try this before easing his relations with Jordan, Saudi Arabia, and even Britain and the United States. In 1959 he restored diplomatic relations with Jordan (only to break them off again in a couple of years and later resume them once more!) and welcomed the King of Saudi Arabia in Cairo. In 1961, shortly before the break-up of the U.A.R., a crisis over Kuwait gave him a pretext to move somewhat closer again to Britain. The British had ended their protectorate over this oil-rich sheikhdom; and once it was independent, Kassim claimed that it belonged to Iraq and prepared to move in. The Sheikh of Kuwait then asked for British help, but the British, wisely for once, withdrew their troops and facilitated the defence of Kuwait against Iraq by an Arab League force including troops from Egypt, Jordan, and Saudi Arabia.

As for the United States, from 1958 the Eisenhower Administration had given Egypt cheap long-term loans to cover the import of surplus American foodstuffs; by the mid-sixties, these loans amounted to about one billion dollars.[81] They were of course given partly in the hope of keeping Egypt out of the Soviet camp. In 1961 President Kennedy exchanged letters with Nasser on Palestine, Israel, and related matters. Here at last, it seemed to Nasser, was an American President who was really trying to understand Egypt. But after his murder relations once more cooled. Cairo and Washington were pursuing conflicting goals in the Congo, and Nasser became convinced that Washington was using its aid to make him change his policies. In April 1967 he renounced further U.S. aid; he could, after all, get food from Russia, and hard currency to buy it elsewhere from oil discoveries in the Red Sea region and the Western Desert.[82]

81. Under PL 480.
82. Mansfield, pp. 151–53. See also John S. Badeau, *The American Approach to the Arab World* (New York: Harper, 1968), *passim*, but esp. pp. 81–97. As U.S. Ambassador to the U.A.R. Mr Badeau was liked and trusted by Nasser, and his retirement was a set-back to relations between the two countries.

Civil War in Yemen. Egyptian Intervention

These were years of ferment not only in Egypt, Jordan, Syria, Lebanon, and Iraq, but also in the North African states of Morocco, Tunisia, and Algeria, as well as in Yemen, Aden, and Libya. They are all part of the essential background to the renewed Arab-Israeli warfare of 1967. In July 1962, after a long struggle that bitterly divided France, Algeria gained her independence from the Government of General de Gaulle, and espoused left-wing policies that brought her into sympathy with Nasser's regime. Four years earlier, Morocco and Tunisia had become independent members of the Arab League. In September of that year, Yemeni officers revolted against the Imam[83] and set up a republic that was at once recognized by Nasser. The Imam escaped, however, and with the help of his northern tribesmen, of Saudi Arabia, and of Jordan, fought to restore his rule. Nasser found himself obliged to back the republicans with arms and other aid in a long and exhausting civil war that drained much of his resources. The Egyptian involvement lasted over five years. In 1965, by agreement with Saudi Arabia, there was a cease-fire which enabled Nasser to bring home a third of his forces, but they could not be finally withdrawn for two more years. By this time the Egyptians had made themselves unpopular as latter-day imperialists in a land they barely understood. Yemen remained a republic, however, and the Egyptians consoled themselves for their costly adventure with the fact that in the same year, 1967, Britain ended her rule in Aden. Yemeni-based terrorism had helped to achieve this, and Nasser took some credit for having hastened Britain's departure.

Britain's Frustrations in Aden

Nasser's propaganda had in fact stirred up nationalist resistance to Britain's plans for the future of the Aden colony and protectorate.

83. The former Crown Prince who had sponsored the union with the U.A.R. in 1958 in the hope of saving the dynasty.

This large area stretching seven hundred miles along southern Arabia, together with the British protectorates over some of the smaller sheikhdoms in the Persian Gulf, were now all that remained of Britain's once imposing presence in the Middle East. Through NATO and CENTO Britain could play her part in defending the area against Communism; yet special measures were needed to safeguard the great oil-producing areas of Arabia and the Gulf. For her share in this task—in which the United States was also keenly interested—Britain had planned to keep naval, military, and air bases in the port and colony of Aden, which had been under her direct rule, though it had gradually acquired some representative institutions. Aden could be reinforced in case of need from British dependencies in East Africa. But British East Africa became independent in the early 1960s, and by that time Britain's presence in Aden itself was endangered by hostile propaganda from Cairo and Yemeni efforts to disrupt British rule over an area they regarded as an extension of their own territory and called South Yemen.

The British authorities tried to check this disruption by forming, in 1959, a federation of the semi-feudal emirates of the surrounding Aden Protectorate,[84] which were largely undeveloped and without resources, and then linking this federation with the Aden port and colony, so that the latter might help to make the combined region a workable whole. This union was set up in January 1963. But the port and colony, with a population aroused by left-wing and militantly trade-unionist, as well as nationalist, ideas, resented being linked with the backward and traditionalist Protectorate. Subversion and violence increased, and eventually two factions emerged as rivals in this agitation: the Cairo-backed Front for the Liberation of South Yemen (FLOSY) and the National Liberation Front (NLF) influenced by the British trade-union movement and Labour Party.

By 1967 the situation was becoming untenable. Moreover, after

---

84. This federation covered only the western states of the Protectorate. The eastern Protectorate, a barren area twice as large as the western region, did not commit itself to the scheme. See Williams, pp. 136–40.

the June war and the closure of the Suez Canal, Aden—which had been one of the busiest oil-bunkering ports in the world—greatly declined in importance. The British withdrew in November, leaving independent Aden in the hands of the NLF, which had managed to outbid its Nasser-backed rivals in the race for power. The new state was renamed, first South Yemen, then the Peoples' Democratic Republic of Yemen, in contrast to traditional Yemen, now called the Yemen Arab Republic, which has not till now managed to take these southern territories over. Britain gave the new state financial aid during its first six months.

As its name implies, the Democratic Republic is Marxist-oriented —and indeed Britain is sometimes reproached by the rulers of Saudi Arabia with having let Communism into the Arabian Peninsula. As in the case of certain other new Asian states, however,[85] the Communist aspect is in fact one of label and style and organization rather than of subservience to Moscow, which is largely precluded in all Arab countries both by passionate nationalism and by Islam. It is true, however, that, in consequence of the help furnished by Moscow to Egypt and certain other Arab countries, and the free use of their ports by the Soviet navy, the Russian fleet is now a factor to be reckoned with not only in the Mediterranean but in the other waters east of Suez.

New Coup in Baghdad. Tripartite Union Tried

Meanwhile, the mid-sixties saw further crises in the Fertile Crescent. In Baghdad in February 1963 a successful coup was launched against Kassim by Arif with the support of the Iraq Ba'athists. Although Kassim had commuted the death sentence of his former colleague, once in power Arif had no mercy on him, and Kassim and his left-wing supporters were put to death. Another coup, in Syria one month later brought to power men pledged to try Arab unification again—in the shape this time of a federation covering Iraq as well as Syria and Egypt. Both Iraq and Syria now had gov-

85. Such as Burma.

ernments in tune with the Ba'athists and their ideas. And the Ba'athists, fired by their double success, had some hope of dominating the new union and thus seizing the leadership of progressive Arab nationalism from Nasser.[86] But after much talk and manoeuvre the new state proclaimed in April 1963, with a constitution broadly on American lines, was stillborn. Nasser was the only conceivable President, but neither the Iraqi nor the Syrian Ba'athists were prepared to give him all the power this implied. There was soon open dissension between Cairo on the one side, and Damascus and Baghdad, both of which, Nasser discovered, were in league against him. Pro-Nasser demonstrations were checked, and in July a coup on his behalf in Damascus was ruthlessly crushed, with twenty-seven executions. Nasser then called the Syrian leaders immoral, inhuman, and fascist; and the union was allowed to lapse.

It seems strange that Nasser should have risked another humiliating failure. A reason was that he had become in a sense a prisoner of his quite exceptional position: he simply could not afford to turn down any offer of union from another Arab state. He also faced a constant dilemma. In countries such as Syria he had the masses on his side, as he knew; yet for reasons of local national pride he could not let his supporters play too prominent a role lest they be labelled stooges of Egypt and lose all their effectiveness. (This incidentally was a reason for the defeat of the FLOSY movement in Aden.) Apart from his own dominating personality, Egypt's size and weight made it hard for her to lead the Arab movement, since she tended to generate feelings of defensive touchiness in the other countries. The presence of the Arab League in Cairo—the one great metropolis of the Arab world—was already liable to produce this kind of complex.

Summit Meetings

Nevertheless the idea of unity refused to die. Arif remained in sympathy with Nasser and in November 1963 managed to oust the

86. "The Iraqis, rougher and more resolute than the Syrians, were always ready to strengthen the Syrians' courage." Mansfield, p. 133; see also pp. 132–38.

Ba'ath, which had tried to isolate him. He then revived plans for union—now between Iraq and Egypt—and a tentative agreement to this end was signed in 1964. Yet this, too, came to nothing. Nasser was by now cautious about such plans; and in 1966 Arif was killed in an air crash. He was succeeded by his brother, who was also cautious, and who wisely concentrated on internal unity by bringing to an end a war with the Kurds then plaguing Iraq. In spite of meagre progress with unification, Nasser remained at the centre of Arab consultations and of other international affairs. This was particularly marked in 1964. Heads of all thirteen Arab states[87] were invited to a summit meeting in Cairo that year to plan reprisals against Israel for her diversion of the Jordan waters. They also agreed to set up a unified Arab military command under an Egyptian general, and a Palestine Liberation Organization with its own armed forces. The person chosen, with some reluctance, to be head of the new Organization was a voluble Palestinian lawyer, Ahmad al-Shukairy, whose sweeping rhetoric was to be easily exploited by the Israeli information services. Although this was not stated publicly, the Arab leaders agreed not to go to war with Israel, but to build up the armies of the states on Israel's borders. They resolved to divert the headwaters of the Jordan in Arab territory; but at a second meeting in Egypt later in the year, Lebanon and Syria were reluctant to carry out the diversion with no better protection than the Arab states could provide.

During this same year, 1964, Khrushchev visited Egypt to celebrate the completion of the first, and inauguration of the second, stage of the Aswan Dam. The speeches made showed how remote the Arabs were from Communism, despite all Moscow's help. Khrushchev hinted that Arab nationalism was an outdated concept and that the true union of the Arabs should be based upon the workers; nationalism was only a stage on the road to Communism. For their part Arif and Nasser stressed the central importance of Arab nationalism and unity without Marxist or class-war implica-

87. Morocco, Algeria, Tunisia, Libya, Egypt, Sudan, Jordan, Syria, Lebanon, Iraq, Saudi Arabia, Yemen, and Kuwait.

tions. The Arab nation, Nasser said, had been united but later artificially divided; yet the Arabs still had one conscience and one mind. Even with Khrushchev present, he voiced his faith in nonalignment.

After Nehru's death in this same year and a meeting, in Cairo in October, of the rulers or delegates of fifty-six non-aligned states, Nasser gained stature as a leader of this group. He did less well in Africa, although the second meeting of the Organization of African Unity (founded at Addis Ababa in Ethiopia, during the previous year) took place in Cairo, again in 1964—one of the peak years of Nasser's career. His problem here was that his close identification with the radical states[88] prejudiced his influence with the African moderates. Moreover, most Africans were outside the charmed circle of Arabic language and culture—so powerful a bond within the Arab world; and it was hard for the Africans to forget the traditional association of the Arabs with the slave trade in Africa. Finally, in significant competition with the Arabs, Israel was exporting her technicians and expertise to many African countries with effect and success.[89]

Nasser Challenged. Libya's Revolution

From 1965 to 1967 Nasser's successes were limited and his problems many. He managed to prevent West Germany from concluding a big arms deal with the Israelis, and induced most Arab countries to break off diplomatic ties with Bonn when the Federal Republic established relations with Israel. But his leadership was now freely challenged in some new quarters. For one thing, President Bourguiba of Tunisia—one of the very few Arab leaders, with Hussein of Jordan, to take a realistic view of Zionism—urged the Arabs to be ready to make peace with their adversary if Israel would discuss a revision of the frontiers and the return of the Palestinian refugees. Some adjustment to the reality of Israel was not far from

88. Notably the Casablanca group: Morocco, Mali, Ghana, Guinea, and Egypt.
89. See Mansfield, pp. 143–51.

the minds of many Arab leaders, even of Nasser, but few had dared to speak of it, and some, jealous of Cairo, rejoiced that Bourguiba had done so, to Nasser's obvious discomfiture. Again, the arch-conservative King Faisal of Saudi Arabia was by no means a friend. Indeed, on a visit to Iran, the King stressed the need for good Muslims to resist "subversive and alien influences"—having, it seems, some fixed idea that there was little to choose between Cairo socialism and Moscow Marxism. And Nasser's influence on still another land—Libya—was to produce in a few years a brash challenge to Cairo's dominant role.

After being liberated during World War II from Italian colonial rule, most of Libya was placed under British military administration. Then in 1951 it became independent under King Idris of the Senussi, as a loosely integrated union of three large provinces—Tripolitania, Cyrenaica, and the Fezzan. Base rights were given to the Americans as well as the British. The sense of protection these bases afforded was at first welcome after a long spell of hard Italian rule, and the rental paid was a substantial addition to the economy of a poor country. While from the standpoint of the West the (American) Wheelus Air Base was important in the Cold War, since it "provided air power near the southern perimeter of the USSR and flanking Europe," it was bound to be seen by Arabs of Nasser's stamp as a last outpost of Western imperialism. In 1963 Nasser's attacks on the American and British installations led to a popular outcry in Libya for their removal.[90] By threatening abdication, King Idris managed to stall this for some years, but he was deposed in 1969, and Wheelus was closed soon after. A Revolutionary Command Council of army officers on the original Cairo model took over.[91] One factor above all inspired the increasing truculence of the Libyans towards the West and towards some of their Arab neighbours. The base rental and other windfalls had ceased to be important, for substantial wealth from oil discoveries

90. See Badeau, pp. 117–18.
91. The R.C.C. had ceased to exist in Egypt when Nasser became President under the 1956 constitution.

gave Libya's new leaders financial freedom and an urge to revitalize the Arab national movement after the sharp setback it was to suffer in 1967.

Nasser's New Egypt

By the mid-1960s Nasser had greatly improved conditions in Egypt, especially for the lower classes from which he had risen. But the R.C.C. and its successors had made no systematic plans, and worked by improvisation and trial and error as they went along. The Government became increasingly Nasser's own regime. Although he seems genuinely to have wanted popular discussion and participation along democratic lines, his aversion to political parties which he blamed for Egypt's ills, his powerful personality, and the country's long acceptance of autocratic rule, meant that he received little constructive criticism of the measures he proposed. When dealing with him, people usually hastened to praise and agree, whatever their private grumbles. Forced constantly to make untried, *ad hoc*, decisions, he landed himself with many tough internal problems.

In the early fifties the land reform had been a vital if partial step towards giving the country a new structure of social and economic power. But the expropriated landowners tended to reinvest in real estate rather than as he had hoped in industry; and many who had been wealthy remained so. He therefore tightened up the intervention of the state. Maximum landholdings were reduced to 100 *feddans,* and income tax was sharply increased. After Suez, the state had seized British and French concerns, and in 1961 hundreds of Egyptian industrial and trading companies were nationalized, among them cotton export firms, banks, and insurance companies. Later the property of many wealthy families—especially from the non-Muslim minorities—was also taken by the state. By 1963 private enterprise had been relegated to a fairly minor role.

In 1962 Nasser had issued a National Charter with guidelines for Egypt's future. Virtually his own creation, it launched a new political system, the Arab Socialist Union. The National Assembly was its parliamentary branch, and half its seats had to be filled by workers and farmers. There were other branches of the Union at all levels and in all spheres of activity up to the Executive, which was reorganized on cabinet lines, with a Prime Minister and Council of Ministers. The Union was to draft a new constitution and to re- cruit cadres of dedicated leaders from the rising generation. The National Assembly elected in 1963 was the most representative Egypt had ever known, and yet its ostensible power to control the Government was bound to be somewhat nominal as long as Nasser lived. The three essential goals he announced were to double the national income, to complete the ASU structure, and to seek Arab unity. But since pursuit of this last goal was one cause of the fiasco of 1967, in a sense it negated the other two. In 1965, meanwhile, there was another trial of strength with the Muslim Brothers, many of them intelligent civilians who resented the army's long spell of power. The economy, too, was in trouble, though to some extent Israel's was as well. Revenues from the Suez tolls and Nasser's dras- tic economic measures had spurred a very high rate of growth and development, not always wisely managed. Wastage and muddle had to be cut down.[92]

Al-Fatah. Egypt's Fatal Commitment to Syria

Meanwhile, between January 1965 and June 1967, there were fre- quent Palestinian guerrilla raids along Israel's borders, largely the work of a body called *al-Fatah* (Conquest), led by one of the Mus- lim Brotherhood, Yasser Arafat. Al-Fatah reportedly had Soviet and Czech weapons, funds from Egypt and Kuwait, its headquar- ters in Syria, and also bases in Jordan. Thirty-one such raids took place in 1965, and in May and September of that year Israeli troops entered Jordan to attack al-Fatah bases.[93] Despite the guerrilla ac- tivity, which his left hand encouraged, Nasser remained most doubtful about another full-scale confrontation with Israel. What-

92. Mansfield, pp. 115–17, 138–43, 156–57.
93. Keesing's Research Report, pp. 10–11.

ever rash words he sometimes used in public before June 1967, he privately said that the Arabs would not be ready for another war with the Israelis for many years. Indeed, his policy was to stop any Arab state, and especially impetuous and volatile Syria, from dragging the rest of them into any such war. To his cost, however, he could not free himself from his earlier commitments or from his towering status in the Arab world.

A fatal sequence of events for Nasser and his fellow Arabs began with a fresh army coup in Syria in February of 1966. The new junta arrested the leading Ba'athists and thus removed the main bar to better relations with Cairo. Nasser could not possibly reject a reconciliation when he had so sharply condemned Damascus for breaking their union; and many of the links between them were restored. Then in November strong pressure from the Syrians forced him into a defence agreement with joint staff meetings and a joint command in case of war. But—still influenced by Ba'athist suspicions—the Syrians refused to have Egyptian bases on their soil; and Nasser's worst mistake was to have accepted this fatal restriction. With such bases he could have helped Syria without having to mass troops on his own frontier with Israel. Without those bases, he was virtually committed to war if Israel seriously threatened Syria,[94] but with one hand tied behind his back.

94. See Mansfield, pp. 160–61, 164, 167, 169.

Chapter 15

Israel:
Triumph and Frustration

Consolidation and Confrontation

During her first two decades Israel forged ahead in pursuit of the unique goals she had set herself. A flood of immigrants, deliberately encouraged, was absorbed in the way we have described. Massive capital imports were used to bridge the constant deficit in trade and balance of payments. Some 70 per cent of this capital came from contributions to the (American) United Jewish Appeal and similar funds, reparations and restitution from West Germany, and institutional and personal remittances. The balance went to repay loans and build up foreign currency reserves.[1]

During these years, as we saw, there was swift and intensive expansion—both industrial and agricultural—with only small regard, in the case of industry, for the special sanctity of the Holy Land. Despite two wars and dependence on imported raw materials, industrial output increased five times between 1950 and 1969. A pipeline from Elat channelled the oil brought from east of Suez to the

---

1. Total capital imports to 1970 were over $10 billion (Israel Ministry of Foreign Affairs, Information Division, *Facts About Israel*, 1971, p. 93). A controversial point in connection with American contributions to funds such as the United Jewish Appeal is that they secure U.S. tax exemption by being classified as charitable.

rest of the country. Also, by 1970 the irrigated areas had been increased fivefold and were producing three-quarters (by value) of the food needed by Israel, which exported quantities of other agricultural produce, with citrus fruit still in the lead. But there was not enough land and water for all the cereals, grain fodder, and fats required, so that some of these still had to be imported.[2] Moreover, security was tight and effective—at some cost to personal rights and freedom in the strategic areas—in a land circled by hostile neighbours who saw in Israel a predatory intruder forced upon them by the Western powers.

Stresses in the Leadership. The Lavon Affair

In the late 1950s and early 1960s, political life was dominated, as ever, by the problem of relations with these neighbours. But the pattern of government coalitions which had emerged after the elections to the first Knesset continued, with periodic reshuffles due to the dissensions, jealousies, and occasional scandals characteristic of politicians the world over. In July 1953 Ben Gurion, then in his late sixties, retired to a remote settlement in the Negev—mainly, it seems, because his Cabinet would not back the belligerent line he urged towards Nasser's Egypt. Before leaving, he appointed Moshe Sharett, the Foreign Minister, as acting Prime Minister, and Pinchas Lavon, a former Minister of Agriculture, as acting Minister for Defence.[3] Both took up their posts definitively at the end of the year, when Ben Gurion resigned after making General Dayan Chief of Staff of the Army. It was said that by installing three men who hated each other in the key posts he could ensure his own return.[4]

2. *Ibid.*, pp. 111, 109, 101.

3. Sharett (originally Shertok) and Lavon were also members of the Israeli east European "establishment," having come respectively from Russia and Poland. Sharett was eight years younger than Ben Gurion and a noted moderate. Lavon, a former Secretary-General of the Histadrut, was almost from a younger generation, having been born in 1904.

4. Uri Avnery, *Israel Without Zionists—A Plea for Peace in the Middle East*, pp. 101–8. Avnery, a former Irgun fighter, is a leading Israel journalist and member of the Knesset, and the outstanding advocate of Arab-Israeli understanding.

Israel was disturbed at the time by Britain's negotiations with Egypt for the evacuation of the Suez Canal and by Washington's apparent hopes—at that stage—of winning Nasser's friendship by aid to Egypt and perhaps lessened support for Israel. In July 1954 members of an Israeli spy ring were arrested in Cairo and charged with arson and sabotage on American and British premises. The assumption of those concerned seems to have been that these misdeeds would be ascribed to the Egyptians and would thus wreck any chance of improved relations between the Western powers and Egypt which might prejudice the West's support for Israel. There ensued a bitter controversy in Israeli public life, where this botched business became known as "a security mishap" or "the Lavon affair." The director of military intelligence claimed that he had acted with his Minister's knowledge and authority. Lavon denied this but was forced, in February 1955, to resign. Ben Gurion returned to the Cabinet as Minister for Defence, and two weeks later Israel launched a fierce attack on Gaza—and this, according to Nasser, was a prime factor in deciding him to turn to the Soviet bloc for the massive supplies of arms he could not get from the West.

Ben Gurion again became Prime Minister after the third general election later in the year, but the Lavon affair was by no means over. After the fourth elections, in 1959, Ben Gurion formed a new government, and one of its cabinet committees cleared Lavon of responsibility for the bungled operation. But the Prime Minister would not accept these findings, which he seemed to think reflected on the military. He demanded a judicial enquiry, and when he failed to win a vote of confidence resigned. He was, however, called back, and Lavon was dropped. Still he insisted on another election in 1961, two years before the normal term; and this did not go too well for him. Mapai lost five seats and the Communists gained two. Ben Gurion finally resigned in 1963, being then 77, and was succeeded not by Sharett (who was to die of cancer two years later) but by Levi Eshkol, the Minister for Finance.[5] Strangely,

5. Another of the Eastern European "old guard," Eshkol was born in Russia in 1895. After piloting Israel through the Six Day War he died in 1969.

the Lavon affair still refused to die. Ben Gurion asked for, and was refused, yet another committee of enquiry. He then left Mapai, which he had helped to found, and set up a splinter party, Rafi (Israel Workers' List). But this group later rejoined Mapai, without him, to form the present Labour Party.

The Eichmann Trial

Another issue, and one that stirred far deeper feelings, was the case of Karl Adolf Eichmann, the former head of the Nazi's Central Emigration Office and of the Jewish Section of the Gestapo. The Emigration Office was the organization responsible for the liquidation of Jews throughout Europe. Thus, though he was not high in the Nazi hierarchy, Eichmann was held responsible for all Jewish deportations and exterminations. In 1945 he had fled to Argentina. Traced there by Israeli agents, he was kidnapped in 1960 and flown to Israel—in breach of all normal international proceedings. In a careful trial before the Jerusalem District Court, in which he was given defence counsel from Germany, he was charged with crimes against humanity and against the Jewish people. The court found him guilty and condemned him to death, this penalty having been abolished in Israel in 1954 save for genocide and high treason. His appeal to the Israel Supreme Court failed, and he was hanged in May of 1962.

Drift to the Third Arab-Israeli War

From 1960 tension mounted on Israel's borders. The year before, ships carrying cargoes for Israel had been seized in the Suez Canal. And in the early sixties there were the disturbing changes we traced in the Fertile Crescent and other parts of the Arab world. In 1961 the U.A.R. had broken up and Syria, leaning farther to the left than Egypt, had become free to pursue her impulsive courses, and, with her claim to be the seed-bed of Arab nationalism, to challenge Nasser's preponderance in the Arab movement. In 1962 and 1963 there were serious clashes on Syria's southern frontier, where Syria alleged that there were Israeli troop concentrations, but an UNTSO investigation revealed nothing special of this kind. Iraq had broken with the Baghdad Pact, and the Communists were influential there under Kassim, until he was replaced and killed by Arif, Nasser's friend, in 1963. In 1962 Algeria had become free under another left-wing regime; and archaic Yemen had established a republic for many years supported by Egypt in a war against the former Yemen ruler, who in turn was helped by Saudi Arabia and Jordan.

Despite leftward trends and marked divergencies between the conservative monarchical regimes such as Saudi Arabia, Jordan, Kuwait, Morocco, and (at that time) Libya, and the radical regimes, the internal influence of Moscow and Marxism, even in radical circles, was limited chiefly to the supply of arms and technical advice, and the adoption of certain economic and political labels and forms of organization. Any risk of genuine Communist revolution was sharply reduced, as we saw, by passionate nationalism and popular faith in Islam; and the Communist party was banned even in some of the most radical countries. On the other hand, from the standpoint of her traditional imperialist ambition to win strategic access to the Middle East, Soviet Russia had gained much by her close relations with Arab countries and the facilities accorded to her navy in their key ports.

Various schemes for Arab unity had been tried between 1957 and 1964, and all of them had failed. The one issue on which all members of the Arab League were united in principle and in public declarations was the need to help the Palestinian Arabs to regain their country. Nevertheless, despite much fiery rhetoric, none of them expected to win another war against Israel at that stage; and Nasser's own attitude to this prospect was distinctly cautious.

Why Did It Happen?

Why then did the war occur? This is still something of a mystery, on which more light may be shed in the next twenty to thirty years.

By then more will have been probed and published and admitted, and some historical perspective may have emerged, as is beginning to happen in the case of the Suez adventure. Certainly one key factor was Syria and what has been called Nasser's fatal decision to make a defence pact with Damascus without the right to have bases on Syrian soil.[6] In this context, the demilitarized zone set up by the armistice agreements on both sides of the Syrian-Israeli border was far more sensitive than those, for example, on Israel's borders with Jordan and Egypt. These other zones had small economic value and were little changed by the swift development of the Israeli economy; whereas the Israeli side of the demilitarized zone with Syria lay astride the river Jordan in one of the richest agricultural areas of Galilee. Again, in the demilitarized zone with Syria lay the only point on the Jordan from which the Israelis could divert the water needed to irrigate the Negev without having to pump it upwards, a point north of Lake Tiberias and some six hundred and fifty feet above sea level.

For the Israelis this zone was vital for agricultural development. For this purpose they had drained Lake Huleh—the Waters of Merom of the Bible—and built up settlements throughout the area. If the Syrians could check this development and block Israel's schemes for irrigating the south it would hit their enemy in a vital spot. The zone between the two countries thus remained an "abscess of permanent tension" for twenty years. From the Syrian side there were guerrilla attacks and infiltration; from Israel, tough reprisals. The settlements somehow survived and, by the end of 1963 Israel was successfully diverting some of the Jordan waters to the Negev, though due to this constant confrontation with Syria they could not do so from the upper Jordan itself. Instead, the pipeline to the south—the Kinneret-Negev conduit—had to run, more expensively, from Lake Tiberias, into which the Jordan flows.[7] At a summit meeting in Cairo in 1964 the Arab leaders decided, as we saw, to retaliate by diverting the northern sources of the Jordan in

6. Mansfield, p. 167.
7. V. D. Segre, *Israel, A Society in Transition*, pp. 156–57.

Syria and Lebanon. Little was in fact achieved, and some of the Syrian works erected were destroyed by Israeli raids.

Raids and Counter-Raids. Rifts in the Arab Ranks

In 1965 and 1966 the acts of force on both sides became more violent and more compromising, especially on Israel's northern borders. Al-Fatah's raids multiplied—at first mainly from Jordan but later increasingly from Syria and Lebanon, the first from Syria being in January of 1966. In November of that year, at the time Nasser signed his one-sided defence pact with Syria, the Israelis launched a strong attack, not on Syria but on three villages near Hebron in Jordan. While this was condemned by the U.N. Security Council, it was still (as probably intended) effective in sowing dissension in the Arab camp. The Palestinians in Jordan blamed King Hussein for not arming and fortifying the frontier villages. The King blamed the Egyptians and the Syrians, accusing the two radical countries of preparing to liquidate the Palestine problem in collaboration with Moscow by handing over Jordan's West Bank to Israel in return for a settlement. He further—most unwisely as the sequel proved—taunted Nasser with hiding behind the protection of the United Nations Emergency Force in Sinai. And this Nasser could not ignore, since it echoed criticisms from other parts of the Arab world he aspired to lead. Why, it was said, if Egypt had the strongest armed forces of them all, as claimed, could she not dispense with UNEF so that the Strait of Tiran and the Gulf of Aqaba could once again be closed to Israel?[8]

In other respects the rifts in the Arab world widened, especially between the radical and traditional countries. The conservatives had resented Nasser's indefinite postponement of their summit conference, to have been held in Algiers in 1966, on the grounds that such meetings were "exploited by the reactionaries for their own ends." As a result Saudi Arabia for a time withdrew all support for joint Arab schemes and the United Arab Military Com-

8. Mansfield, pp. 164–65.

mand virtually ceased to exist. In December former King Saud of Arabia was allowed by Nasser, in defiance of his brother the new King, to settle in Cairo. In February 1967 King Hussein of Jordan slighted Nasser by withdrawing his recognition of the Yemen Republic backed by Egypt; and he renewed diplomatic relations with West Germany before the Arab Foreign Ministers had even met to consider the matter.[9]

Mobilization

By late 1966, significant precautions pointed to a gathering storm. Israel lengthened her military service from twenty-six to thirty months. Jordan brought in conscription for all from eighteen to forty, increased her armed forces, armed her civilians near the Israel border, and fortified her front-line villages. In a new display of conservative solidarity, King Hussein accepted an offer from the Saudi dynasty of Arabia—once the sworn enemies of his own royal house —to put twenty-thousand troops at his disposal. In January 1967, fighting flared up in the critical demilitarized zone between Israel and Syria. This time UNTSO found that there had been a build-up of arms and troops on both sides; and both were told by the U.N. Security Council to restrain their military forces—with small success. In April a ground battle with tanks and guns was followed by an air battle in which the Syrians lost six MIG fighters. At this point Israel accused Syria of organizing the new wave of terrorist attacks. Syria, which alone of the Arab states had all along boasted that the raids came from her territory, now said that they had her full support. In May, Prime Minister Eshkol gave warning that there was bound to be a serious confrontation with Syria if the attacks continued.

The temperature was rising, and with it the rash and infectious impulsiveness that was apt at such moments to beset the leaders of the Arab world. Nasser was bound by his new defence pact to help Syria if she were badly threatened; he now had to honour his blank

9. *Ibid.*, pp. 165–66.

cheque. In April he sent a delegation to Syria, headed by his Prime Minister. In mid-May he declared a state of emergency in Egypt, and Cairo radio proclaimed that all military forces were completely ready for war. The Syrians for their part announced that Nasser's Chief of Staff had been conferring in Damascus on the implementation of the pact; that all their armed forces had been alerted; and that armour and guns were moving into defensive positions on the Israel border. Jordan's forces were also stated to be mobilized and ready if necessary to fight the common enemy.

What Did Russia Want?

On May 17 Egypt and Syria announced a large military build-up by Israel on their frontiers. UNTSO observers found no evidence of this; and it has been suggested that so inflated a rumour was put out by the Russians for reasons of their own. Nasser's resignation speech after the war gives indeed some confirmation of this.[10] The motives of Moscow for such a step have been variously assessed, since it was bound to increase the prospects of a war in which—as they knew and the Arabs knew—their Arab clients were almost certain to be defeated. One authority is convinced that the Russians aimed above all at ensuring that they remained indispensable, and retained access, to the Arab world. They knew that the Arabs were deeply suspicious of Communism and would be glad to be rid of the Soviets if they could get what they needed elsewhere. According to this theory the Russians therefore wished to embroil the Arab states in a war they would lose, hoping that in the process the United States and Britain would be provoked into statements ostensibly supporting Israel. All this would turn the Arabs definitively against the West and towards the Communist bloc, on which alone they would then be dependent for recovery after their defeat.

10. "There was an enemy plan to invade Syria. . . . Our friends in the Soviet Union told the parliamentary delegation which was visiting Moscow . . . that there was a calculated intention" (President Nasser, on June 9, 1967). See in this connection Churchill, *The Six Day War*, p. 28.

Russia could thus hope to secure a dominant and continuing influence in the Near East.[11]

Russia's earlier dealings showed her to be quite capable of a subtle and devious calculation of this kind. Others, however, point out that Russia did at the last moment urge Nasser not to start the fighting, and hence draw the perhaps more obvious conclusion that Israel's victory was in fact a set-back for the U.S.S.R. in terms of resources wasted and damage to Soviet interests far graver even than the Cuban missile crisis.[12] Others again concede that the Russians spread a report they knew to be false, and had been goading Nasser into political moves against Israel. They suggest, however, that, at least after the Arab defeat, many Soviet officials were strongly against any further deep involvement of Moscow in the Arab lands in view of the hostility and unreliability of the Arabs, especially the Syrians and Egyptians. Of course, they say, the Soviets would like to control the Near East but realize that they cannot in fact do so. Until more is known, Russia's true plans and motives before, during, and after the crisis can only be guessed.

Finally, some point to Nasser's faith in what he took to be a pledge by President Johnson that Israel would not attack first, and conclude that Nasser rashly overestimated the capacity of the superpowers, and especially of the United States, to control Israel's actions. A stronger presumption is that in the last days of May, perhaps under the influence of his top generals, Nasser was seized by a kind of euphoria which spread to all Egyptians and seems to have persuaded them that they might perhaps after all be able to settle the Israeli issue for good.[13]

UNEF Dismissed

In any event, war became increasingly certain during the last two weeks of May. On May 18 the Secretary-General of the United Na-

11. Glubb, *The Middle East Crisis: A Personal Interpretation*, pp. 11–13.
12. Churchill, pp. 47 and 192.
13. Mansfield, pp. 168–69.

tions was asked by Cairo to withdraw UNEF from Egypt and the Gaza Strip. U Thant promptly though regretfully agreed, pointing out how much this small force of 3,400 had done to keep things quiet for ten years along the 117-mile border with Israel. Peace, he said, would be threatened by its withdrawal. This soon became clear when UNEF's place was taken by forces of the Palestine Liberation Organization, under Egyptian, Syrian, and Iraqi command. These were of course the principal fire-eaters on the Arab side. But U Thant believed he had no alternative to withdrawing the U.N. force, since Israel had refused to have it on her soil and it was stationed solely in Egypt by agreement with the authorities there. It could not remain without Egypt's consent.[14]

Closing of the Gulf of Aqaba

Meanwhile the Cairo Ministry of Religious Affairs had ordered a *jihad*, or holy war, to regain Palestine for the Arabs, as the Sultan of Turkey fifty years earlier had ordered one against the British just when they were preparing to free the Arabs from the Turks. Various threats were uttered from the Arab capitals as to the grim fate of Israel if she should launch a war.[15] Egypt and Israel called up their reservists. Nasser was offered and accepted Iraqi troops to help him if war should come. Some Iraqi units were also sent to Jordan.

On May 22 Prime Minister Eshkol insisted that Israel had no aggressive designs; that she would withdraw her forces from the

14. U Thant did not feel bound by the essentially theoretical though ostensibly firmer views of his predecessor, Dr Hammarskjöld, who thought that the General Assembly should first judge whether the tasks of the UNEF had been completed. If it did not judge that they had been, and Egypt nevertheless enforced the withdrawal of UNEF, she would have broken her understanding with the United Nations.

15. It is significant that these threats were conditional on an attack being launched by Israel. On May 19 Field Marshal Hakim Amer stated that Egyptian forces had taken up positions from which they could "deliver massive retaliation against Israeli aggression."

Sinai border if Egypt did the same, and that she favoured a general reduction of troop concentrations in the Middle East. On the following day, however, Cairo announced the closing of the Strait of Tiran, Egyptian troops having replaced UNEF at Sharm el-Sheikh—and this meant the blocking of the Gulf of Aqaba to Israeli ships or ships carrying Israeli goods. Eshkol called this an act of aggression against Israel and appealed to the United Nations and the major powers to maintain free navigation. Washington and London condemned Egypt's action on the grounds that the Gulf was an international waterway, basing themselves on the Convention on the Territorial Sea, in force since 1964 and ratified by some thirty countries including Russia and Israel, though not by Egypt.[16] Nasser, however, insisted that the Gulf was Egyptian territorial waters and that the United States and Britain were supporting Israel. Moscow, in tune with Nasser, then accused Israel of being the "overseer for the imperialist powers over the peoples of the Arab East."[17]

There followed a flurry of diplomatic talks. The Israeli Foreign Minister, Abba Eban,[18] flew to Paris, London, and Washington to see whether the governments concerned meant business over keeping the Gulf of Aqaba free. An Egyptian delegation visited Moscow. And U Thant was assured by Nasser in Cairo on May 25 that

16. This lays down that there shall be no suspension of "innocent passage" between one part of the high seas and another, or the territorial waters of a foreign state, innocent passage being that which is not prejudicial to the peace, good order, or security of the coastal state. Nasser contested the validity of this on the grounds that Egypt was at war with Israel, the same argument he had used to stop Israeli ships from using the Suez Canal.

17. Keesing's Research Report, p. 19; see also pp. 10–18. According to General Glubb's interpretation, the statements by Washington and London apparently in favour of Israel were just what the Russians needed.

18. Born in South Africa in 1915 and a former lecturer in Oriental Languages at Cambridge University, Abba (formerly Aubrey) Eban worked for the Jewish Agency after World War II and later represented Israel at the United Nations and in the United States. After serving as Minister for Education and Culture, he became, as Foreign Minister, one of the most skilful and sophisticated exponents of Israel's policies to the world at large.

Egypt would not attack Israel but that Israeli shipping would not be allowed to pass through the Gulf of Aqaba. On May 26 Nasser declared that, if war came, it would be total, and the objective would be to destroy Israel.[19] On the same occasion he called the United States "the main enemy," and Britain "a lackey of America." Three days later the National Assembly granted him full powers to govern by decree.

When Eban failed to secure a commitment from President Johnson on the freedom of the Straits, the Israeli Government announced that it would be entirely within its rights in breaking the blockade as an act of self-defence if the United Nations or the maritime powers failed to do so. It was clear by now that ambition had committed Nasser to another basic mistake. He had known how disastrous war might be, but he had left the Israelis no room for manoeuvre. Those who had gibed at Cairo's leadership when Egypt's confrontation with Israel was shielded by UNEF had forced him to get rid of UNEF and close the Gulf—and this Israel could not accept.[20]

Jordan and Egypt Reconciled. Dayan Minister for Defence

Yet war was still not quite inevitable. A few days later two events made it virtually certain. Before and during the crisis, Jordan and Egypt had been, as so often before, on the worst of terms; and under Nasser's protection the Palestine Liberation Organization had called for the overthrow of Jordan's King. But the Palestinian majority in Jordan were inflamed by the crisis, and on May 30 Hussein suddenly flew to Cairo and signed a defence pact with Nasser. An effective-looking United Arab Command was now restored. An Egyptian general took over the Jordan army. On the face of things,

19. In reference to this speech in Israeli publicity the qualifying "if" was sometimes omitted, so that it looked as though the intention of Nasser and his allies was in all events to attack Israel and destroy her.
20. See Mansfield, pp. 168–69.

Israel was now confronted with a far more formidable threat. For Jordan, reaching near to Lydda and Tel Aviv, would now be definitely reinforced by the far greater resources of Egypt and of all the states that by this time were following Nasser's lead, among them the Sudan, Algeria, and Morocco.[21]

The second event was the appointment on June 1 of General Dayan as Israeli Minister for Defence. This was a controversial choice. Although a popular hero after the campaign of 1956, and a disciple of Ben Gurion, whom he had followed out of Mapai and into Rafi in 1965, Dayan was not on easy terms with the political old guard. A native-born Palestinian with small patience with the game of politics or with most of his fellow men, he seemed to share with other *sabras*—the tough Palestinian-born Israelis—a certain disdain for the elderly European-born founding fathers of Israel and in general for the immigrant Jews, who they alleged, were cowed by their long sufferings and dependence into expecting Israel to rely on protection by other countries. Thus Eshkol's Government was looking to the United States and the strong maritime nations to open the Tiran Straits.

Dayan, an activist, believed that Israel should rely on her own resources, and should deal with any Arab threat by striking first; and this is what Israel proceeded to do. By virtue of his flair for publicity, the lion's share in achieving victory in the war so soon to come has been attributed by many to Dayan. But the core of the Israeli army—which Dayan had been out of for ten years—was now highly professional under an able Chief of Staff, General Rabin, and the new Defence Minister seems to have made in fact only two alterations to the plans already laid for the initial stage. The main factor was his strong charisma, for this was such that his appointment gave an invaluable psychological boost to the morale

21. On May 28 and 29 Sudan and Algeria said they were sending troops to help Egypt; on May 30 Morocco made a similar announcement, but her troops were to be at the disposal of the United Arab Command to "repulse any aggression by Israel." Keesing's Report, p. 21.

of the troops and the nation, and to the conduct of the operations that ensued.[22]

The Arab Alliance

The next few days saw a further sharpening of Arab confrontation with Israel and the West. Kuwait and Saudi Arabia threatened to suspend oil shipments to all Western countries helping Israel. Iraq promised to avenge help to Israel by nationalizing Western oil companies in her territory and breaking off diplomatic relations. Syria undertook to blow up oil pipelines and seize oil installations in the event of war. On June 4, Nasser rejected in advance an Anglo-American declaration which had been presented for signature to a number of maritime nations affirming the right of free and innocent passage in the Gulf of Aqaba, and indicating their intention of exercising it. This, he said, would be an infraction of Egypt's sovereignty and the preliminary to an act of war. On the same day Iraq signed the Egypt-Jordan defence pact, and Libya announced that in the event of war she would fight by Egypt's side, and also deny oil to countries helping Israel; if the United States did so, the Wheelus Air Base would be closed. The number of Arab countries promising to help each other against Israel rose to eleven. By the start of the war it was to reach thirteen.[23]

The Eve of the First Blow

Under the Egyptians alone Israel now faced 80,000 troops with 800 tanks on her Sinai border. Dayan was asked whether, in view of all

22. See Churchill, pp. 56–59; Avnery, pp. 123–45. Avnery stresses the strong influence on him of the British officer Wingate, who trained the Zionists in retaliation raids and had some of those "lone wolf" qualities attributed to Dayan. It was Wingate's creed that soldiers must understand and agree with what they are asked to do. His teaching helped to produce in the Israeli army a special degree of comradeship and mutual responsibility between officers and men.

23. Egypt, Jordan, Syria, Lebanon, Iraq, Kuwait, Saudi Arabia, Yemen, the Sudan, Morocco, Algeria, Tunisia, Libya—i.e., virtually the whole of the Arab world excepting Muscat and Oman, certain states of the Persian Gulf, and Aden.

the adverse measures taken by the Arab states, Israel had not lost the initiative. If this meant, he replied, that she stood no chance in battle, he did not agree. Characteristically he stressed that she wanted to fight with her own troops; that others should not be killed on her behalf. The ground was in fact already being prepared for Israel to strike first and achieve surprise.[24]

Since June 2 fell on a Friday, on that weekend several thousand Israel troops were sent on leave, and photographs of them relaxing on the beaches were widely distributed. Moreover, according to press releases, the latest Israeli Cabinet meeting had been concerned solely with secondary matters. On this same Friday the Defence Minister was asked by a British press correspondent whether the war might not be decided in the air. Dayan assured him that it was most unlikely that either side would achieve total air supremacy. On this, the correspondent, and colleagues from another British newspaper, left for London, convinced that nothing important was going to happen just then. On June 3 the General stressed at a press conference that it was too late for a spontaneous military reaction to the blockade of the Gulf of Aqaba; the diplomatic negotiations started by his Government before he entered it must be allowed to run their course. In view of Israel's skill in masking all immediate warlike intentions, it is hardly surprising that up to the last moment the Cairo atmosphere was relaxed enough for many officers to feel justified in enjoying a normal weekend.[25]

Destruction of the Arab Air Forces

At dawn on Monday morning, June 5, there seemed no special cause for alarm on Egypt's military airfields. Not till some three

24. In the case of Pearl Harbor, Japan was condemned for not observing the traditional formality of a declaration of war before her first strike, and Israel also omitted this formality. But it had been omitted in other more recent conflicts such as the Vietnam War; and Israel could point to the fact that the Arabs in any case regarded her as being at war with them.

25. Churchill, pp. 69–77.

hours later did the Israeli Air Force make its first attacks. By then the precautions normally taken against possible dawn incursions had been somewhat relaxed. During the following three hours the Israelis were able to make three separate strikes on nineteen Egyptian airfields, with their transonic *Mystère* and *Mirage* jet fighter-bombers acquired from France. These had been flown extremely close to the ground to avoid being picked up on enemy radar screens. Previous Israeli air probes toward southern Egypt had hinted at a main attack in that direction. Instead, the attacking aircraft in some of the crucial first strikes flew west over the Mediterranean and then south. Three strikes were possible in the time because of the very short turn-around period—only seven and a half minutes—of the Israel fighter-bombers on returning to their bases. Indeed this seems to have led President Nasser to believe that Israel's air strength must have been supplemented from outside, and to accuse the United States and Britain of helping her with their own carrier-based aircraft.

The massive Egyptian Air Force was regarded as the major threat to Israel. Not until its power had been broken did the Israelis turn, later in the day and again on Tuesday, June 6 to settle accounts with the weaker Syrian, Lebanese, Jordanian, and Iraqi air forces. By nightfall on June 6 the incredible number of 416 Arab aircraft are reckoned to have been destroyed, 393 of them on the ground. The Israelis had lost 26 aircraft and 21 pilots. A great number of the airfields attacked were wrecked by a special penetrative bomb which the Israelis had asked the French to design for them. This could be dropped at low heights and high speeds, but was then slowed by a parachute and driven into the runway by booster rockets. After penetration, a time fuse could produce a series of explosions.[26]

Meanwhile, on this first night Israel's small navy managed to explore Port Said and Alexandria harbours with frogmen and do some

26. *Ibid.*, pp. 78–94. The Arab aircraft losses by country were given as: Egypt, 309; Syria, 60; Jordan, 29; Iraq, 17; Lebanon, 1—the great majority (save in the case of Jordan and Lebanon) of Russian make.

damage. Their activity there and elsewhere helped to discourage the Egyptian navy from raiding Tel Aviv and Haifa. Three Egyptian submarines did approach the coast, but were attacked with depth charges and did not push home their assault. Unfortunately, through their failure to make proper identification, the greatest losses inflicted by the Israelis at sea were in the U.S.S. *Liberty*, a naval electronic intelligence ship, which they attacked with fighter aircraft and motor torpedo boats (MTBS) some fourteen nautical miles north of El Arish on the Sinai coast, causing more than a hundred casualties. The air assaults helped greatly to turn the balance of this short war; so to some extent did the work of the navy. But the first and most decisive victory was won on land, in the Sinai desert, after tough fighting against well-placed and well-defended Egyptian positions.

The Sinai Campaign

For Sinai the Israelis had a triple plan of campaign. They hoped that by speed and dash their three divisions—as against seven Egyptian—would make up for their inferiority in numbers and armour.[27] Two divisions were each to try for a breakthrough at two different and vital points. The first was Rafa, just beyond Khan Yunis at the western end of the Gaza Strip. The chief objective was to try to capture El Arish, on the coast some thirty miles farther to the west, and at the same time to cut off the Gaza Strip. El Arish was an important station on the railway from Qantara on the Suez Canal to Gaza, and was Egypt's main logistic base for supplying her troops in Sinai. The second vital point where the Israelis aimed at a breakthrough was Abu Agheila, among the sand

27. The Israeli army's basic unit was a self-contained brigade group of about 3,000, with its own armour, artillery, support troops, headquarters, and medical units. For the purpose of a campaign two to four of these brigade groups would function as the equivalent of a division. See Churchill, p. 105. I am indebted to this detailed and interesting account of the Sinai campaign (pp. 101–123) and other operations of the war and also to Keesing's Research Report (pp. 25–41) for the short general picture I have given of it.

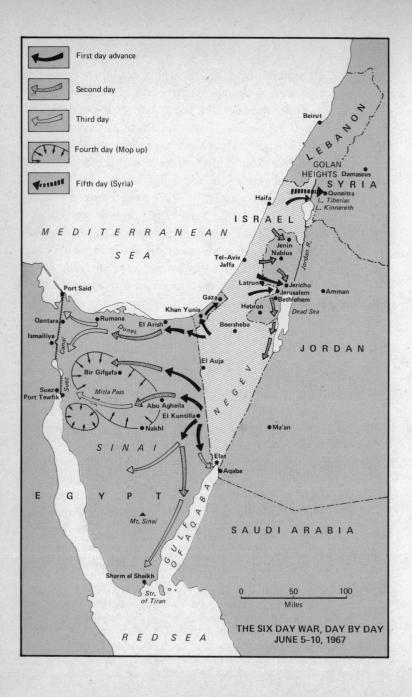

First day advance

Second day

Third day

Fourth day (Mop up)

Fifth day (Syria)

MEDITERRANEAN SEA

LEBANON

Beirut

GOLAN HEIGHTS

Damascus

SYRIA

Quneitra

L. Tiberias

L. Kinnereth

ISRAEL

Haifa

Jordan R.

Tel-Aviv
Jaffa

Jenin

Nablus

Amman

Latrun

Jericho

Jerusalem

Bethlehem

Gaza

Hebron

Khan Yunis

Dead Sea

El Arish

Beersheba

Port Said

Qantara

Rumana

Dunes

Ismailiya

El Auja

Canal

JORDAN

Bir Gifgafa

NEGEV

Suez

Port Tewfik

Suez

Mitla Pass

Abu Agheila

El Kuntilla

Ma'an

Nakhl

SINAI

Elat

Aqaba

EGYPT

Mt. Sinai

SAUDI ARABIA

GULF OF AQABA

Sharm el Sheikh

Str. of Tiran

0   50   100

Miles

RED SEA

THE SIX DAY WAR, DAY BY DAY
JUNE 5-10, 1967

dunes some fifteen miles west of the Egyptian border and thirty miles inland from the coast, and a strongly fortified position with a Russian system of defense in depth. It commanded the junction of the roads from El Arish, from Gebel Libni some twenty miles to the west, and from Kusseima some twenty miles to the southeast near the Israeli border, and thus it blocked any advance by the Israelis from the central Negev into central Sinai.

The third division, mostly of reservists, was committed to something of a gamble. After helping the other two, it was to race westward to Mitla and the other passes in the mountains east of the Suez Canal to block the escape routes of the Egyptian army back to Egypt. Obviously this third division might have been sacrificed if the other two had failed to achieve their objectives or to hold on to them once won. It was Dayan's decision to send all three divisions into Sinai instead of keeping one in reserve as originally planned.[28]

Capture of El Arish, Gaza, and Abu Agheila

The breakthrough to Rafa-El Arish was crucial to the whole campaign, the best of the Israeli armoured corps, with some 250–300 tanks, was assigned to it. The area was mined and also strongly fortified, and extensively covered by artillery. The Egyptians fought well and hard, and the Israelis suffered considerably from the strength and accuracy of their anti-tank fire. The struggle developed into the most massive armoured battle ever fought in the Middle East and, had it not been for the Israelis' initial conquest of the air, and the ability of their army commanders to call on further air strikes as required, the result would have been in doubt. As it was, by dawn on Tuesday, June 6, after a brutal engagement fought by the Israelis regardless of cost, they had taken El Arish as well as Rafa; and Gaza surrendered in the evening of the same day.

28. Avnery, p. 144. In view of the order of these objectives it will perhaps be simplest to refer to these units as the first, second, and third divisions, though they did not specifically bear these numbers.

After this success, part of the division was sent down from the coast towards the Canal. Its commander then moved south with the rest of his troops to join the third division with its fresh forces at Gebel Libni west of Abu Agheila, while the second division from Nitsana in the central Negev set about encircling this second vital breakthrough point.

Having completed their encirclement, the Israelis attacked Abu Agheila during the night of Tuesday-Wednesday June 6–7, dropping a battalion of paratroopers by helicopter inside the defence perimeter to silence the enemy artillery. They had specialized in night-fighting since their training in this form of combat by the British officer Wingate during the disturbances of the 1930s; and the Egyptian troops were less well adapted to it. The Israelis managed to enter the fortifications by 3 A.M. but were then faced with a tank battle inside them from dawn until 6 A.M., when Abu Agheila fell. Part of this second division then advanced southeast toward Kusseima, while the commander with his armoured brigade moved down to Nakhl, sixty miles south of Gebel Libni, in central Sinai, and to this area the Israelis now gained access by breaking through at their two chosen points. More of their armoured forces had advanced from the Negev to outflank Kusseima and Kuntilla—another Egyptian-held point near the Israeli border—from the south. These units then moved on and captured Thamad north of Nakhl, to which the Egyptian forces had retreated. Nakhl itself was captured after another fierce battle in the afternoon of Thursday, June 8.

The Mitla Pass. Bir Gifgafa. Sharm el-Sheikh

The commanders of the first and third Israeli divisions, meeting at Gebel Libni in the early hours of Wednesday, June 7, decided that the first would push on westward to Bir Gifgafa, the main Egyptian headquarters in Sinai, and the third race southwest to the Mitla Pass as originally planned. That same night, advanced units of the third had reached the Mitla Pass, while the first had established itself to the north of Bir Gifgafa, after two of the swiftest advances in the history of mechanised warfare. Meanwhile at the north end of the Sinai front, the detachment of the first Israeli division sent westward after the capture of El Arish had reached the Suez Canal near Qantara. In the south, the Egyptians had abandoned, and the Israelis had taken over, Sharm el-Sheikh; and on that same Wednesday morning, June 7, an Israeli MTB had passed through the Strait of Tiran. By this time there had been dramatic developments in the Jerusalem and West Bank area.

Capture of the West Bank and Jerusalem

Until Hussein's dramatic reconciliation with Nasser, Israel had hoped that Jordan might keep out of this war as she had out of the war of 1956. Even after they had launched their first air strikes against Egypt, the Israeli forces had been told to give no provocation to Jordan and to adopt a purely defensive posture. On the Monday morning, June 5, after their air attack, Prime Minister Eshkol had sent a message to King Hussein through the U.N. representative assuring him that Israel would not start any action against Jordan. But the Jordanians—now under Egyptian command—soon started firing from their side of the border. They shelled in particular the Israeli quarters of Jerusalem, Tel Aviv from Qalqiliya in the Jordan "bulge" only ten miles from the coast, and, in the north, the main Israeli air force base at Ramat David in the Jezreel Valley. The former British Government House—the residence of the one-time High Commissioners—which had become U.N. headquarters, was captured by the Jordanians on the Monday morning but recaptured by the Israelis the same afternoon. On Tuesday, June 6, the heavily fortified Jordanian Police School was taken after the fiercest fighting on this front, and more than half the Jordanian defenders were killed.

The Israelis then linked up with the small force permitted by the 1949 armistice in their Mount Scopus enclave containing the Hebrew University and Hadassah Hospital.[29] They also launched an assault on the Augusta Victoria area between Mount Scopus and the Mount of Olives, in order to dominate the city from the higher ground,[30] but did not take it until the following morning. Then they captured Qalqiliya in the coastal "bulge," Jenin in Samaria, and Latrun overlooking the Tel Aviv-Jerusalem road.

On the Wednesday morning, June 7, advanced units of the Israeli forces entered the Old City of Jerusalem through St. Stephen's Gate. They were met by the Governor of the City and one of the Muslim religious dignitaries, who announced that in view of its holy character the City would not be defended. The Jordanian troops had left, and there was no more organized resistance. In the early afternoon General Dayan, with General Rabin, the Commander-in-Chief, the Commander of the central front, the Chief Military Chaplain of the Israeli army, and many of their soldiers, went to the Wailing Wall to pray and rejoice over this new conquest of Zion. The Chaplain blew the *shofar* (ram's horn) to mark the occasion as one of special festivity. The emotion of the moment seemed to efface two thousand years of history and perhaps overlaid, for those present, the claims of two other great religions— and the nations faithful to them—upon the Holy City. Addressing the troops, Dayan made it plain that the whole of Jerusalem would now be the capital of Israel, and that his people had no intention of being parted from it, or from their holy places, ever again.

On the same day, with the help of strong air strikes, the Israelis conquered Nablus, a key city of Samaria. Lack of air cover had

29. Under the armistice agreement the Israelis were allowed to keep 120 soldiers in this demilitarized zone. A convoy was allowed up once every two weeks with supplies and replacements, a strict check being kept on it by the U.N., particularly as regards the limited amounts of arms and ammunition permitted. 30. Called after the German Empress, consort of William II. The Emperor visited Palestine in 1898, at a time when Germany was becoming increasingly assertive in the Turkish Empire. The name was given to a massive residence, hospital, and hospice for pilgrims subsequently erected in memory of the imperial couple. The first of these was used as the British Government House in the 1920s.

helped to break down a very spirited Jordanian defence. With this capture and that of Bethlehem and Hebron in the south, Jordan's resistance virtually ended. By the Wednesday night, Amman and Jerusalem had accepted a U.N. call for a cease-fire in pursuance of a Soviet resolution adopted by the Security Council. For Jordan the June war had been only a matter of three days. Yet the Jordanians, with a far smaller army and much less modern and sophisticated equipment than some of their Arab neighbours, had shown an aggressiveness far more determined than theirs.

Measures Against the West

Meanwhile, neither the Iraqis nor the Saudi Arabians, nor indeed most of the other members of the Arab League, had made any very noticeable contribution to the military operations. On the Syrian front there had been little activity till then, save for Syrian shelling of Israeli settlements and Israeli air raids on Syrian bases. The war had produced violent anti-American and anti-British demonstrations in Algeria, Libya, Syria, and Tunisia, as well as in Egypt. And the Arab oil-producing nations—Algeria, Iraq, Kuwait, Lebanon, Libya, the Persian Gulf Sheikhdoms, and Saudi Arabia—had banned the export of oil and natural gas to Britain and the United States. On June 6 Egypt had closed the Suez Canal. Cairo claimed that it had been blocked by ships sunk in Israeli air attacks, while Israel accused Egypt of sinking ships to block it. President Nasser's charges—of aid to Israel by American and British carrier-based aircraft—were rejected by Washington and London. Secretary of State Rusk pointed out that the U.S. Sixth Fleet was four hundred miles away; Prime Minister Wilson, that the two British aircraft-carriers in the Near East were at Malta and Aden, each about a thousand miles from the scene. The Soviet Union and its satellites made public statements condemning Israel, but did nothing more effective to help their Arab clients in their hour of trouble.

The Egyptian Collapse. Israel Reaches the Canal

Their trials were by no means over. The Israelis continued to press forward, anxious above all not to be forced into accepting a cease-fire with their other neighbours before attaining all the objectives they now saw to be within their reach. In Sinai they now aimed, first at cutting off, and forcing the surrender of, the bulk of the Egyptian army; then at reaching or dominating the three chief points on the Suez Canal from north to south—namely, Qantara, Ismailia, and Port Tewfik opposite Suez. As we saw, they had already reached the northern part of the Canal. At Bir Gifgafa and the Mitla Pass, forces of the first and third Israeli divisions were seeking to block the main access routes to Ismailia and Port Tewfik.

Meanwhile, forces of the second division had taken Nakhl after a bitter fight in which the Israelis claimed the destruction of some fifty Egyptian tanks. It was now their business to hasten the retreat of the Egyptians towards these two key points—in effect to drive them into a trap. The Egyptians clearly saw the threat, and on Thursday, June 8, with their remaining armour, and the support of some additional tank units from near Ismailia, launched a powerful counter-attack between Mitla and Bir Gifgafa to clear a path for their forces to reach the Canal. This led to some of the fiercest fighting of the war, but ultimately failed. Here again, command of the air by the Israelis was one deciding factor. Amongst other things, they were able partially to block the western end of the pass by air strikes and thus ease the burden on troops exhausted by continuous fighting in an effort to check numbers far bigger than their own.

During the night of Thursday-Friday, June 8–9, the Israeli forces reached the Canal opposite Ismailia, and also at the southern end of the Little Bitter Lake, and opposite Shalufa between this and Port Tewfik. Further south they had also reached the Red Sea coast near the Egyptian oil-fields at Ras Sudr. By this time the morale and organization of Egypt's forces had been broken, and she also had accepted a cease-fire. The Israelis, unable to cope with all the prisoners they could have taken, made arrangements for most of those who reached it to cross the Canal. They retained some thousand senior Egyptian officers to exchange against the few Israeli prisoners taken by the other side. This astonishingly swift and complete victory had been a *Blitzkrieg* (lightning war) in the strict meaning of the word—indeed, the first in history, for the Germans, who invented the term, did not achieve one in World War II in the intended sense of defeating the enemy so swiftly and completely as to end the war. But Israel had now done this.

The Assault on the Golan Heights

Syria's immediate reaction was to announce that she would carry on the war until the destruction of Israel. A few hours later, however, in the early morning of Friday the 9th, she agreed to a cease-fire—to the keen disappointment of most Israelis, who hated to miss the chance of settling accounts with the enemy from whom they had suffered most through the constant shelling of their settlements in the upper Jordan valley. But until that Friday there had been little Israeli action on this front, save air strikes against the Syrian artillery and anti-aircraft batteries. Many were ready to blame Dayan for delaying the attack on Syria until too late. Yet the Syrian positions on the Golan Heights were of formidable strength, a kind of Maginot Line,[31] with concrete defenses so thick that the bombs dropped by the Israelis could not break through them. Dayan wanted to be sure that the attacking forces could be strongly reinforced from other fronts; and these reinforcements needed time for rest and regrouping after the heavy fighting there.

There was a short lull when the cease-fire was due. But very soon the Syrians resumed their shelling and the Israelis their air strikes;

31. The massive defensive complex constructed near France's northern border before World War II. It failed completely to stop the German armoured invasion of France in May-June 1940.

no one knows who broke the cease-fire first. The Israelis then started their ground attacks shortly before noon, and by nightfall had secured two bridgeheads on the heights. The main attack was from the settlement of Kefar Szold at one of the steepest, and therefore less well-defended, points of access to the heights, the way for the armour and mechanized units being cleared by unprotected bulldozers which suffered heavy losses. Subsidiary attacks were made further south, between Gonen and Ashmura. The next morning, Saturday, June 10, with heavy air support, these forces advanced on Quneitra, the principal Syrian town in the area. Attacking at dawn, a new Israeli force took Banias and cleared the enemy from the nearby Syrian-Lebanese border, then joined in the attack on Quneitra, which fell in the early afternoon. Other Israeli units had meanwhile reached the Golan Heights from southeast of Lake Tiberias. In response to repeated calls by the Security Council, a cease-fire was finally enforced from 7:30 (4.30 GMT) on the Saturday evening.

This was the end of the Six Day War. In spite of the strength of their positions, the Syrians' defence had also crumbled once their set plans had been overturned by the dash and determination of the Israeli assault. Lack of flexibility and gift for improvisation and, in the case of many upper-class Arab officers, a lack of regard for, and communication with, their men, seem to have been key factors in this series of defeats.[32]

32. These failings were evident on both the northern and southern fronts. According to the interesting Churchill account, when the Israeli troops approached the Golan Heights, the Syrian artillery continued to shell the settlements in the valley below instead of turning their fire on them, despite being urged (in Russian) to make this change. In Sinai a captured Egyptian general explained that he had abandoned intact his brigade of Stalin tanks because his plans had been upset and he was convinced that he could not resist the Israeli attack. When asked what discussions he had had with his men about their operational plans, he said he would not dream of talking to his men. The Israeli general who took Abu Agheila thought the Egyptian soldiers very good. They were, he said, simple and ignorant but strong and disciplined—good gunners, good diggers, and good shooters—but the officers could fight only according to what they had planned before. Churchill, pp. 186–87, 167–69.

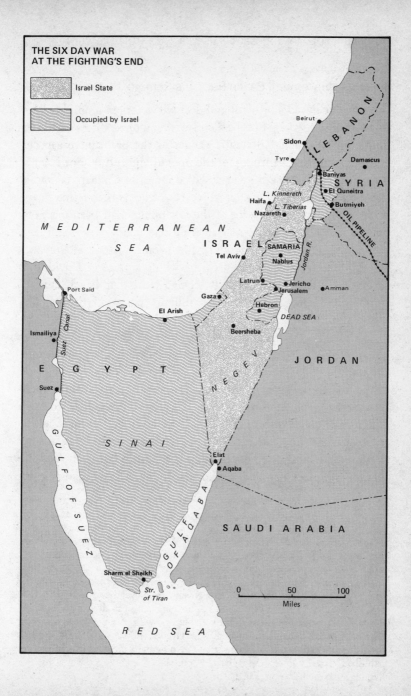

THE SIX DAY WAR
AT THE FIGHTING'S END

Israel State

Occupied by Israel

Beirut

Sidon

LEBANON

Tyre

Damascus

Baniyas

SYRIA

El Quneitra

L. Kinnereth

Haifa

Butmiyeh

L. Tiberias

OIL PIPELINE

Nazareth

MEDITERRANEAN

ISRAEL

SEA

SAMARIA

Tel Aviv

Nablus

Jordan R.

Port Said

Latrun

Jericho

Amman

Suez Canal

Gaza

Jerusalem

El Arish

Hebron

Ismailiya

Beersheba

DEAD SEA

E G Y P T

NEGEV

JORDAN

Suez

SINAI

Elat

Aqaba

GULF   OF   SUEZ

GULF OF AQABA

SAUDI   ARABIA

0   50   100

Sharm el Sheikh

Miles

Str.
of Tiran

RED   SEA

Israel's Achievement. Peace Remains Remote

Israel had achieved a brilliant and decisive victory in a unique campaign against superior numbers and well-equipped forces on three fronts.[33] This brought dramatic echoes of the past and prospects both hopeful and disturbing for the present and future. For Israel's three wars could be seen as a second conquest of Canaan, far more complete than that of Joshua three thousand two hundred years before, only this time the lot of the inhabitants had been mass expulsion instead of simple massacre. Others might feel that these wars had restored the Kingdom of Judah on a vaster scale, or heralded the eventual reconquest of the whole empire of David and Solomon. But for the present it seemed clear that Israel had become, after Turkey, the strongest military power in the Middle East, and certainly the most efficient. With Sinai and the Gaza Strip, the West Bank of the Jordan and all Jerusalem, plus the Golan Heights, Israel had taken an area four times her size before the war.

With such hostages to fortune, her people counted on a swift peace. Surely the Arab nations that had rejected her right to exist would now come to terms, for they must want to recover all or most of what they had lost? But, as we know today, this was an illusion—like most attempts to judge the East in terms of Western logic. The Palestinian Arabs who, rightly or wrongly, had refused

33. The Institute for Strategic Studies in London estimated the total military manpower of the actively engaged Arab countries, before the war, at 440,000 (Egypt 300,000, Jordan 60,000, Syria, 80,000); their combat aircraft at 631 (Egypt 500, Jordan 25, Syria, 106); and tanks at 1,750 (Egypt 1,200, Jordan 250, Syria 300). Against these, Israel had: manpower 275,000; aircraft 300; tanks 800. Out of these, there remained after the war, on the Arab side: 265,000 in effective military formations; 233 aircraft and 750 tanks; on the Israeli side, 272,000; 260; 1000, respectively. In November President Nasser said that 80 per cent of Egypt's army equipment had been destroyed; and that she had lost 10,000 soldiers and 1,500 officers, with 5,000 soldiers and 500 officers captured. Jordanian casualties were given in July as 6,094 dead or missing, 762 wounded, and 463 taken prisoner. No figures for Syrian casualties were published. Israel's losses were given as 679 killed and 2,563 wounded. See Keesing's Research Report, pp. 40–41.

to compromise with Zionism when it was forced upon them—although by doing so they could have kept half their country—saw few grounds for doing so after 1967, when they had lost far more, and Jerusalem—holy to them also—had been proclaimed the permanent possession of their enemies. And the Arab nations whose bid to help them crashed, were far too proud to hasten forward and clasp the hand of those who had humiliated them. Hence Eban's telling phrase. This was the first war, he said, in which the victors sued for peace but the defeated called for their unconditional surrender.

True, it seemed later as though Arab intransigence were being eroded by time, and that there might be some basis for a settlement with her immediate neighbours if Israel were prepared to give up all her conquests in the latest war. It also looked as if the moderate Palestinians might now be prepared to settle for the return to Palestine of those who wished, and a shared Arab-Israeli state. But, as we shall see, Arab intransigence was by no means dead; indeed it was spurred by a new pride—some might say arrogance—on the Israeli side. The defiant Israeli pronouncement on Jerusalem set the tone; and there has been small hope of Israel, in her new mood of self-confident triumph, considering such conditions. Meanwhile, one of the main Palestinian fears has been that their champions among the Arab states might come to terms over their heads with the realities of Israel. The Palestinians might then become, like the Armenians, a half-forgotten people, known to have suffered much, but one whose fate no longer seems to matter to the world or to stir others to fight battles for their cause.

The Refugees. The New Jerusalem. The Canal

One immediate tragedy for the Palestinians was an intensification of the refugee problem. Up to June of 1967 there had been some 700,000 refugees in Jordan, 315,000 in the Gaza Strip, and 300,000 in Lebanon and Syria. After the war, some 150,000–200,000 of the Jordan refugees from the West Bank—about one fifth of its pre-war population—had crossed to the east bank of the river and had become an additional burden on the Government of Jordan in its reduced territory. By an arrangement with Jordan in August, Israel permitted numbers of these people to return to the West Bank provided they applied within a stated time. But, like those in the Gaza Strip, the West Bank refugees now came under the strict rule of those they saw as enemy usurpers. Prisoners of war from all the countries involved were repatriated between June 1967 and January 1968, under the auspices of the International Red Cross.

Jerusalem was officially united and placed under Israeli rule by a law passed on June 27 which also guaranteed that members of all faiths would have access to the Holy Places. The change went smoothly at first, but in July a group of Muslim notables refused to recognize the incorporation of the Old City in the enlarged municipality. Members of the Jordanian municipal council declined to serve on the new council, and there were Arab protest strikes. Early in 1968 the Israelis set about restoring the ancient Jewish quarter of Jerusalem near the Wailing Wall. Most of the synagogues and religious centres in this area of some twenty-nine acres had been destroyed or had suffered during the period of Jordanian rule. A special feature of this restoration was the creation of a large open space for the access of Jewish worshippers in front of the Wall by the removal of intervening buildings (with the exception of mosques and churches), subject to payment of compensation to, and provision for rehousing of, the mainly Arab owners.

Meanwhile the Knesset had authorized the application of Israeli law and administration to any area of Palestine. In July 1967 there were armed clashes across the Suez Canal and in the Mediterranean, where the Israeli navy sank two Egyptian torpedo boats. Each side blamed the other. The U.N. Secretary-General then proposed that an observer force from the United Nations should be stationed on the Canal to prevent such breaches of the truce. The two states agreed, but then argued over the position of the cease-fire line, Egypt contending that it ran along the eastern (Israeli-held) bank, thus leaving the whole Canal in Egyptian hands, and Israel, that it ran down the middle of the channel or along each bank. The United Nations finally ruled that the cease-fire line was the whole Canal. Reopening the Canal was discussed for some two months. The Egyptians maintained that, since it belonged to Egypt, their ships would navigate it as they pleased, but that any attempt by Israeli ships to use it would be met by force. Israel claimed that, if one country used it, Israel too must be allowed to do so. On August 3 both parties agreed temporarily to refrain from using it; and on August 26 this ban on navigation was indefinitely prolonged, to the loss of all concerned.[34]

Nasser Survives, and Rebuilds

On June 9, the day after the Egyptian cease-fire, President Nasser announced that his country had suffered a grave set-back, though Israel had been helped by the United States and Britain and was therefore operating a threefold air force. Still he claimed full responsibility for Egypt's defeat and was therefore resigning all his offices; Zakaria Mohieddin, a former Prime Minister, had been asked to become President. A mass demonstration called for Nasser to stay, however, and this he promised to discuss with the National Assembly. The Assembly voted him full powers to rebuild the country, and his resignation was withdrawn.

Many of Nasser's foes assumed that this was a put-up job, but those who knew him are convinced that his bitter self-reproach was genuine. He was aware, of course, that it would be hard for anyone to replace him; and that the nation must be held together during the months of crucial decisions ahead. He was also concerned to forestall any attempt by the discredited army to install themselves by a self-seeking coup on the Syrian pattern. He became his own Prime Minister and set about a purge of senior officers in the army and military intelligence. His friend Field Marshal Hakim Amer was removed as Deputy Commander-in-Chief under the President, as was the Minister for War. When the Field Marshal tried to re-

34. Keesing's Research Report, pp. 42–45.

cover his position by a coup in September, he was arrested and, not
long after, killed himself.

Russia Trims Her Sails.
Egypt's New Poverty and Relative Weakness

In spite of the disaster, Nasser was still a hero to his own people
and to the masses in much of the Arab world. Yet internationally
he now held a weak hand. After the Cuban missile crisis of 1962
Russia was not going to risk another direct confrontation with the
United States. The Cold War, as such, was over. This explains why
the Soviets gave little more than rhetorical support to Egypt and
her allies in the crisis they had just faced. The U.S.S.R. had agreed
to the United Nations call for a cease-fire without even consulting
the Arabs. The President of the Soviet Union, with his Chief of
Staff, did indeed visit Egypt, Syria, and Iraq in July, while the Soviet navy made demonstrations of friendship in some force at Alexandria and Port Said, at the time and again later in the year. But
Egypt was told that, while the Soviets would help to repair the war
damage, they would only replace the lost weapons with defensive
ones—with fighter aircraft, for example, rather than bombers.

Significantly, a meeting of East European Foreign Ministers in
Warsaw in December resolved that, while peace depended on the
withdrawal of the Israelis from the occupied territories, all the
U.N. member nations in the Middle East should recognize the fact
that each had the right to exist as an independent state and live in
peace and security. Furthermore, "Slowly . . . the evidence accumulated that the Soviets were putting pressure on Egypt to reach
a settlement with Israel through the Americans. This was confirmed
by President Tito when he visited Cairo, Damascus and Baghdad in
August."[35]

The economic outlook for Egypt was also grim. There were few
tourists, the Suez Canal was closed, and Israel had occupied the
Sinai oil wells, which gave the country half its needs. As we saw,

35. Mansfield, pp. 171–78; Keesing's Research Report, pp. 50–51.

the Canal could have been reopened almost at once, as it was after 1956; and to Cairo these tolls would have meant much. But Israel could now insist on its staying closed unless Israeli ships were allowed through like any others. After the stand Egypt had taken for nineteen years, to concede this would have meant a fresh humiliation she was not prepared to face, since it would also have earned her the contempt and resentment of the other Arab countries. As so often, for the sake of pride and politics material advantages were scrapped.

The Khartoum Summit

The Arab nations took the line that the recent fighting was only one more battle in a long war; they now badly needed to close their ranks and consolidate their military strength, and in a few years were to prove that they were capable of doing so. They saw that if the conservative and radical states could sink their differences, this would be a wise step in the right direction. King Hussein had long urged a summit meeting; Nasser, very conscious of the new realities, also wanted one; and both were in dire need of funds. Khartoum was ideally placed and the conference took place there in August of 1967. Prime Minister Mahgoub of the Sudan had been keen to play host, having already helped Egypt and Saudi Arabia to work out a final settlement of their conflict over Yemen.

At this Khartoum meeting it was agreed that all Egyptian troops would be withdrawn from Yemen, and a transitional regime formed, pending a plebiscite. Unlike Nasser's abortive bilateral agreement with the Saudis of 1965, this new pact would be supervised by a three-man Ministerial committee from other Arab states. At the conference, too, Nasser and Hussein promised to continue the struggle against Israel provided all the Arab states would contribute all their resources. The main oil producers, such as Libya, Kuwait, and Saudi Arabia, agreed to give handsomely if they were not financially crippled by having to stop exports to the West. So it was decided that oil exports should be resumed. Libya, Kuwait, and Saudi

Arabia then offered £30 million, £55 million, and £50 million respectively, to compensate Egypt and Jordan for their losses through the war (Egypt was to receive £95 million, Jordan £40 million[36]). Syria and Algeria wanted continued punitive measures against the West, but since neither of their Presidents came, this was not pressed. The meeting led in fact to a kind of bargain between the conservative countries and the moderate radicals such as Egypt and Iraq. For in spite of Nasser's leftward policies for Egypt, his success against the Western imperialists, and Cairo's momentary war fever in early June, in many respects Nasser had always been a moderate, and one who far preferred political to military measures.

The Palestine issue was also discussed at length. The conference decided against recognition of Israel, direct negotiations, or the conclusion of a peace treaty "for the sake of the rights of the Palestinian people in their homeland." One thing, meanwhile, was clear. In spite of all that had been lost, Nasser was still then the leader most capable of guiding the Arab countries towards some kind of solution. Even after his death in 1970, the Egypt to which he had given real independence, a far healthier social structure, and a sense of national purpose after a long history of humiliating subordination, remained a key factor in any eventual settlement with Israel.[37]

The Clashes Continue

As might have been expected, the troops went on firing at each other from time to time across the Canal—where the U.N. observers usually managed to arrange a local cease-fire—and across the Jordan. Around the end of September, the Al-Fatah terrorists resumed their attacks on and within Israel and the occupied West Bank, with the usual severe retaliation by the Israelis and the arrest of many suspects in Israel. In October an Israeli destroyer was sunk by the Egyptian navy with Russian missiles, many aboard be-

36. At the time the sterling-dollar rate was 2.80.
37. Mansfield, pp. 179–82.

ing killed or wounded. A few days later, Egypt's two large oil refineries at Suez were shelled and set ablaze by the Israelis—in reprisal, it was thought, for the loss of their destroyer. This was a further blow to the Egyptian economy. The United Nations increased its observers and observation posts on both sides of the Canal; yet incidents continued for the rest of 1967 and 1968. There were Israeli air raids into Jordan in response to alleged firing from that side; and Arab terrorists did some damage to the Sodom potash works and to the railway to Jerusalem. In December 1967 the Israeli Government announced that three hundred "marauders" had been captured and fifty killed since the end of the June war. The supposed truce was proving a constant drain on the nerves, the resources, and the manpower of all concerned but especially of Israel, still an armed camp without the stimulus of war; and far worse was to come some six years later. Israel's founders had left Europe to escape hatred and violence. In spite of all their achievements, her people now found themselves bitterly rejected and constantly attacked by all their neighbours.

Israel's Choice

Israel might now have attained what she had always longed for—namely, peace and recognition—subject to accepting the basic requirement of her enemies, namely that she renounce her conquests in the Six Day War. These conquests, however, seemed vital to the Israelis as a bargaining counter; and, very naturally, they now saw the chance of permanently improving their strategic and material position by retaining much of what they had won. Such a standpoint would, it is true, defer the hope of peace; but in view of the terrorist excesses and the inadequacy and clumsiness of most Arab publicity, the world could probably be relied on to assume that her enemies were mainly to blame for any continuing hostility and tension. It therefore suited Israel to be intransigent in fact over these basic issues, while showing readiness to seek agreement with her neighbours at any moment.

Thus, in his first post-war statement to the Knesset, Prime Minister Eshkol made it plain, as Dayan had, that Israel would not return to her pre-war frontiers and position.[38] His country would, he said, no longer be "a no-man's land wide open to . . . sabotage and murder"; the Israelis had fought alone for their existence and were entitled to decide how their vital interests should be met. Later he gave warning that, in view of Arab non-recognition, Israel would "maintain in full the situation . . . established in the cease-fire agreements"—i.e., would retain all her conquests. In July the Foreign Minister told the United Nations that Israel saw future peace as the product of "a frank and lucid dialogue" with each of the states that had tried to "overthrow her sovereignty and undermine her existence." Both Jews and Arabs loved the region; they must, he said, "transcend their conflicts in dedication to a new Mediterranean future." In free negotiations with each neighbour, Israel would offer "durable and just solutions redounding to [their] mutual advantage and honour." He later added that there must now be "freely negotiated new frontiers assuring peace and security in the area." With this in view Israel was prepared at any time to meet the Governments of Egypt, Syria, Lebanon, and Jordan.

These well-turned phrases impressed many with the reasonableness and statesmanship of Israel, and yet they offered no concrete concessions of the only kind likely to bring the Arab nations and their Palestinian client eventually to the conference table—namely, some prospect of the more or less complete restoration of the territory Israel had just conquered and, in advance of any negotiations, some genuine and generous offer of reparation and restitution to the Palestine refugees. Nor did Mr Eshkol's statement in December 1967, that Israel sought permanent peace, to be achieved by direct negotiations leading to peace treaties with her neighbours; that her ships must have the free use of the Suez Canal and the Strait of Tiran; and that there must be agreed and secure borders with her

38. This attitude was made even more explicit in General Dayan's television interview with the British Broadcasting Corporation on May 14, 1973, which is dealt with in the final chapter.

neighbours. Then the refugee problem could be settled "within a regional and international context" after the establishment of peace.[39]

Abortive Peace-Making. The British U.N. Resolution. The Jarring Mission

During the second half of 1967 various schemes for a Middle Eastern settlement were urged by other nations. None of them bore fruit. President Johnson laid down "five great principles for peace" of remarkable vagueness. There should be mutual recognition, he said, of the right of national life, justice for the refugees, freedom of innocent maritime passage, limitation of the arms race, and respect for political independence and territorial integrity. Pakistan—an Islamic republic—called on Israel to cancel the altered status of Jerusalem, but when this was adopted by the U.N. General Assembly, the Secretary General was told by Israel that she had no intention of rescinding the measures she had taken. President Tito said he wished to see a solution "favourable to the Arabs," and proposed that there should be no territorial annexations by force, that all the states of the area should be able to live in peace within their national territories, and that the great powers should guarantee their frontiers as they existed before June 1967. Mr Eban immediately retorted that Israel would not allow her rights or interests to be affected by proposals from Yugoslavia.

Finally on November 22, 1967, a British resolution was unanimously adopted by the Security Council. It put forward as bases for the establishment of peace the withdrawal of Israeli forces from the occupied territories, the termination of all claims or states of belligerency, and the mutual acknowledgement of the sovereignty, territorial integrity, and political independence of every state in the area. It also recommended that the Secretary General should appoint a Special Representative to "establish and maintain contacts with the states concerned." U Thant then invited Dr Gunnar Jar-

39. See Keesing's Research Report, pp. 45–50.

ring, the Swedish Ambassador in Moscow, to visit the area as his representative, under the terms of the British resolution. Between mid-December and mid-January of 1968 Dr Jarring had exploratory talks in Beirut, Amman, Cairo, and Jerusalem. But Syria, having rejected the November resolution, boycotted his mission.[40]

Pattern of Events Since the June War

More than a quarter of a century has passed since the foundation of Israel; and after the Six Day War Israel made new and striking gains. Yet the ensuing years were marked by constant tension, disillusion, and frustration ending in a fresh explosion; and there is still no assurance of enduring peace. For some three years a war of attrition went on between the opposing armies—fighting that the Jarring talks were powerless to stop. Then in August 1970 this skirmishing was largely halted on the Egyptian and Jordanian fronts by a new cease-fire agreement sponsored by the United States. But the terrorist incidents and Israeli retaliation continued and became in some ways increasingly vicious and ruthless.

In despair at what they see as the irreparable loss of their homes and homeland, some of the refugee Palestinians have done wild and wicked things and have thus hurt their own cause. On the other hand, those under Israeli rule in the occupied territories, whether bitter or resigned, have been for the most part passive. They know the kind of punishment—perhaps the blowing up of their houses or their expulsion across the Jordan or both—which awaits them at the hands of their new masters should they seem to endanger the security of Israel. And this security has been further ensured in the occupied areas by the establishment of fortified agricultural settlements at certain key points, for example, on the West Bank of the Jordan valley.

During these years Israel's constant policy with regard to the conflict was to seek a direct deal with her Arab neighbours and, despite her dependence on the United States, to reject the interven-

40. *Ibid.*, pp. 51–53.

tion of the great powers. She obviously could not relish the U.N. Security Council's November resolution demanding her withdrawal from the occupied territories, but Dr Jarring's mission was another matter. His talks in 1968 and 1969 were mainly with Egypt, Jordan, and Israel. They led to nothing, and no details were divulged. But they suited Israeli policy insofar as through Jarring confidential views could be exchanged between Israel and countries which deeply concerned her but with which officially she could not speak.

In the first years after 1967 the Israelis had a feeling of great elation and achievement. The number of immigrants swelled from North and South America, from Britain and the British Commonwealth—areas which formerly had sent few. The immigrants felt that Israel had become more completely than ever before a physical as well as a spiritual centre of a Jewish nation. Indeed, some saw the future of World Jewry and Judaism as primarily dependent on the stable establishment of Israel and on the solidarity with Israel of Jews throughout the world.[41] This solidarity had been a constant theme among many Jews while Israel seemed in danger of extinction by the Arabs; and the theme recurred whenever Israel was in danger. Yet not all Jews have felt able to accept Israel, as created and preserved by the sword, as the ideal centre of their national life.

In any case, after 1967 there was clearly small danger of Israel's extinction, and on this score the solidarity between Israel and the Diaspora may suffer. Indeed in the wake of Israel's military triumph in that year the Arabs had grounds to fear that Israel, having reached the Red Sea and the Nile, might feel tempted to reconquer the whole empire of David and Solomon by annexing not only the Golan Heights but much else of Syria, and Lebanon and Jordan as well. Meanwhile six years went by, bringing no real peace— years marked by frequent brief engagements with terrorists or regular Arab forces and a constant but deadly trickle of military and civilian losses of cumulative weight for the strength and morale of a country with so slender a population as Israel's.

41. Norman Bentwich, *Israel: Two Fateful Years, 1967–69*, pp. 15–17.

Indeed, by the 1970s many young Israelis had come to feel a new frustration, a surfeit of eternal armed vigilance against a ring of foes with long and arid spells of military service, a longing for a normal life. Their victorious citizen army with superb morale, dash, and dedication in the lightning battles of the Six Day War had become mostly an occupation force drearily assigned to watching and controlling the lives of a million Arabs, much as the British imperialists in their day watched and controlled the lives of Indians and Egyptians. These young Israelis have learned from the sufferings of their own people in the lands they came from that minorities under alien rule must necessarily claim from those who rule them the respect of all basic human rights. And in dealing with a subjected Arab population some are correspondingly disturbed at having to execute orders which impair or destroy the lives of those now under their control as their fathers used to be subject to the arbitrary dictates of the Pale or ghetto.

The Palestine Liberation Organization. A New Theme

For their part the wiser Palestinians and their main supporters in the Arab nations were well aware after 1967 of the discredit brought on them by the boastful rhetoric of Ahmed Shukairy, the leader of the Palestine Liberation Organization, who had announced beforehand that Israel would be completely annihilated if war broke out. In January 1968 he was replaced by a relative moderate, Yehia Hammouda, who said it was ridiculous to demand that the Jews who had entered Palestine since 1948 should return to their countries of origin. If they wished to stay without giving up Zionism, they should "occupy the areas which had not been exploited before 1948" and return the rest to the Arabs; but the best solution would be an "Arab-Jewish Palestinian state in which both communities would participate according to their rights." There had never, he said, been racial hatred or animosity between Jews and Arabs. They needed each other; but the region must be liberated from an "expansionist state based on . . . racism and . . . neo-colonialism."[42]

Once more, there was a tragic gap in timing. The whole fate of Palestine might have been changed had her Arabs taken such an attitude thirty, or even twenty, years earlier. As it was, the new and moderate Palestinian line produced no response from Israel whatever. After their victories, Israeli leaders saw themselves as sole arbiters of the land they had conquered. Once they had defeated its Arab people and their allies they had no thought of sharing power with those to whom the land had belonged.

Israel's Defiant Pride

After 1967 Israel continued to seek friends and to turn a welcoming face to most of the world. The tourist industry in the Holy Land was now wholly in her hands, and this profited her image and her budget. But her triumph in that year was followed by a stronger note of defiant pride in her public pronouncements and a more marked indifference towards international reactions which did not suit her, as well as towards the feelings of non-Jews within her borders. This was shown in the line she took with the United Nations, and also in Jerusalem and Hebron.

Thus in April 1968 the Security Council unanimously called for the cancellation of a military parade the Israeli Government proposed to hold on May 2, in the Arab as well as the Jewish areas of Jerusalem, including part of the Old City, to celebrate the twentieth anniversary of Israel's independence. The U.N. Secretary General particularly urged that this might adversely affect the search for a peaceful settlement. The response of the Israeli representative to the U.N. was that the parade would take place irrespective of the Council's resolution. Jerusalem, he stressed, was the "crown of the Jewish people," and twenty centuries would march behind the Israeli troops on this occasion. Quantities of captured Egyptian, Jordanian, and Syrian equipment were put on show when

42. Keesing's Contemporary Archives, p. 22475.

the parade was held before a quarter of a million spectators. The Arabs closed their shops; incidents were successfully forestalled.[43]

Then in May the Security Council passed, without opposition but with the United States and Canada abstaining, another resolution condemning the unification of Jerusalem and declaring invalid all Israeli measures that tended to change the legal status of the Holy City. Foreign Minister Eban thereupon rejected this measure as unreasonable, impractical, and an obstacle to peace, and even called it "a sorry chapter in the moral history of the world organization."

Hebron was, after Jerusalem, a place of special sanctity for Jews as well as for Christians and Muslims, as the reputed burial place of the Patriarch Abraham, his descendants Isaac and Jacob, and their wives, Sarah, Rebecca, and Leah. In Crusader times a Christian church had been built by the Tomb of the Patriarchs, apparently on the site of a Byzantine church. After Saladin's reconquest it became a Muslim mosque, and neither Jews nor Christians were normally admitted to the interior. There were further restrictions for Jews during the period of Jordanian rule from 1948 to 1967. Then, after the Israeli conquest, there was a move of religious Jews to Hebron and expansion of the Jewish population in new apartment blocks, in effect under military protection. Jews were now admitted to the mosque for worship at particular times, though the specifically Muslim parts of the building were roped off. But Hebron is still fervently Muslim, and the mosque authorities became disturbed at the possibility of further Jewish encroachments in precincts sacred to their own faith. In the tension of the time the people of the town, where Arab-Jewish relations had formerly been good, were all too easily aroused to fanatical acts. Thus in October 1968 an Arab boy of seventeen threw a hand grenade into a crowd of Jewish worshippers at the Tomb during the Feast of Tabernacles, causing many casualties. The mood of Hebron has since re-

43. There is a vivid picture of this parade, with an analysis of the Zionist background and personal stories of "Israel's aging power elite" and the meaning, for Israelis, of their achievements, in Elon, pp. 7–37.

mained potentially explosive, though Israeli security measures have for the present effectively intimidated the local population and the Muslim religious authorities.[44]

Israeli Peace Plan Offered and Rejected

In this same October of 1968 an Israeli peace plan was presented to the United Nations. It appealed, predictably, for permanent peace "built by Arab and Israeli hands" and contractually guaranteed on the basis of "secure and recognized boundaries," though it did not say what those boundaries would be. The peace treaty should contain an agreed map of the new frontiers, a mutual non-aggression pact, and special security arrangements to avert the outbreak of another war like that of 1967. There must be freedom of movement between the several states, as well as freedom of navigation on international waterways. The refugee problem should be solved by a conference between the Middle Eastern states, the governments contributing to refugee relief, and the U.N. specialised agencies, on the basis of a five-year plan for their integration into productive life. (Again, it did not say where; and the possibility of any return to their Palestine homeland was not mentioned.) The refugee conference could be called in advance of peace negotiations.

On the issue of Jerusalem the plan did not discuss the controversy over Israeli rule, only the Holy Places of Christianity and Islam. Israel, it said, did not seek unilateral jurisdiction over these. She was willing to work out a status to give effect to their universal character, and those who held them in reverence should be responsible for them. The Arab states should withdraw all their reservations about Israel and recognize her sovereignty, integrity, and right to national life. Finally, regional cooperation should "lay the foundations of a Middle Eastern community of sovereign states."

The Israeli plan found of course no favour with the Arab leaders. The Egyptian Foreign Minister described it as "part of a campaign of international deception to undermine the Jarring mission," and

44. Such was the position when the author visited Hebron in October 1972.

demanded Israel's withdrawal from "every inch" of the occupied territories. She could not, he said, have continued her "policy of aggression and defiance of the United Nations and its resolutions without the political and moral support of the United States."

The Big Four Intervene

In the following years the grim story of guerrilla deeds against Israel, and violent retaliation, continued. At the end of 1968 agents of the Palestine Liberation Organization attacked an Israeli airliner at Athens; the Israelis then landed commando troops by helicopter at Beirut airport and blew up thirteen Lebanese airliners, on the grounds that the PLO's headquarters were in Beirut. The major powers now tried to halt this cycle of destruction and bloodshed. In January 1969, following Soviet proposals for a Middle East settlement, the French Government urged a meeting of the four permanent members of the Security Council to explore the possibilities of peace in conjunction with the Secretary-General. Paris had partly stopped arms supplies to Israel after 1967 and now imposed a total ban. France even refused to deliver fifty *Mirage* jet fighters which Israel had on order, or to refund $160 million already paid by Israel for arms not yet delivered.

Following a fact-finding tour of the Middle East on behalf of President-elect Richard Nixon by Mr William Scranton, former Governor of Pennsylvania, Washington accepted the French plan for a meeting of the "Big Four" to discuss the problems of the Middle East, seeing this as a "fruitful and constructive complement" to the Jarring mission. Their meetings started in New York in April 1969. As in the case of the Jarring talks little was divulged, though there were expressions of support by the four powers for the U.N. resolution of November 1967, and Dr Jarring's mediation. Just before the four-power meeting the Israeli Government issued another defiant statement, having, it seems, sent Mr Eban to Washington to try to prevent the four power meeting. Israel would not, it said, become the object of power politics. Nor would she accept any recommendation which conflicted with her vital interests, rights, and security. Israel "entirely opposed" such a meeting, alleging that it undermined the responsibility of the states of the region to attain peace among themselves. She would "maintain in full the situation as determined by the cease-fire" (i.e., would retain all the conquered territories) and would "consolidate her position in accordance with the vital needs of her security and development," unless peace treaties were concluded.[45] A later criticism was that the four-power talks would be useless since "the parties concerned" would not be taking part in them; indeed this intervention had "paralysed" the Jarring mission. Also in April 1969 King Hussein of Jordan, who had been invited to Washington, produced his own peace plan, which purported to be that of President Nasser too. The nub of this was that the Arab countries would recognize Israel and her future frontiers, and would lift all obstacles to Israeli navigation in the Suez Canal and the Gulf of Aqaba, on the sole condition that Israel withdraw from her conquests of 1967 and accept in all other respects the Security Council's resolution of November 1967. There must also be "a just settlement of the refugee problem." Israel responded to this by inviting the King to "come to the conference table" if the Arabs really wanted peace. Meanwhile in March Hussein had announced the setting up of an Arab Eastern Military Command controlling the forces of Jordan, Syria, and Iraq, the three countries forming the eastern front against Israel. It was, however, some years before any effective joint action against Israel was taken.

The Government of Mrs Meir

In the previous month, Mrs Golda Meir had been chosen to succeed Mr Eshkol as Prime Minister after the latter's death. Like her predecessor, she had been born in Russia. Brought up in America, she had settled in Palestine at the age of twenty-three and was over seventy when she became Israel's leader, after being Labour Min-

45. Keesing's Contemporary Archives, pp. 23325–26.

ister, then Foreign Minister from 1956 to 1966. She had been a key figure in Mapai and most of her cabinet (reconstituted as a Government of National Unity in December 1969) were from the expanded and reunified Labour Party. This government was, as always, a coalition including religious elements, in this case three Ministers from the National Religious Party, which, however, did not now include the extreme-orthodox Agudat Israel. There were also two from the more extreme workers' party, Mapam, and one from the Independent Liberal Party which had replaced the Progressives. Her cabinet also included for some time six ministers from the extreme right-wing Gahal bloc, led by Menachem Begin. These however left the government and went into opposition in August 1970, because they rejected the resumption of the Jarring peace negotiations.

Among her ministers were no less than three successful military commanders. These were Yigal Allon, the Deputy Prime Minister and Minister for Education and Culture; Dayan, the Minister for Defence; and Haim Bar-Lev, former Chief of Staff of the Israeli army, the Minister for Commerce and Industry, both the latter, like herself, of east European origin, though Dayan was born in Palestine. Another key figure from Eastern Europe (in this case Poland) was the Minister for Finance, Pinhas Sapir, former Secretary-General of the Labour Party, who has generally been credited with a more flexible and understanding approach than most of his colleagues to the issue of relations with the Arabs.

Renewed Violence of the Palestinian Organization

After its abortive gesture of relative moderation, the Palestine Liberation Organization early in 1969 fell again into the hands of the extremists. At a meeting in Cairo in February of most of the Arab guerrilla organizations, Al Fatah gained virtual control of the PLO, and Yasser Arafat its leader was elected chairman of the Organization's new executive committee. He later visited Moscow as the guest of the "Soviet Afro-Asian Solidarity Committee," and Peking, where, according to his own story, Chou En-Lai assured him that China gave unlimited backing to the Palestine guerrillas. After his return he claimed that there were thirty-two thousand guerrillas in Jordan alone and this was soon to lead to clashes with King Hussein's government that became increasingly serious in the following years. Meanwhile the Cairo meeting rejected the Security Council's resolution of November 1967, and any solution which might emerge from the four-power talks. It was decided to press on with the struggle for Palestine by means of a new plan of military, political, and financial action. After this, and Nasser's announcement in mid-1969 abrogating the cease-fire, it was hardly surprising that the U.N. Secretary-General complained of a "virtual state of war" along the Suez Canal, where, he said, the ninety-two U.N. observers might have to be withdrawn in view of the danger to which they were exposed. Moreover, the toll of grim incidents in the border regions of Jordan, Syria, and Lebanon with Israel, and in Israel herself, went on throughout the year and into 1970.

In the second half of 1969 one group of Arab guerrillas[46] transferred their activities to Western Europe, where bombings of Israeli premises and hijacking of aircraft were carried out. Small wonder that U Thant spoke in September of the "rising tide of violence in the Middle East involving the risk that this great and historic region, the cradle of civilization and of three world religions, would recede steadily into a new dark age." When the Security Council, in yet another resolution, deplored the changes made by Israel in Jerusalem in defiance of all earlier resolutions on this point, the Israeli Foreign Ministry retorted that Jerusalem would remain unified and the capital of the state, because the deep attachment of the Jewish people to the City "transcended all political considerations." The Security Council was, it said, heavily weighted against Israel, since six of its members did not recognize her, and three of the others habitually voted with the Arabs.

46. The Popular Front for the Liberation of Palestine, whose leader, Dr George Habbash, a Palestinian Christian, was a medical graduate of the American University of Beirut. The Popular Front had a stronger Marxist orientation than Al-Fatah.

The American Peace Plan

Meanwhile the four-power talks continued during and after the session of the U.N. General Assembly in September 1969. There had been concurrent exchanges between Russia and the United States, and in October Washington published the proposals it had submitted to Moscow. These in part followed King Hussein's plan, since they envisaged Israeli withdrawal from the conquered territories in return for a binding peace commitment from the Arabs. But, amongst other features, they left open the possibility of "insubstantial alterations" in Israel's pre-1967 borders if these alterations could be agreed with the Arabs. The detailed provisions of the peace settlement could, they suggested, be negotiated under the auspices of Dr Jarring in the same manner as the 1949 armistice agreements at Rhodes. On Jerusalem the U.S. proposals were somewhat unclear. Israel's unilateral absorption of the Jordanian sector was rejected, yet the old boundary between the sectors should not be restored; both Israel and Jordan should have a role in the civic, economic and religious life of the city. All the territory given up by Israel should be demilitarized. The refugees should have the right to choose between repatriation on the basis of an agreed annual quota, or resettlement outside Israel with compensation.

These proposals were promptly rejected by the Russians, by the Arabs, and by Israel. The first two found them too pro-Israeli. The Israelis called them appeasement of the Arabs and insisted that they offered no assurance of the security, peace, and rights of the Israelis "in their own land." They added that Israel "would not be sacrificed by any power or inter-power policy" and would reject any attempt to impose a forced solution upon her. Nevertheless, these proposals were endorsed by President Nixon in his report on the state of the world in February 1970. The President also stressed that the activities of the Soviet Union in the Middle East and the Mediterranean had increased, with consequences far beyond the Arab-Israeli issue. The United States, he added, would "view any effort by the Soviet Union to seek predominance in the Middle

East as a matter of grave concern, for America's policy was to help the freedom of other nations to determine their own future."

How Great Is the Russian Threat?

Here the President touched on a key issue, fundamental to any prospects of future peace. For this threat of Russian power in the eastern Mediterranean and the Middle East has, as we saw, been a live issue for some two hundred and fifty years, and still is at this moment. How real it is in the 1970s, compared with Western strength, is something of a riddle, and, as always, it suits Russia that it should remain one. Since 1967 the main potential threat is a greatly expanded Russian navy challenging Western strength by reason of its access to key ports and facilities in the Arab lands and elsewhere. Could this fleet, composed differently from Western navies, be a match for America's Sixth Fleet in the Mediterranean and those of her NATO allies? For the Russians have virtually no aircraft carriers in the conventional sense. On the other hand, they are strong in under-water vessels, including a new nuclear strategic submarine which can allegedly launch missiles up to four thousand nautical miles. Russia may thus in future be able to threaten all NATO countries from the safety of her own waters, and would have no strategic need of forward positions in the Mediterranean and Middle East.[47]

47. An important analysis of the competition between Russia and the United States in the whole Middle Eastern area is J. C. Hurewitz, ed., *Soviet-American Rivalry in the Middle East*. Another valuable study on the more restricted theme of *Soviet Naval Policy in the Mediterranean* is the research monograph of this title by C. B. Joynt and O. M. Smolansky. The Russian fleet has one or two helicopter carriers, but has been dependent for reconnaissance on aircraft based in Egypt. This last facility has apparently been lost since President Sadat reduced the Soviet military presence in Egypt in July 1972, but not the naval facilities enjoyed by the Russians at Alexandria and Mersa Matruh. According to an intelligence report issued in Brussels in June 7, 1973, on the occasion of the NATO Defense Ministers' meeting, since the Soviet invasion of Czechoslovakia in 1968 Russia has now "practically achieved strategic parity" with the West, her most formidable advances being in submarine strength and long-range ballistic missiles.

Nevertheless apart from strategic goals—which included in earlier years her own protection against nations with far greater resources at sea—Russia had, and still has, good political reasons for acquiring and retaining a stake in the Middle East. By rivalling and challenging the West, and particularly the Americans, in the Mediterranean—even at the cost of some burdensome commitments to her Arab clients—she has come nearer to her main objective, the elimination of Western power and influence in this vital region. Already Washington's position there has been weakened, though of course not solely through Russia's actions. CENTO countries like Iran and Pakistan have been busy normalizing their relations with Moscow and gaining economic, and even political, benefits from this, while Turkey, since the mid-1960s, has tended more and more towards non-alignment. Russia has also been able to make herself felt on two key Mediterranean islands, both former British colonies and both important to NATO. In Malta, NATO tripled its subsidy to the island in return for the continued and exclusive use of its naval and air bases. Yet in December 1971 the Russians managed to secure from Prime Minister Dom Mintoff the right to use Malta for the repair and refuelling of their ships. In Cyprus, in 1972, Russia successfully encouraged President Makarios to reject a solution to the Greco-Turkish conflict over the island which would have greatly strengthened the Western alliance. So effectively in fact has Russia shown the flag and challenged the Western position that between 1968 and 1970 the Spanish, French, and Algerian governments urged that the U.S. fleet as well as the Soviet fleet should withdraw from the Mediterranean so that the most historic and strategic sea in the world should not be used as a focus of confrontation between the two superpowers of the modern age.

While America has no intention of withdrawing, since it would compromise her allies, such demands are necessarily damaging to her status and influence in the region. Russia, on the other hand, asserts that, as a Middle Eastern power, she is in the Mediterranean by right, and point is given to her claim by the massive presence of her fleet. "While the erosion of U.S. influence in the eastern Mediterranean cannot be ascribed exclusively or even primarily to the Soviet fleet, . . . in a number of instances the . . . abandonment of close ties or . . . [reduction] of dependence upon the U.S. has been stimulated by the permanent deployment of the Russian squadron."[48]

The New Cease-Fire

While America's plan to solve the Arab-Israeli conflict, like the plans of other countries, met with small success, another American initiative did manage in 1970 to reduce the tension and costly losses entailed by this long-standing feud. A first move was the visit to the area in April of the U.S. Under Secretary of State for Near Eastern Affairs, Mr Joseph Sisco. Little seems to have been achieved beyond an exchange of views, and in some ways conditions were unpropitious at that moment. The five Arab "confrontation" countries[49] had recently met in Cairo and had been assured by President Nasser that the Arabs had no alternative but to wage their "battle of destiny" against Israel "across a sea of blood and a horizon of fire." Egypt, he said, had recovered from the Six Day War and now had half a million men under arms. Meanwhile, Israel was increasingly alarmed by the fact that the Soviets had installed SAM-3 missile batteries in Egypt and that their pilots were now flying operational missions for the Egyptians. Israel's uncompromising mood was also reflected in her refusal to allow Dr Nahum Goldmann, President of the World Jewish Congress and former President of the World Zionist Organization, to visit Cairo, where, he had been told, President Nasser would be willing to receive him to discuss

48. See Joynt and Smolansky, pp. 25–30.
49. Egypt, Jordan, Syria, Iraq, and the Sudan. Iraq qualified because Iraqi troops were stationed in Jordan, the Sudan because there was a battalion of Sudanese troops on the Suez Canal.

Arab-Israeli relations. According to a government statement, Dr Goldmann was thought to be an "unsuitable emissary"; Israel must reserve the right to decide who should speak for her. In Jordan, demonstrations against the Sisco visit—stirred up, it seems, by the guerrillas and students—were so violent and destructive that he was unable to go to Amman.

In June, however, Secretary of State Rogers announced a new American plan. This was designed, he said, to get the parties to the conflict to stop shooting and start talking. He added that the sovereignty, independence, and integrity of Israel were very important to the United States and described Soviet activities in Egypt as a "very serious new factor." The plan was approved by the Soviet Union, France, and Britain, its main feature being the restoration for three months of the cease-fire between Egypt and Israel and Jordan and Israel, and the revival of the Jarring mission. Views could then once more be exchanged among them within the general framework of Security Council resolution No. 242 of November 1967, which might lead to some eventual peaceful settlement.

All three countries having accepted the plan, the new truce for talks came into operation on August 7, 1970. It at once split the Arab world, since Syria, Iraq, and the Palestinian guerrilla groups would not accept it. The rift had started in June when the American scheme was discussed in Libya at a meeting of leaders from fourteen Arab states to celebrate the withdrawal of the last Americans from the Wheelus Air Force base.[50] Indeed in July Nasser had publicly asked the Iraqi President why his troops and aircraft on the eastern front never fought the enemy; and had closed down two Palestinian radio stations in Cairo which had attacked his acceptance of Mr Rogers' proposals. By this time the Libyan leader, Colonel Muammar Gaddafi, in his newly oil-rich country, was already aiming at a larger role in the Arab world, an ambition he developed considerably after Nasser's sudden death a couple of months

50. The last British units had left Libya in March 1970.

later.[51] Gaddafi tried to heal the Arab rift by calling another meeting of some of the principal contestants but without success. Iraq and Algeria refused to come, asserting that the American plan meant the liquidation of Palestinian rights and the recognition of Israel.

In Jerusalem there were hesitations before the Government decided to agree, and when it did so the truce caused a political split, since, as we saw, the Gahal ministers resigned in protest against any prospect of Israel's withdrawal from the conquered territories. Mr Begin even called it a "calamity and deadly danger for Israel." In replying to Washington Israel explained that if she withdrew from territories occupied in 1967 it must be to "secure, recognised, and agreed boundaries." Her note did not mention withdrawal from *all* these territories, and this was bound to be a crucial point in the negotiations, since both Jordan and Egypt insisted on complete withdrawal as the implied condition of any settlement. In the Knesset Mrs Meir also explained that Washington had been told that Israel would not return to the frontiers of June 4, 1967, and that certain obligations assumed by the United States had made it easier to accept the American plan. Israel would receive aid from America for "the maintenance of her security and of the balance of forces in the region . . . in the light of the Soviet involvement and the flow of Soviet arms to Egypt." But these are of course precisely the obligations to Israel which have made it hard for the United States to increase its friendship with, and influence upon, the Arab nations.

The peace talks which began at the United Nations on August 24, 1970, were soon halted. Having lodged a series of complaints with UNTSO about alleged breaches of the truce by Egypt, Israel announced on September 6 that she would take no further part in the talks until the cease-fire was fully implemented. Against some

51. By mid-1973, with the early prospect of full political union of Libya with impoverished Egypt, Gaddafi was beginning to see himself as a new dynamic Pan-Arab leader in the style of Nasser.

opposition General Dayan had apparently pressed the Israeli Government to break off the talks. The truce agreement had established a standstill zone, fifty kilometres (thirty-one miles) wide on each side of the Canal, in which there was to be no change in the military status quo. Israel's main charge was that, since the truce started, Egypt had been moving missile batteries into the zone and nearer to the Canal.[52] Egypt retorted that Israel had also broken the agreement by putting up military installations in her standstill zone.

The U.S. State Department announced on September 3 that there had in fact been violations on the Egyptian side. In September and October strong words continued to be exchanged. The State Department alleged that U.S. restraint in arms supplies to Israel had not been matched by Russia in her dealings with Egypt. Cairo asserted that the U.S. was primarily responsible for the continuation of the war. It had failed to carry out its own peace initiative by being impartial and even-handed. In particular it had broken an undertaking allegedly given to President Nasser in June not to supply Israel with more aircraft while peace talks were in progress. The Soviet Foreign Minister called the Israeli and American charges of cease-fire breaches a fabrication. Israel was blocking the Jarring talks because she wanted her "aggression" to be rewarded, while the U.S. encouraged Israel by giving her more offensive weapons and holding "naval manoeuvres" in the Mediterranean.[53]

Meanwhile, on September 28 President Nasser died suddenly of a heart attack at 52. For some fifteen years he had been the ruler of a new Egypt. He had rid his country of foreign domination and refashioned it with considerable success on the principles of social justice, in which this descendant of Upper Egyptian peasants passionately believed. In so doing, he had given "a new self-respect and

52. The weapons referred to were SAM-2 surface-to-air missiles, understood to be operated by Egyptians, and SAM-3 missiles, allegedly operated by Russians.
53. This last was apparently an oblique reference to President Nixon's visit to the Sixth Fleet. See Keesing's Contemporary Archives, p. 24322.

dignity to a people who despite their imperial ancestry have been the helots of mankind for over 2000 years."[54] Indeed, by exploiting her unique strategic position, he had managed to raise Egypt's status among nations to that of a major power. After Nehru's death and the fall of Sukarno, Nkrumah of Ghana, and Ben Bella of Algeria, he had become one of the outstanding statesmen of the non-aligned world. And among the Arab peoples he became and remained a leader of towering prestige who showed them what real independence of thought and action could achieve, and set their feet more firmly than ever before on the long and difficult path of inter-Arab understanding and collaboration.

Nasser's prestige among the Arabs survived even such resounding failures as the break-up of the union with Syria, and the strange miscalculations of 1967, when he may at first have hoped for a diplomatic victory without war, though his intelligence and experience must have told him, too late, that Israel would fight if the Tiran Strait were closed. His left-wing views, and the Russian presence in Egypt, led some to suspect him of Communist leanings. Yet he firmly rejected Communism as a creed, and Communists in Egypt got short shrift. He also had a reputation for radical prejudice against Jordan and other Arab monarchies. Yet he worked to the last moment, when already badly overstrained, at helping Hussein to end his strife with the Palestine guerrillas. Indeed an agreement, fragile as it proved but counter-signed by all Arab heads of state, was reached in Cairo on the day before his death. His chief weakness was, in a sense, his strength of character. For although in theory he believed in free criticism and discussion, his dominating personality made it hard for those around him—indeed for most of the country—not to conform. He thus finally created a one-party state instead of a solid political base for his regime. A quieter, less flamboyant successor, who has kept Nasser's system for the present but brought in new men and new ideas, may be going farther in achieving this.

54. Mansfield, p. 201; see also pp. 183–200.

In October Vice President Anwar Sadat[55] was chosen by the National Assembly as Nasser's successor and, after a referendum, sworn in as President. He had been one of the Free Officers who shared Nasser's dedicated nationalism and strong prejudice against the British occupation and who, with him, had dethroned Farouk. In his first press interview, with an American journalist,[56] President Sadat predictably adhered to Cairo's former uncompromising line. Israel, he said, was the only problem between Egypt and the United States, which was using the Israelis as its instrument in the area. If America stopped backing Israel, the conflict would be solved in twenty-four hours. Asked about any possible adjustments to the 1967 borders, he stressed that Israel was already determined to keep Jerusalem, the Golan Heights, Gaza, and Sharm el-Sheikh. These were not minor adjustments; but if the Israelis wanted some minor changes they should explain these to Dr Jarring.

Mrs Meir was equally uncompromising during her visits to America and Britain in September, October, and November 1970, particularly in Britain, where she described a key speech of the British Foreign Secretary, Sir Alec Douglas-Home, as being in parts "unacceptable." He had said in particular that the acquisition of territory by war was inadmissible, and that, subject to minor changes, Israel's future borders should generally be based on the armistice lines before the June war. He had also stressed the justifiable concern and involvement of the major powers because of the risk that they would be involved in any future Arab-Israeli war; and the view of "the international community" that those refugees who wished to return home should be allowed to do so, while those who did not could settle elsewhere with compensation. At her London press conference Mrs Meir was emphatic that the 1967 frontiers had been destroyed by the Arab attack, as she put it. As for the role of

55. Sadat, like Nasser, was of modest family. Unlike Nasser, he was a Lower Egyptian from the Nile Delta, where he was born in 1905.
56. Mr C. L. Sulzberger of the *New York Times*. For the text of the interview see Keesing's Contemporary Archives, pp. 24324–25.

America, Russia, Britain, and France in bringing about a settlement, this, she said, was a forum with no international authority. No group of powers however great had the right to decide the fate of small countries; that belonged to an era of diplomacy that was past and gone. The Soviets were arming the Arabs, France and Britain were hardly objective any more, and only the United States was sympathetic to Israel.

At the end of the year Israel consented to return to the Jarring talks, and these were resumed in New York in January 1971. From Mrs Meir's explanations to the Knesset it was clear that Israel's objections to great power intervention did not apply to the United States. Indeed she freely admitted how much Israel owed to, and was dependent on, Washington. Israel, she said, had asked to be strengthened, and President Nixon had then obtained for her credits of $500 million from Congress. There was a common denominator with America on fundamental issues of politics and security, and the dialogue between them would continue. Israel, on the other hand, could not accept Mr Rogers' proposals of 1969, which called for an almost total reversion to the 1967 frontiers. She stressed once again the Israelis' constant fear that the Security Council or its four permanent members would somehow impose a solution on Israel instead of letting her deal with her weaker Arab neighbours direct. Neither the four powers, nor the Security Council, nor the General Assembly, must interpret or guide Dr Jarring's mission or change his terms of reference in any way. She had "grounds for assuming" that America would not countenance this kind of thing.

When the talks reopened and something became known of the peace plans of Egypt and Jordan, it was clear why Israel was so insistent on this point. For both the Arab countries wanted the participation of the four powers. They insisted on Israel's complete return to her earlier frontiers—including of course the relinquishment of old Jerusalem—and on a "just" settlement of the refugee problem before any general settlement was reached, both points unacceptable to the Israelis. They also wanted a peace force, or supervisory machinery, in which the "Big Four" would take part. Despite successive prolongations, in practice, of the cease-fire[57] and, from time to time, exchanges of preconceived ideas in what had become a largely sterile and repetitive debate, a gulf continued to stretch between the two sides which neither seemed competent to bridge.

57. After seven months of formal cease-fire, the original period of three months having been prolonged first by another three months, then by a further month, which expired on March 7, 1971, President Sadat refused to agree to another formal extension. Actually, however, there was no resumption of hostilities.

Chapter **16** The Latest Phase, and the Future

The Vicious Circle

Between January 1971 and July 1973, much was debated but little achieved in the search for a solution to the Arab-Israeli conflict. The resumption of the Jarring talks led in effect to nothing more than arid restatements of rigidly opposed positions, the main stumbling block being, as before, Israel's future frontiers. In response to feelers from Dr Jarring, Egypt would not hear of peace unless Israel fully implemented Security Council resolution No. 242 of November 1967—i.e., withdrew to her 1967 borders. Cairo conceded that there might again be a U.N. peacekeeping force in Sharm el-Sheikh and free navigation through the Strait of Tiran. There could also be free navigation in the Suez Canal in accordance with the 1888 Convention, but no explicit guarantee was given of free passage for Israeli ships and cargoes. As for Sinai, there should be demilitarized zones astride the border with Israel, covering an equal distance on each side. These should be supervised by another U.N. peacekeeping force in which the "Big Four" would take part. But Israel insisted that there could be no withdrawal to the old frontiers.

This was spelt out by Mrs Meir in a talk with the London *Times* on March 12, 1971. The Israelis, she said, must keep Sharm el-Sheikh and a strip of land linking it with Israel; and also Gaza, which for twenty years had been a base for attacks against her. Israel would now take care of the Gaza refugees. All the rest of the Sinai Peninsula must be demilitarized so that Egypt could not deploy armour, artillery, and missiles there. Demilitarization could be ensured by a mixed force "which must include Israelis and could include Egyptians." (This could not of course be reconciled with the Egyptian plan for demilitarization only astride the frontier). She added that Israel must also keep the Golan Heights and all Jerusalem. As for the West Bank, that was a matter for negotiation. Gahal wanted Judea and Samaria, but against this was the fact that Israel must be a Jewish state with the Arabs only a minority. Six hundred thousand more Arabs in the country would be too much. In any case, the river Jordan "must not be open for Arab troops to cross." And there would have to be changes in the West Bank salient, which had brought Arab forces to within a few miles of the Mediterranean. But the West Bank should not be an independent Palestinian state. It would be too small to be viable, yet big enough to fight Israel. Jordan could have access to Gaza or Haifa as a port, but not with any corridors across Israel.

Washington Tries Again

Meanwhile, Secretary of State Rogers followed up somewhat inconclusively his cease-fire initiative of the previous year. Also in March 1971 he declared that the United States was ready to take part in international guarantees and a peace-keeping force. This last, he said, could give the greatest possible security to both sides: additions of territory were not essential to security. But Israel would not have this. She wanted defensible borders, and was most worried lest the Russians should join in peace-keeping since they were "active allies" of the Arabs. In a bid for compromise, Mr Rogers said that America did not claim that Israel must withdraw from all occupied territory, only that she should not acquire territory "except in insubstantial amounts for security purposes."[1] Mr Rogers' later visits in May 1971 to Saudi Arabia, Jordan, Lebanon, Egypt, and Israel, and his appeals to reason at the U.N. in the autumn, were equally inconclusive. Meanwhile, the Jarring mission lapsed.

One of Washington's main hopes had been to secure an interim agreement for the reopening of the Suez Canal as a useful step towards negotiations on the whole issue, and Mr Rogers had long talks about this and other matters in Cairo and Jerusalem. The Egyptians had offered to reopen the Canal if the Israelis would withdraw from its east bank. Egyptian troops would then move in, but a neutral zone would be set up between them and the Israelis. But Israel rejected this and insisted that if her troops pulled back from the east bank this should not be occupied by Egyptian or Soviet forces. Moreover, Israel must be assured that her shipping could use the Canal. Nothing came of either plan. While Secretary Rogers was in Israel, Mr Ben Gurion told him he personally thought that, in exchange for peace, Israel should return all her conquests except the Golan Heights and Old Jerusalem.[2]

Egypt and Her New Regime

In 1971 President Sadat was establishing his personal power and setting his own style as Egypt's leader. In view of this and the rejection of his plan for reopening the Canal he could hardly afford to be flexible over Israel, even had he wished to be so. In the Canal

1. U.N. resolution No. 242 was to some extent ambiguous in its wording—and this was deplorable from the standpoint of correct diplomatic practice and tradition. The vital part of it, from the angle of Israel's frontiers, was the first principle invoked, which reads: "1. Withdrawal of Israeli armed forces from territories occupied in the recent conflict." The omission of "the" before "territories" has enabled Israel and her sympathizers to claim that the resolution did not require her to withdraw from *all* the conquered territories, an interpretation of course contested by the Arab states and others. Mr Arthur Goldberg, former U.S. Ambassador to the United Nations, stated in October 1973, at the time of the fourth Arab-Israeli war, that the ambiguity had been deliberate.
2. Keesing's Contemporary Archives, p. 24695.

context he accused Israel of seeking a "fragmented" settlement as a springboard for further aggression and expansion. Once again he insisted that all the conquered lands must be given up. In May, alleging a plot to seize power and obstruct his policies, he eliminated a number of prominent associates of President Nasser, including a former Vice-President and a former Minister for War.[3] In the last half of 1971 Cairo's pronouncements became increasingly bellicose, though always with ultimate reservations, so that actual war remained remote. The United States was accused of abetting the occupation of Arab territory by helping Israel, of being in fact Israel's "partner in aggression." Washington, it was said, wanted to replace British and French colonialism in the region, while the Zionists sought a Greater Israel stretching from the Nile to the Euphrates. And this could be achieved only by the downfall of the "progressive" Arab regimes. President Sadat stressed that the crisis must not be allowed to freeze. Political and military moves were needed before the end of the year to remove Israel from her conquests. Later he told Egyptian troops that he had given up hope of a peaceful solution and that Egypt's decision was to fight. Later still, it was announced that "battle unto victory" was the only path to liberation. In a few years the pattern of events would show that this was not just empty boasting. Meanwhile, more cautious than Nasser, Sadat gave himself and others an escape clause. Egypt would continue her diplomatic efforts in spite of everything.

New Paths Are Tried

In November 1971 there were new departures in the search for peace. France tried, without success, to interest China in joining

3. The accused—in all ninety-one—were put on trial and given extremely severe sentences, the former Vice-President and three others being condemned to death, though the sentences were commuted. Significantly, leading members of the Nasser-sponsored official party, the Arab Socialist Union, and of the Socialist Vanguard, founded with his approval to train new leaders, were also involved. One indictment was that some had criticized a new project for federation with Libya and Syria, dealt with below.

the efforts of the big powers to promote a settlement. Shortly before that, four African heads of state, from Senegal, Cameroon, Zäire (the former Belgian Congo), and Nigeria, paid two inconclusive visits to Israel and Egypt on behalf of the Organization of African Unity.[4] The O.A.U. had called for Israel's withdrawal from all occupied territories, and had set up a committee of "ten wise men" to keep track of the Middle East. Israel was of course unresponsive to their main demand.

The Sterile Arms Race

For the rest, both Egypt and Israel sought more arms from their respective patrons. Moscow assured President Sadat that it would increase Egypt's military strength. Thereupon Washington was pressed to send more F4 Phantom fighter-bombers to Israel. As usual, the American response was good. Over three-quarters of the U.S. Senate called for the shipment of these aircraft without delay, and in December President Nixon assured Mrs Meir that the United States would maintain its "ongoing relationship of financial assistance and military supply" to Israel. Despite the build-up, in 1971 and after, the military fronts between Israel and the Arabs on the whole stayed quiet. But there was the usual deadly sequence of terrorism and retaliation. Toward the end of the year the "Black September" group of Palestinian guerrillas[5] came into sinister prominence with the murder of the Jordanian Prime Minister, who, under the King's orders, had dealt the guerrillas a severe blow.

The Guerrillas. Hussein's Determined Fight

Some short-lived pacts had been made by Amman with the guerrillas after severe clashes in 1970, but in the first half of 1971 new,

4. The O.A.U. was founded at Addis Ababa in 1963 to promote unity and international cooperation among African states and to eradicate all forms of colonialism in Africa. Despite regional, political, and linguistic differences, forty-one African states are members. It has largely superseded other more restricted groupings which have been tried.
5. So-called from the month of September 1970, when a strong blow was struck by the Jordan forces against the guerrillas.

fierce fighting broke out between them and the King's forces. The upshot was that the guerrillas were driven out of Amman and eventually from their strongholds in the north. By late July the government claimed that all but two hundred had been captured. It still distinguished, however, between those guilty of trying to overthrow the regime, or other crimes, and those genuinely working for the liberation of Palestine. These last would be released after screening. By this stage, Arafat, the guerrilla leader, was held to have declared war on Jordan.

Other Arab countries, notably those under leftist rule, condemned Hussein's strong measures against the Palestinians. Iraq called for Jordan's expulsion from the Arab League. Egypt termed Hussein a butcher, and again let the guerrillas broadcast from Cairo radio. Syria closed her border with Jordan and later broke off relations with Amman, as did Algeria and Libya. Indeed the young, restless, and ambitious Colonel Gaddafi, Chairman of the Revolutionary Command Council of Libya and in effect President of the country,[6] sought military intervention against Jordan. He sponsored an abortive summit meeting at which only Egypt, Syria, Yemen, and South Yemen were represented. Like most earlier gatherings, this urged Arabs to do all they could to liberate Palestine. But it refused to follow Gaddafi's more drastic anti-Jordanian plans.

A United Arab Kingdom?

A few months later Hussein, strong as ever in the courage of his convictions, was even more widely condemned—by Israel as well as the Arab states—for a plan he devised for the future of Arab Palestine. In March 1972 he proposed that the West Bank should again be linked with Jordan, but in a federation to be called the United Arab Kingdom. Before the Six Day War the West Bank had been simply part of Jordan, but now each area would preserve its separate identity. Jordan proper, or the East Bank, would be called the Region of Jordan. The West Bank would be called the Region of Pal-

6. He was still in his twenties, having been born in 1942.

estine, and would include any other liberated areas of Palestine where the population opted to join it. This was taken as a reference to the Gaza Strip which, it was suggested, might form a natural outlet for Jordan on the Mediterranean if linked with the new state. Amman would be the "central capital" of the U.A.K. as well as the capital of the Jordan Region. Jerusalem would be the capital of the Palestine region. At the same time, there would be considerable decentralization, with separate legislative councils and Governors-General in each Region, the central executive being chiefly responsible for the U.A.K. in international matters, and for ensuring its safety, stability, and development.

Israel was predictably distressed. Mrs Meir had offered port facilities to Jordan at Gaza, but with every intention of retaining Gaza for Israel. It was a very different thing for King Hussein to claim Gaza by implication for the Palestine Region as a natural outlet for the U.A.K. But the strongest and most solemn indignation voiced in Israel was over Jerusalem. Although the most vital and holy parts of the City had only been taken from Jordan and annexed to Israel less than five years earlier, the King was condemned in the Knesset for having "gone so far as to designate Jerusalem—Israel's eternal capital—as the capital of Palestine." On the Arab side, the King's plan was furiously rejected by Al-Fatah and the Popular Front for the Liberation of Palestine. Cairo called it a conspiracy to split the Arabs by the ultimate liquidation of the Palestine issue. In spite of Israel's categorical objections to it, the Egyptians hinted that it had been drawn up in collusion with the enemy, being based on a plan of Allon, the Israeli Deputy Prime Minister. Cairo once again broke off relations with Amman. Syria, Iraq, and Libya called the plan a first step towards a separate Jordanian peace with Israel.

The United Arab Emirates

In 1971–73 new federations and unions in the Arab world were emphatically the order of the day. If words and plans and titles could create unity, the main problem of the Arab peoples—especially vis-à-vis Israel—would have been solved. One of these unions was formed in late 1971 on the eastern fringes of that world by the sheikhdoms of the Persian Gulf. By the withdrawal of her forces from this remote area and the substitution of treaties of friendship with local rulers for treaties of protection, Britain then laid down virtually the last of the responsibilities she had acquired in the Middle East during her period of empire. Through these, and at the price of much hostility, she had for a time shaped the destinies of Egypt, the Sudan, Iraq, Jordan, and other areas, and had taken it upon herself to offer Palestine as a Jewish National Home with no real inkling of what this might become two generations later.

In the Gulf, Britain's new policy meant that a number of other states became, or were about to become, like Kuwait. This had been under British protection, with Britain conducting its foreign relations, but had earlier, as we saw, become completely independent. The other principalities, mostly with actual or potential oil wealth, had also been under British protection, but now became completely independent too. At the same time they joined, or proposed to join, the Arab League, and declared themselves "part of the Arab nation." They also became, individually or collectively, members of the United Nations. The two most important were oil-rich Bahrain and Qatar, both of which kept their separate statehood and membership of international bodies. Of the remaining seven, known as the Trucial States, six formed the United Arab Emirates on December 2, 1971, and in that collective capacity became a member of the United Nations.[7]

7. What have been known as the Trucial States lie between the entrance to the Persian Gulf and Qatar on its south coast. They are Abu Dhabi, Ajman, Dubai, Fujairah, Sharjah, Umm el Quwain, and Ras al Khaimah. Until the early nineteenth century, the area they cover had been known as the Pirate Coast, due partly to their depredations against the neighbouring Sultanate of Muscat and Oman (now the Sultanate of Oman) stretching along the Gulf of Oman and the Arabian Sea, which also came under British protection. Britain then imposed a truce from which the coast afterwards took its name. When the United Arab Emirates were formed, Ras al Khaimah decided not to join for the time being. Britain, however, cancelled her special relationship with this

The Triple Federation

From the standpoint of the conflict with Israel, however, by far the most important, and certainly the most ambitious, of the bids for Arab unity, was the triple federation of Libya, Egypt, and Syria announced on August 20, 1971. This new union had been mooted at a meeting in Libya the previous April, and was largely inspired by President Gaddafi. Before the announcement there had been a conference in Damascus between the Libyan, Egyptian, and Syrian leaders, during which they had also consulted Arafat, the guerrilla leader. The constitution for the new federation was drawn up and signed on this occasion. In a referendum held in each country on September 1, the constitution was approved by massive majorities, though in Syria, which had twice before been disillusioned with unity, the Yes votes were perhaps understandably lower than in the other two.

The new federation was to be the nucleus of a unified Arab socialist society, and any Arab republic believing in such a society could be admitted. Its goal was the liberation of occupied Arab territory, as decided by the Khartoum conference of 1967. The constitution was on predictable lines. The federation would be run by a presidential council consisting of the three heads of states,

---

sheikhdom as with the others. The Sheikh of Abu Dhabi (one of the richest in oil of these small states) became President of the U.A.E., and the Sheikh of Dubai Vice-President. The British-sponsored Trucial Oman Scouts were transferred to the U.A.E. to form the nucleus of a union army. Shortly before the start of the U.A.E., Iran occupied three islands at the entrance to the Gulf, on the grounds that these had once belonged to her. In the case of Abu Musa this was done in agreement with the Sheikh of Sharjah, on the basis of shared jurisdiction and a share in eventual oil profits. The other two, which had been under Ras al Khaimah, were occupied by force. Iraq strongly objected to Iran's action and (rather strangely) to Britain's failure to preserve their Arab character; and broke off relations with both countries. Oman, though now a member of the Arab League, had not, up to the time of writing, rescinded its special relationship with Britain. But it acquired a new and relatively modern regime in 1970, and is likely to follow the general trend to national independence.

one of whom would be elected to preside over the council for two years at a time. This council would appoint a federal ministerial council responsible to it. There would also be a federal legislative assembly with twenty members from each country. Each member state would retain its separate membership of the United Nations and its own diplomatic representation, but the federation would pursue a "unified foreign policy." Defence and military command would be federal matters, and the defense industries of the three countries would be coordinated. There would of course be economic coordination too. The presidential council would ensure the security of the member states. If one of them should appear to be in danger but should not be willing to ask for federal help, the federal authorities would have the right to intervene anyway. There was to be one flag, one capital, and one national anthem, and eventually one political front representing the various political organizations in the member states.

After this step, Egypt, which was still officially the United Arab Republic even after Syria had broken away from their union ten years earlier, resumed her traditional name. She was now the Arab Republic of Egypt. The new federation was formally inaugurated on January 1, 1972, after the appointment of a ministerial council with four Egyptians, three Syrians, and one Libyan. The speaker of the Syrian Parliament became Prime Minister. Foreign Affairs went to Egypt, Economic and Social Affairs to Syria, while Libya was relegated to the less demanding field of Education and Culture. The new flag of Arab unity was hoisted for the first time at ceremonies in Cairo, Damascus, and Tripoli. It was a red, white, and black banner charged with a golden hawk, the emblem of the Prophet's tribe of Quraish.

Gaddafi's Mission

In practice, however, Arab unity remained beset with snags, despite Gaddafi's increasingly obsessive urge to cleanse, revitalize, and direct all the varied Arab peoples, whose strident rivalries blocked the great goal of bringing Israel to her knees. Observers[8] found in him a puritan revivalist demanding a literal return to the Q'uran. This meant the banning of alcohol, usury, gambling, Western music, dancing, and the like. Moreover, Arabic should be the only language, thieves should be mutilated, and adulteresses stoned. In this mood he became the paymaster of the territorists, the organizer of death threats to Arab rulers sluggish in the cause, and of bribes to states in Africa and elsewhere to break off relations with Jerusalem. Even the new federation was marred by Gaddafi's strong antipathy towards Syria and her president, because of their failure to measure up to his exacting Islamic standards.

The Inner Union

In any case, though oil had made her rich, Libya with barely two million people was far too small a base for leadership of the Arab world. The realization of Gaddafi's ambition thus clearly depended upon some link with neighbouring Egypt closer than the triple federation. Hence a new plan announced on August 2, 1972, for full political union between Libya and Egypt by September 1, 1973. As one report put it, ". . . single-handed, Gaddafi forced through the . . . merger, . . . willing to pay any price to buy a place at the top of the Egyptian establishment."[9] Under a "Joint Political Command," mixed commissions would now study how unity was to be achieved in the various governmental spheres: constitutional, political, and economic; legislative and judicial; administrative and financial; educational, scientific, and cultural; and of course in defence, national security, and publicity.

By this union, Egypt, poverty-stricken since the closure of the Canal, would acquire a share in Libya's vast oil income, and a huge

8. See *inter alia*, "Gaddafi the Paymaster" by John Laffin, in the (London) *Daily Telegraph* of April 27, 1973.
9. *Ibid.*

area for the settlement of her overcrowded people. There was already a basis for this settlement, however little it might be to the taste of Libya's tiny middle class. For there was a large Egyptian minority in Libya, controlling much of her economy and providing technical and professional skills which Libya badly needed. Meanwhile on the international plane the prospect of this new union of neighbours seems to have emboldened Cairo to loosen Egypt's dependence on the Soviet-Communist regime so repugnant to the God-fearing Gaddafi, though he too had received arms from Russia. Egypt's reliance on Moscow had in fact been formalized in 1971—the year in which the Aswan High Dam was finally completed with Soviet help—by a fifteen-year treaty of friendship and cooperation with the U.S.S.R. In spite of this, on July 18, 1972, President Sadat ordered the immediate withdrawal of Soviet military advisers and experts from Egypt, and placed Soviet bases and equipment under the exclusive control of the Egyptian forces. The reason he gave—namely, Russia's "excessive caution" as an ally—seemed again to reflect the pressure of Gaddafi's youthful impetuosity. Those in the West who saw in Communism the root of all evil were briefly cheered; for them, Sadat might be on the road to virtue and salvation. But for those who prayed for peace, the influence of Gaddafi was no very happy omen. For one of the main dangers to Egypt of the new union was that the prudent Sadat might be swept against his real judgement into another clash with Israel, a clash that could bring further humiliation. Indeed, as the time for this inner union drew near, the risk emerged that in a new and sudden crisis there might be less unity among the Arabs than in 1967, and certainly not more.

By May 1973 King Hussein had apparently decided that Jordan would not join a new war against Israel at this juncture. It would be premature while the Arabs were still so inadequately prepared, and could only lead to a fresh catastrophe. With his usual clear-sightedness he also condemned another Gaddafi plan for denying Arab oil to America. For this would only make Washington strongly anti-Arab and more determined than ever to support

Israel.[10] Mainwhile union with Libya promised Egypt other risks
and tensions. One was the probable insistence of Gaddafi on imposing his brand of Islamic fundamentalism on the easygoing, cosmopolitan, hedonistic Egyptians. Another, more immediate and
personal, was that with his wild views but charismatic appeal Gaddafi might manage to supplant Sadat.

The Unchanged Risk of War

Meanwhile, the risk of war was undiminished for other reasons.
Some five thousand Soviet advisers and experts were due to leave
under Sadat's ban. But Soviet training personnel were not affected;
and naval facilities would still, apparently, be granted to the Russian fleet. At the same time it was by no means clear whether
Egypt had wanted to expel the ten to fifteen thousand Russian
combat forces manning the advanced anti-aircraft-missile emplace-
ments, and the two hundred-odd pilots flying the latest MIG-23
fighters, and whether these were actually withdrawn. Did Moscow
in fact remove them also, as has been suggested, out of resentment
at Sadat's order; and, if so, was the removal total or partial, permanent or temporary? What in any case was certain was that the Soviets were not ceasing to supply arms and advisers to the Arab
world, including countries which had fought in the war of 1967
and might, as we shall see, be planning to fight again, and that
Soviet hardware and expertise would therefore still be available
within the triple federation and outside it. Thus, according to press
reports,[11] Syria had received Russian aircraft, tanks, missiles, and
other arms to a value of $150 million in 1972, and of no less than
$185 million merely in the first half of 1973, with teams of Soviet
technicians to help her use them. By then Syria had in fact become
the largest recipient of Soviet aid.

But the Arabs also had other, non-Communist, sources of sup-

10. See "Jordan will not join Arab War," by Elias Nawas, Beirut, in the (London) *Daily Telegraph* of June 1, 1973.
11. *Newsweek*, July 9, 1973.

ply, some with specially effective weapons. Thus France, from the days of President de Gaulle, had reforged her links with the Arab nations. So, to some extent, had Britain in recent years. Although France had placed an embargo on arms supplies to Egypt, Israel, Jordan, and Syria since the war of 1967, on the ground that these were "battlefield countries," she had supplied arms to other Arab nations in return for an assurance that they would not be made available to the "battlefield" group. Subject to this somewhat tenuous safeguard, France had agreed in 1969 to sell to Libya a hundred Mirage fighter-bombers, and some fifty of these had been delivered by the time the new Libyan-Egyptian union was announced. These were aircraft which had been decisively helpful to Israel in the Six Day War, but were now denied her. Moreover the restrictions on sales imposed by France would clearly be meaningless when Libya and Egypt were in effect one. All this was disturbing to Israel, but by stressing her vulnerability she had, as we saw, managed to get nearly all she wanted from America, including Phantom jets in quantity in place of French Mirages. Indeed in the United States it was reckoned in mid-1973 that Israel had over a hundred Phantom jets, was getting more at the rate of two a month, and—not least in view of the high skill and training of her pilots—was in no danger of losing command of the Middle Eastern skies.[12] Moreover it appeared that, in his first three years in office, President Nixon had given Israel more aid than all previous Presidents combined. This again was remarkable for a President who, before he took office, had sent Governor Scranton to the Middle East to explore the possibilities of an even-handed policy as between the Arabs and Israel.

America and the Arabs

Nevertheless the United States did not—could not—ignore the importance of the Arab lands and peoples. And this was not just a matter of oil, though oil counted. For those in the United States

12. *Ibid.*

who had studied the question in depth there were other less material considerations. As we saw, from the days of the early nineteenth-century missionaries, who launched what became the American University of Beirut and similar institutions, there had been a fine tradition of cultural exchange and beneficial and disinterested American work among the Arabs in all modern fields. At the same time there were memories of President Wilson's King-Crane Commission and its grave doubts about the wisdom and justice of Palestine becoming a Jewish state. There was also, for many, a not always articulate sense of shame. Despite Jewish suffering and Israel's achievements, and the crimes of some terrorist gangs, such Americans remained conscious that what had happened to the Palestinian Arabs was, at the lowest, bitterly unfair. Therefore, whatever might be possible should be done for them and for the Arabs in general—so long, that is, as it did not prejudice the task of upholding Israel which America's leaders had chosen to assume. In practice, therefore, U.S. policy towards the Middle East, with its frequent divergence of purpose between the White House and the State Department, was less one of evenhandedness than of embarrassed compromise. In the process U.S. arms were made available to some Arab countries as well as Israel. Thus Jordan gets some $30 million annually in such arms from America, besides generous financial aid to keep the state viable, in acknowledgement of the King's realistic attitude towards Israel. And Saudi Arabia, leader of the Arab oil states and field of work of key American corporations, also receives U.S. arms. When the Saudis were recently promised thirty Phantom jets and the Israelis asked for more, for fear lest these jets might end up in Egyptian hands, Israel was told, it seems, not to worry; her American friends judged her to be strong enough already.[13]

The Final Year

Meanwhile much of 1972 and early 1973 was marred by outrages committed by a few desperate and unbalanced men, and followed

13. *Ibid.*

as always by fierce retribution. Many who did these things were young fanatics enrolled by the terrorists and brought by unscrupulous leaders to believe that they would be serving the cause of Palestine by violence, murder, and destruction—a cause to which in fact they did nothing but harm. Sometimes gunmen were hired from abroad. The Arab terrorist leaders in turn were often financed and supported by extremist rulers in the Arab world. Such rulers had accumulated large stocks of heavy armament of the most sophisticated kind, yet for several years they preferred to back the criminal activities of the desperate few rather than to coordinate with their Arab fellow rulers a well-planned, purposeful, joint campaign of legitimate warfare to reverse the humiliations of 1967 and recover from Israel if possible all or most of what they had lost. As it was, by sponsoring courses condemned by human society, they sent a few wild men to sow, and reap, death at no risk to themselves.

A Spate of Terrorism

Such was the general background of tragedies with which the world is shockingly familiar. The first was the indiscriminate killing of passengers at Lod (Lydda) airport in Israel on May 30, 1972. A second was the murder of eleven Israeli athletes at the Olympic Games in Munich in the following September. A third was the killing of the American Ambassador together with his Counsellor, and of the Belgian Chargé d'Affaires, at Khartoum in March 1973. The airport assault, which caused twenty-five deaths, was not even the work of the guerrillas themselves but of three Japanese gunmen hired and trained by the extreme left-wing Popular Front for the Liberation of Palestine. One of the gunmen committed suicide, a second was killed, the third captured and sentenced to life imprisonment, there being, as we saw, no death penalty in Israel save for treason in war-time, and genocide, for which Eichmann was hanged.

The second and third assaults were the work of the Black September group and were both, according to press reports, carried out with the support and encouragement of President Gaddafi.[14] In both these cases the victims were seized as hostages—at Munich in the Olympic Village, at Khartoum in the Saudi Arabian Embassy —in an attempt to secure the release of terrorists held by the opposing governments. In the Munich case the gunmen demanded the freeing of two hundred Arab guerrillas held by Israel. In the Khartoum coup they insisted on the release by Jordan of guerrillas held there; by the United States, of Sirhan Sirhan, the murderer of Robert Kennedy; by West Germany, of German anarchist-terrorists who allegedly supported the Palestinian cause; and by Israel, of all women guerrillas. No concessions were made to these demands, and the murders were carried out.

At Munich, in trying to prevent the murder of the Israeli hostages, the German police tricked and killed some but not all of the assailants.[15] In Khartoum the gunmen surrendered to the Sudanese Government after the murders, and face the death penalty there. But even had the demands been met, apart from the encouragement this would have given to further terrorism, it is doubtful whether it would have saved the lives of the hostages. For at Munich two of the Israelis were shot dead as soon as the gunmen burst into their quarters. And in Khartoum the Saudi Arabian Ambassador—also a hostage together with the Jordanian representative

14. See Laffin. According to this account, the Libyan President was making an annual payment to Al-Fatah of $75 million, plus a bonus for outstanding operations; and the Black September group received some $7½ million as a reward for the Munich murders. President Gaddafi also took credit for sending arms to help the insurgents in Ireland, because Britain, too, was one of the enemies.

15. Five were killed and the remaining three eventually captured. But in October the survivors were released by Germany—to Israel's indignation—in order to save a German airliner, its passengers and crew, which the Black September group had hijacked and threatened to blow up with all aboard. The freed gunmen were flown to Tripoli in Libya, where the bodies of their colleagues had already been sent and buried as "martyr heroes."

—said that both of them knew at once that the two Americans and the Belgian would be killed as "enemies of the Palestinian cause." Their own lives were spared on the ground that they were Arabs.

Hijacking and Letter Bombs

Hijacking of passenger aircraft to secure hostages was a constant device of the guerrillas. In September 1970 three international airliners had been brought down and blown up by them in Jordan. Some guerrillas had by then been released in exchange for passengers, and the aircraft were empty at the time. This may have led the terrorists to expect results from all similar coups; but by no means all were successful. In May 1972 a Belgian airliner on its way to Israel was hijacked by a Black September gang, of two men and two women. At Lod they demanded the release of their people held in Israel; otherwise the plane would be blown up with all on board. In this case Israeli special forces disguised as mechanics managed to approach the aircraft ostensibly to work on it. They then stormed it, shot or captured the hijackers, and released the passengers. The terrorists had another and double failure at Nicosia in Cyprus in April 1973. Those making an explosives raid on the Israeli Ambassador's apartment were caught, and their intended victim remained unharmed. On the same day, others who had started to shoot up an Israeli airliner at Nicosia airport were beaten off, and one was killed.

There was yet another failure, in Thailand in December of 1972. In a coup foreshadowing the tragic incident in Khartoum, gunmen —again from Black September—had captured the Israeli Embassy in Bangkok and held the staff as hostages in the Ambassador's absence, demanding as usual the release of their people in Israel. This time, with the help of the Egyptian Ambassador, the Thai authorities talked them into surrender, and they were flown to Cairo under Thai escort. Another tragedy, due in part to the nervous tension bred by hijackings and other violence, was the shooting down by the Israelis, over Sinai in February 1973, of a Libyan airliner bound for Cairo, with the loss of one hundred and four lives. The French pilot apparently thought he was over Egypt and that the aircraft ordering him to land were Egyptian; since he was already starting his descent to Cairo he ignored them. The Israelis claimed that they had been expecting a terrorist move to crash a plane loaded with explosives into Tel Aviv, that since this one did not obey their orders they suspected a hostile mission, and that they did not realize that there were passengers aboard. Another device exploited by the terrorists—letter bombs of innocent appearance addressed to their intended victims—also killed a number of Israelis. The same sinister weapon was subsequently used to some extent by Israelis against Arabs they suspected.

Arab Disillusion with the Terrorists

By early 1973, even those countries which had upheld the Palestine guerrillas in spite of their misdeeds, and had condemned Hussein's firm line, seemed to be changing their views. In spite of Gaddafi's alleged encouragement of the Khartoum conspiracy in March, after the event none of the Arab states tried to defend or condone the murders. Indeed, no reference was made to them in the press or on the radio even in Libya, Syria, or Iraq—all countries which had been strongly for the guerrillas in the past. In Egypt the leading, and semi-official, newspaper criticized the Black September operations, describing the Khartoum killings as "the latest in a series of mistakes" by the Palestinian organizations. And such organizations were now banned in the Sudan.[16] By late April 1973—as if to admit that Hussein had after all been right—the Lebanese Government virtually went to war with the guerrillas in their own country— guerrillas who had poured into Lebanon and Syria after their defeat in Jordan. Before this, however, there had been many months of tense and bitter conflict with Israel in the border regions of Syria and Lebanon. For the Lebanese this was a most unwelcome turn of fate. Devoted, like their Phoenician ancestors, to finance and trade,

16. Keesing's, p. 25806.

they had tried for years to stay more or less neutral in the Palestine conflict. Now it was tearing them apart.

Israel Strikes Northward at Al Fatah

The main concentration of guerrillas after their expulsion from Jordan was in the part-Syrian, part-Lebanese, region around Mount Hermon known to Israel as "Fatahland." In early 1972, attacks on Israel by rocket and armed raids led to strong Israeli air strikes and troop penetrations into Syria and Lebanon and the destruction of houses of those suspected of harbouring or helping Al-Fatah. Lebanon then requested and received more U.N. observers on her border with Israel. Later in the year, the Munich murders were followed by the heaviest air strikes yet made by Israel against guerrilla bases in the two countries, which acknowledged that there had been hundreds of casualties. Between September 1972 and February 1973 the Israelis carried out further extensive military operations across their northern borders. They invaded Lebanon from the sea as well as from the land and air, inflicting heavy casualties not only on the guerrillas but also on the Lebanese army. The Beirut Government then ordered Al-Fatah to stop operating on the Lebanese border with Israel, and was told that this would be done. In November, and again in December and January, there were air and ground clashes between Israeli and Syrian forces in the region of the Golan Heights. Israel alleged that, in the case of Syria, the terrorist raids were carried out in full cooperation with the Syrian army.

The Israelis in Beirut. Lebanon Tackles Her Guerrillas

In December there was a first clash between the Lebanese army and the guerrillas who, although they had evacuated the frontier areas when ordered to do so, soon returned in force. Then in April 1973, within a day of the abortive coups in Nicosia, the Israelis carried out their most daring and irregular raid against the terrorists. A specially trained Israeli unit, disguised in the most casual civilian clothes, and one of them apparently as a woman, was landed by launch on a deserted strip of beach near Beirut. Here they were met by cars hired by Israeli agents who had entered Lebanon beforehand, three of them on forged British passports. Knowing just where to find the homes of certain top guerrilla leaders, a detachment went there and killed them, together with one of their wives. Another went to one of the guerrilla headquarters and despatched a number more of the Palestinians there. After street battles with Lebanese soldiers and police in which two of these raiders were killed, the rest managed to get back to their launch and leave with two of their wounded men. Arafat alleged that the operation had been mounted in consequence of liaison arrangements between U.S. and Israeli intelligence, a charge briskly denied by Washington. Far more sober criticism was voiced elsewhere but, as so often in the past, Israel showed small signs of being impressed by objections to her actions in the world.

After the raid, the Lebanese Government fell. The next one did its best to deal with the guerrillas. There could not, it said, be a state within the state. After some three weeks of heavy fighting with several hundred casualties, and the mediation of Egypt and Kuwait, an agreement was reached with the Palestinian organizations on May 17, and the state of emergency was lifted soon after. It was then clear that the guerrillas faced no such drastic eradication in Lebanon as had been their lot in Jordan. The agreement was said to "guarantee Lebanon's sovereignty and the security of the Palestine revolution." Heavy weapons were to be withdrawn from the refugee camps, and these camps were no longer to be used as training grounds for guerrilla operations. The impression left was that Hussein would have done it differently, and that the task might have to be done again. But at least it showed increasing realization by the Arab nations that, deeply though the Arabs of Palestine had been wronged by the creation of Israel, their strong-arm men had chosen a false path for their redemption, and one which could only besmirch their name.

Whither Israel's Neighbours?

One key to the future of Israel's neighbours is the enigmatic Colonel Gaddafi. As we saw, after Khartoum even he seems to have become disenchanted with the Palestine terrorists. Will this wealthy and charismatic young leader gain in his thirties more wisdom and balance under the impact of events, or perhaps under the influence of two older and shrewder neighbours?

One such neighbour is President Bourguiba of Tunisia, with which country, as with Egypt, he tried to bring about a union. This Bourguiba declined. When he visited Tunis in December 1972, Gaddafi stressed, fairly enough, that Arabs should abolish the artificial frontiers of colonialism; then, in the context of Arab unity, he attacked Britain and America. Bourguiba retorted that he had fought for Tunisia's freedom for fifty years, and had not become his nation's leader through a military coup, as had Gaddafi; moreover, Gaddafi had been born in the very year in which Britain and America had freed Libya from her colonial masters. As for Arab unity, what was needed was a transformation of the Arab mentality. The Arabs must recover the scientific intelligence they once had when Europe came to learn from them.

In the Palestine conflict Bourguiba, like Hussein, is brave and realistic. Unlike the approach of Jordan, Egypt, and Syria, however, his attitude is basically disinterested, for Tunisia has no lost territory to recover. There could thus be real value in his recently expressed readiness to meet the Israelis and discuss Palestine with them, on the basic condition that Israel would be recognized by the Arab states provided that Israel for her part recognized the right of the Palestinians to a homeland of their own.[17] The suggested meeting found a ready response in Israel, but did not have an easy passage with other Arab leaders, and Bourguiba has qualified his bid in some respects. But it is one sign of a new outlook,

17. See, e.g., William Coughlin, "Bourguiba-Meir Meeting Possible," *Los Angeles Times*, June 24, 1973.

and at least he has not been promptly killed, as might earlier have been the case. In 1965 Nasser had angrily thrown out a suggestion of Bourguiba's for a settlement with Israel on somewhat similar terms. It was therefore a gain that the present offer was not instantly rejected by President Sadat.

Sadat's Egypt. Can Union with Libya Really Work?

In March 1973 Sadat became his own Prime Minister while remaining President, as Nasser had done after the war of 1967. This, he said, was to "unify responsibility for a limited period and a specific purpose." From one aspect the aim was clearly to get a firmer grip on internal affairs, since, as he complained, students were trying to promote revolutionary violence "in the name of Neo-Nasserist-Marxism, although Nasser was not a Marxist." This was another sign that Egypt in future was to bear Sadat's imprint, not that of the past leader. He also, characteristically, spoke of "total confrontation" with Israel, and the military moves this would need, while again promising that Egypt would continue her diplomatic efforts for a peaceful settlement. He then set about trouble with a firm hand. When students demonstrated, the universities were temporarily closed, and there were many arrests. There was also a purge of journalists and intellectuals. They were dropped from the Arab Socialist Union and thus lost their jobs. The charge was that they had given the foreign news media an impression of Egypt's instability.

Instability was, it seems, Sadat's main worry, faced as he was with the scheme for integration with Libya in September—a scheme which neither he nor many Egyptians really wanted and one which was to prove more a matter of form and façade than of substance. Even in July 1973 Gaddafi's cavalier attitude to Egyptian susceptibilities, and his open talk of basic disagreements, did not promise a happy union—indeed cast doubt on whether there would be a real union at all. During an uninvited visit to Cairo,

Gaddafi talked of giving up in Libya if union were not achieved when planned, even though the committees supposed to be working out the implementation of the union were in effect bogged down. The merger must go through, he said, "even if it meant civil war." On the question of Israel, from recent press accounts of his views,[18] he and Sadat were poles apart. He complained that Egypt and Syria paid lip service to, and exploited, the Palestinians' cause, but that their real interest was in Sinai and the Golan Heights; also that Sadat talked of total confrontation with Israel and then went on with diplomatic talks. But he, Gaddafi, claimed to reject all measures short of war. He also condemned Egypt's night clubs and alcohol drinking as nasty colonial habits, even though wine and dancing had in fact been Oriental pleasures since the dawn of history.

At the same time, Gaddafi was extremely casual about a number of hard, concrete issues demanding a solution, such as the future currency and banking system of the union. These, he implied, were just administrative details to be settled in due course. The vital thing was the union itself. Why should it be so urgent for him to bring this about, however poorly the ground might have been prepared? The conclusion reached by some is that the impatient colonel is interested above all in the extent to which his own position, and the scope for his activities, will be enhanced by a post near the centre of Egypt's power structure, and by constant access to the mass media of Cairo, the metropolis of the Arab world.[19] Whatever exactly that may portend, in the early 1970s Gaddafi seemed to see it as his mission to "keep the flame of the Arab Revolution alive," with the possible prospect already mentioned, that he might in the process supplant Sadat. But further revolution was by no means an aim of some of his weightier fellow rulers,

18. See, e.g., Henry Tanner, "Gaddafi Concedes Differences with Egypt on Merger," and "Gaddafi Giving Egyptian Leaders Foretaste of Difficulties under a Merger," *New York Times*, June 30 and July 8, 1973; also John Bulloch, "Egypt's Dilemma after Beirut," London *Daily Telegraph*, April 25, 1973.
19. *Ibid.*

including Bourguiba and King Faisal of Saudi Arabia. Moreover, there was no certainty that even countries of revolutionary outlook, such as Syria and Iraq, would accept Gaddafi as their leader in the long run.

Are There Alternatives?

In this dilemma, Sadat set about widening and strengthening the circle of his friends, and seeking, it seemed, reinsurance and alternative support, as well as funds comparable to those Egypt might share with Libya under union. He renewed his ties with the Sudan, recently resentful of Egypt's somewhat patronising line, and mediated between Syria and Lebanon during their latest troubles. Even more significant was the visit paid to him by King Faisal in Cairo in May. For the King was a Muslim puritan with even better title than Gaddafi, since Mecca and Medina are in his charge. And Arabia was even richer than Libya from oil. Moreover, as an autocrat, Faisal was against revolution, and strongly disliked the modern republican socialism Gaddafi had forced upon Libya. Even Nasser's fairly moderate regime in Egypt had been most unwelcome to the Saudis, though they had helped in common Arab causes and had given funds to make up some of Cairo's losses when the Canal was closed. Gaddafi's ambition to be a second Nasser had therefore made him one of King Faisal's least favourite people. Thus the King's rapprochement with Egypt and his announcement that he would give Sadat sizable financial help was specially important at that juncture.[20]

The Nixon-Brezhnev Summit. What Did It Imply?

A decisive development in the story of the Arab-Israeli conflict may well have been the visit to Washington in June 1973, of Leonid

20. Tanner, *New York Times*, July 8, 1973.

Brezhnev, First Secretary of the Communist Party of the Soviet Union and as such Russia's most powerful leader. The communiqué issued after his meetings with President Nixon was terse on the Middle East but significant, not least by its omissions. While conceding that the two leaders had differences about the area, it said that Russia and America would "exert their efforts to promote the quickest possible settlement in the Middle East," a settlement which "should be in accordance with the interests of all states in the area, should be consistent with their independence and sovereignty, and should take into due account the legitimate interests of the Palestinian people." There was no reference either to Security Council resolution No. 242, or to the Jarring mission, around which diplomatic negotiation had revolved during the last six years. The Israelis were on the whole elated, the Arabs depressed, by Russia's "soft line."

In spite of all the help Moscow has given them since 1967, the Arabs could find in this announcement no Soviet commitment to forcing Israel out of their conquered lands, as the Security Council had ordered. Indeed, as Gaddafi pointed out, Soviet military help seemed to have been coupled with some pressure to avoid a new war with Israel. Indeed a Russo-American détente implied a conflict between Soviet and Arab interests. The Syrians responded by saying that they would have no Soviet bases in their country unless and until Russia took a tougher line with Israel. And Egypt, understandably, had fresh thoughts about her treaty with Moscow of 1971. Meanwhile, as a result of this new understanding between the giants of East and West, the Arab countries seemed to feel more than ever the need for greater self-reliance, the urge to free themselves from their humiliating and historic dependence on the whims and ambitions of this or that combination of great powers. In spite of the collapse—actual or potential—of so many dramatic and mainly paper schemes for unity, the determination had not faltered to give some real meaning to the phrase "the Arab nation." Many Arabs looked to the prospect at least of more effective military collaboration, and meanwhile saw the potentialities of step by step practical integration between Arab states, beginning in some of the most basic economic and social fields. For all Arab leaders could observe that, just at the moment when genuine coordination had become vital to their world, Western Europe—which did not even have, as the Arab peoples had, a common language and culture—was showing through the European Economic Community how valuable a degree of integration could be attained by gradual, practical steps.

Israel's reaction to the summit was simple. As she saw it, the Arabs now knew that the great powers would not force Israel to give back her conquests. Therefore they would have to sit down with the Israelis and work out some compromise.[21] Her leaders have always wanted a minimum of international intervention in what they see as *their* problem with *their* neighbours. They were therefore happy that the Security Council resolution and the Jarring mission had been ignored. At the same time they knew that there was in fact small chance of any direct talks with those neighbours without some outside mediation. And for that they pinned their faith partly on the new U.N. Secretary General, Dr Waldheim (despite their cavalier treatment of certain U.N. resolutions) and, as ever, on the United States. Even so, their hope was dim that any swift progress would be made. Too often since 1967 this long-awaited bargain with the adversary had eluded them. For the Arabs knew full well that, in any direct diplomatic deal, Israel might play by far the stronger hand.

Our story pauses, inconclusively like all stories in the life of nations. In dealing with the immediate present some dramatic turn of events may suddenly confound whatever final judgements we try to pass. The meaning of the past is a different matter. We have covered in outline a unique story beginning nearly four millennia ago. We can hardly end it without seeking to assess what the re-emergence of a Jewish state in the Holy Land has meant to those who lived there, to the Jewish people, and to the whole world.

21. For an account of the reactions to the summit of both sides see Juan de Onis and Terence Smith, *New York Times*, July 10, 1973.

Israel. Prospect and Retrospect

The central fact of our story is the creation of Israel in defiance of those peoples, now generally called Arabs, who lived in and around Palestine before and during the two and a half millennia of the Jewish Diaspora.[22] The wider background is the efforts of successive empires from the dawn of history to the present to grasp a foothold in this immensely strategic area of the Fertile Crescent and Egypt.

Some will feel that the emergence of a militarily strong, efficiently run, aggressively modern, Israel—a potential example of advanced technological development but presently a source of fear to her Arab neighbours—is a manifestation of God's Providence. This is because there was a Jewish state in Palestine two thousand and more years ago and because, after the ancient migration of Abraham and his family from Mesopotamia and the conquest by the ancient Hebrews of the land which they believed the Lord had promised them, the unique religion of Judaism evolved there and in its turn inspired both Christianity and Islam. But, for most other people, Israel has been essentially a product of human forces and individuals, some unswervingly dedicated to the achievement of this goal, others moved by well-meaning but confused statesmanship, and others again by destructive instincts of the most sinister kind.

The First Two Creative Factors:
The Zionist Movement and Britain

The first and basic factor in the emergence of Israel was of course the dynamic work of the Zionist movement, which we have described. Some twenty years after this started, Britain conquered Palestine. She then, for a variety of motives by no means clearly thought out—in which imperialism, idealism, and war strategy all played their part—officially sponsored a Jewish National Home in

22. As many authorities now agree, this is properly reckoned from the Babylonian Captivity in 587 B.C.

this crossroads of southern Syria which had been ruled for centuries by the Muslim Turkish Empire. Britain did this without consulting the Arab inhabitants of Palestine who formed nine-tenths of the population, and without providing, as she could have done, effective safeguards for their interests.[23] One of the ironies of history is that, if Britain, against her strongest wishes, had not been forced into war with Turkey in 1914, Israel might never have existed, and certainly not in the form she has assumed today.[24]

As we know, the National Home became the embryo of a Jewish state in part of the country; and this nucleus eventually conquered the rest of it and a wide area beyond. But in the early years this was by no means a foregone conclusion. It was definitely not within the thoughts or plans of the London Government when it at last officially defined—in 1921–22—what it regarded as the proper meaning of the loosely-worded Balfour Declaration and the Mandate for Palestine; and from then onwards this excluded for Britain any vision of what was actually to happen—namely, a Jewish state ruling the whole country after the flight of most of the Palestinian Arabs to whom it had belonged. But the general belief of the Zionists, from the first arrival of their Commission in Jerusalem in 1918 —and of many Jews who were not Zionists—was that Palestine was to be more or less completely theirs.[25] They therefore promptly as-

23. That is, safeguards for their political and economic rights.

24. The author discussed this point with Mr Amos Elon in Jerusalem in November 1972. Elon maintained, though without convincing the writer, that the Zionists would somehow have taken over Palestine even if it had remained under Turkish rule.

25. In fairness it must be said that the British Government, in its casual and lofty manner of the time, did in 1917 give some encouragement to these Zionist views. It appears from Prime Minister Lloyd George's memoirs that the Imperial War Cabinet did not think of setting up a Jewish state in Palestine immediately after the war without reference to the wishes of the majority of the inhabitants. They had in mind, however, that "when the time arrived for according representative institutions to Palestine, if the Jews had meanwhile . . . become a definite majority of the inhabitants . . . Palestine would . . . become a Jewish Commonwealth." President Wilson took a similar view. But these were not government decisions and were in no way contractually binding on their successors after the war. See Weizmann, pp. 265–66.

sumed that any British actions to slow down or soften this process out of fairness towards, or consideration for, the Arab Palestinians were a devious betrayal of Britain's promises to the Jewish people, which should take precedence of all else.

The diplomatic skill, charm, and political flair of Dr Weizmann managed for years to mask this fundamental cleavage, although he personally shared the general Zionist purpose and belief. He could not, however, avert the bitter clashes between the Zionists, with their wilder supporters, and the Palestine administration, which grew increasingly violent in the 1930s and 1940s. Apart from divergent views on the future of Palestine, these were largely due to a psychological barrier, a lack of understanding between two almost totally different groups of people. In a land poised between Asia and Africa, British officials trained in the creditable but somewhat slow-moving and phlegmatic traditions of Britain's overseas administration found themselves faced with the restless, explosive, dynamism of immigrants dominated by Eastern Europeans often of keener intelligence than themselves, but also often lacking in those qualities of restraint, patience, and consideration for the rights and problems of others which the British had been taught to value and respect. These new arrivals were men who dealt in absolutes and who were conditioned by ill-treatment to claim and grasp from life what they could.

Hitler's Fateful Contribution

The third chief factor in the creation of Israel as she is today was the Nazi holocaust. As we have seen, this greatly intensified the pressure on Palestine through a flood of European Jews, many—perhaps most—of whom would have been content in normal times to stay in their countries of adoption. It also of course intensified a bitter determination on the part of the Yishuv to resist any British policies or counsels of moderation designed to avert the displacement and victimization of the Arabs, who were, however, in no way to blame for the tragedy of the Jews. It must also be said that the ruthlessness and sinister efficiency with which the Nazis dealt with their Jewish victims was ultimately reflected in the ruthlessness of certain Zionist attitudes and actions when dealing with their Arab neighbours. At the time they saw themselves faced with a life and death struggle for survival, though in the event this proved to be far less grim than they had thought. The Arabs were of course themselves violent in much they did, but far less efficient and thorough than those who had learned in the hard school of Central European terror to meet and survive the Nazi system of destruction.

If Hitler Had Never Happened

In any case, to judge by the lack of tension in the middle twenties under the Plumer administration, and the moderate dimensions of the National Home at the time, without Hitler a balance of the Arab and Jewish populations might gradually have evolved which in time would have been tolerable and even beneficial to both communities. It is of course quite impossible to say whether this would have taken the form of a unitary Arab-Jewish state, independent but under the general protection of Britain and other Western powers, with one representative assembly covering the whole country; or of some federal system based on cantonalization; or whether the country would have had to be divided into two separate but not irrevocably hostile states. There might well have been unpleasant outbreaks of violence from time to time—as there were in 1929, and as there are in other countries of varied ethnic background such as Malaysia or India. But the Holy Land has been specially conditioned throughout its history to the confrontation and interpenetration of rival peoples on its soil. It might thus well have become in time a land of peaceful coexistence between Arab and Jew, with neither of these two major communities harming, displacing, or subjugating, the other. And this is broadly what the British Government, when it had settled down to the operation of the Mandate, would have regarded as a fair and proper solution of the thorny burden of Palestine which it had so casually taken on its shoulders.

This vision of the might-have-beens bears of course some resemblance to the White Paper Plan of 1939 which the Zionists so fiercely rejected. But the main grounds for this rejection were that the flight from Hitler to Palestine was already assuming the proportions of a flood which British officials were vainly trying to dam. Had there been no flight and flood from Europe there need have been no unconquerable bitterness between the Yishuv in Palestine and the British, nor between the Yishuv and the Arabs, many of whom were prepared, reluctantly, to make the White Paper work. Nor, given a gradual growth of goodwill on both sides, need the Jewish proportion in Palestine have remained as low as one-third. But given the explosively dynamic, strongly self-centred qualities of the European (especially east European) elements which still dominate Israel, with their restless drive for achievement, a National Home making up one-third or one-half of the population of Palestine would almost certainly have insisted on the exclusive management of its own affairs, even if it were prepared to collaborate or coexist with the Arabs of Palestine in the interests of the country as a whole.

Israel: the Accomplished Fact

In any event, Israel is now an accomplished fact. It is therefore important to assess what her creation and achievements have meant for the Jewish people and for the world at large, and what is likely to be her future. It has certainly given to many Jews in other countries a sense of pride that numbers of their once sedentary people should have been brought back and resettled on the hard soil of the land of their ancient patriarchs and prophets, and that they have since, with outstanding success, made a new life there by the sweat of their brow. Many, too, have been deeply impressed by the mastery these men of Israel have acquired of the harsh and arid arts of modern war. And most Jews in the world look forward to that elusive day when Israel may be at peace with her neighbours and live with them in mutually beneficial understanding.

But there are still, between Israel and World Jewry, and between Israel and the non-Jewish world, some unresolved problems of identity, definition, and understanding. Israel's founders and citizens have often spoken and written of her as if she were identical with, or the sole legitimate representative of, the Jewish people as a whole; or at least as if her needs and goals and interests were essentially the same as theirs. Indeed, often no clear distinction is made—especially by Americans—between the terms Zionist, Israeli, and Jew; yet these differences are still important. On the other hand, the implied identification of World Jewry with Israel is, not unnaturally, a key theme in Zionist and Israeli publicity, since it offers a constant and convincing justification for the creation of Israel, despite the grave problems this has caused for her and others. It also helps to explain and justify the sacrifices which have been, and still are, regularly demanded of Jews throughout the world to build Israel up and keep her materially solvent; though these may of course diminish as she becomes more intensively industrialized and is able to create more wealth by using and exporting her highly varied and sophisticated human skills.

Israel and World Jewry

There is in fact still a distinction to be made between World Jewry and Israel. This is firstly because Israel only contains a fraction of the Jews in the world. While the complete "ingathering" of all Jews is one of Israel's proclaimed goals, it is hardly within the bounds of practical attainment. One reason is that, unless more land is conquered, Israel is far too small to hold them all, however developed she becomes. Another is that many Jews do not in fact regard their adopted countries as an unwelcome exile which they long to leave and, whatever pressures are brought to bear upon them, as they sometimes are today, they can hardly be forced to renounce the lives they have chosen in favour of mass emigration

to Israel. It can of course be argued in favour of the thesis of identification that there are also more Irishmen outside Ireland, and
more Lebanese outside Lebanon, than in their own countries. But
these last two peoples have had a continuous base throughout history in the land of their name. Moreover, in contrast to them, the
number of Jews in Israel is far smaller in proportion to those outside.

A second and more important factor requiring some distinction
to be made between Israel and World Jewry is that Israel, despite
all her successes, is not in fact universally accepted, even by Jews,
as the crown and centre of the Jewish people. And to some extent
those who doubt the validity of Israel as representing the true
Return to Zion in fulfilment of the Messianic promise, or for other
more secular reasons, reflect the old divergence between the uni-
versalist message of some of the greatest Jewish prophets, including
Elijah, Amos, and Isaiah, and the narrower, more exclusive, creed
of Jewish nationalism which evolved from the teachings of the
scribe Ezra, and others, after the Babylonian captivity.

Doubts and Criticisms

The Jewish critics of Israel are broadly the successors of those who
in earlier years had felt uneasy about the whole Zionist programme.
They were formerly numerous in America, Britain, and Western
Europe—even in Germany before Hitler—especially in the years of
the Balfour Declaration and the early 1920s. For the most fervent
followers of Zionism were, as we saw, those from Eastern Europe,
where conditions for Jews had been long and notoriously bad; and
it is of course still mainly those of Eastern European descent who
form the leadership in Jerusalem. With the holocaust and the establishment of Israel the number of critics inevitably dwindled.
Many were converted by the urgent appeals for aid to a beleaguered Israel and her refugee immigrants. This campaign had a clear
humanitarian appeal, but it also served the political purpose of the
Zionists of invoking help for the new state. And this purpose was
strengthened, especially in the United States, by the powerfully

developed instincts of most Americans for social and group conformity.

But some of the critics, with appreciable moral, and even physical, courage, held their ground. They had not been convinced even
by the holocaust that grave discrimination or persecution was the
probable lot of Jews generally in their adopted countries, or that
settlement in Palestine or Eretz Israel was the only proper destiny
for the whole Jewish people. Some have inevitably been more vehement, others more measured, in their views. One of their main
objections to Israel is on the religious and ethical grounds indicated above. Their view could perhaps be summarized as follows.
The God of Israel is a God of Righteousness for all mankind, not
just for the Jewish people; therefore the only fitting Return to
Eretz Israel would have been one which would further the creation
of the Kingdom of God on earth, and thus fulfil the true mission
of the Jewish people. With Ahad Ha'am, whom Weizmann had
once revered, they feel that the National Home should have been
above all a cultural-religious centre of outstanding quality, express-
ing and diffusing the highest spiritual and ethical values of Judaism. Instead, in their view, Judaism has suffered grave damage
from the creation, by people many of whom were indifferent to
religion, of an Israel based ultimately on force and with the values
and much of the aspect of a thrusting, modern, industrial state.
They also deplore as an affront to Jewish ethical standards—as do
some citizens of Israel—the damaging injustice its creation has done
to the Arab inhabitants of the land.[26]

26. Three of the more prominent critics of Israel in the United States are
Moshe Menuhin, Alfred Lilienthal, and Rabbi Elmer Berger. The first, father
of the famous violinist, Yehudi Menuhin, is the most vehement; Rabbi Berger
and the American Council for Judaism take a more moderate line, with
Lilienthal somewhere in the middle. Menuhin, born into an orthodox Jewish
family in Russia, has personal experience of Palestine, having been at school
there. His *Decadence of Judaism in Our Time* was published in 1965 at his
own expense in America. Perhaps Lilienthal's best-known book is *What Price
Israel?* (Chicago: Henry Regnery, 1953). One example of European criticism
is that of the left-wing French-Jewish scholar, Professor Maxime Rodinson, in
his *Israel and the Arabs*.

These critics further object to the formidable pressures still exerted on Jews throughout the world to make them accept and support Israel, as if to do otherwise were a betrayal of their Jewish heritage; and to the severe and humiliating sanctions sometimes inflicted upon dissenters. For in this way many who had remained doubtful were brought into line. Pressure of this kind, the critics claim, is a denial of democracy and freedom of choice; it can also create dangerously divided loyalties. To avoid this last risk, the United States had always set its face against any of its citizens having dual nationality. Yet every American Jew is a potential Israeli, and some who have lived in Israel have in fact acquired Israeli nationality without being forced by the United States to give up their American citizenship. Moreover, the risk of divided loyalty now exists, say the dissenters, because Israel has made it plain from her earliest years that she looks for help to all with Zionist sympathies abroad whatever their nationality, even if this should put them out of line with their own Government. One example of this occurred in relation to Britain in 1948. In that year, Britain's economic stability was important to Washington so that she might become the pivot of the Marshall Plan for the recovery of Europe. Yet just then the tensions in Palestine induced American Jews to boycott British goods. Why, say these critics, should a new nation, whatever the historic significance of its origin, which has become just another small Middle Eastern state, have a claim in perpetuity on the active loyalties of millions of citizens of other sovereign states throughout the globe? By all means let Americans who put Zionism first become citizens of Israel; but let them cease to lead double lives.

Dissent in Israel

Dissent of course exists also in Israel; and this is inevitable in the case of her Arab citizens. But there is, too, as we have shown, some criticism of Zionism and of government policies on the part of Jewish Israelis. We have already mentioned Uri Avnery, whose

Israel Without Zionists urges a federation between Israel and a new Arab-Palestinian republic, leading hopefully to a larger confederation of all the states in the region. Amongst other dissenting groups is that of the Black Panthers, called after the protest group in the United States in the hope of shocking the government into action. These are Sephardic Jews, mainly from North Africa and the Middle East, who strongly resent the secondary status to which they feel they are confined in Israel. They complain that the mainly European Israeli establishment is supported by and represents the wealthier classes, and that many of the Sephardic immigrants live in conditions no better, and often worse, than those in which they lived in the Arab countries. Zionism, they say, may have solved problems for the Eastern European Jews; but it has done nothing for them.

Another example of protest is found in a small fringe group of ultra-pious Jews called Neturey Karta, which refuses to recognize the state of Israel at all, alleging that the Talmud forbids an independent Jewish state, or massive Jewish immigration into the Holy Land, or any artificial steps to advance the coming of the Messiah. These extremists have no official authority to perform valid religious ceremonies, since they are quite separate from the regular Rabbinate of Israel, which they regard as heretical. They condemn Israel's attitude to the Arabs and complain that her leaders have substituted hatred of the Arabs for belief in God.

The Arabs and Israel

This brings us in conclusion to the key factor in Israel's present and future—namely, her relations with her neighbours. In view of the nature and purpose of this book I have tried to give the broadest possible picture of an immensely complex question, leaving it to readers to draw their own conclusions, rather than to present any special thesis as the only proper interpretation of so highly controversial an issue. For this reason also I am suggesting no particular solution to the prevailing conflict. Many solutions have already been put forward by persons far better qualified than myself.

Nobody now seriously questions—not even her bitterest enemies —that Israel is in the Middle East to stay. She has won for herself in battle a position of great strength and almost certainly of ultimate security. But, precisely in view of her outstanding achievements in this and other fields, a time would seem to be near when she can afford frankly to face certain hitherto unpalatable facts and, not least in her own interest, to respond to them with human understanding and creative generosity, however much she may believe in the strength of her own case. This is far likelier to bring peace nearer than any continued insistence on her claims in a mood of injured, self-righteous pride.

One fact is that the Arabs of Palestine have suffered a great injustice, and mostly through no fault of their own. And for this, in time, some comprehensive and healing reparation must be made, even though the earlier situation of those in exile clearly cannot in general be restored.[27] This is of course not just a debt of Zionists and Israelis, though many of them have a bad conscience on this score. Britain, too, is heavily responsible. For her original decision to sponsor a Jewish National Home was made with no reference to the Arabs of Palestine whose land, predominantly, it was. And this Home became in time a dominant Israel by which the Arabs were displaced. The hard fact is that the Palestinian Arabs were treated as of small account by the original Zionist settlers, as they were by the authors of the Balfour Declaration, and as to some extent they still are by the Israelis today. The United States, on whom Israel is so dependent for her survival, has also a debt to pay. Violent and cruel though many Arab actions were in the years before and during their displacement, it can hardly be denied that, against this background, those for example who took part in the Arab Revolt of the 1930s had every right to fight for their land and

27. Even the partitions of Poland in the eighteenth century—though on a much larger scale—were a less serious injustice than the fate of the Palestinian Arabs since, although the Poles came under alien rule, they remained in their own country. And for the far more terrible holocaust, the West Germans at least made reparation in respect of finance and property.

homes. Even Ben Gurion in recent years has conceded that, were he an Arab, he would have done the same. If peace is ever to come, here is an open reckoning which must be squared; and not from any lofty standpoint of charitable help to the poor and defeated, but in candid recognition of a wrong done.

Another fact—but one more freely acknowledged—is that Israel must one day be able to stand on her own feet. For she cannot afford to be permanently dependent on massive and repeated injections of foreign funds and external support of other kinds. She will always enjoy certain special advantages internationally by reason of the strong tradition of voluntary mutual help among Jews the world over. But it will do much for Israel's image and dignity if, as her economic and political stability develops, she can abandon the present campaigns for her unqualified acceptance by all Jews, the intensive fund drives, and all the abnormal techniques of high pressure salesmanship, and in this respect attain another of her proclaimed goals, that of being "a nation like any other." But here again much must depend on her relations with the surrounding Arab states. What is the future of these to be?

Will there be some visible change of attitude by Israel towards the Palestinian exiles? Hitherto she has insisted that any settlement with them can only follow, not precede, a political settlement with the surrounding Arab states; in other words, they should remain a kind of bargaining counter between the two sides. But, if Israel could bring herself to make a really generous offer of reparation to these people in advance of a political settlement, much could be changed. Especially if the manner and content of the offer were such as to convince the mass of the exiles, apart from a few extremist agitators, that those they had been taught to regard as implacable enemies were genuinely extending their hands in friendship and regret. Only comparatively few of these Palestinians might in practice be able to return to the areas in Israel where they had lived—and where their homes might have been destroyed or taken over—and many might not want to go there. But if these few were resettled where they came from in a generous and welcoming manner, the others being offered substantial compensation to help them start a new life in other Arab countries, this could have great symbolic value. And if Israel took the initiative, as would be important, other countries such as America and Britain which share responsibility for the exiles' fate could be relied on to give all support within their power.

Again, if nearly all the West Bank is handed back in accordance with the Allon plan,[28] with more intensive farming and some industrialization, many of the Arabs who originally fled from other parts of what is now Israel could be settled there. The sources which already have an obligation to help the refugees could probably find the substantial funds needed. Such moves could one day do much to prepare the ground and mood for really constructive peace talks between Israel and her Arab neighbours, since, to right the wrongs of the Palestinians and ensure that Israel is not once again a threat to the Arab countries are still their chief reasons for continuing to fight. Moreover, there is now nothing to be gained for Israel by her not coming to terms over the refugees. As a bargaining element in peace talks these unhappy people have long since been superseded by something of far more immediate concern to Israel's neighbours—namely the territory conquered and occupied in the Six Day War.

Dayan and the Possible Future

Unfortunately for the prospect of any such conciliatory moves, the most powerful figure in the Israeli Government, General Dayan, is not conspicuous for humility. This is no doubt one consequence of his fine military record and charismatic character. But, with his present influence, there is no great hope of any really understanding and flexible approach to peace by Israel over the refugees, the frontiers, or any of the other matters in hitherto barren dispute.

As Minister for Defence he is already a key figure in the country and one of renowned intransigence. Many think he may become

28. See below.

the next Prime Minister after Mrs Meir. That he denies any such ambition, or even the possibility of his succeeding her, on the grounds that he would be unwelcome to some of the party leaders, is not convincing, for the same political doubts existed before he was made Minister for Defence. It is in any case a lesson of history that soldiers (and lawyers) are by no means ideal as diplomat-negotiators or statesmen. For the soldier and lawyer are above all concerned to win. The true statesman, on the other hand, in peace negotiations as in other matters, tries at all times to find ground for compromise, to avoid unduly humiliating his adversary, and to put him as far as possible in a mood to accept and effectively operate whatever peace arrangements are worked out because they have given something even to the defeated side.[29]

In a recent interview with the British Broadcasting Corporation in May 1973, General Dayan stressed his conviction that the Arabs do not want a genuine and lasting peace with his people. Moreover, none of their leaders would face the responsibility of being the first to recognize Israel. Therefore, whatever the risks, she must rely on herself and not on any outside power for protection. He would hate any outside guarantees. And he would rather not have peace than accept the condition required for it by the Security Council and the Arab states—namely, withdrawal to the old pre-June 1967 frontiers. Israel would have to keep the Golan Heights, Sharm el-Sheikh, Gaza, and of course Jerusalem, "which is Israel." There should also be some changes all along the old Sinai-Israel border. But Egypt could have the Suez Canal back. And, whether or not Sinai were formally demilitarized, there should be no "foreign"—i.e., international—forces there. Rather than that, he would prefer to have Egyptian forces near to Israel.

As for the former Jordanian West Bank, he was against the plan of the Deputy Prime Minister, Yigal Allon, which was supported

29. This is a favorite, and still highly pertinent, theme of the late Sir Harold Nicolson and other writers. See in particular Nicolson's *Evolution of Diplomacy* (New York: Collier, 1966); *The Congress of Vienna* (New York: Viking, 1963); and *Peacemaking 1919* (New York: Grosset & Dunlap, 1965).

by most of the Cabinet. Under this plan the West Bank would be given up save for a strategic military perimeter of some twelve miles. Rather strangely, Dayan thought that Israel should keep control of the West Bank, but that this should remain part of Jordan, with its people Jordanians. He was not much perturbed by the quicker increase of the Arabs compared to the Israelis, provided the Arabs did not have political rights in Israel. He did not want another million Arabs as Israeli citizens. And he did not favour making a miniature Palestinian state out of the area; it was too small. Its capital should in any case be Amman; it could not be Jerusalem.[30] Judea and Samaria—i.e., the West Bank—were, he said, Israel's homeland. Israelis should therefore have the right to settle and stay there for ever. But they would not expel the Palestinians—there was room enough for both—nor actually take over Nablus or Hebron. He praised King Hussein's courage and firmness in suppressing the terrorists in Jordan, but he did not think that the Lebanese would have the political courage to do the same. In any case, should Syria take over part of Lebanon so as to back the terrorists more effectively, then Israel should intervene. He was not moved by international condemnation of the recent Israel raid on Beirut to kill terrorists. What else, he said, could the Israelis have done?

There is a boldness and defiance here which some may admire but many will regret. For the future of Israel would seem to depend on whether such attitudes prevail indefinitely among her leaders. It must also hinge on whether power remains concentrated in an elite of mainly Eastern European descent. Even when born in Palestine these leaders have somehow inherited from the Jewish record in Europe and the repeated successes of their new state a certain condescending—if unacknowledged—contempt for the Middle Eastern peoples who surround them and even to some extent

30. The Gahal plans for the West Bank are a good deal more logical than those of General Dayan and in some ways fairer to the people concerned if they have to remain under Israel. These are that the occupied territories should be annexed outright, but with the grant of political rights to the Arabs there.

for their fellow Jews from the Orient whom they have been at pains to gather into their midst. But many of the young Israelis are, as we saw, becoming restive under the long predominance of their aging, Europe- and America-oriented establishment. This is necessarily marked among the Oriental Israelis, who for years have formed a majority in the state and who, in a country taking its stand upon democracy, insist that they must have their share of power. But it is not confined to them. In what is still basically an unmilitaristic society, the children of Europe, too, have small taste for repeatedly serving and often dying as the watchmen of an eternal armed camp partly because, as they see it, those in power have become set in prideful, stiff-necked ways.

The new Israel was conceived in Europe and America, but inspired by the Oriental kingdoms of David and Solomon, of Israel and Judah. In this writer's view, if there is ever to be stable peace and fruitful understanding between Israel and the rest of Western Asia and North Africa, she must in time become what those ancient Jewish kingdoms were—namely, a Middle Eastern state. For all the supreme values of religion and ethics by which Jews have sought to live were created in this Middle Eastern setting, and were then somehow upheld in Europe through centuries of a part-brilliant, part-tragic, fate. But, whatever new skills and outlook they may have acquired in the West, it is right that the children of the Dispersion who have chosen to return to the Eastern land where their people learned to be Jews should gradually become adjusted to the conditions and spirit of that ancient region. There are already signs that Israel's elder statesman, David Ben Gurion, in his years of retirement and reflection close to the soil and people, has come to appreciate this truth. In modern terms, Israel should free herself from her present artificial and abnormal dependence upon her Western launching pad and enter resolutely into Middle Eastern orbit.

This will not of course preclude more voluntary immigration from Europe, America, and elsewhere; and the imprint of the West will remain strong. But, as those born in the country around the time of statehood, and those originating in the Arab lands, assume their due share of power, so the new leaders of Israel are likely, at last, to treat their neighbours as themselves—and not as exotic and inferior beings. With this new spirit and approach much that is now bitterly contested could be resolved.[31] Meanwhile, by returning most of the conquests of 1967 and clearly showing her determination to repair within practical bounds the wrong to the Palestinians caused by her creation, Israel could at least start to convince the Arab states that she is a potential friend and helper, not a threat. And this could one day lead to the postponed fulfilment of the main points of the Faisal-Weizmann pact of fifty years ago, which failed when the Arabs were denied the independence they have since attained. As envisaged by this, Israel, in friendly cooperation with the other states of the Middle East, could became a valuable seedbed and example of the latest methods and technology, and one more potential source of East-West understanding.

Yet if any settlement is ever to be reached it will almost certainly have to be guaranteed by the four major powers, however much Israel's intransigents—so long as they are dominant—may dislike this. At present they would doubtless prefer to keep all options open. But the Arab states are sure to insist on a great-power guarantee, particularly of Israel's future frontiers. For, however accommodating the Israeli approach to them may become—and so far there are small signs of this—the Arabs have not unnaturally an obsessive fear that she will seek to expand further. This is, after all, the programme of Gahal. They will therefore want to be sure

31. The exact points on which agreement might be reached, and how, are outside the scope of this study. In any case, as regards the areas conquered by the Israelis in 1967—so long as these remain in their hands—much could be achieved by a new flexibility on the Israeli part. One idea, the author understands, has already been considered in official circles in Israel, but rejected at government level. "Face" being of exceptional importance in the Middle East as in other parts of Asia, Egyptian sovereignty could continue to be recognized at Sharm el-Sheikh and perhaps at other points in Sinai which Israel feels she should continue to control. Egypt might consent to lease these points to Israel for an indefinite period, though her consent is by no means certain.

that, if there is ever any move in this direction, Israel will be restrained by those powers which helped to create her. If certain face-saving devices are adopted, such a guarantee could also make it easier for the Arab leaders to stop insisting on the return of every inch of conquered territory as the condition for Israel's recognition. For even the most dove-like Israeli leaders would find it hard to accept this now. And, in spite of General Dayan's pessimism, King Hussein may prove to be the Arab ruler with sufficient realism and courage to take the lead in proposing somewhat easier conditions for acceptance of the fact of Israel. His grandfather was a victim of such realism, but Hussein has already risked his life for the same clear-headed sense of realities in his campaign against the Palestine guerrillas, and survived.

Perhaps rather more realism may be needed by the Israelis, too, as a final inducement to moderation. They freely acknowledge the courage of individual Arab fighters. But they would be rash to assume that, despite their far greater numbers and rich resources, the Arab armies could not now be a threat to Israel because some of them have lacked efficient and disciplined organization, and close reliance between officers and men. For the Jews themselves, under their mainly Eastern and Central European leadership, only recently developed, or revived, astonishing military qualities which had in general been foreign to them for centuries. The defeat and humiliation inflicted on the Arabs, like the kind of suffering the Jews endured in Europe, could be a hard but effective school for producing fighting qualities of a remarkable kind. Arab political integration may be far off. But it is not impossible that a leader of real statesmanship could one day inspire the rulers of the Arab world to consent—as an effective weapon of Arab unity—to the formation of a supra-national Arab army, financed by the oil-rich countries, composed of the toughest fighting types from all areas, and meticulously trained, if necessary with outside help, in an Arab version of the Wingate-Dayan tradition. And meanwhile, if the Arab armies can at least succeed in establishing more effective fighting methods and greater coordination, much could be changed.

Indeed, if such armies managed later to inflict even a minor reverse on the forces of Israel, this could have a truly sobering effect upon a people whose success has for the present frankly mounted to their heads.

In spite of the (now unofficial) cease-fire, the Middle East remains potentially explosive, with Israel as the main source of ferment. As long as this continues, it could spark off a third world war involving all the larger powers. These cannot therefore stand aside, as the present Government of Israel would wish. Both in the United Nations and outside they must watch and, if necessary, help and act. One precaution which already to some extent exists is a tacit understanding between Russia and America, thanks to the Washington-Moscow "hot line," to stop any flames from spreading in case of another conflagration. Meanwhile there is a more immediate and restricted issue between Israel and the world at large, on which she could be more sensitive to the views and feelings of others. This is Jerusalem itself, all of which she has defiantly annexed as an integral part of Israel, despite twenty-five years of U.N. rulings that the Holy City should be international. Here then, say the critics, is a government which invokes and relies on the United Nations when its decisions suit her, but ignores or rejects them when they do not. Jordan would have preferred the U.N. solution and respected Jerusalem's international status throughout the 1948 war. But when the new city was annexed by Israel, Jordan felt obliged similarly to take the Old City over. Just for that reason, however, it could have been a skilful and inspiring move on Israel's part, which would have given her wide prestige, had she offered a measure of internationalization after conquering it all in 1967. Instead, General Dayan's proud and unbending proclamation held the field. It fired the imagination of his people, and it is almost certainly too late to make any major changes, or to efface the international impression caused.

There might however still be room, in a city of such sanctity, to silence some of the criticism to which Israel is exposed from eight hundred million Christians and Muslims in the world. In the early years Israel was prepared to consider some kind of extraterritorial status for the Holy Places. This, too is hardly practicable any more. But something could perhaps still be done to ensure that neither the Holy Places, nor the general aspect of the City, remain at Israel's sole discretion. Nearly all these shrines are sacred to more than one of the world religions. It would therefore be fitting that some international authority should at least have the right to be consulted on arrangements affecting all but purely Jewish shrines, and also on any further erection of unlovely modern buildings on sites and areas held sacred by half mankind.

Jerusalem is after all the centre and symbol of a Land where the Jews evolved a uniquely inspiring faith in the oneness and righteousness of God, and a system of ethics of transcendent quality. Their greatest figures believed that they had been chosen by God to help in the diffusion of His message, which was meant not just for themselves but for all men. And in due course His Word was in fact carried to all corners of the earth, in part directly—by Jews of the Diaspora—but mostly by the daughter faiths of Christianity and Islam which Judaism inspired. Despite the strong hostility faced by Jews at tragic moments during their Dispersion, and all the undeserved suffering this entailed, men of goodwill have always acknowledged the world's deep debt to the great moral and religious legacy of Judaism.

In recent years Zionism has been accomplished in the shape of Israel, not according to the Scriptures, but as a largely secular movement with political goals and a fierce concentration on what its leaders believe to be for the benefit of the Jewish people—admittedly after they had passed through one of the most terrible crises in their history. But in this new process much, frankly, has been done to others which belies those high standards of spiritual and moral integrity set by Jewish precept and doctrine in the past. This has already taken a bitter and dangerous toll. For the children of the new Israel are now faced with fresh destructive hatreds in regions and among people where these had been largely unknown, and especially in parts of the Middle East. Yet the new Israel is there to stay, as we and they know; and demands to be seen in historical perspective.

The ancient Israelites conquered Canaan in a savage tribal age. Yet eventually their descendants evolved a Jewish religion and way of life which inspired many of the finest values by which we live. In our time, after the Jews had suffered under Hitler the far more devastating cruelties of the modern age, the Israelis have achieved a dominance in the Holy Land never before attained by Jews save during the short-lived empire of David and Solomon. This was won mainly by the sword and at grave cost to those whom they conquered and displaced. Yet the new masters of the Land, with a leadership predominantly of European stock, are from what has become during the Diaspora the world's most gifted and long-suffering people. Will they too, in time, set new standards of justice and righteousness in dealing with their neighbours, and especially with those who have been subjugated and driven from their homes? This must surely be part of the price of peace, whatever new attitudes may also be needed from Israel's foes. Is it not also a debt which the new Israel owes to all that through the ages has been a source of pride for Jews—the incomparable legacy of their faith, their traditions, and their creative achievement?

Epilogue

Soon after this book was written, the fourth Arab-Israeli war put to the test, and confirmed the validity of, some of its conclusions. Paradoxically, despite the losses and suffering, in the long run this latest clash may prove to have been a disguised blessing rather than a misfortune for Israel. As a result of the new struggle, certain realities have been brought home to both sides more clearly than ever before, and by early 1974 Egypt and Israel had reached an initial understanding. Unless this promise of a better future should be wrecked by human folly or some perverse fatality, it could at last lead, through compromise and concession and the sacrifice of many illusions, towards Israel's long-sought goal of safe and peaceful acceptance by her neighbours.

The October War: General Background and Implications

The course of the fourth war and its sequel can only be briefly told here. Until time permits some historical perspective, the full im-

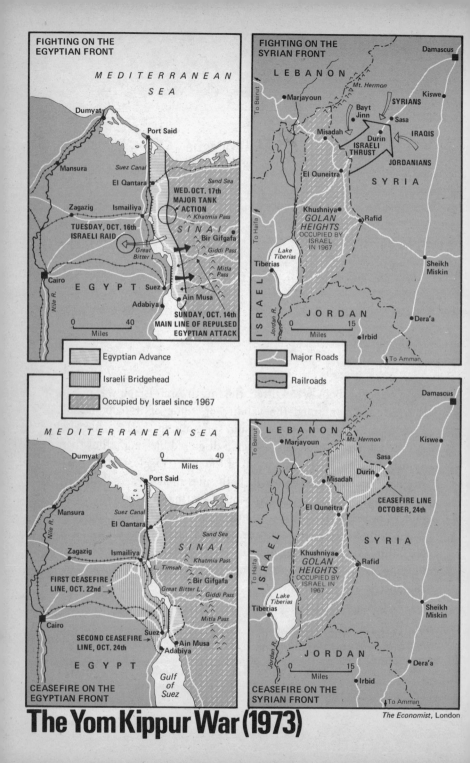

FIGHTING ON THE EGYPTIAN FRONT

MEDITERRANEAN SEA

Dumyat
Port Said
Mansura
Suez Canal
El Qantara
Sand Sea
Zagazig
Ismailia
SINAI
WED. OCT. 17th MAJOR TANK ACTION
^ Khatmia Pass
TUESDAY, OCT. 16th ISRAELI RAID
Bir Gifgafa
^ Giddi Pass
Great Bitter L.
^ Mitla Pass
Cairo
Nile R.
E G Y P T
Suez
Ain Musa
Adabiya
SUNDAY, OCT. 14th MAIN LINE OF REPULSED EGYPTIAN ATTACK
0   40
Miles

FIGHTING ON THE SYRIAN FRONT

Damascus
L E B A N O N
To Beirut
Marjayoun
Mt. Hermon
SYRIANS
Kiswe
Bayt Jinn
Sasa
Misadah
Durin
ISRAELI THRUST
IRAQIS
El Quneitra
JORDANIANS
S Y R I A
Khushniya
GOLAN HEIGHTS OCCUPIED BY ISRAEL IN 1967
Rafid
To Haifa
Lake Tiberias
Tiberias
I S R A E L
Sheikh Miskin
Jordan R.
J O R D A N
Dera'a
0   15
Miles
Irbid
↑ To Amman

Egyptian Advance	Major Roads
Israeli Bridgehead	Railroads
Occupied by Israel since 1967	

MEDITERRANEAN SEA

Dumyat
0   40
Miles
Port Said
Mansura
Nile R.
Suez Canal
El Qantara
Sand Sea
Zagazig
Ismailia
SINAI
L. Timsah
^ Khatmia Pass
FIRST CEASEFIRE LINE, OCT. 22nd
Bir Gifgafa
Great Bitter L.
^ Giddi Pass
^ Mitla Pass
Cairo
Suez
SECOND CEASEFIRE LINE, OCT. 24th
Ain Musa
Adabiya
E G Y P T
Gulf of Suez
CEASEFIRE ON THE EGYPTIAN FRONT

Damascus
L E B A N O N
To Beirut
Marjayoun
Mt. Hermon
Kiswe
Sasa
Misadah
Durin
CEASEFIRE LINE OCTOBER, 24th
El Quneitra
S Y R I A
To Haifa
I S R A E L
Khushniya
GOLAN HEIGHTS OCCUPIED BY ISRAEL IN 1967
Rafid
Lake Tiberias
Tiberias
Jordan R.
J O R D A N
Sheikh Miskin
Dera'a
0   15
Miles
Irbid
↑ To Amman
CEASEFIRE ON THE SYRIAN FRONT

The Yom Kippur War (1973)

The Economist, London

plications of the war—even the exact details of just what happened and how—will be in doubt. What does seem clear is that Israeli intelligence reports showed that Arab attacks were impending, but not when they might occur. It then appears that in weighing the situation the Israeli Cabinet, with a general election in the offing and on the eve of a specially sacred festival—and out of concern for Israel's image abroad—rejected their Chief of Staff's plea for another pre-emptive strike against the Arab forces like that of 1967. This decision was to cost them dear. Although orders were issued placing the Israeli forces on full alert by October 4–5, there was evidently some breakdown in the chain of command, since many of the troops on the actual fronts had no previous warning of the Arab attacks. The Arabs thus achieved a large measure of surprise and important initial gains.

Ultimately and after intense fighting, the Israelis in turn achieved successes that secured afresh most, but not all, of their gains in the 1967 war. But the price was heavy. Although Arab losses were considerably higher than those of Israel, Arab manpower was far larger, too. Israel with her small population lost in soldiers killed more than three and one-half times the number killed in the 1967 conflict.[1] Furthermore, the Arab states, despite their military setbacks in the later stages of the war, afterwards succeeded—through the use of the oil weapon and in other ways—in partly isolating Israel and reducing for the time being her influence in the world.[2] The

1. In June 1967 Israeli deaths in action had been 679. In October 1973, according to figures issued by the Israeli General Staff on December 8, they were 2,412. This was apart from wounded and prisoners. See Keesing's Research Report of 1968, p. 41, and Keesing's Contemporary Archives, p. 26176.

2. There has been a bewildering stream of reports on the war in the American and British press and elsewhere, including some vivid and stimulating analyses of particular issues in, e.g., *Newsweek* (November 5: "The War that Nobody Won"; December 3: "The Oil Recession"; December 17: "Dr K.'s Mid-East Gamble") and the *New York Times* (October 19, James Reston: "The Hidden Compromise"; November 24, Arthur Waskow: "A Time for Terms in the Mid-East"; and December 7, Flora Lewis: "Peace Talks a Dilemma for the West Bank Palestinians"). In December the British press produced on successive Sundays some of the first over-all accounts of the new conflict. Thus the

war also had significant consequences for the superpowers. It imposed a new strain on relations between Washington and Moscow, which Mr Brezhnev had recently been at such pains to improve in the hope of economic and technological exchanges profitable to the Soviet Union.[3]

The war was launched on the holiest day of the Jewish year: Yom Kippur, the Day of Atonement, which fell on October 6—a solemn occasion normally entailing a pause in nearly all activity and concentration on certain traditional and religious observances.[4] Cairo has made it clear that this day was chosen for good military reasons (amongst others the existence of a full moon and a favourable state of current in the Suez Canal) and not from any evil determination to disrupt a sacred occasion. Indeed, although the lull

---

(London) *Observer* of December 9 and 16 contained a two-part assessment of "The Yom Kippur War" by Winston Churchill, co-author of *The Six Day War*; the (London) *Sunday Telegraph* of December 9, 16, 23, and 30, a four-part account by Christopher Dobson and Ronald Payne called "Why the Arabs didn't Win"; and the (London) *Sunday Times* of December 9, 16, and 30, a three-part analysis by their Insight Team on "How Egypt caught Israel napping," "The Victory that Egypt Threw Away," and "The Battle of Chinese Farm." There is also a useful record of events in Keesing's Contemporary Archives for November 5–11, 1973, pp. 26173–77. Finally, there is a valuable preliminary analysis of the meaning and lessons of the war, and the prospects created by it—from both United States and British sources—in *Survival*, vol. 16, no. 1, for January-February 1974, published by the International Institute for Strategic Studies, London. Under the general title Strategic Forum: The Middle East Conflict 1973, this contains three important articles: "The Superpowers," "The Military Lessons," and "The Prospects for Real Peace" by Marshall D. Shulman, Kenneth Hunt, and Sydney D. Bailey, respectively. The Institute's Strategic Survey, 1973, to be published in early April 1974, will contain further studies of "The Middle East War and its Implications" and of "Oil as a Weapon."

It is impossible in a very brief summary of this kind to do justice to the wealth of good material now becoming available, but this Epilogue is an attempt to clarify, on the basis of it, what seem to be the most essential points.
3. This is one of the main themes of Mr Shulman's article (cited in n. 2, above).
4. The emphasis of the Day of Atonement is on cleansing from sin. As traditionally observed, it required abstention from all work as well as from food, drink, and sexual intercourse.

in normal Israeli activity on Yom Kippur may marginally have helped to catch the Israelis unawares, the fact that most of them were concentrated in their synagogues and homes speeded up final mobilization once the war started.[5]

Of greater value to the Arabs in achieving surprise was their remarkable skill and discretion in publicly masking their intentions. There were none of the boastful threats that had preceded the Six Day War; and it soon became clear, as the Israelis later admitted, that the Arabs had learned in other ways from their earlier humiliations, and notably how to fight in a tougher, more coordinated, and more effective way.[6] By the end the Israelis had largely redressed the military balance. Yet the war had in no sense been a walk-over for them. There had been no repetition of the swift and sweeping triple victory of 1967; and by the end of 1973 the Israelis' dangerously intoxicating mood of self-approval that had followed that earlier victory had evaporated. Moreover, Israel found herself faced with the uncomfortable realization that the Arabs now knew how to recover from defeat and to draw from this the lessons that could lead to a steadily improving military performance in the future. Indeed, with Soviet arms, superior numbers, and vast control or potential wealth from oil, the Arab states might be capable of launching every few years assaults no less damaging—and perhaps even more so—than those of October 1973. And these could be assaults that a nation of Israel's size and population might find it progressively harder to resist.

The Actual Fighting

The course of the fighting is of less importance than its consequences. On October 6 the Israelis found themselves suddenly at

5. See the Dobson and Payne article in the (London) *Sunday Telegraph* of December 9, 1973 (see n. 2).
6. See Eric Silver's report from Jerusalem: "Israel sees a Ray of Hope in Peace Talks," in the (London) *Observer* of December 2, 1973. In it he says: "Israel's first grudging response to the Algiers summit [of Arab leaders in late November] is that the Arabs seem to have learned as much about diplomacy as they have about fighting since 1967."

war when the Egyptians and Syrians simultaneously attacked them in force, the Egyptians across the Suez Canal and the Syrians in the Golan Heights area. Yet, predictably, these were not the only Arab forces involved. As before the 1967 war, King Hussein of Jordan— so often at loggerheads with his neighbours—had been brought back into the Arab fold, and had aligned himself with Egypt and Syria as the result of earlier talks in Cairo. This time, however, instead of opening a third front with a thrust towards Jerusalem, he eventually sent his troops to fight on the northern front under Syrian command. The Syrians were also in due course supported by armoured and air forces from Iraq as well as by units from Morocco and Saudi Arabia. There was bitter fighting for over two and one-half weeks, with tank battles on a formidable scale and heavy losses of material as well as men.

The Arab armies did not attempt to match the highly sophisticated *Blitzkrieg* tactics used by the Israelis in 1967. Instead, they endeavoured to inflict maximum losses on their enemy by wave after wave of attack pressed home with small regard for their own casualties.[7] Despite military errors on the Arab side and serious reverses in the end, these methods achieved for a time partial and disturbing success in a struggle lasting three times longer than that of 1967.

On October 22 there was an initial cease-fire on the Egyptian front, in response to a resolution of the U.N. Security Council. This broke down and fighting was resumed for two days. Then on October 24, in response to a second Security Council resolution, a more or less effective cease-fire came into operation on both the Syrian and Egyptian fronts.

The Syrian Front

On the northern front the Syrians, in considerably greater numbers than the Israelis and supported by some Moroccan motorized units earlier stationed in that country, managed to recover in the first few

7. Described as the "meatgrinder" technique.

days much of the Golan Heights lost to Israel in 1967. The new war was a highly technological one, and on the Syrian as on the Egyptian front the Arabs made effective use of Russian missiles, including some lethal new ones.[8] Indeed, these missiles and extremely concentrated ground fire seem to have caused more losses to the skilful Israeli air force than the aircraft of the Arab states. In the north these missiles also damaged Israeli kibbutzim in Galilee. For their part the Israelis bombed Damascus and other parts of Syria, killing, it seems, some civilians in the Syrian capital, among them a U.N. observer and his family.

On October 10 Mrs Meir announced that by a counter-offensive the Israelis had completely reoccupied the Golan Heights. On the same day Baghdad reported that an Iraqi armoured force and some 200 Iraqi aircraft had joined the battle on Syria's side. On October 13 Jordanian forces and some 3,000 Saudi Arabian troops (apparently units stationed in Jordan since 1967) also joined the Syrians. By this time the Israeli land forces were advancing on a fairly nar-

---

8. Churchill (see n. 2) writes: "The Egyptians . . . had learnt that they were unable to compete tank-for-tank in ground battles and aircraft-for-aircraft in close combat with the Israelis. . . . The Sagger anti-tank missile and increasingly sophisticated SAM missile systems which the Soviet Union was perfecting were tailor-made to remedy these defects." He later explains that Israeli pilots immediately found themselves faced with the highly mobile SAM-6, the newest anti-aircraft missile in the Soviet armoury and one to which no Western nation had yet developed an answer. Moreover, Soviet FROG surface-to-surface missiles were launched against the Galilee agricultural settlements round Ramat David, one of Israel's principal air bases in the area.

A more professional analysis of the missiles and weapons used in this war, and the military conclusions to be drawn from it, will be found in Brigadier Hunt's article (see n. 2). This brings out the fact that the Soviet-built tanks of the Arabs were outranged by the British- and American-made tanks used by the Israelis, but that Israeli tank casualties were caused by a whole variety of Soviet anti-tank missiles, both wire-guided and hand-held, in response to which the Israelis were able, belatedly, to use an American anti-tank missile. Indeed, it makes it clear that the new effectiveness of such weapons has now enhanced the role of infantry and for the time being somewhat diminished that of tanks. Equally, the role of the fighter-bomber has been to some extent reduced by the effectiveness of ever more sophisticated air-defence missile systems (including a man-portable or vehicle-mounted heat-seeking SAM-7) and anti-aircraft guns.

row front from Quneitra, at the edge of the Golan Heights, towards Damascus. Against strong resistance they eventually penetrated Syrian territory to a depth of some fifteen miles.

On their left flank the Israelis efforts to thicken their salient were contested by the Syrians attacking southward from the foothills of Mount Hermon, on the right flank by the Iraqis, and to a lesser extent the Jordanians.[9] Although the Iraqis seem to have been badly mauled and Syrian losses were very heavy, by the time of the cease-fire on October 24 the opposing forces were still deadlocked south of a town called Sasa, the main defensive position covering Damascus, at a distance of some twenty miles from the capital of Syria. Towards the end of these operations the Israelis recovered an important observation post high in the Mount Hermon range which the Syrians had taken in their first attack.

The Suez Front

On the Suez front a far more complex situation developed. In their initial attack the Egyptian forces managed to cross to the east bank of the Suez Canal at five points and in the first full day of operations brought over some 400 tanks on pontoon bridges, along with other troops. They reoccupied Qantara, the former provincial capital of Sinai, and fanned out north and south along the whole hundred-mile length of the Canal and beyond, from the Mediterranean coast to Ain Musa south of Suez. Strengthened by a substantial flow of reinforcements, in the next few days the Egyptians penetrated several miles into the Sinai desert and overran the so-called Bar-Lev Line,[10] constituting the flexible advance system of Israeli defence in Sinai. This was in fact not a line but a series of loosely-linked strong points, the last of which surrendered on October 13. These initial setbacks produced ugly recrimination and controversy among the Israeli generals on this front. On October 14, in num-

9. See "To the Rescue of Damascus," by the Levant Correspondent of the (London) *Economist* of October 20, 1973, p. 38.
10. Named after Gen. Hayyim Bar-Lev, former Israeli Chief of Staff.

bers estimated at 100,000 and with powerful armoured support, the Egyptians drove forward into the desert, their main thrust being launched from the area between Suez and the Bitter Lakes towards the Mitla Pass in central Sinai, where they had met so painful a defeat six years earlier.

The Egyptians could gain no decisive victory unless this thrust succeeded. Yet by making it they ran a grave, and in the event fatal, risk; for their armies were forced to abandon the protective screen afforded by their missiles in the Canal Zone, and expose themselves to the deadly effectiveness of the Israeli air force. With this new advantage, the Israelis managed to repulse the Egyptian advance, having meanwhile also been strengthened by reinforcements from the Syrian front, where they had regained the initiative and driven the Arabs back. Between October 14 and 19, somewhat farther to the north in the desert east of Ismailiya, one of the biggest and fiercest tank battles in history was fought. As a result, Egypt's eastward drive was checked, and from October 17 the tide of battle started here, too, to turn in Israel's favour. Her generals were able to seize the initiative on this southern front as they recently had in the north.[11]

Egypt's Weak Spot

It was also unfortunate for the Egyptians that they had left something of a gap in their forces in the region between Ismailiya and the Great Bitter Lake. Their Second Army was operating to the north of Ismailiya, their Third Army to the south of this city and down to the area of Suez. At this weak point in the Egyptian centre, near the northern end of the Great Bitter Lake, the Israelis on October 16 managed to cross into Egyptian territory on the west bank of the Canal.

This risky operation was conceived and commanded by a dashing if controversial general, Ariel Sharon, who in his own estimation and that of many Israeli soldiers and civilians was the hero of the

11. See Keesing's Contemporary Archives, pp. 26173–74.

October War. His military seniors frankly dispute some of his pretensions. They have resented his unsparing criticism of them, and his tendency to despise planning and logistics and to ignore orders. Sharon, a man of right-wing views in political opposition to the government, had been commander of the Egyptian front during the war of attrition between 1969 and the U.S.-sponsored cease-fire of August 1970. At that time he had planned an Israeli incursion into Egypt at roughly the spot where this was eventually made. Meanwhile, having lost hope of becoming Chief of Staff, he had left the army in July 1973, and, like many Israeli generals, made himself a power in politics. He helped to recast the main opposition to Mrs Meir by welding together the two main constituents of *Gahal* (his own Liberal Party and *Herut*) with two smaller right-wing groups (the State List and the Free Centre) under the new label *Likud*. Recalled to the colours at the outbreak of the new war, he had to serve under a former subordinate on the Egyptian front and was indignant at being debarred by the top leaders—for good reason— from launching his planned Canal crossing in the first anxious days. When this was at last authorized he went his own flamboyant and impetuous way and sought the maximum credit for an operation that ultimately succeeded thanks chiefly to the efforts of others, though at one point it came near to disaster.

This new and highly charismatic figure on the political and military scene is clearly a man to watch. With his brash self-confidence and swashbuckling conviction that Israel can defeat all comers, he may, unless restrained, be a greater potential danger to the future of his country than any Olympian notions of General Dayan. Indeed Dayan—his star somewhat dimmed by the Government's unpreparedness for the Arab attacks—is now a key supporter of Mrs Meir's policies of comparative moderation, while Sharon, his new rival in public esteem, is aligned against the Cabinet with the ex-Irgun leader and Israel's arch-imperialist Mr Menachem Begin.[12]

12. For the character and political activity of General Sharon, see Henry Stanhope: "The 'King of Israeli' in Search of His Crown," in the (London) *Times* of December 27, 1973. As regards the delay in authorizing his expedition

Having eventually crossed the Canal in force against stubborn Egyptian resistance, the Israelis gradually expanded their bridgehead on the west bank, chiefly to the west and south. These advanced forces then concentrated on destroying or "taking out" as many as possible of the missile sites and missiles in the area, so that the Israeli air force could operate with progressively more effect on this part of the Egyptian front. Despite Egypt's complex and carefully organized command structure and military machine, no accurate intelligence of this Israeli operation seems to have reached the Cairo High Command in good time; but it was soon clear that this was far more than a small-scale commando raid, as the Egyptians at first claimed. By October 20, according to Tel Aviv, the Israeli air force had achieved total superiority on the Egyptian

---

across the Canal, his seniors seem rightly to have judged that it was important first to defeat the Egyptian armoured force that had exposed itself in Sinai beyond the protection of its missile screen.

For a careful analysis of the ups and downs of the Israeli invasion of Egypt, see "The Battle of Chinese Farm," in the London *Sunday Times* of December 30, 1973 (see n. 2). From this it appears that, as a result of strong Egyptian resistance, the Israeli scheme fell far behind schedule. Nevertheless in the early hours of Tuesday, October 16, Sharon crossed the Canal with only 200 men, leaving to others the harder essential task of keeping a corridor open to the Canal so that a proper bridgehead could be established. He then, ignoring his orders to dig in around the bridgehead, split his tiny force into separate raiding parties, which dispersed into Egypt with the task of "taking out" missiles and doing what damage they could. Through the cumbersome nature of their military bureaucracy, habit of working to set plans, and lack of adequate military intelligence, the Egyptians failed to destroy these small parties, as they could easily have done had their reactions been quicker. In the event, Sharon's gamble came off, but only *just*. The removal of some missiles by his people made an "opening" for the Israeli air force; and the troops at the bridgehead held on long enough for substantial reinforcements of Israeli men and armour to get across. Thus "a plan which had originally failed dramatically was essentially . . . baled out by the fighting ability of the Israeli rank and file."

The complete text of their interesting analysis of the Yom Kippur war by the *Sunday Times* Insight Team has been published in London in book form by André Deutsch under the title *Insight on the Middle East War*. Around this time the Israeli authorities charged Sharon with defaming the army and, according to the press, were contemplating an investigation of his conduct on grounds of insubordination and disclosure of confidential military matters.

front, and the Israeli ground forces had pushed to within some seventy miles of Cairo. In the process their bridgehead had been enlarged to a length of twenty-five miles and a depth of twenty. Israeli reinforcements were still being brought over with all possible speed, so that by the time of the first cease-fire in the early evening of October 22, there were some 12,000 troops and 200 tanks in the Israeli bridgehead, which had been lengthened to thirty miles. Moreover, the direct Cairo-Ismailiya road had been cut, though alternative routes to Ismailiya were still available farther north; and the Israelis had reached the edge of the Cairo-Suez road.[13]

The First Cease-Fire

Meanwhile, the Egyptians had retained a long strip of territory east of the Canal, running southwards from Port Said to the area of Ismailiya, and another strip from a point east of the Great Bitter Lake to the Gulf of Suez—in all, some 400–450 square miles of Sinai. But the two strips were separated by the Israeli bridgehead, and the Egyptian Third Army was in imminent danger of encirclement. A clear objective of Israel's military leaders was to complete the encirclement and defeat of this Third Army, while the Egyptian leaders were equally determined that their army should break out of Israeli encirclement if it could.

The cease-fire on October 22 was a check to both plans. It was especially resented by the Israelis, who were in sight of achieving a decisive victory, and whose government had been forced to stop fighting chiefly as the result of Great Power pressure through the Security Council. And this in turn had been caused by the Soviets' determination to save their Arab clients from any really disastrous collapse such as that of 1967.

The Second Cease-Fire

There was thus on both sides of the Egyptian front a strong urge to bring matters to a quick decision; and this caused heavy fighting

13. *Ibid.*, p. 26174. See also *The Economist* (London), October 27, 1973, p. 48.

to recur for another two days, each side putting the blame upon the other. The upshot was a further marked gain for Israel, whose forces west of the Canal were able to reach the Gulf of Suez south of Adabiya and complete the encirclement of the enemy forces in the Suez area. But at this point, on October 24, with the Egyptian Third Army trapped but not destroyed, a second cease-fire was imposed through the U.N. Security Council by the same international pressures that had brought about the first. It required the Israeli forces to withdraw to the line they had reached by October 22.

The War at Sea

Meanwhile, the war had also been fought at sea. The Israeli navy with air support had attacked points on the Syrian and Egyptian coasts, including Latakia, Tartus (where a Soviet supply ship was sunk), Banias (a terminal of the pipeline from Iraq where oil storage tanks were fired), the Bay of Aboukir, the approaches to Alexandria, and the Gulf of Suez.[14] Farther to the south, however, the Egyptian navy, with support from the Yemen, imposed a blockade of the Strait of Bab el Mandeb leading from the Red Sea to the Gulf of Aden, the Arabian Sea, and the Indian Ocean—thus partly neutralizing Israel's ability to gain access to Africa and the Orient through the Gulf of Aqaba and the Strait of Tiran. Both the Soviet and United States fleets in the Mediterranean were reinforced. The Soviet fleet was reported to have been increased to over eighty warships, the largest number it had ever sent into the area.

The Superpowers Supply Both Sides with Arms

As early as October 10, Washington was disturbed by a Soviet airlift of military supplies to Egypt and Syria. On October 15 the U.S. Government announced that, since the Russian airlift had become "massive," the United States, to offset this, would make an "appreciable" airlift of similar supplies to Israel. This would prevent the

14. Keesing's Contemporary Archives, p. 26176.

Soviet supplies from "unsettling the military balance in the area."
On October 18, 220 U.S. Representatives and 67 Senators called
for unlimited aid to Israel, and on the following day President
Nixon sent an emergency request to the Congress for immediate
military aid to Israel to a value of $2,200 million.[15]

Implementation of the Cease-Fire

After October 24, Egyptian-Israeli talks on the implementation of
the cease-fire took place under U.N. supervision at the point of
junction of the two forces some sixty miles (101 kilometres) from
Cairo on the Suez-Cairo road. These led to the signature on November 11 of a formal cease-fire agreement providing for discussions on the return of the Israeli forces to their positions of October
22 within the framework of a wider agreement on disengagement
and separation of forces under U.N. auspices. It formalized arrangements for the supply of non-military necessities to the encircled
Egyptian Third Army; and for the replacement of Israeli by U.N.
checkpoints on the Cairo-Suez road as a preliminary to the exchange of all prisoners of war.

By the end of October the International Committee of the Red
Cross had been given the names of nearly 6,000 Arab prisoners by
Israel, and of some 450 Israeli prisoners by Egypt. The Israeli-
Egyptian exchanges were eventually carried out. The Syrians, however, were charged by Israel with supplying no lists and with murdering some forty of their Israeli prisoners.[16] The talks later became
deadlocked; and discussion of the key issues of disengagement and
Israeli withdrawal as a step towards some permanent political settlement was in effect transferred to the Middle East conference
that opened at Geneva on December 21 under the chairmanship of
Dr Kurt Waldheim, Secretary-General of the United Nations. Of
the main protagonists only the Egyptians, Jordanians, and Israelis
were present; the Syrians had refused to attend.

15. *Ibid.*, pp. 26176–77.
16. *Ibid.*, pp. 26203, 26320.

Political Repercussions in the Arab World and Africa

A remarkable aspect of the war and its sequel was the passive role during the conflict, and subsequent eccentricities, of the fire-eating Colonel Gaddafi; and it became clear that the ostensible union between Libya and Egypt was more nominal than ever. On October 8 Gaddafi announced that he did not agree with the strategy of the campaign against Israel, nor with the battle plan drawn up by Egypt and Syria—on which, it seems, he had not been consulted—and he did little more than pledge support to the Arab cause in money and oil. Later he boycotted and tried to wreck a summit meeting of the Arab heads of state held at Algiers November 26–28 on the initiative of Egypt and Syria, alleging that this was designed to ratify a "capitulation" by these two countries.

The meeting was boycotted also by Iraq, despite the fact that Iraqi troops had taken part in the war. Baghdad declined to endorse "unilateral decisions" by Egypt and Syria in regard to the conflict. Arab unity evidently still had some way to go.

These absences did not deter the leaders at Algiers from issuing a number of far-reaching declarations. Their chief political pronouncement, while insisting on Israel's evacuation of all occupied Arab territories and on the "full national rights" of the Palestinian people, in fact implicitly authorized President Sadat to negotiate with Israel once the Geneva conference had been arranged. Another document referred to the previous week's decision by the Organization of African Unity to call for an economic, especially an oil, embargo on Israel, South Africa, Portugal, and Rhodesia; and announced an ambitious programme of Arab help to the African countries. Yet another endorsed the use of oil as a political weapon of world-wide scope, with which to punish Israel's alleged champions and gain supporters for the Arab cause. The Algiers meeting incidentally drew a protest from King Hussein of Jordan when it recognized the Palestine Liberation Organization as the sole legal representative of the Palestinian people.

President Gaddafi was again conspicuous after the Geneva conference opened. He urged the Palestinian guerrillas and the Arab "revolutionary regimes" to launch a revolution in Egypt to stop President Sadat from making peace with Israel. He was also widely suspected of encouraging Syria's boycott of the conference (Syria being still nominally federated with Libya and Egypt) and of supporting fresh terrorist actions by the guerrillas, one of which led to the massacre of thirty-two airline passengers at Rome airport in mid-December.[17] Another of Gaddafi's surprising initiatives—but one unlikely to have much future—was the announcement in January 1974 of a union between Libya and Tunisia, a plan earlier rejected by President Bourguiba. As might have been expected, after the fiasco of the Libya-Egypt union and earlier attempts at formal Arab unification, this new move was coolly greeted in the Arab world. Moderate, luxury-loving Tunisia was in any case even more out of tune with Gaddafi's fundamentalism than Egypt. Soon afterwards Bourguiba had obviously been having second thoughts.[18]

Another consequence of the October War was Israel's increasing isolation in Africa, where she had made special efforts to gain friends by programmes of aid, training in Israel for Africans, and provision of Israeli experts for African countries. Conversely, Arab-Muslim influence had gained ground and, as we saw, the Organization of African Unity had supported the Arab posture, not only in regard to an economic embargo on Israel, but earlier by calling on the Israelis to give up their conquests of 1967. In 1972 and early 1973 seven African countries—Uganda, Chad, Niger, Mali, the

17. According to Christopher Dobson: "Arab Terror Gang Bungled Rome Mission" in the (London) *Sunday Telegraph* of December 23, 1973, the discovery of the gang's weapons by metal detectors and subsequent shooting seem to have panicked the terrorists into destroying a Pan-American Boeing 707, which they had really intended to hijack. Thirty-two of its passengers were thus burned to death.

On Colonel Gaddafi's eccentric courses, see Keesing's Contemporary Archives, p. 26176 and, e.g., Paul Martin: "Libya Calls for Revolt in Egypt to stop Peace Pact with Israel," in the (London) *Times* of December 29, 1973.

18. See John Bulloch, Beirut: "Arab World lukewarm to Libya-Tunisia link," in (London) *Daily Telegraph* of January 14, 1974; and "Shipwreck in Tunisia," in *Newsweek* of January 28, 1974.

(former French) Congo, Togo, and Burundi—had broken off diplomatic relations with Israel. Then in October 1973 sixteen others took the same step: Zaïre (the former Belgian Congo), Dahomey, Rwanda, Upper Volta, Cameroon, Equatorial Guinea, Tanzania, the Malagasy Republic (Madagascar), the Central African Republic, Ethiopia, Gambia, Nigeria, Zambia, Ghana, Senegal, and Sierra Leone. Indeed, after the October War the only members of the Organization of African Unity to retain diplomatic relations with Israel were Botswana, Lesotho, Malawi, Swaziland (all four more or less within the orbit of South Africa), and Mauritius, an island in the Indian Ocean. The Israeli Foreign Minister conceded that these were "heavy blows."[19]

Economic Repercussions: Oil

The decision of the Arab leaders, formally announced at Algiers, to use oil as a political weapon—and the way this was implemented during and after the October War—was to have not only political consequences but also a deeply disturbing economic impact on the rest of the world, particularly on the industrially advanced nations. Even before October these nations, with steeply rising fuel consumption, faced the prospect of an over-all oil shortage. At the same time it was often rashly assumed in the West that the Middle East producers for whom this was the major, and in some cases the only, source of wealth, had virtually no choice but to sell their oil at prices generally acceptable to their Western customers, on whom in any case they were largely dependent for aid and technology as well as for the manufactures and capital goods needed for development. Now, however, the October War spurred these Middle East producers to impose cutbacks in production and steep price rises, to which producers elsewhere had broadly to conform.

These moves seriously endangered the economic targets of the European nations and of Japan; and caused deep concern even to the United States, which, with substantial resources of its own, was

19. Keesing's Contemporary Archives, p. 26188.

far less dependent than Europe on Middle Eastern oil. Meanwhile, as a result of the war Israel was even more heavily dependent on the United States for funds than before. And yet one more consequence, among many, of the October conflict was that, through their price increases, the Arab oil-producing states managed to recoup themselves from the West, and especially from Europe, for much of the cash cost of their fight with Israel.

Since World War II, oil had been a factor in Middle Eastern nationalism. Some of the producing countries had increasingly exploited it to assert their independence of the West, whose alleged "economic imperialism" had replaced the basically colonial pattern of the past. As we saw from Chapter 14, in 1951 Iran had nationalized her oil industry in defiance of Britain; Iraq, too, went far along this path in later years. Following this general pattern, between December 1971 and September 1973 the Libyan Government had either nationalized completely, or had acquired a majority holding in, the foreign oil companies operating in Libya. These included British, Dutch, and Italian oil interests, but the main target was the United States. In mid-1973 the U.S. Government had become specially unpopular with the Arab majority members of the Organization of Petroleum Exporting Countries (OPEC) as the result of its veto of a U.N. Security Council resolution deploring Israel's continued occupation of her 1967 conquests despite Council Resolution No. 242. Indeed, Colonel Gaddafi had stridently voiced the hostility of the Arab extremists to American power, wealth, and sponsorship of Israel, and this became increasingly, with the October War, the political basis for Arab manipulation of oil resources to the detriment of the West.[20] Also before the October War,

20. For details of these Libyan moves, of the Western oil companies involved, and of the Libyan President's accusations of the United States, see Keesing's Contemporary Archives, pp. 26194–96. In particular Colonel Gaddafi said, "No power on earth can take away from us the right to nationalize our own oilfields. . . . The Americans think that they dominate the world with their fleets and military bases. . . . America continues to support Israel in order to humiliate the Arabs. American imperialism now takes the form of limitless aid to monopolistic oil companies." The OPEC has eleven full members, of whom seven are Arab (Abu Dhabi, Algeria, Iraq, Kuwait, Libya, Qatar, and Saudi Arabia), and four non-Arab (Indonesia, Iran, Nigeria, and Venezuela).

other producers—notably Kuwait, Abu Dhabi, and Nigeria—were seeking early or eventual majority participation in their national oil industries. Moreover, OPEC resolved in September that its members should negotiate substantial price increases, since existing prices were "no longer compatible with prevailing market conditions as well as galloping world inflation."[21]

The new war gave a sudden, explosive impetus to all these trends. On the day after its outbreak, Iraq took further nationalization measures, alleging that a blow must be struck at "American interests in the Arab nation so that Arab oil may be a weapon in our hands and not in the hands of imperialists and Zionists." Baghdad also called on Arab oil producers to ban exports to the United States. On October 17 the Organization of Arab Petroleum Exporting Countries (OAPEC)[22] met in Kuwait to draw up a common Arab oil policy, and resolved to reduce petroleum production by at least 5 per cent progressively each month, with effect from October, on the basis of the previous month's production. This was to be continued "until Israeli forces had withdrawn completely from the territories occupied in the June 1967 war and the legal rights of the Palestinians had been restored."

Most members of OAPEC took this step forthwith; some indeed cut back production by 10 instead of 5 per cent. They also implemented the ban on exports to the United States, as well as to the Netherlands because of manifest Dutch sympathy with Israel. Iraq had reservations, being against "indiscriminate" reduction. In Baghdad's view more drastic action was needed, but action directed specifically against those supporting Israeli; preferential treatment should be given to countries that backed the Arab cause. A further Arab meeting early in November decided that, in place of the additional 5 per cent cut due that month, there should be one of 25

21. *Ibid.*
22. Apart from the seven Arab members of OPEC, OAPEC included also Egypt, Syria, and Bahrain. It had formerly included Dubai, but when in June 1973 the Organization approved plans for building a dry dock for supertankers at Bahrain, Dubai withdrew, from pique (it seems) at not being allotted the site for this dry dock. The Organization had earlier decided to establish an Arab tanker fleet.

per cent of the September level of production, taking into account "the amount reduced as a result of not supplying America and the Dutch market with oil."

Later in November the Arab states resolved to go ahead with the next 5 per cent cut due in December, but to exempt from it all members of the European Community except the Netherlands in response to a statement by the Foreign Ministers of the Community on November 6 that broadly supported the Arab standpoint.[23] The Western countries and other hard-hit nations had small hope of filling from other sources the gaps thus created in their oil supplies. Iran, said the Shah, would not join in embargoes, but also would not increase production to take advantage of the shortages caused by the Arab cuts. Nigeria and Venezuela followed the same line; while Indonesia's production was largely committed to Japan.[24]

Hardly less serious than the reduction in supplies was the sharp increase in oil prices, by Arab and non-Arab producers, before, during, and after the October War. Indeed, OPEC members were allegedly responsible for raising the price of oil by some 370 per cent in 1973. All this was a double blow, not only at economic growth but, more cruelly, at the living standards of ordinary men in countries rich and poor, nearly all of which were forced to impose severe restrictions on the consumption of scarce fuel, with consequent dearth and cost inflation of a whole range of daily necessities.[25] Although strictly just a local war, the October conflict was truly one that shook the world.

23. The European Community is now the correct title of the three Communities that were merged in 1967, namely the European Economic Community (loosely known as the Common Market), the European Coal and Steel Community, and Euratom. The present nine members are France, West Germany, Italy, Belgium, the Netherlands, Luxemburg, the United Kingdom, Denmark, and Ireland, the last three having joined in 1973.

For the foregoing Arab oil moves see Keesing's Contemporary Archives, pp. 26224–25. According to Newsweek, January 21, 1974, Iraq and Libya, despite their formal acquiescence in the oil cutbacks decreed by OAPEC, went on producing flat out, where possible, to take advantage of the inflated prices.

24. Ibid., p. 26225.

25. Ibid., pp. 26225–28. For the increase in oil prices and their probable future consequences, see Newsweek, January 21, 1974, pp. 18–20.

The oil crisis was a paradox in other ways, for conservative Saudi Arabia, until then Washington's good friend, played the leading role. More important, for once Arab conservatives and radicals made common cause. Thus, in spite of all the rifts that still persist, some now believe that a new superpower may be emerging in the shape of a unified Arab nation, one ultimately able to defend itself and capable of projecting its power on a global basis. Meanwhile, for the West to try to unlock the Middle East oil resources by force, as has been suggested, and impose its will upon the Arab peoples, would be a hopeless task. For these peoples now know only too well how to resist by terrorism and sabotage as well as by regular warfare those whose intrusions they resent.[26]

A further paradox is that the cuts in Arab oil production were not, as they have sometimes been presented, a sacrifice for political reasons in the anti-Zionist cause. There was in fact little if any sacrifice involved, since the price increases of earlier years and 1973 amply made up for any potential loss in revenue to the oil-producing countries, which had been rapidly acquiring more money than they could usefully spend without boosting inflation to ever more unprofitable levels. Cuts and freezes in production had in fact been made by Libya and Kuwait in the years before the war for the sound economic purpose of preserving oil resources that must inevitably dwindle, their effect being masked by large increases in Saudi Arabian production. Further cuts would almost certainly have been needed by the end of 1973, especially in such countries as Saudi Arabia, even without the pretext of a war with Israel.

In any event, by early 1974 one final conclusion seemed to be emerging from the effective joint action over oil taken by the Arab producers around the time of the October War. This was the probable futility of the developing scramble by the advanced industrial countries to make separate deals with particular producers to ensure

26. See "Mideast: The New 'Superpower'" (letter to the *New York Times* of December 7, 1973, from T. A. Heppenheimer). This suggests that, should a powerful and united Arab nation emerge, Israel might still have an assured existence as a protected enclave, guaranteed by the United States, within the orbit of this Arab nation, on the analogy of enclaves such as West Berlin that already exist on a basis of international guarantees.

their own supplies; for this could only strengthen the bargaining position of the oil-rich states. On the other hand, the advanced countries are themselves in a position of considerable strength in their dealings with the oil producers. The vast wealth of these Middle Eastern states is held in a few Western currencies and cannot be taken out of the Western monetary system.

Moreover, these states depend for nearly all their essential non-military imports—and for many military ones as well—on the industrialized nations belonging to the Western-oriented Organization for Economic Cooperation and Development (OECD),[27] which affords them a potential framework for joint action. It follows that, if the oil needs of the advanced world are subjected to restrictive pressures by their Middle Eastern suppliers, the equally essential needs of these producing states could also, if necessary, be subject to scrutiny and restriction by the advanced countries, which are in effect their bankers and suppliers of sophisticated goods. Apart from sending arms, the Communist bloc is in no position to fill the gap, the Arab peoples being, as we saw, strongly hostile to any undue dependence on religion's most notorious foes. In Washington, as in the European capitals and other centres of the world's economic growth, it was becoming clear that the only effective response to the dictation of terms by oil producers in the Middle East would be for the major consumers themselves to show their strength by forming a united front.[28] This was one of the many problems receiving a new impulse from Henry Kissinger, America's dynamic new Secretary of State.[29]

27. The Organization for Economic Cooperation and Development started in 1961 as an extension and replacement of the Organization for European Economic Cooperation (OEEC), which had been the main instrument of the Marshall Plan for the recovery of Europe after World War II. Designed to embrace the advanced non-Communist nations outside Europe, OECD originally included the United States and Canada, and later Japan and Australia.
28. See in this connection the interesting article by Mr Shmuel Yaari, Director of the Israel School of Petroleum Studies in Tel Aviv: "Is Israel Irrelevant to Arab Oil Policy?" in the *New York Times* of December 9, 1973.
29. Henry Kissinger, born in Germany in 1923, came with his family to America at 15 in 1938 as refugees from Hitler Germany, and completed his educa-

The Wider International Dimension

In his pursuit of a Middle Eastern settlement Kissinger's chief goal was to get the adversaries round a conference table; and the Geneva conference was brought about only after several weeks of intense and urgent diplomatic activity in which he played the principal part. The aftermath of the war, and its implications, were, he found, unique. There had been more effective Arab coordination, and the Egyptians and Syrians had given a far better account of themselves, than ever before. Yet the military performance of the Israeli forces—considering their initial disadvantages and the strength of their adversaries—had been in some ways even more striking than that of 1967. On the other hand, the war's aftermath bore some resemblance to that of the Suez crisis in that the Arabs gained more internationally than they had on the field of battle. But what was, again, unique was that the consequences, as we saw from the oil crisis, were felt by nearly all the world instead of just by the countries immediately involved.

In his role as peacemaker in this Middle Eastern conflict Dr Kissinger—of German-Jewish antecedents—inevitably called in question Israel's claim to the special loyalty of Jews throughout the world.[30] For at a time of President Nixon's weakness of authority Kissinger had become the United States' leading policy-maker in international affairs and as such proved to be more truly "even-handed" in his dealings with the Arabs as well as with Israel than the President had ever been. He was made warmly welcome in Cairo—anxious as ever to elude too close an embrace of the Russian-Communist bear—and it was on him that President Sadat came

---

tion in the United States. He had a distinguished academic career at Harvard, eventually as Professor of Government. Appointed Special Assistant to President Nixon for National Security Affairs in 1969, he became in effect his adviser on foreign policy as well, and U.S. Secretary of State in succession to Mr Rogers in August 1973.

30. So in a sense did the part played by the (also Jewish) Austrian Chancellor, Dr Bruno Kreisky, in closing the transit camp at Schloss Schönau for Soviet Jews on their way to Israel, in response to Arab threats and pressure.

mainly to depend for the extraction of acceptable concessions from Israel. Gone were the days when Israel felt able to insist on settling her affairs with her neighbours without Great Power intervention.

At the same time, for the superpowers who had already taken the risk of re-stocking their clients with arms, the war had brought a more crucial test. Washington and Moscow clearly grasped the risk of a far wider conflict. Russia was almost certainly just as anxious as the United States to avoid a third world war. Yet the Kremlin seems at one point to have been tempted to apply its own form of brinkmanship in order to test the nerve and resolution of its principal rival for world power.

The United States Grapples with the Post-War Problems

On the day after the Arab attack, President Nixon called for a meeting of the U.N. Security Council. Two weeks later, on October 20–21, Dr Kissinger visited Moscow at Mr Brezhnev's invitation, and subsequently Tel Aviv. The upshot was the Security Council's Resolution No. 338 leading to the first cease-fire. This ordered all parties not only to stop fighting but also to start implementing the Council's resolution No. 242 of 1967 calling on Israel to withdraw from her conquests of that year. At a news conference on October 25, after the second cease-fire, Dr Kissinger mentioned the need for more external forces to stabilize the military situation now created, since it was clear that the ninety U.N. observers stationed along the Suez Canal before the war would no longer be adequate. Moreover, he said, U.S. forces had that morning been placed on precautionary alert throughout the world.

A Potential Confrontation with the Soviet Union?

The Secretary of State explained that President Sadat had asked the Soviet Union and the United States to send troops to ensure the observance of the cease-fire, but that Washington opposed this. There could be no question, he said, of transplanting this Great Power rivalry to the Middle East, or of the two superpowers' establishing a military condominium there. But it was equally important to avoid the unilateral introduction of military forces into the Middle East by any Great Power, and especially by any nuclear power. This problem was settled that same evening when the Security Council resolved to set up a U.N. Emergency Force to be drawn from member states other than the five permanent members of the Security Council. Two days later the Council approved a plan of Dr Waldheim for a U.N. Force of 7,000 to serve in the Middle East, initially for six months. Its main task would be to supervise a full cease-fire on the Suez Canal and to ensure a return to the positions held by both sides on October 22.

Meanwhile, the long-established U.N. Truce Supervision Organization (UNTSO) would continue to operate here and elsewhere, including the Syrian front, where there would be no special peacekeeping force. Although they would not be sending troops, the Soviet Union and the United States offered to contribute thirty-six observers each to UNTSO, this being the size of the largest existing national contingent in the observer group.[31]

On October 26 President Nixon and the U.S. Defense Secretary, Dr James Schlesinger, announced that the specific reasons for the U.S. alert had been the Soviet alert to their paratroops in Eastern Europe, the doubling in size of the Soviet fleet in the Mediterranean, and the apparent preparation of large Soviet aircraft for the transport of troops. Its purpose had been to indicate to Moscow that any such unilateral move of Soviet forces to the Middle East was unacceptable to the United States. The point was promptly taken by Moscow; Mr Brezhnev at once criticized the "fantastic rumours" about the intentions of the Soviet Union, which he implied was firmly wedded, in accordance with U.N. resolutions, to a policy of peace in the Middle East.[32]

The Diplomatic Chessboard

In November and December 1973 and January 1974 Dr Kissinger was more indefatigable than ever in the search for peace in the

31. Keesing's Contemporary Archives, pp. 26197–202.
32. *Ibid.*, pp. 26200–201.

Middle East and elsewhere. It is, however, beyond our scope to assess here the style and general achievement of this remarkable man during his five years at President Nixon's side.[33] On November 5 he embarked on a world-wide diplomatic mission, starting with Morocco, Tunisia, Egypt, Jordan, and Saudi Arabia, but also embracing Iran, Pakistan, China, and Japan. In Egypt he paved the way for the restoration of diplomatic relations with Washington, severed since the Six Day War; and negotiated the cease-fire agreement on the Egyptian front signed on November 11. His proposals had been conveyed to Israel by Mr Joseph Sisco—the U.S. Assistant Secretary of State who accompanied the Kissinger mission—and accepted by the Israeli Government. By now President Sadat had publicly indicated his willingness to take part in an international conference with the Israelis.

The Arab leaders, and those of Israel, were no less active in pursuing in other quarters their own vision of a satisfactory Middle East settlement. Within the Arab world (independently of the summit conference at Algiers) visits were exchanged between the rulers of Egypt, Syria, Kuwait, Saudi Arabia, Algeria, Jordan, Bahrain, Oman, Qatar, and the United Arab Emirates. As for the Western world, Washington was visited by Mrs Meir; Paris, London, and Washington, by the Egyptian Foreign Minister; and Israel sent Mr Eban to Bucharest for talks with the Roumanian leaders. Since Roumania was the only Communist country to retain

33. It is also invidious to select from all that has been written on Henry Kissinger in the United States and other countries. Two excellent articles by Michael Davie may, however, perhaps be mentioned: "The Peace Doctor" and "The Kissinger Doctrine," in the (London) *Observer* of November 11 and 18. There is also in the (London) *History Today* for January 1974 an interesting review of Kissinger's (1957) study of Metternich: *A World Restored; Europe after Napoleon* (Magnolia, Mass.: Peter Smith). This points out that, when historians start making history, their works throw light upon themselves. It then stresses Kissinger's special interest (in the Metternich tradition) in equilibrium—that is, in a general equilibrium that makes it risky for one power or group of powers to try to impose their will on the remainder; and a particular equilibrium defining the historical relation of certain powers among each other. The review suggests that he has striven for both, in their appropriate context, in the Middle East as in Southeast Asia.

diplomatic relations with both Israel and the Arab states, she had obvious potential value as an intermediary between the disputants.

So far as the Middle East is concerned, the climax to Dr Kissinger's diplomatic activities came, as we saw, with the opening of the Geneva conference in December. This, however, merely created the traditional framework of international negotiation within which a binding treaty settlement of the Arab-Israeli conflict might perhaps one day be reached. For the present this seemed likely to be achieved only between Egypt and Israel—and even this was far from certain. Yet for the first time since the creation of Israel, representatives of these two enemy countries were dealing directly and publicly with one another across a conference table in formal and dignified debate. The hope was that, if their deliberations were successful, a pattern might be set which could inspire and pave the way for comparable settlements between Israel and her other Arab neighbours. Of course the most vital points at issue would still have to be thrashed out not at Geneva but at or near the scene of recent action, and in the Egyptian and Israeli capitals. By mid-January 1974, direct talks on the Suez front were still limited to arguments between the military at the point of contact of their forces, arguments embittered by breaches of the cease-fire—some, it seems, deliberate on Egypt's part.

Meanwhile the real focus of negotiation on the key issues was the still untiring Henry Kissinger, flying repeatedly between Cairo and Tel Aviv, urging, proposing, persuading, and eventually succeeding in bringing the two foes to terms over the first stage in the mutual disengagement of their forces. Such was the background of the Israeli-Egyptian agreement signed on January 18, 1974, under the auspices of the U.N. Emergency Force Commander, at kilometre 101 on the Cairo-Suez road.[34]

34. Dr Kissinger's high-speed diplomacy was not of course to everyone's taste. In Israel's anxious mood some there called him "Hustling Harry." He knew, however, how vital speed was. Despite the style imposed by the fantastic speed of modern communication, it would perhaps be fairer to value his achievement in the traditional nineteenth-century terms he understands so well. Indeed, in this instance his role was essentially that of "honest broker," the title claimed

Egyptian-Israeli Disengagement

The published agreement was in general terms, much remaining
confidential. Authoritative statements, e.g., by General Dayan and
the Egyptian leaders, have, however, indicated some vital details
not included in the text. It was soon clear that one Israeli concession was the absence of any statement formally terminating belligerency between Egypt and Israel. Earlier Israel had insisted that
there would be no withdrawal without this. Nevertheless the
agreement did state, not only that the cease-fire would be scrupulously observed, but that both sides would refrain in future from
all military or para-military actions against each other, this being
generally interpreted as committing the Egyptians to stopping
terrorist attacks against Israel from Egyptian territory.

On the other hand, Cairo had also made an important concession, for previously Egypt had insisted that no partial agreement
would be made with Israel unless the Israelis first undertook to
evacuate all the territory taken in 1967. This point was skated
over in the final clause of the pact, which stipulated that it was
not a final peace agreement, merely a first step towards a final, just,
and durable peace in accordance with Security Council Resolution
No. 338 (establishing the first cease-fire, of October 22, and calling for the implementation of Resolution 242 inviting Israel to
withdraw from her conquests of 1967) and within the framework
of the Geneva conference.

The key parts of the agreement were, however, clauses B and
C. Clause B provided for the separation of the military forces of
Israel and Egypt by a "zone of disengagement" policed by the
U.N. Emergency Force. The agreement then referred to lines on
maps, the purport of which was that, once the Israeli forces had
withdrawn from their bridgehead on the west bank of the Suez

---

and deserved by Bismarck as chairman of the Berlin conference of 1878 (see
Chapter 6), which also settled an explosive situation on the fringes of the
Middle East—that one arising out of Russia's disastrous defeat of Turkey in
that year.

Canal, an eighteen-mile strip east of the Canal would be established, sliced into three approximately equal bands to be manned respectively by Egyptian, United Nations, and Israeli troops. The U.N. zone of disengagement was to be pinched to about half its width at the point where it cuts the road eastwards from Ismailiya, thus leaving the Israelis in control of the important El Tasa crossroads on the way to their military and air force base at Bir Gifgafa in central Sinai.

As we saw, the U.N. Emergency Force was to be about 7,000 men. This would also be the approximate size of the Egyptian and Israeli forces permitted under the agreement in their zones to the west and east of the central U.N. disengagement zone. In military terms the Egyptians and Israelis could each have eight battalions—seven infantry and one armoured—in their zones; with about thirty tanks and six artillery batteries in each force. The artillery would thus have some thirty-six big guns, but with an agreed limit of around four miles range. No missiles would be allowed up to nineteen miles west of the Canal for the Egyptians and up to nineteen miles east of the Mitla Pass for the Israelis. These limitations would be inspected by the U.N. Emergency Force on the ground and in the air, with the attachment to the Force of Egyptian and Israeli officers. The air forces of both countries would have the right to operate up to their respective lines without interference from the other side.[35]

The stages of withdrawal and its detailed implementation would be settled by military representatives of both sides within five days, and actual disengagement would start two days later—i.e., within a week of the signature of the agreement. After this, disengagement would be completed within forty days. The Israeli

35. The general terms of the agreement are taken from the (London) *Times* of January 19, 1974; the additional details given above regarding the size of the zones, the actual limitation of forces, etc., from statements by General Dayan and other Israeli military sources quoted by Eric Silver, Jerusalem, in the (London) *Observer* of January 20. The particulars regarding missiles are from a report by Guy Rais in Tel Aviv on General Dayan's announcements, in the (London) *Daily Telegraph* of January 19.

withdrawal in fact started on January 23, the agreement having been approved by the Knesset the previous day after a stormy debate lasting seven hours, only the Likud voting against the Government.

There were good reasons for this acceptance. The Israeli army was left with a good defence line, one that Dayan regarded as stronger than the Suez Canal. On the one hand, Israeli forces were left in control of the narrow Mitla and Giddi passes through the first range of hills in Sinai, and would be able to keep as heavy a concentration of forces as they wished on the western slopes of these hills. And farther north, between the hills and the sea, the Israelis could operate if necessary in open tank country ideally suited to their style of swift, flexible, armoured warfare. Meanwhile, for both sides UNEF would provide a valuable trip wire against surprise attack.[36] It seems also that for the present the Israelis will be able to keep their heavy weapons some eight miles west of the passes on a line from Balouza on the Mediterranean to the Gulf of Suez, and to retain the Egyptian oilfields at Abu Rodeis as well as the strategic point of Sharm el Sheikh, ensuring their control of the Strait of Tiran. At the same time the Egyptian heavy artillery will be pulled back to some ten miles west of the Canal. A point in the agreement not publicly revealed is understood to be a guarantee of freedom of navigation for Israeli shipping through the Strait of Bab el Mandeb at the southern end of the Red Sea.[37]

The Future of the Suez Canal

The reopening of the Suez Canal was not mentioned in the agreement. President Sadat seems to have told Dr Kissinger that repair work could go ahead, but that navigation would not be resumed until a definitive peace settlement was achieved. Meanwhile, shipping experts reckon that the Canal could be reopened with its

36. Eric Silver, *op. cit.*
37. *Daily Telegraph* (London), January 19, 1974.

present limited depth and size within six to eight months. But these permit it to take ships of only 38 feet draught, while the giant supertankers increasingly used for oil have a draught of at least 65 feet, and before the Canal's closure in 1967, some were already using the route around South Africa's Cape of Good Hope. So there are plans for deepening, widening, and straightening the channel; but this would take eighteen months to complete if the waterway remains temporarily free of shipping, and several years if it is used by ships while the alterations are being made. Foreign firms are, it seems, bidding for the clearance contract, which would have to cover the removal of the wrecks blocking the channel and of fourteen ships stranded in it when the Canal was closed. Unofficial reports state that Washington has promised Egypt massive aid to restore the Canal; in return Egypt will let Israeli cargoes through it, so long as they are carried in foreign ships.[38]

Can There Be a General Arab-Israeli Peace?

In making a separate Egyptian-Israeli pact in advance of any corresponding deal between Syria and Israel, President Sadat had chosen a "lonely and potentially perilous path."[39] He risked being pilloried as a traitor to both Arab solidarity and to the Palestinian cause. Indeed, even though Arafat was present at the signing ceremony, the compromise over disengagement split the Palestine Liberation Organization wide open. In defiance of their leader, the wilder elements in the Organization rejected the pact—as did the Popular Front for the Liberation of Palestine and other extremist

38. See Robert Bedlow, Shipping Correspondent: "Suez Canal Reopening Could Start 'In Weeks,'" in the (London) *Daily Telegraph* of January 19, 1974; Eric Silver, Jerusalem: "Canal will be Open to Israeli Goods," in the (London) *Observer* of January 20; and John de St Jorre, Cairo: "The Great Suez Renaissance," in the *Observer* of February 3. Of the three firms reported to be bidding for the Canal clearance contract, one is American, one West German, and one Yugoslav.

39. St. Jorre, *op. cit.*

groups—and were in turn condemned by Arafat. Nevertheless, Egypt's President remained determined that the Palestinians should be represented at Geneva; and this could hardly be unless and until the main groups came around to backing Arafat in accepting the pact. Sadat was equally determined that there must also be a disengagement agreement with Syria before any resumption of the Geneva talks.[40]

In early February, despite visits to Damascus by Dr Kissinger and his hint of "constructive proposals" on disengagement from President Assad, Syria was still sulky and intransigent, having talked at one moment of breaking off diplomatic relations with Egypt; and Iraq, hostile to Egypt's move, was even asked by Assad to send some troops back to Syria. Thus, at a time when Sadat had become the advocate of United States policies of compromise, and favoured a relaxation of the oil embargo in recognition of Washington's role in securing concessions from Israel, he faced widespread opposition not only in the Fertile Crescent but also in other parts of the Arab world, such as Libya—his nominal associate—and Kuwait, a strong champion of the oil weapon, with a population two-thirds Palestinian.

For her part, Jordan was concerned chiefly with the liberation of the West Bank and East Jerusalem; and King Faisal of Saudi Arabia, with being able to pray as of old in the Dome of the Rock. King Hussein discussed his plans for the West Bank when Dr Kissinger visited Jordan, and Israel's response to them seems to have been conveyed to the King by President Ceausescu of Roumania during a visit he paid to Damascus and Amman in February, in the footsteps of President Tito of Yugoslavia. It appeared, however, as though Israeli annexation of the Old City of Jerusalem might prove to be the hardest barrier of all to a general settlement between Israel and the Arab states. As for the Yugoslavian connection, the main purpose of the visit to Damascus by the two East European leaders was evidently, with Moscow's encouragement, to add Communist bloc pressure to that of the United

40. *Daily Telegraph*, January 22 and 24, 1974.

States in the hope of persuading Syria to compromise with Israel over disengagement as Egypt had done. It seemed a hopeful sign that the two superpowers were acting in unison over the next move.[41]

With all the risks involved, why have Egypt, under the normally cautious Sadat, and Israel, with Dayan still prominent at the controls, been so swift and resolute in adjusting their relations, with Washington's help and Russia's acquiescence? The apparent reason is that, quite independently of tension and hostility elsewhere, Egypt and Israel stand to gain substantially from making peace between themselves. For most Egyptians Palestine is a long way off; and Egypt's traditional patriotism has been that of the Nile Valley. It is clear now that Sadat never fully shared Nasser's Pan-Arab ideals, which brought Egypt so much loss and suffering in the name of liberating Palestine from Jewish occupation. Now that he has largely expunged the shameful memory of 1967, Sadat seems determined to grasp this chance of extricating the Nile Valley as far as possible from the ruinous penalties of further Arab-Israeli wars; and to rely on negotiation and the pressure of the superpowers to achieve what is still needed for Egypt, for the other Arab states at war with Israel, and for the Palestinians themselves.

First and foremost he means to rebuild and restore his country, starting with the Suez Canal and the ruined cities along its banks. Freed from further wars, and with the hope of funds from conservative Saudi Arabia, from Kuwait (both of whom he has

41. According to John Bulloch, Beirut: "Tito Starts Communist Peace Drive in Syria," in the (London) *Daily Telegraph* of February 6, 1974, King Hussein's plan for the West Bank was that Israeli forces would withdraw to the hills overlooking the River Jordan while maintaining check points at the river bridges; Jordanian forces would also withdraw, leaving check points; and U.N. troops would patrol both sides of the river. The West Bank would be returned to Jordanian civil administration, but corridors would be established from Israel within her new borders to the main Israeli settlements near the river. In return, Israel would agree to Palestinian representation at the Geneva conference, so long as this was confined to the relatively moderate Palestine Liberation Organization.

just approached), and from Suez tolls, Egypt can regain her prosperity, and her people the chance of higher living standards of which they were cheated for so long, mainly by the bitter feud with Israel. His new course also promises a long-desired gain in independence from his Communist patrons.

For the Israelis, peace with Egypt may be an even greater prize and one well worth pursuing despite the present dubious chances of stable and permanent peace with Syria, or even with Jordan so long as the tangled fate of the West Bank, Gaza, Old Jerusalem, and the Palestinians, remains in the balance. The Egyptian regime is far more secure and widely accepted than those in Damascus and Amman, and internal factors in Egypt should strengthen rather than weaken the prospects of peace. In Syria and Jordan there is always the risk that those favouring peace with Israel might suddenly be overthrown by fanatical advocates of a harder line. Nevertheless, were it not for political instability, the chances for Syrian-Israeli disengagement might be relatively good. Though much was destroyed in the war, Syria has a well-balanced and resilient economy and, like the Egyptians, her people have a real desire for peace. Unlike the Egyptians, however, there are not too many of them. The 6.7 million Syrians have land and water enough to feed themselves and export agricultural produce; and this capacity should be doubled from the end of 1974 when the Euphrates Dam (built after 1968 with Russian aid) is due to be completed.[42]

Against this, Syria since independence has been a land of tension and repeated revolutions. The regime, based on the Ba'ath

---

42. The Euphrates Dam is also supposed to quadruple Syria's electrical output. This should permit considerable industrial expansion in a country that already has an encouraging light-industrial base. (In Egypt, on the other hand, the population explosion largely nullified the benefits expected from the Aswan High Dam.) In Damascus in early 1974 there was something of a thaw towards the West, and the Government has liberalized the economic system so as to attract foreign investment as well as exiled Syrian capital. See Michael Field: "Syria Still Stands Firm," in the (London) *Daily Telegraph* of February 7, 1974.

party and the army, seeks to combine Marxist Socialism with strong Arab nationalism; and only now is the fact of Israel starting to be accepted as a disagreeable necessity. At the same time, the extensive reliance of the country on the Communist bloc in recent years is checked by the strong Islamic loyalties of the mass of the people. President Assad is something of a pragmatist, and his (reported) "constructive proposals" to Dr Kissinger are not unreasonable.[43] It is thus unfortunate that his position is potentially weakened by his being an Alawi who has placed his fellow Alawis in key government positions and thus fired the resentment of the Sunni Muslim majority of 70 per cent in the country.[44]

The Israelis reckon that these new Arab divergencies will play into their hands. For they can hope in future to deal with the other Arab states through and with the help of Cairo as well as of Washington. Meanwhile, given Sadat's policy, some stable adjustment of Israel's relations with Egypt should not be insuperably hard. Save for some oil, and Sharm el-Sheikh, Sinai has little value for Israel once her security is assured by the arrangements just concluded and—if and when she is forced into further withdrawals —by some future demilitarization of the rest of Sinai under U.N. supervision. At the same time, the Israelis will do all they can to

43. *Ibid.* According to Michael Field, the Assad proposals would require the Israeli troops to leave the pocket of Syrian territory conquered in October 1974, and be replaced there by a mutually agreed number of Syrians. The Israelis would then have to abandon all the Golan region except the 2½-mile strip of the Heights bordering Israel. U.N. forces would then move into this area, which would be demilitarized but returned to Syrian civil administration. The 20,000-odd Syrians who fled from the war zone in October would then be permitted to return home. In exchange, Syria would deliver the list of Israeli prisoners now held (believed to be about a hundred) and take her seat at the Geneva conference.

For the complex story of the Ba'ath party's fortunes and activities in Syria and Iraq, and also to some extent in Lebanon and Jordan, see "Middle East Survey," pp. 83–90.

44. The Alawis live in the northern highlands of Syria and form only 10 per cent of the population. In religion they are an offshoot of the Shi'is but "carry the Shi'i tendency to its ultimate extreme and believe that Ali was an incarnation of God." "Middle East Survey," p. 35.

keep Sharm el-Sheikh, at least until they feel reasonably sure about Egypt's intentions. They realize that a watch on the Strait of Tiran cannot by itself ensure the free passage of Israeli ships to and from Elat, since this can be blocked farther south in the Bab el Mandeb Strait. But they seem to think that an Israeli presence at Sharm el-Sheikh will help to guarantee good relations with Egypt since it would enable them to blockade a reopened Suez Canal,[45] should Cairo default on its obligations.

The Holy Land and the Aftermath of the October War

The October War may have greatly strengthened the prospects for peace in the Middle East. By February 1974, it looked as though the Egypt-Israel disengagement agreement could be a vital and genuine step towards ending the long and deadly Arab-Israeli strife, towards the eventual if reluctant acceptance by the states of the Fertile Crescent as well as by Egypt, and by Arabs generally, of Israel in their midst. Of the implied conditions for this acceptance, one has already been fulfilled. This is the abandonment by Tel Aviv of the dreams of some Israeli leaders after 1967 of Israel's becoming the dominant power in the Middle East.[46]

The other conditions—hard though not insoluble—have still to be tackled, it is hoped in an enlarged Geneva conference if the present Kissinger-Sadat-Dayan trend towards peace can be kept moving. One condition is of course some just and generous settlement of the rights of the Palestinians—both those who have been displaced and those living on the West Bank and in Gaza under Israeli rule. Another is the relinquishment by Israel of most of her conquests of 1967, subject to really effective international guarantees of her security, and formal acceptance by her Arab neighbours

45. See *Daily Telegraph* special article of January 31, 1973: "Why General Dayan Counts on Egypt; Israel Takes Risks for a Separate Peace."

46. "The October war stripped Israel of its confident assumptions . . . when Israeli military superiority was a safe long-term assumption." *Daily Telegraph* special article of January 31, 1974 (see n. 45).

of the new Israeli frontiers, wherever they may finally be fixed. This in turn will require some adjustment of the status of Jerusalem —whether by internationalization or otherwise—so that Muslims and Christians will once more have access as of right to the Holy Places on the same footing as those of Jewish faith.[47]

Thus the Great Powers will once again, as throughout history, have the final voice in determining the fate of the Holy Land. This time, however, any intervention on their part will have to be acceptable, not only to a still militarily imposing, dynamic, and progressive Israel, but to the key leaders of what may be a newly emerging major power, the Arab nation. For such is the name in which the often discordant peoples of the Arab world take pride, not just on the strength of a splendid but distant past, but of a newly discovered capacity for military achievement and economic leverage based on their ownership of so large a share of the oil resources vital to the world's economic development.[48]

At this juncture can Sadat, having taken the first bold step, keep up the momentum of the drive he has launched, with Washington's and Israel's support, to bring about a more general settlement of the Arab-Israeli conflict? Failing this, his own standing with his fellow Arabs, with Israel, with the Soviet Union, and with the West, must suffer. Yet he can keep things moving only if he can persuade President Assad of Syria—with a domestic base far weaker than his own—to take the risk of implementing disengagement with Israel along some such lines as those discussed with Kissinger in Damascus; and this is not yet sure. Accordingly, one of the chief goals of a mid-February conference of key Arab leaders in Algiers was, it seems, to convince Syria that she can count on Egypt in her new-found military strength, and on Saudi Arabia, leader of the oil-producers' bloc; and thus to encourage her to face

47. There may possibly be encouragement and inspiration in the solution in 1929 of what seemed an equally insoluble problem—that of the rights of the Holy See in Rome and the former Papal States—by the creation of the independent state of Vatican City.

48. See "Arab Pride and Power," in *Newsweek* of February 18, 1974, pp. 12–18.

a deal with Israel. The Egyptian and Saudi Foreign Ministers were then despatched to Washington for talks with Dr Kissinger in the (reported) hope of reaching a compromise agreement on future oil supplies and of inducing Israel, through him, to withdraw from her recent new conquests in Syria and from nearly all of the Golan Heights.[49]

There is small hope of any resumption of the Geneva conference unless and until Syrian-Israeli disengagement is achieved. If it is not or if, once agreed, the scheme breaks down through some new Syrian revolution, some fresh reversion to bitter intransigence towards Israel, Sadat will be tempted to seek Egypt's interests first. He may then abruptly renounce his efforts for a united Arab front in dealing with Israel and pursue the obvious mutual advantages of peace between Israel and Egypt. Whatever the delays and setbacks elsewhere, a stable understanding based on self-interest linking these two ancient lands could be the creative first step towards comparable adjustments between Israel and her other neighbours.

Nevertheless, the road to a general peace will still be long and hard. Despite public intransigence, Israel and Syria may yet agree on troop disengagement and a new regime for the Golan Heights. Syria and Egypt may then give first importance to their own affairs, to regaining their lost territory and repairing the damage of the years of strife. Yet no Arab state—and certainly not Jordan, the most vitally concerned of all—will be able to evade the pledges

49. The meeting was held in Algiers rather than in Cairo as originally planned, on the insistence of President Boumedienne of Algeria, who has assumed some weight in Arab councils. Also present were King Faisal of Saudi Arabia and Presidents Assad and Sadat. Colonel Gaddafi was significantly absent. See John Bulloch, Cairo: "Can Egypt build on her Success?" and Harold Sieve, Algiers: "Arabs keep up Oil Embargo but send Envoys to U.S." (*Daily Telegraph*, February 14 and 15, 1974).

The visit of the Egyptian and Saudi Arabian Foreign Ministers to Washington came just after the Washington Energy Conference of thirteen major oil-consuming nations. Over French objections, this achieved a qualified success in setting up machinery for coordinated action and plans for later meetings with the oil-producing states and the underdeveloped countries.

repeatedly and solemnly given to the Palestinians to uphold their rights. Should these be abandoned, the Palestinian terrorists would at once seek retribution, with aid from the more fanatical Arab chiefs, from those they considered had betrayed them. Far more valid is a traditionalist Arab attitude that regards the fate of the Palestinians, and of Jerusalem, as a matter of honour on which there can be no dispute. Such is the outlook of leaders like King Faisal of Saudi Arabia, who holds the oil weapon in his hands. And these are factors that Mrs Meir, however much she may question the legitimacy of the Palestinians' case, and even their identity as a people, will not be able to ignore.

Meanwhile the Palestinians themselves are perforce bitterly divided. For the acceptance of Israel even by their Arab supporters is coming to be an accomplished fact; and the most they can hope for is a miniature Palestinian state based on the West Bank and the Gaza Strip, internationally recognized and free from Jordanian or Egyptian rule. The moderates, including Arafat, would now be prepared reluctantly to accept this compromise, subject to safeguards for the Arabs in Israel and for those who might wish to return to their former areas and live under Israeli rule. Yet this compromise, which might give them back one-fifth of former Palestine, would consecrate the defeat of their cause—i.e., what they see as their right to recover the whole of the land taken from them by the Zionist movement and the pro-Zionist policies of the Western powers. Here as in all aspects of the Arab-Israeli conflict the moderates will be hard put to it to bring the extremists into line.[50]

In early March the prospects of securing Syrian-Israeli disengagement were evenly balanced. Syria had rejected Israel's offer to

50. See "Why the Arabs rallied to the Cause of Palestine" and "Why PLO will not settle for Half-Measures" by Edward Mortimer, in the (London) *Times* of January 29 and 30, 1974. See also "A Palestinian State must be Created," in *Newsweek*, February 25, 1974, p. 18. This last article quotes an interview with the new editor of the semi-official Cairo newspaper *Al Ahram*, who claims that "the establishment of a country the Palestinians can call their own will mean, finally, that the Arab countries and Israel can bury their differences."

withdraw only from her conquests of 1973, and insisted that there must also be withdrawal on the Golan Heights. On the other hand, Damascus had produced counter-proposals and made it plain that disengagement negotiations would continue. Moreover, Dr Kissinger had at last been able to bring to Israel a list of sixty-five Israeli prisoners of war held by Syria, and permission for the Red Cross to visit them. The Israelis were, however, gravely disturbed over the fate of many others who may have lost their lives. Talks on the Syrian-Israeli issue were to be resumed in Washington towards the end of March.

Meanwhile, under the disengagement agreement with Egypt, Israeli withdrawal to the Sinai passes was punctually completed. Although the pact enshrining this retreat had been presented to the Knesset by a caretaker government, it was, as we saw, promptly accepted. Predictably, the further withdrawals Egypt will be bound to require from Israel will have a far rougher passage. Nevertheless, they are likely to be carried through in the long run for the sake of the prize that peace with Egypt can mean for an Israel still perhaps beleaguered on her other flanks. Again, in early March Dr Kissinger reportedly discussed with King Hussein in Amman the Palestinians' future and Jordan's own problem of disengagement with Israel. Yet among Israelis any proposal to give up the West Bank, as a step toward adjusting relations with Jordan and the Palestinians, is sure to kindle further acute controversy, stirred up by the traditionalists and extreme right wing. For the land of ancient Judah is far more precious than all of Sinai to those who dwell on the past.[51]

Israel has also been deeply worried by Moscow's recent determination to reassert itself in the area by sending the Soviet Foreign Minister, Andrei Gromyko, in Kissinger's footsteps to Damascus and Cairo; and especially by a joint Syrian-Soviet warning issued on March 7 that there was danger of a new explosion in the Middle East unless Israel withdrew from all her conquests of 1967.

51. "To the religious and chauvinistic . . . the West Bank is integral to the historic 'Land of Israel.'" Eric Silver, "Road to Peace grows harder for Israel," in the (London) Observer of March 2, 1974.

There was fear that this kind of sabre-rattling might imperil the careful advances towards peace that Kissinger was contriving to achieve. In fact the Soviet Union, having gained little enough from the Arab-Israeli wars, does not seem to have abandoned its new goal of limited superpower cooperation to bring peace to the Middle East. It has been chiefly concerned over the decline of Russian influence in countries such as Egypt and Syria—due to the clumsy high-handedness of Kremlin dealings and general Arab rejection of the Communist creed—and the marked growth in the influence of the United States. In Egypt, after all, Sadat's plans for rebuilding his country have assumed a distinctly capitalistic tinge. With the new trends in the Middle East the Russians, it may be guessed, are just determined not to be left out.

With many dark clouds still on the horizon, it is fortunate for Israel that, nine frustrating weeks after the elections at the end of 1973, Mrs Meir was at last able to form a government with a small but assured majority. This was another coalition of the Labour Alignment with Religious and Independent Liberal elements of the kind somewhat wearisomely familiar since the birth of Israel. Indeed many, especially younger, Israelis would like to revise the present electoral system that produces a kaleidoscope of parties through proportional representation. They see this as a bar to badly needed fundamental reforms, and favour a partial change to majority voting by districts as in most Western countries. Nevertheless, with the support of the now controversial but still powerful General Dayan, who had at one moment threatened to withdraw, of four other former generals, most of the National Religious Party, and the moderately conservative Independent Liberals, the new cabinet is probably the best that could be devised under the existing system and, it seems, the one best fitted to keep the wilder elements at bay.[52]

52. See pages 433, 475, and 520. Apart from the Labour Alignment, embracing the combined Labour Party and Mapam, the new cabinet is to contain four Ministers from the National Religious Party (against three in Mrs Meir's former government) and two from the Independent Liberals (against one). General Dayan remains as Minister for Defence; General Yitzhak Rabin, Chief of Staff during the Six Day War, enters the cabinet as Minister for Labour. Formation of

Israel has at the moment new prospects of peaceful acceptance in her Middle Eastern setting and of creative coexistence with some—perhaps one day all—of her Arab neighbours. Only now more than ever she needs outstanding and nationally accepted leadership to steer her through the phase of limitation and partial renunciation on which she has been forced to embark. With all his rough edges and eccentricities, Ben Gurion was a great leader during the years of strife when the National Home and eventually the state of Israel were thrust upon a hostile Palestine and finally displaced or subjected most of its people; but he died at 87 on December 1, 1973. To some extent his father figure has been replaced by Golda Meir, but at 75 she is nearing the end of her time. It is hard to be nationally accepted in so deeply diversified, so fiercely individualistic, a society as that of Israel. Perhaps fortunately Mr Begin and General Sharon are not; General Dayan no longer is; and there is no other truly national figure immediately in sight. A shift of power may well be at hand from the entrenched East European Old Guard to younger, more tolerant and flexible leaders reflecting the ethnic composition of Israel today, with its Oriental majority, and the new realities of Arab power. These must be leaders consciously and generously seeking not dominance but conciliation and understanding in their relations with the peoples surrounding them in this unique corner of the Orient that has absorbed and bequeathed so much—and especially with those who have been injured by the rise of Israel. Whence such leaders will come and who they will be is still unknown. That they will emerge, however, must be an act of faith for all who have witnessed through the centuries how the descendants of the children of Israel have suffered, recovered, created, and survived.

---

a government was held up by hair-splitting controversies provoked by the religious parties over the exact definition of a Jew, and by right-wing pressure to form a government of national unity (as had been done in 1969) by the inclusion of the Likud extremists. Mrs Meir judged—almost certainly correctly—that the inclusion of such hard-line elements as Mr Begin would endanger the prospects of the policy now pursued by Israel, with Washington's and Cairo's support, of peace with her Arab neighbours.

Appendix

Mandate for Palestine, together with a Note by the Secretary-General relating to its application to the Territory known as Transjordan, under the provisions of Article 25.

The Council of the League of Nations:

Whereas the Principal Allied Powers have agreed, for the purpose of giving effect to the provisions of Article 22 of the Covenant of the League of Nations, to entrust to a Mandatory selected by the said Powers the administration of the territory of Palestine, which formerly belonged to the Turkish Empire, within such boundaries as may be fixed by them; and

Whereas the Principal Allied Powers have also agreed that the Mandatory should be responsible for putting into effect the declaration originally made on November 2nd, 1917, by the Government of His Britannic Majesty, and adopted by the said Powers, in favour of the establishment in Palestine of a national home for the Jewish people, it being clearly understood that nothing should be done which might prejudice the civil and religious rights of existing non-Jewish communities in Palestine, or the rights and political status enjoyed by Jews in any other country; and

Whereas recognition has thereby been given to the historical connection of the Jewish people with Palestine and to the grounds for reconstituting their national home in that country; and

Whereas the Principal Allied Powers have selected His Britannic Majesty as the Mandatory for Palestine; and

Whereas the mandate in respect of Palestine has been formulated in the following terms and submitted to the Council of the League for approval; and

Whereas His Britannic Majesty has accepted the mandate in respect of Palestine and undertaken to exercise it on behalf of the League of Nations in conformity with the following provisions; and

Whereas by the afore-mentioned Article 22 (paragraph 8), it is provided that the degree of authority, control or administration to be exercised by the Mandatory, not having been previously agreed upon by the Members of the League, shall be explicitly defined by the Council of the League of Nations;

Confirming the said mandate, defines its terms as follows:

Article 1
The Mandatory shall have full powers of legislation and of administration, save as they may be limited by the terms of this mandate.

Article 2
The Mandatory shall be responsible for placing the country under such political, administrative and economic conditions as will secure the establishment of the Jewish national home, as laid down in the preamble, and the development of self-governing institutions, and also for safeguarding the civil and religious rights of all the inhabitants of Palestine, irrespective of race and religion.

Article 3
The Mandatory shall, so far as circumstances permit, encourage local autonomy.

Article 4
An appropriate Jewish agency shall be recognised as a public body for the purpose of advising and co-operating with the Administration of Palestine in such economic, social and other matters as may affect the establishment of the Jewish national home and the interests of the Jewish population in Palestine, and, subject always to the control of the Administration, to assist and take part in the development of the country.

The Zionist organisation, so long as its organisation and constitution are in the opinion of the Mandatory appropriate, shall be recognised as such agency. It shall take steps in consultation with His Britannic Majesty's Government to secure the co-operation of all Jews who are willing to assist in the establishment of the Jewish national home.

Article 5

The Mandatory shall be responsible for seeing that no Palestine territory shall be ceded or leased to, or in any way placed under the control of, the Government of any foreign Power.

Article 6

The Administration of Palestine, while ensuring that the rights and position of other sections of the population are not prejudiced, shall facilitate Jewish immigration under suitable conditions and shall encourage, in co-operation with the Jewish agency referred to in Article 4, close settlement by Jews on the land, including State lands and waste lands not required for public purposes.

Article 7

The Administration of Palestine shall be responsible for enacting a nationality law. There shall be included in this law provisions framed so as to facilitate the acquisition of Palestinian citizenship by Jews who take up their permanent residence in Palestine.

Article 8

The privileges and immunities of foreigners, including the benefits of consular jurisdiction and protection as formerly enjoyed by Capitulation or usage in the Ottoman Empire, shall not be applicable in Palestine.

Unless the Powers whose nationals enjoyed the afore-mentioned privileges and immunities on August 1st, 1914, shall have previously renounced the right to their re-establishment, or shall have agreed to their non-application for a specified period, these privileges and immunities shall, at the expiration of the mandate, be immediately re-established in their entirety or with such modifications as may have been agreed upon between the Powers concerned.

Article 9

The Mandatory shall be responsible for seeing that the judicial system established in Palestine shall assure to foreigners, as well as to natives, a complete guarantee of their rights.

Respect for the personal status of the various peoples and communities and for their religious interests shall be fully guaranteed. In particular, the control and administration of Wakfs shall be exercised in accordance with religious law and the dispositions of the founders.

Article 10

Pending the making of special extradition agreements relating to Palestine, the extradition treaties in force between the Mandatory and other foreign Powers shall apply to Palestine.

Article 11

The Administration of Palestine shall take all necessary measures to safeguard the interests of the community in connection with the development of the country, and, subject to any international obligations accepted by the Mandatory, shall have full power to provide for public ownership or control of any of the natural resources of the country or of the public works, services and utilities established or to be established therein. It shall introduce a land system appropriate to the needs of the country, having regard, among other things, to the desirability of promoting the close settlement and intensive cultivation of the land.

The Administration may arrange with the Jewish agency mentioned in Article 4 to construct or operate, upon fair and equitable terms, any public works, services and utilities, and to develop any of the natural resources of the country, in so far as these matters are not directly undertaken by the Administration. Any such arrangements shall provide that no profits distributed by such agency, directly or indirectly, shall exceed a reasonable rate of interest on the capital, and any further profits shall be utilised by it for the benefit of the country in a manner approved by the Administration.

Article 12

The Mandatory shall be entrusted with the control of the foreign relations of Palestine and the right to issue exequaturs to consuls appointed by foreign Powers. He shall also be entitled to afford diplomatic and consular protection to citizens of Palestine when outside its territorial limits.

Article 13

All responsibility in connection with the Holy Places and religious buildings or sites in Palestine, including that of preserving existing rights and of securing free access to the Holy Places, religious buildings and sites and the free exercise of worship, while ensuring the requirements of public order and decorum, is assumed by the Mandatory, who shall be responsible solely to the League of Nations in all matters connected herewith, provided that nothing in this article shall prevent the Mandatory from entering into such arrangements as he may deem reasonable with the Administration for the purpose of carrying the provisions of this article into effect; and provided also that nothing in this mandate shall be construed as conferring upon the Mandatory authority to interfere with the fabric or the management of purely Moslem sacred shrines, the immunities of which are guaranteed.

Article 14

A special Commission shall be appointed by the Mandatory to study, define and determine the rights and claims in connection with the Holy Places and the rights and claims relating to the different religious communities in Palestine. The method of nomination, the composition and the functions of this Commission shall be submitted to the Council of the League for its approval, and the Commission shall not be appointed or enter upon its functions without the approval of the Council.

Article 15

The Mandatory shall see that complete freedom of conscience and the free exercise of all forms of worship, subject only to the maintenance of public order and morals, are ensured to all. No discrimination of any kind shall be made between the inhabitants of Palestine on the ground of race, religion or language. No person shall be excluded from Palestine on the sole ground of his religious belief.

The right of each community to maintain its own schools for the education of its own members in its own language, while conforming to such educational requirements of a general nature as the Administration may impose, shall not be denied or impaired.

Article 16

The Mandatory shall be responsible for exercising such supervision over religious or eleemosynary bodies of all faiths in Palestine as may be required for the maintenance of public order and good government. Subject to such supervision, no measures shall be taken in Palestine to obstruct or interfere with the enterprise of such bodies or to discriminate against any representative or member of them on the ground of his religion or nationality.

Article 17

The Administration of Palestine may organise on a voluntary basis the forces necessary for the preservation of peace and order, and also for the defence of the country, subject, however, to the supervision of the Mandatory, but shall not use them for purposes other than those above specified save with the consent of the Mandatory. Except for such purposes, no military, naval or air forces shall be raised or maintained by the Administration of Palestine.

Nothing in this article shall preclude the Administration of Palestine from contributing to the cost of the maintenance of the forces of the Mandatory in Palestine.

The Mandatory shall be entitled at all times to use the roads, railways and ports of Palestine for the movement of armed forces and the carriage of fuel and supplies.

Article 18

The Mandatory shall see that there is no discrimination in Palestine against the nationals of any State Member of the League of Nations (including companies incorporated under its laws) as compared with those of the Mandatory or of any foreign State in matters concerning taxation, commerce or navigation, the exercise of industries or professions, or in the treatment of merchant vessels or civil aircraft. Similarly, there shall be no discrimination in Palestine against goods originating in or destined for any of the said States, and there shall be freedom of transit under equitable conditions across the mandated area.

Subject as aforesaid and to the other provisions of this mandate, the Administration of Palestine may, on the advice of the Mandatory, impose such taxes and customs duties as it may consider necessary, and take such steps as it may think best to promote the development of the natural resources of the country and to safeguard the interests of the population. It may also, on the advice of the Mandatory, conclude a special customs agreement with any State the territory of which in 1914 was wholly included in Asiatic Turkey or Arabia.

Article 19

The Mandatory shall adhere on behalf of the Administration of Palestine to any general international conventions already existing, or which may be concluded hereafter with the approval of the League of Nations, respecting the slave traffic, the traffic in arms and ammunition, or the traffic in drugs, or relating to commercial equality, freedom of transit and navigation, aerial navigation and postal, telegraphic and wireless communication or literary, artistic or industrial property.

Article 20

The Mandatory shall co-operate on behalf of the Administration of Palestine, so far as religious, social and other conditions may permit, in the execution of any common policy adopted by the League of Nations for preventing and combating disease, including diseases of plants and animals.

Article 21

The Mandatory shall secure the enactment within twelve months from this date, and shall ensure the execution of a Law of Antiquities based on the following rules. This law shall ensure equality of treatment in the matter of excavations and archæological research to the nations of all States Members of the League of Nations.

1. "Antiquity" means any construction or any product of human activity earlier than the year A.D. 1700.

2. The law for the protection of antiquities shall proceed by encouragement rather than by threat.

    Any person who, having discovered an antiquity without being furnished with the authorisation referred to in paragraph 5, reports the same to an official of the competent Department, shall be rewarded according to the value of the discovery.

3. No antiquity may be disposed of except to the competent Department, unless this Department renounces the acquisition of any such antiquity.

    No antiquity may leave the country without an export licence from the said Department.

4. Any person who maliciously or negligently destroys or damages an antiquity shall be liable to a penalty to be fixed.

5. No clearing of ground or digging with the object of finding antiquities shall be permitted, under penalty of fine, except to persons authorised by the competent Department.

6. Equitable terms shall be fixed for expropriation, temporary or permanent, of lands which might be of historical or archæological interest.

7. Authorisation to excavate shall only be granted to persons who show sufficient guarantees of archæological experience. The Administration of Palestine shall not, in granting these authorisations, act in such a way as to exclude scholars of any nation without good grounds.

8. The proceeds of excavations may be divided between the excavator and the competent Department in a proportion fixed by that Department. If division seems impossible for scientific reasons, the excavator shall receive a fair indemnity in lieu of a part of the find.

Article 22

English, Arabic and Hebrew shall be the official languages of Palestine. Any statement or inscription in Arabic on stamps or money in Palestine shall be repeated in Hebrew, and any statement or inscription in Hebrew shall be repeated in Arabic.

Article 23
The Administration of Palestine shall recognise the holy days of the respective communities in Palestine as legal days of rest for the members of such communities.

Article 24
The Mandatory shall make to the Council of the League of Nations an annual report to the satisfaction of the Council as to the measures taken during the year to carry out the provisions of the mandate. Copies of all laws and regulations promulgated or issued during the year shall be communicated with the report.

Article 25
In the territories lying between the Jordan and the eastern boundary of Palestine as ultimately determined, the Mandatory shall be entitled, with the consent of the Council of the League of Nations, to postpone or withhold application of such provisions of this mandate as he may consider inapplicable to the existing local conditions, and to make such provision for the administration of the territories as he may consider suitable to those conditions, provided that no action shall be taken which is inconsistent with the provisions of Articles 15, 16 and 18.

Article 26
The Mandatory agrees that, if any dispute whatever should arise between the Mandatory and another Member of the League of Nations relating to the interpretation or the application of the provisions of the mandate, such dispute, if it cannot be settled by negotiation, shall be submitted to the Permanent Court of International Justice provided for by Article 14 of the Covenant of the League of Nations.

Article 27
The consent of the Council of the League of Nations is required for any modification of the terms of this mandate.

Article 28
In the event of the termination of the mandate hereby conferred upon the Mandatory, the Council of the League of Nations shall make such arrangements as may be deemed necessary for safeguarding in perpetuity, under guarantee of the League, the rights secured by Articles 13 and 14, and shall use its influence for securing, under the guarantee of the League, that the Government of Palestine will fully honour the

financial obligations legitimately incurred by the Administration of
Palestine during the period of the mandate, including the rights of public servants to pensions or gratuities.

The present instrument shall be deposited in original in the archives
of the League of Nations and certified copies shall be forwarded by the
Secretary-General of the League of Nations to all Members of the
League.

Done at London the twenty-fourth day of July, one thousand nine hundred and twenty-two.

Certified true copy:

For the Secretary-General,
RAPPARD,
Director of the Mandates Section

Note by the Secretary-General
relating to Transjordan

This transmits to the members of the League of Nations a memorandum of the British Government approved by the Council of the League
on September 23, 1922. The memorandum cites Article 25 of the Mandate for Palestine and requests the Council to pass the following resolution:

"The following provisions of the Mandate for Palestine are not applicable to the territory known as Transjordan, which comprises all
territory lying to the east of a line drawn from a point two miles west
of the town of Aqaba on the Gulf of that name up the centre of the
Wadi Araba, Dead Sea and River Jordan to its junction with the River
Yarmuk; thence up the centre of that river to the Syrian frontier."

Preamble. Recitals 2 and 3

Article 2. The words "placing the country under such political administration and economic conditions as will secure the establishment
of the Jewish national home, as laid down in the preamble, and".

Article 4.

Article 6.

Article 7. The sentence "There shall be included in this law provisions framed so as to facilitate the acquisition of Palestinian citizenship
by Jews who take up their permanent residence in Palestine."

Article 11. The second sentence of the first paragraph and the second
paragraph.

Article 13.

Article 14.

Article 22.

Article 23.

In the application of the Mandate to Transjordan, the action which, in Palestine, is taken by the Administration of the latter country, will be taken by the Administration of Transjordan under the general supervision of the Mandatory.

3. His Majesty's Government accept full responsibility as Mandatory for Transjordan, and undertake that such provision as may be made for the administration of that territory in accordance with Article 25 of the Mandate shall be in no way inconsistent with those provisions of the Mandate which are not by this resolution declared inapplicable.

Chronology

* See p. 1, n. 2.

167–165	Hasmonean (Maccabean) revolt against Hellenistic rule
37	Hasmonean dynasty supplanted by Herod
37–4	Rule of Herod the Great; the Temple rebuilt

A.D.

26–36	Pontius Pilate Roman Procurator of Judea
(?)33**	The Crucifixion
66–70	Jewish revolt against Roman rule
70	Destruction of Jerusalem by Romans
132–35	Revolt of Bar Kochba; Hadrian completes destruction of Jerusalem, renamed Aelia Capitolina
(?)313	Edict of Milan; Constantine proclaims equality of all religions in Roman Empire, and later adopts Christianity
330	Constantine establishes Constantinople (Byzantium), at junction of Europe and Asia, as his capital
395	Roman Empire divided; Western empire, based on Rome, soon invaded by barbarians (Huns, Goths, Vandals); Eastern empire, based on Byzantium, survives for another thousand years (till 1453)
425	Jewish Patriarchate in Palestine abolished; centre of Jewish life shifts to Babylonia
476	End of West Roman empire
ca. 400–750	Completion, first of Palestinian, and later of Babylonian, Talmud
ca. 570	Birth of Muhammad in Mecca
622	Flight of Muhammad from Mecca to Medina; the Hijra becomes basis of Muslim calendar
632	Death of Muhammad
632–61	Rule, from Medina, of the four Orthodox Caliphs (Abu Bekr, Umar, Othman, and Ali); Arab conquest of Syria and Palestine, Egypt, Mesopotamia, and Persia
661–750	Umayyad Caliphate, capital Damascus; Muslim conquest of Afghanistan, parts of Central Asia, Sind and the Indus valley, North Africa, and Spain
711	Muslim invasion of Spain and later southern France
732	Defeat of Muslims by Charles Martel, ruler of the Franks, at Poitiers

** Various authorities have assigned different dates to the Crucifixion, such as 29 and 30.

750–842	Abbasid Caliphate (early phase); period of Caliphs' effective rule; final phase of Arab imperial greatness
755	Umayyad Caliphate established at Córdova; "Golden Age" of Jews in Spain begins
771–814	Reign of Charlemagne, grandson of Charles Martel, first as King of the Franks, then (from 800) as Roman Emperor of the West; contemporary of Baghdad Caliph Harun al-Rashid (786–809)
827–1061	Arab rule in Sicily
842–1258	Abbasid Caliphate (later phase); Turkish troops gain power and gradually reduce Arab Caliphs to impotence
910–1171	Fatimid Caliphate in Egypt
1055	Capture of Baghdad by Seljuq Turks
1071	Battle of Manzikert; Byzantines defeated by Seljuq Turks
1085	Spanish Christians recapture Toledo
1096–1149	First and Second Crusades; conquest of Palestine
1099–1187	The Latin Kingdom of Jerusalem
1187	Battle of Hittin; Crusaders defeated by Salah al-Din (Saladin)
1100–1243	Disintegration of Seljuq Empire; their defeat by Mongols paves way for rise of the Ottoman (Osmanli) Turkish Empire
1189–1270	Third to Eighth Crusades
1236	Spanish Christians recapture Córdova
1252–1517	Mamluk rule in Egypt
1258	Mongols capture and destroy Baghdad
1260	Mamluks defeat Mongols and add Syria to their dominions
1291	Fall of Acre; end of the Crusades
1290–1326	Rule of Osman, traditional founder of Ottoman Empire
1453	Constantinople captured by Ottoman Turks; end of Byzantine Empire
1492	Spanish Christians recapture Granada; end of Muslim rule in Spain; discovery of New World by Christopher Columbus; all Jews unwilling to be baptized expelled from Spain and later Portugal; converts face persecution by Inquisition
1517	Ottoman conquest of Fertile Crescent, Egypt, and

	Arabia; under Turkish suzerainty Mamluk rule in Egypt continues; Turkish Sultans eventually assume Caliphate of Islam
1534	Turks conquer Iraq, with Baghdad
1571	Battle of Lepanto; Christian powers defeat Ottoman fleet
1683	Turks besiege Vienna for second time, fail to capture it
1699	Peace of Carlowitz; as Ottoman power declines, European imperialism gains ground in Middle East
1764	Poland abolishes Council of Four Lands
1772	First partition of Poland
1774	Treaty of Kuchuk Kainarji; important gains by Russia in Black Sea region
1789–1815	French Revolution and Napoleonic era, following German Aufklärung, brings emancipation to Western Jews
1793	Second Partition of Poland
1795	Third Partition of Poland; most Eastern European Jews come under harsher rule of Russia
1798–99	Napoleon in Egypt
1807–39	Mahmud II, Sultan of Turkey, introduces many reforms
1811	Muhammad Ali suppresses Mamluks in Egypt
1820–75	Expansion of Western Christian missionary education in Syria and Lebanon contributes to rise of Arab nationalism
1821	Greek revolt against Turks
1826	Suppression of Janissaries in Turkey
1827	Battle of Navarino; defeat of Turkish-Egyptian fleet
1830	London Protocol secures independence of Greece; France occupies Algeria
1831–32	Ibrahim Ali defeats Turkish armies; occupies Palestine, Syria, and part of Anatolia
1833	Treaty of Unkiar-Skelessi places Turkey virtually at mercy of Russia
1839	Britain occupies Aden
1839–61	Tanzimat reforms in Turkey during reign of Sultan Abdul Mejid
1840	Convention of London; European great powers back

Sultan of Turkey against Muhammad Ali; Russia gives up advantages under Treaty of Unkiar-Skelessi

1841   Second Treaty of London embodies Straits Convention regulating passage through Bosphorus and Dardanelles; Muhammad Ali confirmed as hereditary ruler of Egypt and Sudan

1848   Year of European revolutions

1853   Russia again tries to dominate Turkey; outbreak of Crimean War

1854–69   Building of Suez Canal

1856   Treaty of Paris ends Crimean War, checks Russian ambitions

1860–61   Disturbances in Syria (conflict between Druses and Christian Maronites); French military intervention; Lebanon given special constitution

1866   Austria defeated by Prussia

    Syrian Protestant College (afterwards American University) founded in Beirut

1869   Suez Canal opened

1870   France defeated by Prussia; creation of German Empire

1875   Britain acquires Khedive's Suez Canal shares

1876–1909   Abdul Hamid Sultan of Turkey

1876–77   Constitution for Turkey proclaimed, then revoked

1877–78   Russo-Turkish War; Russia's successes checked by Congress of Berlin

1878   Treaty of Berlin; Britain takes over Cyprus

1881   France annexes Tunisia

1881–98   Mahdi and Khalifa gain control of most of Sudan

1882   Britain occupies Egypt

1883–1907   Sir Evelyn Baring (Lord Cromer) controls administration of Egypt

1883–1914   German influence grows in Turkey, especially in military training and railway construction (Baghdad railway, Hejaz railway)

1885   Capture of Khartoum by Mahdi; General Gordon killed

1888   Suez Canal Convention regulates navigation through this waterway

1889   Turkish Committee of Union and Progress formed

1890–97	Armenian revolutionary movement; subsequent massacres of Armenians by Turks
1897	First Zionist Congress organized by Theodor Herzl
1898	German Emperor visits Istanbul and Palestine; proclaims Germany's friendship for all Muslims
1898	Battle of Omdurman; British defeat Khalifa and establish Ango-Egyptian rule in Sudan
1904	Anglo-French *Entente*; this and Britain's subsequent *entente* with Russia result in allied alignment against Central European powers when World War I breaks out, it ending Anglo-French conflict in Egypt
	Death of Herzl, followed by interregnum and influence of "practical Zionists." Weizmann gradually acquires leading role
1906	Act of Algeciras gives France predominant position in Morocco
1907	Anglo-Russian Entente
1907–14	Gorst and Kitchener continue British control of Egypt
1908	Young Turk Revolution; Husain ibn Ali becomes Sharif of Mecca
1909	Abdul Hamid attempts counter-revolution, but is deposed
1911–12	Italo-Turkish War; Italy occupies Tripolitania, Rhodes, and Dodecanese Islands
1912	Greece annexes Crete
1912–13	Balkan Wars; further territorial losses by Turkey
1913–18	Turkey ruled by Enver-Jemal-Talat triumvirate
1914	Outbreak of World War I; Kitchener becomes Britain's War Minister; Egypt made a British protectorate; Turkey joins Germany against Britain, France, and Russia
1915–16	Correspondence between British High Commissioner in Egypt (MacMahon) and Sharif Husain of Mecca; Britain promises support for Arab independence
1916	Arab Revolt; Sykes-Picot Agreement divides Fertile Crescent into French and British spheres of influence in conflict with Britain's promises
1917	United States declares war on Germany; March and October revolutions in Russia; Bolsheviks assume power, publish Sykes-Picot Agreement; Balfour Declaration; Jerusalem captured by British

1918	Defeat of Turkey; Amir Faisal's forces and British army enter Damascus; Anglo-French Declaration assures peoples of Fertile Crescent of self-determination; Zionist Commission arrives in Palestine
1919	Paris Peace Conference; Faisal-Weizmann Agreement; U.S. King-Crane Commission visits Syria, Lebanon, and Palestine
1920	San Remo meeting of Allied Supreme Council assigns mandates for Syria and Lebanon to France and for Palestine and Iraq to Britain; expulsion of Faisal from Damascus, and start of mandatory rule by France and Britain in Fertile Crescent; Arab Revolt in Iraq; humiliating terms inflicted by Allies on Turkey through Treaty of Sèvres
1921	Faisal becomes king of Iraq; Reza Khan (army colonel) assumes control of Iran; first anti-Jewish disturbances in Palestine; Amir Abdullah becomes ruler of Transjordan, thenceforward excluded from area assigned under the mandate for establishment of a Jewish National Home
1922	Mandates assigned to France and Britain in Middle East approved by League of Nations; British White Paper defines mandate for Palestine—no domination of Palestinian Arabs by Jews contemplated; Turks defeat Greeks in Anatolia
1923	Treaty of Lausanne recreates a strong though diminished Turkey, eventually as a republic under Kemal Ataturk
1924	Ibn Saud, ruler of Nejd, defeats King Husain of Hejaz and takes over most of the Arabian Peninsula, which becomes Saudi Arabia
1925	Hebrew University at Jerusalem opened by Lord Balfour; Reza Pahlevi becomes Shah of Iran
1925–27	Druse insurrection in Syria
1926	French create Greater Lebanon
1927	Britain recognizes independence of Iraq
1928	Britain recognizes independence of Transjordan
1929	Serious attacks by Arabs on Jews in Palestine
1930	British Passfield White Paper suggests restrictions on Jewish immigration into, and land purchase in, Palestine

1932	Iraq admitted to League of Nations
1936	Outbreak of Arab revolt in Palestine
1937	Peel Report on Palestine, suggesting separate Arab and Jewish states, rejected by Arabs and Zionists
1939	British White Paper on Palestine laying down strict limitations on Jewish immigration—acceptable to most Arabs, strongly opposed by Zionists Outbreak of World War II
1940	Collapse of France; Battle of Britain; defeat of Nazi air attacks on, and invasion plans for, British Isles. During ensuing year Britain remains only major power fighting Hitler
1941	Axis powers occupy Yugoslavia and Greece; Germans invade Russia; Allies occupy Syria and Lebanon, but Germans advance in North Africa; revolt in Iraq suppressed United States at war with Japan, Germany, and Italy
1942	Germans reach northern Egypt but are defeated at El-Alamein; American and British forces occupy French North Africa; Russians defeat Germans at Stalingrad Zionist Biltmore programme; Hitler holocaust intensified
1943	Axis resistance ends in North Africa; Allies invade Italy
1944	Irgun joins Stern Group in terrorism against the British in Palestine; foundation of Arab League; murder of Lord Moyne; Allied invasion of Normandy
1945	Surrender of Germany and, later, Japan; Labour Government in Britain; appointment of Anglo-American Committee of Enquiry into problems of Palestine; Harry S. Truman becomes President of the United States
1946	Anglo-American Committee report recommends admission of 100,000 Jews to Palestine yet on basis of binational solution; immigration proposals strongly backed by President Truman
1947	Britain refers Palestine problem to U.N. judgement; appointment of U.N. Special Committee on Palestine; UNSCOP partition plan passed by United Nations; large-scale hostilities between Arabs and Zionists; flight of Arab Palestinians from Palestine begins

1948 End of British Mandate for Palestine; proclamation of State of Israel; start of first Arab-Israeli War; murder of Count Bernadotte, U.N. Mediator; remainder of Arab Palestine incorporated in Jordan

1949 Armistice agreements between Israel and Egypt, Lebanon, Jordan (with Iraq), and Syria; Arab refugees increase to nearly one million

1951 Murder of King Abdullah of Jordan

1952 Revolution in Egypt; King Farouk dethroned; Naguib-Nasser Military Council takes over

1954 Anglo-Egyptian agreement for British troop withdrawal from Suez Canal Zone; Nasser gains control in Egypt and increasing prestige among the other Arab nations

1955 Baghdad Pact aligns Iraq, Iran, Pakistan, Turkey, and Britain with United States; Egyptian arms deals with Communist bloc

1956 Failure of Western negotiations to finance Aswan High Dam; Nasser nationalizes Suez Canal
Second Arab-Israeli War; Israel aligned with Britain and France against Egypt

1958 United Arab Republic created by Egypt and Syria; UAR and Yemen become United Arab States; Iraq and Jordan form Arab Federation
Baghdad Revolution; Iraq drops Arab Federation and Baghdad Pact, subsequently renamed Central Treaty Organization (CENTO)
U.S. troops sent to Lebanon; British troops to Jordan

1961 Dissolution of UAR and UAS

1962 Algeria gains independence from France
Civil War in Yemen; Nasser supports republican regime against Imam's forces

1963 Abortive scheme for federation between Egypt, Syria, and Iraq

1967 Third Arab-Israeli (Six Day) War. U.N. Security Council Resolution No. 242 calls on Israel to give up conquests in return for mutual acknowledgment of sovereignty and territorial integrity by Israel and Arab neighbours; start of Jarring Mission
Arab summit conference at Khartoum
End of British rule in Aden; inauguration of South

Yemen Republic (later: People's Democratic Republic of Yemen)

1969   Revolution in Libya, King Idris dethroned and republic proclaimed, Colonel Gaddafi becomes Chairman of Revolutionary Command Council; Mrs Golda Meir becomes Israeli Prime Minister

1970   U.S. cease-fire proposals accepted by Egypt, Jordan, and Israel

End of civil war in Yemen

Death of Nasser; Anwar Sadat becomes President of Egypt

U.S. Wheelus Air Base in Libya closed

1971   King Hussein suppresses Palestinian guerrillas in Jordan

United Arab Emirates formed from seven small Sheikhdoms (the Trucial States)

Triple federation of Libya, Egypt, and Syria proclaimed

1972   Full political union between Libya and Egypt announced, to take place the following year

1972–73   Peak of Palestinian terrorism: massacre at Lod airport, murder of Israeli athletes at Munich Olympic Games, murder of Western diplomats at Khartoum

1973   Israeli raid on Beirut; murder of Palestinian guerrilla leaders

Libyan-Egyptian union nominally in force; Sadat's rapprochement with King Faisal of Saudi Arabia

Summit meeting between President Nixon and Leonid Brezhnev, First Secretary of U.S.S.R. Communist Party

Fourth Arab-Israeli (Yom Kippur, or October) War

Bibliography

Although there is a vast amount of good writing in the wide field covered by the present work, in view of the essentially introductory nature of this book I have in general chosen shorter and more recent works giving a clear and readily comprehensible insight into the issues involved—and, where possible, those available in paperback. Certain longer and highly detailed studies of outstanding quality are of course indispensable and have been included; but I have purposely omitted some other excellent works that are found in the fuller standard bibliographies. These will be valuable to readers interested in gaining a deeper and more profound knowledge of this many-sided and fascinating subject. Many of the issues are highly controversial, and, in the interests of a balanced judgement, the works I have listed approach these issues from widely varying standpoints.

An asterisk before the entry marks a title either originally published in paperback or currently available in paperback. The numerals in parentheses after each entry refer to the chapter(s) in which the work is cited or discussed.

Abrahams, Israel. *Jewish Life in the Middle Ages*. New ed., rev. and enl. London: Goldston, 1932. (5)

*American Friends Service Committee. *Search for Peace in the Middle East*. Greenwich, Conn.: Fawcett Publications, 1970. Short, forceful, clearly written presentation of both Israeli and Arab standpoints, as well as their own, Christian, plea for peace. (16)

Anglo-American Committee of Enquiry. *Report of the Anglo-American Committee of Enquiry Regarding the Problems of European Jewry and Palestine*. London: H. M. Stationery Office, Cmd. 6808, 1946. (13)

*Antonius, George. *The Arab Awakening*. New York: Putnam/Capricorn Books, 1965. (4, 6, 7, 10, 11, 12)

Armajani, Yahya. *Middle East, Past and Present*. Englewood Cliffs, N.J.: Prentice-Hall, 1970. A useful teaching text with a helpful introductory section. The Islamic period is its starting point. (2, 3, 4, 6, 7, 8, 10, 12, 13, 14, 15, 16)

*Atiyah, Edward. *The Arabs*. Baltimore: Penguin/Pelican, 1958. (3, 4, 7)

*Avnery, Uri. *Israel Without Zionists: A Plea for Peace in the Middle East*. New York: Macmillan, 1968. A former Irgun fighter, now a journalist and member of the Knesset, argues forcefully for a more understanding approach by Israel to the Arabs. (15)

*Badeau, John S. *The American Approach to the Arab World*. New York: Harper/Colophon, 1968. An authoritative work, published for the Council on Foreign Relations by the former U.S. Ambassador to Egypt. (13, 14, 15)

*Bailey, Thomas A. *The Art of Diplomacy*. New York: Appleton-Century-Crofts, 1968. (13)

*Barbour, Nevill. *Nisi Dominus*. London: Harrap, 1946 (in U.S., *Palestine: Star or Crescent?* New York: Odyssey, 1947). Criticism of some aspects of Zionist expansion. (11, 12, 13)

Begin, Menachem. *Revolt: The Story of the Irgun*. London, W. H. Allen (New York: Schuman) 1951. (13)

Bentwich, Norman. *Israel*. London: Ernest Benn, 1952. (14)

———. *Israel: Two Fateful Years, 1967–1969*. London: Elek, 1970. (15)

*———. *The Jews in Our Time*. Baltimore: Penguin/Pelican, 1932. (5, 9)

———. *Palestine*. London: Ernest Benn, 1934. (9, 11) One of the younger disciples of Weizmann in Britain, Bentwich fought in the Palestine campaign of World War I and was Attorney-General in the British administration there in the early years of the Mandate.

Blunt, Wilfrid Scawen. *The Secret History of the English Occupation of Egypt.* London: Fisher, Unwin, 1907 (New York: Knopf, 1922). Sharp and candid criticism of London's policies by a great Victorian liberal who strongly defended the rights of the Egyptian nationalists. (8)

Burt, Alfred Leroy. *The British Empire and Commonwealth.* Boston: D. C. Heath, 1956. (8)

Butler, R., J. P. T. Bury, and M. E. Lambert, eds. *Documents on British Foreign Policy, 1919–1939.* Vol. 13 (1920–21). London: H. M. Stationery Office.

Cambridge Medieval History. Cambridge: Cambridge University Press. Vol. 2 (1913), (2); vols. 3 (1922), 4 (1966–67), 5 (1926), 6 (1929), (5, 6)

Cambridge Modern History. Cambridge: Cambridge University Press, 1934. (6)

Cattan, Henry. *The Arabs and Israel.* London: Longmans, 1969. By a distinguished British-Palestinian lawyer who has defended his people's case at the United Nations. (14).

————. *Palestine: The Road to Peace.* London: Longmans, 1970 (New York: International Publications Service, 1971). (16)

*Churchill, Randolph S., and Winston S. Churchill. *The Six Day War.* London: Heinemann (Boston: Houghton Mifflin). Detailed and vivid account of background and operations of the 1967 war by the son and grandson of Sir Winston Churchill. (15)

*Churchill, Sir Winston. *My Early Life.* London: Collins/Fontana (New York: Manor Books), 1972. (8)

Cohen, Aharon. *Israel and the Arab World.* London: W. H. Allen (New York: Funk & Wagnalls), 1970. Study in depth by an Israeli writer who shows marked understanding of the Arab position. (16)

Cohen, Israel. *The Zionist Movement.* London: Frederick Muller, 1945. (12, 13)

Commission on the Palestine Disturbances of August, 1929. *Report of the Commission* . . . British Government White Paper. London: H. M. Stationery Office, Cmd. 3530, 1930. (12)

Cooley, John E. *Green March, Black September: The Story of the Palestinian Arabs.* London: Frank Cass, 1973. By the *Christian Science Monitor* correspondent. (14)

Correspondence between Sir Henry McMahon, His Majesty's High Commissioner at Cairo, and the Sherif Hussein of Mecca, July, 1915, to March, 1916. British Government White Paper. London: H. M. Stationery Office, Cmd. 5957, 1939. (10)

Correspondence with the Palestine Arab Delegation and the Zionist Organization. British Government White Paper. London: H. M. Stationery Office, Cmd. 1700, 1922. (11)

Cromer, Lord. *Modern Egypt.* 2 vols. London: Macmillan, 1908

(New York: Macmillan, 2 vols. in 1, 1916). Magisterial account of his stewardship by the man who ruled Egypt for more than twenty years. (8)

*Davis, John H. *The Evasive Peace*. New York: New World Press, 1970. (16)

*Davison, Roderic H. *Turkey*. Englewood Cliffs, N.J.: Prentice-Hall, 1968. (7)

Dodd, C. M., and M. E. Sales, eds. *Israel and the Arab World, 1914–1968*. Cranberry, N.J.: Barnes & Noble, 1971. (16)

Dummelow, J. R., ed. *Commentary on the Holy Bible*. New York: Macmillan, 1955. (1)

Eban, Abba. *My People: The Story of the Jews*. London: Weidenfeld & Nicolson (New York: Random House), 1969. Monumental, attractively printed and illustrated history by Israel's Foreign Minister. (5, 9)

*Elon, Amos. *The Israelis: Founders and Sons*. London: Sphere Books, 1972 (New York: Holt, Rinehart & Winston, 1971). Frank and vivid, if somewhat impressionistic, picture of contemporary Israel, her origins and manifold problems. (11, 14, 15, 16)

Emanuel, Muriel, ed. *Israel: A Survey and Bibliography*. London: St. James' Press, 1971. Particularly valuable for its full statistics and bibliography. (15)

*Epstein, Isidore. *Judaism: A Historical Presentation*. Baltimore: Penguin/Pelican, 1959. (1, 2, 9)

Fisher, Eugene M., and M. Cherif Bassiouni. *Storm Over the Arab World*. Chicago: Follett, 1972. (16)

Frank, Gerold. *The Deed*. London: Cape, 1964 (New York: Simon & Schuster, 1963). (13)

Friedman, Isaiah. *The Question of Palestine, 1914–1918: British-Jewish-Arab Relations*. London: Routledge & Kegan Paul, 1973. (10)

*Gervasi, Frank. *The Case for Israel*. New York: Viking, 1967. (16)

Glubb, Sir John. *The Empire of the Arabs*. London: Hodder & Stoughton, 1963. (4)

———. *The Great Arab Conquests*. Englewood Cliffs, N.J.: Prentice-Hall, 1967. Clear and vivid account of rise and early triumphs of Islam among the Arabs of Arabia and neighbouring lands they conquered, by an author who lived and worked with Arabs most of his life. (3)

———. *The Middle East Crisis: A Personal Interpretation*. London: Hodder & Stoughton, 1967. Analysis of the Six Day War's consequences, by the general most deeply and effectively involved on the Arab side in the 1948 war (he sees Russia as the nation that gained most from the 1967 war). (15)

———. *Peace in the Holy Land*. London: Hodder & Stoughton (Mystic, Conn.: Verry), 1971. (3)

————. *A Short History of the Arab Peoples.* London: Hodder & Stoughton (New York: Stein & Day), 1969. Valuable for reference, this work draws important distinctions between the original Arabs—the nomads of Arabia—and the many peoples now called Arabs who, after being conquered, assimilated Arabic language and culture. ('3, 4, 7, 13)

————. *A Soldier with the Arabs.* London: Hodder & Stoughton, 1957. Candid and fascinating account by the British officer who built up and for many years commanded Jordan's army (the Arab Legion), the only Arab force to fight effectively in the 1948 war. (13, 14)

*Glueck, Nelson. *Rivers in the Desert: A History of the Negev.* New York: Norton, 1968. (1)

*Goitein, S. D. *Jews and Arabs: Their Contacts Through the Ages.* New York: Schocken, 1964. (1, 3, 4, 5, 7, 9)

*Guillaume, Alfred. *Islam.* Baltimore: Penguin/Pelican, 1964. (1, 3)

*Haim, Sylvia G., ed. *Arab Nationalism: An Anthology.* Berkeley: University of California Press, 1962. (7)

*Harden, Donald. *The Phoenicians.* Baltimore: Penguin/Pelican, 1971.

Halpern, Manfred. *The Politics of Social Change in the Middle East and North Africa.* Princeton, N.J.: Princeton University Press, 1965. (14)

Harkabi, Y. *Fedayeen Action and Arab Strategy.* Adelphi Papers No. 53. London: Institute for Strategic Studies. By the former Chief of Israeli Military Intelligence. (15)

*High Commissioner on the Administration of Palestine, 1920–25. *Report of the High Commissioner . . .* British Government White Paper. London: H. M. Stationery Office, Colonial No. 15, 1925. (11)

*Hitti, Philip K. *History of the Arabs, from the Earliest Times to the Present.* New York: St. Martin's, 1967. This detailed, scholarly work concentrates on Arab history before the expansion of Western imperialism in the 19th and 20th centuries. (1, 3, 4, 6, 7, 8)

*Holt, P. M. *Egypt and the Fertile Crescent 1516–1922.* Ithaca, N.Y.: Cornell University Press, 1969. (6, 7, 8)

————. *The Mahdist State in the Sudan, 1881–1898.* Oxford: Clarendon Press (New York: Oxford University Press), 1970. (8)

*Horowitz, David. *The Economics of Israel.* Oxford/New York: Pergamon Press, 1967. By the Governor of the Bank of Israel. (16)

*Hourani, Albert. *Arabic Thought in the Liberal Age, 1798–1939.* London/New York: Oxford University Press, 1970 (1962). (7)

* Hurewitz, J. C. *Middle East Politics: The Military Dimension.* New

York: Praeger, 1968. Although covering a wider field than the Fertile Crescent and Egypt, valuable for its analysis of the swiftly expanding role of the military in the countries of this area after World War II. Published for the Council on Foreign Relations. (14, 15, 16)

*————, ed. *Soviet-American Rivalry in the Middle East*. New York: Praeger, 1969. A useful analysis of this vital theme. It somewhat neglects, however, the significant fact that Russian rivalry with the Western powers in Asia Minor and the eastern Mediterranean (in the past mainly with France, Austria, and Britain) is nothing new, but a centuries-old tradition, stemming from what Russia regards as the demands of her geographical position and strategic needs as a great Eurasian power. (14, 15, 16)

Hyamson, A. M. *Palestine under the Mandate*. London: Methuen, 1950. The author, a British-Jewish scholar, was Director of Immigration of the Palestine Government. (11, 12)

Ingrams, Doreen. *Palestine Papers 1917–1922: Seeds of Conflict*. London: John Murray, 1972. (10, 11)

*Israeli Ministry of Foreign Affairs, Information Division. *Facts about Israel*. A yearly publication, useful for reference, in which the facts, as in the above Survey and Bibliography, are (understandably) presented in the most advantageous light. (15)

Izzeddin, Nejla. *The Arab World*. Chicago: Henry Regnery, 1953. (4)

*Jiryis, Sabri. *The Arabs in Israel*. Beirut: Institute for Palestine Studies, Originally published at Haifa by the author (a former Israeli citizen) in Hebrew, and based on official Israeli sources. (14)

John, Robert, and Sami Hadawi. *The Palestine Diary*. Vol. 1, 1914–45. New York: New World Press, 1971. Foreword by Arnold Toynbee. Documented history of Palestine during the two world wars, and critical both of Britain and of Zionism. (10, 11, 12, 13, 14)

Joynt, C. B., and O. M. Smolansky. *Soviet Naval Policy in the Mediterranean*. Bethlehem, Pa.: Lehigh University, Department of International Relations, 1972. (15)

Keesing's Contemporary Archives (1948–73). London: Keesing's Publications. Well-written and reliable summary of important current developments in the different parts of the world, compiled from all public sources, available in most American and British libraries, and particularly useful for checking more recent events when they have not yet been fully dealt with in published works. (14, 15, 16)

Keesing's Research Report: The Arab-Israeli Conflict. London: Keesing's Publications (New York: Scribner), 1968. Clear and concise study, by the organization responsible for *Keesing's Contemporary Archives*, of the origins and course of the Six Day War. (15)

*Keller, Werner. *The Bible as History*. London: Hodder & Stoughton (New York: Apollo Books), 1956. (1)

*Kerr, Malcolm H. *The Arab Cold War*. 3rd ed. London/New York: Oxford University Press, 1971. Study of the interplay of personal ambitions and the pursuit of national goals in Arab world, with particular reference to relations, after Suez, between Egypt, Syria, Iraq, and Jordan, and their various abortive attempts at unification. (15)

Khadduri, Majdia D., ed. *The Arab-Israeli Impasse*. Washington, D.C.: Luce, 1968. Series of studies of the origins and course of present conflict by prominent Western writers of moderate views. (4, 13, 14, 15)

Khalidi, Walid, ed. *From Haven to Conquest*. Beirut: Institute for Palestine Studies, 1971. Another anthology critical of Zionism and British policy, in the form mainly of key documents and quotations from British, Jewish, Arab, and other sources, and concentrating on the period 1897–1948. (10, 11, 12, 13, 14)

*Khouri, Fred J. *The Arab-Israeli Dilemma*. Syracuse, N.Y.: Syracuse University Press, 1968. (16)

Kimche, Jon, and David Kimche. *Both Sides of the Hill*. London: Secker & Warburg, 1960. Illuminating analysis of the 1948 war by a participant and a press observer (on the Israeli side), who judge that Britain, not the Arabs, was the main loser. (14)

*Kirk, George F. *A Short History of the Middle East, From the Rise of Islam to Modern Times*. New York: Praeger, 1970. (3, 4, 6, 7, 8, 10, 11)

Kirkbride, Sir Alec. *An Awakening*. Tavistock: University Press of Arabia, 1971. A far shorter and more down-to-earth account of the Arab Revolt than that of T. E. Lawrence, by another British participant. A convincingly factual and at the same time vivid and humorous picture of this extraordinary campaign. (10)

———. *A Crackle of Thorns*. London: Murray, 1956. Autobiography with penetrating observation and dry humour, covering early years of the Mandate with particular reference to Transjordan and northern Palestine. (11, 14)

Koestler, Arthur. *Promise and Fulfilment: Palestine 1917–1949*. London: Macmillan, 1949. One of the best-known Jewish writers analyses Palestine problem in a strongly pro-Zionist, anti-British sense. (10, 14)

Kohn, Hans. "Theodor Herzl." *Encyclopedia Britannica*, vol. 11

(1971), pp. 459–60. (9)

Kollek, Teddy, and Moshe Pearlman. *Jerusalem, Sacred City of Mankind*. Jerusalem: Steimatzky's, 1968. Brilliantly written, if occasionally provocative, history of Jerusalem, written in aftermath of Israel's triumph in Six Day War. (1, 2, 5, 9)

Laqueur, Walter Z. *A History of Zionism*. London: Weidenfeld & Nicolson (New York: Holt, Rinehart & Winston), 1972. The most recent comprehensive work on the subject; ends with creation of Israel in 1948. Readers wishing to explore the subject even more thoroughly should consult also Nahum Sokolov's two-volume *History of Zionism* (London: Longmans, 1919), as its author played a key role in the development of the movement. (9, 11, 12, 13)

*———, ed. *The Israel-Arab Reader: A Documentary History of the Middle-East Conflict*. London: Weidenfeld & Nicolson (New York: Bantam Books), 1970. (9, 10, 11, 12, 13, 14, 15)

Lawrence, T. E. *The Seven Pillars of Wisdom*. New York: Doubleday, 1938. Although in places inaccurate, a fascinating if highly subjective account of the Arab Revolt by one of its most famous participants. (10)

League of Nations: Mandate for Palestine, Together with a Note by the Secretary-General Relating to Its Application to the Territory Known as Transjordan. London: H. M. Stationery Office, Cmd. 1785, 1922. (11) Reproduced in Appendix.

Lenczowski, George. *The Middle East in World Affairs*. Ithaca, N.Y.: Cornell University Press, 1952. (6, 10)

*Lewis, Bernard. *The Arabs in History*. 4th ed. New York: Harper & Row/Torchbooks, 1966. (3, 4, 7)

*———. *The Emergence of Modern Turkey*. 2nd ed. London/New York: Oxford University Press, 1968. (7, 10)

*———. *The Middle East and the West*. New York: Harper & Row, 1966. (6, 7)

Mansfield, Peter. *The British in Egypt*. New York: Holt, Rinehart & Winston, 1971. The outstanding recent work on the subject. (8, 12)

———, ed. *The Middle East: A Political and Economic Survey*. 4th ed. London/New York: Oxford University Press, 1973. (14, 15, 16)

*———. *Nasser*. London: Methuen, 1969. (14, 15)

Marlowe, John. *The Seat of Pilate*. London: Cresset Press, 1959. Candid British critic examines Britain's policies and performance as Mandatory for Palestine. (11)

Marriott, Sir J. A. R. *The Eastern Question*. 4th ed. Oxford/New York: Oxford University Press, 1940 (1956). (6, 7, 8)

*Monroe, Elizabeth. *Britain's Moment in the Middle East*. London: Methuen/University Paperbacks, 1965. (10, 11, 12, 14)

Mousa, Souleiman. *T. E. Lawrence: An Arab View*. London: Oxford University Press, 1967. Both Mousa and Antonius (but especially Mousa) are more critical of Lawrence than most Western writers. (10)

*New English Bible. Old Testament. Oxford University Press/Cambridge University Press, 1970. A translation of high value in view of its exceptionally clear and dignified modern language. There are of course many other first-rate modern versions, such as the "Jerusalem Bible," which some readers may prefer. (1)

*Nicolson, Sir Harold. *Peacemaking, 1919*. New York: Grosset & Dunlap, 1966. (10)

*Nutting, Anthony. *The Arabs: A Narrative History from Mohammed to the Present*. New York: Mentor Books, 1964. The author, a scholar and also a Minister of the British Government, resigned his office in 1956 in protest against its policies at the time. He stresses the extraordinary extent to which personal leadership has been responsible for the successive triumphs and setbacks of the Arabs. (3, 4, 7, 10)

Oxford Bible Atlas, ed. Herbert G. May. 2nd ed. London/New York/Toronto: Oxford University Press, 1974.

Palestine Royal Commission: Report. British Government White Paper embodying Peel Report. London: H. M. Stationery Office, Cmd. 5479, 1937. (12)

Palestine: Statement of Policy. British Government White Paper. London: H. M. Stationery Office, Cmd. 6019, 1939. The famous White Paper to which the Zionists so strongly objected because it would have restricted their immigration in such a way as to make it probable that they would remain a permanent minority in Palestine. (12)

Palestine: Statement of Policy by His Majesty's Government in the United Kingdom. British Government White Paper. London: H. M. Stationery Office, Cmd. 3692, 1930. (12)

Pares, Bernard. *A History of Russia*. London: Cape, 1958. (6)

Parkes, James. *The Conflict of the Church and the Synagogue*. Cleveland/New York: World/ Meridian Books, 1961. (2)

———. *Whose Land? A History of the Peoples of Palestine*. Baltimore: Penguin/Pelican, 1971. (1, 2)

*Peretz, Don, ed. *Israel and the Palestinian Arabs*. Washington, D.C.: Middle East Institute, 1968. (15)

*Perowne, Stewart. *The Life and Times of Herod the Great*. London: Arrow Books, 1960 (Nashville: Abingdon, 1959). (1, 2)

Raisin, J. S. *Gentile Reactions to Jewish Ideals, with Special Refer-

ence to Proselytes. New York: Philosophical Library, 1953. (2)
Rand McNally Bible Atlas, ed. Emil G. Kraeling. Chicago: Rand-McNally, 1969. (1)
*Rodinson, Maxime. *Israel and the Arabs.* Baltimore: Penguin/Pelican, 1968. Clear and significant analysis of the past and present destinies of the Jews, and the conflicts they face, from the standpoint of a French-Jewish scholar of left-wing views who is conscious not only of the recent achievements of Zionism but also of the injustice suffered by the Palestinian Arabs. (5, 10, 11, 14, 15, 16)
*Roth, Cecil. *A History of the Jews, from Earliest Times Through the Six Day War.* New York: Schocken, 1961. (1, 2, 5, 9)
———. *History of the Jews in England.* Oxford: Oxford University Press, 1964. (2)
———, and Geoffrey Wigoder. *The New Standard Jewish Encyclopedia.* New rev. ed. London: W. H. Allen (New York: Doubleday), 1970. There are well-established and authoritative Jewish encyclopedias in several volumes, but this recent compilation contains in compact form most of what a student or general reader will require. (1, 2, 5, 9, 14)
*Roux, Georges. *Ancient Iraq.* Baltimore: Penguin/Pelican, 1972. (1)
*Sachar, Abram Leon. *A History of the Jews.* 5th ed., rev. and enl. New York: Knopf, 1965. (4)
*Safran, Nadav. *From War to War: The Arab-Israeli Confrontation, 1948–67.* New York: Pegasus, 1969. (16)
*Schweitzer, Frederick M. *A History of the Jews Since the First Century A.D.* New York: Macmillan, 1971. The work of a Christian scholar who, like Parkes, has made an understanding and sympathetic study of Jewish history. Professor Schweitzer has taken specially into account the Second Vatican Council documents. (2, 3, 5)
Segre, V. D. *Israel, a Society in Transition.* London/New York: Oxford University Press, 1971. (16)
Seton-Watson, Hugh. *The Russian Empire 1801–1917.* The Oxford History of Modern Europe, vol. 3. Oxford: Clarendon Press, 1967. (6)
Stein, Leonard. *The Balfour Declaration.* London: Valentine, Mitchell, 1961. A major work in considerable detail, primarily for those wishing to study the subject in depth. (10)
*Stevens, Georgiana G., ed. *The United States and the Middle East.* Englewood Cliffs, N.J.: Prentice-Hall/Spectrum, 1964. Prepared as a background study for the Twenty-fourth American Assembly in New York. (13, 14)
Storrs, Sir Ronald. *Orientations.* London: Nicholson & Watson, 1945. (8, 11)

Swain, J. W. *The Ancient World*. New York: Harper, 1950. (1)

*Sykes, Christopher. *Crossroads to Israel*. London: Collins (Cleveland/ New York: World), 1965. Vividly written account of the Mandate period, and the time following, by a British writer sympathetic to Zionism and, like many others, critical of Britain's policies towards both Jews and Arabs. (10, 11, 12, 13)

*Trevelyan, Lord. *The Middle East in Revolution*. Boston: Gambit, 1970. Clear-headed and authoritative study of three of the most unstable areas of the Arab world, the author having served as British Ambassador to Egypt and Iraq and as Governor of Aden in the last stages of British rule there. (14, 15, 16)

*Tuchman, Barbara (Wertheim). *Bible and Sword*. New York: Minerva Books, 1968 (1956). Penetrating historical study of British attachment from ancient times to Palestine and the Bible —an attachment leading eventually to the Balfour Declaration and the Palestine Mandate. (2, 5, 9, 10)

*———. *The Guns of August*. New York: Dell, 1971 (1962). (10)

*———. *The Proud Tower*. New York: Bantam Books, 1967 (1966). (10)

*———. *The Zimmermann Telegram*. New York: Bantam Books, 1966 (1958). (10) Although lacking to some extent in scholarly profundity, the three above Tuchman works are written with vividness, clarity, and distinction, and form an excellent introduction to the complex tragedies of World War I and the stable, over-confident, hierarchical world that preceded it.

*U.S. Department of State. *Issues in U.S. Foreign Policy. No. 1. The Middle East*. Washington, D.C.: U.S. Government Printing Office, 1969. Brief, very helpful summary of the main questions, with emphasis on the Arab-Israeli conflict. (15)

Vatikiotis, P. J. *The Modern History of Egypt*. London: Weidenfeld & Nicolson (New York: Praeger), 1969. (6, 7, 8)

Vilnay, Zev. *The Guide to Israel*. Jerusalem: Ahiever, 1971. Not just a travel guide, but a scholarly work with considerable coverage of archaeology, history, flora and fauna, and other topics. The same considerations, however, apply to some extent as to *Facts about Israel*; and, significantly, it covers the territories conquered in 1967 (with no separate marking on the accompanying map) as though they were part of Israel. (15)

Weisgal, Meyer, and Joel Carmichael, eds. *Chaim Weizmann: A Biography by Several Hands*. London: Weidenfeld & Nicolson, 1962 (New York: Atheneum, 1963). (13)

*Weizmann, Chaim. *Trial and Error*. New York: Schocken, 1966. Extremely significant and revealing autobiography of the main architect of the Balfour Declaration, later first President of

Israel. (9, 10, 12)

Westminster Historical Atlas to the Bible, ed. G. E. Wright and V. F. Filson. Rev. ed. Philadelphia: Westminster Press, 1956. (1)

*Williams, Ann. *Britain and France in the Middle East and North Africa.* New York: St. Martin's, 1968. (10, 11, 14, 15)

Woodward, E. L., and R. Butler, eds. *Documents on British Foreign Policy, 1919–1939.* Vol. 4 (1919). London: H. M. Stationery Office, 1952. (10)

Zeine, Zeine N. *Arab-Turkish Relations and the Emergence of Arab Nationalism.* Beirut: Khayats, 1958. Published in U.S. as *The Emergence of Arab Nationalism, with a Background Study of Arab-Turkish Relations in the Near East.* 3rd ed. Delmar, N.Y.: Caravan Books, 1972. (7, 10)

———. *The Struggle for Arab Independence.* Beirut: Khayats, 1970. (7)

Index

Index